TOOL INTEGRATION

WILEY SERIES IN SOFTWARE BASED SYSTEMS

Series Editors **Colin Tully**, *Colin Tully Associates, UK*
Ian Pyle , *SD-Scicon Ltd, UK*

KRONLÖF (ed): Method Integration: Concepts and Case Studies

THOMÉ (ed): Systems Engineering: Principles and Practice of Computer-based Systems Engineering

SCHEFSTRÖM and VAN DEN BROEK (eds): Tool Integration: Environments and Frameworks

TOOL INTEGRATION

Environments and Frameworks

Edited by

D. Schefström
Telia Research, Sweden
and
G. van den Broek
Philips Research, The Netherlands

JOHN WILEY & SONS
Chichester • New York • Brisbane • Toronto • Singapore

Other Wiley Editorial Offices

John Wiley & Sons, Inc., 605 Third Avenue,
New York, NY 10158-0012, USA

Jacaranda Wiley Ltd, G.P.O. Box 859, Brisbane,
Queensland 4001, Australia

John Wiley & Sons (Canada) Ltd, 22 Worcester Road,
Rexdale, Ontario M9W 1L1, Canada

John Wiley & Sons (SEA) Pte Ltd, 37 Jalan Pemimpin #05-04,
Block B, Union Industrial Building, Singapore 2057

British Library Cataloguing in Publication Data

A catalogue record for this book is available
from the British Library

ISBN 0 471 93554 9

Produced from camera-ready copy supplied by the editors
Printed and bound in Great Britain by Bookcraft (Bath) Ltd

Contents

Preface

This book is about System Development Environments, that is the use of computers to support the development of computer based systems. From very little activity ten years ago, the subject has grown to an independent area, with dedicated conferences and publications. The fact that we talk about System Development Environments should be noted, since the background includes support for Software, Hardware, and technology independent activities. However, since software is an increasing and often dominant part of systems, much of the material will be oriented towards the software domain. The target audience of this book is researchers and practitioners in systems engineering, particularly those concerned with developing or otherwise establishing computerized support for large scale development efforts.

Large investments have been made over the last decade in this area: in product developments, generating a market of tools and toolsets often referred to under the name Computer Aided Software Engineering (CASE), and Computer Aided Design (CAD); in a multitude of university research projects; and in a number of national and international joint research and development projects and consortia, an important examples of which is the ESPRIT-II project ATMOSPHERE [1]. The work and experiences reported here were mostly developed within this latter context, and were concentrated and refined within the group called ATMOSPHERE Environment Integration Taskforce. The personal background experience of the authors is however even wider, including other ESPRIT efforts, Eureka projects like EAST and ESF, as well as various kinds of CASE product developments.

A special characteristic of ATMOSPHERE is its pragmatic attitude, the goal of which is to ensure concrete useful results. In the choice between describing general approaches, with the risk of being vague and imprecise, and reporting on actual designs, with the risk of overemphasizing the particular, we have usually chosen the latter. The material collected here is however rich enough so that abstract principles, and case studies and experience reports will covered.

The ATMOSPHERE project started in 1989 with an initial ambition of creating a single and tightly integrated development environment, intended to simultaneously meet the requirements of the rather wide range of companies and cultures involved. It was however realized that those differing needs and goals should not be viewed as problem, but as a source of strength. Instead of creating a single environment, it was therefore decided to build four different ones, each targeting a different application

---

[1] The ATMOSPHERE project was partly funded by the European Community under the European Strategic Programme for Research and Development in Information Technology (ESPRIT) ref. number 2565.

domain. In this way, the designs could be optimized with respect to the special needs, culture, habits, and technology of the particular domain of application.

The approach chosen in this book is to emphasize architectural principles and underlying technology, discussing what technological means are available, and how these can be used to meet different requirements. There are however many design-choices and trade-offs that must be made, and there is usually no single "right" solution. Therefore, the book contains a number of examples of real environments: those that were built, or significantly extended, within the ATMOSPHERE project.

The overall layout consists of five parts, an initial general overview of the field and four case studies:

System Development Environments: Contemporary Concepts. As the title suggests, we here get an overview of the subject, pointing out important results and discussing design alternatives. Much of the work in environments has concentrated on the problem of *integration*, that is the principles and mechanisms that help us make the tools of the environment cooperate efficiently towards a common goal. Therefore, this part goes into some depth on what are the innermost secrets of this issue.

With some minor variations, each of the five parts has a similar structure, where the supported development process is described, followed by an overview of which tools are included. Finally, the used technology and internal design is desribed, based on an extended version of the three dimensions of integration, that is Control, Data, and Presentation.

Each of the four examples have been written with the various issues discussed in the first part in mind. In this way we hope to further increase the uniformity, ensuring a complete coverage of each environment example. The checklist contains use of database technology, configuration management, process modelling, support for cooperative work, integration across life-cycle phases, distribution, host-target support, scalability and support for large projects, object-orientation, and many other aspects.

Not all issues have been relevant to all environments, but together they represent a probably unique coverage of principles, technology, and practice in the area of System Development Environments.

The Aerospace Systems Software Engineering Environment is based on the Portable Common Tool Environment, called PCTE [BMT88] and the EAST project [SFG91]. This ambitious effort achieves integration mainly by means of a common framework dominated by a common datastore. In terms of ambition on overall coordination, by means of a common framework, it is probably fair to say that this is the most ambitious of the efforts described here. But therefore also the one with the highest risk.

The Aerospace environment as presented here is an excellent example of pursuing the most classical of goals in environment construction: the unification of all tool's data by representing it within a single homogeneous datamodel. This datamodel is then to be represented using the PCTE environment database. The consistent orientation towards using the persistent data objects as the focus for integration is here very visible even in the approach to user interfaces: the user interface integration is to a large extent viewed as a problem of providing a consistent and uniform view of the object base. Consequently, the architecture includes central components for object visualization.

Even though doubt has occasionally been raised concerning the very approach of a single data model, and especially single database, the environment presented here is one of the best examples of large scale data integration in existence today. Because of its wide scope, the description of this environment touches upon most issues, services, and problems that will face an environment architect. Therefore this chapter is well worth reading. In fact, it should be standard reading for anyone interested in large scale data integration and frameworks.

The range of tool support described covers requirements capture, design and early simulation, programming, documentation, and configuration management. Special attention is given to the problem of integrating tools that correspond to different lifecycle phases, and keeping their respective data consistent.

The Process Control Systems Software Engineering Environment is centred around the specification and description language SDL, but does also emphasize the importance of early requirements phase, by means of an technique called AKL inspired on SA and SADT. The integration between those tools is here especially interesting because it also represents an integration between development phases. In fact an important part of the rationale of the design of AKL was to make the transition to the design phase easier.

The Process Control environment is also a nice example of consistent internal design and integration. The various editors, for several aspects of SDL and one of AKL, are based on the same underlying technology for graphics manipulation and user interface construction.

This sharing of basic mechanisms does in fact extend all the way down to data object management. Although this environment does not use a single database, and has chosen not to provide many of the features usually associated with CASE database technology, such as transactions, general queries, configuration management, various indexing strategies, distribution, etc., it does impose a common datamodel. While each tool maintains its own database, the sharing of software and datamodel makes it relatively easy to exchange information between them, that is to integrate in the data dimension.

The subsystem responsible for this data management is furthermore both based on the object-oriented paradigm, and oriented towards supporting even the finest granularity of data. The similarity in concept and direction with the emerging market of Object-Oriented Databases should therefore be noted.

Finally, there is also a good example of Control integration, where services of the SDL toolset are made available by means of a communication protocol. As is described in this section, this allows other tools to integrate with and use the functionality of the SDL server in a very flexible and non-intrusive way.

The Communication Systems Software Engineering Environment has similarities with the process control one in that SDL has a central role, around which support for both specification oriented tools, and later-phase code generation facilities are grouped. It may be fair to say that the SDL language here acts as an integrating factor. It includes examples of tool support emerging from combined use of different languages or methods, such as LOTOS, SDL, the protocol data specification notation ASN.1, and the hardware description language VHDL, and, of course, C. The situation is a good illustration of the need for "Method Integration", that is the planning and adaption of formalisms so that they work well together. This issue is however addressed by a separate book in this series: Method Integration: Concepts and Case Studies [Kro92].

The architecture is very different from the Process Control one, and is also to a larger extent built with non-proprietary tool-sets and framework technology. Depending on the viewpoint, it can therefore be called either more heterogeneous and less integrated, or more open and flexible.

This environment does not attempt any integration through unification of data. Exchange of data is instead performed by means of transformations, undertaken "when needed", but usually stored in the domain and format of its originating tool. There are also a few very good examples of control integration. The SDT toolset, which is supporting parts of the SDL work, is internally integrated by means of its so called Postmaster model. This model is a nice example of integration based on a broadcast message server mechanism. The overall framework is however based on another message based system, HP SoftBench. The systems coexist and work well, but the usual question arises: should one impose a single mechanism, or is there room, or even need, for multiple solutions to the same problem. In the example above, one could view it as the Postmaster specializing in coordinating a single toolset, (SDT), while HP SoftBench provides the support for the next level of abstraction. The question of "levels of granularity" occurs here, just as in the data management area.

The Hardware Engineering Environment is of special interest since it is the only one of our four environment examples that is primarily built to support the design of hardware.

From an architectural point of view, this environment does however show strong similarities in approach with the other environments, and maybe especially the Aerospace one, in that it is based on an ambitious and clearly identifiable framework, Jessi Common Frame [JCF91], and in its rather strong orientation towards data integration.

The design process for hardware does differ from that of software. However, as can be observed by reading the relevant chapters, the difference is not at great as might be initially perceived. The same concerns for integration among tools and development phases occur here, and is well exemplified by the coordination between the synthesis, verification, and performance evaluation toolsets.

Another way of seeing the commonalities between software and hardware environments is by observing the requirements for data management developed here, which result in a similar set of conclusions about the need for multiple levels of abstraction and granularity of data, multiple views, "alternative realizations" (versions), and support for complex objects.

Further commonalities can be found in the user interface dimension, where it is quite obvious that the basic mechanisms for efficient production of various graphical editors is a very generic need. And indeed, the Hardware Design environment includes a User Interface Management System with a strong emphasis on graphics support. It provides a "graphical datastructure" with definition and manipulation routines, as well as software for its visualization on the screen. The interested reader may compare it to the corresponding component of the Process Control environment.

The idea of utilizing the commonality between hardware and software design to develop a common framework has been proposed several times before. This truly common Hardware/Software environment has however not yet gained complete acceptance. The relevant part is an excellent opportunity for anyone who wants to seriously evaluate the viability of this approach.

What was then, in essence, the conclusion of this effort? What should have been done differently, and what are the most important single results? Why were at least four different approaches and technologies developed? Is there not a single "right" one?

The maybe evasive answer to these questions is that there are no simple singular conclusions. The subject is so complex, including aspects ranging from basic technology to organizational issues and human behaviour, so that single answers just do not exist. The questions must be more specific. On the positive side, one can however conclude that common understanding of the intricate nature of increasing automation in system development has increased significantly. A major advice is therefore: read the book and explore its broad menu of concepts, ideas, advices, case studies, and conclusions. Each of the five parts also have their own chapter of perspective, conclusions, and future work.

Some personal remarks

System Development Environments are large systems with an unusually broad interface towards humans and organizations. It is also a very young area, with no more than a decade since it was recognized as a seperate discipline. Comparing with the long experience gathered in other fields that produce large computer based systems, such as telecom, process control, command and control, business processing, flight control, etc., the System Development Environments area has had little time to grow a tradition of agreed concepts and architectures. Consequently there have been rather few experienced environment architects available, which of course is necessary before a widely accepted and mature common culture can emerge. This is however slowly changing, and the efforts and experiences represented by this book will hopefully prove to be part of this.

The question on why four different environment approaches where produced, and not a single one, is not only because of actual differences in needs. It is easy to accept that differences in application domains must lead to differences in tools and notations at higher levels, but there is much less reason to expect differences in lower level basic support mechanisms. It is however also important to note the surprisingly big cost and high risk involved in any technology transfer and technology absorbtion. Many large organizations have developed their own basic environments technology over a long period of time. The thereby mature understanding of the particular technology's characteristics and limitations makes operation and usage very efficient. This sometimes hidden body of knowledge about the internal technology is usually larger and more important than initially thought. Although everyone in principle agrees that standardizing in a larger scope should be economical - buying someone elses basic solutions - there is always a suspicion that the cost of internalizing that other technology can be so high that it off-sets the advantages. To this add the risk that this technology would prove no better at closer inspection. Therefore, the process of eliminating "unnecessary" technology differences is rather slow. In the project underlying this book a number of large organizations have been presenting their internal solutions to each other, and now do so for a larger community. This book therefore represents a contribution to the global technology harmonization process.

Among important general observations we also have the need for supporting different working styles and organizational cultures. An environment that tries to impose a different approach to running projects than the users feel comfortable with, is probably going to fail. The problem here is that there are so many ways and styles of doing development, ranging from projects in new areas that need a high degree of exploration, to developments in mature areas where much is already known. The former needs a less rigid process supporting change, innovation, and much interaction, while in the latter case it is possible to apply stricter specialized roles and more formality. The currently most dominating answer to this problem is what is called "Process Modelling", that is the desire to factor out a formalization of the development process and thereby make it easy to change. In this way, environments would be possible to quickly adapt to different working styles.

It turns out, however, that assumptions about process are hiding in a large number of places: in configuration management, in basic data modelling, in selection of notations and tools, in the emphasis on which tools are most important to integrate better, and even in the selection of requirements on the very basic support technology. As just a single example, one can note that those who need a process which includes many and frequent changes to design items (such as more exploratory projects) have another need for database transaction and version handling capabilities than those who expect a rather stable waterfall approach with few and infrequent changes. A benefit of this book is that it points out a number of such tensions and options, and therefore facilitates communication between different schools of thought.

Concerning approaches to integration, one conclusion is that data integration can be rather expensive, and closely interacts with both process modelling and configuration management in sometimes intricate ways. The part on the Aerospace Environment is a good illustration of this, but also the Hardware Engineering and to some extent the Process Control ones. It is, however, a most valuable form of integration once completed. The complexity of data integration has lead to an increased interest in "communications oriented" approaches, usually labelled control integration. It is believed to be less expensive since it allows for a rather loose coupling between components, and the Communication Systems Environment is an example of this. It is however not completely clear whether the apparent simplicity is real or just a sign that the harder problems of standardizing on semantics of messages has just begun. The user interface integration area has reached a certain maturity and seems to be the one currently causing the least problems. User Interface Management Systems, that are toolsets dedicated to the efficient production of user interfaces, seem to be in use in most places. A major new phase of development in this area is however showing up with the request for Multimedia support. System Development Environments must both use this technology and support its production.

Finally it deserves pointing out one direction where Environments should be fruitfully strengthened in the future, namely support for distributed collaborative work on the less formalized side. That is, making it possible for developers to meet, argue, plan, comment, and maybe even "chat" while not necessarily leaving their Environments and workstations. A large part of a developer's day is dominated by work related to meetings, reviews, and discussions, especially in the important early phases of projects. Sometimes possibly boring travelling is needed for meetings; sometimes needed meetings do not take place because it would require travel. The combination of Environments, Distribution, and general Computer Supported Cooperative Work is a promising blend addressing important needs.

To conclude, the material in this book provides a probably unique insight into problems, solutions, and approaches in the area of System Development Environments, that is furthermore not only theoretical, but is rooted in real practice and the construction of environments that are in actual use. It provides a breadth of scope, viewpoints, and experience that are hard to find in any other place.

Acknowledgements

SYSTEM DEVELOPMENT ENVIRONMENTS: CONTEMPORARY CONCEPTS

As author of the part SYSTEM DEVELOPMENT ENVIRONMENTS: CONTEMPORARY CONCEPTS, Dick Schefström, states that the daily context at the Section for Software Technology at Telia Research in Lulea was an essential contribution to the material in this part of the book. Many of the ideas and opinions presented have its real roots there, and he would like to thank all the people working there. At a more detailed level, the material was commented on at various stages by Johan Bengtsson, Petter Bengtsson, and Johnny Widen of Telia Research, as well as by Christer Fernstrom at CGInn, Grenoble, France.

AEROSPACE SYSTEMS SOFTWARE DEVELOPMENT ENVIRONMENT

As author of the contribution on the AEROSPACE SYSTEMS SOFTWARE ENGINEERING ENVIRONMENT, Ian Simmonds, would like to thank Fanny Camilleri, John Cheesman, Philippe Desanois, Sylvie Lavabre and Pierre Montminy amongst others for helping him to work out which features of the EAST framework were truly important and in finding the best ways of explaining them to others. His understanding of PCTE and configuration management on PCTE has been built up over several years through discussions with many other people who were also seeking such an understanding. Notable amongst these are Karima Berrada, Françoise Lopez, Régis Minot, Gilles Pitette and Ian Thomas.

The production of the Aerospace Environment within the ATMOSPHERE project also benefited from the presence of many of the people mentioned above. In addition Ian would like to thank Paolo Bonissone, Agustín Cuenca-Guevara, Gianfranco Del Duca, Christian Negri, Alessandro Orlandi and Giancarlo Savoia for introducing him to the methods and tools of the Aerospace Environment and for coordinating its development.

Finally, for the production of this book Ian would like to thank the authors of the other chapters, the editor of the ATMOSPHERE series and Alan Brown, all of whom provided invaluable review comments during the production of his contribution.

PROCESS CONTROL SYSTEMS SOFTWAE ENGINEERING ENVIRONMENT

The author Gerd Höfner, wants to thank Dr. Hans Delfs for the valuable contribution of the "Data Integration" chapter and Gerhard Gries for his initial ideas and contribution to the "Control Integration" chapter. Special thanks go to Michael Eike who prepared the early drafts of this part.

They thank also to the people who discussed and reviewed our work during the long period of creation: Arne Westpfahl, Hans-Günter Tempel, Max Raff and Wilhelm Gruber.

A special thanks to all the people who have developed and realized the tools and toolsets of the Siemens Environment.

COMMUNICATION SYSTEMS SOFTWARE ENGINEERING ENVIRONMENT

As author of the part on COMMUNICATION SYSTEMS SOFTWARE ENGINEERING ENVIRONMENT, Ger van den Broek, would like to thank his collegues from the section IST of Philips Research for their contributions and support. Especially: Ben Gorissen, Con Holzscherer, David Kamp, Monique Roosen, Marc Stroucken, Menno Treffers, Rob Vader, Rob Wieringa all from Philips Research. The auuthor also wants to thank Gert Nilsson from Telelogic and Tuomas Lamminpää from Nokia for their contributions.

HARDWARE ENGINEERING ENVIRONMENT

The authors of the contribution on the HARDWARE ENGINEERING ENVIRONMENT, Maria Brielmann, Elisabeth Kupitz and Susanne Rudolph, want to thank Ferdinand Bunte (Cadlab) and Gerd Kachel (Cadlab) for their contribution to the description of the JESSI Common Framework, and Martin Büttner (University of Dortmund), David Mallon (University of Strathclyde), Detlef Manske (Siemens Nixdorf Informationssyteme AG), Franz–Josef Stewing (Siemens Nixdorf Informationssysteme AG) and Norbert Weißenberg (University of Dortmund) for valuable discussions concerning the data schema, for the descriptions of the tools and for proof reading. The authors also thank the members of the Synthesis Group at Cadlab, especially Bernd Kleinjohann, for their contribution to a first version of the data schema.

Editors

The editors Dick Schefström and Ger van den Broek thank the reviewers of this book, especially Christofer Fernstrom and Joachim Lenzer for their effort in reviewing the material. We would like to thank our co-authors, the members of the ATMOSPHERE Environment Integration Taskforce, for an interesting, educating, and fun time together. Finally we thank all the people who contributed to the ATMOSPHERE project, this book describes only one specific view of their work.

List of Authors

Maria Brielmann

CADLAB [2]

Bahnhofstraße 32
W-4790 Paderborn
Germany

Ger van den Broek

Philips Research
Information and Software Technolgy

Prof. Holstlaan 4
5656 AA Eindhoven
The Netherlands

Gerd Höfner

Siemens AG
ZFE BT SE 54

Paul-Gossenstr. 100
W-8520 Erlangen
Germany

Elisabeth Kupitz

CADLAB

Bahnhofstraße 32
W-4790 Paderborn
Germany

Susanne Rudolph

CADLAB

Bahnhofstraße 32
W-4790 Paderborn
Germany

Dick Schefström

Telia Research

Aurorum 6
S-95175 LULEÅ
Sweden

Ian Simmonds

Société Française de
Génie Logiciel

14, rue de la Ferme
92100 BOULOGNE
France

[2] Joint Venture of Siemens Nixdorf Informationssysteme AG and University of Paderborn

Trademarks

ADA is a trademark from US Governement (Ada Joint Program Office)
AdaNICE is a trademark from Intecs Sistemi SpA
Apollo is a trademark from Apollo Computer Inc.
Domain is a trademark from Apollo Computer Inc.
DSEE is a trademark from Apollo Computer Inc.
East is a trademark from SFGL
Emeraude is a trademark from GIE Emeraude
Encapsulator is a trademark from Hewlett Packard
Ethernet is a trademark from the Xerox Corporation
FrameMaker is a trademark from Frame Technology Corporation
GNU is a trademark from Free Software Foundation
HP/UX is a trademark from Hewlett Packard
KeyDoc is a trademark from LPS srl
KeyOne is a trademark from LPS srl
Motif is a trademark from Open Software Foundation
NFS is a trademark from SUN Microsystems Inc.
OPEN LOOK is a trademark from Unix System Laboratories
OSF/1 is a trademark from Open Software Foundation
POSIX is a trademark from IEEE
PostScript is a trademark from Adobe Systems Inc.
SADT is a trademark from SoftTech
SDT is a trademark from Telelogic
SIGRAPH is a trademark from Siemen Nixdorf Informationssysteme AG
SoftBench is a trademark from Hewlett Packard
SORIX is a trademark from Siemen Nixdorf Informationssysteme AG
SPARC is a trademark from Sparc International Inc.
SUN is a trademark from SUN Micro Systems Inc.
TeleUSE is a trademark from Telelogic
TPS is a trademark from Interleaf
Ultrix is a trademark from Digital Equipment Corporation
UNIX is a trademark from Unix System Laboratories
VAX is a trademark from Digital Equipment Corporation
VMS is a trademark from Digital Equipment Corporation
X Window System is a trademark from Massachusetts Institute of Technology

Series Preface

Among the many series of books on professional software issues, the *Wiley Series in Software Based Systems* is out of the ordinary. It would be hard to justify the series if its titles were interchangeable with those of any other software-related series. They are not, however. The series is quite distinctive in its origin and purpose.

The origin of the series lies in two international collaborative projects, ATMOSPHERE and COMPLEMENT, and their desire that some of their results should be shared with a worldwide readership. Of the first five titles in the series, ATMOSPHERE contributes three and COMPLEMENT two. Both projects are part of the ESPRIT programme of the Commission of the European Communities.

It is not intended, however, to limit the series to outputs from those two specific projects. Later titles may come from other ESPRIT projects, or indeed from any other source whatever, provided only that they conform to the purpose of the series.

(Because this volume is an output from the ATMOSPHERE project, brief descriptions of ATMOSPHERE and of ESPRIT are included at the end of this preface.)

The purpose of the series is to present new ideas and experience from the frontiers of practice in building software-based systems—to offer conceptual advances applicable to practising engineers. That description of purpose places equal emphasis on three things: *conceptual innovation* (which marks the series out from the general run of practitioner books), *applicable experience* (which marks it out from the general run of academic books) and a *systems perspective* (which marks it out from the general run of software books, whether for practitioners or academics).

CONCEPTUAL INNOVATION

Practitioner texts generally describe in detail how to perform a specific kind of task or how to solve a specific kind of problem: they are essential for those needing well defined techniques based on well understood concepts. By contrast, this series addresses hard practical problems for which ready-made methods and techniques do not yet exist; and the justification for presenting conceptual innovations is that in those circumstances they help practitioners organize their thinking about the problems, and to take decisions in a more orderly manner. These conceptual innovations, if sound, will be the basis for the next generation of theory (nothing is of more practical use than a good theory) and of methods and techniques.

APPLICABLE EXPERIENCE

In any case, none of the books in the series is wholly conceptual. Each contains a significant (if not predominant) proportion of case study or other empirical material, drawn either from the direct experience of the authors or from their observation of others' experience. It is this firm rooting of concepts in applicable experience, from which the concepts are developed and which they are intended to illuminate, that distinguishes the series from the conceptual treatment usual in academic texts.

SYSTEMS PERSPECTIVE

The term "software based systems" in the series title is carefully chosen. It is meant to indicate the ever-increasing extent to which software is the critical element in the large and complex systems which we seek to engineer, and the extent to which software engineering alone is inadequate to deal with the systems problems inherent in such advanced engineering projects. So while there are many software based systems which can be successfully dealt with by software engineers, there are many others which cannot, and which demand a distinctive systems engineering approach.

It is not necessary or appropriate to develop this point further here: different books develop it in their own ways. One point should be made, however: the term "software based systems" was chosen in preference to the wider term "computer based systems", because software really is the predominant theme running through the series; nevertheless, several books (notably those originating from the ATMOSPHERE project) pay significant attention to issues in VLSI engineering, which are distinct from software, though related to it.

A NOTE ON ESPRIT

ESPRIT is the European Strategic Programme for Research in Information Technology. It is the largest single programme within the European Community R&D Framework Programme, which defines strategic goals and funding levels for collaborative R&D among the member states of the Community. ESPRIT has three objectives: to promote European transnational cooperation in information technology; to provide European IT industry with the technologies it needs to meet the competitive requirements of the 1990s, and to contribute toward the development and implementation of international standards. In the domain of software, PCTE is to date probably the best-known outcome of ESPRIT.

ESPRIT is a programme of precompetitive R&D. Projects are carried out by consortia which must minimally include two industrial partners, and may include any additional number of industrial and academic partners. The Commission funds up to 50% of the total value of approved projects, the remainder coming from the participant organizations.

ESPRIT was launched in 1984. The first batch of over 220 projects was launched during the period 1984-1988, retrospectively known as ESPRIT 1. ESPRIT 2 covered the period 1988-1992, and ESPRIT 3 was launched in 1992.

A NOTE ON ATMOSPHERE

ATMOSPHERE started in 1989, and ESPRIT funding was provided for its first three years. At the end of that phase, in mid-1992, the partners agreed to establish an ATMOSPHERE Special Interest Group (SIG), as a short-term mechanism for continued collaboration, and as a means of putting in place longer-term structures and funding for the work of the consortium.

The six main partners are CAP Gemini Innovation (lead partner, France), Bull (France), Philips (Netherlands), Siemens (Germany), Siemens Nixdorf Informationssysteme (SNI, Germany) and Société Française du Génie Logiciel (SFGL, France). Over twenty other companies and universities are or have been involved, as associates or subcontractors, from ten countries. At peak activity the project deployed the equivalent of about 120 people full-time.

ATMOSPHERE was one of a special category of ESPRIT 2 projects, called Technology Integration Projects (TIPs). As such, its mission was not, as it is for other ESPRIT projects, to carry out technological innovation, but rather to achieve innovation in the understanding and practice of existing technology.

ATMOSPHERE's essential area of concern is what, since the project's inception, has become known as computer-based systems engineering (CBSE). In the late eighties and early nineties, CBSE has emerged as a necessary discipline to address a level of problems above those of software engineering, in just the same way as software engineering itself, in the late sixties and early seventies, emerged to address a level of problems above those of programming. Arguably (and many people certainly argue), software engineering is not yet established as a defined, reputable and teachable discipline, corresponding to the vision of its early champions. After only two decades, however, that is perhaps not wholly surprising; certainly it would be a mistake to expect CBSE to establish itself any faster, or with any less opposition. Processes of this kind are fundamentally sociological, and therefore slow and inherently subject to resistance.

At this very early stage in the life and growth of CBSE, ATMOSPHERE is asking questions such as: what is CBSE? what does it have in common with, and how is it distinct from, related engineering disciplines such as (especially) software and VLSI engineering? what does it have in common with, and how is it distinct from, other areas of systems engineering? what processes constitute it? what are the methods which support those processes? what are the tools (on the one hand) and the theories (on the other hand) which support those methods? and how can the diversity of methods and tools be integrated effectively so that they can be combined with the maximum synergy and the minimum frictional cost? These questions can be summarized as the reflection of two predominant concerns: the first is, how can we improve our *understanding* of CBSE? and the second is, how can *integration* help us construct better configurations of methods and tools, to improve our practice of CBSE? Of the three ATMOSPHERE books to appear in the series in 1992, one is concerned with understanding CBSE, and the other two with integration (of, respectively, methods and tools).

The critical characteristic which pervades ATMOSPHERE is that all its work is rooted in the current understanding and practice of the industrial members of the consortium, and in the improvements that those organizations regard as desirable and cost-effective. The aim of the project is to assist in making those improvements, and to share the results to the benefit of the whole consortium.

Colin Tully

Part I

System Development Environments: Contemporary Concepts

Dick Schefström
Telia Research
Aurorum 6
S-95175 LULEÅ

Sweden

Tool Integration: Environments and Frameworks, Edited by D. Schefström and G. van den Broek

1

System Development Environments: Contemporary Concepts

The goal of this book is to be practical and concrete, presenting examples of working systems rather than general reasoning and speculation. However, a certain amount of more abstract discussion is still needed. In this chapter, we will therefore introduce a few general ideas that we believe are important, such as the "three dimensions of integration", and which have been used to direct the structure and contents of the following chapters.

Without claiming a complete coverage, we will then also develop some reasoning around a few of the many design trade-offs that are faced by the support environment architect.

1.1 THE DREAM OF AN ENVIRONMENT

Many visions have been presented in this area, and most of them will have been touched upon before the end of this book. However, to set an initial tone it seems appropriate to start out with a couple of them.

Let us first take a look at environments from the *Information Management* viewpoint. The philosophy behind this approach is that the key to automation in systems development is in systematically capturing and structuring the many different "objects" that are produced: requirements, design specifications, meeting records, software modules, test specifications, plans, etc.

According to this view, the state of a project is defined in terms of the state of the objects it has produced at a given point in time. The progress is then measured in terms of the growth, in quality and quantity, of the objects in this information base. The idea is illustrated by figure 1.1.

An important part of the vision is that all this information - concerning all aspects of the system under development - should in principle be available to everyone in the daily interactive situation. Sometimes a hypertext/hypermedia metaphor is used to

Tool Integration: Environments and Frameworks, Edited by D. Schefström and G. van den Broek

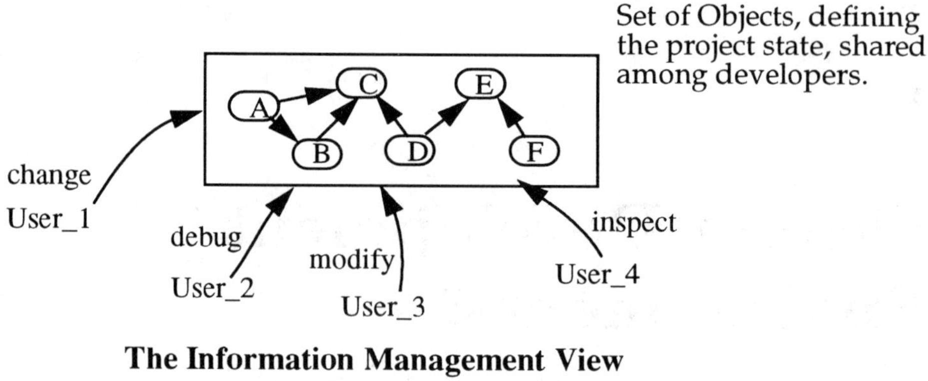

Figure 1.1

emphasize the information browsing and navigation ability. Such immediate availability of accurate information is believed to be the key to productivity increase. This view has naturally led to database-centred approaches to environments.

There are, however, a few very difficult problems to solve before reaching this goal. The first is *managing change*, that is maintaining consistency and functioning of the information base in the face of continuous modification. The other major obstacle is *information gathering*, that is how to ensure that this information really is getting to the right place and in a format that allows for a level of automatic processing. A central solution idea, for both problems, is the integration of tools, so that they more or less automatically store and update the necessary information, mostly as a side-effect of the activities the user performs anyway.

Another approach to Environments takes the *Process Support* view, according to which we should first define a precise development process, which identifies the necessary steps, actions, roles, and information flows throughout the complete life-cycle. The role of the Environment should then be to support this specified process, manifesting as much of it as possible in executable software and computer stored structures. This development process, often called the Process Model in this context, now takes the role of a kind of blueprint for the environment.

The vision sometimes takes the form of trying to introduce a special element, the Process Engine, which conceptually would "execute" the process model. It would continuously receive state change information and be guiding users and tools by monitoring state changes, drawing conclusions based on the actual state and the process model, and finally emitting guidance and directives to users and tools (figure 1.2).

The implementation of this vision meets similar problems to the Information Management view, and the same essential element of the solution is present: tool integration. For any kind of process execution (the word "enactment" is usually used in this area), the state changes and other information must be gathered automatically, and in a form that lends itself to mechanical manipulation.

On the path towards these visions, and several alternative formulations, a rich body of principles and technologies has been developed. The aim of this book is to take a closer look at a number of these.

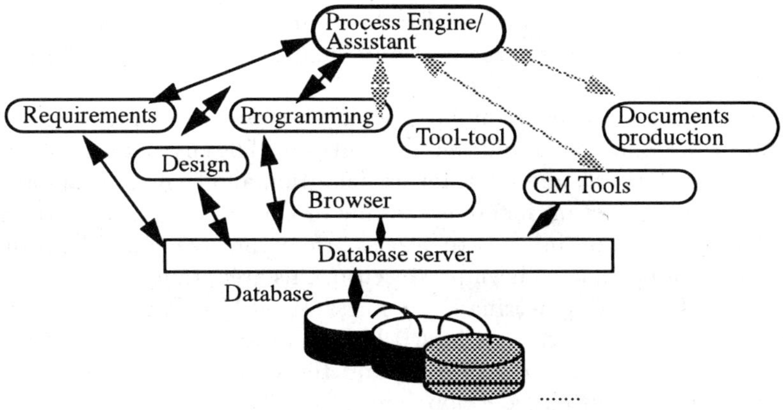

The Process Support View

Figure 1.2

1.2 THE NEED FOR ABSTRACT CONCEPTS

For the purpose of this document, we use the following definitions:

> The *Architecture* of a system is an identification of (1) its main subsystems, objects, or otherwise important parts, and (2) a description of the ways they interact, exchange information, or otherwise affect each other.
> The *Principles* of an Architecture are the guidelines and rationales used in developing the Architecture.
> The area of *Integration Technology* is then the task of identifying and further developing these principles, with the ultimate goal of manifesting them in executable pieces of software.

The need for continuously evolving and refining our knowledge about these concepts is a major reason for this book. We need the concepts for the following reasons:

- *Understanding.* Systems described in terms of principles are easier to understand.
- *Comparison.* Superficial differences between systems can be eliminated while essential ones are clearly noticed.
- *Standardization.* If we clearly formulate the principles, and even implement some of them in a reusable way, technology fragmentation decreases. The ultimate goal is a "standard", which usually proves to be very economic.
- *Reuse.* Closely related to standardization, however at a smaller scope, less formality, and less bureaucracy. Standardizing within a project or an organization rather than within Europe, America, or the world.

1.3 MODELS OF DEVELOPMENT PROCESSES

Before getting into the area of Support Environments, it deserves remembering that underlying all computerized support for development there is always some organizational idea of how the working process should be. It may be rigid and formal, or flexible and free. It is, however, always there.

In fact, one could view the main purpose of any support environment as to manifest this working process in executable pieces of software. The environment should make the process visible, enforce it, and allow for its definition and change. Defining the *Process Model* is therefore important before describing or constructing a support environment. It therefore seems relevant initially to discuss briefly the area of development processes.

Numerous documents have been produced in this area, ranging from text books like the classical "Software Engineering Economics" [Boe81], over procedures as developed by many companies, to standards issued by organizations like the IEEE (IEEE 830-1984, IEEE 730-1984, IEEE P1016/D4), and the famous US Department of Defense standard for software systems development, often called "2167".

The titles of the documents may differ: "Standards for Software Development (or Engineering)", "Recommended Practices for Design", "Quality Assurance Plan", "Specification Practices", etc. The purpose is however always to establish a certain level of uniformity for parts of the work involved in producing computer and software intensive systems. Although uniformity has its advantages, all projects just do not have the same characteristics - a fact that puts a definite limit on the value of general documents such as the ones referred to above.

1.3.1 The classical model of development

Most of the documents above are based on some variant of the so called Waterfall Model of development. The idea is that any project will pass through a number of *phases*, the structure of which is independent of the project contents. Boehm [Boe81] identifies the following phases:

- *Feasibility study.*
- *Requirements specification.*
- *Product Design.*
- *Detailed Design.*
- *Coding.*
- *Integration.*
- *Implementation.*
- *Maintenance.*
- *Phaseout.*

For each phase, a number of tasks to be performed are then prescribed. These may include the production of documents with certain names; the undertaking of certain meetings and reviews; and the application of certain methods, tools, or standard formats in performing those tasks.

The *Plan* for a project is then, in its simplest form, a statement of when the project is expected to start and finish a certain phase and what resources will thereby be used.

In principle, the *monitoring of progress* can therefore be reduced to the almost trivial task of checking whether the project has completed a given phase at the planned time, consuming the stated resources.

1.3.2 Limitations of the Waterfall model

In its most clean and rigid form, the Waterfall model is based on the following assumptions:

- *Phasing.* Each phase must be completed before the next can start.
- *Subtask synchronization.* All parts of the project move through phases synchronously.
- *Context independence.* Projects are dominated by new developments.

In this form, the Waterfall model has received a lot of well deserved criticism. In the following sections we discuss, for each of those points, how the pure Waterfall must be changed when the assumptions are not valid.

1.3.2.1 Phasing

The assumption that each phase must be completed before the next one can start implies that all essential characteristics, properties, and solution alternatives of the end product must be known in early phases. This is obviously in direct conflict with many people's experience that quality insights cannot be gathered without reference to some of the work associated with later phases. For example: to produce a good Product Design it is often necessary to do some Coding and Integration. *Prototyping* should therefore not only be allowed, but be part of the standard approach to development.

In practice, we therefore allow ourselves a more iterative application of the Waterfall model. The phases exist, but we have very legitimate reasons to go back and forth between them to a considerable extent.

1.3.2.2 Subtask synchronization

The second assumption similarly implies a sometimes unrealistic level of determinism. It is based on the early existence of a *Work Breakdown Structure*, which identifies the subcomponents of the final product. A phase of the whole project is then performed by finishing the corresponding phase for each of the components in the Work Breakdown Structure.

The problem here is that this structure most often evolves as a result of progress, and that different parts of the product have different characteristics, risks, and delivery time requirements. Therefore, we must in practice often treat different Work Breakdown Structure parts as if they were separate projects with respect to phase transitions and work methodology. Consequently, it is less trivial to know exactly in which phase the complete project is and, hence, the progress achieved.

1.3.2.3 Context independence

Finally, the strongly phased approach of the Waterfall model does not match well with the continuous improvement and bug fixing that is typical of software intensive products. In such cases, the system is never finished but will evolve over time as successive releases. In terms of the waterfall model, we have two alternatives:

- Call it all "maintenance".
- Treat each release as a new waterfall project.

The first approach seems to represent the official Waterfall answer to the problem. It does however not contribute much to structuring the actual work: it is hidden inside a single phase. For work that can clearly be characterized as pure error correction, this is reasonable, although the exact process of doing the work must then be developed. The Waterfall model does not do that.

The second approach is more useful as the work involved has a larger content of new development. In those cases when an existing application is significantly extended, it is usually possible to identify the traditional phases of the Waterfall model. It must however be adapted with respect to the constraints imposed by the fact that we are now essentially repeatedly going through development phases that have been performed several times before for the same software. It is then important not to lose the results and conclusions from those earlier iterations. The Waterfall model does not prescribe any procedures for doing this.

1.3.2.4 Conclusion

Most people should agree on the Waterfall phased view of development, in the sense that we start with the fuzzy and unclear but end up with the concrete and well specified. But, the path between those extremes is seldom a monotonic evolution towards the goal. It is however worthwhile to make it look that way afterwards. It is furthermore necessary at some points in time to produce documents reflecting the current state of work, as a way of securing intermediate results and facilitating human communication.

As a consequence of the above observations concerning phasing, subtask synchronization, and context independence, the Waterfall must be changed in at least the following ways:

- We must account for iteration between phases, and that documents produced in a phase may be changed at, in principle, any time.
- We must allow different parts of the work to be in different phases at a given time.
- We must initialize new developments (this may in some cases be called maintenance) with the constraints of existing requirements, designs, and implementations. That is, essentially, reuse of existing results.

Several alternative process models have been presented. A well known one is the *Spiral Model* [Boe88], triggered by similar observations as above. The spiral model is a "risk-driven" approach, where development is structured as a number of smaller but complete cycles (as each cycle adds to the total cost and completeness, we get an explanation of the name "spiral"). At the start of each cycle, an analysis is made to

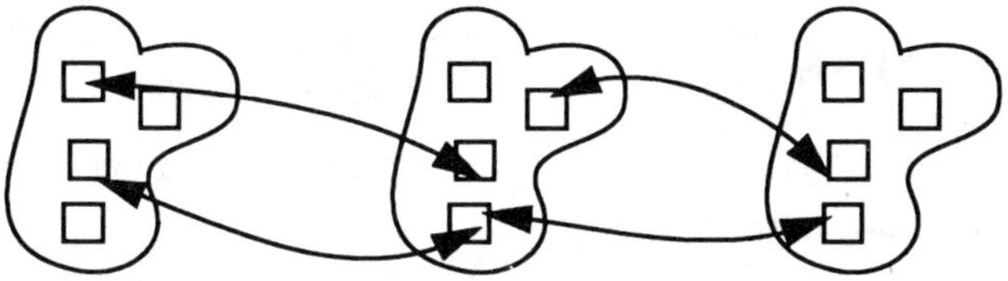

Figure 1.3 Inter-phase traceability

identify the major "risks" at hand. The goal of the cycle is then to eliminate or decrease those risks, by means of prototyping or special investigations. After an evaluation of the outcome, a new round of risk-analysis starts the next cycle. In this way, work is continuously focused on quickly getting to the bottom of the most high priority issues. Variations on this theme are also developed under the label of *Concurrent Engineering.*

Rejecting the pure Waterfall model is not controversial in any way. Many authors and publications have expressed their frustration with this view of software development. The following is a citation of one such source, picked from many possible [Per89]:

> The entire life-cycle is iterative: requirements grow and evolve as understanding of the problem increases; the design evolves as design decisions constrain the solution space; these design decisions have backwards-reaching effects on the requirements, both from finding inconsistencies and lack of clarity as well as indicating costs that may generate reconsiderations of the requirements and changes to them; and so on throughout the remainder of the cycle. A system evolves in all its parts from beginning to end. Trying to force this evolutionary process into neat, distinct and independent phases only serves to obscure the reality of software development.

A somewhat philosophical writing on the same subject is [Sch88], which discusses the tension between creation and determinism by picking examples from several different aspects of life and society.

1.3.3 Implications on Environments: inter-phase traceability

Development environments, being responsible for reflecting this development process in executable software, therefore have a delicate task. They must, among other things, provide for several styles of working and, especially, account for very flexible iteration among any kind of "phases" that they try to impose. This problem is one of the most central, and occurs in many shapes. It is often talked about in terms of "traceability", referring to the need for tracing "back" to the source of problems or decisions: which program module caused a certain error report, which design object caused a certain program module to be created, which requirements lead to a certain design object (figure 1.3). This vision of global information navigation ability is essential to the Information Management view of environments.

As the figure above suggests, different objects can be attributed to different phases of the development cycle. The problem of tracing dependencies between such objects we here call the *inter-phase traceability problem.* Compared to the problem of achieving

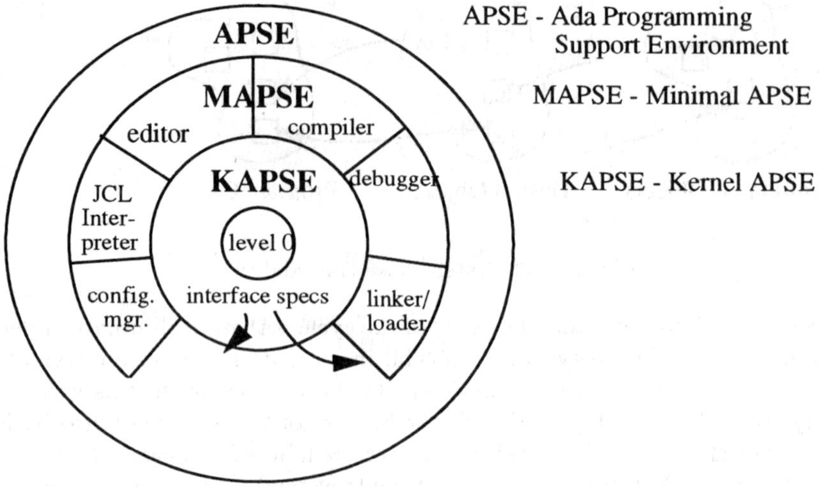

Figure 1.4 The APSE model

integration and traceability among objects belonging to the same phase, this problem is significantly more challenging. The reason is that specialized and largely incompatible notations have often been developed for the roles corresponding to these different phases, which in turn lead to different toolsets, developed by different organizations.

Just the first step, of combining and harmonizing notations, is a special and large problem. It is sometimes called "Method Integration", and is the subject of a separate book in the same series as this one [Kro92].

1.4 MODELS OF DEVELOPMENT ENVIRONMENTS

Several generic models of environments have been suggested, at varying levels of abstraction and detail. More as an example than as a complete survey, we will describe a few such proposals below.

1.4.1 Data orientation: the APSE

An early example, and one which has also had significant impact, is the *Stoneman* document [Bux80, Bux84]. This requirement specification for an Ada development environment established the APSE/MAPSE/KAPSE model, shown in figure 1.4.

Although Stoneman emphasized requirements rather than architecture, two central citations had important implications:

> "The toolset must not only support the appropriate functions, but must be integrated into a consistent environment."
>
> "The APSE must provide a well coordinated set of useful tools, with uniform inter-tool interfaces and with communication through a common database which acts as the information source and repository for all tools."

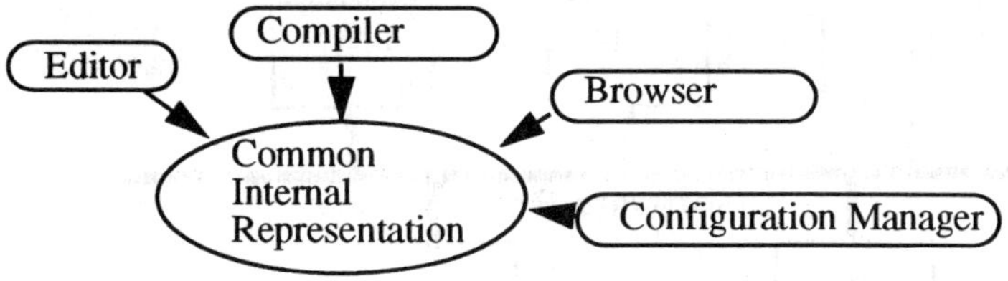

Figure 1.5

The first of these sentences emphasizes *integration* - the recognition that for significant progress to be made, tools must cooperate towards a common goal to a higher degree than was currently the case. The second sentence introduces the idea of the *environment database*, the all-encompassing structured data storage, which would act as the most important integrating factor in the environment. All this was placed in the three level KAPSE/MAPSE/APSE model, with the database at the very kernel KAPSE level.

Consequently, Stoneman can be viewed as an early example of an environment reference model. Because of its focus on the environment database, it was heavily oriented towards data integration.

1.4.2 Language orientation: Rational

An effort that closely adhered to the original vision of an APSE was the Rational Environment [Inf85, Rat86, Mor88], [Rip88]. It combined the larger scale project support attitude of Stoneman with ideas from early environments work, such as Interlisp, Smalltalk, and language oriented editors, and implemented a tightly integrated development environment dedicated to software development in Ada. Integration, and tailoring for the purpose, was taken far, originally with a special purpose hardware supporting an operating system that was completely dedicated towards production of Ada software. The compiler was built to be incremental, with most tools working against the internal representation of the (Ada) programs. The language, Ada, acts as the major integrating factor, resulting in a major example of the language oriented approach to environments.

Another central idea that was carried on in the Rational environment was that of the *unified internal form*, the idea that all data should be stored in a common format suitable for automatic processing. In this case, being strictly Ada oriented, this internal form emerged out of an abstract representation of Ada, the *Diana* representation, [MS]. All tools should access this common representation, and thereby achieve both simplicity and uniformity, as indicated in figure 1.5.

While most language oriented editors provided mainly syntax oriented support, whose importance in a broader perspective can be questioned, the Rational environment could provide further services like interactive cross referencing and semantic completion. Using the same language oriented and tight integration approach, services for configuration control and documentation support were provided.

The properties that contribute to exploring the benefits of tight integration can however at the same time be viewed as a problem. Requiring special purpose hardware

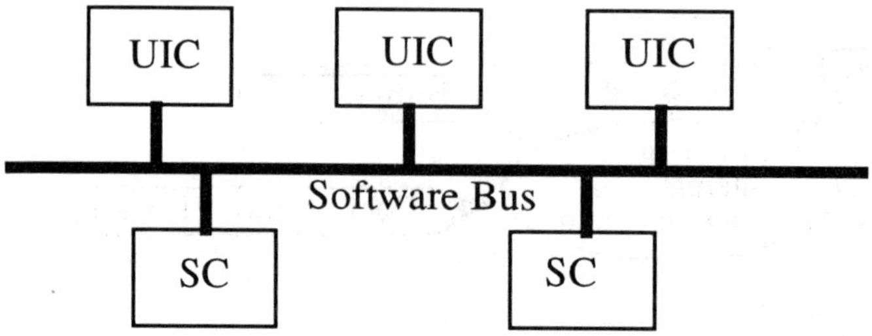

Figure 1.6

and a proprietary operating system is from some viewpoints very negative with respect to integration, since it may separate the environment from the continuous evolution of the rest of the world. The Rational environment is however one of the few novel environments that has reached the state of a stable product in industrial use.

1.4.3 Communication orientation: ESF

One of several later approaches is represented by the European multi-company co-operation *Eureka Software Factory*, ESF [CF88, FO89]. Among other characteristics, (such as an emphasis on process modelling), ESF suggests a communications oriented architecture, where components communicate with each other over a *software bus*. This approach more or less rejects the idea of the central database, partly on the basis that a large number of companies are unlikely to agree on a single standard database and schema.

Although not giving the full picture, the idea has come to be associated with the picture shown in figure 1.6. The User Interface Components (UIC) should contain the user interface, while the semantics of a tool, accessible through procedural interfaces, should be provided by the Service Components (SC).

1.4.4 Process orientation: ISTAR

Few concrete environment examples of strong process orientation have been reported. An early example of an environments effort with a strong "process orientation" was, however, ISTAR [Dow87]. Here, the programming aspect of environments was de-emphasized, claiming that we should instead provide support for the orderly management of projects, with all it implies in terms of visible organizations, responsibilities, project plans, and contracts. The latter word, *contract*, was made a basic concept, around which any project should be organized. ISTAR therefore supported the organization of a hierarchy of contracts, which defined what was the input and constraints, and what defined the expected deliverables. Figure 1.7 was used to illustrate the idea.

The holder of a contract was free to establish subcontractors, and, around this organizationally oriented structure, the rest of the environment should be grouped. Traditional programming support was treated by loosely integrating existing products into the ISTAR framework.

Experience showed however that it required a lot to express the ideas on project

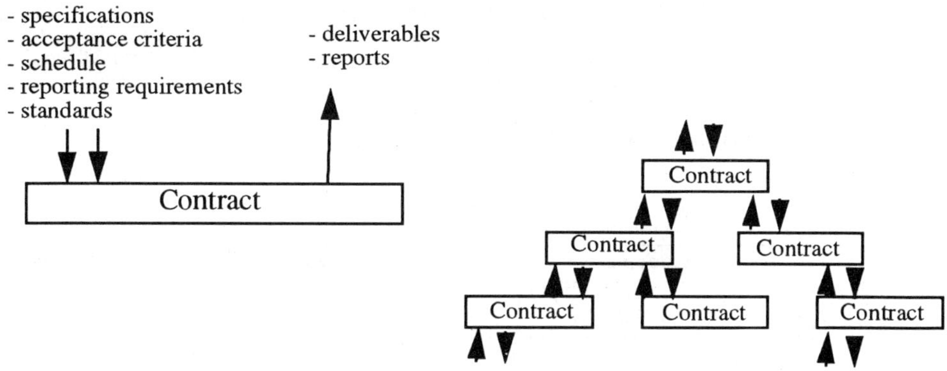

Figure 1.7

organization with a detailed enough semantics, so that conclusions and support could be automatic. As a commercial product, ISTAR was less successful.

1.4.5 A standards attempt: ECMA

An even more recent model-oriented work related to environments is finally the so-called *ECMA Reference Model for Frameworks of Software Engineering Environments*, which is a quite extensive enumeration of services that can be expected to be present in a CASE framework. It has recently been further developed in a cooperation with the US standardization organization NIST [ECMer]. Here, the model now incorporates a wider combination of approaches, getting close to the three dimensions of integration as originally introduced in [Sch89a].

- Data, that is intuitively understood as the degree of data representation uniformity among tools.
- Control, within which some, like ECMA/NIST, include both inter-tool communication and message passing mechanisms, but also the integrating effects achieved by the use of a common process model.
- Presentation, that is the extent to which the "user interface" is uniform among tools in an environment.

In addition, the ECMA/NIST model also addresses access and security issues, as well as administration of the environment (framework). Figure 1.8, which has evolved through a number of slight variations, has come to be associated with this "ECMA-model". As it is general and broad, the ECMA model provides less problem solutions. Since it is aiming at a standard, it has a rather singular flavour and does not analyze the multitude of actual architectures that may be built, and their advantages and drawbacks.

It is strong on elaborating the Data aspect - as it has evolved out of work related to the PCTE standard [ECM90], but is less developed in the Control and especially User Interface domains. It furthermore provides a single level of abstraction of tools. In fact, the ECMA/NIST document explicitly states that it does not discuss architectures and design alternatives.

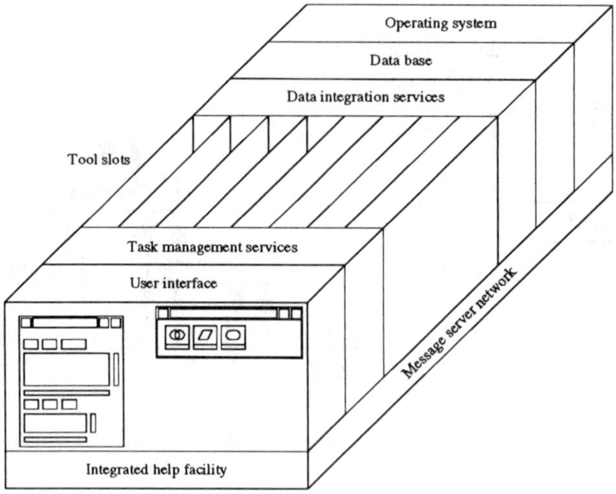

Figure 1.8 The ECMA "Toaster Model"

The work here therefore intends not to replace or debate the ECMA model, but to complement it in the following ways:

- providing examples and rationales
- identifying real problems of environments design
- pointing out multiple solutions and approaches
- pointing out different opinions
- using concrete ATMOSPHERE design and implementation work as the basis

Architectural design principles for development environments is a young but very fruitful discipline. It embeds the essentials of how to design large integrated systems while maintaining modularity and flexibility. The findings here can, and will, also have impact far outside the pure environments area.

1.4.6 The two CASE cultures

Most of the discussion above has its roots in the culture and approaches related to the Stoneman document. In parallel, however, another trend has more emphasized the design phase, providing support for drawing of dataflows, architecture diagrams, programme decompositions, etc. Much of this work can be traced back to practices and methodologies as documented in books such as Structured Design, [YC79], and Jacksons work on JSP and JSD [Jac75, Jac83]. Originally emerging in the telecommunications area, the SDL language [Roc85] evolved into an accepted standard for graphic description of software systems. In the Ada context, the so called Booch- [Boo87] and Buhr diagrams [Buh83] became well known and the basis for many tools.

Even though the methods included much reasoning about design principles, using concepts like Coupling, Cohesion, Object-Orientation, etc., the initially most important aspect was the graphics.

From initially being design methods, illustrated by more or less informal hand drawn diagrams, there evolved a need for easy maintenance of those drawings, and for mak-

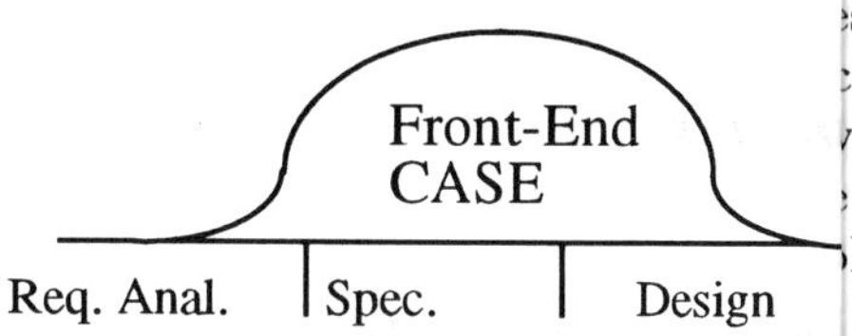

F

focused in on the earlier requirement
they correspond to Back-End CASE

Fast turnaround time in the edit-co
the Environments culture, while the
this issue, based on the assumption
the coding trivial. The Environment
prerequisites for allowing fast protot
the Diagramming tools culture fully

Mutual influence, and the fact tha
ually decreased the differences. The
attempting integration with code-ger
originally rather programming orient
into broad concerns for full project su
of integration ambitions.

The characteristics of these two cult
is further developed in [Sch90]. A re
[WM92].

1.4.7 Inter-phase traceabilit

Partly as a consequence of the differ
certain discontinuity in the support
identify islands of internally reasona
connect to each other to any extent
achieved within them. Exemplifying
the problem can be illustrated by fig

It seems to be inherent in the basic
behaviour of the programme can not
could execute it. If we had such a "des
itself a programming language, creati
software. Therefore, our definition of
incompleteness and abstraction at a l

As a partial remedy, many design-t
that parts of a program are generate
pler applications, much detail must st
outside the control of the design tool
nothing guarantees that the program
ment is that when further developme

sign representation and generate new
ways of incorporating the refinement
ious cycle.
general problem of inter-phase trace-
lutions can be developed. Progress this
a configuration management problem,
cise solution; and direct pairwise inte-
lifferent objects. Approaches classified
ation of earlier phases, such as design
such as code.

MENT ENVIRONMENTS

opposed to a set of independent tools,
ity that we associate with the former
re valuable and efficient than the sum
usly frustrating attempts at definition.
when we see it.

tion

hould remind ourselves what is the ul-
level it should meet little objection to

ffort is to increase the productivity of

e role of tools is most often in providing
doing so with short response time and
ne or context breaking dialogues with
efine the exact quantitative value of a
tive to its cost, the latter of which has

knowing about its need, finding it, and

e the computer is working.
g the result of the service in the context

d *time*, and a purpose of integration is

ound time of currently identified atomic
any typical pattern of the work process.
l interface is a common task, one could
aditional environment since it probably
ystem, explicitly locating a file holding

the interface, studying the interface and remembering it, and then returning to the first point of editing without any other result than what could be memorized during the break. Similarly, the user should with minimal effort have information on changes or new versions of the interface that have been, or will be, produced by his colleagues.

Given the above view of the goal, it is clear that cooperation among tools is a key issue. The first and third components of the turnaround cost can obviously be very effectively attacked by utilizing context information - making one tool explicitly utilize knowledge about the detailed state and context of the other tool. As will be described later, it also turns out that much less computer resources are consumed in a carefully built integrated system, making it effective in reducing even the second cost component.

Integration efforts have a cost, however. It is more complex, and require significantly more overview and architectural skill to create an integrated system than a non-integrated one. And, as will be discussed from several viewpoints later, there is an inherent tension between the desire to integrate components, in order to make the system more helpful, and the need to keep them separate and independent, in order to decrease overall complexity.

Any integration effort should therefore be carefully considered: whether it has a clear purpose and a high enough value and whether the increased complexity can be managed. This difficult judgement is the major responsibility of the environment architect.

1.5.2 Integration models

In recent years, it has gained increased acceptance to discuss the subject of dimensions of integration in terms of three "dimensions" usually called control, data, and user interface. Using the original version of [Sch89a], the definitions are as follows:

> The **control** integration aspect of a tool determines its communicational ability, i.e. the degree to which it communicates its findings and actions to other tools, and the degree to which it provides means for other tools to communicate with it. This includes the *temporal* aspect of immediate notification; the *selective* aspect of communication with a particular tool; and the *granularity* aspect of communicating changed circumstances with high precision.
> The **data** integration aspects of tools determines the degree to which data generated by one tool is made accessible and is understood by other tools.
> The **user interface** integration aspect is the degree to which different tools present a similar external look-and-feel, and behave in a similar way in similar situations.

The idea that those three aspects can be viewed as reasonably independent dimensions of the same underlying concept of integration is sometimes emphasized by presenting them as a three dimensional diagram (figure 1.11). As we shall see later, most aspects of environments can be accommodated within this model.

1.5.2.1 Process support

From the discussion earlier it is clear that the *human*, and the direct and indirect interaction among humans, is a major part of the turnaround time, and is therefore a

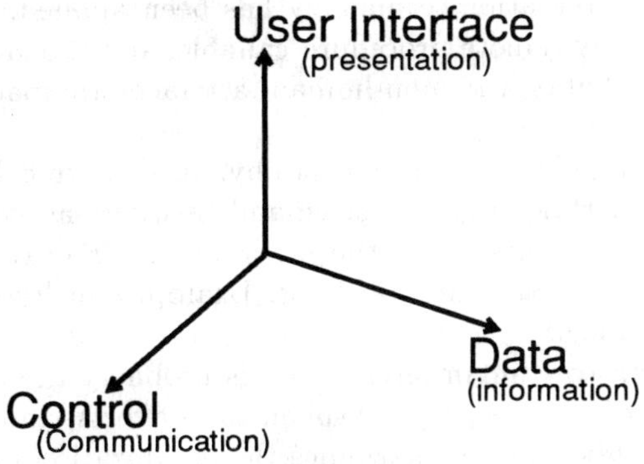

Figure 1.11 The three dimensions of integration

		Message Destination	
		Tool	**Human**
Message Origin	**Tool**	Communication	Process Guidance/ Notifications
	Human	Action	Cooperation

Figure 1.12

central part of the integration problem. It is then often proposed that the support for guidance of users and their collaboration *as a team* is incorporated into the model.

The addressing of these issues represents a major source of potential results, and is currently dealt with within areas like *Process Modelling* [IEE91] and *Computer Supported Cooperative Work* [CAC91, BRS91].

From certain perspectives, it is natural to include these aspects into the Control dimension, since it is an extension of the need for communication between tools and components into communication between different humans, and between humans and a computerized representation of a work organization. In the latter case, the word Control also carries an intended flavour of the human being (partly) guided by the environment.

Further refinements of this line of thought are achieved by making an explicit distinction between the various actors involved. The reasoning above has identified two such actors: humans, which together make up the organization, and "software components", which we for the current purpose just call Tools. The idea is summarized by figure 1.12.

The Tool to Tool communication is the most basic aspect of control integration, and where much previous integration technology has been applied. The provision of procedural interfaces, possibly remote procedure callable, and broadcast message systems are examples of this. Automatic, non-human, artefacts are made to utilize each other's services.

The Human to Tool communication is the most obvious and typical situation, where the user has decided to undertake a given action and therefore activates a Tool.

The Tool to Human case occurs when the environment is drawing more or less automatic conclusions to notify or guide the user. Examples include change triggers and enacting of process models.

The final case, of Human to Human interaction, is probably the most common. It is here that significant parts of large projects spend their efforts, and the efficiency by which this communication takes place determines the organization's overall efficiency. The Human to Human interaction may, of course, utilize the environment as a medium. This is in fact one of the most promising ways of increasing software productivity: by improving *team* efficiency. The ultimate software development environment should therefore include a large element of support for human to human cooperation. The generality of this issue makes it coincide with what previously was called Computer Supported Cooperative Work.

To conclude, we can accommodate the issue of Process into the control dimension, if we so desire. The key difference is the explicit inclusion of the Human as a party in the communication, and where the "highest" level is achieved when team efficiency is increased by humans cooperating better with each other.

1.5.2.2 Distribution

Another aspect of environment integration that may be addressed here is *distribution*. It is considered important because the very concept of an "environment" bears in it an ambition of supporting large projects. Since project size often makes centralization and co-location physically impossible, an environment architecture should provide for distribution while maintaining the benefits of integration.

While the Control dimension has an inherent distribution readiness, and the UI dimension is neutral in this aspect, the Data dimension requires explicit care for addressing distribution.

An easy way out of the problem would be to claim that data distribution is "hidden", that is we assume the existence of a data store that allows us for all interesting purposes to ignore the problems of distribution while assuming the advantages. A database that logically gives the impression of a single localized space, but which underneath is distributed as needed.

While results in distributed database technology do exist, it must still, as is the general lesson on applying database technology in environments, be adapted to the special requirements and characteristics of this application domain.

Therefore, distribution will here be addressed within the data dimension, rather than as an independent aspect of integration. As will be further discussed in the chapter on Data integration, the question is also related to version handling and concurrency control.

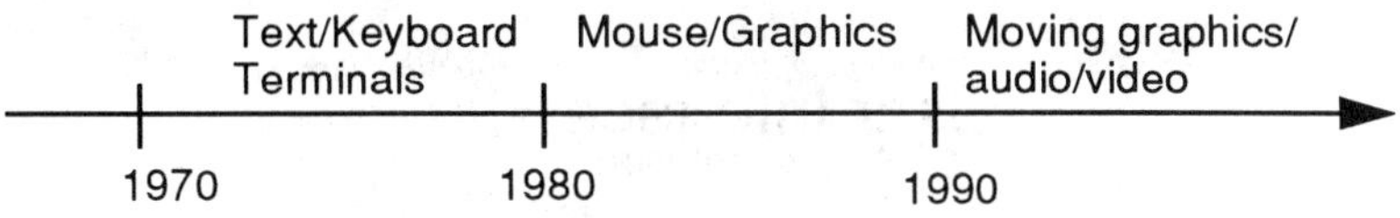

Figure 1.13

1.5.2.3 Integration dimensions revisited

We have now showed how to incorporate new issues of environments within the original definition of the three dimensions of integration.

The user interface area is similarly evolving, with new technology and approaches emerging. Just as user interfaces made a major step forward during the eighties, with the mouse, menu, and graphics interface replacing the limitations of purely text and keyboard based terminals, the next phase will extend into the use of even more advanced moving 3D graphics, audio and video (figure 1.13).

This latest area is usually called *Multimedia* [Com91], since it integrates many different media (such as graphics, video, audio) to make the human interaction more efficient. The area of *Hypermedia* [CAC92], is related, but focuses on providing efficient means for navigation and access in large, shared, distributed, information bases.

To be competitive and successful, environments must utilize those new technologies as they mature. Since the theme for this section is integration, it deserves pointing out that Multimedia may just as well be called Media Integration, since the really new aspect about it is the integration of previously independently existing technologies into a coordinated new whole. Its further integration and use in the development environment is a fruitful area for further research.

Having added this point to the user interface dimension, we can now revisit the three dimensional diagram with each axis annotated by increasingly rich and complex technologies and approaches. The result is shown in figure 1.14.

In retrospect, we can see that projects and proposals in the area of development environments have often had a different focus with respect to the dimensions above. Some of the large European efforts are good examples of this: while the Eureka Software Factory project has stressed aspects of the Control dimension with its emphasis on a Software Bus, other joint European efforts, such as the PCTE/PACT and EAST projects, have mostly worked in the data dimension. The "market" mostly addressed the user interface dimension by means of the standardization around X-windows and associated toolkits like OSF/Motif and OpenLook.

However, in a well balanced environment all three dimensions must be explicitly cared for.

Having seen that User Interface, Control, and Data really represent robust and important aspects of integration, we can already draw a simple conclusion with respect to the architecture of tools, as indicated in figure 1.15.

To support integration, tools should consequently provide open interfaces corresponding to all these dimensions. This is the basis for a tool being a good citizen in the environments community.

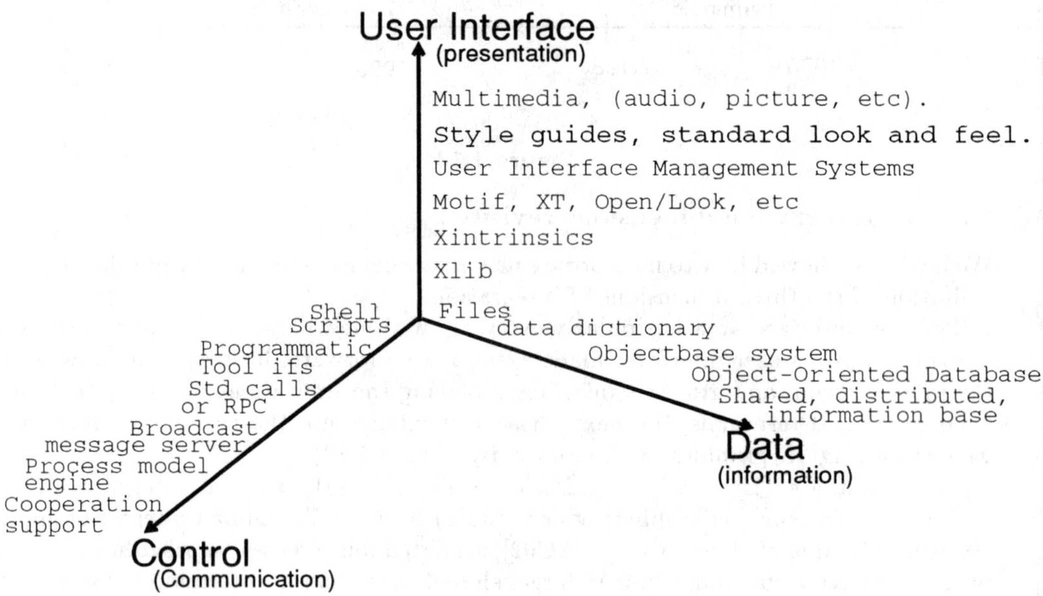

Figure 1.14 The three dimensions of integration

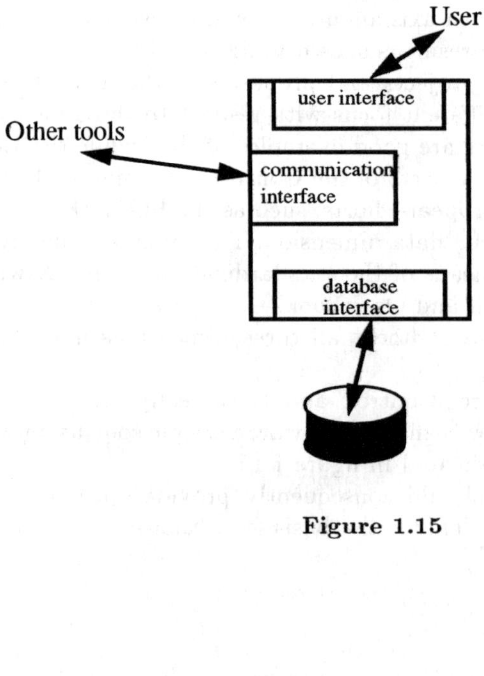

Figure 1.15

1.5.3 Levels of abstraction

Most thinking about environments has assumed that they consist of a set of tools that are assumed to cooperatively support the development. There is, however, in almost every environment a much richer structure, where multiple levels of abstraction can be identified, and where the requirements for cooperation/integration differ depending on the level. In this section we will develop this view in some more detail.

1.5.3.1 A multiple level tool model

The smallest entity of concern is called a *service*. The concept does not need to be further defined except that it should be an action performed by the computer that is of interest to a system developer. The services are partitioned into subsets that are called *tools*. Each tool should provide a well delimited set of services that are regarded as strongly related to each other while showing little overlap or dependency on other tools. The problem of designing tools is therefore similar to that of designing software modules in general, and we now arrive at the following definition:

> A *Tool* is a set of services that show strong internal cohesion and low external coupling.

The concepts of cohesion and coupling are well known and have been used before within the area of software design [YC79]. While not having a strong formal basis, they do correspond to an intuition about modularization criteria that is accepted within the software community. Here, we say that *cohesion* is a measure of the strength of the arguments on why certain entities should be grouped together, while *coupling* denotes the extent to which entities that we choose *not* to group together anyway depend on each other. In this sense, they describe the trade-off that always has to be made when modularizing systems.

In the context of development environments, the word integration is often used in the role of cohesion, while the requirement for low coupling is often talked about in terms of pluggability, extensibility, and composability. Examples of tools are editors, formatters, graphics design tools, compilers, etc.

Just as related services are grouped into tools, certain sets of tools are more closely related than others. Examples include a compiler and its associated debugger; a project planning tool and its critical path analyzer; a graphical design editor and its associated analyzer and code generator; a document editor, its spelling checker, and picture drawing subsystem, etc. Although being clearly identified as distinct tools according to the definition above, they are made to work closely together with certain other tools. We call this a toolset, and define it in a way similar to that of tools:

> A *Toolset* is a set of tools that shows strong internal cohesion and low external coupling.

The concept of an environment can now be explained in the same way:

> An *Environment* is a set of toolsets that shows strong internal cohesion and low external coupling.

There are fewer examples of environments than of tools and toolsets. The reason being that the task is bigger and therefore more expensive.

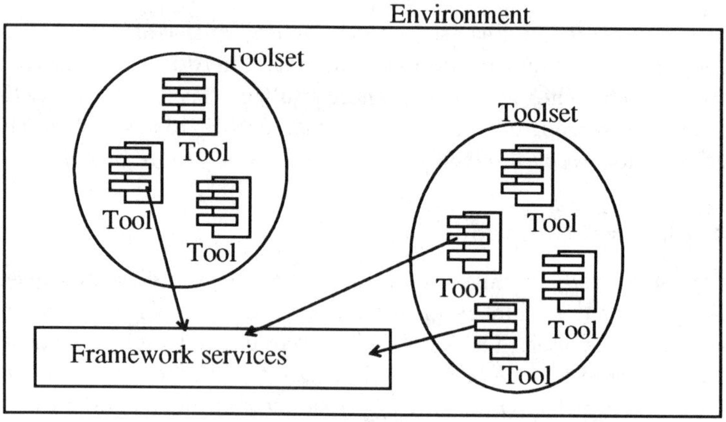

Levels of abstraction in development environments

Figure 1.16

As in every system, it is always a good thing to factor out common routines into separate reusable modules. This idea, of avoiding duplication of code, has always been one of the most basic driving ideas behind any system design. Tools are no exception in this case, and we therefore need an element in our model that explicitly identifies such basic pieces of software that we expect to be of use to many different tools. We call this part the framework.

> A *Framework* is a set of software modules that is expected to be of interest to several tools, and is therefore especially well documented and supported.

Utilizing a framework has the same advantages as reuse of software in general: it is economic and imposes uniformity among its users. The model is summarized graphically in figure 1.16.

So, we now have a hierarchical view of system development tools, consisting of *services, tools, toolsets*, and *environments*, where a latter entity is composed of a set of former ones. Parts of the tools are implemented by reusing services provided by a *framework*.

1.5.4 The integration dilemma

The definitions above embed a potential contradiction: the requirement for low external coupling at one level, such as between tools, is at the next higher level contradicted by the requirement on strong internal cohesion, such as within a toolset. We call this problem the *Integration Dilemma*, since it reflects the eternal tension between the desire to make independent modules while meeting the need for close cooperation between the same modules. The technical complexity, and thereby cost, increases as we try to satisfy both those requirements while addressing ever larger systems. The word integration has even sometimes come to represent this problem, and the area of integration techniques is emerging as an independent subject where systematic solutions are sought.

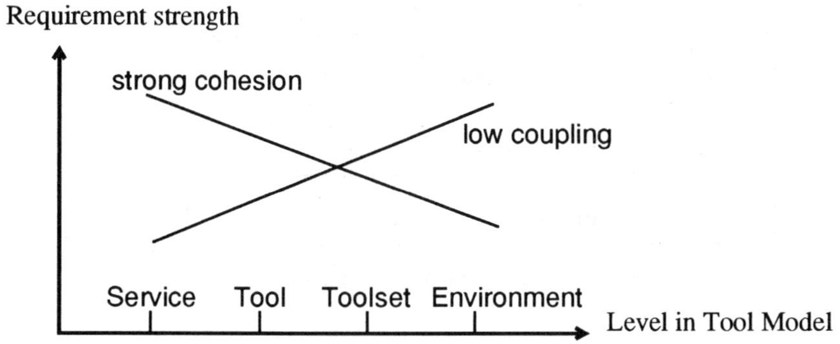

Figure 1.17

At first sight, the complexity of satisfying both the cohesion and coupling requirements seems overwhelming when scaling up the ambitions into large environments.

Part of the solution to this dilemma is in observing that the concepts of coupling and cohesion are relative, having slightly different meanings depending on which level they are applied. The "strength" of the requirement on cohesion is usually higher at lower levels in the model, while the need for low coupling is increasing at higher levels (figure 1.17).

This observation can be used to draw a number of further conclusions:

- It is possible to construct a full environment while still keeping overall complexity under control. Assuming that the total complexity is proportional to the sum of cohesion and coupling, (satisfying both at once), the above diagram indicates that this sum could be kept constant while scaling up from simple services to full environments.
- The increasingly strong requirement on low coupling at higher levels in the model fits well with an expected increase in diversity of implementation work organization. Different toolsets will be designed by different organizations.
- The difference in requirement emphasis at the different levels in the tool model makes it possible to use *different technologies* depending on the level.

The last point is of special concern to this document, since it points to the need for identifying not only a single, but multiple, problem definitions and solution techniques in the area of integration.

1.5.5 Relationship to development process and organization

The levels of the tool model identified above have correspondences with levels or entities that can be found within organizations. A single service or procedure corresponds to a single action or subtask performed by an individual. The gathering of a set of actions into a tool then corresponds to supporting a particular task or activity. Similarly, the toolset corresponds to a method or role, such as programmer, designer, documenter, etc. Finally the environments level corresponds to a complete development process or organization. The correspondences are shown by figure 1.18.

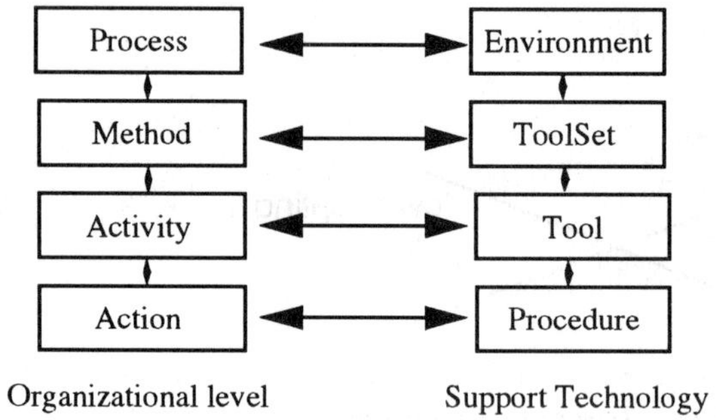

Figure 1.18

With this observation in mind, it is clear that in addition to managing the risk of significantly increased technical complexity, we must address the increased organizational complexity as we move upwards in the model.

Although not being the main subject of this document, it is clear that part of the reason why few successful environments are in use, is the increased need for education; adaptation to specific organizational needs and development culture; and the fact that an environment could disturb the often touchy political, managerial, and sociological patterns of the organization. The awareness of such issues become urgent at the environments level.

1.5.6 Openness

In recent years there has been a growing tendency to emphasize the importance of "openness", and due to its positive connotations the concept has been used to characterize a large number of things. System Development Environments should of course also be open, but the problem is that it is not completely clear what is demanded for a system to be "open". Usually, it includes ingredients such as building on standards, the ability to work together with other systems, adaptability, and the availability of some of the internal interfaces for public use.

General broad interfaces to basic mechanisms are however quite costly to publish, since they expose much of the internal structure (contrary to ideas of information hiding), and imply rather high maintenance costs. They must also be kept very stable, which introduces further limitations on the system's evolution. It is furthermore a rather passive way of stimulating integration, since it is the responsibility of the user of the interfaces to provide the added value.

In the context of Environments, openness has often been discussed in terms of how easy it is to adapt it to new needs, new tools, and new technology. It seems to be expected that an open environment should allow for any of its constituent parts to be replaced with other or newer technologies. Although a user needs an environment, he may want to use his own editor, configuration management system, or user interface style.

Based on this observation, we suggest the following definition:

> The *openness* of an environment is an inverse measure of the cost of replacing any of its subsystems with a new, external, one, without losing the original functionality.

The problem is therefore to find integration mechanisms that are easy and cheap to use, but which still provide the quality and depth of integration that was the original goal.

1.5.7 Conclusion

The "real" meaning of integration in Environments has continuously puzzled its developers. Many other views on integration have been presented, although the three dimensions used here seem to be the currently most stable and accepted.

A number of alternative and possibly more refined proposals are found in [IEE92], where several articles address this issue. Just to mention a few keywords, one can conceive Process integration , Framework integration, Interface integration, Tool integration, Team integration, and Management integration. As we have also noted here, integration can be addressed, preferably in different ways, at different levels. In [WM92], the Lexical, Syntactic, Semantic, and Method levels are proposed. In [BFW92], the levels of Mechanism, End-user service, and Process are instead suggested.

Since little can be proven in this area, work will continue until a model is developed that corresponds to most people's viewpoints and intuition about the subject.

2

Control Integration

At the core of the goals underlying control integration we find a desire to reuse tool functionality in ever new ways. It should therefore be possible to utilize the abilities of tools not only through the packaged end user interface, but through more basic procedural interfaces.

If this was the case, every tool would not only be representing a service available to an end user, but a library of reusable routines. In constructing a new tool, the functionality of others would be utilized, creating a pattern of communication/reuse (figure 2.1).

It seems intuitively clear that the amount of cooperation in the tool population is now increased, and thereby the level of integration. Tools could be viewed as basic building blocks, to be combined in new ways as needed by the circumstances.

Another rationale for the interest in control integration came from a reaction to the somewhat centralized nature of data integration. The hope was that by "communicating" instead of sharing a single database and schema, the benefits of integration would be achieved while not sacrificing the independence of tools. The communications approach also seems inherently more distributed, not even logically requiring any central point of definition and coordination.

When putting this idea into large scale use, at least two subjects present important problems that must be addressed in a systematic way:

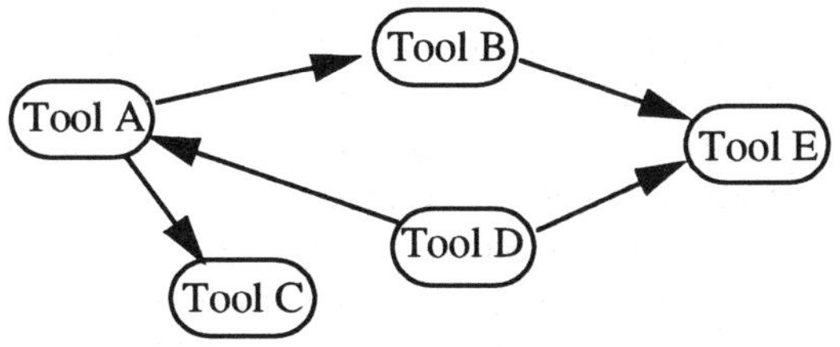

Figure 2.1 Communicating tools

Tool Integration: Environments and Frameworks, Edited by D. Schefström and G. van den Broek

- *Interprocess communication.* The standard technology for reusing software relies on simply linking the reused software into the client's code. In the case of large scale tool cooperation, this may result in an undesirable monolithic architecture. A possibly better approach would be to keep tools in separate processes, and provide programmatic access across processes. This technology is however more complex and computing intensive. Functions must also be developed to pack, convert, and unpack datastructures.
- *Interface/Component description.* The services and datastructures involved in a tool interface must be described in a way that is conveniently accessible to external tools. This has generated the development of various proposals that can be categorized as interface or component description languages. Here a number of sometimes very complex requirements must be met, such as language independence, expressive power, data typing, consistency checking, and naming and scoping. It is usually also expected that given such interface descriptions, it should be possible to generate the software for undertaking the conversions and data transfer operations.

Much work is being done to solve those problems. The ESF Software Bus [ESF91], and the ATMOSPHERE CIDL project [dV92] address both issues. Another example of an interface description language is the proposal of the Object Management Group [OMG91b]. Early work in this area was also performed around the Interface Description Language, IDL [SS]. The result is that a role similar to that played by the database schema in the data integration case will be played by the component description languages.

To further refine the picture, we will now turn to discussing a few concrete problems that often occur, and principles that can be used, in the area of control integration in development environments.

2.1 NOTIFICATIONS

Although one of the most basic of all design principles tells us that all the operations on a particular "object" or datastructure should be grouped into a single package, we can seldom maintain this principle in practice. It is usually possible to do so at lower levels, but since different higher level modules often provide different views of the same lower level object we get a consistency maintenance problem.

Consider, for example, an environment that consists of an Editor, a Compiler, a Database that holds information about the complete system, and a Browser that graphically presents an overview of module interrelationships (figure 2.2).

The Browser is used to graphically present how modules are connected, and allows the user to interactively explore the system at this level. The Browser reads the information from the Database.

The Editor is used to change source code, which is then analyzed by the Compiler which in turn stores information about the module, and its relationships to other modules, in the Database.

The Editor/Compiler and the Browser present different views of the same thing, and we all expect them to be consistent. When the Compiler changes the database, we expect the Browser to immediately reflect this.

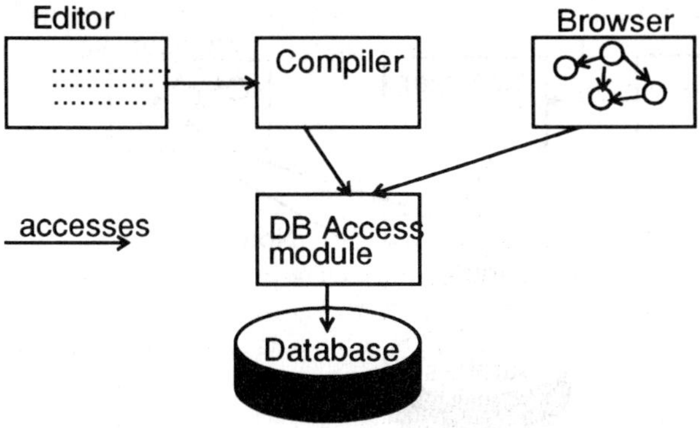

Figure 2.2

In this situation we have two extreme approaches with respect to modularization:

- Put the Editor/Compiler and the Browser in the same tool/module since they have an important datastructure in common (the Database).
- Accept the quite natural view that a Browser is a distinct module from the Editor, and consequently minimize their coupling.

Applied rigidly, the first rule would probably lead to a single but very large and complex tool, while the second rule does not tell us anything about how to achieve the coordination/exchange between the Editor/Compiler and Browser that we know *is* necessary.

The above is one example of the more general case when we have a need for temporal control integration, i.e. an immediate notification of a state change. We define it as follows:

> A *Notifier* is a mechanism for immediate passing of state-change information between modules/tools for which we otherwise want to minimize the coupling.

The very reason we distinguish this case from others is because it breaks an otherwise clean dependency structure. By clearly identifying the case, we can limit its negative impact, and maybe even find a special technique for its implementation.

Being the highest common module, the "DB Access Module" should notify all depending tools when any of them change the database, creating the access pattern shown in figure 2.3.

As will be later discussed, the notifier does not need to be implemented that way. Examples of techniques that are related to this problem are *triggers*, as discussed in the context of object management systems, and *broadcast message servers*, as provided in environment frameworks like HP SoftBench [Cag90].

2.2 DUAL USER INTERFACES

Assume that we want to use an existing text editor in the integrated environment described in the previous example. While utilizing this editor's standard text manipulation features, we would still like to have language sensitive services like interactive

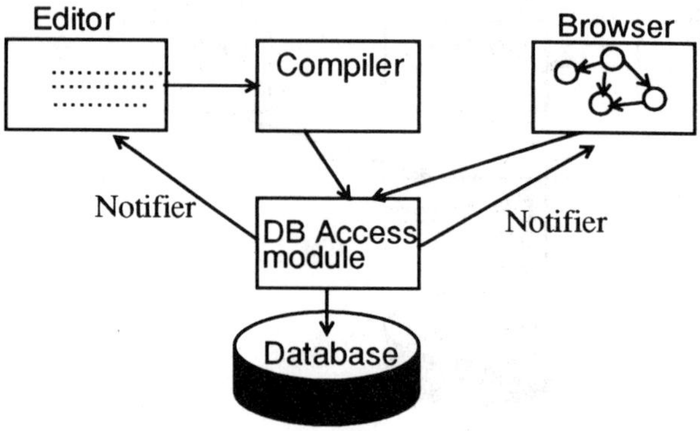

Figure 2.3

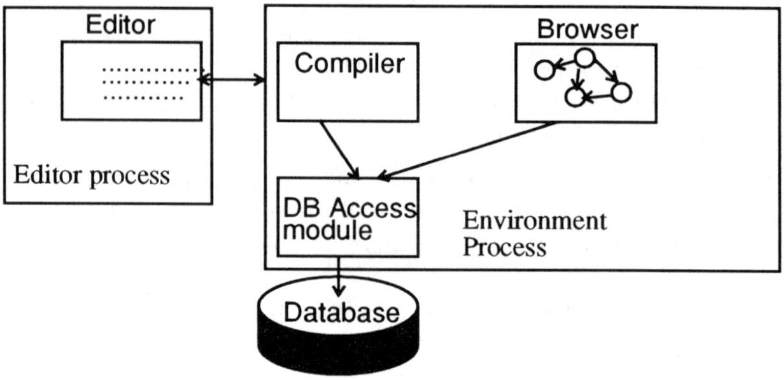

Figure 2.4

cross referencing, automatic template insertions, and a tightly integrated compilation service. Furthermore, we would still like to use the Browser and other non-editor parts of the environment. Extensible editors, such as Emacs, are available, but providing all basic functionality within the scope of the extension language is usually not realistic. Rather, the editor should communicate with another system that can provide it with the extra information needed to implement the desired services.

In terms of operating system processes we then end up with the configuration shown in figure 2.4.

From a user's point of view, the total system must be experienced as a homogeneous system. The user will sometimes interact with services managed by the editor and sometimes with the rest of the programming environment. It will even be the case that an action initiated while working in the editor will cause user interactions at the Environment process side. Some of the many examples are the following:

- When initiating a compilation from the editor, the error messages should pop up in a separate window allowing the user to point at an error and the editor to show that location in the program.

- The same pattern can be observed with services like semantic completion and interactive cross referencing: the editor has a user interface for text editing, while the Environment process already knows how to interact with the user to support other related services.
- The Browser, part of the Environment process User Interface, is used as a way of telling which unit to edit.

Some important conclusions can be drawn from the above examples:

- It must be possible to implement different parts of the same user interface as distinct tools, even as separate processes when needed from a product management point of view.
- Components must have the ability to respond to both interactive user actions *and* requests from other systems and processes.
- The initiative of a communication may originate at any place, pointing out a need for a very flexible architectural support.

2.3 COMPARING SOLUTIONS

As a small exercise we will now compare a few alternative solution principles in the light of the problems stated above. The three principles chosen are the following:

- Standard procedure calls, that is the simple way in which most current software modules are integrated.
- The Software Bus concept, as once proposed within the ESF project [ESF89, ESF91].
- The Broadcast message server, as exemplified by the Field environment [Rei90b], the Postmaster of the SDT toolset [GM90], and within HP SoftBench [Cag90].

As a guideline for comparing these principles, or architectural concepts, we must have some criteria. Here, we propose the following four:

- *Visibility.* The principles applied must be easy to observe in the software. There must be written documentation describing the principles and their application to different aspects of the design.
- *Efficiency.* The architecture must not impose any significant performance degradation. Rather, a good architecture should make the system more efficient.
- *Extensibility.* It must be easy to add new subsystems and functionality to the system. Ideally, this should be possible to do without changing existing parts.
- *Suitability.* The architecture must allow us to meet all functional requirements, and must therefore not impose limitations on needed internal communication between modules.

A good principle should compare well in all four aspects.

2.3.1 Standard procedure calls

Control integration closely corresponds to the most basic and natural way of combining independent modules in any software system: by means of direct calls of each other's procedural interfaces.

In general software, this way of combining modules is so self-evident that it is sometimes even not identified as an independent means for integration. Just define the procedural interfaces as needed, define the calls as needed, link the application into an executable, and run.

The benefits of utilizing another module by calling some of its externally visible routines is self-evident: it is very efficient, we get close control over error conditions and special cases, we get immediate response, and the interfaces are usually rich enough that we can achieve all our purposes.

Strange enough, it has not always been possible to use this most basic form of integrating software pieces for building environments. The reason is that the tools that we want to combine into toolsets and environments have seldom been thought about as modules in a larger system. Rather, they have been manufactured as "final" packaging attempts by independent organizations.

Referring back to our evaluation criteria on an architecture, we conclude the following with respect to "standard procedure calls":

- *Visibility.* This is maybe the weakest point since, as an integration technique, it is too obvious. It has no special and easily recognized name, but its presence is just assumed when nothing else is said. It is visible only by means of the interfaces that may be called.
- *Efficiency.* Standard procedure calls are the most efficient way known for communication between modules.
- *Extensibility.* The existence of procedural interfaces for a tool is a basic means for extensibility. When building new tools, existing tools can now be reused and be made part of a larger system. The extensibility is in other words good.
- *Suitability.* Standard procedure calls as such do not impose any restriction on intermodule information flow and access patterns.

We can conclude that standard procedure calls are a very attractive approach to integrating tools, since they are efficient, extensible, and suitable. The approach is however not clearly visible as an independent integration mechanism.

In terms of the levels in the tool model, it seems like standard procedure calls are most suitable in those cases where the involved components are manufactured by the same organization or team and will always be sold and used together. Since the technique requires a single virtual space, it also has a tendency to generate few and large processes.

2.3.2 Software bus

The name "software bus" has been used in a number of contexts, usually with the purpose of emphasizing the pluggability aspect of a software design. Because of the generality of the concept several different interpretations are available, we shall here concentrate on an interpretation used within the Eureka Software Factory project, and prototyped within subprojects like EASE [Con89].

The ESF software bus builds on the recognition of the need for programmatic interfaces to software tools. Consequently, all tools within the project should present programmatic interfaces.

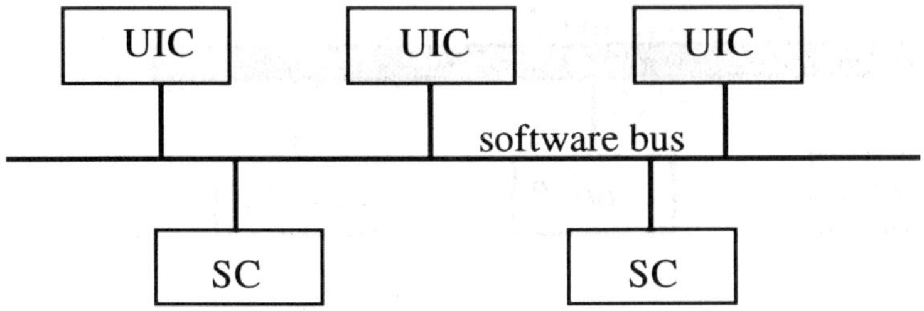

Figure 2.5

In addition to this probably well accepted need, the ESF interpretation of Software Bus and the ESF Architectural Guidelines impose a number of further requirements:

- The procedural interfaces are located in *Service Components*, (SC), and should not perform or initiate any user interface actions.
- All user interface actions should be implemented in *User Interface Components* (UICs), which in turn call Service Components for semantic actions.
- The User Interface Component and the Service Component should be put in separate processes.

The term Software Bus has therefore in this context come to represent the facilities used for implementing the calls from a UIC to a SC. Figure 2.5 has often been used to illustrate this architecture.

The ESF Software bus is not yet completely defined, and several interpretations and alternative approaches are available. Some of the interpretations impose further restrictions and principles, while others take away some of the requirements mentioned above. The separation into UIC and SC components can be argued to be a property of the ESF Architectural Guidelines rather than the Software Bus itself. They have however always been presented and used together in a way that makes it natural to treat them interchangeably in this context.

An initial evaluation of this idea against our architecture requirements is as follows:

- *Visibility.* This is maybe the strongest point about this interpretation of a software bus. It delimits options and thereby creates contrast. It has a nice graphical look. It provides a strong correlation between abstract architectural entities (UIC and SC), and easily recognizes computing elements like processes.
- *Efficiency.* Here, the requirement on UIC-SC process separation is the major risk. There is not necessarily any performance degradation if care is taken to avoid high frequency or bulk data utilization of the software bus. There are, on the other hand, no reasons to believe that performance will be improved. The requirement on process separation has furthermore indirect effects in that there are many kinds of references, like pointers, open files, etc., which are bound to the memory space of a particular process and cannot be directly utilized in a different one: process separation has a tendency of forcing interfaces to be "value"-oriented rather than "reference"-oriented.
- *Extensibility.* The provision of procedural interfaces guarantees a basic support for extensibility. In terms of practical use, the software bus does however introduce both

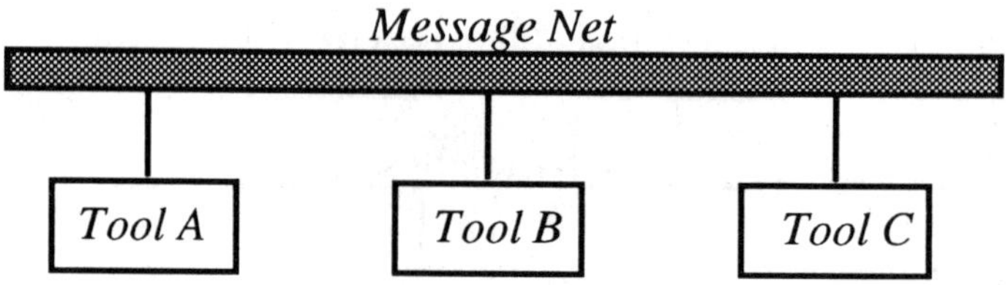

Figure 2.6

advantages and drawbacks relative to the more basic standard procedure call case. On the positive side, the separation into different processes automatically removes the potential problems involved in the use of different programming languages. On the other hand, more complex software is involved both at the caller and client sides to make use of the bus possible.

- *Suitability.* Depending on the interpretation, this is probably the weakest point, since there are several known important cases where needs are identified that are in conflict with Software Bus principles: the requirements on separation into different processes and the unidirectional control structure. This can be seen from the problem examples (sections 2.1 and 2.2), which identified the need for a quite unrestricted communication pattern.

The conclusion is that one must either extend the concept of a Software Bus, or if some interpreter of the concept has already done so, further emphasize and explore flexibility.

The tendency is that process separation is better suited at higher levels in the model than at lower levels. The extra complications relative to the straightforward standard procedure call solution must be motivated by some other aspects, which are probably easier to find at larger granularity of components. As will be discussed later under the section on "Tool Granularity", a requirement on distribution should be present to fully motivate process separation.

In addition, it is believed that the control mechanism, such as the communication bus, must be de-coupled from other ideas on how to design tools, such as User Interface-Application separation.

2.3.3 Broadcast messages

If we like, we can probably view any need for communication between tools as an instance of the *notification* problem described above. The solution idea that this problem points to, is to invert the control flow and responsibility for initiating the right calls, and leave this to the consumers of information rather than the producers. Following the always very seductive temptation of uniformity, one could even suggest that the whole environment should be built around such a communication mechanism. In its simplest form this idea, called *Broadcast Messages*, can be illustrated by figure 2.6.

The idea here is that tools report their results, actions, and state-changes by sending out a message on the net, with the expectation that if someone is interested he should

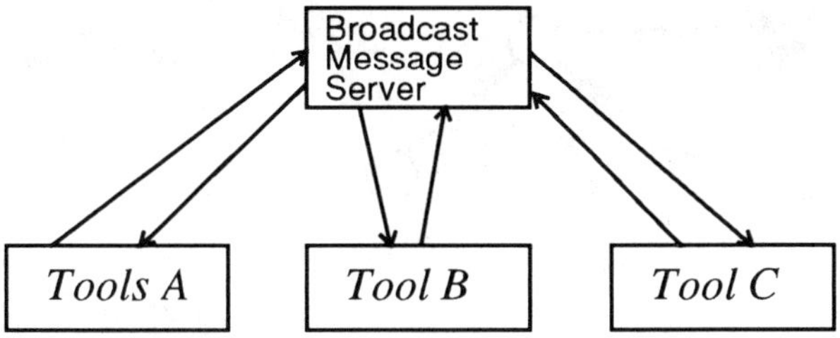

Figure 2.7

listen, somewhat like a common ether. This simple idea has several advantages in this context:

- Since we do not address other tools directly, we are not dependent on them.
- The extensibility is good, since the very idea embeds the property that adding a new tool does not disturb the ones already connected.

Notification and regular calls are now unified and are handled by the same mechanism. This does not remove deeper semantic dependencies between tools - waiting for a needed response is a dependency - but the mechanism as such is rather minimal in this sense. When implementing this idea, one discovers that at the level of software technology we do not have any convenient raw material corresponding to that of an electrical Ethernet. Therefore, on implementation the Message Net is usually replaced with a software component that provides a similar functionality.

The idea also seems to have strong aspect of non-determinism: the tools should be able to "listen" and send messages like concurrently executing entities, leading the thoughts to processes. However, as will be discussed later and also elaborated in the chapter on User Interface integration, solutions to a very similar problem are standard within user interface technology without using multiple processes. With these remarks in mind, we can develop a probably more realistic architecture, shown in figure 2.7.

Tools call the Broadcast Message Server for two reasons:

- Sending of a message, whose further delivery is the responsibility of the Server.
- Subscription on a certain kind of message.

The Server calls tools when delivering a message.

Again, it is worth noting that the pattern is similar to the style developed in the area of User Interfaces where the widget library takes the role of the Message Server, and the tools correspond to the applications. In this case, the applications call the widget library to register "callbacks", which are then called by the widget when a corresponding event occurs. The analogy should be clear. However, this established solution seldom utilizes, and definitively does not require, separate processes.

Similar ideas have been developed in the area of database technology under the name "triggers". From the point of view taken here this is the same thing as discussed above, but applied in a different context. We therefore do not develop that aspect further here. We should now match this solution against requirements and tool model:

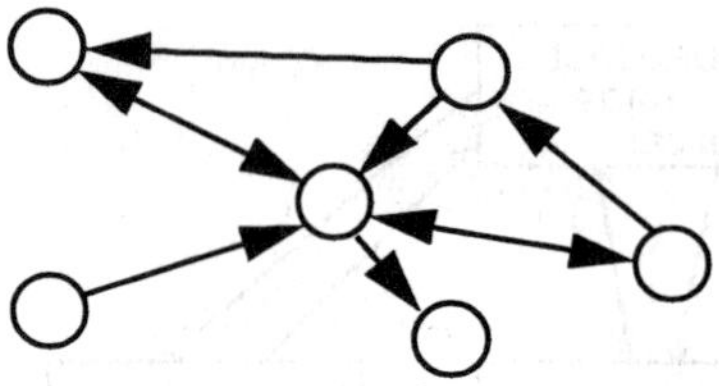

Figure 2.8

- *Visibility.* At the abstract level the visibility is very good. The principles and advantages are easily explained from a simple figure. However, when moving into practical implementations it may be hard to maintain this clear structure, since, as we noted above, implementations of the same ideas can here look very different. An accepted standard at the more implementation oriented level is probably required.
- *Efficiency.* The UI style of callback implementation is basically standard procedure calls and is therefore very efficient. If the implementation instead moves to a process level mechanism more care is needed to keep the performance.
- *Extensibility.* This is the strongest point about this technique. It imposes minimal technical dependencies.
- *Suitability.* No principal limitations can be observed. A multiprocess implementation may impose the general restrictions that are connected to virtual space separation.

The same basic principle can be used at several levels in the tool model, possibly in different implementations. At lower levels, the widget style callback, single process, implementation is suitable. At higher levels, the organizational and product managerial aspects indicate that a multiprocess implementation should be used.

2.4 TOOL GRANULARITY

Communication oriented integration techniques bear with them a suggestion that the message receivers/senders are implemented as separate processes, implying a network of communicating components (figure 2.8). As with all models, there is a temptation to utilize it uniformly in as many cases as possible. On the other hand, experience has shown that there usually is a limit where such unification efforts cease to contribute, and instead start generating drawbacks.

A classical example is the data granularity problem of tools where unification desires suggest that the same data model and database should be used for all kinds of objects, "large" as well as "small". Practice indicated, however, that the needs for data modelling, and especially the implementation techniques, were different at different levels of abstraction.

In the same way, one could suspect that pushing the interprocess communication model too far will experience similar problems. A comparison with the database approach shows several similarities:

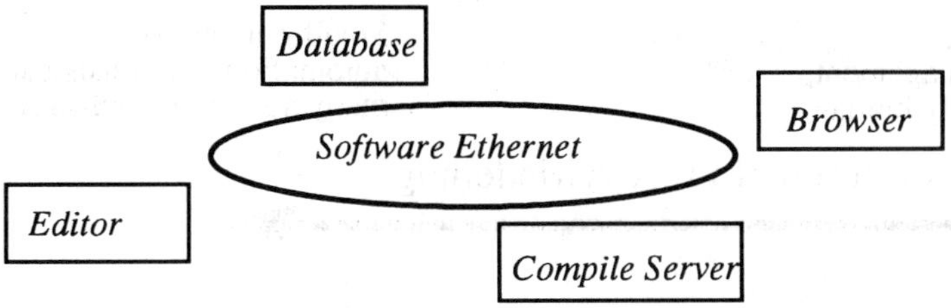

Figure 2.9

	Database	Control
Unifying vision	Single model for all data (size and type).	Single communication technique for all components (size and type).
Advantages	Common access, semantics, and implementation	Common principle and implementation.
Drawbacks	Bulkiness and inefficiency when used outside intended size range.	Virtual space separation, communication overhead, and code duplication may cause similar problems.

As with all modularization or object identification work, it is not obvious how to find the "right" objects with respect to the criteria at hand. Even a simple example illustrates some of the trade-offs (figure 2.9).

What are the objective reasons for selecting either a multiprocess solution or another technique, like standard procedure calls, for integrating two components?

- Why not view the Compile Server, which provides translation, checking, and query facilities, and the Database, which provides the storage and access, as a single component?
- Why not make the Editor and Browser a single component? They probably share a lot of input data, and should together make up a seamless editing/viewing service over a range of software abstraction levels.
- Why not view them all as a single component, since they are anyway intended to be used together in a closely cooperating way?

These larger components could still send and receive messages with other similar components, while using another technology for their internal communication. Different rationales could be developed for choosing one or the other, and the following includes some of the arguments that can be used. Use multiprocess solutions, such as the broadcasting, in the following cases:

- The component has a genuine end-user value independent of other components.
- The component must be implemented and maintained by an organization or groups different from those having responsibility for the other components.

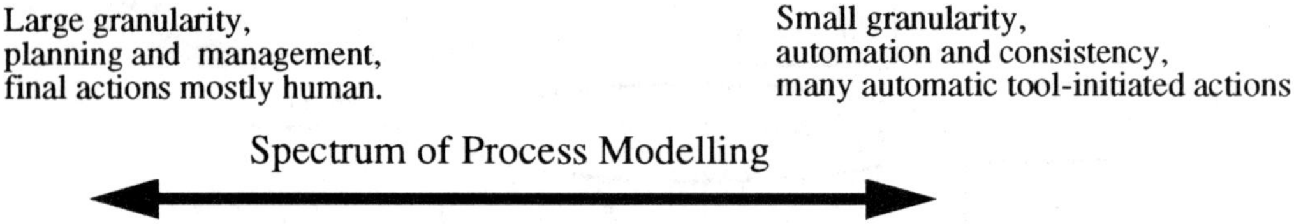

Figure 2.10

- The component has technical needs or potential for parallel execution, such as a debugger or a system for parallel distributed compilation.
- The data communication needs between components is moderate with respect to access frequency, volume, and data structure complexity.
- There is little shared code between components, or the sharing can be managed in some other way (such as "shared libraries", "dynamic linking", etc.).
- Replacement of components is likely and frequent.

2.5 PROCESS MODELS, ENGINES, AND ENACTMENT

The idea of process modelling is ultimately to execute, or "enact" , a model of the development process. In its interaction with the environment, the user would get hints, guidelines, and directives to support and direct his work. Just as we will see with several other subjects, there exists a spectrum of approaches, ranging from viewing the process model as a rather abstract specification at the level of typical project plans, with relatively little pure automation potential, to rather detailed workflow control with a high degree of automation.

The observation is illustrated by figure 2.10. Let us call the left side of the spectrum "management oriented", and the right side "automation oriented". The management oriented approach has less of a detailed automation ambition, but is instead trying to extend and integrate the traditional project plan into the environment, to make it more available and visible to the project members. Viewing this component as a "Process Engine", it would integrate in a rather loose way, mostly interacting with humans (figure 2.11).

The user is supplied with a list of "tasks" to be performed, and when finishing a task he reports this back to the process engine. In this case, the process engine could be viewed as a groupware variant of a developed project planning tool.

Because of the limited interaction between tools and the process engine, this level of functionality requires less integration, and is therefore less complex to implement. A number of systems of this kind have been built, where the "Task manager" of the DSEE environment [LC84] can be viewed as a simple early example. A recent example of a product dedicated to this area is Process Weaver [CAP92].

At the other extreme, at the Automation oriented part of the spectrum, there is envisioned a higher level of automatic conclusions and direct interaction between the process model and various tools. The picture shown in figure 2.12 may be more relevant in this case.

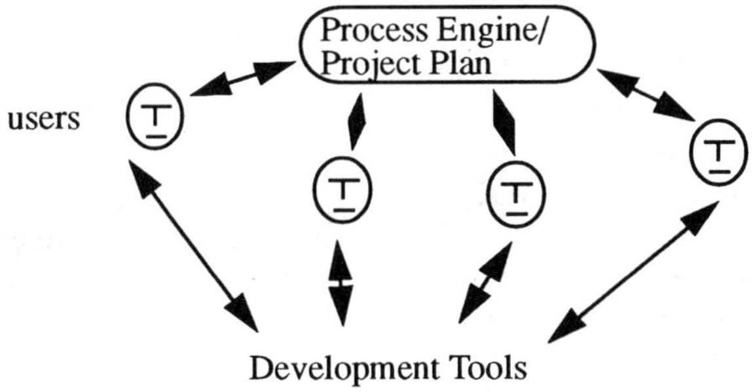

Figure 2.11 Management oriented view of process modelling

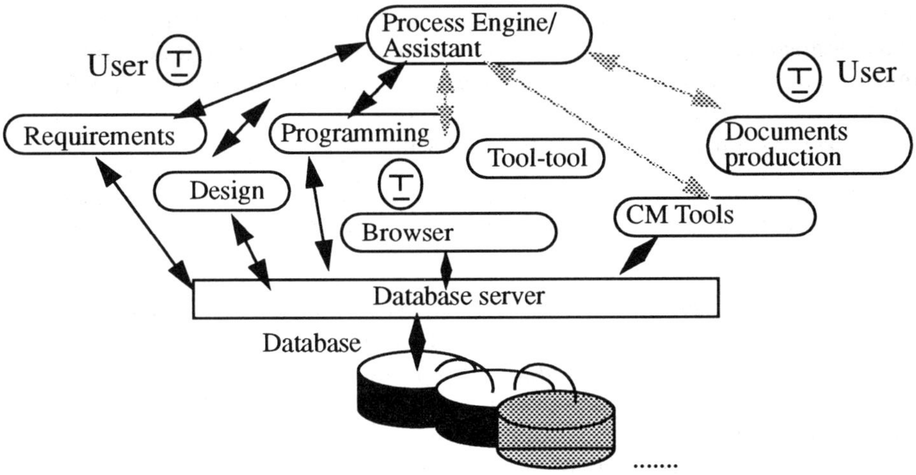

Figure 2.12 Automation oriented view of process modelling

In this scenario, the process engine continuously receives state information from the actual process by means of the tools implicitly reporting about it. The engine uses this information to draw conclusions, (as programmed into the process model), and responds with directives to the tools and/or the user.

This approach has, obviously, a higher ambition in terms of automation, but is also more complex to implement, since it requires a rather tight integration with the various tools. This presents a similar dilemma to that in data integration: tools must to a large degree now be engineered for openness, and be involved in cooperation in ways that are not easy to plan for beforehand.

The desire towards automatic conclusions creates two tendencies within this approach. The first is that, for automation to be possible, one must go down to a rather detailed and mechanistic level of the work process, such as keeping track of the fact that certain modules have been made obsolete by the change of some central interface, or that a certain tool should be invoked after the application of another one. In those cases, the process modelling overlaps what is otherwise regarded as configuration management or general consistency handling.

A second trend, while currently less emphasized, is trigged by the inherent complexity of being able to automatically draw intelligent conclusions on what to do next. In such cases the experimentation with Artificial Intelligence related rule-based techniques for expressing the process model has been proposed.

2.6 COMPUTER SUPPORTED COOPERATIVE WORK

Outside the pure environments area the same problem, of imposing computerized support and structure on human cooperative activities, has been addressed. The emphasis has been more general, and less oriented towards formalizing a specific process. Rather, the development has oriented itself towards general human interaction patterns, and technology for supporting less strongly structured information exchange. A few recent publications in this area are [CAC91], [ECS91], and [Uni91]. A typical definition of this area, usually named CSCW, is the following:

> The use of computers and communication to improve the means for cooperation between people, by elimination of differences in place and time, while adding extra value and quality to the process.

A number of techniques and approaches can contribute to this goal, like computerized meeting systems, electronic bulletin boards, meeting schedulers, multimedia electronic mail, computer integrated video and audio systems (sometimes called "picturephones"), and workflow management software [Ovu91].

The area has relationships to Multimedia [Com91], in that it will make use of many different media to make the human interaction efficient, and to Hypermedia [CAC92], in that a main focus will be on providing efficient means for navigation and access in large, shared, distributed information bases.

The term *Groupware* is often used in this context as the name of a distinct piece of software that provides services in the area of CSCW.

In defining the concept, some authors especially stress the information sharing aspect, such as [EGR91]:

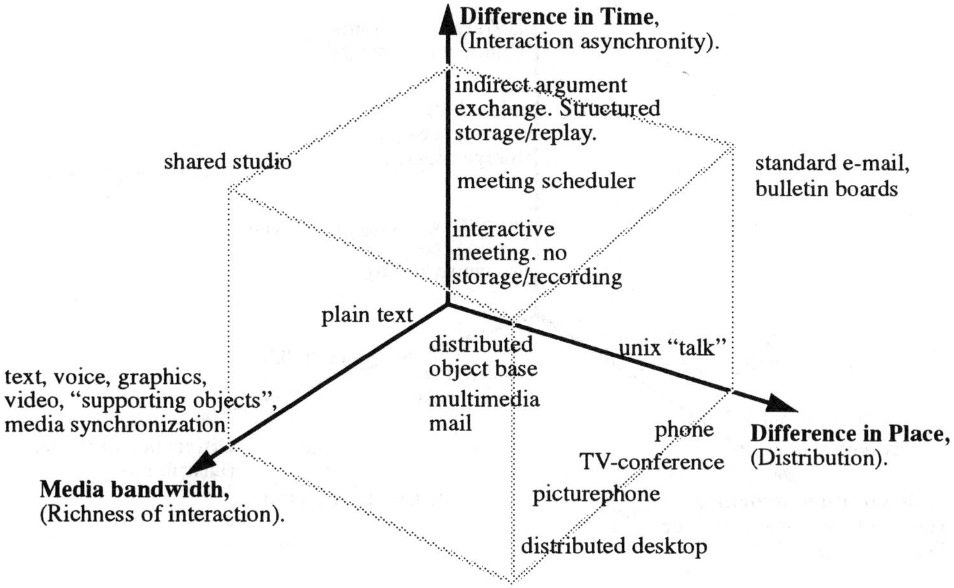

Figure 2.13 Dimensions of CSCW

> We define *Groupware* as computer-based systems that support groups of people engaged in a common task (or goal) and that provide an interface to a shared environment.

The idea is relying on communication technology and distributed systems, in that the important usages of CSCW will be those where it connects geographically separated people.

The fact that the necessary infrastructure, in terms of computers and communication, is largely established, while project sizes and therefore probability of physical separation is increasing, makes distributed CSCW solutions increasingly interesting.

A number of technologies have been developed which can be used to address this area. In figure 2.13 we categorize some of these by evaluating them with respect to essential CSCW characteristics such as *Difference in Place, Difference in Time*, and *Media Bandwidth*. The reader is invited to characterize his favourite tool or technology with respect to these dimensions. After some analysis, one can however identify a few basic building blocks:

- The asynchronous building block, typified by the Multimedia Mail tool, which allows for people to differ in both time and place.
- The synchronous building block, typified by the Distributed Desktop, which allows for real-time but distributed interaction around shared documents.
- The distributed object-base, which is a necessary precondition for most activities.

Instead of using the Media Bandwidth as the third dimension, we can also characterize CSCW approaches with respect to how rigid a set rules for collaboration they impose (figure 2.14).

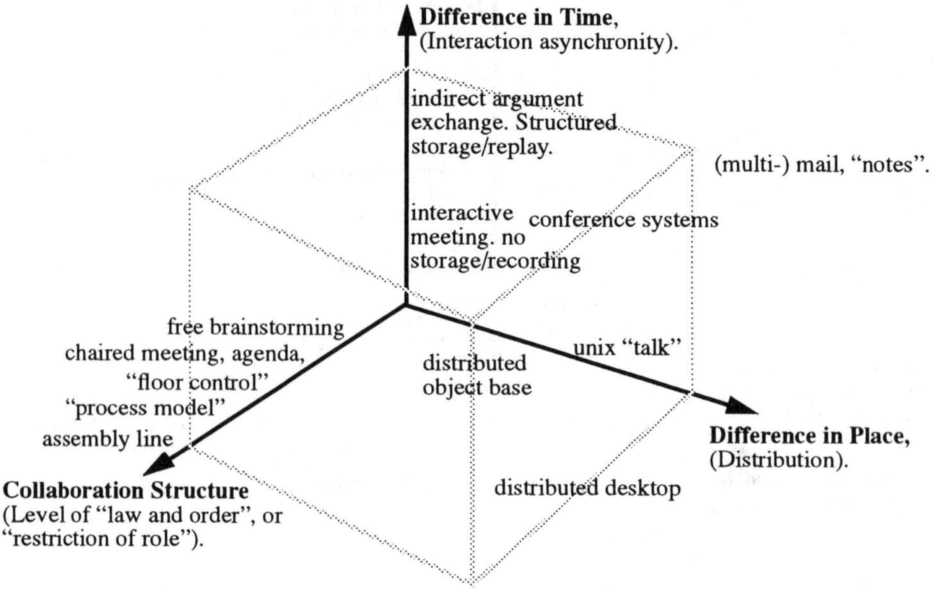

Figure 2.14 Dimensions of CSCW, alternative.

In this diagram, we instead emphasize the range of interaction possibilities that exist, from free brainstorming over highly structured development processes up to the specialized but inflexible assembly line.

2.7 COORDINATION TECHNOLOGY

It seems clear that similar visions of creating a computer based framework for working in teams have been developed both within the environments and CSCW communities. The wordings have been just slightly different:

CSCW		**Environments**
"shared environment"	<—>	Information management
view "common task or goal"	<—>	Process management view

The CSCW community is however, more than environments, emphasizing distribution, to eliminate difference in place and time, and multimedia, to increase the human interaction bandwidth. But the similarities are large enough to envision a combined approach, which may be referred to under the name *Coordination Technology.* This will be an important future direction for system development environments.

3

Data Integration

One of the original ideas of support environments is that of the *environment database*. In this place, all relevant information of a project should be stored. Tools and users would then benefit by utilizing the now complete availability of information to draw the right conclusions, answer questions correctly, and in general increase the level of automation.

The environment database has often been thought about as a network of information pieces, jointly explored by users and tools, as indicated by figure 3.1. This mental picture has made it natural to talk about "objects" and "entities" as the information pieces, while the various dependencies and references between them, often drawn as arrows, have been called "relations".

An environment database becomes interesting and important to the extent it is a complete and reliable definition of the project state. From the data oriented viewpoint, the progress of a project can even be defined by the growth, in amount and quality, of the objects it produces. The state of the environment database should reflect exactly this.

Given the presence of this database, a number of challenging visions could be realized. Every user would in principle have online access to all information, speeding up

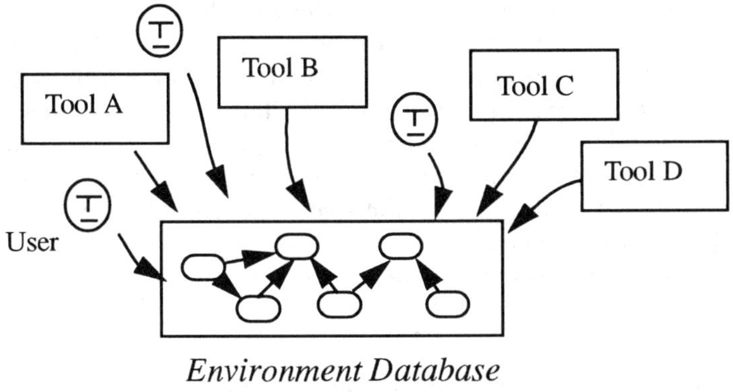

Figure 3.1

Tool Integration: Environments and Frameworks, Edited by D. Schefström and G. van den Broek

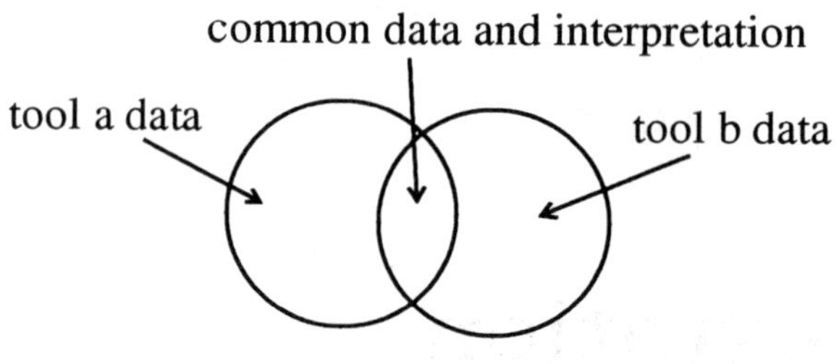

Figure 3.2

decision making and problem understanding. A small information revolution seems possible, where the user can, in more or less structured ways, browse around in the data, similar to the way it has been envisioned within the area of Hypermedia [CAC92]. In [Sch91], the vision is expressed as the creation of a "Software Hypertext Engine", with a complementary "Disorder Combat Engine" to deal with change. In [CR92] a similar hypertext-based approach to environments is described.

Tools would benefit in a similar way from this information availability. Various conclusions could now be drawn automatically, since data generated by one tool would be available for use by other tools. This is now close to the core of the idea: tools utilizing each other's data represent an increased level of coordination and information reuse, and a potentially very efficient division of labour in the tool society. We say that tools *integrate*.

The road there is however not an easy one. First, we must ensure that the information is stored in a way that makes it suitable for automatic manipulation, and in a format that is understood, to the degree necessary, by all involved. This is usually dealt with under the label of *Data Models*.

We must then also plan for how to collect the data in the first place, and how to maintain it in the face of change. This fact, that the data discussed here is continuously changing, is an extremely complicating factor, and is the most distinguishing point of the environment database when comparing it with other information access problems, like the Hypermedia paradigm mentioned above. Change is in fact one of the most characteristic attributes of software, and can not be avoided. Rather, change is the sign of life and progress, and should be supported, not hindered. All this is addressed by various techniques and approaches within *tool to database integration, consistency control*, and *configuration management*.

These are the issues to be addressed over the next sections.

3.1 DATA MODELS: A WAY OF IMPLEMENTING COMMON ASSUMPTIONS

For integration to take place, components must understand each other. This may be done by accessing the same piece of data with some level of common interpretation. In fact, the degree to which two tools are data integrated can be said to be proportional to the degree their interpretations of data intersect (figure 3.2).

The larger the intersection, the more data integrated the tools are, arriving at the following alternative definition of Data Integration:

> The degree of *Data Integration* among a set of tools is proportional to the extent their interpretation of data intersects.

This definition does not say anything about the quality, relevance, or value of such shared interpretations. Therefore, it states the necessary preconditions although they are not sufficient in themselves.

We now need a way to manifest clearly and enforce those common assumptions, both at a conceptual and implementation level. A natural way of doing this, that has been used many times before, is to introduce a Data Model. Those parts of the tool data that are expressed in terms of this Data Model will then automatically achieve a level of commonality with those other tools that have also used it.

More precisely, a Data Model can be defined as consisting of three parts:

1. A set of *Object Types*, which are the basic building blocks available in expressing data.
2. A set of *Operations* on the Object types and combinations of them.
3. A set of *Construction Rules*, constraining the way Object Types can be combined.

A set of tools using the same data model therefore also agree on the corresponding set of Object Types, Operations, and Construction Rules. This, therefore, defines the extent of their data integration. Sometimes points 1 and 2 merge, emphasizing the view that operations are really part of the type. In some cases, such as with non-navigational operations, (like "give me all objects such that condition C is satisfied"), it is however less natural to group this way.

Besides conceptually defining data integration among tools, the data model has an obvious software engineering implication: the software corresponding to the Operations can be factored out from the tools and implemented in a single place, rather than be repeated in every tool. This also applies for all further operations that can be built in terms of the initial ones. In this way, we standardize not only concepts, but also implementation. The economical advantages of this should be obvious.

The issue of meta-models, meta-meta-models, etc, is ignored here. Instead we take the view that any given data model always acts as a kind of meta model for anyone who wants to add new information. The existing rules (model) must be obeyed, but is on the other hand extended into a new model by addition of information. From this point of view, the issues of "meta" are completely relative, and less interesting for the purposes here

It should also be understood that the reasoning in the following is qualitative rather then quantitative. Precise numeric measures will seldom be possible. However, as with any models it fills an important role in sharpening our conception of important facts about reality, and helps in defining names for what is observed.

3.2 REPRESENTATION CONVERGENCE

We have concluded that to achieve data integration, the various tools must represent at least part of their internal datastructures in terms of a common data model. The fact

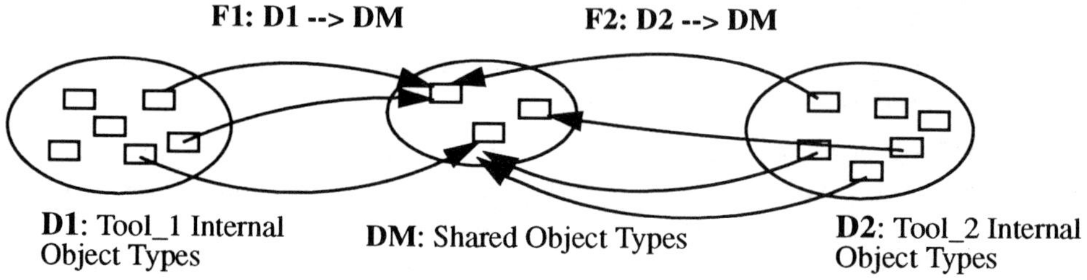

Figure 3.3

that this data model is shared makes tool more unified and integrated. The process of data-integrating tools can therefore be viewed as providing a mapping from the domain of internal object types to the domain of shared object types. This is illustrated by figure 3.3.

The functions (mappings) are restricted, in that not all of their domains, D1 and D2, are mapped, but just parts of them.

Most benefits are obtained in those cases when internal object types of different tools are mapped into the same shared object type, since we can then immediately prove that two object types that were previously unrelated now share a number of operations. A more precise measure of the degree of data integration is therefore obtained by the cardinality of the set for which the mapping functions give an equal result. For a given size of the involved data models, this can be expressed as follows:

$$R = Card(\{d \in DM \mid \exists d1 \in D1, \exists d2 \in D2, d = F1(d1) = F2(d2)\})$$

This expression, R, is called the *Representation Convergence*, since it describes how well the data representations of a set of tools converge when being mapped to the same data model.

Since we have defined the shared data model to be the only shared information between tools, the mapping functions $F1$ and $F2$ can be viewed as otherwise uncorrelated. This implies that R depends only on the cardinality of the domain of shared Object Types, DM, since the larger the cardinality of DM, the smaller is the probability that $F1(d1) = F2(d2)$.

This result suggests that data models should always be made very small (simple), so as to maximize the Representation Convergence. However, each time two internal object types are mapped to the same shared object type, there is a risk that this new object type does not completely cover the intended semantics. The extent to which it does is called the *Semantic Fit*. A decreased Semantic Fit affects data integration negatively.

Since a small domain of shared object types leaves us with lower mapping resolution, we must conclude that, on average, semantic fit decreases with the size of DM. We can then assume that the amount of data integration is proportional to the sum of Representation Convergence and Semantic Fit, leaving us with the function characteristics shown in figure 3.4.

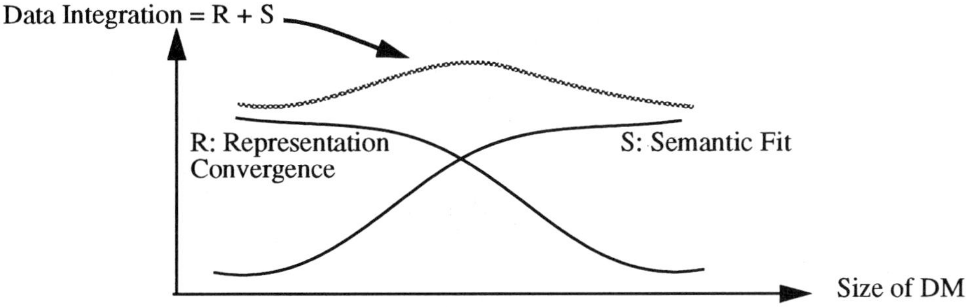

Figure 3.4

The goal is, in other words, to find a data model as small as possible, without losing too much of the semantic fit. The maximum of the summary function above may be possible to calculate precisely. For now, however, we believe that it must be sought by applying "Sound Engineering Judgement".

3.3 DATA GRANULARITY

Experience in trying to achieve data integration in development environments has many times shown that important simplifications can be made by distinguishing between different levels of granularity of data. "Large" objects have different characteristics and relevance than "small" objects.

In many cases we already have a natural distinction between large and small granularity of objects. Most programming languages have a "module" concept which summarizes the inner structure and the relationships to other modules. In fact, many believe that every language or design notation that is intended for serious large scale use must have a module concept. In C++, there are classes, and maybe files; Ada has its packages; SDL provides process blocks; documentation systems and formatters provide chapters and sections.

Another way of finding the border between small and large is to look for the smallest object that it is reasonable to change and work on independently. In configuration management, this is often called the Configuration Item (the smallest object of which independent versions are made). Quite often, this will coincide with the concept of a module. In database and object management systems a decision must also often be taken on which is the smallest object for which to support locking and independent access rights. Again, a border between two sizes of objects can be found.

The conclusion is that every notation that is used in describing aspects of software development can be expected to have a "module". In finding the "large" level of granularity, we should select what is a natural module of the notation at hand.

Another important observation is that Representation Convergence is often more important at a large granularity level, while Semantic Fit is a critical issue for most kinds of small objects. This is quite natural, since larger objects are usually also more

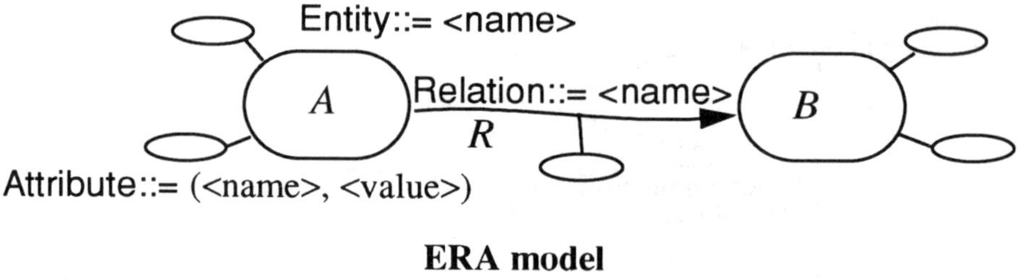

Figure 3.5

abstract, and need less specific representations than the small granularity data. The latter are more numerous and varied in structure, and therefore need more specialized representations to be efficient.

To conclude, we should use a smaller and simpler data model for large granularity objects, to ensure Representation Convergence, while smaller objects need a bigger and more complex data model to ensure Semantic Fit.

A remaining problem is now to select and integrate these two data models, corresponding to large and small object granularity, without creating an unproductive discontinuity.

3.4 SELECTING DATA MODELS

There are many well known examples of data models. The Entity-Relation-Attribute (ERA), Rational, and the C++ Type System will be used here as concrete examples. These examples are, however, quite arbitrary.

The Object Types of the ERA model [Che76] are Entities, Relations, and Attributes, while its Construction Rules state things like "an attribute can be associated with exactly one entity" and that "relations can only be placed between two entities". Examples of Operations are "give me the entities reached from entity E, following relation R". Figure 3.5 tries to summarize this model.

The Object Types of the Relational model [Cod70] are the Relation, Tuple, and Attribute, (sometimes called Table, Row, and Column). The Construction Rules say things like "all tuples within a relation must have the same number of attributes", while the Operations include the well-known select, project, join, union, and difference.

The Object Types of the C++ type system [ES90] are finally all the constructors, records, arrays, pointers, etc., together with predefined types, while the Construction Rules state the many ways in which these may and may not be combined, rules of compatibility, etc. The Operations are, as we know, numerous.

There should be little objection that the C++ Type System is a much larger data model than the others, and therefore represents a point on the right part of the diagram in figure 3.4, generating little representation convergence. It does, however, allow for a very good semantic fit. It is therefore well suited for small granularity objects. For the

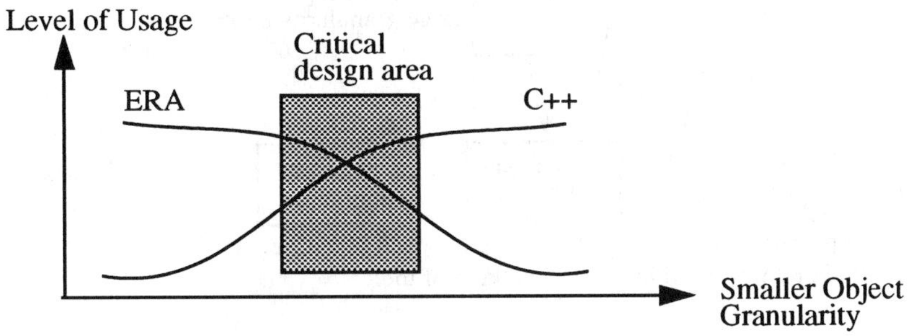

Figure 3.6

large granularity side, we propose the ERA model, because it meets the requirement of simplicity, and thereby good representation convergence.

The ERA model is furthermore very well known, and seems to be the intuitive way many people reason about data at a higher level. One should note the fact that most abstract design notation proposed, as provided in many development environments, are basically slight variations of ERA.

Because of its widespread use in many areas of the information industry, we will later briefly return to the relational model, and its suitability in environment applications.

3.5 INTEGRATING DATA MODELS

The problem to be solved is how to integrate the two data models of ERA (large objects) and C++ (small objects), so that they can be used together in a smooth and convenient way. At the same time, we must ensure efficient use of available technology. The situation can be summarized by figure 3.6.

A range of solutions exist, of which the following two may be the end-points of a spectrum.

- *Separated type systems*, where the small and large levels are strictly separated.
- *Type specialization*, where we utilize inheritance and specializations to achieve a continuous type system from the large to the small.

In the first, separated, case, entities at the large level are made to have special "attributes" that may contain an arbitrary inner structure.

There are operations to read and write bytes from and to this "attribute". At the level of the ERA model, the data inside this attribute are just a sequence of bytes, similar to how the file system views a file. Just as with the file example, the program performing this read and write is responsible for imposing any further structure or semantics on those data.

The advantage with this solution is that it is simple and is known to work. It leaves complete freedom for tools to use any means for representing the small granularity data. The drawback is that we impose a discontinuity between the data models which

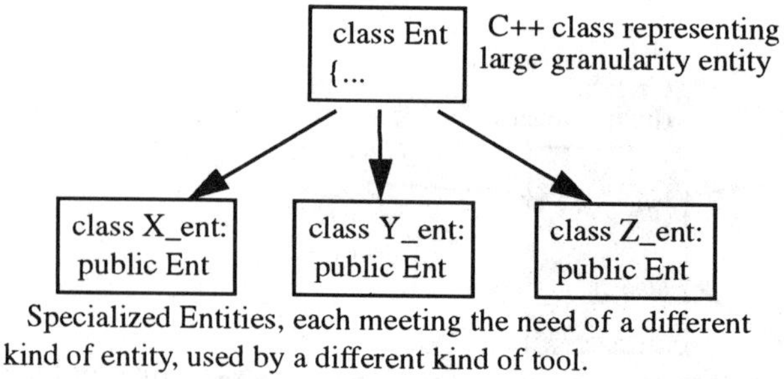

Figure 3.7

is felt conceptually annoying. In addition, this may result in the loss of certain benefits of Object Oriented Databases (assuming such is used in the implementation).

In the second approach we attempt to maintain a single continuous type system by utilizing the C++ ability of type extension by specialization, (inheritance). The idea is to represent Entities by C++ classes, which may then be inherited in the creation of arbitrary other classes (figure 3.7).

The parent class, Ent, provides all operations that are needed to make it an Entity (insert and delete relations and attributes, investigate relations and attributes, etc.). This behaviour is inherited by the children classes (which make them all Entities at this level). They may add arbitrary datastructures and operations. The full freedom and power of C++ is available. We have however still a single type system, and get the convenience and power of polymorphism and dynamic binding without limitations. The presence of this specialization hierarchy also invites further categorization of entities and tools.

Obviously, the highest level of the class hierarchy corresponds to the large granularity shared data model (ERA) while the lower levels correspond to what we have called the small granularity level (full C++).

3.6 SEMANTICS OF SMALL GRANULARITY DATA

We do not expect, per definition, that tools will be able to understand and interpret each others small granularity data. This is defined to be the domain of the large granularity data model. This does however not stop one tool for utilizing information, and asking queries, that require knowledge about this finer granularity level. It just says that the only one who can produce the answer is the tool which maintains those fine granularity data, and questions must therefore be directed there.

This very reasonable and practical division of responsibility results in the architecture shown in figure 3.8. It means that tools must provide public interfaces that summarize the operations they offer on private data. It also means that other tools must know about, and explicitly address those interfaces, and therefore to some extent depend on them. This is unavoidable if services concerning the level below the shared datamodel are needed. Tools do still not, however, need to know about each other's internal representations.

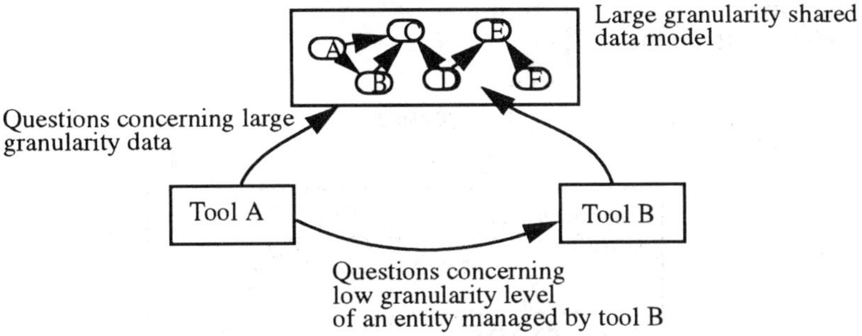

Figure 3.8

3.7 DATA CREATION AND MAINTENANCE

As discussed earlier, the environment database is interesting only if it contains relevant, accurate, and up to date information. A major problem is how to collect this data and maintain it.

A central requirement is that we want this to happen as automatically as possible. We do not want a system with significant delay or extensive manual procedures between the original creation of results by project workers, and its storage in the database. To ensure the vision of the database being the true reflection of the project state, the distance between working action and database should be short.

This can however only be achieved by tools integrating rather tightly with the database, making information flow into the database as a side-effect of users working with the tools. To achieve this, tools must express the data for which they are responsible in terms of the agreed-upon data model, and ensure that those objects are always stored in the database. In the context of data management, we now make the following assumptions about Tools:

- Every tool creates, modifies, and maintains data objects.
- The data objects are persistent, in that they must maintain their state between independent invocations of the tool.
- The data objects are usually not accessed all at once, but in convenient pieces or aggregates called *modules*.
- There are *relations* between modules, describing how they depend on, or otherwise refer to, each other.

To integrate with the database, the tool must represent its modules and dependencies in terms of the agreed data model. The work can be divided into two categories:

- *Statics*, that is structuring of persistent data in terms of modules/entities and relations.
- *Dynamics*, that is the insertion and maintenance of modules/entities, relations, and attributes to reflect the user's work.

The static modelling of data in terms of ERA must be performed on a case by case

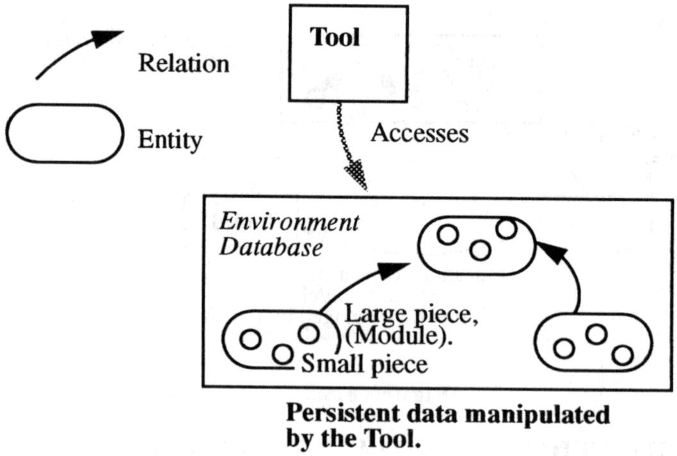

Figure 3.9

basis, depending on the characteristics of the data or notation involved. The general idea is however the identification of large granularity pieces of data, which are then represented by entities. The small granularity part is considered part of the entity's inner structure, and is left outside this ERA modelling work.

Attributes should be used as a way of summarizing important aspects of entities. Although the inner structure of an entity is the private domain of the tool, one can in many cases find ways of summarizing its state or properties in a way that is suitable for representation as an attribute, and thereby making it accessible to everyone. The attributes can therefore act as one way of creating a bridge between the private small granularity data and the public world of large data. It is therefore the responsibility of the tool to maintain the attributes so that they reflect the change of the entity as performed by the user.

Similar to attributes, the relations should be used as a way of summarizing important aspects of entities. However, while attributes describe properties of the entity itself, as seen in isolation, the relations are used for summarizing how the entity relates to other entities. Just as with the attributes, this information must often be derived from the private inner, and small granularity, data structures. It is therefore the responsibility of the tool to maintain the relations so that they reflect the change of the entity as performed by the user.

The relations are however more complex in that they are also often central in dealing with the concept of consistency, as will be developed later. The resulting situation is illustrated by figure 3.9.

To summarize, the cycle when using a tool is as follows:

- Accessing of an existing module for change or further development.
- Alternatively, creation of a new module.
- Checking and validation of the changed, (or new), module.
- Persistent storage of the result.

At each step, the tool interacts with the database.

3.8 REQUIREMENTS ON ENVIRONMENT DATABASES SYSTEMS

The special requirements and characteristics of environment databases have now been thoroughly investigated for several years. It has been concluded that the needs for this application domain are different enough to require the development of a specialized technology. Among many others, [Ber87] is reasonable argumentation concerning this question.

Here we will summarize some of the points that are currently felt to be the most important, and claim that environment databases must provide the following:

- *Data Model and Schema Management.* The datamodel offered should be close, preferably equivalent, to what an application program would anyway use. The database datastructures should naturally fit as runtime datastructures of the application. The database must also accommodate change in its basic structure, its schema, in a flexible way.
  Some of the trade-offs involved here were discussed in the initial sections on data integration, such as model complexity, data granularity, and object/entity orientation issues.
- *Distribution and Multidatabase architecture.* The overall database must be possible to build up through pieces that can be independently accessed and distributed.
- *Long transactions.* It must efficiently handle a granularity of change that is quite large, and that can be extended over time.
- *Version and configuration management.* It must be possible to introduce, maintain, and track multiple versions of what otherwise should be considered as the same entity. This then implies that larger sets of such versions must be possible to manage systematically, that is, support for configuration management.
- *Multiple views.* Different users must be able to have different views of the same collection of data. That is, be able to independently work on different configurations without replicating parts that are still shared.
- *Change and consistency management.* The Environment database is to act as the foundation for a highly dynamic and changing process: that of software development. It must be possible to allow change in a controlled way, and to propagate changes to depending entities and even to other users.
- *Support for work process and cooperation.* There must be support for systematically re-integrating the changes implied by the many and parallel long transactions in a way that maintains control over consistency and makes cooperation among users smooth.

Several other proposals exist for finding the essential issues of environment databases. For example, [Kat90] identifies a related set of concerns, named Organization of the Version Set, Configurations, Dynamic Configuration Mechanisms, Version Grouping, Instances versus Definitions, Change Notification and Propagation, and finally Object-Sharing Mechanisms. Although Katz's point of view is emerging in the CAD database community, it is easy to relate his points to the ones proposed above. In both cases the need for a basic version concept is identified. While Katz talks about Dynamic Configurations, we approach the same problem in terms of the more general concept of a "view". There is a similar concern for managing change and consistency.

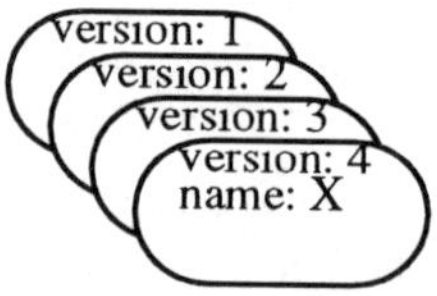

Figure 3.10 Multiple versions

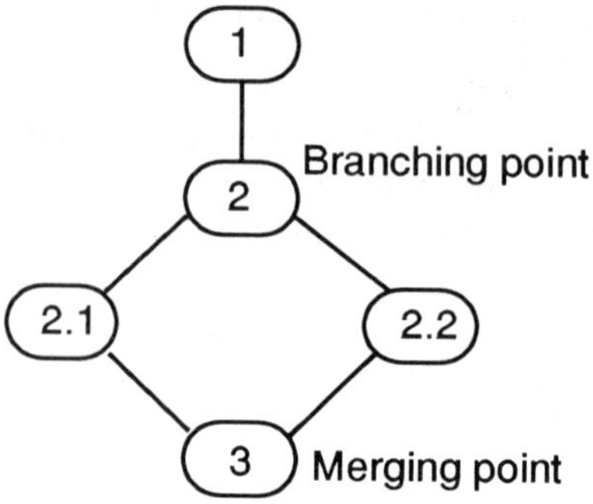

Figure 3.11 Version graph

Katz does however not emphasize distribution, nor configuration management as part of a cooperative process, the latter of which relates it to process modelling and computer supported cooperative work. The conclusions show however very clearly that environments for CAD and CASE share a lot in their needs for data management.

In the following sections, we will take a closer look at the above issues.

3.9 VERSIONS AND CONFIGURATIONS

The systematic management of different *versions* of objects has always been central to development environments. The reason is the well-known special characteristic of software development: *change*.

By changing objects, while saving a previous state, we end up with multiple versions of the "same" object. We will not attempt to provide any precise definition of what makes certain objects versions of each other. For the purpose here we accept they are so if the user says it, and view the role of the development environment as to reflect and maintain this stated opinion. We also assume that the concept of versions is tied to what we previously have called the large granularity level. It presents little problem conceiving multiple versions of Entities. We cover the intended semantics by just allowing them to have the same "name", distinguishing them by version numbers (figure 3.10).

The set of entities that are considered versions of each other are called a *version set*. Most often we also need the ability to express parallel versions, *branching*, as well

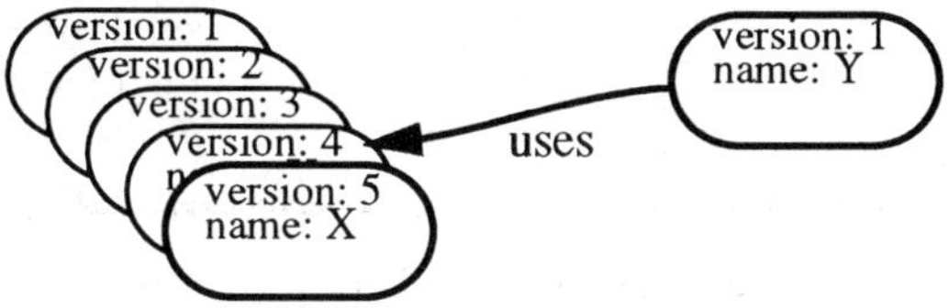

Figure 3.12

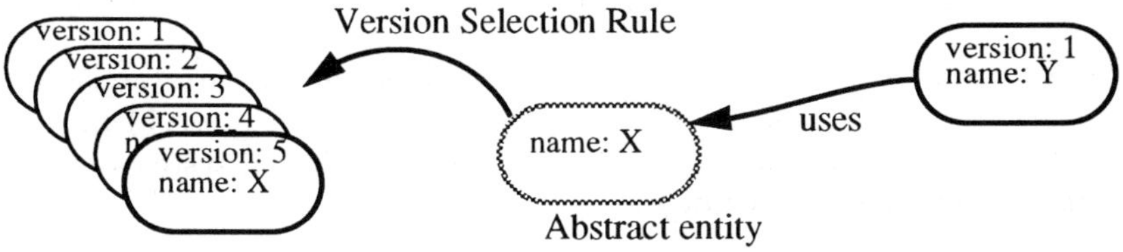

Figure 3.13

as the corresponding joining of such parallel paths, *merging*. The result is a directed acyclic graph as shown in figure 3.11.

Successive versions are sometimes called *revisions*, where a later one is usually assumed to replace an older one. Parallel versions are usually called *variants*, and are assumed to have independent reasons for simultaneous existence. In the following we will however mostly abstract from these issues, and mainly talk about versions.

Since the concept of versions is fundamental to many issues in development environments, it is a reasonable requirement that the database provides support for it.

The *relations* do however require more concern. The reason is the role of relations as the basis for reference and navigation between entities, in combination with a desire to easily change which entity version to "see" at a given moment. The issue will be clarified in the following. Consider the case that an entity Y is using services provided by version 4 of entity X, and that a new version, "5", is created (figure 3.12).

In some cases, it is desirable that Y still uses X version 4. It is however just as often desirable that the relation should point out version 5 instead, for example, as a way of automatically referring to what is most recent. Both behaviours must be supported, and many database systems provide mechanisms for doing it. Some recent object oriented database systems provide such solutions [LLOW91, Ver91]. The name *floating relations* has been used to denote the latter behaviour. The database underlying the Arcs environment [Sch91] also provides this facility. Although basic PCTE does not address this, similar functionality can, and has, been built on top of it.

From an abstract point of view, we could see it as introducing an extra level of indirection between a relation and the entity it targets (figure 3.13).

It could be viewed as if relations are no longer going to particular versions, but to the version set as a whole. The choice of which version of (version set) X to target is delayed, allowing different users to apply different rules in different contexts. We call

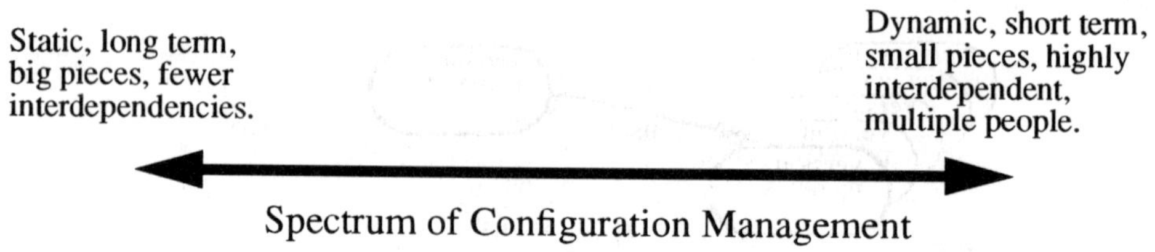

Figure 3.14 Accessing a common baseline of data.

this the *Version Selection Rule*, and it also provides a basic mechanism for supporting *views*.

As a direct consequence of the introduction of versions, we get into the issue of how to maintain a certain level of order in this potential chaos. The problem is that of knowing which versions of entities to combine so that meaningful systems emerge. We can now define the concept of a configuration:

> A *Configuration* is a set of Entities, where for each relation the Version Selection Rule has been applied.

The process of doing this is called Configuration Management, and will be further discussed later.

3.10 CONFIGURATION MANAGEMENT DYNAMICS

In trying use a database to support environments, we end up with a number of questions on how to organize the data stores with respect to work in large teams, versions, views, concurrent access, and work process. This is the level above the basic database technology, and there is no established name for it. However, it is the author's belief that all these issues can be categorized under the label *Configuration Management*. It turns out that, in actually using the environment database, almost any action can be viewed as part of the configuration management process. The key to the overall dynamics of environment data management can therefore be found here. This view, that CM is an important focus for addressing even definition and guidance of the Work Process, is also taken by some other researchers [CLO$^+$90, BEM91].

There is however a rather wide spectrum of configuration management, spanning from the long term management of seldom changed product parts down to support for the frequent change of heavily interdependent objects developed by a group of people (figure 3.14).

Without ignoring the importance of the left side of the spectrum, it is believed that the most demanding requirements are exposed by the right side, which is supposed to solve the high frequency change and teamwork problems. This is also where the majority of Tools will have to integrate. We therefore concentrate mainly on this side. Similar observations on the surprisingly wide spectrum of functionality that is commonly grouped under configuration management have been made by other authors [Dar91, Fei91].

Every significant piece of software takes a *team* to develop. Large systems take large

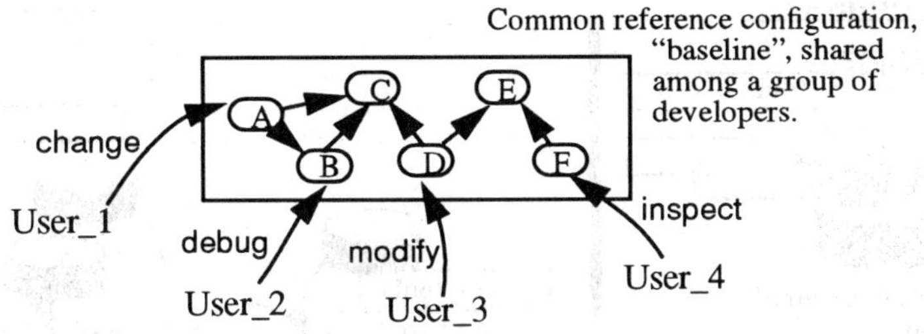

Figure 3.15

teams. In other words, we have a number of individuals that develop and change different parts of the same software system. The situation can be visualized by figure 3.15.

The boxes with arrows between them can be thought of as the large granularity representation of the software system the team is jointly developing. Different users have different needs: some only inspect the software, while others add further components to it. Most of them have a working situation which consists of a mixture of investigating the system and changing/adding to a part of it.

This observation, of the need for adding own parts while at the same time investigating unchanged shared ones, is important. It leads to the requirement that different users must be able to have slightly different configurations of the same otherwise shared configuration. In the following, we call this shared common software - the goal and purpose of the developers work - a *Baseline*. It acts as the reference point relative to which progress is measured, and its change is governed by a set of known and formal procedures.

Since configuration management is a process rather than an isolated mechanism, we should describe this overall process rather than providing a number of pieces. In the following sections we will therefore provide a scenario to show the position and interrelationship of the more basic aspects of underlying database technology.

3.10.1 Decentralization

The first requirements express a need to avoid the centralized approach to databases, and that physical distribution is required for creating a practical system.

- The database should be built out of multiple subdatabases, here called *segments*, that can each be accessed and distributed independently.
- It should, however, be possible to view the universe of all such segments as a single whole when needed, with full reference ability between them.

Figure 3.16 indicates that different users, running different instances of maybe the same tool, should not be forced to access the same database instance. As we will see, a mixture of reading shared segments and writing into private ones is a model that has good opportunities to work well. Past experience on using single central databases is negative, because of the performance problems of imposing a single bottleneck, and

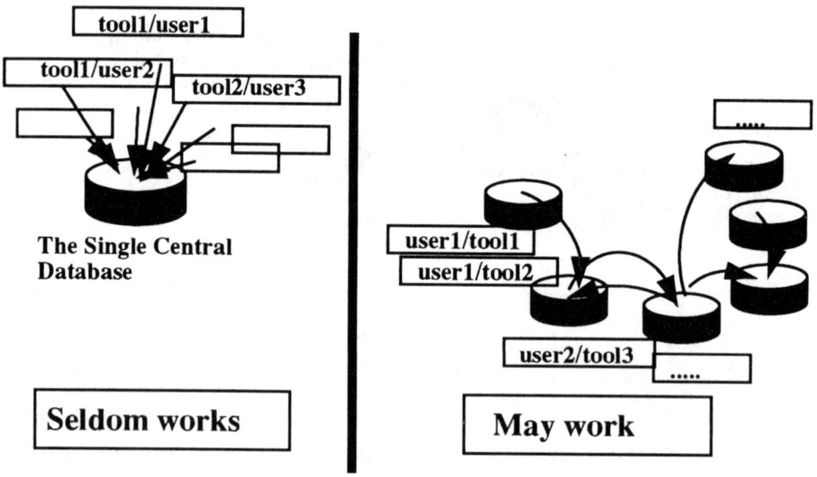

Figure 3.16 Decentralization of data

because of the difficult technical problems involved in managing a massive parallel update.

The multi-database architecture indicated above also has a high inherent distribution potential. Different segments can naturally, and with less disruption or extra work, be managed by different computers.

3.10.2 Multiple views

Different persons must be able to have different views of an otherwise shared common configuration of objects. The decentralized architecture can be used to provide this as figure 3.17 suggests.

As discussed in the section on decentralization, the complete database for a particular user is built by combining a number of different segments. In figure 3.17, Dick's view is the combination of the shared one at the top, and his private one, (down to the left). Johnny's view is similarly constructed, but includes an own private database segment.

The principle is easily generalized in an arbitrary number of levels, however usually with a tendency that segments "higher up" are shared by more people then the one at the "bottom". This last segment should typically be accessed by a single person, motivating the name "private" segment.

The desired difference in view can be achieved by imposing a particular Version Selection Rule as follows:

> Given a specified ordering of segments in the database, always select the version of an entity that belongs to a segment as early as possible in this ordering.

In terms of a typical tool, the updates or creation of new data should then always go into the first, private, segment, while the reading of unmodified objects would be performed against the shared segment. In this way we get a pattern where the shared

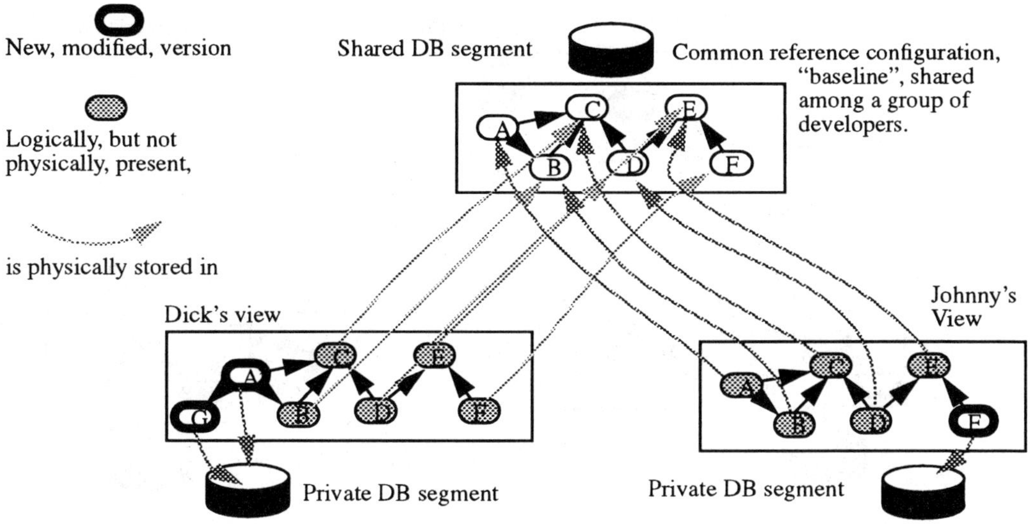

Figure 3.17 Multiple views of data

segment is seldom written into, which simplifies database management and improves efficiency.

The difference in view between the users then tends to be largely defined by the changes and additions they have made, as stored in the private segments.

Writes usually take place into the private segment, which because it is private does not need the complex locking and concurrency support otherwise required. The private segment can furthermore be localized closer to the user (even at his local computer), while the shared segment is on a common and possible remote server.

The conclusion is that this model of utilizing databases both supports the need for multiple views, and allows for practical and efficient use of the computer resources.

3.10.3 Multiple versions

One should be able to introduce and maintain multiple versions of the same object. This requirement, illustrated by figure 3.18, more or less follows from the requirement on multiple views, because we already had different versions of the same object in the private and shared segments.

At some point, it is however necessary to merge versions, as evolved in different database segments, into the same database segment. The need occurs because otherwise there is no good way of keeping track of all versions of an object. We say that we *publish* the entity.

Although being "versions" in both cases, there is an important distinction to be made in this model between an entity version in the private and shared segments. We therefore introduce the following definitions:

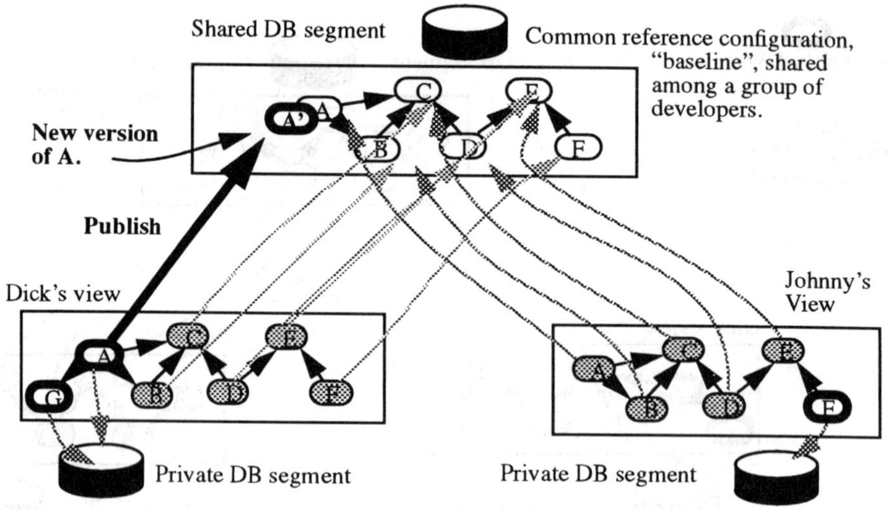

Figure 3.18 Multiple versions of entities

A version is said to be in its *transient* state of versions state after having been created, but before having been published.
A version is said to be in its *stable* state after it has been published.

Different protocols for performing these transitions are available. According to the *pessimistic* coordination strategy, entities should be locked before entering the transient state to prohibit parallel change. When using the *optimistic* strategy, we instead try to resolve possible conflicts at the time of re-entering the stable state, (that is when the publish operation is performed).

Advantage can be taken of the tendency that frequent change is local to a single user and therefore usually takes place in private segments. A simplified management of private segments may include less concurrency control overhead and simply overwriting changed entities rather than providing version set capability.

In shared database segments, objects are however typically not overwritten, but new versions are instead created. Besides simplifying concurrency control, this is required to avoid having users disturb each other's views at unpredictable times.

The concept of a *long transaction* (sometimes also called *design transactions*) can furthermore now be seen to directly correspond to the contents of the private database segment. Aborting a long transaction can then be made to correspond to just forgetting about the segment contents.

3.10.4 Change and Consistency Management

It must be possible to define what is a "consistent" configuration, and to compute and propagate the effects of changes on such configurations (figure 3.19). Configuration management is not only the problem of ensuring constant consistency, (which is rather

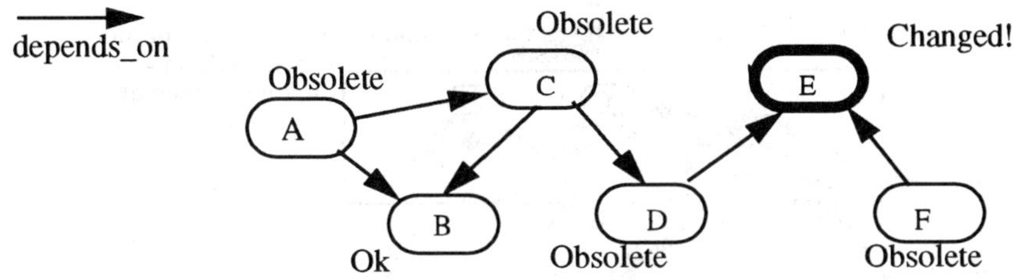

Figure 3.19 Consistency Management

easy by just forbidding all change), but more importantly the one of computing and controlling the effects of change.

The environment database should therefore provide means for catching and propagating consistency breaking changes to the affected users and tools. The role of the environment database is here probably best defined as providing the basic mechanisms, delegating to other tools to draw detailed conclusions. In the case that the environment includes a central coordinating element, such as has previously been called a "process engine", this is the natural receiver of such information. This mechanism is therefore closely related to what have been called triggers in some database proposals.

The change information mechanism is necessary at all levels of configuration management, from the highest level of knowing what would be the effects of replacing a given subsystem in a large product delivery, down to supporting the individual programmer with automatic computation of actual recompilation needs.

Further refinements and example solutions will be provided in later sections.

3.10.5 Support for Cooperative Work

The advent of a new public version should be made known to other users and provisions be made for those users to include, if so desired, such new versions into their views (figure 3.20).

Although users do not want to be immediately disturbed by colleagues creating new versions of objects, they do want to know about their existence. The fact that the version was published by introducing it into the shared segment creates the necessary precondition for other users to include it into their views, if they wish.

Users should have the possibility to "subscribe" on the publishing event, and should then be notified.

Observe that including a new version into the view also has to take into account the direct and indirect effects of relationships. References that previously were to the old version, should now go to the new version, however with the appropriate actions taken with respect to consistency checks and recompilation needs. One should also observe that the new unit may depend on other objects, that may in this view be of different versions than in the view where it was originally created. The same caution must be taken here with respect to consistency checks and recompilation needs.

In any case, the shared segment, "baseline", acts as the natural point of information exchange and coordination between users.

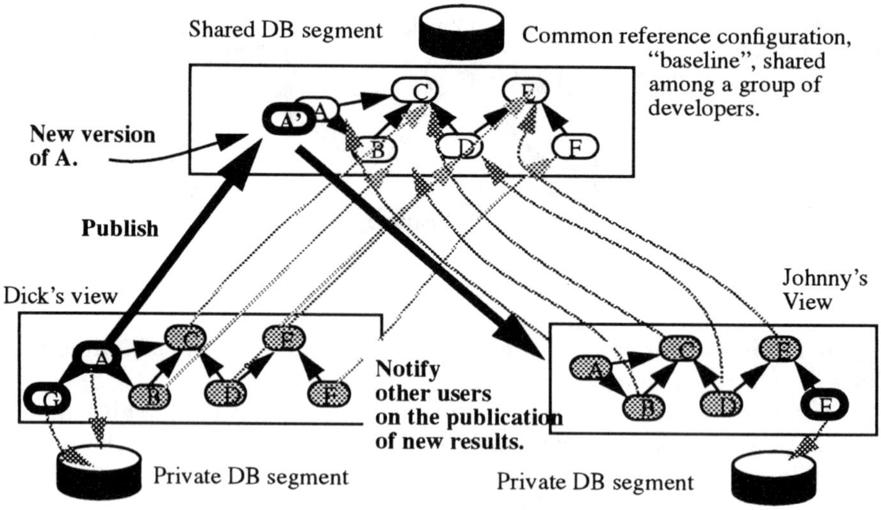

Figure 3.20 Cooperative Work

3.10.6 Work process support

There must be support for systematically restoring a common baseline against which to measure further progress and tests (figure 3.21).

After some time of working, the team has probably arrived in a situation with many new versions, and widely different views among the team members. This makes communication and consistent testing harder. One must therefore reestablish a situation where all members again refer to the same baseline, so that a new step in teamwise software development can take place.

The process of doing this can be automated to a large extent. We call it the *Baseline Update* step, since it updates the common baseline to reflect the sum of parallel change. The automation potential comes from the fact that all the necessary information is in place for a tool, call it the Baseline Processor, to automatically establish the most recent versions as the defaults and undertake the sometimes necessary recompilations and consistency checks. As a side effect, various statistics can also be produced telling what has happened since the last Baseline Update: Which objects were changed? Who changed which object, and why? What is the complete list of the version numbers of objects at which the new Baseline starts?

After the Update process, all users should in principle have the same view, with empty private database segments.

3.10.7 Conclusion

The approach to configuration management presented above is obviously one of several possible processes. It is believed, however, that it corresponds well to an emerging consensus in the environments community. Its basic structure is taken from the Arcs 2.0 system [Sch91, Wid91] but a very similar process can be observed with the NSE acquire-resynchronize-reconcile cycle [SUN89]. NSE however shows few typical

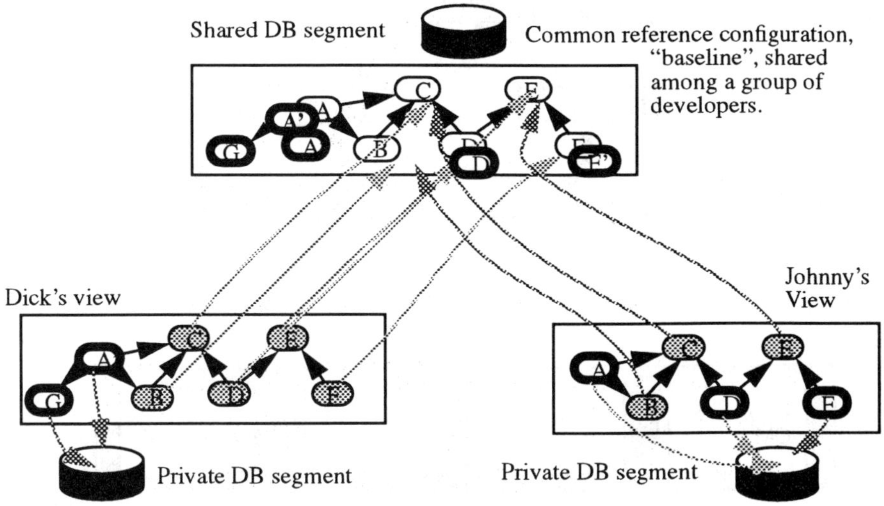

Figure 3.21 Work process support

database properties, and its data model is basically the file system. It has taken the optimistic approach to coordination, and does not explicitly provide the Baseline Update step. Instead, every user must include all published entities in his view and ensure that the common baseline is consistent, as a whole, before his publish operation can succeed.

The relationship between this aspect of configuration management and cooperative work has been noted previously. In for example [Hon88], a presentation of NSE is made in a conference session dedicated to Cooperative Work.

The utilization of multiple database segments to achieve multiple views and cooperation among parallel workers was also pointed out in [Kat90]. His closely related model of configuration management confirms the feeling of emerging consensus around the issues above.

The multiple segment approach lends itself very naturally to a structure that corresponds to different organizational levels. This idea seems to be inherent in the subject, and with little variation both NSE and [Kat90] suggest at least three levels, usually called Private, Project, and Company (figure 3.22).

The idea is that entities flow upwards as they gain in stability, gathering with others to produce larger and larger systems. The related observation, that there exists a related spectrum of configuration management concerns and corresponding styles and techniques, is also made by [Fei91] who use a figure close to 3.23.

Change and consistency management have usually been addressed by different mechanisms at different levels. At the corporate level, configuration management has often been treated as the problem of statically determining which versions of which entities went into which configurations, and to which customers they were was delivered. At the individual level, tools such as UNIX Make have typically taken on the role of con-

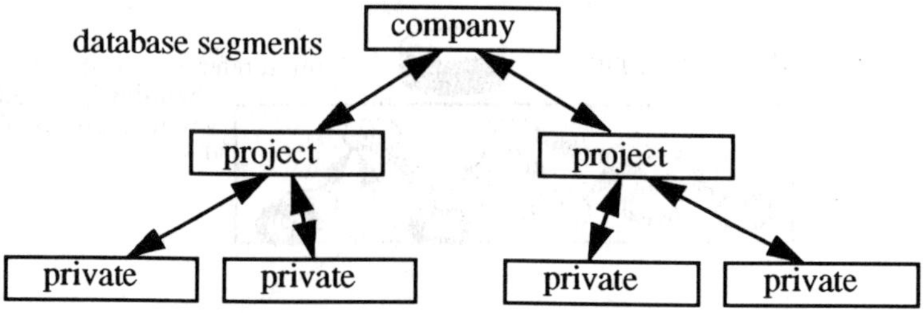

Figure 3.22 Levels of database segments

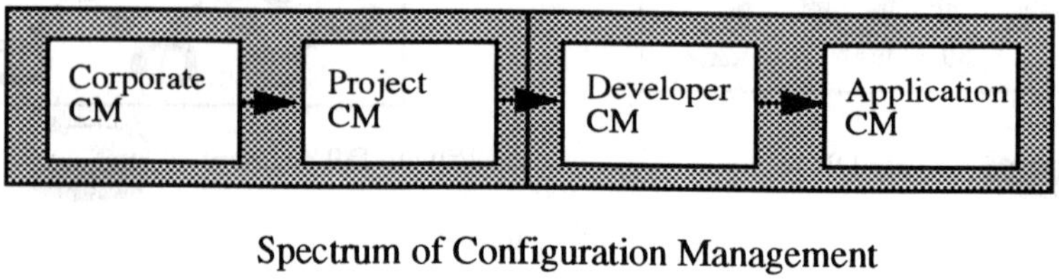

Figure 3.23

sistency control and change propagation. In some systems, such as Arcs 2.0 [Sch91], a single mechanism is used, combined with continuous incremental maintenance of recompilation and change impact lists.

With the above reasoning we have addressed parts of several important areas, such as:

- Application sensitive use of database technology.
- Configuration, version, and change management.
- Support for Cooperative Work, and
- Work Process Support.

The model above not only solves the problem of exploring the benefits of databases without sacrificing teamwork, but also imposes a partial structure on the way a group of people should coordinate their work. Among several remaining questions is the one of how to find a good balance between what is the domain of the configuration management system, and what should be extracted into a separate process model definition.

3.11 CONSISTENCY CONTROL MECHANISMS

To be able to reason about this problem, we must first define what it means for a configuration to be "consistent". The model we have worked with this far has assumed that configurations are networks of entities, where different configurations can be obtained by selecting different versions of entities. Since it seems like the concept of

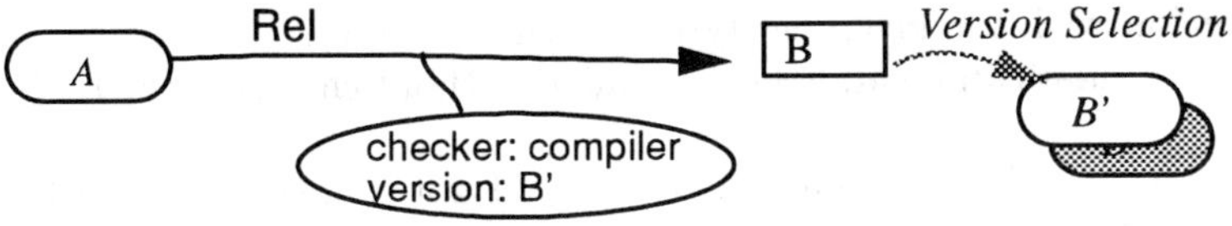

Figure 3.24

consistency is tightly coupled to how we decide to connect entities to each other, we should be able to use the relation as the basic building block. This, together with the requirement that tools are responsible for introducing and maintaining relations, leads us to the following definition:

> We say that a relation A → B is consistent if it has been checked by an authorized tool after any of A or B has changed.

This means that in a completely consistent configuration, all relations have been guaranteed correct by some tool, usually the one that introduced the relation. "Tool" should be understood in a very broad sense, ranging from a compiler that checks that an imported module is used according to the language rules in the importing module to the tool that asks for human confirmation that the protocol of the last meeting has been reviewed. However, as soon as a different version of either A or B is introduced, we have a potential inconsistency. It may still be consistent, but we do not know. A repeated check is needed.

We now need a mechanism so that inconsistencies can be detected as quickly, and with as high precision, as possible. An example of a basic mechanism (illustrated by figure 3.24) that meets those needs is, associate with every relation zero or more attributes that state:

- The name of the tool that is responsible for the check.
- The version identification of the destination of the relation.

The Version Selection process is now extended to check, for each attribute of the relation, if the relation is still bound to the particular version of the entity for which the given tool performed the check. In other words: whether the relation is still consistent. For later reference, we call this set of attributes the *Consistency Rule.* This is a basic mechanism. It imposes little of policy, but does just provide for the efficient catching of change process information, so that higher order tools can draw conclusions. It matches well to a number of practical needs:

- Dependencies between entities can be controlled. Assuming that, in A → B, the B is a newly changed module that is referred to from the function A, the check results in an inconsistency that implies that we must recompile A (because B has changed since the compiler checked the relationship).
  Obviously the same need occurs in most languages and datastructures be it the code depending on its design diagram, or the design depending on its requirements document. There are almost always such dependencies between the many objects occurring in a software development project.
- An arbitrarily fine level of consistency control can be introduced: a relation may be consistent according to tool X but inconsistent according to tool Y.

- If no attribute is present, the relation is considered to be always consistent if just *some* version with the given entity name can be found.
- Consistency rules can be added or extended without changing the underlying mechanism.
- The information about an inconsistency need not be explored directly, but can be sent to a special tool, such as a "process engine", or be broadcast to all tools, for further conclusions.
- The mechanism is at the finest granularity possible within the context of the ERA model. Inconsistencies are detected incrementally, and can therefore be fixed incrementally.

The user may now feel safe to experiment with any context: he will always keep control of what is consistent and what is not. The change is caught at the finest level of granularity allowed by the data model, and is furthermore enriched with information on which tool is responsible for reassuring consistency.

3.12 MAKING TOOLS SUPPORT CONSISTENCY CONTROL

The state of complete consistency is a static situation where all data is complete, correct and tested. Everything is under control. Our system is consistent. This safe but slightly boring world is only threatened by change. Therefore, we must carefully plan for controlling its effects.

With respect to entities, change (and therefore inconsistency) comes in two varieties:

- *Internal change*, in which case the inner structure of an entity has been changed, with a corresponding risk that the attributes and relations are not correctly reflecting it.
- *External change*, in which case another entity has changed and therefore possibly invalidates the first entity.

To cope with *internal change*, the tools must ensure that before committing a transaction, the small and large grain datastructures are saying the same thing: the attributes and relationships must have been updated to reflect the properties of the small grain data objects. In many cases, this process can be very naturally coupled to the validation of the change. The purpose of the tools is often to support the use of some design or programming language, in which case there is a rich and sometimes complex set of rules to check. The successful passing of those checks should, if not before, lead to the update of the large grain objects of the ERA world. In some cases, entities must be left in a state where they have not passed the checks. The minimal requirement on the tool is then to register this situation by inserting an attribute noting the incomplete state. General configuration management tools can then easily find entities that are internally inconsistent.

In the case of *external change*, one or more other entities have changed, on which the consistency of a first entity depends. A major use of relations is to register and track such dependencies.

A typical example are the relations between *interface, user*, and *provider* entities as shown in figure 3.25. We have at least two consistency rules here:

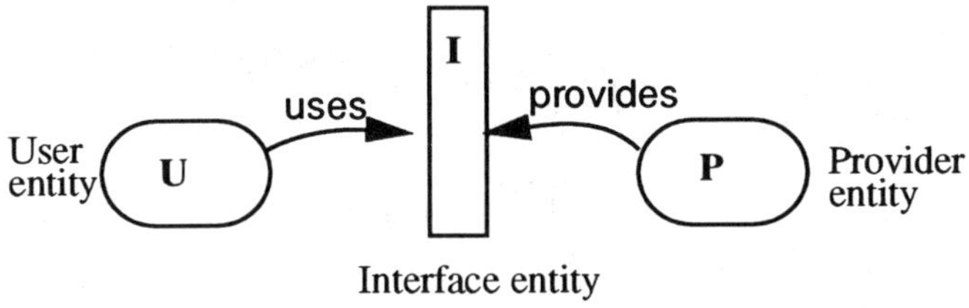

Figure 3.25

- The user U must make correct use of exactly those services provided by the interface named I.
- The provider P must implement what is promised in the interface I.

These rules must be checked by someone, man or machine. To achieve a high level of automation and productivity, it is however highly desirable if the checks can be performed by the machine, that is "tools". In such cases, it then seems very natural to put this responsibility on the tool that processes the entity that is dependant (the relation "origin" entity).

When a tool accesses and lets a user change U, it should as part of the consistency control ensure that U makes use of the services in I according to available rules. When this is ensured, the tool introduces the relation "uses" to I, as well as the tool identification and the version id of I. Whenever I is changing, and thereby gets another version id, we know that U must be re-checked by the tool whose identification we have.

A similar scenario exists for the provider. The conclusion is anyway that tools must introduce relations, together with the "destination" entity version id and its tool identification, in all cases when the correctness of an entity depends on other entities. This work is probably best performed at the same time as ensuring the internal consistency of the entity.

3.13 INTER-PHASE TRACEABILITY

Initially, we identified the problem of tracing dependencies between objects that traditionally have been developed in different project phases. We called it "inter-phase traceability" and pointed out its importance and difficulties. A major problem in this case is that the different objects seldom belong to a single coordinated notation system, making automatic consistency checks hard if not impossible. The creation of such coordinated notation systems is the subject of another book in this series [Kro92]. Here we can just point out how some of the mechanisms discussed above can be used to address parts of the problem.

The role of the database/configuration management system is in this case to register dependencies, directed by tools or human users, and to detect and make available changes that may violate constraints of those dependencies (figure 3.26).

The mechanisms described above perform exactly this. It is just that in examples like the one in the figure above, including dependencies that usually emerge out of human

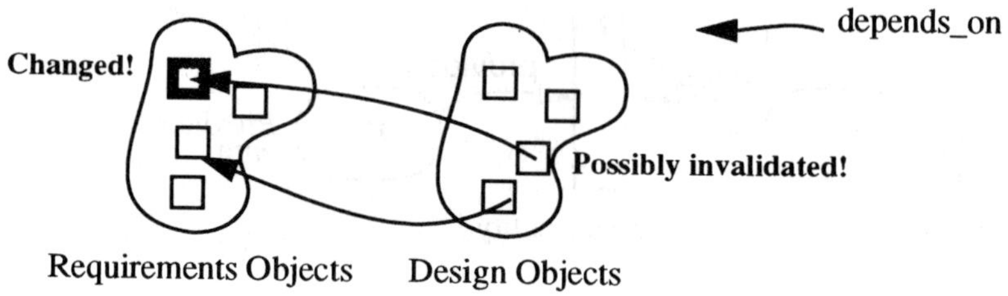

Figure 3.26

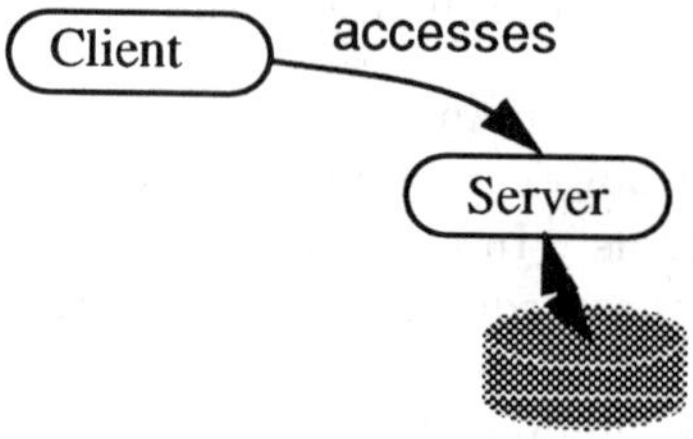

Figure 3.27

creativity and informal decisions, the Consistency Rule is simple: "the designer said so!". The contribution of the environment is then to help the user track all those decisions, and be aware of when changes possibly invalidate his previous work.

3.14 DATA SCHEMAS

A database always provides a data model, which imposes rules on how the user is to express his data. The way this structure is expressed varies between systems, ranging from conventions largely built into client programmes to clearly separated specialized data definition languages. In all cases, however, the word "schema" can be used to denote the assumptions made about database structure. For our purposes, we therefore use the following definition:

> A *schema* is a description of the structure of the data kept in a database system.

Such a description is needed for at least two reasons:

- *Access checking.* It ensures that the raw bits stored are interpreted in a consistent way: that floats are not mistakenly treated as booleans, that the extent and layout of records is maintained, etc.
- *Semantics definition.* It contributes to catching and documenting the assumptions about, and meaning of, data.

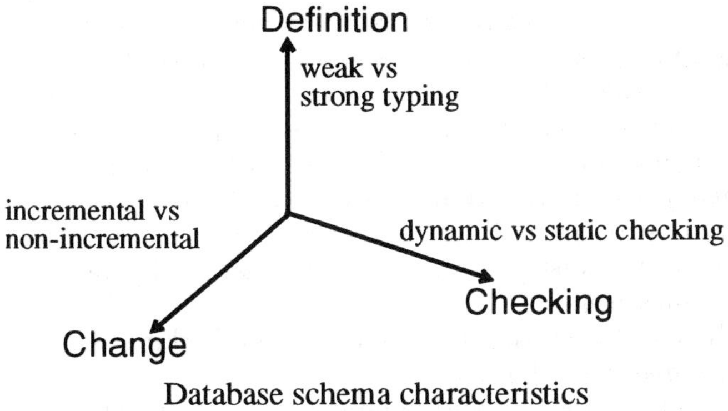

Figure 3.28

One should note that these are the same reasons why we use type systems in programming languages. And indeed, the similarity of schemas in database systems, and type and instance declarations in programming languages, is real. From using this analogy, it is clear that there exist several valid ways and styles of imposing schemas/types. There are always two parts in any data access situation. Let us call them "client" and "server" (figure 3.27). The Server provides data, and defines its structure and allowable operations. The process of *checking* means in this case to ensure that the Client does not violate any of the rules that the Server has established. It provides access checking and contributes to maintaining the semantic contents.

To express the schema, we must furthermore have a "language". In the database community this is sometimes called a *data definition language*, and is often different from other languages. This difference can in many cases be viewed as a drawback, since it creates a "semantic gap" between the natural way of expressing data in the world of the Client and the Server. Different "language bindings" are then sometimes developed to bridge this gap.

In programming languages, and in some recent Object-Oriented databases, the language for expressing the schema is equivalent or made part of ("well integrated with") the language of the Client. This is usually considered an important advantage.

Another important issue is that of how *Schema Change* is accommodated. It is desirable that a small change in schema (that is in the server) should cause a small change in the client. This is especially important in CASE environment databases, where addition of new tools, and therefore schema change, is not an exception but part of the core idea. Using the definition of *openness* that defines it as an inverse measure of the cost for introducing a new, or replacing an existing, subsystem, we see that making schema change easy is also important for promoting openness.

As there are three important aspects, it is tempting to once again use a three dimensional diagram as shown in figure 3.28.

Without claiming that definition, change, and checking represent completely independent, or orthogonal issues, we can observe that there exists, for each aspect, a range of possibilities.

The *Definition* aspect of schemas is closely related to the discussion on different datamodels. In fact, schemas are really the manifestation of the Datamodel. However, taking a more programming language oriented view, we can this time discuss it from the viewpoint of *weak* vs *strong typing*.

Weak typing, is usually associated with a small and simple datamodel, which forces the user to represent many different real world objects with the same type. The classic example is Lisp, where most things end up as lists. It is also well known that there are both advantages and drawbacks with this approach. It imposes a certain uniformity and generality on the way datastructures are handled, although we lose some of the semantic definition expressiveness.

Weak typing, as discussed here, can still provide access checking. There will however be a less centralized semantics definition.

Strong typing is usually associated with a large and complex data model. Different real world entities are expressed as different data types. Ada is an example among programming languages. The advantage is a clearly visible mapping between real world and datastructures, while the possible drawbacks lie in the increased multitude of options.

The *Checking* aspect can likewise be discussed in a programming language oriented way, by observing the options of *dynamic* vs *static* checking.

With static checking, we mean the ability to check at client construction time. The tool responsible for this is often called a compiler. The advantage is that once checking is done, it does not need to be performed again unless the Client or Server is changed. The drawback is exactly the same: when the Client and Server are frequently changing, repeated checking must be performed. This kind of checking is furthermore often very labour intensive and requires human intervention. Quite often it consists of possibly massive recompilations and reinstallations.

Dynamic checking defers Check until access time. The component responsible is sometimes called an "interpreter". The drawback is decreased runtime performance, since we have to pay the price of checking at every access. The advantage is that Client and Server can be changed without extra checking being imposed. The needed runtime checking is there anyway.

Quite naturally, there has been a tendency that weak typing systems are implemented using dynamic typing, while strong typing systems are implemented using static typing.

We also note that different granularities of data have different requirements on schemas. Larger granularity data have less problems with weak typing and dynamic checking than fine granularity data. This is because when modelling more abstract objects, the need for a complex datamodel is less expressed.

Ultimately, we want high scores in all three characteristics of database schemas: strong typing, static checking and incremental change. Current technology has however a tendency to force a trade-off between the first two issues and the last one. In Environments, we do however believe the ability to perform low cost changes to be most essential, since environments have an unusual need for reconfiguration and adaptation to new needs.

As a final reflection concerning the semantics definition aspect, it deserves remembering that however powerful the schema definition language is, a majority of "semantics" will anyway be in the way the client interprets the data.

3.15 EXISTING TECHNOLOGY FOR ENVIRONMENT DATABASES

A large number of proposals on environment databases have been presented over the last decade, some of which have even been implemented. Without providing a full survey of the many proposals, it seems appropriate to identify three types of systems:

- *ERA-oriented databases.* These systems provide a network-like datamodel, with variations around the entity-relationship-attribute model. Well-known examples include the US proposal CAIS [MOPT88], and the European standards PCTE [BMT88, ECM90].
- *Relational databases*, based on the relational model as originally proposed by [Cod70], but which have been significantly evolved over two decades, and have been described in most text books on database systems. There is a large number of product quality implementations available, in wide spread production use.
- *Object-oriented databases*, which are an emerging class of systems that may be characterized as a combination of ERA approaches and persistent implementation of object oriented programming languages (usually C++, but also Smalltalk and proprietary languages).

We will conclude this chapter with a few remarks on theese alternatives.

3.16 OBJECT- AND ERA-ORIENTATION

The emerging class of systems labelled Object-Oriented Databases can usually be viewed as persistent implementations of some programming language. This is a very natural approach, since the very idea of object orientation is to provide a rich datamodel *together* with operations, just like modern programming languages.

A number of products are already available. One of the first examples was GemStone [Ser90], which supports a slight variation of Smalltalk, while the most recent over all trend seems to be towards C++ [Ver91, Obj91]. Although these databases were originally developed to meet the needs of applications like CAD and CASE, and indeed represent a significant step forward, the reasoning above indicates that the full freedom of, say, C++ is not the perfect solution. The freedom and power leads to less uniformity and common structure; lower representation convergence; and therefore less integration. While the work of implementing a single isolated tool is probably rather free of problems, and is much helped by the OODB, the construction of a complete environment requires special care in using all the flexibility.

Most of these systems have adopted a Multidatabase architecture, and support many of the mechanisms discussed above, such as aspects of version and configuration management.

A major concern of environment databases has always been that of schema management. It is important that additions to the schema can be done incrementally, that is without invalidating or unnecessarily disturbing other clients. The object-oriented databases are here confronted with an even greater challenge than previously.

First of all the “data definition language” is unusually large and complex, in fact more or less equivalent to a programming language like C++ or Smalltalk. Implementing an incremental approach to its change is of course even harder than for a simpler language.

Secondly, the operations, "code", is now conceptually very tightly integrated into the schema. This, together with the presence of inheritance and dynamic binding, imposes yet another dimension of concerns. In principle the object oriented approach could be used in very elegant ways, for example using dynamic binding to make common operations available independently of actual type. Assume that we have implemented all our different objects, be it C++ code or SDL design diagrams, by specializing a common class:

```
class Entity {
    virtual void Edit;
    ....
};

class SDL_Entity: public Entity {}...

class C_Plus_Plus_Entity: public Entity {}...
```

The Edit function must be provided by the specializing classes, invoking different editing tools depending on their actual type. However, other tools do not need to know the actual type, but can view them as of the (parent) type Entity, and just call its Edit function.

The extra complication with respect to schemas is that although the "other tool" does not need to have the schema of "SDL_Entity" or "C_Plus_Plus_Entity" in their scope, the *code* to be called must come from these schemas. This creates an extra and somewhat invisible dependency between what should otherwise be unrelated tools. This, and similar issues, still largely remain to be solved. Object-oriented databases are a very active area of both research and commercial developments. Numerous papers have been published. A recent publication, giving an overview of current issues, is [BM91].

The ERA approach of PCTE is then more well known and mature in many respects. It does also address another level of abstraction, and was built to make the entities of its ERA model correspond to a level of granularity corresponding to that of "files". Infact, the original approach of PCTE was to view it as an extension of the UNIX file system, where the fixed hierarchy of directories and files, and fixed number of file attributes, was generalized into a network of files with arbitrary relationships and attributes.

Schema management is central to PCTE, and additions can in principle be made incrementally. The mechanism is called Schema Definition Sets (SDSs) which allows for the combination of several schemas into a set which together make up the schema of a process. However, allowing free combinations of sub-schemas does not automatically solve the underlying problems. Viewing them as modules of a (proprietary) language, they must still together make up a consistent definition.

Therefore it is not clear to what extent the schema handling of the ERA example PCTE is in principle more flexible than what is typically provided by object-oriented databases, nor whether it is essentially different.

Having noted the orientation of PCTE towards large granularity data, and the

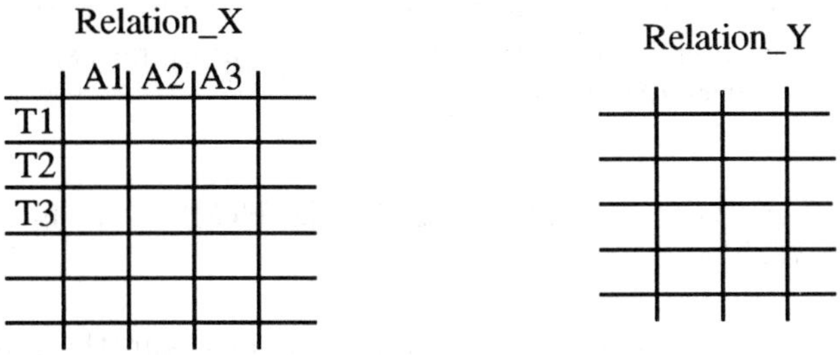

Figure 3.29 Relational Model example.

object-oriented system's tendency towards finer granularity, a natural thought is that a combination of the two in principle provides a complete solution, leaving however a certain discontinuity between the two types of systems.

There are several examples of environments built on ERA and Object Oriented Databases, some of them are described in other parts of this book. The Aerospace Environment is built on PCTE, the typical ERA example providing a further description of this alternative. The Environment for Process Control utilizes a (proprietary) object-oriented database, and the Hardware Engineering Environment is based on the JESSI Common Frame Object Management System, which maybe could be classified as an in-between.

Since the ERA and Object-Oriented models have been at least initially discussed previously, and since they will be exemplified by use in real environments in later parts of this book, we here complement the presentation with a brief discussion of relational databases.

3.17 RELATIONAL DATABASES

The relational model gains its power from its extreme simplicity; its suitability for many business oriented applications; and its direct and obvious correspondence to "a file of records".

A database implementing the Relational model provides a set of tables, as shown in figure 3.29. Each Relation (table) consists of a set of Tuples (Rows), T1, T2, etc. Each such tuple furthermore has a set of Attributes (Columns), A1, A2, etc. The type of an attribute was originally defined to be of a non-complex kind, usually constrained to things like integer, real, and string. This constraint was originally called "first normal form". Manipulation of the Relations is now performed using the well known Relational Algebra operations of Select, Project, Join, Union, and Difference.

The main advantages of this model were mentioned initially. In addition, one sometimes also claims its perfect orthogonality as an advantage: the ability to equally well respond to any query. One should note that the same word, "Relation", may now be used with very different meanings. When speaking about the ERA-model, the word means something else than when working in the so called "Relational Model". One should note this difference in the discussion below. The relational data model may be viewed as the Lisp of datamodels: a single concept, the "Relation", is used to represent what in the ERA model is distinguished as Relations, Attributes, and Entities. In those cases when the ERA model is felt closer to the application needs, the Relational model makes certain semantics disappear.

3.18 USING RELATIONAL DATABASES FOR CASE APPLICATIONS

It has been concluded many times that the relational model, and the approach that used to be applied in its implementation, does not meet the CASE requirements very well. This is, of course, one major reason we have seen the large number of CASE database proposals in recent years.

However, relational databases are, as most implementations of notations, in principle "Turing complete", in that every function or datastructure can be realized. The difference will come in convenience, efficiency, and cost.

We now evaluate the relational model according to some typical environment database requirements:

- *Long transactions.* Relational databases do not include direct support for this concept. Rather they are usually made for short and small transactions, including typically at most a few dozen tuples. The transaction time is assumed to be short, in the order of seconds.
  Long transactions can be built on top of a relational database. But this is then extra work, which furthermore will experience both performance and functionality problems since the underlying mechanisms are usually not built to support it.
- *Distribution and Multidatabase architecture.* The extent to which this requirement is met will vary between implementations. There is no standard.
  One can however assume that multiple relational databases can be defined, and that it is possible to build a program that "integrates" those different databases, and performs access and manipulation across those subdatabases.
  This "integrating" program is however, from the database point of view, just another application program, and gets no special support in its work. The result is again extra implementation work and potential performance problems.
- *Minimization of semantic gap.* For most application programs in the CASE environment, it is not natural and convenient to define its datastructures in terms of "relations" as defined above. Therefore, inconvenient and inefficient packing and unpacking operations can be expected.
  A relational database should therefore probably not be used for storage of what has been called "fine-grain" data. The negative experience is especially well documented in this case.
  For the large granularity level, the problems will be less urgent. There is, however, still the case that we, in a somewhat unnatural way, represent both Attributes, Entities, and Relations as, yes, Relations.
- *Object/Entity-Orientation.* The CASE applications have consistently come to the conclusion that data is naturally Object or Entity oriented. Therefore, the ERA model suits well. The Attributes are always accessed in direct connection to its Entity, just as its Relations. With the Relational model, this cannot be modelled, while at the same time allowing new attributes and relations to be added. The

latter requirement, of dynamic introduction of new attributes and relations, is of extreme importance.

Besides scattering data that we feel logically belong together, this may create inefficiency. This is because it does not allow us to utilize the localization of access that is made possible by already at the conceptual level grouping certain data with a given entity. Computation of "transitive closures" of relations, that is a typical need in environments applications, is not well supported and usually inefficient.

The Relational model does in fact not provide any of the properties usually associated with object orientation: no identifiable "object" around which related data can be gathered; no polymorphic type system and inheritance; no associated operations.

- *Version and configuration management.* The concept of a version is not an important one in the area where relational databases are usually applied.

  One can, of course, simulate versioning. Using database jargon one could "make the key of the entity relation consist of two attributes: its name and its version". However, this implies that similar version tags also must be put on other data associated with this entity. Smarter solutions may exist, but it is probably hard to find ones that are felt to be truly natural and straightforward.

  The concept of a version is so fundamental, but also complex, that most designers have come to the conclusion that it must at least to some extent be supported at a lower level.
- *Multiple views.* Different users must be able to have different views of the same collection of data. Many relational databases provide a view concept, but a closer look at what is provided will probably show that it has a different meaning from what is needed in the CASE context.

  In CASE, the concept of a view is tightly interacting with the concept of versions, which returns us to the problem of providing versions within the relational model.
- *Support for work process.* Teamwork, check-in and check-out, exchange of information among views as known in the CASE area are typically not supported in the relational database. It may suffice to point out that the cooperation between people in the CASE environment is built upon the long transactions, entity-orientation, multiple views, and version management, all of which we have concluded as less well supported by relational databases. Although a concept of consistency is usually provided, it is not at the ERA level that seems to be so natural to the CASE application.

The conclusion is that the requirements of CASE databases can be fulfilled by relational database technology only if substantial extra software is added to it.

Taking this idea further would however mean that we use the relational database mostly as a very basic search, storage, and access machine, on top of which several more layers of semantics are added. Viewed as a provider of such very basic mechanisms a relational database may be less suitable, because it will probably not show the performance profile that is expected from what is now considered as low level primitives.

4

User Interface Integration

As has been observed several times, integration often takes the form of making solutions more similar, increasing their level of commonality and homogeneity. In terms of software, it is then natural to factor out commonalities in separate and distinguishable modules.

In the area of user interfaces, this idea has been applied for a long time, to a varying degree and style. A basic decomposition into *user interface*, and *application* parts has however reached wide acceptance (figure 4.1).

This figure, which is used in many variations, suggests a simple architecture to be applied to every tool. Many discussions about user interface technology, at least those concerned with architecture, have their roots in this idea. The model-view-controller paradigm of Smalltalk, as well as research and numerous products often labelled User Interface Management Systems [Hix90, IEE89]. Much of this work goes back to the Seeheim model [Pfa85], which identifies components for Appearance, Dialogue, and Application Interface.

In some cases, as in the Eureka Software Factory project, major parts of the architecture are built around the idea of making this separation [FO89]. The names used in that case are "User Interface Component" (UIC), for the UI part, and Service Component (SC), for what we have called the application part.

The arguments on why this design is a good idea can be summarized as follows:

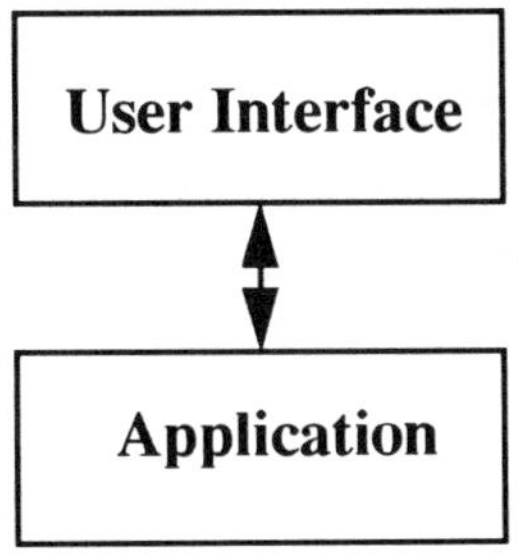

Figure 4.1 Separation of UI from Application.

Tool Integration: Environments and Frameworks, Edited by D. Schefström and G. van den Broek

- *Separation of concern.* It provides an early separation of concern which allows specialists to develop the user interface independently of the application.
- *Module independence.* It allows changes to the user interface while leaving the application undisturbed. What is sometimes called "look and feel" can to some extent be changed by replacing only the user interface part.
- *Investment sharing and standardization.* Having separated the issues, specialized high-quality, (and expensive), software and tools can be developed for the user interface part, to be shared among several developers, groups, and even companies. Sharing of a common basis promotes standard solutions, which usually turns out to be very economical.

This last point is probably the most important driving factor in achieving user interface integration.

As with most simple models, many questions still remain, or need further refinements. In the following, we will therefore touch upon some of these questions, and survey a few of the technical considerations that are involved.

4.1 USER INTERFACE TECHNOLOGY IN DEVELOPMENT ENVIRONMENTS

The need for carefully designed user interfaces and efficient associated technology is not limited to environments and tool production. Is it a very general concern. There are, however, a few special characteristics of this area that can be observed:

- Development environments are often large, covering several tasks and therefore involving several tools. It is therefore in the very concept of an "environment" that the desired UI uniformity must extend over a large population of tools. This makes the problem larger, but also creates a larger "market" to share the cost of a well designed underlying UI technology.
- There are almost always several tools and notations that are graphically based. In fact, for some time the concept of CASE was heavily dominated by various graphics drawing support systems. Software development environments therefore have a clearly identified need for a generic support of graphics, allowing for efficient production of graphics editors and browsers.

The first point loosely corresponds to the need for standardizing "look and feel". Part of this is today achieved by providing libraries of basic building blocks (called various things like "widget", "interactor", "UI-object", etc.). As will be discussed later, many libraries of this kind exist, some even widely accepted, as well as tools for making their utilization simpler. For the second point, generic graphic editor support, the supply of widely accepted standards does not seem to be quite as extensive.

4.2 ENCAPSULATION APPROACHES

A special problem concerns the encapsulation of existing tools. Much software has been built, and is still being built, with very simple assumptions concerning input/output devices:

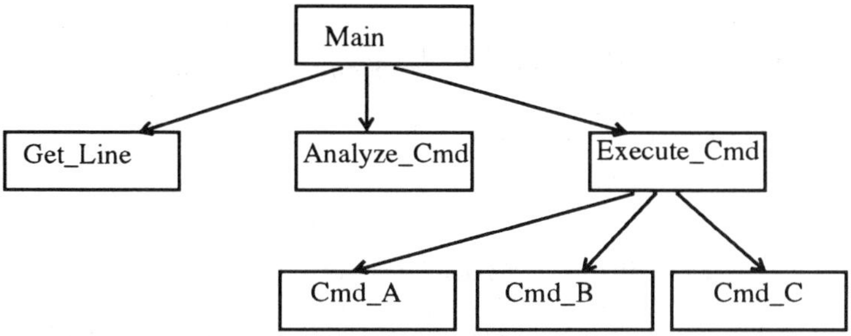

Figure 4.2 Typical architecture of tty-oriented tools

- A single window.
- A single input device, (the keyboard).

This is sometimes called the "tty-assumption", and does of course severely limit the opportunities in creating an easy-to-use user interface. A common need, therefore, is to find ways of improving the UI of such tools in a way that is not unreasonably expensive.

However, the internal architecture of a tty-based tool can be very different from that of tools built for taking advantage of graphics UI. In most tty-oriented applications, the input/output structure consists of a simple loop describing a "Get Line - Analyze Command - Execute Command" cycle (figure 4.2).

The point of input in the program is known and localized - in the domain of the application programmer - and each command runs until it admits to return the control to "Main", which then once again starts waiting for input. There is no way to switch back and forth between different locations of input, such as is expected in a windowed/graphics application.

With the usage of windowing and graphics user interface systems, the responsibility for managing input-focus is taken over by the UI software, which in turn, based on the actual event, activates the application. The structure of the resulting program is, as will be discussed later, completely different. Here it suffices to conclude that even in case modification of a tty-based tool is possible, it is not necessarily simple to give it a graphics user interface. In [EG91], the experience from a few such efforts is reported.

Therefore, it is in such cases often an economic solution to build a simpler "encapsulation", which leaves the tty based tool undisturbed, but provides at least some of the benefits of a graphics UI. The most straightforward way of doing this is to build a "shell" or front-end that utilizes menus and buttons as a way of injecting commands into (the basically unchanged) tty-oriented application. This architecture is shown figure 4.3.

This kind of architecture is attractive because of its low price and simplicity. It gives a feeling of "workstation-like interface" without having to change the existing code. In its simplest form, communication is unidirectional: the Shell provides the user with menus and buttons, and sends the corresponding commands, expressed in the old command language, to the standard input of the old application. Output from the application is still just written on a tty (emulating) window. The application is not changed, and need not know about any windowing code or conventions.

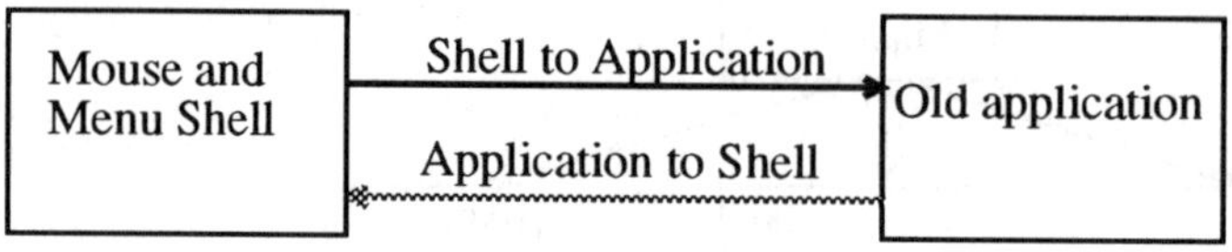

Figure 4.3 Encapsulation of a tool

In the slightly more ambitious case, attempts are made to catch the application output, either by redirecting its standard output to a file or communications channel, or by doing some smaller changes to the application. In this case, the output is still the same but can be presented in a different way. At this point it is usually also necessary to make the application communicate auxiliary information to the Shell, so that it knows the application state.

Most of the first generation workstation tools utilized this technique, such as "dbx-tool", "emacstool", "mailtool", etc. The suffix "tool" has almost come to represent this kind of approach to user interfaces.

Although simple to implement, the above approach has limitations that become more acute with higher ambitions:

- Multiple and dynamically created overlapping windows are troublesome to implement since the underlying application doesn't know about them and therefore cannot give them a strong semantics.
- Direct-manipulating and context sensitive graphic interfaces become hard to implement since, again, the distance between the application semantics and the user interface representations increases.
- Attempts to meet these issues within the above architecture increase the need for communication bandwidth and the complexity of datastructures passed. The application must now furthermore be significantly extended to support a communications protocol, with the risk of taking away some of the original advantage and reason for the architecture: simplicity and keeping the application unchanged.

Early usages of UIMS systems often consisted of building the Shell part of this architecture. Some systems, like HP SoftBench [Cag90], provide specialized support for this kind of encapsulation. The EDL (Encapsulation Description Language) can here be used for controlling the Input and Output to the tty tool, (such as pattern matching over its output), managing the interprocess communication, and for making the graphics presentation.

Although having limited potential, the encapsulation approach has often proved to provide a cost efficient solution in practice. Having dealt with this basically migration oriented solution, we now turn our attention to those cases when tools are purpose built for modern graphics user interfaces.

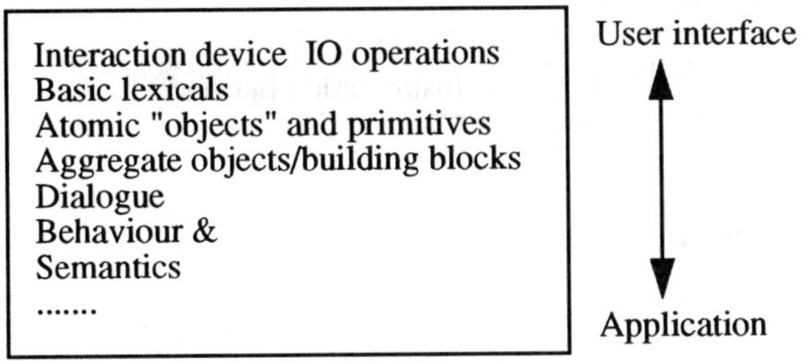

Figure 4.4 UI layering

4.3 THE USER INTERFACE AND APPLICATION SEPARATION PROBLEM

The model introduced initially suggests that there is an obvious or at least very natural way of extracting the User Interface (UI) part from the "rest". The latter has been named "application", "model", "logic", "service component" and sometimes even "semantics".

At closer inspection, the task is not that straightforward. According to the initial arguments above, we want to make the UI independent and less reliant on the application. At the extreme, tools would then all behave similarly to a very large degree, since their user interfaces have rich and important lives no matter which application they are to support. On the other hand, common sense tells us that the whole purpose of a user interface is not to be "general" and independent, but to provide precise control over the application. So, it is not clear how far we really want to push this separation.

Similar problems occur in trying to define what really constitutes the UI part. From one point of view it can be argued that we, in the concept of a user interface, must include most aspects of how a tool responds to user actions. The way it "behaves" in its interaction with the user. This behaviour is, however, most often determined by the computations, transformations, and logic of the application. Using this wide but hard to reject definition, a majority of any tool's code ends up in the UI part. Since this threatens to degenerate the original modularization goal, it is probably not what we want.

It therefore turns out that the initial model with a sharp border between UI and application in practice is much more continuous, ranging from the basic input/output operations, over purely lexical issues of size and shape of buttons, to style of interaction and what finally is user perceived genuine characteristics of the application. This layering of software according to a perceived distance to the basic operations of the interaction device, we call the *UI layering* and is shown in figure 4.4.

It must therefore be concluded that it is hard to find a strong and general definition of what constitutes the UI part of a tool.

But what if we nevertheless see benefits in finding some kind of separation, where do we draw the line? What remains is to put in the UI part those pieces of software that can be expected to be reused, suggesting the following definition:

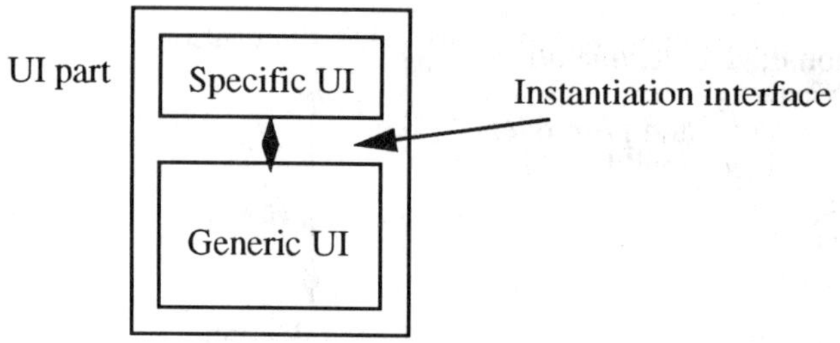

Figure 4.5

We call the *User Interface Component* of a tool, the upper parts of its UI Layering such that we expect them to be economically shared with, or reused in, other tools.

In terms of the three reasons for modularization: Separation of Concern, Module Independence, and Investment Sharing and Standardization, we have thereby chosen the last one as the real foundation criteria from which the others should follow.

4.4 UI INSTANTIATION

According to the reasoning above, the UI part of a tool should contain software that is of a very general character. For economical and standard software engineering reasons, it should be built out of standard pieces. However, at some point this standard common software must be specialized and made to behave in various ways to meet the requirements of the particular application.

This final parameterization into the desired behaviour should be possible with little effort. It should also be clearly identified, separated from the basic software, and easy to change. What we get here can therefore be viewed as another important interface: just as the UI component as a whole interfaces to the Application, there is an internal interface between the specific and generic parts of the UI (figure 4.5).

The specific part should be small, high level, and will often be changed, while the generic part is expected to be larger, complex, and less frequently changed.

Several products and standards exist addressing the generic part, ranging from globally accepted standards like X-windows, libraries of building blocks (called "widgets", "interactors", "presentation objects", etc.), like Motif and OpenLook, graphics packages like PHIGS [HHHW91], to a multitude of company internal systems of varying acceptance and extent.

Various technologies have been developed to support this model. The simplest and most straightforward approach is the direct procedural access to interfaces as provided by the systems above. In this case, the instantiation interface consists of standard procedure calls, often using a call-back style of programming. Although this is a well proven and efficient technology, it may require rather large amounts of sometimes very complex programming, interfacing to large and intricate generic UI packages.

Many systems categorized as "UIMS" have addressed exactly this problem. A common approach is to avoid some of the instantiation programming by providing a special UI-editor which allows for interactive design of the final user interface. This style seems

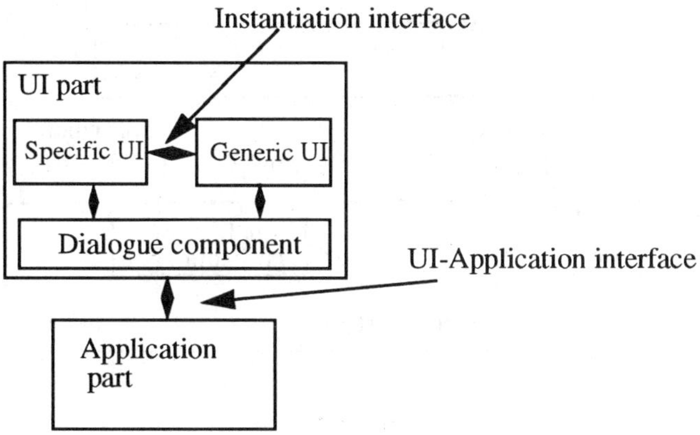

Figure 4.6

to be especially suitable for interfacing to widget libraries, that is those systems that provide a large collection of basic "things" (widgets), like windows, frames, buttons, menus, text fields, etc. The user can then by directly manipulating corresponding graphic objects, combine them into more complex aggregates. The underlying software is then generated from this "specification". An example of this kind of product is TeleUSE [Tel92, Hix90]. Ibuild [VB], which is part of the Interviews distribution [LCI+91], is another example. Several important examples are also described in the other parts of this book, where each of the Environment examples have included the development or usage of user interface management systems.

Similar technology can be used for production of graphic editors, exemplified by Unidraw [LV89], and SemDraw, an ongoing subproject of the Eureka Software Factory effort.

4.5 UI TO APPLICATION COMMUNICATION

Whenever a modularization has been found, we have to find a way of re-connecting the separated components. However separated, the UI and the application need to communicate. The problem is to achieve this in a way that is clearly identified, efficient, and does not blur the original separation.

Of the components identified by the Seeheim model, the Dialogue and Application Interface address this. In the ESF architecture, the Software Bus and the associated component interaction description language also suggest solutions in this area [ESF91]. Related work, especially on how to describe the interfaces of components and how to perform transfer of complex datastructures in a distributed and heterogeneous environment, has been explored and exemplified in the ATMOSPHERE project [LHKB91]. A more complete picture of the UI part of a tool can now be drawn, (figure 4.6). Two components are of special concern here:

- UI-Application interface, and
- Dialogue.

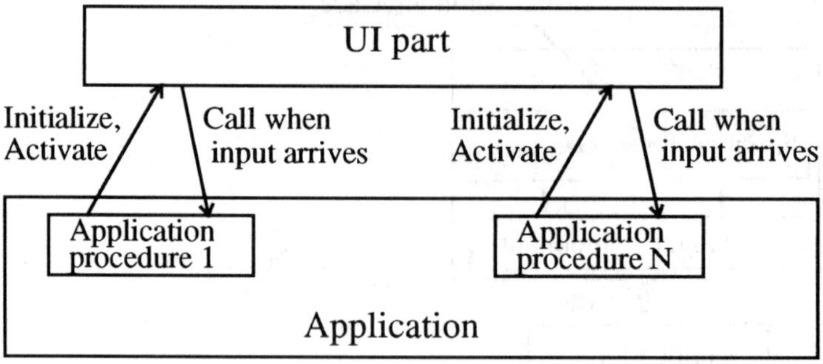

Figure 4.7

The UI-Application interface should provide procedural access to the basic computations of the application. It should provide a complete interface, much in the style of an abstract data type declaration.

In the cases where the UI and Application parts can be put in the same process, the connection of the two need not differ from how software modules are put together in general by means of standard linking operations and "call-backs". In this latter style of programming, the linking consists of specifying a procedure in the application (often by providing a pointer to it) to be called when given events occur at the UI side. This may be the user pushing a button, or selecting a certain menu entry. In this way, we get an application that is driven by events of the UI part, as is illustrated by the figure 4.7.

Several variations of the same theme exist. In Ibuild [VB], the Application Procedure is connected to the UI by utilizing the dynamic binding and inheritance capabilities of C++ [ES90]. Taking a simplified view, each interaction object is represented by a class, as with the "button" below:

```
class Button {
    virtual void Push();
};
```

The UI system calls the Push routine when the user pushes the given button. By declaring a subclass, where the virtual function Push is implemented (the Application procedure), we have connected the UI to the Application by means of inheritance in an object oriented language.

```
class Application_Action: public Button {
    virtual void Push;
};

Application_Action::Push() {
    cout << ''Button pushed!\n'';
};
```

The technical solutions are less straightforward when UI and Application are to be implemented in different processes. The complications stem from two facts:

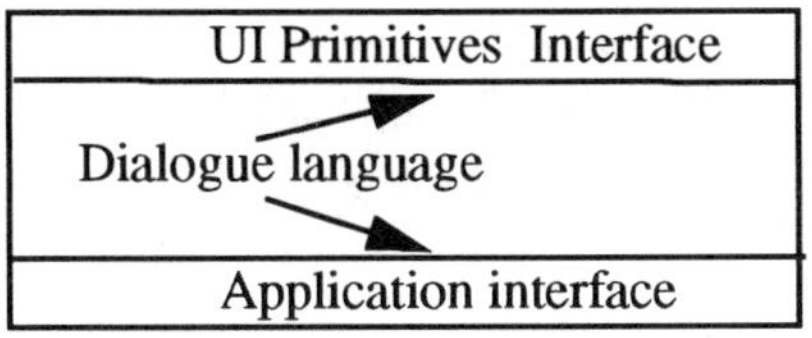

Figure 4.8

- *Communication overhead.* An inter process communication is many times more expensive than a simple procedure call.
- *Virtual space separation.* Data passing between separate processes can, obviously, not easily include pointers and references, since those are valid only in the virtual space of their original processes.

This means that this solution cannot be used unless special care is taken, and that the benefits obtained must be known to be substantial to pay for the drawbacks.

On the other hand, it can be argued that in heterogeneous environments, where UI and application parts are implemented using widely different technologies, software as well as hardware, conversions must anyway take place. The communications channel then provides a natural place for solving that problem.

Another reason for choosing this solution may be the desire to provide for distribution, making it possible to run the UI and Application parts at different computers. Technology addressing these problem is under development at several places, among them within ATMOSPHERE [dV92] and the ESF project [FO91].

In the *Dialogue* part of the UI, we try to isolate those parts of the UI software that determine the sequence of interactions that takes place between the user and the tool. This is the place where many UIMSs have hoped to provide an easily accessible and simply modifiable representation. In some cases, special "high-level" languages have been developed to ease the expressing of the dialogue.

Because of its central position, and flavour of specification of behaviour, the design of such a language has resulted in many proposals, including rule based, grammar oriented, and other special purpose approaches.

The role of the dialogue language in an architecture is illustrated by figure 4.8. From a communications oriented viewpoint, the Dialogue can be said to be the place where the (high level) protocol between the UI and the Application is implemented. It has interfaces both "downwards" to the Application, and "upwards" to the basic UI software providing the basic primitives of interaction.

5

Retrospective

5.1 THE CLASSICAL IDEALS OF ENVIRONMENTS

A wide interest in environments construction has existed for at least a decade. The visions and ideas may have changed slightly over time, but we will here take a brief look at some of the original ones, such as...

- Unification through a central database
- The environment viewed as a single tool
- Tight integration
- Homogeneity

Occasionally, those ideas are today criticized, often using less positive valued words like "monolithic approach" and "lack of modularization". To better understand the issues, one should take a look at what generated the original ideas and what may have been experienced this far.

The original rationale for pursuing the idea of *unification through a single database* was that it would enable tool information exchange by representing as much data as possible in a similar, and therefore open, way. Using a single datamodel would make more tools understand each other's data, and therefore communicate better. It would also allow us to standardize on the basic data storage and access technology, thereby saving implementation efforts.

The objections experienced seem to be that the database seemed to be harder to implement than expected, and that the needed standard consensus did not arrive. The very idea also seems to contain a bottleneck, since the benefits of the database probably come only when used on a rather large scale by many tools. This makes incremental introduction hard, and requires concentration and coordination of efforts that are not always possible to achieve. The cost of adapting existing tools to a common database also turned out to be rather high, with too small short term gains. Finally, one should also notice that the vision of the central database covers only one of the three dimensions of integration that we have identified.

The idea of viewing the *environment as a single tool* was motivated by the obvious user reaction of not wanting to deal with different user interfaces, conventions and system behaviour. The fact that many tools are internally well engineered and productive to use also stands in contrast with their inability to work together. Extending

Tool Integration: Environments and Frameworks, Edited by D. Schefström and G. van den Broek

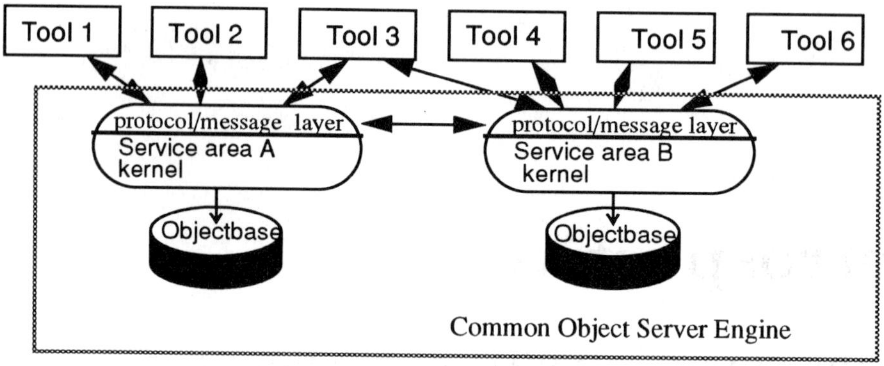

Figure 5.1 A principal environment architecture

the concept of what a "tool" is then seems natural, since it per definition removes the actual troubles.

The objections or problems experienced were then that this approach has a tendency to generate single supplier solutions, with rather closed toolsets and environments, which in turn generate some market resistance. It is also hard to implement since it requires full control over a large product line, something which few organizations have. A very large "tool" may finally overwhelm the user unless presented as a distinct subsystem at the user interface level.

The high expectations on *tight integration* came from the quite obvious observation that there was too little integration between tools, and that increasing the interface between tools would allow for richer flow of productive information. There were furthermore several positive examples showing the way, such as integrated editors-compilers, documentation-drawing, spreadsheet-graphics, etc.

The objections heard after a while claimed that tools were now less independent, which sometimes also was misinterpreted as less well modularized. Tools were also getting harder to use without also using certain complementary, integrated, tools. The difference between a set of integrated tools and tools outside the set now also became very visible, a difference that can be misinterpreted as a lack of "openness".

The demand for *homogeneity* was finally a reaction to the excessive heterogeneity that caused part of the problems. An emerging homogeneity around operating systems, such as UNIX , seemed to be very productive, since it avoided lock in into certain suppliers and helped in achieving reuse and portability.

It seems, however, that a certain level of heterogeneity is tightly coupled with the very concept of a "market". It was furthermore not clear at which level the homogeneity was to be implemented. Although a single basic operating system would be an attractive and realistic goal, it went too far to expect a single approach to development environments.

5.2 AN EXAMPLE ARCHITECTURE

The model and definitions discussed in this document do not imply a single actual architecture. Rather, a number of different ones fit into the picture. In this section, we will discuss one such architecture, and select a few points for further discussion. Figure 5.1 gives an overview of the involved components. One could note the following points:

- Each "service kernel" implements a closely related set of operations, managing its own most central objects and acting as message server for a set of tools.
- The service area kernels are utilized both by each other, but maybe more typically by a number of tools. The kernels may include finally packaged functionality, but are also communicating with the tools using *specialized tool protocols.*
- The kernels, and most often also the tools, are permanently activated. This avoids the otherwise quite inefficient and state destroying start-process-terminate cycle.
- Although there is not a single global database, there is a strong need for unifying the object access implicit in the tool protocols. The commonalities together make up the *common object server engine.*

The "kernels" in the architecture are a response to the practical need for parallel work with less coordinated developments. Functionality and tools should be brought tighter together only after developing a strong "integration idea". Before that, they are probably better evolved in isolation. Within a kernel, the traditional idea of database integration can be applied with success. To approximate, the "kernel" and the tools accessing it correspond to the level of a toolset in the model of the previous section.

In addition, it may in many cases be a simplification to bring the message server responsibility into the realm of the kernel. Although arguments for separation of concern would point at separating the message broadcast server from the service and object kernel, this could be viewed as a question of tool granularity as discussed previously. The following points should then be noted in the direction of a combined solution:

- The set of tools accessing the same objects, the *object set*, will often be the same as the one communicating with the same message server, the *message set.*
- *Requests* are different from *info/events.* While the former in practice involves addressing a known provider of a service, it is the latter that truly utilizes the broadcast properties. Requests may therefore be handled in another way than by means of the message broadcast service.
- Info/events are most often the same as what are known as database triggers, i.e. the notification of when an object in the database is modified or otherwise accessed. A close relationship between data access and message delivery would therefore be natural.

Some experiences indicate that general and broad public tool interfaces often require high bandwidth, are complex to specify, expose more of the lower level services, and are hard to maintain [Sch91]. The problems are especially obvious when tools and the kernel are implemented in separate virtual spaces, in which case it seems even more of an advantage to use specialized high level protocols that are close to the end user functionality desired. The specialized nature does however generate a need for quick

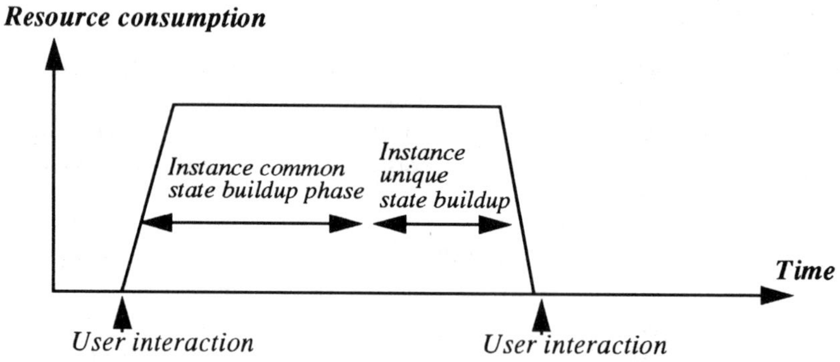

Figure 5.2

and even user-implementable new protocols, leading to the need for providing both kernels and tools with an easy to access extension facility for doing this work.

It also seems clear that future environments and operating systems will have to leave the traditional start-process-terminate cycle, and instead invoke services by sending messages to already activated instances of components. In many cases, the repeated start-process-terminate has been one of the most serious reasons for efficiency losses and lack of interactiveness. The reason could be visualized by the diagram shown in figure 5.2.

Many tools repeatedly perform the same operations and build up the same datastructures each time they are invoked. We call this phase the *instance common state buildup*. As an often smaller part of the work, the purely *instance unique* work is performed, followed by a throw away of the state at termination. In addition to repeatedly wasting the energy corresponding to the area of the first part of the diagram, the opportunities for user interaction are usually limited to before start and after termination.

Future environments can gain much from avoiding this cycle. When the compiler used in the Arcs [Sch91] system was integrated to work this way, the response time was in most cases improved by an order of magnitude.

The architecture above avoids imposing a single central database as the means for integration and unification. This is not because the idea of the central database can be shown to involve any principal flaws, but is rather a recognition of the fact that it has proven to be hard to implement it in practice. The central database has a tendency to become a development bottleneck and often experience continuous problems in reaching the extremely high quality and maturity that is required by such a central basic component.

Therefore, it may be more practical to accept a certain heterogeneity among databases, although the final goal of a single homogeneous one remains. It also seems clear that the needs for unifying the way we access the now different databases will have to be addressed, causing a return of the global database concerns at the level of the tool protocols. Experience will show whether it will be easier to deal with this time.

What is clear, however, is that there is now a wide awareness that multiple integration technologies, in several dimensions, must be addressed. The most recent aspect to explore here has been the Control dimension, which therefore was the main theme of this part of the book.

5.3 REUSE

The area of (Software) *Reuse* has received a fair amount of interest in recent years (a rather early compilation of papers dedicated to this area is [Tra88]). Most people believe that reuse is important, and may be a key factor in finally realizing the long expected increase in development productivity. There are, however, many that also believe that support for reuse shares most aspects with more general software engineering and support environment issues: that it is an *objective*, and not an independent technology.

It is indeed hard to identify an independent reuse technology, and this is also reflected by the fact it was not obvious where to discuss reuse within this book. The tendency in recent years has however been to view reuse as more of an organizational problem, of making projects produce more general software and finding incentives and organizational support for this. To see the economical benefit of making software more reusable, one must calculate over several projects and complete organizations. It therefore requires global planning depending on higher level management decisions and support.

The focus here is however on technological support, and we will therefore discuss a few approaches to reuse that have a close relationship to support environments, the *Database, Browsing*, and *Evolution* approaches.

5.3.1 The database approach

Initial work on reuse viewed the problem as the one of finding the appropriate candidates given a large collection of existing software modules. The simple model of the reuse process was the following:

- The user perceives a need for a certain kind of module, and expresses this in terms of a *database query*.
- The query is processed over a large existing database/repository of modules.
- The answer to the query is presented to the user who now returns to work with the module he needed.

According to this approach reuse is a database problem, which is then solved in the traditional database way by focusing attention on finding an appropriate *query language* and a suitable *database schema*.

However, further investigations reveal that there is more to be addressed before reuse takes place. Although the database approach has a role, it is probably not the case that the major obstacle on the road to large scale reuse is that we are getting lost in vast repositories of valuable reusable modules.

On the other hand, the integration of a database, and the thereby associated query capabilities, has been a central part of the general environments culture since its very start.

Obviously, the database in which reuse-searches are to be made, should be the same as the database we use for storing any objects, for access by other kinds of tools like compilers, editors, browsers, configuration managers, etc.

It seems equally obvious that the query mechanisms utilized by the reuse subsystem should not be different from the one we use for other searches, such as all modules that refer to a given one, all modules that have been changed since the last release, all modules that depends on a module that is written by a given person, etc.

Basic software engineering principles now tell us that the database support for reuse must be the same (reuse the same facilities) as developed for the general context. The reuse aspect is therefore a special emphasis integrated into a larger existing picture.

5.3.2 The browsing approach

Much of previous de-facto reuse has taken place by designers inspecting existing systems, learning from them and borrowing all, parts, or just the over all structure of the solution. The availability of actual source code, and means for overviewing and browsing in it is therefore important. A paper arguing for the importance of this view is [Wei87]. The systematic borrowing of fragments of source code is a most important part of many programming cultures.

This model of the reuse process is less structured, but probably close to reality. It also corresponds well to many people's own practical experience.

One could note the similarity with how most of us gather information and publications when entering a new area. Some of us go to the library an ask for a search in any of the literature databases. In doing so, we specify a number of search criteria, usually in terms of a list of index terms. The expectation we have now is to get the full list of those publications that are important.

However, many people have the experience of not being completely satisfied with such results: we do not always get the "right" references nor the latest ones. Instead, we ask colleagues whether they have read anything interesting; we read one article and there find references to further publications; we go to conferences; and we browse around in book stores and the journals circulating at work. The conclusion is that although the centralized repository has a role, it is far from a complete description of the knowledge reuse process. To the untrained observer this process may look somewhat unstructured, building on a seemingly stochastic browsing approach. However, most professionals work this way and master it in a way that makes it a reliable and efficient method in practice.

The conclusion with respect to reuse of software modules is that support for browsing is central, and a most fruitful areas to address. Just as with the database we can however observe that such services are already part of the more general development environment approach: "software hypertext" - the ability to quickly navigate in and grasp software structures at different levels of abstraction is not particular to reuse, but is a central part of the general development environment idea.

Basic software engineering principles now tell us that the browsing support for reuse must be the same (reuse the same facilities), as developed for the general context. The reuse aspect is therefore, again, a special emphasis integrated into a larger existing picture.

5.3.3 The evolution approach

It is rarely the case that the right interfaces or subsystem decompositions are found at the first try. Rather, we refine the design of systems as our experience and understanding matures as a result of actually using it. Therefore, reusable modules are probably not developed, but are evolved. This is not a deficiency in the way of working, but a reflection of the inherent nature of the development task.

As a consequence of this observation we must provide support for this process to take place in a systematic way: it must be possible to modify so called reusable modules, and reintegrate them into the reuse library; versions and configurations of modules must be tracked and maintained; information on who is changing and why; gathering of statistics on the amount of reuse of different modules. Finally, it must be possible for all those accesses and modifications to take place in parallel by different people.

The picture above has once again obvious similarities with the corresponding support for system development in general. The same requirements on cooperative work and configuration management are present without especially emphasizing reuse. And indeed, solutions to those problems have been developed within the general software development environment area and are in productive use in many places.

Self-evident software engineering principles now tell us that the support for reuse in this area must be the same (reuse the same facilities) as developed for the general context. The reuse aspect is therefore, again, a special emphasis integrated into a larger existing picture.

5.3.4 Conclusion

In the above sections, we have shown that reuse is really a special emphasis applied to technology that is well established and understood anyway. Technology or services that can be argued to support reuse often already have other independent reasons for existence.

Since we thereby have taken the view that "reuse is an objective, not a technology", the truly reuse specific support must be made part of the development process. It should therefore be imposed in the environment by means of a process programme that takes it into account.

Part II

Aerospace Systems Software Engineering Environment

Ian Simmonds
Société Française de Génie Logiciel
14, rue de la Ferme
92100 BOULOGNE

France

Tool Integration: Environments and Frameworks, Edited by D. Schefström and G. van den Broek

6

Introduction to the Aerospace Environment

Aerospace systems are characterised as computationally complex and highly reactive real-time embedded systems.

While the ATMOSPHERE project investigated support for the Systems Engineering community, systems developed within the Aerospace application area can be described as *software intensive*. Many parts of these systems cannot yet be sensibly supported by specific hardware (such as ASICs—Application Specific Integrated Circuits) due to the complexity of their algorithms, and the difficulty of testing modules on the final target systems. Systems must be correct before deployment, due to their mission criticality. Support for systems development in this application domain is therefore largely concerned with supporting the software development activity. The sub-discipline of systems engineering related to the production of software intensive systems is *software engineering*.

The European Aerospace industry has adopted a number of software development methods and languages as *standards*. There use is encouraged by the European Space Agency (ESA)—IDEF0 for functional specification, HOOD [Gro89a, Gro89b] for architectural design, and Ada for coding. IDEF0, based upon SADT, has been widely applied in many application areas and is equally appropriate within the aerospace domain. HOOD and Ada have been developed to directly support certain sound engineering principles, both with significant financial aid from major aerospace and defence system suppliers and procurers. Considerable efforts have been made to define and choose compatible methods, illustrated by the particularly smooth boundary between the HOOD architectural design method and the Ada language.

Despite a strong desire to use Ada, the C language is still heavily used in the aerospace domain. Because of this, a major objective of the developers of the Aerospace Environment was to adapt the HOOD method so that it targets C. In order to thoroughly explore the implications of this evolution of HOOD, the Aerospace environment is primarily concerned with developing C language applications, although most of the tools of the environment support both C and Ada variants.

An additional weakness of the standard IDEF0, HOOD, Ada methodology is in the area of performance evaluation and design verification, both of which are eased by the ability to simulate the developed system during the architectural design process.

Tool Integration: Environments and Frameworks, Edited by D. Schefström and G. van den Broek

To this end a design simulation technique (GSED) was integrated with the HOOD method, and toolset support for the resulting GSED/HOOD method was investigated.

The technologies supporting the Aerospace Environment are based upon a long term vision of computer-aided software engineering. This vision is that of the East project [Bou90], a major European project that has developed a range of generic facilities for supporting the systems engineering activity across a wide range of application domains and life-cycle methods. East is itself based upon PCTE [ECM90], an environment framework component offering important data and control integration services.

Brown and McDermid [BM92] have criticised efforts in the systems engineering environment world saying that integration efforts that concentrate purely on basic integration technology typically achieve only a 'lexical' or 'syntactic' level of integration. They went on to say that effort should be focused on the development of environments in which tools might even have 'knowledge' of the development process in which they are being used.

The breadth of the ATMOSPHERE project's mission—to further the understanding of systems engineering, integrate methods together, extend existing methods, investigate tool integration techniques and technologies, increase industrial awareness of systems engineering techniques and technologies, etc.—meant that the desire to develop a tightly integrated and complete environment had to be balanced against our strong goals in other areas of the project. A consequence of this was the sharing of research efforts between the various aspects of ATMOSPHERE's mission: it was equally valid to develop and extend tools to support extensions to existing methods as to concentrate on the integration of pre-existing tools to produce a tightly integrated environment.

The ATMOSPHERE project provided an opportunity for gaining further experience in applying this vision and checking the validity of the approach as well as performing innovative research. Within the context of ATMOSPHERE, tools were brought into the East Environment to support the life-cycle specific needs of the aerospace application domain, and improvements were made to the general support offered by East for large scale software projects. Specific overall improvements to the East framework resulting from work in ATMOSPHERE were to support the general engineering issues of *configuration management* and *process management*. However, the ATMOSPHERE project's mission ensured that this work on improving tools and framework was part of the larger systems engineering domain pointed to by Brown and McDermid, making it of industrial as well as academic interest.

figure 6.1 gives a brief overview of the application domain-specific parts of the Aerospace Environment, showing supported methods and the names of tools that provided that support.

6.1 OVERVIEW OF THE DESCRIPTION OF THE AEROSPACE ENVIRONMENT

The goal of this description of the Aerospace Environment is to show that environment development is a multi-faceted process. Firstly, there is a need to understand the development methods to be supported and how these methods can be given appropriate tool support. Secondly, the existence of many methods leads to a need to

chapter 6 is a simple description of the a
allowing the integration task to be seen
Further chapters go on to describe this
velopment environment.

The Aerospace Environment is based
extensible. This is achieved through the
the most fundamental of which is the u
number of conventions for its use. This i
affecting the design of presentation and
chapter 8 and chapter 9 describe the b
control and process integration, give ex
to exploit these technologies, and descri
Examples are also given of the encapsu
that they can be used in the environmen

An attempt has been made to descri
users, tool developers and environment
viduals should be aware of the needs of t
ends with a summary of these issues.

6.2 METHODS SUPPORTED ENVIRONMENT

This section describes the basic method
expanding on the general overview of fig
engineering issues of *configuration* and *p*
section are to act as an introduction to r
understanding how these methods can b

6.2.1 Requirements capture

The goal of this phase is to establish a do
of the users of the developed system. E
simply by gathering together the short pl

The simple method supported by the
possible requirements capture with two e
that seem to be aspects of some larger
related requirements.

Ensuring that a non-functional requir
quirement. Process related requirements
adopted for the project, while others m
tation language chosen; hardware platf

6.2.2 System specification

A complete specification of a system sho
and performance, as well as any other

ely. Miscellaneous issues are typically similar
d in a similar style of documentation to user
ent includes no specific methodological sup-
rformance specifications, although they can,
m as miscellaneous issues. However, there is
al specification through the presence of the

IDEF0

(Structured Analysis and Design Technique),
ysis of a set of requirements in a top-down
ar functional specification. This specification
tended system, and the data flows between
decisions made during the definition of a
description of the function itself.

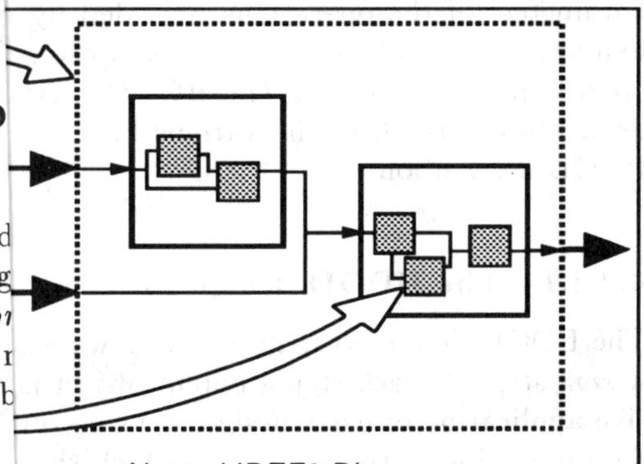

Nested IDEF0 Diagrams

del represents a piece of functionality, with a
gst other things). No control flows are shown.
ore elementary functions giving a more detailed
n (left hand diagram). The components of a
nputs and produce the same output as their
position in the right hand diagram.

ion methodology', where ICAM stands for
g, the programme under which the IDEF0
IDEF0) as part of the wider IDEF method-
nitial phase in this wider methodology.
tem model is the *diagram*. Each diagram
a single function—indeed, there is a clear
Diagrams can, at least in theory, be nested
n (as shown in figure 6.2). The fact that
with a clearly defined unit of modularity,

means that the analysis of a system can be divided amongst a number of individuals, with each individual refining a different set of diagrams within the specification.

6.2.4 Architectural design—HOOD

HOOD (Hierarchical Object Oriented Design) is the European Space Agency's standard architectural design method. HOOD is a combination of abstract machine and object oriented design concepts and was originally oriented towards Ada program development.

Following Booch's definition, an object is a model of a real world entity which combines data with the operations working on that data. Objects are the basic unit of modularity in HOOD: a software system is modelled as a set of interconnected objects. The HOOD method provides rules to identify objects and to organise them into a well-structured decomposition hierarchy.

HOOD has both a graphic and a textual description language. As a rule, the graphic formalism is used to give the overall description of the architecture of the modelled system, while the textual formalism is used to refine this with details such as the parameters of the operations provided by each object, the description of a resource managed by an object or the description of the algorithms used to implement the operations of an object. The HOOD methodology defines when and through which description formalism the various kinds of information have to be inserted into the HOOD description.

6.2.4.1 The HOOD design process

The HOOD design strategy is top-down and consists of the execution of a set of *basic design steps*. In each step a parent object is decomposed into its child objects. Successive application of basic design steps to objects of the design results in a hierarchical decomposition of the system in which the root object corresponds to the functionalities provided by the modelled software system, and leaves correspond to elementary objects. Each basic design step is used to decompose a single HOOD object into child objects, and consists of four phases:

Definition and analysis of the problem Aims at clearly identifying the problem that the object has to solve. This is done through the organisation of the information already gathered during the previous requirement analysis phase of the software lifecycle, which for the lifecycle supported by the Aerospace Environment is IDEF0. While there is no clear methodological support for converting IDEF0 requirements and functions into HOOD objects and operations, there is a clear need to support some kind of traceability between them. Indeed the IDEF0 method expects each function of the IDEF0 model's hierarchy of functions to be assigned to an identifiable architectural component of the resulting system—the function's 'mechanism'. Such traceability allows verification that the designed system meets its intended requirements.

Elaboration of the informal solution strategy An informal, natural language description of the functionalities provided by the object is given in this phase.

Formalisation of the strategy Here the informal solution strategy is analysed in order to identify the objects and the operations that implement the strategy. The result is an initial decomposition of the object into a set of child objects.

This phase may be further decomposed into four subphases: (i) identification of objects (for example, taken from the set of nouns of the informal solution description); (ii) identification of operations (taken from the set of verbs of the informal solution description); (iii) grouping objects and operations; (iv) graphical description.

HOOD is deliberately open-ended at this point, allowing design documentation to be enriched with whatever characteristics may be appropriate. The GSED method, described in § 6.2.5, is an example of an addition of performance evaluation techniques to HOOD.

Formalisation of the solution This phase converts the results of the previous phase into a more formal format—the Object Definition Skeleton (ODS).

The phase produces the 'child-mode' ODS (ie an ODS with only the provided and required interface section fully described) of each newly identified child object and completes the 'parent-mode ODS' (ie an ODS with all sections fully described) of the parent object.

The parent-mode ODS includes a definition of the control behaviour of each of the operations the object provides and, in the case of a so-called *active object*, of the overall behaviour of the object. The behaviour of an operation is described in an *OPeration Control Structure* (OPCS), and the behaviour of an object in an *OBject Control Structure* (OBCS). It is these two classes of control structure that are further specified in the GSED formalism (§ 6.2.5).

A number of HOOD concepts are illustrated in figure 6.3.

6.2.4.2 HOOD and cooperative work

HOOD supports cooperative work quite naturally, in that successive refinement partitions the system into a number of components, each of which may be refined independently. However, the partition of work based on the allocation of branches of the design to different teams really requires explicit support. The HOOD toolset of the Aerospace Environment (AdaNICE) adds a notion of *subproject* to formalise this separation of work on different branches of the design.

6.2.5 Design verification and performance evaluation—GSED

A major goal of the architectural design of a system is the imposition of constraints on the components of the system to ensure that the integrated system will behave as required. If the architectural design is correctly performed, the developers of distinct design objects may be allowed to proceed largely independently of one another, as long as they respect their given constraints. However, deciding upon appropriate performance constraints for design objects is an intrinsically difficult task. While constraints for the overall performance of a system may be easily identified, decomposing the performance constraints associated with an operation of one design object into constraints on the operations of child design objects that will combine to perform this operation, requires assumptions to be taken on the relative amount of time taken to perform each child operation. Such assumptions are difficult to make.

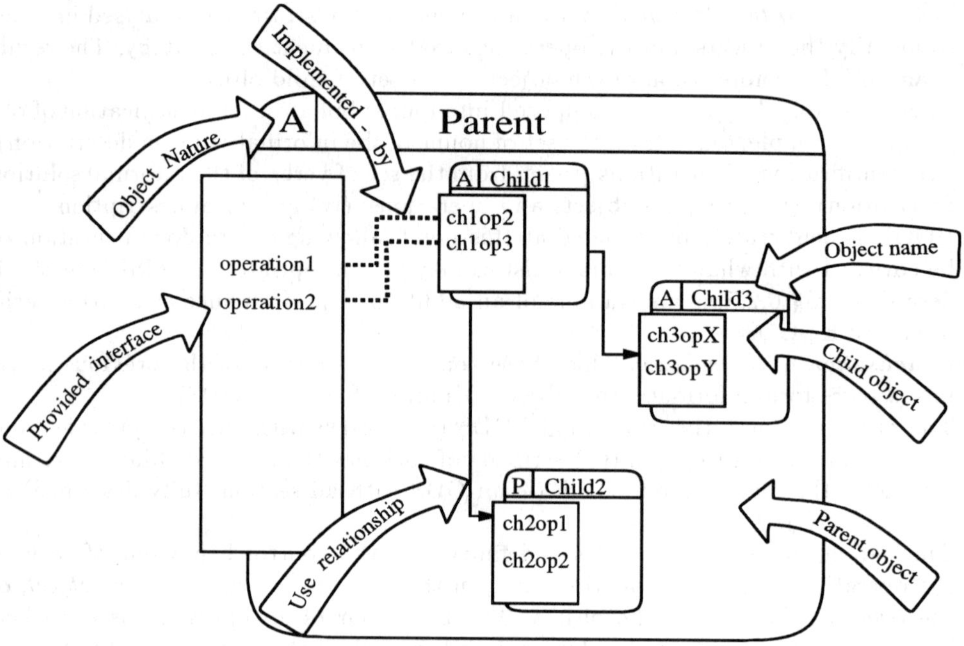

Figure 6.3 This diagram shows the decomposition of the object 'Parent' into three child objects—Child1, Child2 and Child3. Each object provides a number of operations as part of its *provided interface*, and has a *nature* indicating whether it is active ('A') or passive ('P'). Systems designed with HOOD may be parallel, and an object that is active corresponds to an independent thread of control. A *use* relationship records the calling of operations provided by one object from another object. Each *implemented-by* relationship records the fact that a particular provided operation of a decomposed object will actually be provided by a particular child object.

GSED (Discrete Event Simulation Generator) is a general purpose description technique supporting design simulation. To fulfil its role within the Aerospace Environment this was adapted to allow the analysis and description of the behaviour of active HOOD objects. Interest in this is easy to understand since HOOD, which was originally targeted at Ada (a language used primarily for real-time, embedded systems), offers no explicit support for the assurance that desired real-time behaviour constraints will be met.

The GSED method allows the description of the behaviour of the objects and operations of a HOOD design and allows these descriptions to be combined to generate a simulator for the design which may be used to increase understanding of the behaviour of the design. This process is applied iteratively, yielding a better understanding of the behaviour of the system, an assessment of the overall timing requirements to be imposed on each design object, and the refinement of behavioural requirements for lower-level design objects. This leads to an early identification of performance critical operations, the impact of operation performance being seen before coding is started.

It also allows the verification of the system's ability to handle external events, which are modelled as interrupts.

6.2.5.1 Time modelling in HOOD

The GSED method is based on the notion of Time Behaviour Objects (TBOs). Each TBO is a finite state machine and captures the behaviour of a single HOOD entity—an object or an operation. A HOOD object's (operation's) TBO is a restatement of its HOOD object (operation) control structure in a way that is sufficiently precise to allow the generation of a simulator for the design.

Like any finite state machine, a TBO is defined as a number of states, together with transitions between these states. Each state corresponds to a state that the design entity could be in at any one time, and each transition to a means of passing between states. Each transition has an associated action to be taken during a simulation, together with a means for evaluating the time that the action should take. Simple actions, such as the assignment of a variable or the evaluation of a condition allow the simulation of loops and conditional behaviour, and can be given fixed times. Other actions, such as calls to operations provided by other objects, interrupt handling, transition synchronisation, or exception raising and handling, correspond to specific semantics of the HOOD method, and act as a basis for *combining* TBOs.

TBOs must be specified for each object and operation of the part of the design to be simulated, and can be automatically combined following the implicit semantics of the HOOD formalism to give a single finite state machine—a *composite TBO*—capturing the joint behaviour of this part of the system.

6.2.5.2 Running a simulation

A complete simulator for a design consists of both a specification of the behaviour of the system—a composite TBO—and the definition of a means for *driving* the simulation. The way of driving a simulation specified by the general GSED method is not always completely defined. For example, a state may exist in a composite (or simple) TBO that requires a choice to be made between two equally valid transitions. However, the HOOD method brings semantics allowing all ambiguities to be automatically resolved. This has allowed the development of a generalised driver for simulating HOOD designs.

It should be noted that the solution that HOOD provides for the example of ambiguity in a choice of next transition is to make an arbitrary choice, removing a category of 'starvation' from the designed system. However, the presence of such ambiguities in a design is normally a result of an inadequate definition of the control structures of some objects or operations. By animating HOOD's arbitrarily made choice, GSED/HOOD shows designers the *actual* behaviour of the system they have designed, *complete with any design faults that they have made* in their definition of object and operation control structures. The recognition that a simulation of a design should capture all faults of the design being simulated was a significant step in the establishment of the semantics of a generalised driver.

The combination of a simulator and its driver gives a prototype system that exhibits a design's specified behaviour, including those aspects of the system that result from both good and bad design. This prototype may be executed and interacted with—interaction being in terms of interrupts.

6.2.6 Detailed design and coding—Ada and C

The HOOD method supports the architectural design of a system by providing a formalised hierarchical decomposition of a system into components. Each elementary decomposition within this hierarchy effectively groups several child components into a larger package.

While it is intended that source code will be supplied only for leaf objects: Objects that are not decomposed using the HOOD formalism—a goal of HOOD is to maintain and formalise the interfaces between *all* objects. Given this goal, HOOD is sufficiently rich to allow the complete generation of *interfaces* for the code modules implementing each HOOD object. The format of the interface depends upon the language used for coding the system.

For the Ada language, the concept of HOOD object maps into the concept of *library package*. Ada itself makes a clear split between the specification (interface) and body (implementation) of a package. Moreover, there is a clear notion within Ada of one package being built up of other packages. The mapping between HOOD and Ada is particular clean since HOOD was developed as a design methodology for Ada development.

For the C language, however, a mapping had to be newly developed in the ATMOSPHERE project. There is less of a distinction between specifications and bodies within C (although similar concepts appear in the related language C++). Such a separation was made by introducing additional semantics for C source files, which became bodies, and header files, which became specifications. The nesting of specifications for non-terminal objects was mapped into the nesting of include files. The result is similar to Ada, with a header file for each HOOD object, but with source code only for leaf objects. Logically the body of a non-terminal HOOD object can be considered as the C library that would be generated from the source code of all HOOD objects beneath this node in the design.

While there is a natural mapping between HOOD concepts such as active objects, exceptions and interrupts in HOOD and constructs of the Ada language, these concepts do not exist in C. Consequently the HOOD/C method assumes the existence of a HOOD/C run-time library which supports these missing concepts.

6.2.7 General support for detailed design and coding

The Aerospace Environment made use of a tool called KeyOne which supports the step-wise refinement of code from an 'empty' architectural component to final, compilable source code. It is based upon the principles of syntax directed editing, and aimed at not only easing the development of code, but guiding the developer to produce well structured, easily understood code that can be relatively cheaply maintained.

The gap between an architectural design and compilable source code is considerable and a great deal of creativity is normally required to bridge that gap. Coding is a design activity, often described as being achievable through step-wise refinement, starting with an element of the architectural design, and arriving at compilable code, passing through a number of intermediate levels of *abstraction* that consist of so-called *pseudo code*—a mixture of coding language specific syntax and natural language.

The motivation behind KeyOne is that it is precisely these intermediate levels of abstraction that help in the *understanding* of a program. Programmers usually establish an understanding of a program by identifying which lines are clearly related to one another, and can be seen to combine to perform some useful task. They mentally group lines into 'bundles', and then 'bundles' into larger bundles, an activity which can seen to be the reverse of the process of refining a design into code. KeyOne seeks to simplify program understanding by capturing the refinement process followed during detailed design. With knowledge of the hierarchical refinement of source code that took place during detailed design, it becomes possible to view the code from this design perspective, viewing as many levels of refinement as required for an understanding of the code, or even replaying the design process.

The benefits of this approach become particularly clear during the maintenance of software developed using KeyOne. Maintenance engineers are able to view the detailed design of the code as recorded by KeyOne, thus dramatically reducing the time they must spend to understand the code as well as risk of them misunderstanding the rationale behind the code.

6.2.8 Version and configuration management based upon the Adele model

Each of the methods and languages presented above has a clear notion of *modularity*—the means by which a system is broken down into smaller, potentially independently defined and developed pieces. Each module of a system may well be developed incrementally and be subsequently modified or evolved to correct bugs or introduce new features. The tracking of changes to modules of a system gives rise to the subject of *version management*, while the combination of selected versions of modules to give a complete system gives rise to *configuration management*.

6.2.8.1 Versions, packaging, and configurations

The model of configuration management supported by the Adele [Est85] configuration management system had been previously used by one of the companies participating in the ATMOSPHERE project. The model seeks to formalise the notion of *module*, and to use this to allow the automatic generation of configurations based upon knowledge of functional dependencies between modules.

The Adele approach makes use of the fact that modules can be characterised by the services that they provide to introduce a distinction between *interfaces* and *realisations*. An *interface* captures those characteristics of a module on which a user of the module depends. In this way, each *realisation* (implementation) of a module can be made to depend upon the services that it expects another module to provide, independently of how that other module is implemented. This replaces the *tight binding* together of specific versions of modules with a *loose binding* that can be evaluated to construct particular configurations.

Figure 6.4 shows how functional dependencies can be expressed between modules, and illustrates the notions of *interface*, and *realisation*.

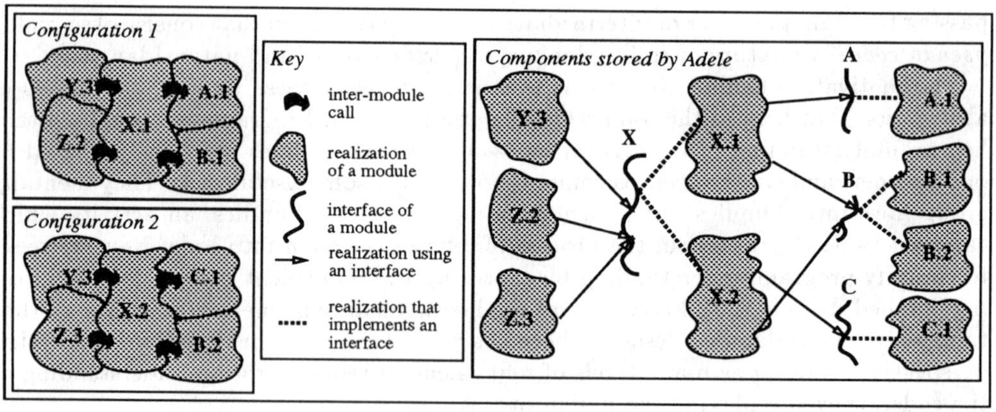

Figure 6.4 *Configuration 1* consists of a system of five modules, two of which make use of subsets of *X.1*, and two of which are used by *X.1*. However, the fact that *X.1* makes use of *A.1* and *B.1* is completely hidden from the modules that use *X.1*. Indeed, *configuration 2* shows a different version of *X* offering the *same interface* but being used by a different version of *Z* and itself making use of different modules (*C.1* and *B.2*). Rather than storing these modules tightly bound into configurations 1 and 2, Adele encourages the storage of well-packaged modules which are related to the *interfaces* of the modules that they call. This now makes clear the fact that other potential configurations could have been built based upon the same modules, such as one consisting of *Y.3*, *Z.3*, *X.1*, *A.1* and *B.2*.

The identification of interfaces as independent entities means that each version of a module is *packaged* as a unit which is known to provide certain services and to make use of other services. The consumer of a service need not, in general, be aware of the way in which that service is implemented. Moreover, both realisations *and* interfaces may be versioned, allowing control over the impact of changes which affect the interface of a module.

6.2.8.2 Application of the Adele model throughout the environment

The Adele model can, at least in theory, be applied to any product of the systems engineering development process, with many different notions of 'module' and 'relationships between modules' being managed in a *loose bound* manner. Such relationships may be inter- or intra-method, with the possibility of the modules at the ends of a relationship being versioned independently of the presence of the relationship.

6.2.8.3 Classical configuration management

Classical configuration management usually takes place in a world of versioned *configuration items*, lists of which form *configurations*, and a central role is given to the identification of *baseline* configurations. A baseline is a snapshot of a system at a particular moment in its life, typically at the moment of its release to its users. Future corrections to the system are strongly controlled through *change control* procedures, an area that overlaps with process management (§ 6.2.9). A variety of approaches to configuration management are presented in [Fei91].

In short, there are a large number of issues related to the provision of good configuration management in a software engineering environment. However, the technical problem of integrating tools together to form a useful, scalable environment with strong configuration management support, primarily involves ensuring that all tool's are able to manipulate and maintain appropriate *components* of the 'descriptions' they are used to define. The majority of discussions of version and configuration management within the Aerospace Environment are therefore related to the identification of *well-packaged* components to which the disciplines of more classical version and configuration management can be applied.

6.2.9 Process management

Each of the methods supported by the Aerospace Environment (and shown in figure 6.1) defines or infers a number of elementary 'process steps' to be integrated into the overall process model of an aerospace development project. For example, we may infer that there should be steps to 'code a C module', 'debug a C module' or 'analyse the client's non-functional requirements', as well as the explicitly defined 'basic design step' of the HOOD method (see § 6.2.4.1). These elementary process steps typically correspond to the performance of an action related to a single *component* of a specification, design or implementation, as mentioned in § 6.2.8.

However, these elementary process steps are merely part of the syntax of the methods involved, and any additional aspects of the systems development process—those typically found within a Process Definition Manual (frequently called a Quality Assurance Manual)—usually fall outside the scope of the methods themselves, being *policies for the application of a development method* within a particular organisation. Such policies include those related to requesting and authorising change, review and inspection cycles, and more general management activities.

Process management is part of the general vision of software engineering behind the Aerospace Environment and East, and reflects the widely perceived need for understanding and managing software processes [Hum89] rather than merely keeping track of the results of these processes. In East this need is introduced through the provision of formalisms for the definition of process models; means for viewing the process being followed, ensuring that users of East are continually reminded of the process they are following; and means for guiding developers by 'subsetting' the environment to those parts necessary for the completion of their tasks.

While a description of these mechanisms is beyond the scope of this book, the subject of producing tools and other environment components that match the needs of an organisation's software processes is frequently raised.

6.3 THE AEROSPACE ENVIRONMENT

This section describes the tools that form part of the Aerospace Environment. The Aerospace Environment brings together a range of prototype and commercial tools and framework technologies to support the development methods and processes introduced in § 6.2 and summarised in figure 6.1.

Each tool present in the Aerospace Environment existed in some form before the

ATMOSPHERE project and had to be modified to a greater or lesser extent in order to be consistent with the evolutions made in ATMOSPHERE to the method that it supports. In addition, a number of changes were made to each tool in order to integrate it into the environment: for the pairwise cooperation of tools, or for the general use of framework technologies. This latter class of integration is described in § 6.4.

6.3.1 Requirements capture and non-functional specification—RMT

RMT (Requirements Management Tool) offers simple means for the creation and viewing of *requirement trees*. Each requirement is represented as a *node* within a tree of requirements, and may make reference to other requirements within its requirement tree or within other trees.

The precise semantic use of the tree structure is left to the user of the tool, but typically non-leaf nodes are used to group together the nodes beneath them in the tree. The ability to make references between requirements allows this structure to be overcome when richer groupings of requirements is required than a strict hierarchy, or to allow the inclusion of useful pointers throughout the tree for constructing and following chains of related requirements. The central tree structure was maintained, however, since it is this that imposes sufficient structure for the generation of paper copies of a requirement tree.

The toolset supports several *views* (see § 8.1.1, § 8.2) of each requirement node as well as summary views of an entire requirement tree or sub-tree. Textual and graphical views of each node exist, showing the *attributes* of the node and which other nodes relate to this node—either by being referenced by it, or by making reference to it. Each node may also have an associated document attached to it containing a so-called *content*. This content is managed by an independent document editor and so is displayed and edited in a separate view.

RMT supports the generation of paper documentation which combines all details of a requirements tree together with the attributes and content of each requirement.

RMT was developed to use all elements of the East framework and so, in particular, supports all standard features of a tool that uses the East-UIMS (see § 8.1).

Although originally developed for capturing user requirements, RMT is quite generic and could be used to support a number of text-based activities, such as analysis of non-functional requirements or storing the results of a document review. Within the Aerospace Environment it is used for its original purpose—capturing user requirements—and for storing miscellaneous results of non-functional requirements analysis.

6.3.2 Functional specification—how the IDEF Toolset supports IDEF0

The IDEF Toolset supports the IDEF0 method. As described in § 6.2.3 the basic unit of the IDEF0 method is the diagram, each of which represents a function in terms if its input and output data flows and its decomposition into more elementary functions. The functional requirements of a system are analysed by hierarchically decomposing the functionality of the system, thus resulting in a hierarchy of functions.

The IDEF Toolset allows the editing of individual diagrams and the maintenance of trees of diagrams. An entire tree is referred to as a *model*. figure 6.5 shows how the three tools of the toolset (the IDEF0 shell, model editor and diagram editor) relate.

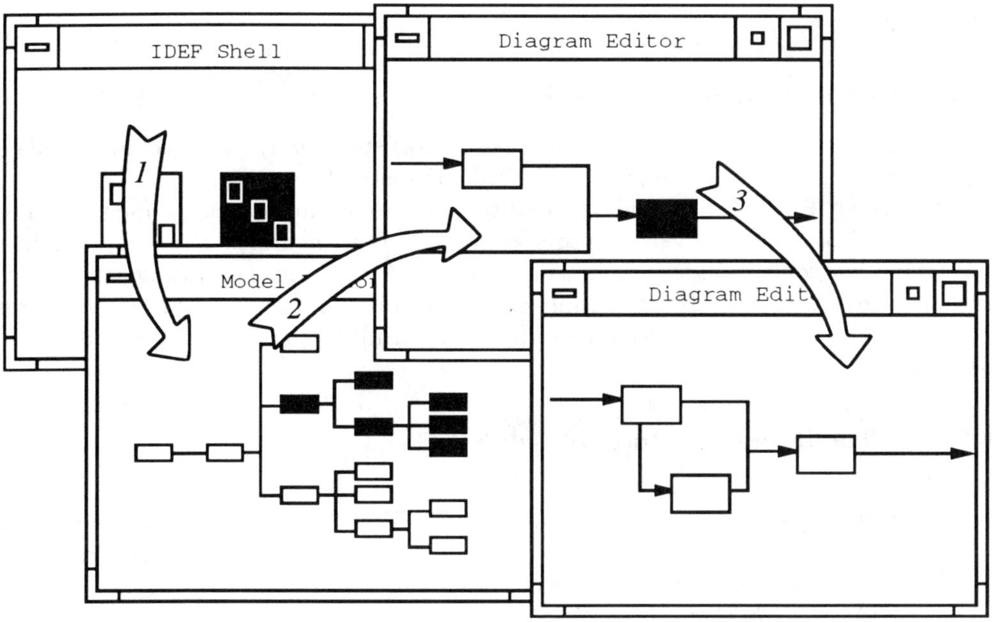

Figure 6.5 The tools of the IDEF Toolset: The user starts the IDEF0 shell within the context of an IDEF0 project. Then (1) they open a model, starting the model editor, which shows a hierarchical view of the diagrams within the model. The user may then (2) open a diagram, which is presented by the diagram editor. Finally, (3), the diagram editor may be used recursively to view the diagrams associated with child functions

The *diagram editor* supports the editing of a single diagram, allowing its function to be defined in terms of child functions and the data flows between them. It also assures that data flows of the function being decomposed are used and provided by child functions. The added value of the *model editor* is that it allows certain manipulations of the diagram tree such as cutting and pasting of branches around the tree. The *shell* provides a graphical entry point to the toolset. As will be seen later in § 8.5, the shell tool is only relevant when the IDEF Toolset is used outside a graphical user interface. Consequently there was no need to bring the shell into the Aerospace Environment.

A number of constraints are implied by the IDEF0 method, such as:

- since many functions appear as a child function in one diagram and as the parent function in another, the data flows of many functions are represented twice. Double representation introduces a risk of inconsistency.
- there are minimum and maximum limits on the number of child functions within a decomposition

Constraints localised within a single diagram (that each input flow is used, and that all functions are reached, ...) are checked by the diagram editor when the diagram is saved, as well as on user demand. Constraints that can only be checked by consulting several diagrams can be validated upon demand from the model editor.

The toolset was developed to support many users working on a single model, but with the restriction that only one user may be editing a particular branch of diagrams at any one time.

6.3.3 Architectural design—how AdaNICE supports HOOD

AdaNICE is a tightly integrated set of CASE tools specifically designed to provide a high degree of automated support to the HOOD method.

The AdaNICE tools are classified into interactive tools and command line tools. The interactive tools cover the various parts of the HOOD ***basic design step*** (see § 6.2.4.1). Command line tools include a document generator, a means for generating source code skeletons from a HOOD design, facilities for exporting and importing HOOD designs by means of a standard interchange format, and utilities to manage the AdaNICE's database.

6.3.3.1 The interactive tools of AdaNICE

HDE: The HOOD Diagram Editor

This is a graphical editor that supports HOOD's graphical formalism, with each window based upon a single HOOD object and its decomposition. The user interface of this editor is described in more detail in § 8.3.1.

ODSE: The ODS Editor

This tool supports the specification of objects using the textual formalism of the HOOD method, the ODS (Object Definition Skeleton). Besides supporting simple text editing based upon an initial template, the editor allows the syntactic and semantics correctness of a resulting ODS to be checked.

ISSE: The Informal Solution Strategy Editor and Analyser

This tool provides a text editor to edit the informal solution strategy text of an object and an analyser to analyse supporting the identification of objects and operations indicated within the informal solution strategy text.

The text attribute editor

This is a general purpose free text editor allowing the editing of the text attributes of HOOD objects. The set of text attributes of a HOOD object can be extended by configuring a *document template* (see document generator below). The standard configuration supports the unextended HOOD method.

6.3.3.2 The command line tools of AdaNICE

AdaNICE provides a large number of command line tools to perform non-interactive design activities such as the generation of documentation and source code as well as basic perform database management functions such as the creation, deletion and duplication of HOOD projects.

The Document Generator

This tool allows the generation of design documentation. The document generation is driven by a user-defined *document template* which defines the content and the format of generated documents. A design document consists of a set of chapters, one chapter per object. The content of each chapter is defined in terms of which of an object's attributes should be presented and how they should be formatted. Documents can be generated with different internal representations to allow the subsequent application of a variety of popular publishing tools, such as FrameMaker, TPS and Ptroff.

The code extractor

This tool allows the generation of Ada or C source code from a HOOD design. The code extractor generates a set of source files for each object together with a separate file representing the main unit of the program. In the case of C code an appropriate build structure is also generated. On UNIX this is in the form of a *makefile* [Fel79] while on PCTE it is a structure suitable for the use of the East Build toolset [Sim91a]. The rules for mapping HOOD constructs into target language constructs are not embedded in the code extractor but are described in a user customisable template.

The SIF generator and compiler

Tools are provided for the importation and exportation of HOOD designs using the HOOD method's Standard Interchange Format (SIF).

The rule checker

Many of the constraints of the HOOD method are not sensibly enforced during the design activity. However, these constraints must be satisfied by a completed design. The rule checker analyses a design and generates a report in which all constraint violations of these rules are listed. The rule checker can be applied both to complete designs and more locally within a design.

An example of a constraint assumed by the HOOD method is that each object in a completed design must provide at least one operation.

6.3.4 Design verification and performance evaluation using GSED

The GSED/HOOD toolset provides facilities for defining the behavioural characteristics of a HOOD design and for performing a simulation of a design that was enriched in this way.

The toolset was developed to work closely with AdaNICE for a number of reasons. Firstly, a GSED/HOOD toolset naturally displays a simulation by animating a hood design. Secondly, if GSED/HOOD is to be used in the same environment as a HOOD tool then it is desirable that the layout of HOOD diagrams between GSED and that tool is similar, if not identical. Finally, since the development of a tool to display HOOD designs is a significant piece of work, it made sense to reuse AdaNICE—a tool that was already available within the Aerospace Environment.

The complete toolset supporting the GSED/HOOD method within ATMOSPHERE appears to the user as an extended AdaNICE, with an extra couple of windows allowing access to the operations of GSED.

6.3.4.1 Defining Time Behaviour Objects (TBOs)

As mentioned in § 6.2.5, GSED/HOOD enriches the formalisms for describing control flow within and between objects (OBCS: Object Control Structure), and within and between operations (OPCS: Operation Control Structure). This formalism—Time Behaviour Objects (TBOs)—is based upon the notion of finite state machines.

The GSED/HOOD toolset allows the user to edit the TBO associated with each HOOD entity (object or operation), the selection of the HOOD entity whose TBO is to be edited being made within the design displayed by AdaNICE. The TBO editor provided by GSED is a simple text editor. Syntax of TBOs is only validated when the design is compiled to generate a composite TBO. Ideally the TBO editor would be replaced by a syntax-directed editor.

6.3.4.2 Preparing a simulation

As mentioned in § 6.2.5, a prerequisite for running a simulation is the generation of a composite TBO from the TBOs associated with each object and operation of the design. The composition of TBOs is the composition of finite state machines, and is an algorithmically simple procedure. However, being recursive, its application to even small designs is time consuming and error prone if done by hand. For this reason, the GSED/HOOD method is only realistically usable with full tool support.

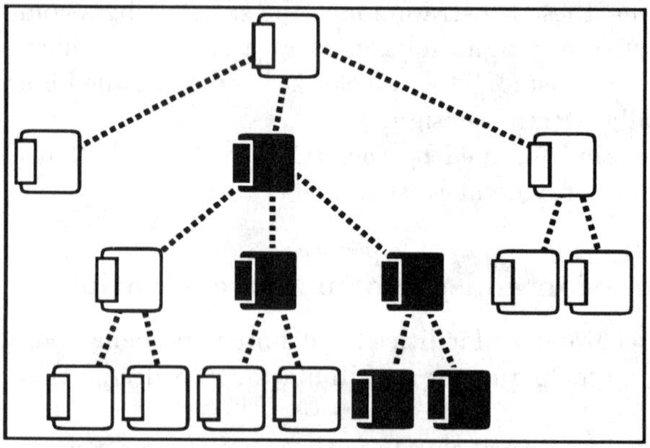

Figure 6.6 A subtree of a HOOD design: a subtree is any connected subgraph of a tree of HOOD objects. The subgraph to be simulated must be connected for otherwise control flow would be restricted to within each connected subgraph—the HOOD method only captures control flows between parent and child objects, and between sibling objects.

It is frequently useful to generate a simulator for a *subtree* of a HOOD design. This allows the simulation of a particular part of the design when the behaviour of other nodes is undefined, or allows a simulation that concentrates on debugging a part of the design. figure 6.6 illustrates the definition of a subtree. When preparing a simulation, the user selects those HOOD entities whose TBOs should be included in the simulator.

The resulting composite TBO will be based upon the TBOs of whichever objects and operations have been selected, although only those operations and states that can be reached from an identified entry point need appear in the generated composite TBO.

6.3.4.3 Running a simulation

A simulation can be started from any object for which a composite TBO has been generated. As the simulation proceeds, the HOOD design displayed by AdaNICE is animated, with each operation and object that is active (undergoing state transitions, rather than active in the HOOD sense) being highlighted.

The interaction of the system with the world is simulated through interrupts. These are either user inspired, found within a predefined script (*simulation scenario*), or a combination of both. Interrupts are processed (or not!) as defined within the original HOOD design. Usually a range of scripts is defined to perform a number of test scenarios for an object. A single script may be run with several different simulators containing differing degrees of detail, corresponding to different subtrees of the design.

6.3.5 Detailed design—the KeyOne toolset

The KeyOne toolset offers facilities for the structured editing, browsing and printing of a variety of programming, design or other sufficiently well-defined languages. This is enriched with direct support for capturing the refinement process, and the viewing, editing and printing of code in a manner that reflects the refinement process.

6.3.5.1 KeyOne in general

KeyOne formalises the notion of the *abstraction*, and introduces the notion of a *Program Description Language* (PDL). A PDL is a conventional programming, design or other language whose syntax has been extended with abstractions. An abstraction may be used to represent any element of the programming language (expression, statement, condition, loop, block, declaration, etc.), allowing syntax compliant pseudo code to be developed.

The structured editing offered by KeyOne not only allows code to be developed directly within KeyOne, but also the introduction of a design structure into code developed elsewhere. This second point supports reverse engineering.

KeyOne includes a documentation package called KeyDoc. This package can produce a large range of documentation from a single source file, ranging from pretty printed source file listings, to design-oriented documentation of each abstraction. In preparation for this, the user may associate textual descriptions with any abstraction, statement, expression or identifier. These descriptions not only appear within printed documentation, but are available on-line: for example, the description of a variable is available wherever the variable is displayed.

6.3.5.2 The role of KeyOne in the Aerospace Environment

KeyOne supported the structured editing of a number of the languages supported by the Aerospace Environment. In addition, the environment benefits from the ability to use KeyOne abstractions in each of these languages, and produce KeyOne-quality documentation.

KeyOne is used in the detailed design and coding phases in variants supporting the C and Ada languages, as well as in the architectural design phase where it is used to support the HOOD ODS language.

6.4 GOALS WITHIN THE ATMOSPHERE PROJECT

The ATMOSPHERE project was part of an on-going effort towards achieving the long term goal of integrated, yet modular, process-centred environments. Several significant steps were taken down this road, but the quest remains far from finished.

This section sets the integration work performed in ATMOSPHERE into an overall integration scheme. This work can be split into three categories:

Tool-Framework integration
: The central hypothesis for basing environments on a specifically developed framework that factorises commonly required facilities of an environment is that this allows the production of cleaner, more modular tools which may more easily cooperate than those based upon different base technologies. Moreover, such an environment should be more easily extended and customised than one built without a single rich underlying technology.
Consequently, since the Aerospace Environment is a framework-based environment, all tools have been either developed, reengineered or encapsulated to use the framework.

Tool-Tool integration
: Wherever there is a relationship between two activities or entities at either a methodological or process level that are themselves supported by software tools there will be at least an opportunity, if not a need, for those tools to cooperate to support that relationship. That is to say that Tool-Tool integration is a means for achieving method-level and process-level integration.

Environment building
: A significant part of the functionality of an environment need not be supported by functionality-specific tools. An environment framework such as East contains a number of generic tools that can support additional functionality upon the provision of *models*—a document editor driven by *documentation models*, process support tools driven by *process models*, etc.. A role of an environment builder is to identify what functionality is not provided by tools and supply appropriate models to complete the environment, bringing the environment into a state where it is 'ready to be used'.

While it is believed that two tools that have each been integrated within a common, rich framework may be more deeply and easily integrated together than similar tools based on differing technologies, it is clear that however good the framework is tool-tool integration requires significant extra effort. The pairwise integration of two tools may require important changes to be made to the functionality offered by each tool so that they come to share a common view of the subject of their cooperation. One way of reducing such work is by improving tool modularity, thus allowing much integration work to be done during environment building without a need for tool modification.

6.4.1 Tool-Tool integration

Figure 6.7 shows and labels the opportunities for integration between the lifecycle tools and methods of the Aerospace Environment. Two classes of inter-method integration

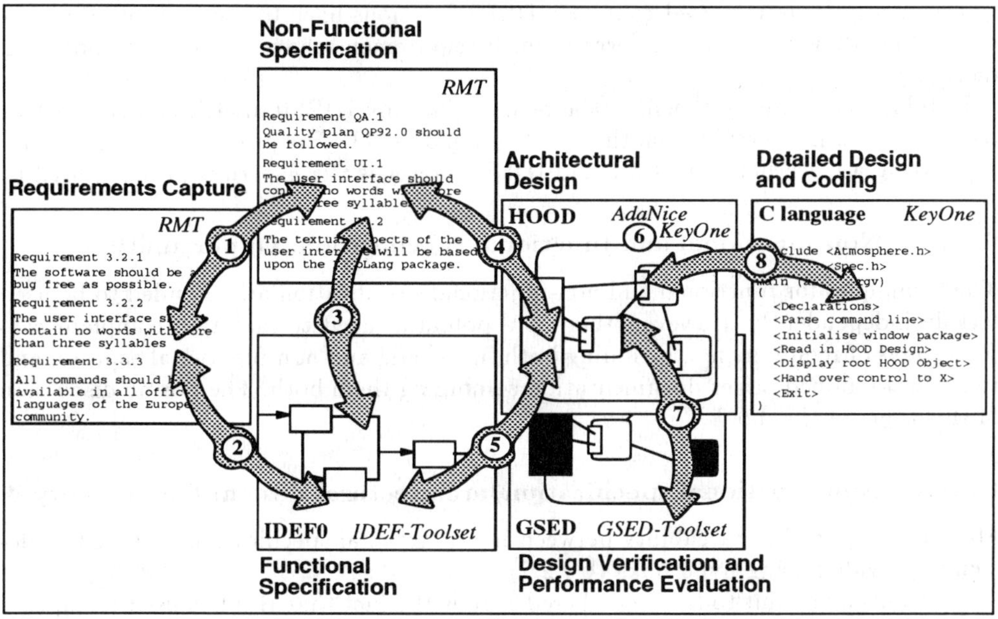

Figure 6.7 The majority of integration opportunities between tools correspond to the integration between underlying methods. The exceptions were opportunity 6: the use of a sophisticated syntax directed editor to replace a minimal text editor within the HOOD toolset; and opportunity 7: the extension of one method with another.

that imply tool-tool integration have been factorised out as tool-framework issues: these are version and configuration management and process integration.

6.4.1.1 Requirements capture/non-functional specification: Opportunity 1

The principal need for integration between these two development phases is to ensure that all customer requirements are analysed, even if some are eventually turned down after customer/developer negotiation. This class of integration is often termed *traceability*.

The support of traceability between these two phases is significantly simplified in the Aerospace Environment since a single tool is used for both requirements capture and non-functional specification, namely RMT. Indeed, the fact that requirements in one requirements tree (see § 6.3.1) can be related with requirements in another requirements tree means that the desired traceability is already present: a 'requirement' in the non-functional specification can refer back to the customer requirement(s) that it corresponds to. Consequently this main integration opportunity was met.

6.4.1.2 Requirements capture/functional specification: Opportunity 2

Traceability between captured requirements and functional specifications is also important, the goal being to check that all customer requirements have been considered.

Consequently there is a need to relate IDEF0 functions back to the customer requirements that they fulfil, and to record which requirements have deliberately not been met.

Unfulfilled requirements will not appear within any IDEF0 model, and so must be recorded elsewhere—clearly another application of RMT. The proposed mechanism for supporting a trace between RMT and IDEF Toolset is the *hyperlink* (§ 9.2, § 9.2.2).

6.4.1.3 Non-functional and functional specification: Opportunity 3

The techniques for functional and non-functional specification are intended to be used largely independently. However, there is a potential need to maintain complete *configurations* of requirements, including both functional and non-functional aspects, and to generate unified paper documentation combining them both. There is no discussion of this topic in this book.

6.4.1.4 Non-functional specification/architectural design: Opportunity 4

Minimal support for traceability between non-functional specification and HOOD design is provided using hyperlinks (§ 9.2.2).

An additional point to be remembered here is the fact that RMT is used to capture behavioural and performance specifications in addition to the miscellaneous specifications for which it is more ideally suited. If a more appropriate method had been used for capturing these specifications then there would have been scope for integrating that with the GSED-HOOD method, allowing a trace down to the environment's support for modelling behaviour and verifying performance constraints.

6.4.1.5 Functional specification/architectural design: Opportunity 5

As described in § 6.2.4.1, there is no formal method for passing between an IDEF0 model and a HOOD design. Consequently, the best form of integration that could have been supported without extending either the HOOD or IDEF0 method was one based upon hyperlinks—simple traceability between methods.

6.4.1.6 Internal to the HOOD method: Opportunity 6

An integral part of the HOOD design method is the textual description of HOOD entities in the Object Definition Skeleton language. The AdaNICE toolset provides a minimal text editor for editing object ODSs. However, the ATMOSPHERE project offered the opportunity to replace this with the structured editor KeyOne.

The GSED method is based upon a language for defining Time Behaviour Objects, which could also, like most languages, benefit from a language specific structured editor. Unlike HOOD, GSED was a proprietary, non-standardised method, and so the investigation of a version of KeyOne adapted to this language was seen to be a much longer term goal.

All three toolsets are able to generate paper documentation based on the information that they manipulate: AdaNICE can generate a print-out of a HOOD design including all aspects of each HOOD object; KeyOne is able to provide a range of pretty-printed formats related to each language that it supports, and HOOD-ODS in particular; the

GSED description of the time behaviour of each HOOD entity is currently stored in a textual format. A complete integration of the toolsets might imply the generation of a single document containing all of this information, and fully benefiting from the presentational advantages of each toolset.

6.4.1.7 Architectural design/performance evaluation: Opportunity 7

The GSED/HOOD method leads to a means of animating HOOD designs, through the representation of the control structures of HOOD objects and operations in terms of time behaviour objects. Consequently, there was considerable scope for integrating the AdaNICE HOOD tool with GSED/HOOD:

- reusing AdaNICE's graphical capabilities as the sole means for browsing HOOD entities, and selecting them as the subjects of GSED's operations
- extending AdaNICE's graphical capabilities with means so that GSED could animate diagrams displayed by AdaNICE
- sharing common data representing the HOOD design in the PCTE object base, resulting in a single HOOD editor (AdaNICE), a single graphical formalism, and avoiding the need for tools to convert the data format of AdaNICE into the data format of GSED
- the production of unified documentation containing the HOOD design enriched with GSED time behaviour objects representing the control structure of each HOOD object and operation.

6.4.1.8 Architectural design/detailed design and coding: Opportunity 8

One result of architectural design with HOOD is a complete definition of the *packaging* of a software system: that is, each HOOD object should map to a clearly defined module to be developed in the target programming language. There is a considerable potential for exploiting this mapping:

- It is possible to generate package specifications for all HOOD objects, and code skeletons for all leaf HOOD objects. This facility was provided for both the C and Ada languages but is not described in detail here. For C it resulted in the creation of a structure that both stored the generated source code and allowed this code to be built with the East Build toolset ([Sim91a]).
  It should be noted that there are many version and configuration management issues to be addressed here. In particular, if a design is updated after code has been generated from it, care should be taken to make sure that any manual changes made to the previously generated code are not lost.
- Code generation satisfies the needs of forward engineering, but there is also a clear need for reverse engineering, generating a HOOD design reflecting existing code.
  The major difficulty in this area is that code developed using HOOD has a number of structural properties that are not satisfied by all code. While code packaging notions within Ada force most properties of HOOD designs to be respected, the C language is almost as famed as FORTRAN for its ability to support arbitrarily badly structured code. In general, therefore, it is difficult to imagine completely automatic tools for regenerating a HOOD design from source code.

- An intermediate solution for integrating architectural design and coding is the provision of tools to verify that a code module has a specification consistent with a given HOOD object.
- A HOOD design includes a pictorial representation of the packaging of source code. Potentially, a HOOD tool could be used for browsing Ada or C source that had been designed using HOOD.
  This is actually quite a difficult integration opportunity to exploit, for a number of reasons. It is not easy to maintain consistency between a design and code: changes to design can have a large and potentially undesirable impact on underlying source code; and the automatic reflection of changes made at code level at the design level generalises to the problem of reverse engineering.

An additional area of study would be code generation from GSED Time Behaviour Objects. The combination of HOOD and GSED provides a design similarly detailed as SDL (see § 11.5 and § 17.4), for which code generators have been produced (see § 11.7.4.2 and § 21.3). While the target applications of SDL (in telecommunications) tend to be highly parallel, they are computationally sufficiently simple and similar that complete target applications can be generated directly from SDL. However, this is not the case for HOOD (typically aerospace) applications, in which computationally complex calculations are prevalent and, in the vast majority of cases, difficult to generate.

6.4.2 Tool-Framework integration

As will be described in § 6.5, the Aerospace Environment is built on top of four main components: PCTE, X/Motif, East-UIMS and East-Process. PCTE offers facilities for data and low-level control integration while X/Motif offers low-level presentation integration. The prime role of East-UIMS is to support a higher level of presentation integration and it has secondary roles related to control and process integration. East-Process, as the name suggests, offers basic process integration mechanisms, and combines with generic facilities of East to allow the building of an environment reflecting the user's detailed development process.

Process integration is often considered to be related to issues at a higher level of abstraction than those addressed at framework level. While the tools for the definition of process models are precisely that, tools written above the framework, certain environment-wide conventions need to be followed to allow the degree of process support envisaged for East. Similarly, the provision of pervasive version and configuration management require a number of conventions to be adopted and followed throughout the environment. Although not strictly part of the framework, these conventions are as pervasive as 'style guides' for user interface development, and may imply changes to tools which seek to become 'good citizens' of the environment.

6.4.2.1 Data integration using PCTE

PCTE ('A basis for a Portable Common Tool Environment') [ECM90] includes an object management system (OMS) for the maintenance of objects and relationships between objects stored within a distributed object base. The facilities of the OMS are complemented by those services essential to the maintenance and use of a distributed, multi-user, multi-tool, concurrently accessed object base. Some of these complementary services can be categorised as supporting control integration between tools.

PCTE was developed as a replacement for many of the medium to coarse grain data storage mechanisms present in existing CASE tools, to promote the sharing of data between tools through its storage in a common object base, and to allow the development of common utilities and mechanisms that would be applicable to all data stored within the object base, such as version and configuration management.

Within the Aerospace Environment all data that relate to the *intended products* of the development process and those that leave a *record of the process itself* are stored in the common PCTE object base. In addition, the base is used to store what is often termed 'metadata': that is, objects representing users, tools, process models and the data schemas of the object base.

All tools of the environment have been either developed, reengineered or encapsulated to allow their data and metadata to be stored in the object base. § 7.6.2 presents an example of the encapsulation of a UNIX tool for use in PCTE and describes some of the inherent difficulties and limitations of encapsulation.

6.4.2.2 Configuration management on PCTE

Basic use of the data integration mechanisms of PCTE can result in a simplification of individual tools, and may allow easy integration between certain tools, such as that between AdaNICE and GSED and KeyOne-ODS. However, this simple level of integration supposes that tools are used in a single user manner, without any real support for some essentials of significant development projects: version and configuration management.

As suggested in § 6.2.8, the Adele model could, at least in theory, be applied to any product of the systems engineering development process, with many different notions of 'module' and relationships between 'module' being managed in a *loose bound* manner. As soon as the modules at either end of a relationship are independently developed it becomes likely that they will each exist in many versions, and the simple maintenance of relationships between specific versions will be inadequate: loosely-bound relationships should be established that have a precise meaning within the context of a single configuration, yet do not overly constrain the way in which versions can be combined to make up configurations.

The large variety of such relationships between modules maintained by a single tool, or even by different tools, gives rise to a large number of places where a true configuration management discipline could be applied. The results of *each of* the methods of figure 6.7 may be developed as a number of independent modules, so version and configuration management disciplines could be applied within each method. The relationships maintained between the results of successive methods need also to be maintained under a version and configuration management discipline.

The long term goal of integrating existing CASE tools into East is to *factorise out* explicit support for cooperative and parallel working from the tools, as well as any support they may have for version and configuration management. By removing these mechanisms from individual tools and relying upon common, environment-wide facilities, the tools become themselves much cleaner modules, and become available for the support of a wider class of software processes.

6.4.2.3 Tight control integration based upon PCTE

PCTE supports an operating system-like notion of *process*. This is required to support the multi-user facilities of PCTE including access control, security, concurrency control and transparent distribution. Given this, it is also natural for PCTE to provide uniform mechanisms for communication between processes whether they are on the same machine or on different machines of the local area network. This communication is primarily based upon message queues.

PCTE also supports a *notification mechanism* that allows processes to monitor certain objects for certain events such as the modification or deletion of the object. The occurrence of a monitored event results in a message being sent to all processes interested in monitoring the event. At the time of writing no implementation of PCTE supported the notification mechanism although many clear usages for it had been identified. For example, all tools that display information from the base *without using locks to prevent its modification* need to use this mechanism to update the display of data that is modified by other tools.

The prime use of message queues for control integration within the Aerospace Environment was to implement communication internally to the East-UIMS. PCTE message queues were also used internally to the GSED toolset.

The other example of communication between tools was that between AdaNICE and the tools with which it was extended: GSED and KeyOne. However, this communication was upon a mechanism in X/Window rather than PCTE message queues (see § 9.1).

6.4.2.4 Loose control integration within East: process guidance

Increasing levels of process support are being introduced into East environment. The initial conceptual model of East was as an environment to which the user gained access by giving not just their login identifier and password but also by selecting the task on which they intended to work. This entry point would then be used by East to establish a working context for the user, consisting of the types of data and operations needed to perform the task, as well as guiding the user towards the particular objects needed for the performance of a task. All this would be controlled by higher level process management facilities which would be used for defining generic 'task templates' and the way that they guided the developer, as well as controlling the scheduling and availability of tasks.

The East environment, therefore, has an entry point which is used to select the task on which the user is to work. The choice of a task allows the environment to select a *process-related subenvironment* which restricts the working schema (§ 7.1.4) of the user to providing an appropriate subset of all types in the object base, as well as the subset of operations needed for the performance of the task. Unfortunately these mechanisms are not further described in this book.

6.4.2.5 Loose presentation integration based upon X/Motif

As for all of the ATMOSPHERE environments, the basic technology for presentation integration in the Aerospace Environment is X/Motif. Common use of the lowest layer of this—X/Window—ensures that tools are capable of running and displaying information simultaneously in separate windows on the bitmapped display of a UNIX workstation. This is the basic form of integration possible, requiring a simple, but essential choice of windowing technology.

The next level is Motif, which offers a common toolkit of dialogue elements that if uniformly used can lead to a common 'look' and 'feel' across all tools of the environment. All interactive tools of the Aerospace Environment are now available in variants based upon X/Motif, many having been reengineered to use it within the context of ATMOSPHERE.

6.4.2.6 Tight presentation integration based upon East-UIMS

The East environment is based upon a common user interface management system (UIMS). Besides supporting the development of the user interface component of tools, the East-UIMS provides important run-time support for East.

The East-UIMS is itself built upon X/Motif and so tools developed using it may run alongside other X/Motif tools. However, East-UIMS-based tools support a number of *user-level abstractions* (§ 8.1.1) that increase the perceived integration between tools. For example: the notion of *dragging* allows parameters of the operations of one tool to be filled in terms of objects displayed by other tools; and the menus displayed after the designation of a displayed entity may combine operations of many tools and not just of the tool displaying the entity. At the time of writing these abstractions were only supported for tools that were written using the East-UIMS. The *hyperlink service* was also at its best for tools built using the East-UIMS (§ 9.2.1).

All tools that may be called within a particular *configuration* of East must be registered with the East-UIMS (§ 8.1.3). Each registered tool must be at least partly based upon the East-UIMS in order to respect certain conventions, notably those that allow the tool to be started. In order to allow *foreign* tools—tools not built upon the East-UIMS—to be used within the environment, it is necessary to provide a capsule. This *capsule* is itself an East tool, and is free to start the foreign tool itself. Typically, one capsule must be supplied for each *entry point* of a tool. Simple encapsulation can be used to bring non-interactive command line tools and interactive tools maintaining their own X/Windows into East.

The list of entry points identified for the foreign tools of the Aerospace Environment, together with the basic principles of encapsulation, are given in § 8.5.

6.4.2.7 Tight presentation integration—common syntax-directed editing

Many methods are based upon textual formalisms with sufficiently well-defined syntax and semantics to be supported by syntax-directed editors. In order to limit the time needed to become proficient in the use of the environment, it is desirable to base all classes of editing upon a common interaction paradigm, and this suggests the use of common technology. The common syntax-directed editing technology within the Aerospace Environment is KeyOne.

The languages within the environment that are defined sufficiently well to be supported by syntax-directed editors are Ada, C, HOOD ODS, and the language used for defining time behaviour in GSED. § 7.6.1 describes some of the issues of using KeyOne to edit the ODS of HOOD objects.

6.5 ENVIRONMENT AND TOOL ARCHITECTURE

This section gives a brief overview of the integration problem by showing the high-level architecture of each tool or toolset of the Aerospace Environment. Particular attention has been made to whether or not X/Window, Motif, East-UIMS, PCTE or UNIX is used by each tool.

6.5.1 Overall architecture

figure 6.8 gives a simple overview of the architecture of the Aerospace Environment, including the principle toolsets of the environment. The basic technology supporting the environment—the environment 'framework'—is a UNIX-based implementation of PCTE, and an X/Motif-based implementation of the East-UIMS.

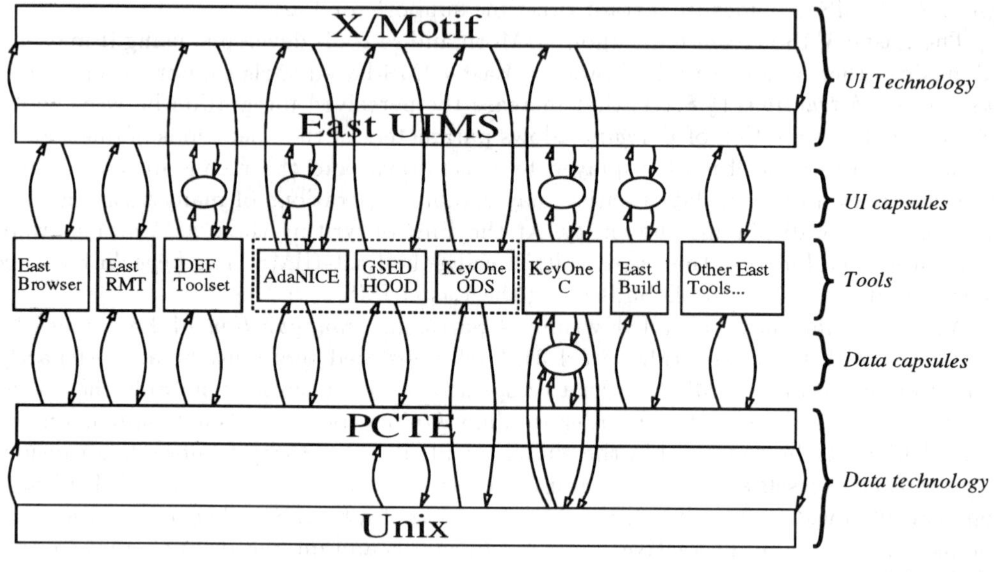

Figure 6.8 This diagram shows how tools use the framework components of the Aerospace Environment: X/Motif, East-UIMS, PCTE and UNIX. Tools such as RMT, that are fully developed using the East framework, make direct use of only PCTE and East-UIMS. Other tools may be brought into the environment by means of encapsulation: tools which provide there own user interface based upon X/Motif must be encapsulated so that they may be called from the East-UIMS, while tools expecting data to be stored in UNIX may by 'integrated' with the PCTE object management system by means of a *data capsule*. GSED/HOOD and KeyOne/ODS have been grouped together with AdaNICE since they are only indirectly available through the East-UIMS: AdaNICE can be called from East, and GSED/HOOD and KeyOne/ODS may be called from AdaNICE. This group also relies upon the use of a common control integration mechanism—IPCP.

Without the direct dependencies of many tools on X/Motif, the porting of the user interface aspects of the environment to other frameworks would have only involved the provision of a new implementation of the East-UIMS. With so many dependencies on X/Motif, porting to a non-X/Motif framework component would involving modifying each tool that directly depends upon X/Motif. The situation for porting data aspects to non-UNIX environments is better, requiring a special case to be made only for two variants of a single tool. The reliance of some tools on the communication mechanisms of X/Window is not shown in the diagram.

6.5.2 Architecture of the IDEF Toolset

The architecture of the IDEF Toolset toolset is shown in figure 6.9. Each of its three tools supports a single window, and is packaged as a separate executable. The toolset

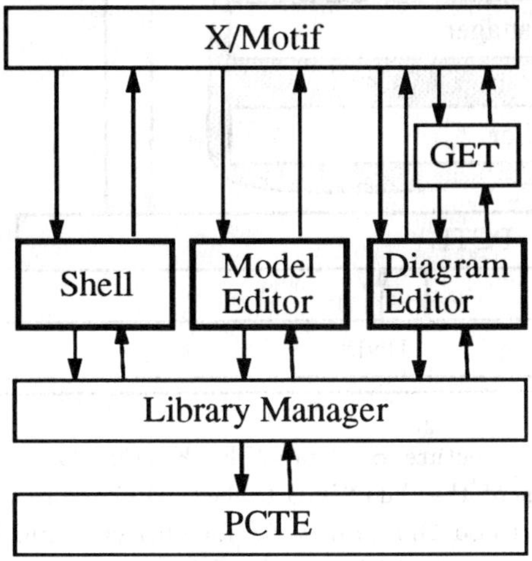

Figure 6.9 The architecture of the IDEF Toolset. Each of the tools of the IDEF Toolset has an interface based upon X/Motif. In addition, the most complicated of the tools, the diagram editor, uses a commercial graphics package that was developed to simplify the creation of a number of similar graphical editors. All three tools access data through a common module called the *library manager*. This acts as a portability layer—porting the toolset to a different database would require a reimplementation of the library manager only. Within ATMOSPHERE a library manager was developed for storing data within PCTE.

has been redeveloped on a number of platforms, databases and user interfaces. This was the first version to be developed to use X/Motif or to run in a UNIX environment, as well as being the first version built for PCTE. This made it desirable to rewrite the toolset in C.

6.5.3 Architecture of AdaNICE, KeyOne-ODS and GSED

The architecture of the combined AdaNICE, KeyOne-ODS and GSED toolset is shown in figure 6.10.

The dialogue manager handles interactions with the user and provides all the presentation and dialogue services needed by AdaNICE's interactive components and acts as a portability layer.

The data handler manages all accesses to the database, making its implementation on different platforms (UNIX or VMS file system, PCTE OMS) transparent to other

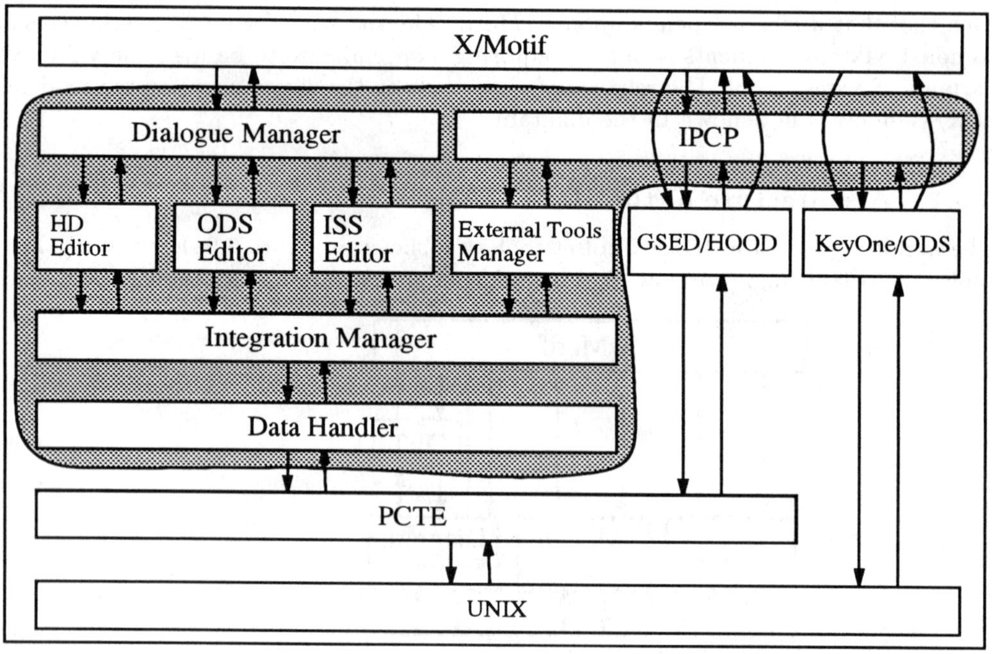

Figure 6.10 The combined architecture of AdaNICE, KeyOne-ODS and GSED. The shaded area identifies components of the AdaNICE toolset. IPCP stands for InterProcess Communication Protocol; HD for Hood Diagram; ODS for Object Definition Skeleton; ISS for Informal Solution Strategy. The command line tools of AdaNICE are not shown.

components of AdaNICE. It is responsible for providing a particular set of data access, concurrency control and transaction management services to the integration manager and other components that are independent of the database technology on which a particular variant of AdaNICE is built. The activity carried out in the context of the ATMOSPHERE project included the implementation of this component of the toolset on the PCTE OMS. This implementation successfully exploited the OMS at a fine level of granularity, representing HOOD objects and operations as PCTE objects, and their relationships as PCTE relationships.

The integration manager has the purpose of providing control integration facilities and consistency check services to interactive components. Before performing an operation, a component must ask the integration manager for permission: if the operation is allowed, the integration manager broadcasts the request of performing the operation to all the active components to which the operation is relevant allowing the simultaneous update of the different views of the design.

The AdaNICE components are classified into interactive components and command line tools. Interactive components are provided to support the HOOD *basic design step* (see § 6.2.4.1). These components use the dialogue manager for managing the presentation of information and dialogue with the user. The command line tools provided include tools for generating printed documentation, generating source code from the design and exporting and importing HOOD designs via a standardised interchange format (SIF), as well as tools for the administration of AdaNICE.

In the PCTE/X/Motif variant of AdaNICE, the three interactive components are packaged within a single executable, together with the integration manager and other AdaNICE components. Previous variants have had to be packaged differently, for example, when the windowing technology imposed overrestrictive limits on the number of windows that could be maintained by each tool process.

A special component is the external tool manager, which has the purpose of managing the interaction with external tools, namely tools that are executed as separate processes and that do not use the data handler to access the database. AdaNICE provides mechanisms for activating external tools and for interacting with them through the IPCP package (InterProcess Communication Package), a package which has been built upon the interprocess communication mechanisms of X/Window (see § 9.1).

The integration of tools using IPCP required the establishment of a message protocol between the tools. Such protocols were developed to allow AdaNICE to communicate with KeyOne-ODS and GSED/HOOD. Part of the protocol between AdaNICE and KeyOne-ODS averts the need for KeyOne-ODS to be ported to PCTE: AdaNICE is able to transfer the ODS files needed by KeyOne from PCTE to UNIX, thus allowing KeyOne to continue working as a UNIX tool.

7

Data Integration

A major goal of the East framework, and hence of the Aerospace Environment, is to provide a high degree of data integration. The prime means for achieving this was to base East upon PCTE which acts, as the acronym suggests, as a basis for East as a *Portable Common Tool Environment.*

This chapter starts with an introduction to the object management system of PCTE, in which the PCTE model is introduced together with a description of certain characteristics of a PCTE object base. This introduction also includes a brief introduction to the ideas behind producing data schemas for an extensible software engineering environment.

Next follows a description of a number of approaches towards the provision of tools for use within East. PCTE is intended to be used by tools as their only repository, and to support cooperation by tools by the sharing of commonly understood data. § 7.2 describes the development of a data schema for the PCTE tool RMT.

However, there are many tools that are already in use and that are not based upon PCTE. For these a variety of strategies can be adopted, all of which are part of a steady migration towards PCTE. At opposite ends of the spectrum of migration strategies are the near reimplementation of a tool, as described for the IDEF Toolset in § 7.3, and the encapsulation of an unaltered tool, as presented for KeyOne/C in § 7.6.2. A much more radical and ambitious approach is that adopted for AdaNICE, and presented in § 7.4. This toolset was completely reengineered so that as much of the toolset as possible became independent of the underlying repository, with only those parts closest to the repository—in this case PCTE—being implemented when a new repository needs to be supported.

PCTE has explicit support for schema extension, allowing tools and types to be added to an environment without stopping the environment from being used. Tools developed for a PCTE environment should expect their data types to be extended to include additional functionality and the integration of their functionality with that supported by other tools. A specific example of the enhancement of one tool with another tool that is partly supported by schema extension is the addition of the design simulation capabilities of GSED/HOOD to AdaNICE. This is presented in § 7.5.

Finally, when building a PCTE-based environment based upon a selection of PCTE-based tools there is often a need to complete the overall schema with schema pieces

Tool Integration: Environments and Frameworks, Edited by D. Schefström and G. van den Broek

that are not directly assumed by any of the environments tools. Examples of this are given in § 7.8.

7.1 THE PCTE OBJECT MANAGEMENT SYSTEM (OMS)

This section provides an overview of the object management system of PCTE [ECM90]. It is intended to illustrate some of the issues in developing tools and services to be used in a PCTE-based environment rather than to provide a comprehensive description of PCTE—such a description would require a book of a similar size to this one.

The section starts by describing a PCTE object base in terms of how it is spread ('distributed') across a local area network in order to suggest the intended large scale usage of PCTE. This is followed by a basic introduction to the data model of PCTE, showing how the support for typed data not only governs the structure of that data but also the ways in which that data can be manipulated. Next comes a discussion of PCTE's support for the extension of the object base's data schema. The section concludes with a discussion of how the process of building an environment is supported by the categorisation of data schema fragments as being either 'functional' or 'organizational'.

7.1.1 The infrastructure of a PCTE object base

A PCTE object base may be physically distributed across the workstations of a local area network, with data physically located on the PCTE *volumes* of each machine. Volumes would be called *file systems* in a conventional operating system such as UNIX. It is also possible to have diskless machines that are registered to use the object base. This degree of distribution of data allows the resources of a network to be shared, both for physical storage space and for processing power.

An important characteristic of an object base is its resiliency to *network partitioning*. In UNIX, if one machine becomes inaccessible (due to a power failure, or the network crashing), then it is still possible to continue working on other machines: the most serious loss in capabilities is due to the unavailability of the data that is stored on the inaccessible machine. PCTE supports a similar level of resilency to network partitioning as UNIX.

To support this resiliency, PCTE is based upon two prime assumptions: that each machine with associated PCTE volumes is able to access that data itself, implying that PCTE implementations are based upon a 'multi-server' architecture; and that sufficient data is *replicated* on each machine to allow it to be meaningfully used 'standalone'. Examples of replicated data include the basic tools required to manipulate the object base, and the basic parts of the data schema needed to allow these tools to be used.

Data replication is an important feature of a distributed system—not only does it increase the resiliency of the object base, but it increases the performance of the environment, allowing frequently and widely accessed objects to be consulted locally. Unlike UNIX, where the replication of many essential bits of data must be done largely by hand, PCTE explicitly supports a notion of a logically unique yet physically copied object—the *replicated object*. Each replicated object appears on all machines of the environment that support PCTE volumes.

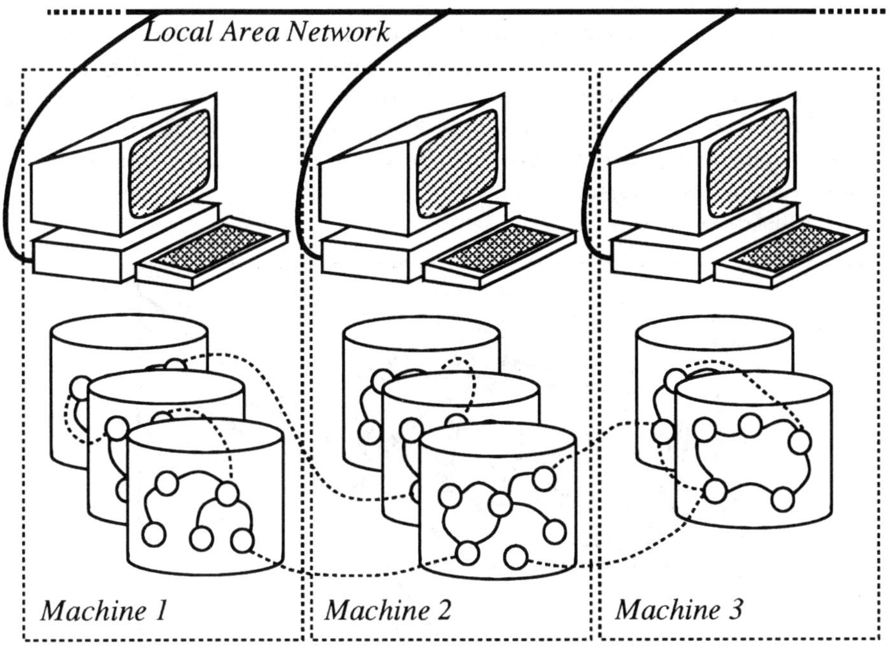

Figure 7.1 This diagram shows three machines that form part of a local area network. Both machine 1 and machine 2 have three volumes, while machine 3 has only two. Each volume stores a number of objects (circles), and there are links between objects (arcs). Some links join objects that are physically located on the same volume, while others pass between volumes.

As far as users and tools are concerned, the physical location of objects within a PCTE object base is largely irrelevant. The most common time when the physical location of an object becomes clear is when a PCTE volume becomes full. In this case objects may be physically relocated onto other volumes of the object base. Such a relocation of an object does not change the object in any meaningful way since objects are not primarily accessed in terms of their physical location.

Figure 7.1 shows a sample PCTE object base.

7.1.2 PCTE's object model

7.1.2.1 Basic elements

The basic unit of storage within a PCTE object base is the *object*. Objects may be related to one another using *links*. The characteristics of both objects and links may be defined within their *attributes*. The attributes of a link are used to store information that is neither an intrinsic property of the link's origin object or of its destination object, but is a property of the *relationship* between the objects that is modelled by the link.

In order to guarantee the *referential integrity* of links, they are normally created in *mutually inverse pairs* or *handshakes*—in this case, it is impossible to have a link leading from one object to another object without there being a corresponding link leading in the reverse direction.

Links also provide the standard means of gaining access to objects. This is through *paths of links* starting from well known starting points—so-called *reference objects.* Each pathname is given relative to a reference object, and consists of concatenated *link names.* This style of access is known as *navigational access.* Examples of reference objects include a central root object of the whole object base—the *common root* object—and a user's *home object.*

Figure 7.2 illustrates these concepts.

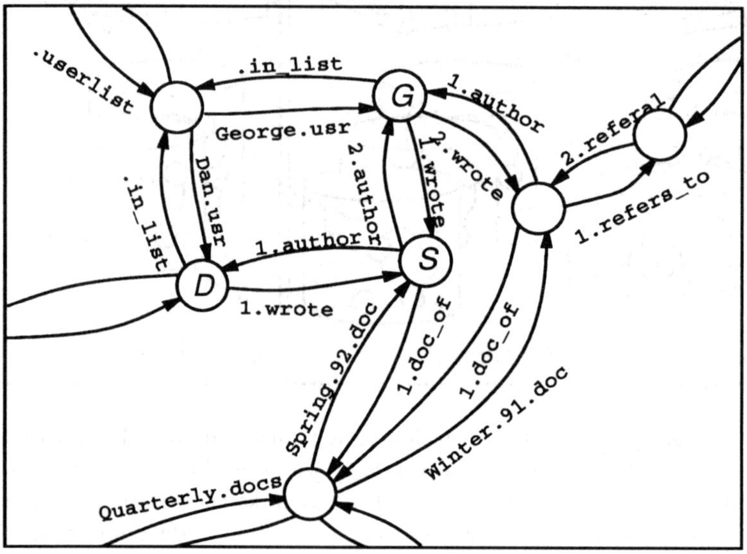

Figure 7.2 Each circle shows an object, and each arrow a link. Notice how links exist in pairs, and how each link has a name and a direction. This diagram illustrates how tools and users can *navigate* around the object base: object *G* is the *home object* of George. He can navigate from the object in terms of paths of links: *1.wrote* leads him to object *S*—a document that he has helped write. From there he can follow links *1.author* and *2.author* to objects that represent the two authors of this document, one of which returns to his home object. The link *Spring.92.doc* arriving at object *S* provides one of several possible names for the object: 'Spring.92'.

Objects may also have an associated content, which may be used to store such things as pure data, an executable image, ASCII text, or other persistent, but fine-grained data. It might also be logically associated with some more dynamic or physical notion, such as a communication channel (message queue or pipe) or a logical device (printer, window, etc.).

7.1.2.2 Basic manipulation model

The common object base supporting a project will store information belonging to many different people. Just as in an operating system, it is important that all data is clearly owned by somebody, and that this owner is able to decide who else is able to read or update his data. The granularity of ownership in PCTE is the object, and each attribute, link, or content falls into the *access control domain* of a single object.

Each object has an associated *user identifier* that indicates which user *owns* the object. This user is able to decide which other users may read or modify the attributes and links falling within the access control domain of the object. In general, the access control domain of an object includes:

- most of the object's attributes
- all of the links leaving the object
- all attributes of the links leaving the object
- the object's content, communication channel or device, if it has one.

By granting another user permission to read (update) an object, this user can then read (update) all things within the access control domain of the object.

The fact that links are maintained in pairs and that each link within a pair falls within the access control domain of a different object, seem to suggest that a user would only be able to create a link between two objects when he had permission to modify *both* objects. This is one reason why PCTE distinguishes between different *categories* of link: for some links we really do want the creation or deletion of a link to be a significant event for its origin object, but for others we do not. This gives rise to the so-called *significance to the origin* link property. Links without this property can be created or deleted without permission to update their origin object. All links without this property are known as *implicit links.*

An implicit link is so called because it can only be created or deleted *implicitly* when its reverse link is created or deleted. figure 7.3 illustrates the notion of access control domain, highlights the importance of link categories, and underlines the fact that the choice of link categories constrains the way that these links may be manipulated.

Several other link properties are known to PCTE: a link with the *composition* property can lead from an object to another that is to be logically considered as a component object; a link with the *stability* property guarantees that the destination object cannot be *significantly changed* without removing this link; etc.. These and other properties are built in to PCTE because it is the PCTE object management system that ensures that the properties are enforced. For example: the *composition property* must be respected by all PCTE operations affecting composites; *referential integrity* must be respected when an object is moved to another physical location; objects can only be created at the ends of links with the *existence property.*

Some combinations of link properties have little real value: for example, a link which had the composition property but not the referential integrity property might result in an object with a link to a component object that no longer existed. Rather than supporting all possible combinations of link properties when some are considered nonsensical, PCTE supports a restricted number of combinations, each of which is known as a *link category.* table 7.1 summarises the PCTE link categories.

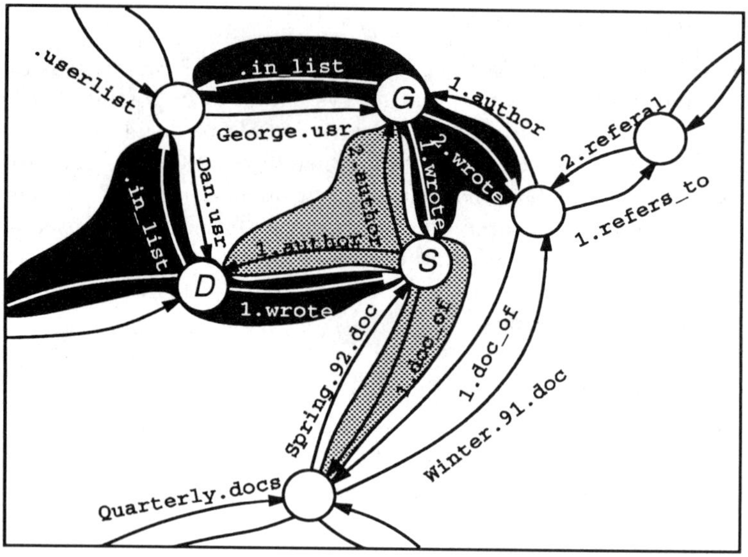

Figure 7.3 The access control domains of three of the objects of figure 7.2 have been highlighted. Notice how the access control domain of each object only covers the object itself and the links that *leave* the object. Object *S* is a document and has been written by George and Dan. Authorship is shown in terms of a *.author/.wrote* relationship. It is instructive to see the effect of various combinations of link category for these two links. If *.wrote* links were significant for user objects and *.author* links implicit, then any user would be able to declare himself the author of any document, without any control, and this seems undesirable. On the other hand, if *.author* links are significant and *.wrote* links implicit, then only those users with permission to modify the document can decide who the authors really are, which seems to be much more appropriate.

Category		*Property*: *Referential integrity*	*Significance to the origin*	*Existence*	*Composition*
Composition	c	Yes	Yes	Yes	Yes
Existence	e	Yes	Yes	Yes	No
Reference	r	Yes	Yes	No	No
Implicit	i	Yes	No	No	No
Designation	d	No	Yes	No	No

Table 7.1 PCTE link categories as combinations of link properties

7.1.2.3 Strong typing

The PCTE data formalism is based on Chen's Entity Relationship model [Che76] with *strong typing.* Every PCTE entity (object, link or attribute) is an instance of a particular type, and this type has a specific set of *properties* associated with it (we have already seen various properties appropriate for links). The advantage of strong typing is that every instance of a particular type is guaranteed to have the same set of properties—tools can be written to recognise certain types of objects and can assume that all types that they have been written to recognise will have the properties that they need.

For example: an attribute representing a percentage may be an integer with default value 100; an object type representing a requirements document may be defined as a specialisation of the type *document* so that it inherits an *author* link type and so that it has a *content*. Link types are defined in pairs, for example: a link type author making reference to a *user* object modelling the document's author, reversed by an implicit link type leading back to the document.

The object base of a software development environment may be required to store a range of different classes of information, varying in size, numbers of instances, and the rate at which instances must be accessed. For example, some classes of information may be accessed individually, and rarely in large numbers, such as projects, users, architectural design elements or change requests, whereas others may be accessed in large numbers and rapidly, such as words within documents, and statements within source code. Although the Entity Relationship model underlying PCTE can be used to model most types of information, PCTE was primarily designed to address problems of multi-user working and cooperation between tools rather than rapid access to large quantities of *fine grained* data. Such fine-grained data is intentionally left as *hidden detail*, and can be stored within the contents of a special category of object called a *file*. Although PCTE offers no direct support for extending the typing structure to fine-grain data stored in the content of a PCTE object, such an approach can be built on top of PCTE. In particular, all PCTE tools that access file contents must assume something about the format of these files: this format can easily be referred to as a *content schema*. An example of this is given in § 7.7.

7.1.3 Type definitions and process assumptions

figure 7.4 introduces the graphical formalism used for showing fragments of PCTE data schemas throughout this book. With practice it becomes possible to read a PCTE data schema and learn not only the types of data the schema supports, but the way in which that data is intended to be manipulated. Given that decisions as to who can manipulate which data and in what ways govern the way that people work, a data schema can be said to support a number of built-in *process assumptions*.

7.1.3.1 Examples of inadequate and excessive process assumptions

An example of a design choice that could have led to a schema with inherently bad process assumptions has already been given. This was illustrated in figure 7.3, and related to the way in which the authorship of documents should be modelled. The choice was between two definitions for a pair of link types, each of which had a different set of process assumptions. In both cases links of type *.wrote* led from *user* objects to *document* objects and were reversed by links of type *.author*, and the decision to be made was which of the two links should be significant to its origin object.

In the first definition *.wrote* links were significant to their origin objects—*user* objects—while *.author* links did not have this property. Consequently authorship could only be established for those with permission to make significant changes to *user* objects. However, in the Aerospace Environment at least it was assumed that the only

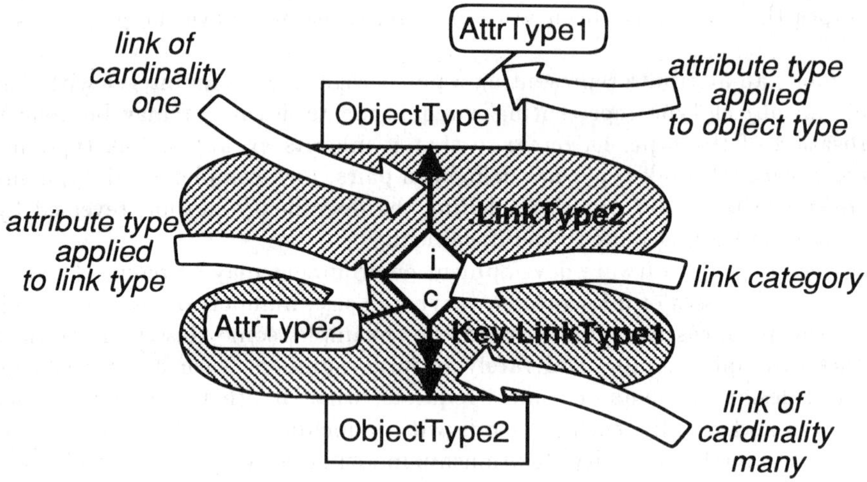

Figure 7.4 The conventions used for data schemas in this book. Object types are represented as rectangles and attribute types in rounded rectangles with a line leading to the object or link type to which they are applied. Link types are always shown in pairs, since all link types shown with this book have the *referential integrity* property. The two shaded regions of the diagram show how the category, name and cardinality of each link type is placed on the destination side of the link. So, for example, *LinkType1* is a link type of category composition and cardinality many leading from *ObjectType1* to *ObjectType2* and with the applied attribute *AttrType2*.

user who would have permission to make such changes would be the user modelled by that object. The process assumptions implicit in this choice would therefore have been:

- in order to establish the authorship list of a document, each of its authors would have had to have created a *.author* link to declare itself to be an author
- at the same time, there would have been no protection against absolutely anybody deciding that they wished to be an author of any document
- moreover, there would have been no way of 'freezing' the content of the document and at the same time 'freezing' the list of authors.

The second definition differed from the first in making the other link significant. In this case, the content of the document and the list of authors were a part of the significant information of a single object:

- only those who could change the content could decide which users were the authors
- only those who could decide which users were the authors could change the content
- moreover, if the document was 'frozen' upon completion then the content of the document and its list of authors would be 'frozen' together.

So, schema design involves ensuring that a set of modifications that should be commonly controlled are modifications to significant data falling within the access control domain of a single object. Failing to ensure this can be described as making *inadequate process assumptions*.

It is also possible to make *excessive process assumptions*. It is often the case that a first attempt at designing a tool's schema leads to excessive process assumptions, and the data schemas for some of the prototype tools of the Aerospace Environment suffer in this way. The assumptions built into the schema of one of these prototypes are described in § 7.5.2, together with an alternative schema that resolves most of the associated problems.

7.1.3.2 Versions, packaging and configurations

An entire class of excessive process assumptions has to be avoided when a lifecycle tool is developed to make the tool compatible with the needs of version and configuration management.

§ 6.2.8 introduced the idea of packaging components of *modules* in such a way that they could later be assembled to produce configurations of larger modules or entire systems. In this case it is important to distinguish between properties that a packaged component intrinsically has before being placed into a configuration and the additional properties that it has within each configuration in which it is placed. In particular:

- placing a packaged component into a configuration should not modify that component
- the component may be placed into many different configurations and have an independent set of configuration-specific properties within each one

The separation between a packaged component and a component appearing in a configuration is reflected by the notion of *surrogate*.

A *surrogate* object is an object that represents another object in a specific context. Surrogates are linked to the object they represent by a link of a type that ensures that the represented object need not be modified simply to be represented in another context.

The notion of *surrogate* was introduced in [Sim91b], although the term used there was 'duplicate'. The ATMOSPHERE project investigated the development of a PCTE-based configuration management system based upon the Adele model and surrogates. This is described in [BLM91].

7.1.3.3 Process assumptions *vs* process choices

While the goal of a tool designer is to avoid unnecessary process assumptions, that of the environment builder is to reflect their organisation's *process choices*. The ability to break down a PCTE environment's data schema so that its parts can be developed by different individuals is described in the next section to prepare the way for a description of two classes of schema definition sets—*functional* and *organizational.* The goal of this separation is to distinguish between the schema fragments provided by tool developers, with their inherent process assumptions, and those provided by environment builders, which reflect and support an organisation's process choices.

7.1.4 Schema definition and environment extension

Software Engineering Environments differ from many other systems in being highly modular, and being built from components developed by several different individuals and companies including the environment's end users. An environment should be adaptable to support the changing needs of the software development process of the organisation that it is supporting, even offering many competing means for achieving essentially common goals such as change management. Moreover, if an environment is to be used by a significant number of people, it is important to be able to add new tools (and their data schemas) to the environment without disrupting those using the environment.

The means for defining the data schema for such an environment should be supportive of the specific nature of software engineering environments. In order to meet this goal, PCTE has chosen to replace the notion of an overall data schema for the entire environment with one of many Schema Definition Sets (SDSs), each of which defines *some* of the properties of the types of the environment. The overall data schema exists only as the sum of all pieces of schema reflected in the environments schema definition sets. Users and tools view the object base through a *working schema* made up of the pieces of the overall schema that they need, and thus do not constrain the evolution or addition of pieces that they are not directly using.

The total set of properties of a type is a combination of all the properties assigned to the type within all of the environment's SDSs. These properties are split between *applied properties* and *inherent properties*. The applied properties of a type are defined within the context of an SDS: the set of attributes applied to an object or link type; and the set of origin and destination object types of a link type. Other properties are inherent to the type independent of the SDSs in which the type appears and fixed when the type is created: the category of value that an attributes stores (integer, string, boolean, ...); whether an object has a content or not; whether the instances of a link type are significant to their origin objects or not; etc..

As well as being a place where types are extended with applied properties, SDSs also allow the association of names with types. Within an SDS, each type can be given a *local name*. If a type has a local name in several SDSs, the resulting (*SDS name, local name*) pairs act as *synonyms* for the type. It is in this way that tools that access similar types, written by different vendors, each using different names for the types, can be integrated without modifying the tools. Each tool views the types through its own SDSs, but because their SDSs have been installed to *share* certain types, the tools can cooperate without even being recompiled.

7.1.5 Two classes of schema definition set: functional and organizational

The previous section introduced the need for the maintenance of a data schema for an environment as a number of pieces—SDSs—each of which contributes some properties to the types to which it makes reference. This ability to define an environment's data schema as a patchwork of many pieces encourages the design of the schemas of individual tools so as to maximize the potential uses of the tools: any type whose presence is assumed by a tool imposes constraints on the way that environment builders and other tools would wish to model similar data. Schema (and consequently tool) design should therefore be done within a spirit of a 'separation of concerns' to limit the number of peripheral process assumptions made by the tool.

The guidelines for defining PCTE schemas for use in the East environment [Eas92a, Eas92b] suggest that individual schemas should be classified as being either *functional* or *organizational*:

- a functional SDS is one whose type applications are directly assumed by a particular tool
- an organizational SDS is one whose type applications are not directly assumed by any particular tool

These definitions are both phrased in terms of type applications rather than types because the provision of a complete schema may involve the inclusion of all properties assumed by the tools that manipulate them plus others properties that are manipulated using more generic tools (such as a graphical shell), but are still an integral part of the environment. The only sense in which a type could be talked of as being either a functional or organizational type would be if all of its properties were applied to it in functional (respectively organizational) SDSs. However, in an evolving environment it is unlikely that any type would maintain such a classification.

The distinction between organizational and functional is illustrated by the following example. Given a pathname to an object of type *HoodObject*, a HOOD design tool may be able to work quite happily without caring how the pathname was supplied to it or precisely which object and link types were used to construct the pathname. The presence of the type *HoodObject* with certain attribute and link types applied to it would be quite sufficient for the HOOD tool to be used to create a hierarchy of HOOD objects, while the place where its objects were stored would be of little direct significance to the tool. Nonetheless there would have to be a means for creating the HOOD object—a link type with the existence property which allowed objects of type *HoodObject* to be created. *HoodObject* is therefore an object type with both functional and organizational properties.

The choice of the term 'organizational' as the converse of 'functional' is actually multi-faceted. One justification comes from the fact that specific environment functionality is almost always applied to 'small corners' of the data schema, and these corners are fastened together using conceptually higher level organizational types. Another is due to the fact that 'organizational' parts of the data schema are only minimally constrained by the tools within the environment; consequently they can be left to the organisation using the environment to define these parts of the schema to match their own needs.

It is worth noting that using 'organizational' as the converse of 'functional' also detracts from the value of organizational SDSs. All PCTE types and type applications are subject to the same manipulation model (see § 7.1.2.2)—each property falls within the access control domain of a particular object. This implies that organizational schemas can be defined with in-built process assumptions reflecting the organisation's *process choices*—a *design document list* object type could be defined so that only the owner of the list object could add design documents to the list, ... In this sense organizational SDSs themselves correspond to end-user functionality, even if they are not directly manipulated by any particular tool.

The provision of organizational schemas is amongst an environment builder's most important tasks. Examples of the organizational needs of the Aerospace Environment are given is § 7.8.

7.2 DEVELOPMENT OF A FUNCTIONAL DATA SCHEMA FOR PCTE—RMT

As in classical database theory, the first stage of developing a PCTE data model is to produce a conceptual model. The requirements management tool (RMT) maintains trees of requirement nodes, each node of which potentially has not only child nodes but an associated document outlining the requirement and a number of references to other requirements either in the same requirement tree or in other trees (see § 6.3.1). Each requirement also has a title, and all relationships between requirements are assigned a *class* and *comment* defining how the child or referenced node is to be interpreted by viewers of the parent node. It is also clear at a conceptual level that requirement trees do not exist in complete isolation—they may be created by users or act as reference documentation for entire projects. However, given the desirability of making RMT as widely applicable as possible, all associations of requirements to other types in the environment are left as organizational issues.

The next step is to convert these concepts into PCTE types and type applications. The most obvious object type is one to represent a node in a requirement tree. There are clearly also two link types corresponding to the storage of the child nodes of a node, and for making references to other nodes. Both link types are to be considered to be significant to their origin requirement node—the addition of a child node to a requirement should be restricted to those with permission to modify the requirement object. Both link types should carry referential integrity, and neither is of significance to its destination object—a requirement should be sufficiently stand-alone to be referenced from another requirements tree by those who could not otherwise modify it. The only difference between these links that has an impact on the choice of their link category is that child nodes are logically a part-of their parent objects, while references do not carry this semantic.

Consequently, the decomposition of requirements is modelled by the composition link type *child_req* which is reversed by the implicit link type *parent_req*. References between requirements are represented by the reference link type *refers_to* which is reversed by the implicit link type *referred_to_by*.

The cardinalities of most of these links are clear: a requirement may be broken down into an arbitrary number of sub-requirements; a requirement may make reference to an arbitrary number of other requirements; a requirement may be referenced by an arbitrary number of other requirements. The only choice that is difficult to make is the cardinality of the *parent_req* link type. Initially it seems that it should be cardinality one, since requirements form a strict tree. However, as soon as the question of version and configuration management of requirement nodes is considered it seems useful to be able to place a single version of a branch of a requirement tree within many separate configurations of a tree simultaneously. A complete consideration of version management issues for requirement trees was not done during the ATMOSPHERE

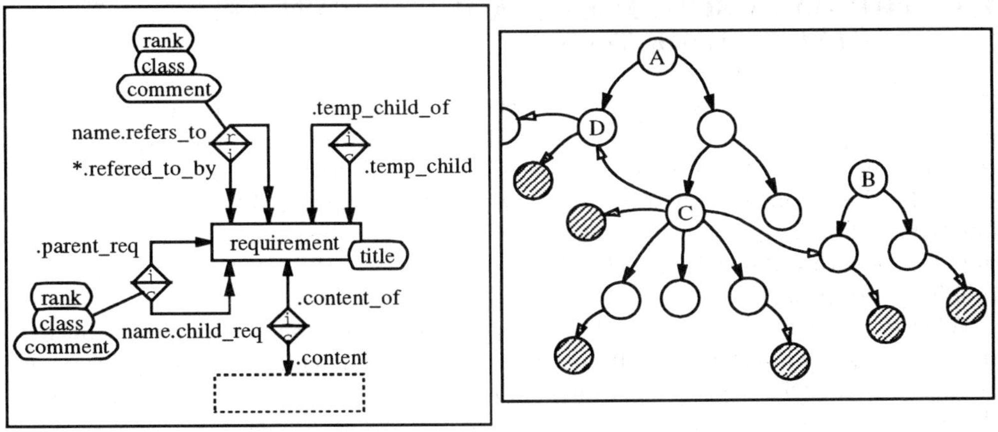

Figure 7.5 The left hand diagram shows the data schema of RMT, the other some objects respecting this schema. White objects are of type *requirement*, and shaded objects represent requirement contents. The shading of arrows indicates the use of the three principal types of link. (Links of type *temp_child* are intended only for temporary use so do not appear here; all implicit links are also left out of the diagram) Objects A and B are root nodes within requirement trees, object C makes reference to object D within the requirement tree rooted at A and object E within the other requirement tree.

project and the possibility of sharing 'versions' in many configurations was precluded by making *parent_req* a cardinality one link type.

Figure 7.5 shows the SDS of RMT. There are several features about this SDS that have not yet been discussed:

- the attributes *class* and *comment* were intended to be attributes of these relationships.
- both *refers_to* and *child_req* links have an attribute called *rank*.
  These attributes are used to define an ordering amongst the child objects of a specific requirement. Note that this attribute is a property of the relationship between two nodes and not of the child node. This clearly associates the rank with the child node while leaving the ordering of the child nodes of a requirement under the control of those who can write to the parent node.
- a requirement's content is stored as a separate object, but its type is not restricted by RMT.
  This was done primarily for reasons of open-endedness: to ensure that a variety of document editors could be used to maintain the contents of requirement objects, or even several document classes of a single document editor such as DOCS (see § 7.7). The responsibility for ensuring that organizational SDSs exist which provide object types modelling requirement contents is left to the environment builder. The way in which this was done for the Aerospace Environment is described in § 7.8.1.

RMT is a just a small example illustrating several issues of schema design for PCTE. However, even a small example shows the way in which the basic manipulation model of PCTE (access control domains, link categories, etc.) can be used to impose a way in which objects are to be manipulated.

7.3 THE DATA SCHEMA OF A REENGINEERED TOOLSET—IDEF Toolset

The IDEF0 model of a system consists of a hierarchy of functions, and the decomposition of each function includes both child functions and data flows between these children. As described in § 6.2.3, each decomposition is described graphically as a diagram. The hierarchical decomposition of the system's functionality into a hierarchy of functions naturally gives rise to a tree of diagrams. The diagram is the natural unit of modularity within the IDEF0 method, and consequently the IDEF Toolset's principal tool is the *diagram editor*.

When designing a data schema to support the IDEF0 method, the duality between the functions and diagrams becomes especially clear. If a medium grain representation of an IDEF0 model is chosen, then the PCTE objects stored would model diagrams and there would be no explicit representation of data flows. In a finer grain representation both child functions and data flows would be represented as objects. This contrast is shown in figure 7.6. A coarse grained solution might store an entire IDEF0 model in a single file.

For the purposes of the prototype produced in ATMOSPHERE the medium grained solution was adopted, being a more direct evolution from the previous representation used by the tool than the fine grained representation. Even a medium grain representation allows several users to have simultaneous access to different diagrams within a single model, and results in an explicit representation of the diagram hierarchy.

The principal types within the IDEF Toolset's data schema are the object type *IDEF0_diagram* which models an IDEF0 diagram, and a *.parent/.child* relationship which is used to represent the diagram hierarchy. Other types include:

- an object type modelling an IDEF0 model, and a link type supporting the creation of diagrams (*has_diagram*). These links have a key attribute that assigns an identifier for each diagram. The value '0' is used to identify the root diagram of a model.
- a link type supporting the identification of roots of *secondary hierarchies.* Secondary hierarchies are described below.
- an object type that is used to store graphical details for each diagram. This information is generated by the GET graphics package (see figure 6.9).

Figure 7.7 summarises the IDEF Toolset's data schema.

It is important to notice that the *.child* relationship is of category 'reference', and so does not have the existence property. Instead, diagrams are created using *.has_diagram links*, and attached to an object of type *IDEF0_model.* This allows diagrams to be created either as part of the decomposition of another diagram, or as the roots of standalone *secondary* hierarchies which can be later integrated into the primary IDEF0 model. This should be contrasted with the data schema of AdaNICE which imposes stricter adherence to a top-down design method. IDEF Toolset's support of secondary hierarchies is more flexible, allowing both top-down development and middle-out development. Secondary hierarchies can also be created by pruning off a branch of another hierarchy and can be grafted back into place in another hierarchy.

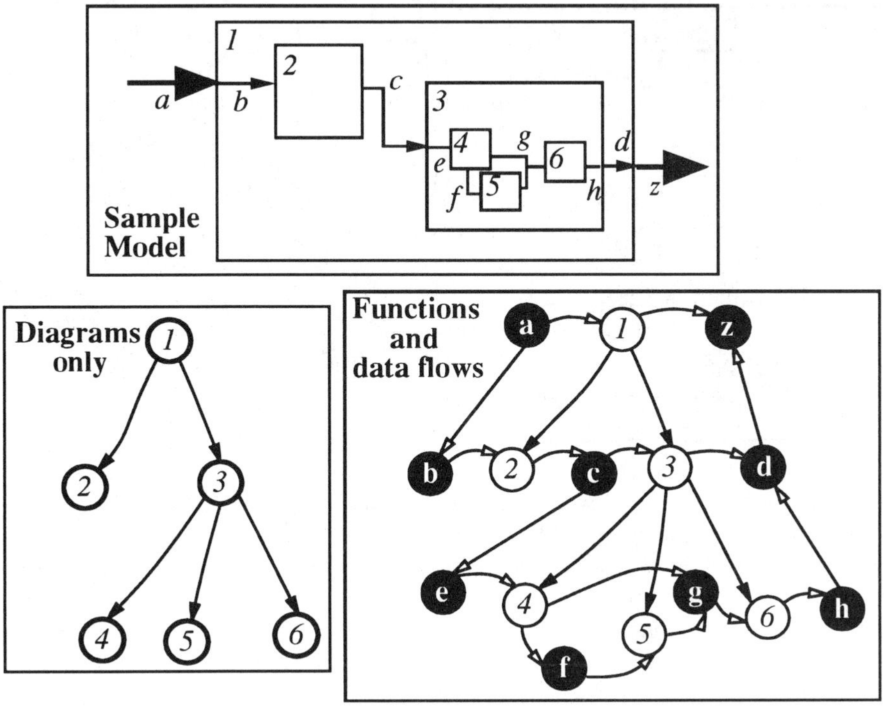

Figure 7.6 These diagrams show medium and fine-grain representations of a sample IDEF0 model, in which *functions* are labelled with numbers and *data flows* with letters. In the coarse grained representation an object is used to store each diagram, with all internal structure of the diagram being hidden in the content of each diagram object. In the finer grained representation both functions (white objects) and data flows (black objects) are represented. In this case it is possible to see in the object base that all data flows of a parent function are consumed and provided by child functions. For example, function *3*'s input flow *c* maps onto input flow *e* of function *4*.

7.4 REENGINEERING A TOOL FOR PCTE—AdaNICE

Being a commercially available toolset, it is important that AdaNICE is both available on a wide variety of platforms, and at the same time easily maintained. Before the start of the ATMOSPHERE project, AdaNICE existed in variants for a number of operating systems, including VMS and several variants of UNIX. Each variant of AdaNICE was based upon essentially the same database technology—the HOOD Project Library (HPL)—which was developed specifically for AdaNICE. This component required only minimal changes to be ported to a new filesystem, thus ensuring that the majority of the code of AdaNICE was common to all variants. However, the goal within the ATMOSPHERE project was to port AdaNICE to another database—the object base of PCTE—in such a way that AdaNICE's data was well-modelled in PCTE terms. This implied that AdaNICE started to exist in versions that *did not use* the HPL database.

In order to continue to have an easily maintainable toolset it was necessary to

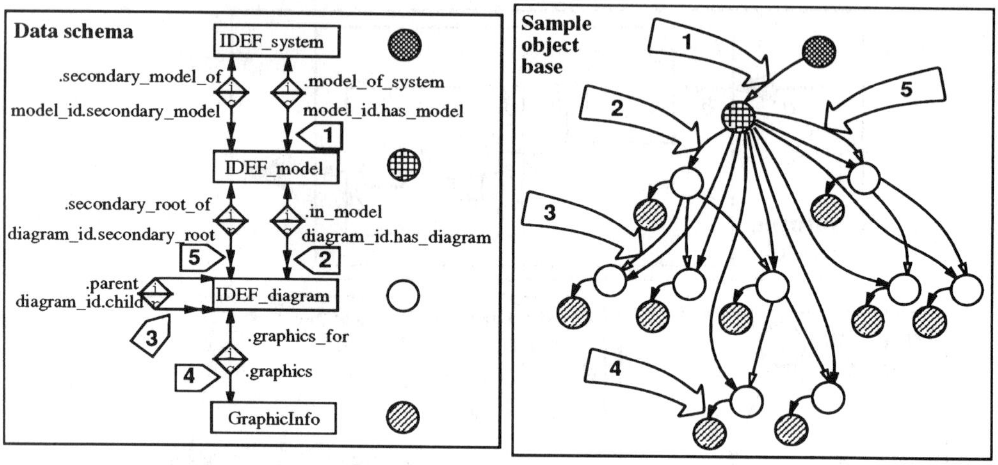

Figure 7.7 The left hand diagram shows the data schema of the IDEF Toolset. The right hand diagram shows a collection of objects in the object base following this schema In the instance diagram, black headed arrows are composition links while white headed arrows are reference links. No implicit links are shown—each link in the diagram actually has a corresponding implicit reverse link. All attribute types have been omitted from the data schema diagram. *IDEF_system* objects gather together a number of models (1) produced during the analysis of a system. A model consists of a set of diagrams, each of which has an object identifier (2). Each diagram models an IDEF0 function, and the hierarchical decomposition of these functions is modelled by links between the diagrams (3). The details of a diagram are stored in the content of the object modelling the diagram, and additional graphical information is stored in an associated file (4). As well as the primary hierarchy of diagrams (headed by the object with diagram identifier '0') it is possible temporarily to store secondary branches (5).

introduce a new internal interface within AdaNICE—that of the data handler (see figure 6.10)—which ensured that as much of the AdaNICE toolset as possible could be kept free of platform specific features. With this architecture it not only became possible to produce variants of AdaNICE based on a class of HPL-like data handlers, but also on data handlers built using a wide range of databases including the object base of PCTE.

7.4.1 The architecture of AdaNICE before ATMOSPHERE

The AdaNICE HPL was not only developed to allow the storage of HOOD data but to support a certain style of concurrent access to the data of a single project and a per session transaction mechanism.

The means of supporting concurrent access was the HOOD *subproject*, which allowed a hierarchy of HOOD objects to be broken down into independently editable subtrees, as illustrated in figure 7.8. Declaring an object to be a subproject 'froze' its interface, ensuring that it could be subsequently reintegrated into its parent subproject, and established a 'subcontract'—the goal of the subproject being to provide a

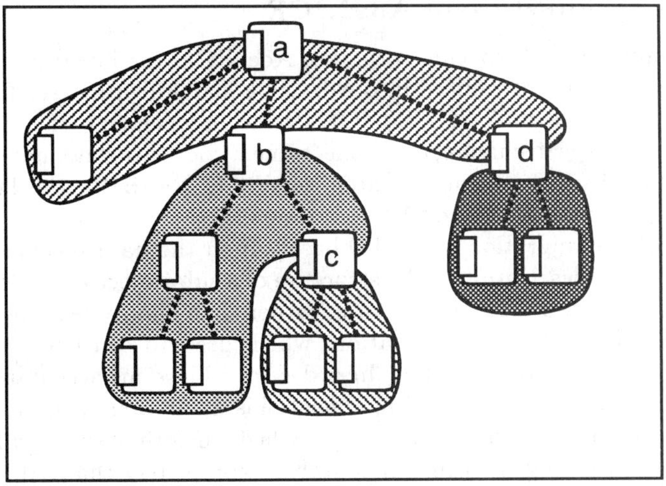

Figure 7.8 Each shaded region corresponds to an AdaNICE subproject. The border of each of the three nested subprojects has been drawn to pass through the centre of its root object. This is because most HOOD objects appear in two diagrams: in one diagram they are a *child object*, and in the other they are a *parent object.*

decomposition of the given object, and the 'frozen' interface acting as the statement of this subcontract.

The subproject was the unit of concurrency within AdaNICE. At any one time a HOOD subproject could be opened either by one user in write mode, or by many users in read mode. Facilities also existed for signing off a subproject, which merged the subproject's subtree back into its parent subproject.

The HPL was implemented as a set of directories within the filesystem, each of which corresponded to a subproject and contained the files of a subproject-wide HPL database. Each subproject directory included a *master file* which contained all information manipulated and presented by the HOOD diagram editor. Additional pieces of information, notably the 'attributes' of a HOOD object—informal solution strategies, operation control structures, etc.—were stored in secondary files, their filenames combining an object identifier with a filename extension which indicated the file's 'kind' (ISS, ODS, OPCS, etc.). When the HOOD diagram editor was activated on a selected subproject the master file for that subproject was loaded resulting in an in-memory 'run-time database'. The diagram editor was then able to continue without accessing the file system until either the user requested the 'save' operation or a save was automatically triggered by the tool. The save operation reconstructed a master file, but saved it in a separate directory known as the subproject's *work area.*

The work area was used to implement AdaNICE's transaction mechanism: at the end of a session the user could choose either to commit the transaction, resulting in an overwriting of the original files with those stored in the work area, or to abort the transaction, which involved merely removing files from the work area. All updates to secondary files were also done on copies within the work area, ensuring that these updates were also subject to the transaction mechanism.

7.4.2 The new architecture of AdaNICE

Rather than producing a PCTE-specific variant of AdaNICE, the integration manager and data handler layers were introduced into AdaNICE's architecture (see figure 6.10) with the aim of making the bulk of AdaNICE's code independent of the choice of an underlying data storage technology. At the same time, two data handlers were developed based upon PCTE and an updated version of the HPL, the latter itself being used as a basis of both UNIX and VMS variants.

A major impact of the migration to PCTE based upon the data schema of § 7.4.3 was that the retrieval of a description of the structure of a subproject involved scanning a subgraph of objects in the PCTE object base, rather than simply reading a file (the 'master file'). Hence the initial load operation, which used to construct a run-time database, had to be completely rewritten. In order to achieve an acceptable level of performance, it was found necessary to implement this as an incremental load, with objects only being read and their associated data cached when they were really needed.

Also, the approach to saving the run-time database completely changed. The 'master file' was a well encapsulated, closed world, that could be completely overwritten at the end of a transaction. However, the PCTE object base is not expected to be used in this way—its goal is to allow the integration of tools, which typically means that extra information may have been added to AdaNICE's data, restricting the modifications that AdaNICE may make to what it previously considered to be its own data. Consequently, the update of a cached copy of the object base without verifying that each individual update will actually work was totally unacceptable—each modification to the run-time database must be immediately reflected in a change to the underlying object base, thus ensuring that all cached states correspond to reachable states of the object base.

This last point did interfere with the provision of design transactions to the user. Rather than AdaNICE implementing its own transaction mechanisms, as it did in the pre-ATMOSPHERE version, AdaNICE merely coordinates the use of PCTE transactions. By opening a PCTE transaction wherever it would have previously started working in a 'work area', all direct modifications to the object base that the data handler makes are subject to roll-back through PCTE mechanisms. It is worth noting that the abort of a PCTE transaction forced the data handler to reestablish its cached copy of the object base.

7.4.3 The data schema of AdaNICE on PCTE

It was a deliberate goal when developing a PCTE data handler for AdaNICE to attempt to model as many HOOD and AdaNICE concepts in PCTE terms as possible.

At a conceptual level, the principal entities within a HOOD design are HOOD objects and operations. HOOD objects are related to one another by two relationships: the *include* relationship which models the decomposition of HOOD objects, and the *use* relationship which records the fact that one object makes use of the operations of another object. Operations are related by a single relationship—the *implemented_by* relationship which shows how operations provided by a decomposed object are actually provided as operations of the object's child objects. Finally, the *use* relationship is n-

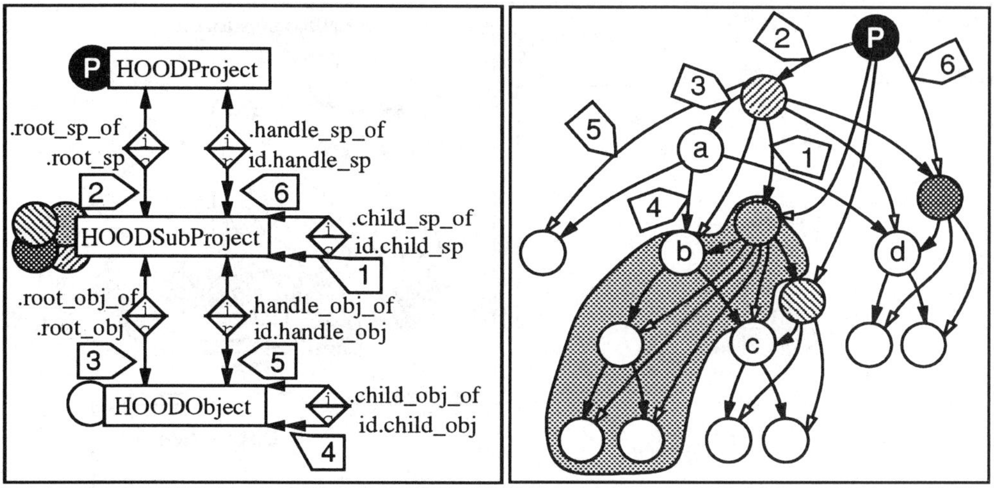

Figure 7.9 The high-level organisation of HOOD subprojects and objects in AdaNICE's data schema. Every HOOD project has a hierarchy (1) of HOOD subprojects attached to it, the root of which (2) is linked to the HOOD project. Every HOOD subproject is attached (3) to a branch of the project's hierarchy (4) of HOOD objects. For example the HOOD project shown in figure 7.8 has four subprojects. These govern the subtrees of the HOOD object hierarchy rooted at *a*, *b*, *c* and *d*. The internal identifiers that AdaNICE associates with HOOD objects are assigned within the context (5) of a HOOD subproject, ensuring that objects have unique identifiers at least within a subproject. The identifier of the root object of each subproject is assigned within the parent subproject. Each subproject is itself given an identifier (6) in the context of its project. One subproject and its subtree (with root at *b*) have been highlighted to help illustrate these constraints.

ary, recording not only *consumer* and *used* objects but also the set of operations of the used object that the consumer uses.

AdaNICE itself brings the additional concepts of HOOD project and subproject, and the notions of *object identifier*, *operation identifier* and *subproject identifier*. Finally, both objects and operations are qualified by a number of attributes: a HOOD object has (amongst others) an 'analysis of the problem', an 'informal solution strategy', an 'object definition skeleton' and an 'object control structure'; a HOOD operation's attributes include an 'operation control structure' and a 'signature'.

The data schema of AdaNICE (see figure 7.9, figure 7.10) represents each of these conceptual entities and relationships. The following points are of particular interest:

Management of subprojects and access control

There was an implicit assumption in AdaNICE that all PCTE objects that formed part of the representation of a subproject were equivalent from a PCTE access control point of view. That is, all objects had not only a common owner but similar access permissions so that a user who was allowed to start working on a subproject in 'write' mode would be able to manipulate all data of the subproject in a uniform manner.

PCTE allows the owner of an object to *give* that object to another user. The

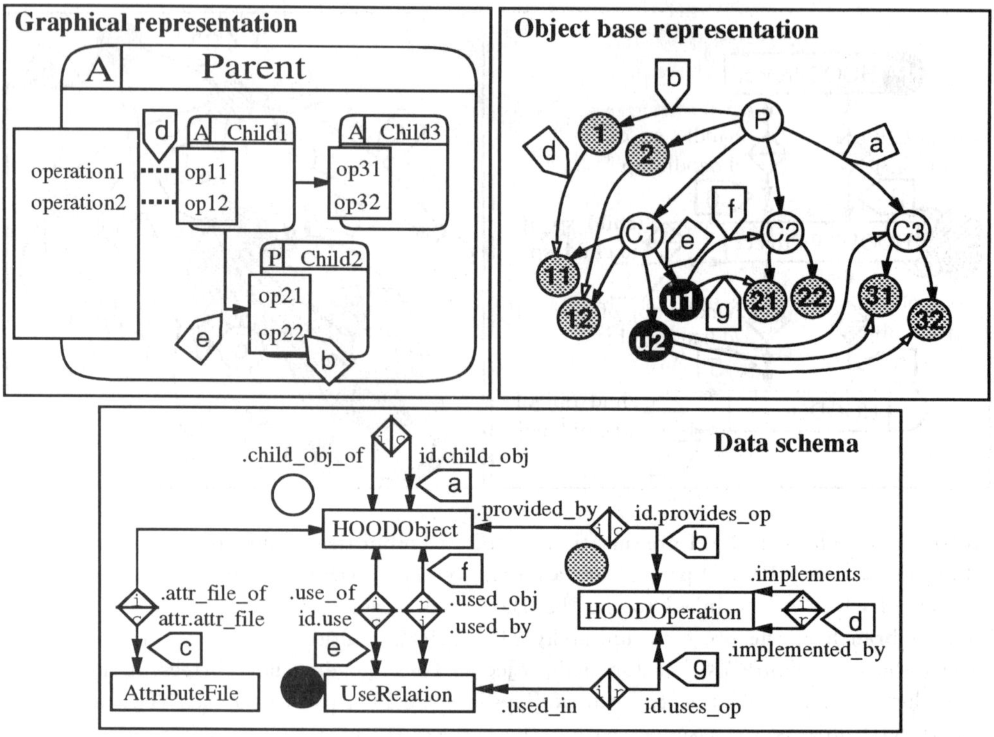

Figure 7.10 The fine-grained organisation of HOOD objects and operations. The top left hand diagram shows the graphical representation of a single decomposition of the HOOD object *Parent*, the top right hand diagram the underlying object representation and the bottom diagram the data schema respected by these PCTE objects and links. As before, HOOD objects (a) form a hierarchy. Here details of the *operations* (b) provided by each HOOD object have been added, together with the way (c) in which a HOOD object's *attributes* are stored. HOOD *implemented_by* relationships (d) are modelled as PCTE links of type *.implemented_by*, and use relationships are modelled by the introduction of another type of object—*UseRelation*—which sits between the consumer object (e) and the used object (f), and allows each of the operations of the used object that is actually used to be referenced (g). For example, while object *Child1* uses all of the operations of *Child3*, it only uses one of the operations of *Child2*. This information is not visible within the graphical representation.

creation of a subproject was based upon this possibility: the creation of a subproject object followed by handing over the ownership of all of the PCTE objects which represented the subproject and its HOOD objects to the user who would perform the subproject. Finishing a subproject involved giving the updated objects back to the owner of the enclosing subproject.

The assumption of uniform access control was a relic of the previous filesystem versions, where the majority of a subproject was stored in a single file and so had a single owner and set of access permissions. Supporting the full possibilities of PCTE access control—where each PCTE object's ownership and permissions were independent—would have required changes not only within the data handler, but the introduction of additional user-level concepts.

Modelling n-ary relationships as objects

A HOOD *use* relationship connects not only two HOOD objects but also some of the operations of its 'destination' HOOD object. PCTE 'handshakes' are inherently *binary*—connecting a pair of objects—and so an alternative means is required for modelling such *n-ary* relationships.

The solution adopted in this case was to model *use* relationships as objects. Each HOOD object had not only component objects representing HOOD attributes and operations, but also objects modelling *use* relationships. The resulting object type—*UseRelation*—had three *roles*: the first being filled with the origin HOOD object of the relationship; the second being filled with the destination HOOD object; and the third being a 'cardinality many role' filled by operations of the destination object.

Representation of object, operation and subproject identifiers

An additional feature required for compatability with non-PCTE versions was a link type to provide a 'handle' on each object of a subproject. The programmatic interface of the data handler was specified in terms of these identifiers and the majority of operations took identifiers as parameters, rather than paths down the HOOD object hierarchy. It therefore seemed natural to model this direct access within the object base, simplifying the development of the data handler and removing the need to perform relatively expensive tree scanning in order to find given objects.

Figure 7.9 shows how each HOOD object of a subproject was directly attached to the subproject with a link whose key was the object's identifier. Similar approaches were taken for the identification of subprojects within a HOOD project, and operations and use relationships within the context of a HOOD object

§ 9.1.2 and § 9.1.3 describe how AdaNICE was integrated with two other tools through the use of a communication mechanism. AdaNICE supported a set of *requests* that allowed other tools to cooperate with it. The majority of these requests had parameters that refered to HOOD objects and operations for which object and operation identifiers were used rather than the 'names' of the objects and operations concerned. Despite being relics of former filesystem-based variants of AdaNICE, object and operation identifiers found at least a temporary place in the prototype PCTE variant of AdaNICE.

7.5 EXTENSION OF A TOOL USING A COMMON SCHEMA—AdaNICE AND GSED/HOOD

The GSED/HOOD toolset offers a means for describing the time behaviour of HOOD design objects, and the simulation of HOOD designs based upon this prescribed behaviour (see § 6.3.4). Tool support for the GSED/HOOD method was provided by extending the AdaNICE HOOD toolset in order to minimise the effort of producing a running prototype. This removed the need for the development of several of the major components of a complete simulation package that were provided by AdaNICE and that are likely to be provided by any HOOD toolset.

7.5.1 The schema extension

Having chosen to make an extension to AdaNICE as a means of developing and viewing HOOD designs it was natural to simply extend AdaNICE's data schema so that it allowed the storage of whatever data was required for GSED/HOOD. Defining a data schema for GSED/HOOD without considering the design decisions taken by the designers of AdaNICE would limit the degree of integration achieved between the tools. Consequently, a large proportion of the PCTE data types used by GSED/HOOD are precisely those of AdaNICE.

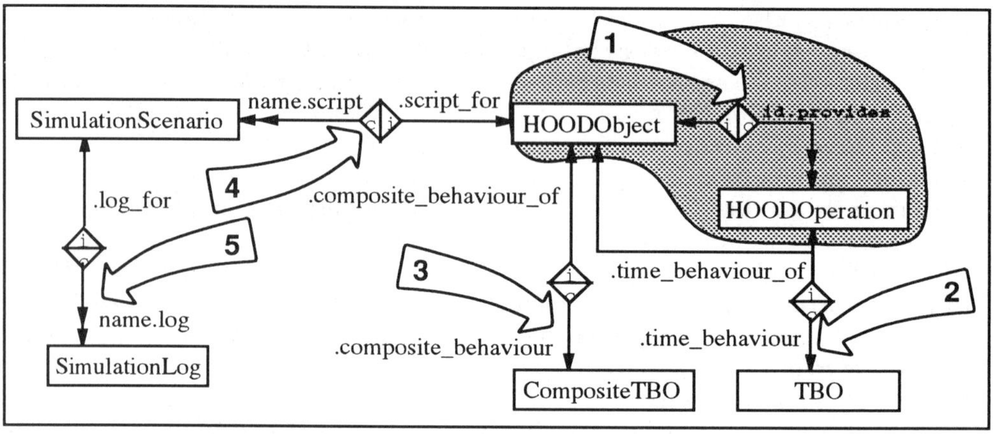

Figure 7.11 The data schema additions for extending AdaNICE with GSED. The shaded area shows some of the types from AdaNICE's data schema that GSED-HOOD reuses, including (1) the link type that relates HOOD operations to the HOOD objects that provide them. A PCTE object of type *TBO* (2) is used to store the GSED time behaviour of each HOOD object or operation, while composite behaviour (see § 6.2.5.1) can only be generated for HOOD objects (3). Simulation scenarios (scripts) can be defined for an object (4), and the result of performing a simulation based upon a particular scenario may also be stored (5). As elsewhere, TBO stands for Time Behaviour Object.

At a conceptual level, GSED/HOOD adds a number of issues to those previously addressed within AdaNICE's data schema. There is a need to store: time behaviour objects (TBOs) for HOOD objects and operations; simulation scenarios for any HOOD object which is to be simulated; and composite TBOs for any object to be simulated. The results of simulations may themselves be stored to allow subsequent analysis. Finally, all fine grained details of TBOs, simulation scenarios and simulation results have been left as hidden detail within the contents of PCTE objects. Figure 7.11 shows how these conceptual issues were modelled at a PCTE level for the purposes of the prototype.

7.5.2 Process assumptions of the prototype

The PCTE data schema of the GSED/HOOD prototype is known to be overly restrictive in terms of some of the process assumptions it makes. While these restrictions might be serious for a commercial product, they were reasonable for a prototype that was developed primarily to determine the true value of the integrated GSED/HOOD method, rather than as an exercise in modular tool design. However, it is still informative to see what some of the process assumptions of the prototype are.

The following statements of process assumptions make reference to the PCTE types shown in figure 7.11.

People who can define time behaviour for a HOOD object can also change that object
This assumption is reflected in the fact that the PCTE link type *.time_behaviour* is of category composition, and so is significant for its origin objects—HOOD objects and HOOD operations. Consequently, the creation of a TBO object to store the time behaviour of a particular HOOD object represents a significant change to that HOOD object, a change that can only be made by someone who has permission to modify the HOOD object itself.
The same is true for the creation of TBO objects for HOOD operations.

People who are able to generate a composite TBO for a HOOD object are also able to change that object
This is true because *.composite_behaviour* links are significant for HOOD objects.

People who develop simulation scenarios for a HOOD object are also able to modify that object
This is true because *.script* links are significant for HOOD objects.

Only people who can modify a simulation scenario are able to record the results of a simulation based upon that scenario
This is true because *.log* links are significant for simulation scenario objects.

Of these, the assumption that time behaviour is defined by the same people who are allowed to modify HOOD objects seems the least restrictive. It does seem quite natural that successive versions of a HOOD object would contain progressively more detail, and that such extra detail would include a definition of the object's time behaviour.

The other assumptions may be inappropriate for some organisations, especially if design validation is performed by someone other than the original designer. An example of a data schema which makes different, less restrictive process assumptions is given in figure 7.12. It should be noted that while this alternative schema is less restrictive, it implies slightly more work on behalf of users of the tool, both at environment building time and at run time. Unlike the prototype's schema, the alternative schema does not contain links with the existence property leading to objects of type *SimulationScenario*, *SimulationLog* or *CompositeTBO*. This means that there is no *functional* means for creating these objects, and that an *organizational* schema must be defined for this purpose.

Secondly, all information for the creation of objects of each of these types was explicitly known to the operations that created them. For example, to create a composite TBO object the only information required was the HOOD object whose composite behaviour was to be stored. Given that, a composite TBO object could be created using a *.composite_behaviour* link leaving this HOOD object. With the alternative schema, both the type of the existence link to be used for creating the composite TBO, and the origin object of that link must be parameters of the composite TBO creation operation.

Although both of these points appear to give the end user of the tool more work to do, the gain in process flexibility easily outways both points.

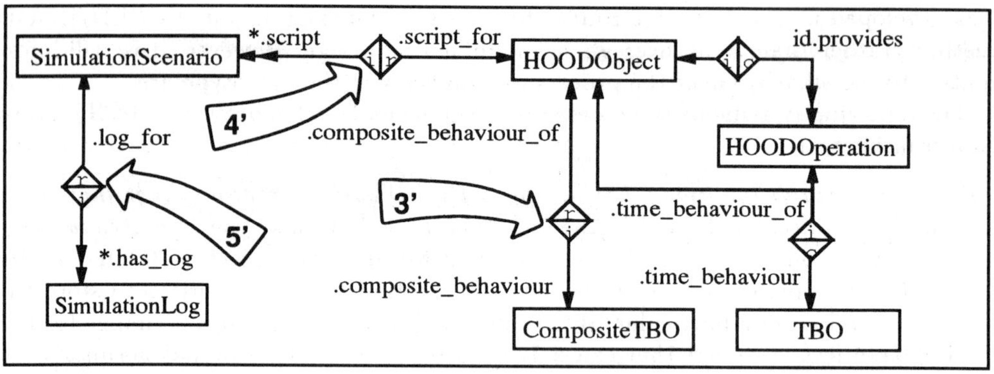

Figure 7.12 Each of the category boxes pointed to by arrows (3'), (4') and (5') shows the reference category in one direction and the implicit category in the other direction. In figure 7.11 each of these category boxes has the composition category where this figure has the implicit category, and the implicit category where this has the reference category. Unlike implicit links which are not considered significant, both reference and composition links are considered to be a significant part of their origin objects. So in the schema shown in figure 7.11, the creation of a *.composite_behaviour* link implied the modification its origin *HOODObject*, while here it involves the modification of the *CompositeTBO* object at the origin of the reference link *.composite_behaviour_of*.

7.6 ENCAPSULATION OF A TOOL FOR PCTE—KeyOne

The syntax directed editor KeyOne is used in the Aerospace Environment to provide support for editing both HOOD-ODS and C language source files. KeyOne-ODS was brought into the environment through its tight integration with AdaNICE, while KeyOne-C was brought in through the development of a data capsule.

7.6.1 Integration of AdaNICE with KeyOne/ODS

The goal of this integration is to replace the simple text editor that AdaNICE provides for editing object definition skeletons (ODSs) with a KeyOne-based structured editor—KeyOne-ODS.

Since KeyOne-ODS simply acts as a replacement for AdaNICE's existing ODS editor, the PCTE data schema of AdaNICE already included an object type to store the ODS of each HOOD object. Consequently, no changes to were made to AdaNICE's data schema to support the integration of KeyOne-ODS into AdaNICE.

However, a number of finer-grained data representation problems had to be solved. The most significant changes required to achieve full data integration were as a consequence of a number of ambiguities in the syntax of the HOOD method's ODS language. The existence of a complete and unambiguous syntax of a language is a prerequisite to its use as a common format to be used by a number of tools. The adoption of a common syntax resulted in changes to both AdaNICE and KeyOne/ODS.

Since KeyOne is a UNIX-based toolset which assumes that each source file that it edits is stored as a UNIX file, a means had to be found by which KeyOne could be made to access and update files stored elsewhere—that is, in the PCTE object base.

This access was provided as part of KeyOne-ODS's integration with AdaNICE, rather than by introducing specific mechanisms into KeyOne to allow it to use PCTE.

The integration between AdaNICE and KeyOne-ODS is achieved primarily through control mechanisms. Whenever KeyOne needs to access the ODS of a HOOD object, AdaNICE creates a UNIX copy of the PCTE file containing this ODS. KeyOne then edits this file as if it was permanently stored there and, after finishing editing the file, KeyOne tells AdaNICE that it has finished using the file, and AdaNICE copies the file back into the PCTE object base. Further details of this communication are given in § 9.1.3.

7.6.2 Data encapsulation of KeyOne/C

The C language variant of KeyOne was brought into the Aerospace Environment without being modified through the development of two capsules. The first of these, a data capsule allowing the data on which KeyOne works to be stored within a PCTE object base, is described in this section. The second, a UI capsule allowing KeyOne to be called from the East-UIMS, is mentioned in § 8.5.4.

The object base of PCTE is intended to be used as the common repository for CASE tools. Tools gain access to this repository through a standardised programmatic interface [ECM90] which is supplied as part of each PCTE implementation. However, early PCTE implementors and environment builders recognised the need for easing the use of non-PCTE tools within a PCTE environment, and primitives were included within the PCTE interface to allow the importation and exportation of files from PCTE to foreign file systems to support this and other needs. However, the integration of tools into PCTE-based environments using such mechanisms was seen as a short-term, although necessary, evil—eventually, with the widespread adoption of PCTE as an international CASE standard, native PCTE versions of CASE tools would be widely available, and data encapsulation would become redundant. File import and export mechanisms would then be used as a basis of other necessary services, such as for the exportation of executables for use in the underlying operating system.

7.6.2.1 Emeraude's implementation of PCTE files and '*ContentsAccess*'

The PCTE implementation used as the basis of the Aerospace Environment (Emeraude [Eme90b]) represented PCTE files as UNIX files. That is to say, each PCTE volume (see § 7.1.1) resided on a UNIX *filesystem*, a portion of which being devoted to a database storing all objects of the overlying PCTE volume. The content of any of the volume's objects that had a content was stored as a UNIX file. This implementation of PCTE contents assured that PCTE tools gained access to files stored in the underlying operating system with a similar degree of performance as tools that made direct use of the operating system.

Emeraude provided a primitive (*ContentsAccess*) which given a pathname to a PCTE object and a desired access mode (read or write), created a UNIX *symbolic link* to the UNIX file containing the contents of the named PCTE object. This symbolic link could then be used by a native UNIX tool to access the contents of the PCTE object as a UNIX file, unaware of the fact that this file was actually stored within a PCTE object base.

The goal of specifying the access mode with which the data was to be accessed was to allow Emeraude to check whether the capsule had PCTE permission to access the object in that manner. This was necessary since UNIX tools accessing PCTE files through UNIX are beyond the control of PCTE access mechanisms.

Data encapsulation of UNIX tools implies the transfer of PCTE-resident knowledge to the UNIX world in the format that the UNIX tool expects it to appear in, and the subsequent restoration of modified data into the object base. This could be achieved, in a limited way at least, especially for file-based tools—tools for which the majority of information is stored in the content of files.

7.6.2.2 Example of the use of *ContentsAccess*—KeyOne/C

While UNIX has no explicit support for data schemas, and is based on a few very elementary types of entity which include *file* and *directory*, file naming conventions have long been established for indicating the nature of the content of many 'classes' of file. Being a UNIX-based tool, KeyOne/C respects the standard UNIX/C conventions, namely, that C source files are stored in a file whose names ends with the characters '.c' and the final letters '.h' are used to indicate header files. Corresponding PCTE conventions were formalised in the link types within the C development schemas of PACT [PAC89] and East, where object types exist to model source and header files. A small part of the East C development schema is shown in figure 7.13.

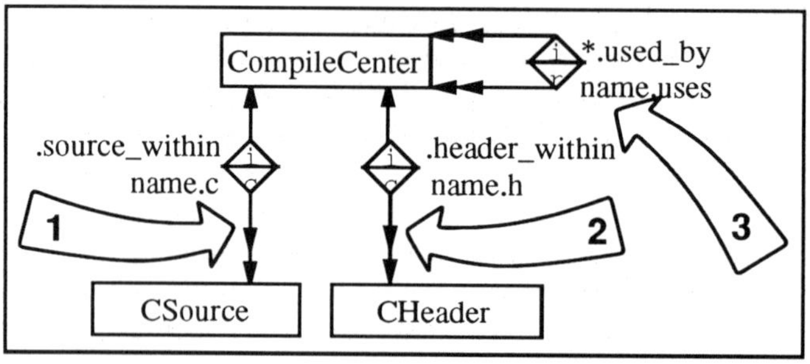

Figure 7.13 Files of type (1) *CSource* and (2) *CHeader* are grouped together to form *CompileCentres*. The names of these link types—'.c' and '.h'—mimic UNIX file extensions. A compile centre is used to model a certain size of module within a system, and (3) may make use of functions that are implemented within other compile centres.

For KeyOne to be used to edit the source and header files of a compile centre, its data capsule must predict which files KeyOne and its user may need to access during the forthcoming KeyOne session and then prepare a temporary UNIX directory in which KeyOne will be started. This UNIX directory must contain a symbolic link to the UNIX file underlying each of the potentially accessed PCTE objects. The preparation of this directory is shown in figure 7.14.

The capsule is also responsible for ensuring that each object that KeyOne accesses is protected against concurrent access. It therefore places locks on each of the objects, and so completely represents KeyOne as far as PCTE is concerned. Once KeyOne has finished executing, the capsule cleans up the UNIX directory in which KeyOne has been working.

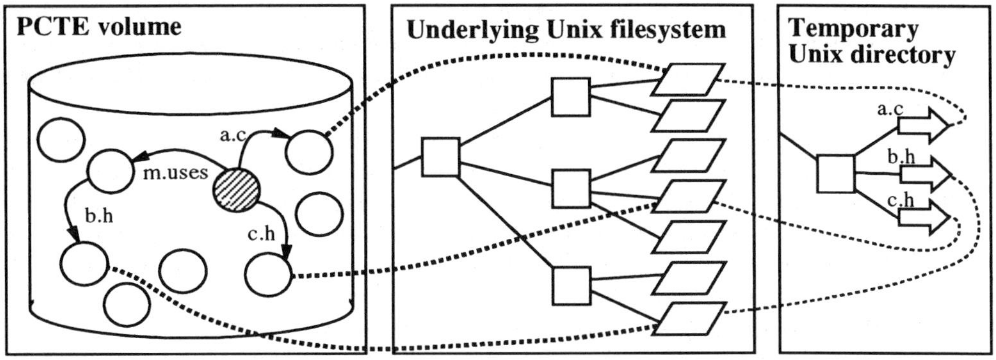

Figure 7.14 This diagram shows an object of type *CompileCentre* within a PCTE object base. The compile centre has a source file *a.c* and a header file *c.h* attached to it, and makes use of functions supplied by another compile centre *m.uses* and that are declared within header file *b.h*. Objects *a.c*, *c.h*, *b.h* each have an underlying UNIX file. Before starting KeyOne, its capsule creates a symbolic link to each of these underlying files from a temporary directory in UNIX. It names each symbolic link with the same name as the corresponding PCTE link to ensure that file names presented to the user by KeyOne correspond to those appearing within the PCTE object base and displayed by native PCTE tools.

7.6.2.3 Limits of the use of encapsulation

The use of the *ContentsAccess* primitive, and hence the development of capsules, is based upon a number of assumptions, each of which can easily break down for even the simplest of foreign tools.

The encapsulated tool's data needs can be predicted
In order to make data available to the encapsulated tool before calling it, the capsule must *predict* what data will be of interest to the tool. For the encapsulation of KeyOne the prediction made was that the user would only wish to view source code and include files within the local compile centre, and include files within directly referenced compile centres.
The encapsulation of KeyOne involved no communication between the capsule and KeyOne, merely the preparation of data on which KeyOne was to be started. The development of communication-based capsules is also possible, and is illustrated by the integration of KeyOne-ODS and AdaNICE (see § 7.6.1 and § 9.1.3).

The encapsulated tool can be called in a restricted form
The tool should confine itself to working on the data which it is asked to use, and respect access controls that it is told exist on the data, despite the tool's apparent UNIX permissions on the object. For example, the UNIX editor 'vi' allows a file to be edited even when the user has no read permission on the file. Although the original UNIX file cannot be overwritten, the user can choose to create another file containing the modified file. In this case, the capsule is unable to predict where such a file was created, and so cannot easily recover it and store it in the object base. It is inadvisable, therefore, to encapsulate 'vi' as a tool for displaying text files.

KeyOne/C, as described above, works upon a list of files, all stored within a single UNIX directory. It neither adds files nor removes files from this list so the capsule can easily tidy up the UNIX filestore and the PCTE object base at the end of a session.

However, a tool for whom the object base representation was large and complicated, and that could be used to perform arbitrary restructuring of this collection, would present significant algorithmic difficulties for the capsule developer, and include many cases where changes made in the UNIX world could not be easily reflected in the PCTE world. As seen in the case of AdaNICE (§ 7.4.2) it is highly desirable to immediately act upon user manipulations that affect object base structure.

The encapsulated tool fulfils a well-defined, precise function

This is strongly related to the ability to call tools in a restricted form. The tool 'vi' allows you to switch to another file at any time. However, since this tool works in UNIX, by simply switching to another file the user starts navigating within a world that is completely independent of the PCTE object base, and any semblance of a well-integrated tool is lost.

Many tools satisfy these assumptions, but many others do not. KeyOne/C is an example of a tool that neatly fitted these assumptions.

7.7 TYPE DEPENDENT OBJECT CONTENTS—DOCS

The goal of this section is *not* to describe the functionality of the document editor DOCS (DOCumentation Service) but rather to point to the way that DOCS is customised, how this customisation is modelled in the PCTE object base, and how DOCS recovers customisation information when used to display or edit a document.

7.7.1 Concepts behind a customisation of DOCS

DOCS was based upon the document editor Grif [Qui87]. DOCS allowed the definition of templates, each of which was used to describe the generic structure of a class of documents. Such a template-based document editor then acted as a means for defining and supporting project-wide documentation standards.

Each document class was defined in terms of two *schemas*:

a structure schema

which defined what elements were needed within each of the class's documents (for example: a title, a date, a glossary).

one or more presentation schemas

defining how the content of the document was formatted in a final paper copy of the document as well as when displayed by the DOCS editor itself. A presentation schema allowed uniform formatting decisions to be made, such as fonts to be used for displaying the various elements identified in the structure schema, page layouts, invariant text, etc..

It was therefore possible to talk of 'requirements documents' or 'meeting minutes' or 'progress reports' as specific classes of document, and to predict the formats used for each class.

7.7.2 Use of the PCTE metabase for customising DOCS

As mentioned earlier, in the description of PCTE's object model, PCTE has no direct support for defining the internal structure of an object's 'content'. However, a widely used convention is that it should be possible to predict the internal structure of an object's content simply by knowing the object's type—that is, each object type should have an associated *content schema*. For example, the content schema of objects of type *CSource* would be the syntax of the C language; an object storing a table may have a fixed record structure; etc.. DOCS already had a notion similar to contents schema—*document class*.

The need, therefore, was to represent document classes in the object base and to somehow associate these with object types. PCTE supports this kind of association through the provision of a *metabase*.

The *metabase* is a part of the PCTE object base that provides a PCTE representation of its own types and schema definition sets, as well as objects known as *types-in-SDS*. A type-in-SDS is an object that represents a type within a particular SDS, and is therefore an example of a *surrogate* object. These objects are used as a basis of a representation of the properties assigned to a type within a particular SDS. Amongst the various types within the so-called *metaschema* is an object type whose instances represent object types. These objects are accessed by following well known paths—the object modelling a particular object type is found by using one of the type's names (see § 7.1.4). Generic tools such as DOCS may associate type-dependent information with a PCTE object type by attaching it to the object that represents this type within the metabase. Figure7.15 shows DOCS' data schema and how DOCS used the metabase to find the document class for an object that has the local name *Results* in the *Review* SDS.

7.7.3 Document classes and environment building

The definition of document classes is part of the task of building an environment. The environment builder must identify those types of document used to support their organisation's development process and not supported by more specific tools and then may create a new object type to model this type of document and prepare the structure and presentation schemas for its document class.

As might be expected, the development of document classes relates strongly to the provision of organizational data schemas. Indeed, the creation of a new document class implies the creation of a new object type which itself must be created within an organizational data schema. The principal example of a document class produced for the Aerospace Environment was one used to structure the contents of the requirement management toolset's requirement objects. § 7.2 introduced the need for this object and the following section shows how it was added.

7.8 COMPLETING THE DATA SCHEMA—ORGANIZATIONAL ISSUES

§ 7.1.5 introduced East's policy towards the high-level management of data schemas, and how this balances the needs of packaging the data schemas of individual tools

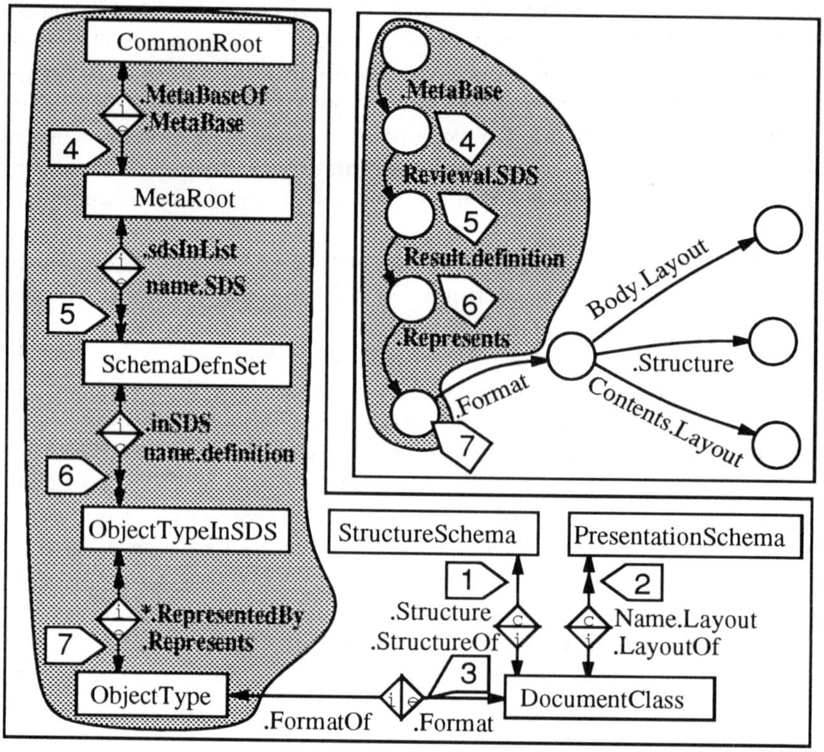

Figure 7.15 A *document class* consists of (1) a *structure schema* and (2) a set of presentation schemas. A document class is associated with a particular *object type* to act as its *content schema* (3) using a link of type *.Format.* The object modelling a particular object type is found relative to the *common root* object of the object base by navigating (4) along the root of the *metabase*, and three other links (5,6,7). Shaded areas indicate parts of the metabase and metaschema.

against those of the environment builder. This section describes some of the *organizational* types that could be used to join together the schemas of the Aerospace Environment listed above. The goal of this section is to illustrate what it means to build an environment from existing, packaged PCTE tools, rather than to give an exhaustive list of the organizational types of the Aerospace Environment.

The introduction of new types within organizational schemas also has an impact at the user interface level, both for the association of *operations* with each type, and for the provision of *forms*. These needs are discussed in § 8.5 and § 8.4.

7.8.1 Bringing together tool fragments—RMT and DOCS

RMT supports the creation of trees of 'requirement nodes' for each of which there may be an associated 'content'. However, RMT itself does not provide any explicit support for the display or editing of such a content and relies instead on other tools of the environment to do so.

The data schema of RMT (figure 7.5) reflects this by separating a requirement's content from the requirement itself, and by allowing the definition of an object type for each class of requirement content and an implied selection of an appropriate editor. RMT is therefore left as an incomplete tool fragment that must be complemented with other tools before it can be completely used. Given the intended use of RMT within the Aerospace Environment to support requirements capture and the recording of behavioural, performance and miscellaneous specifications, it seemed appropriate to have three different classes of document content reflecting these different classes of requirement.

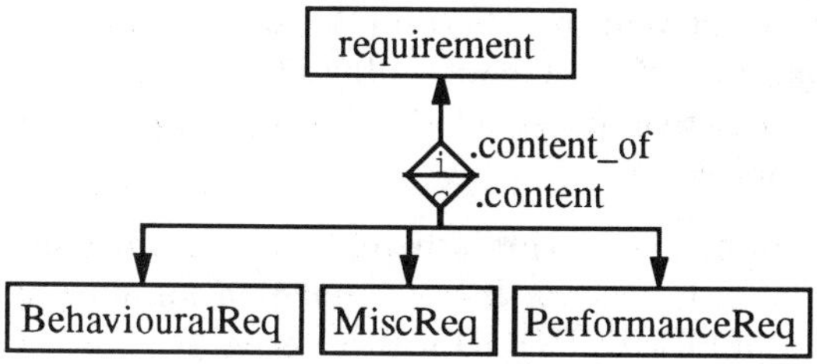

Figure 7.16 The link type *.content* has simply been extended to three new object types.

Each of these document classes was supported by the document editor DOCS and so for each class it was necessary to create a new PCTE object type as well as supplying the elements of this type's document class (see § 7.7.3). It was also necessary to complete RMT's data schema by extending the link type *.content* to each of the newly created object types. This is shown in figure 7.16.

7.8.2 Organising existing functionality

§ 7.5.2 described some of the process assumptions inherent in the data schema of GSED/HOOD and proposed an alternative schema which, while removing some overly restrictive process assumptions, introduced a need for additional organizational data types. This section describes one of the many possible organizational schemas that would fill this role.

The organizational needs identified above were to allow the preparation of simulation scenarios, the performance of simulations and the generation of composite time behaviour objects. One possible way of organising this is:

- to allow the creation of *design tests*, each of which would involve the identification of a simulation scenario as well as the composite TBO to be tested, and would be used to generate a single simulation log
- while a simulation log would be the result of a single design test, both composite TBOs and simulation scenarios would be reusable for a number of tests
- finally, to allow the independent creation of lists of simulation scenarios, each of which could be used for many design tests and in combination with many composite TBOs.

This schema is shown in figure 7.17.

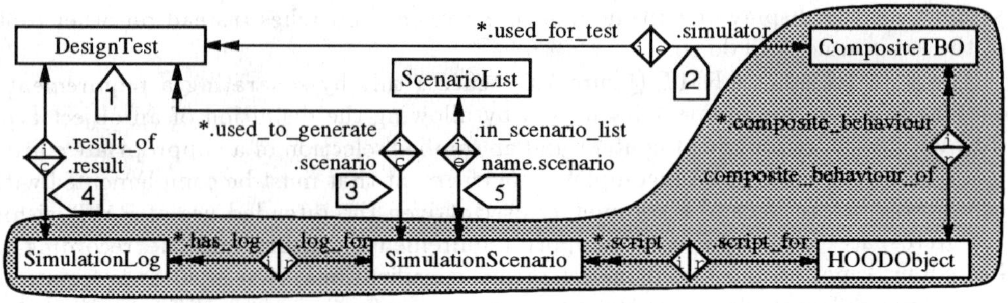

Figure 7.17 This diagram shows a part of the data schema of GSED/HOOD (shaded) and several additional types. The object type *DesignTest* (1) has been introduced to allow the specification of a design test in terms of a composite TBO (2) and a simulation scenario (3). It also supports the subsequent creation of a simulation log (4). Finally, simulation scenarios can be created within a scenario list (5).

Note that even with the addition of this schema there is no means for creating design tests or scenario lists. This schema merely makes a number of choices about the way in which the objects of GSED/HOOD's alternative schema would be created as components of objects modelling concepts at a higher level of abstraction. These types of object themselves must be created by using the types of another schema, and so on recursively until the schema is well 'anchored' within the environment's overall schema.

7.8.3 Organising a user's workspace and provision of 'reference areas'

The highest level of organizational schema is that used to define what can be described as 'user workspaces' and 'reference areas'.

A user's workspace is centred around his 'home object'—an object modelling the a user and acting as their entry point into the object base. The user may also use this object for the creation of other objects using link types which have the existence property. Such links rarely have any functional meaning and exist purely to allow objects to be created 'somewhere'.

For example, a HOOD design may be developed by a design team and so is naturally found attached to an object that models that team. Once completed it may be considered as a major result of a project and so may merit being attached to a more widely known object. Figure 7.18 gives an example of a few type definitions that would support the storage of AdaNICE HOOD projects and GSED/HOOD test scenarios, based upon the organizational schema shown in the previous section.

The set of organizational schemas given in this section supported one of many possible sets of process choices. It is overly simple in that it makes no provision for the storage of multiple versions of produced components and ignores many other issues. However, this section should have demonstrated the degree of freedom given to the environment builder when tool and schema designers make an effort to limit the number of process assumptions that they build into their tools.

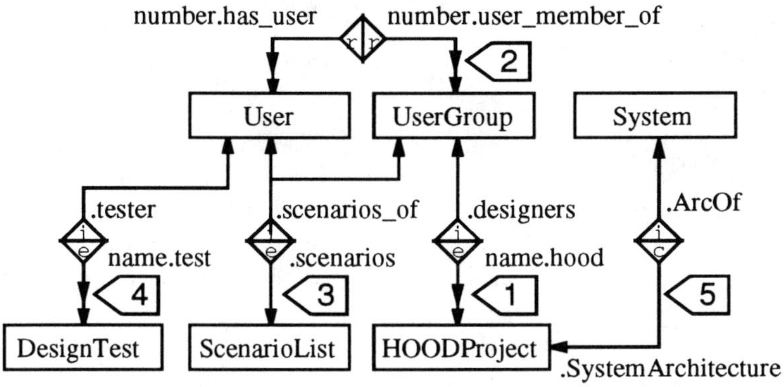

Figure 7.18 Rather than being produced by specific individuals, HOOD designs are typically developed cooperatively be a design team. Consequently the sensible place for creating objects of type *HOODProject* is (1) attached to an object modelling a group of users. *User*, *UserGroup* and the relationship between them (2) are predefined types within PCTE. Unlike a *HOODProject* which is to be worked on by a team, each user may develop test scenarios (3) and perform tests (4). Particularly successful test scenarios may be moved to a scenario list that is common to all members of the team. Finally, once a complete HOOD design has been produced it may be attached to an object modelling the system under development (5).

8

Presentation Integration

Like the majority of modern CASE tools and software engineering environments, the Aerospace Environment has a largely graphical interface. This interface is based upon *de facto* industrial standards (X/Window and Motif) which provide the most basic of presentation integration—the possibility of using several tools simultaneously on a workstation's bit-mapped display.

However, this level of presentation integration is clearly minimal. The developer of new tools should benefit from the facilities of a user interface development system (UIDS), and the end user from basic concepts built into the user interface management system (UIMS) that relate to the nature of the software system that they are using: an integrated, yet extensible, software engineering environment. Moreover, the environment builder—the person responsible for selecting tools and fitting them together to form a complete environment—can benefit from a uniform means for registering tools into the environment. It is for these reasons that a major architectural component of East is East-UIMS which, although primarily present to ensure a tightly integrated user interface for the end user, also supports the tool developer and environment builder.

§ 8.1 presents an overview of the East-UIMS, and § 8.2 illustrates the way in which a tool developer makes use of its user interface development features. The chapter concludes in § 8.5 with a description of how the environment builder registers tools into the environment, based upon examples taken from the Aerospace Environment.

Just as in the case of the use of a common repository, an environment based upon a common UIMS must allow the use of tools that were not developed to use its features. In order to be used within East, tools must be surrounded by *UI capsules*, which are themselves tools built using the East-UIMS. § 8.5.2 describes the production of UI capsules. AdaNICE is an example of an encapsulated tool which, being based upon X/Motif and PCTE, was a natural candidate for use within the environment.

Finally, two of the tools of the environment are not directly accessible through the East-UIMS since they are only naturally used in combination with AdaNICE. § 8.3 describes how the graphical editor of AdaNICE was used to animate design simulations driven by GSED, and how KeyOne-ODS was made available from AdaNICE.

Tool Integration: Environments and Frameworks, Edited by D. Schefström and G. van den Broek

8.1 THE East-UIMS

Keller *et al* [KCTT91] stress the difference between the notion of a UIDS and a UIMS. The purpose of a *User Interface Development System* is to ease the development of user interfaces for new tools, while a *User Interface Management System* is to support the user interfaces of tools at run-time. The East-UIMS has both UIDS and UIMS facilities.

East is essentially a data centred environment. The provision of a user interface management system for a data centred environment presents some novel issues, mostly due to the fact that the data within the environment does not belong to any one tool—objects are available to be accessed by several radically different tools:

- each tool is interested in different properties of an object
- several different tools may be used simultaneously to allow a user to view a set of objects from many points of view
- there will be many key objects that many users will need to view simultaneously

The availability of a range of tools for accessing and displaying a single object is naturally complemented by an appearance of the environment as a 'single tool', with a single space of dialogue, and tool boundaries largely unknown to the user. This has led to the adoption of an 'object-oriented' dialogue style for East.

This section gives a brief overview of the East-UIMS. Its run-time (UIMS) aspects are described in § 8.1.1. The (UIDS) support given to the tool developer and environment integrator is described in § 8.1.2 and § 8.1.3. Finally, § 8.1.4 describes the architecture of the East-UIMS.

8.1.1 Run-time user interface—basic user-level abstractions

The East-UIMS is based upon a number of high level abstractions related to the concepts of the PCTE object base. The inclusion of these abstractions simplifies the development of tools (a UIDS capability), and increases the uniformity of the environment for the user (a UIMS capability). The basic abstractions of the East-UIMS are illustrated in figure 8.1, and include:

views: Within East the general concept of *window* has been specialised to the more specific notion of a *view*. A *view* is a *window* onto the object base. Most views are centred upon a central PCTE object and present that object and its locality within the object base—displaying some of the object's attributes and links, and some of the objects related to that central object. Different views of an object relate to different ways of understanding this object and its neighbouring objects, and adopt presentation styles best suited to each understanding of the object.

entities: Within a view there are always a number of selectable *entities*. Most entities are UI *representations* of underlying PCTE objects and links, and the East-UIMS recognises them as such.

operations and *menus:* Associated with each type of UI and PCTE entity there is a *set of operations*. The set of operations for a particular type of entity is, on demand, presented to the user as a *menu* that is largely *independent of the view in which the entity is displayed.*

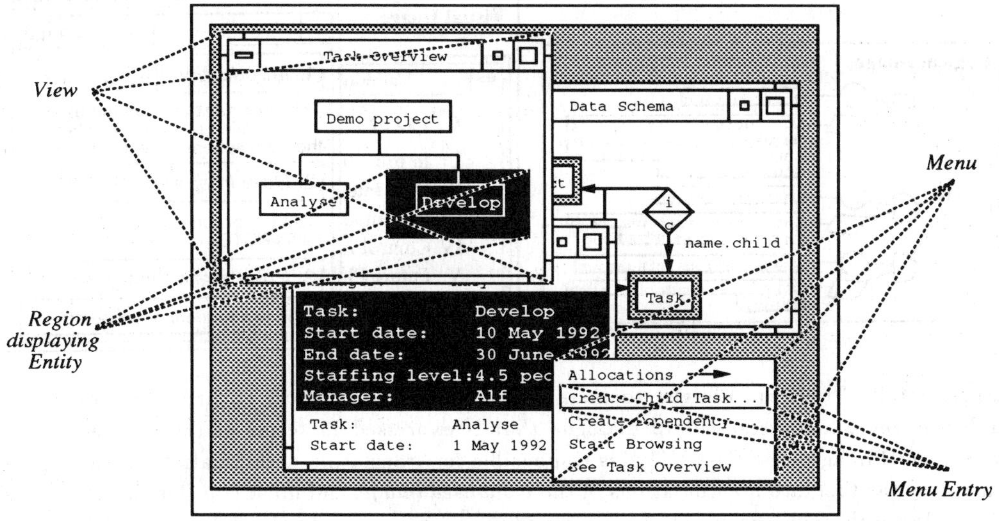

Figure 8.1 A typical screen managed by the East-UIMS. An entity, highlighted in black, has been selected and a menu requested.

dialogue boxes and *dragging:* Some operations require a number of parameters to be provided. These parameters may be completed through a specialisation of a window called a dialogue box. Many operations have objects as parameters, and, in a UIMS in which displayed entities are known to correspond to objects in the underlying object base, it is natural to be able to use these displayed entities when supplying parameters. The East-UIMS *dragging* mechanism fills this need.

The role of tools in such a world is to provide views and to support *operations* that manipulate the object base. Frequently a modification of the object base will imply a change to the presentation of data within a view, although since most views only display some properties of an object, not all views of the object need to be updated each time it is changed. The problem of making sure that views accurately reflect the current state of the part of the object base that they display is termed *view coherence.*

The object-oriented dialogue style relies on the association of operations with each entity type, and the definition of menu structures not on a per tool basis but on an environment-wide basis. This means that East needs to maintain a centralised register of operations.

8.1.2 Supporting the tool developer: the logical UI

The primary goal of the *logical UI* is to simplify the development of user interfaces. The logical UI hides the low-level graphical facilities of the windowing system and presents the developer with a simpler image to manipulate, free of lower level graphical issues.

A tool developed using the East-UIMS manipulates a so-called *logical image.* This is a collection of *logical entities*, each of which may be rendered as a region within a view. This rendering is specified independently as a set of *presentation rules.* The East-UIMS is therefore responsible for replacing the need for tools to directly maintain *visual images* with the need to maintain *logical images*, thus considerably reducing the

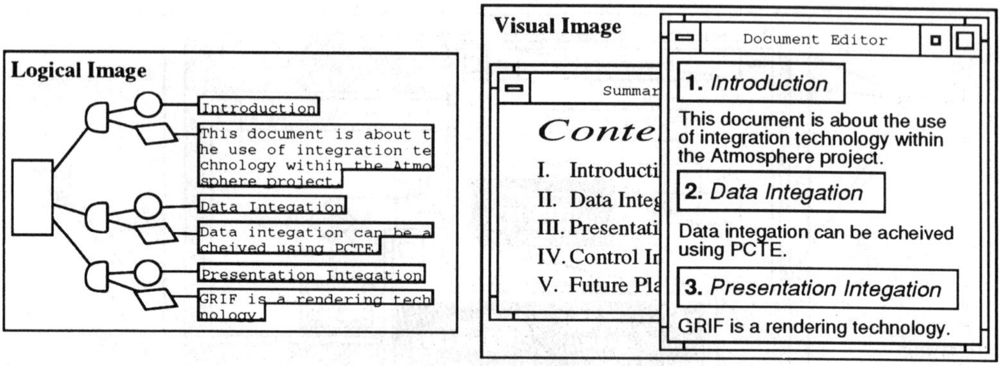

Figure 8.2 Tools are obliged to maintain a hierarchy of logical entities that constitute a *logical image*, and respond to dialogue that is expressed in terms of the entities within that logical image. The East-UIMS is responsible for translating manipulations of the logical image by the tool into manipulations of the *visualised image*, and must translate user requests for dialogue through *regions* of the *visualised image* into requests about logical entities to be answered by the tool. An advantage of making the separation between logical and visualised images is that this allows the support of several radically different views to be based upon the same underlying logical image, as shown here.

effort to produce the user interface part of a tool. The distinction between logical and visual images is shown in figure 8.2.

Examples of views built using this approach are given in the description of the user interface of RMT in § 8.2.

8.1.3 Representation and the entity/operation model

Certain logical entities can be declared as being *representations* of underlying PCTE entities (objects or links). Representation supports two user-level abstractions: *object-oriented menus* and *dragging*.

The menus of operations requested by users are automatically generated by the East-UIMS, and are the primary graphical means by which operations can be requested. In illustrating the basic user-level abstractions of the East-UIMS, figure 8.1 showed, amongst other things, the menu of operations for a particular entity. Figure 8.3 shows the way in which this menu is produced based upon the East-UIMS's knowledge of what data is represented by the visualised image.

Each operation is provided by a tool, and is defined as being an operation of either a logical or a PCTE entity type. The addition of a tool to the environment involves deciding what operations are provided by the tool, and deciding to which entity types the operations apply. Each operation must be written to expect a principal operand—the entity upon which it has been selected—as well as having a number of additional parameters. Parameters may themselves refer to PCTE objects or links, and are supplied by means of the *dragging* dialogue:

- a certain combination of mouse buttons can be used to obtain a reference to any represented PCTE object or link

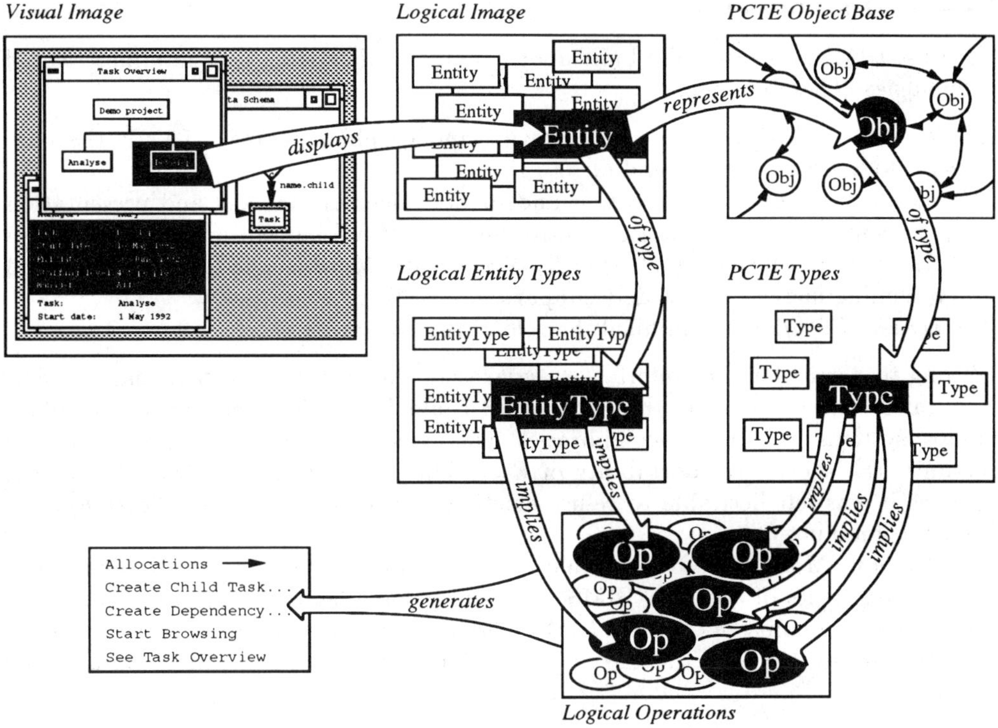

Figure 8.3 This diagram shows the relationship between an image presented to a user, the *logical* image known by a tool, the data stored in the PCTE object base, and the operations available in a menu requested in that region. Each *region* within a *view* corresponds to an underlying logical entity, which is known to, and maintained by, the East-UIMS. The East-UIMS is also aware of the role that the logical entity plays within the logical image (the *type of the entity*), any entity within the PCTE object base that the logical entity may *represent*, and the type of that PCTE entity. The set of operations that would be presented as a menu for a designated region can therefore be generated automatically.

- this reference may then be *dragged* across the screen (using the mouse) and *dropped* into a dialogue box to fill a parameter.

Consequently, representation supports not only the provision of menus of operations, but the supply of parameters for these operations.

The entity/operation model is the central pivot of East, combining both PCTE objects and links (*entities*) and the functionality (*operations*) of an environment built upon the East framework. It is the means by which tool designers specify their tools—as a set of operations upon particular data types—and through which environment builders fit together environments—taking the data schemas and operations of the tools they have acquired and complementing them with organizational data schemas (§ 7.8) and forms (§ 8.4) to give a complete environment.

§ 8.5 describes how the entity/operation model was applied to build the Aerospace Environment, and how the *entry points* of the environment's foreign tools (IDEF Toolset, AdaNICE and KeyOne/C) were encapsulated to give usable East operations.

8.1.4 UI architecture

The East-UIMS was originally built upon a number of existing user interface related technologies. These include:

X/Window Toolkit: a low level windowing and graphics package. This is the base technology used by Motif and Grif.

Motif: which supports the creation and management of dialogue and presentation components such as menus and control buttons. Motif is itself implemented on top of X/Window. The combination of X/Window and Motif is a de-facto standard and is becoming increasingly widely supported.

the kernel of Grif: which fulfilled the role of the logical UI.

Tying to particular user interface standards in this way was, in fact, unnecessary. It is quite conceivable that the East-UIMS could be implemented on top of other window systems and/or dialogue libraries. The initial choice of X/Motif was made to maximise the short-term portability of East. The initial choice of Grif [Qui87] was made as it was felt desirable to re-use existing logical-UI technology rather than to develop something new.

X/Window, Motif and Grif are enabling technologies that act as a foundation of major components of the East-UIMS. Additional modules were added to completely cover the functionality of the East-UIMS, and to coordinate the use of Motif and Grif. The relationship between the East-UIMS's architectural components is summarised in figure 8.4.

8.2 DEVELOPMENT OF A FULLY INTEGRATED TOOL INTO THE East-UIMS—RMT

RMT is used within the Aerospace Environment to support the capture of user requirements and the storage of any non-functional specifications that are identified during the analysis of these requirements. It is based upon the East-UIMS and so respects many of the design prinicples associated with such tools.

RMT supports three *views*, the first being of a tree of requirement nodes, and the others offering alternative views of a single node. These last two views are actually based upon a common *logical view*.

8.2.1 The requirement tree view

The nodes of a single requirements document form a tree. A natural means of viewing this tree is as precisely that: as a tree of nodes.

Looking back at the data schema of RMT (figure 7.5) it can be seen that there are two types of PCTE object stored in the base—*requirement* and *req_document*—and that there are two principal relationships between requirements, modelling the decomposition of a tree of requirements (*child_req/parent_req*), and references between requirements. Visually, therefore, while it is natural to present a view of a requirements tree that displays not only the requirements in the form of a tree but also the requirements referenced by each requirement node, it is important to be able to visually distinguish these two types of relationship. Also, it is natural to want to display

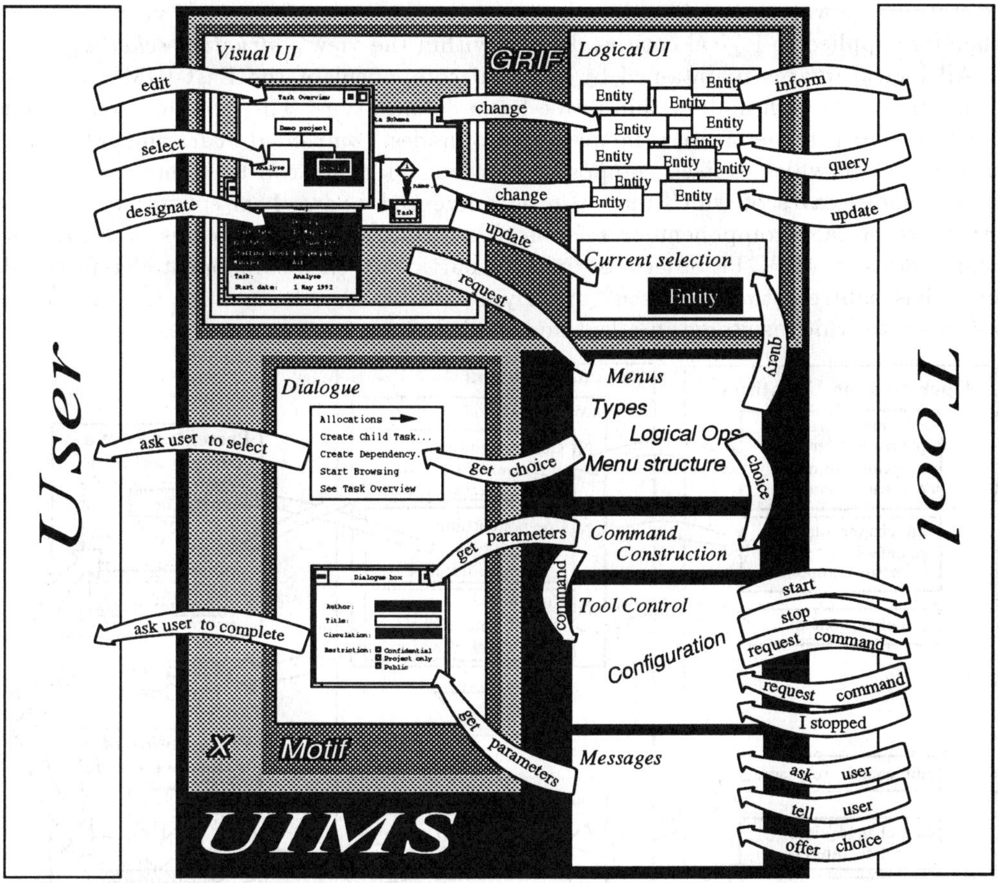

Figure 8.4 The architectural components of the East-UIMS. It can be seen that Grif supports the logical and visual images; Motif supports dialogue; and X/Window acts as a basis for both of them. Other components support menus, basic editing and tool dialogue. The East-UIMS also has a number of dependencies on PCTE which are not shown here.

at least some minimal information about each requirement to ease the browsing of the requirement tree structure.

The tree view forms a major part of the user interface of RMT. It is through the views of a tool that much of a user's dialogue with the tool is initiated. Following East's entity/operation model, the operations supported by the tool are applied to specific PCTE or UI entity types. The application of an operation to a PCTE type implies the availability of that operation whenever a representation of that object appears on the screen. So, if applied to the object type *requirement*, certain operations of RMT (such as *display_tree*) will be available whenever a representation of a requirement object is displayed. This operation is a means by which RMT is started—an object of type requirement is selected in a view of another tool and its associated menu will contain the operation to view the requirement as a part of a requirement tree. Other operations, however, are directly related to the presence of the tree view, and are therefore applied to logical entities defined within the view's *structure schema*.

All logical images maintained by the Grif component of the East-UIMS are tree structured, and each node within a tree has a definite type. The structure schema for the tree view is made of two principal types of nodes: *component nodes* and *referenced nodes*, each of which is itself composite. Component nodes can be combined to form a tree, some leaves of which may also be referenced nodes. Leaf entities within the structure of each component or referenced entity are strings, integers, booleans or representations of PCTE objects or links. In particular, each component or referenced node has subtrees that represent underlying PCTE objects or links (see § 8.3), a reference to which is stored in a leaf node called *Represents*.

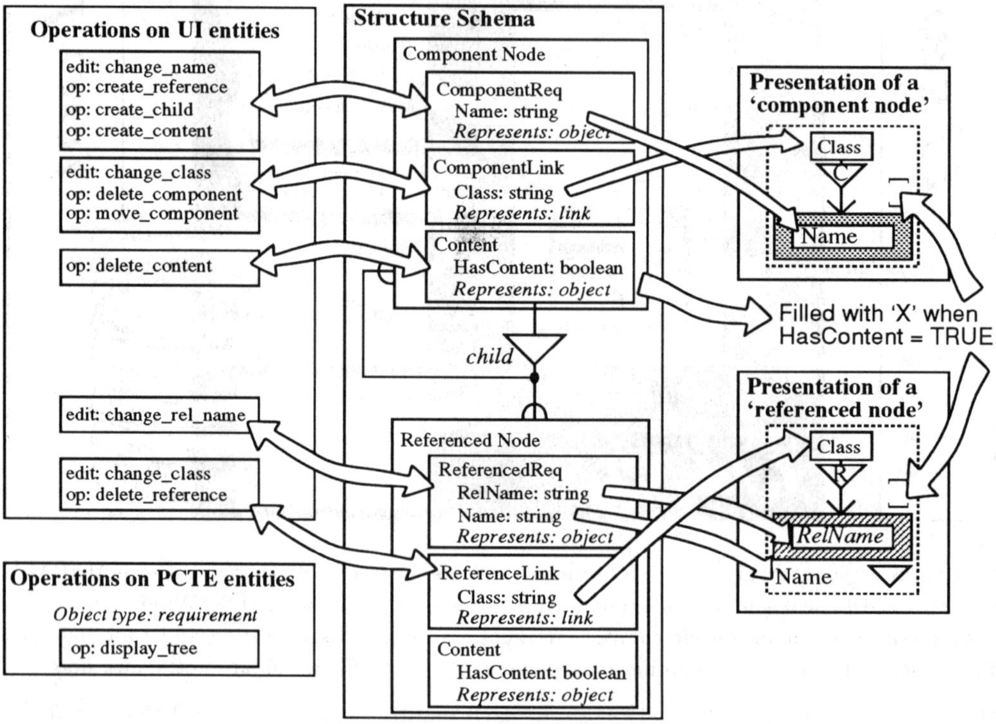

Figure 8.5 The structure schema, presentation rules and operations of RMT's tree view. The difference between operations classified as *edit* and those labelled as *op* is that *edit operations* can be started simply by the user trying to edit displayed text, while the latter must be requested through a menu.

The structure schema of the logical image that RMT manipulates is shown in figure 8.5, together with some of the presentation rules used by the East-UIMS to construct a view from the logical image and the operations supported by RMT for manipulating the tree. The only operation related to this view that is applied to a PCTE entity type is that for starting the RMT tool—*display_tree*. Figure 8.6 shows a sample logical image built up by RMT following the structure schema, and the corresponding visual image displayed by the East-UIMS.

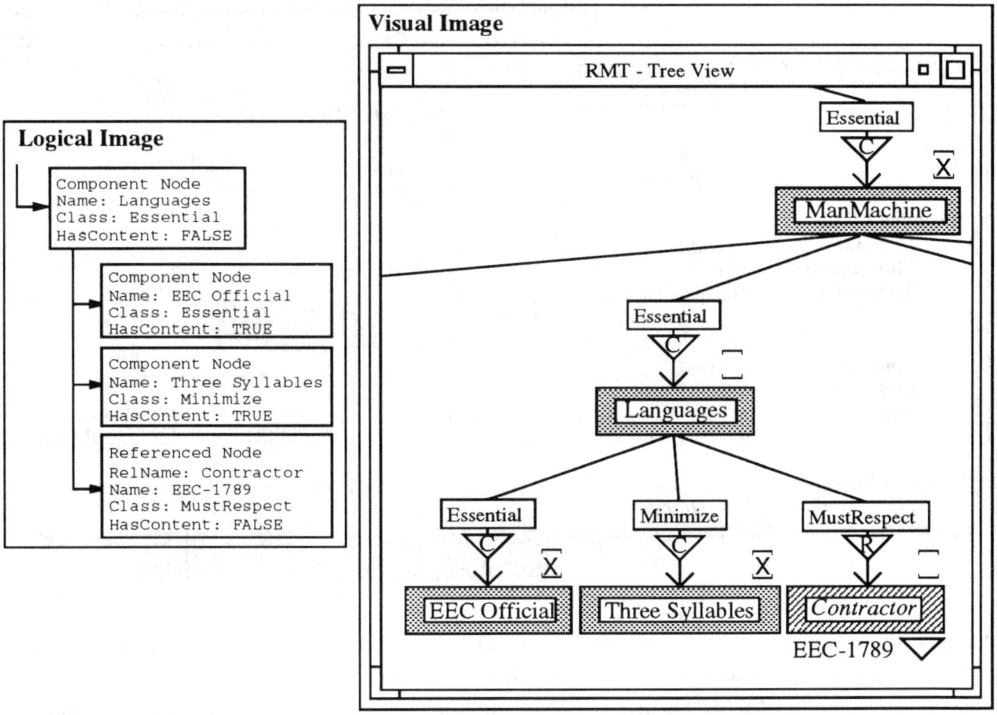

Figure 8.6 Sample logical and visual images based on RMT's tree view. Note that the logical image reflects the structure schema given in figure 8.5, although the object references of the *Represents* and *Content* elements of each component have been omitted.

It is worth noting that RMT has no operation for allowing the content of a requirement to be edited. This is a typical example of the modularity achievable for environments built using the East-UIMS. The fact that there is a region in the tree view that displays UI entities of type *Content* that themselves are used to represent *req_document* objects means that an operation for editing documents can be provided by another tool and available within the menus displayed for this region, even when RMT offers no direct support. A similar approach can be used to leave RMT open to use with a variety of editors: either by allowing several different editors to be used to edit *req_document* objects, or by allowing the creation of many different types of object using *child_req* links, each of which supports a different editor or customised editor.

8.2.2 Single requirement views

The two single requirement views are built using similar principles to the tree view, the major difference being that here two views exist based upon a common structure schema. Figure 8.7 shows examples of these views, illustrating how a single logical image can give rise to two very different visual images.

There is naturally a set of operations associated with the manipulation of these views, as well as two primary operations—*display_text_view* and *display_single_node*—

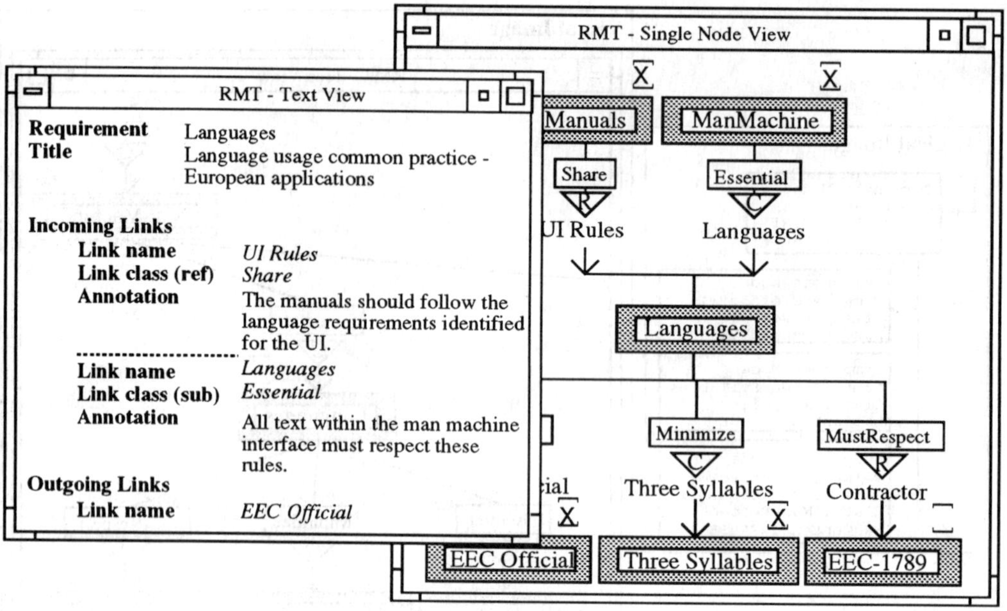

Figure 8.7 This diagram shows two views of a requirement object called *Languages* that are based upon a common logical image. Both views show all links arriving at and leaving this central requirement object. The *Single Node View* offers a clearer overview of the requirement, showing below the viewed node all child nodes (triangle containing a 'C') and all referenced nodes, and above the viewed node the parent node (*ManMachine*) and another node that makes reference to this one (*Manuals*). The fact that the windows can be scrolled is not shown. It is worth noting that each view contains some information that is not available in the other. All information that is used in either view must be stored in the underlying logical image.

applied to the PCTE object type *requirement*, each of which displays one of the two single requirement views. Once again the operation for viewing the content of a requirement is made available by ensuring that a part of the view corresponds to an underlying representation of the requirement's content object.

8.2.3 Cheap integration with other tools

A major goal of the development of tools using the East-UIMS is to achieve as much representation as possible: that is, to assure that whenever a region of a view has been derived from information stored as a PCTE object or link the East-UIMS is aware of this.

It has already been mentioned that this allows the integration of the tool used to edit the content of requirement documents with RMT at almost no cost to the tool developer, and that RMT is itself made available to the user by applying its primary operations (*display_tree*, *display_text_view* and *display_single_node*) as operations of the PCTE object type *requirement*. All PCTE entities represented within the views of RMT are also available to be used as parameters of operations (using the *dragging* mechanism), and are valid origins and destinations of hyperlinks (see § 9.2.2).

8.3 EXTENSION OF AdaNICE WITH GSED AND KeyOne

The development of a graphical interface for a toolset frequently consumes a significant proportion of the overall effort required for the production of the toolset. The ATMOSPHERE project gave the opportunity for the development of a tool for simulating HOOD designs that reused the user interface of a pre-existing HOOD design tool.

8.3.1 The user interface of AdaNICE

AdaNICE, like many other graphical design tools, offers facilities for the display of those portions of the design that are meaningful in the context of the design method that it supports. Since HOOD is a hierarchical method, a natural means for viewing and browsing a HOOD design is in terms of the elementary decompositions of the hierarchy—an object and its immediate children. The design hierarchy of HOOD objects can then be navigated by opening windows to view either the decomposition of an object that is currently displayed as part of the decomposition of another object, or the parent object of an object whose decomposition is currently displayed.

The primary means for viewing a HOOD design with AdaNICE is by using the HOOD Diagram Editor. This presents a graphical view of a HOOD object and its immediate decomposition into child objects. The HOOD diagram editor allows the user to view the decomposition of several objects at once in separate windows. Other secondary views exist supporting the editing of the other attributes of each object (the informal solution strategy, object definition skeleton, etc). In combination these views cover the various formalisms of the HOOD basic design step (see § 6.2.4.1). The basic layout and use of the HOOD diagram editor's primary view is shown in figure 8.8.

The HOOD diagram editor can be used to navigate a HOOD design, and acts as the backbone of the toolset. All other editors can be started from within this tool, being accessed through the menus attached to a *menu bar*. A subset of the operations in this menu bar are also available from other AdaNICE editors and views. Of particular interest here are the *Tools* and *External Tools* menus.

The *Tools* menu is the means by which other AdaNICE editors are started. This menu contains an entry for each editor, with the editor being started upon the selected object—either the parent object or a child object of the currently shown decomposition—depending on whether the editor takes an object as parameter or not. Some operations also take operations as parameters.

The *External Tools* menu was added within the ATMOSPHERE project to allow non-AdaNICE HOOD-related tools to be made available to the user though the AdaNICE interface. The two tools that were added into this menu are GSED/HOOD and KeyOne-ODS. Although KeyOne-ODS was offered as an alternative to the standard object definition skeleton editor of AdaNICE, AdaNICE's tool was *not* removed from the *Tools* menu. The KeyOne-ODS editor is started to edit the ODS of the currently selected object and, like the HOOD diagram editor, is able to support windows for several HOOD objects at once. The control integration issues of this integration are described in § 9.1.3.

The integration of GSED with AdaNICE is more elaborate than that of KeyOne with AdaNICE and is described in the next two sections. The first section describes

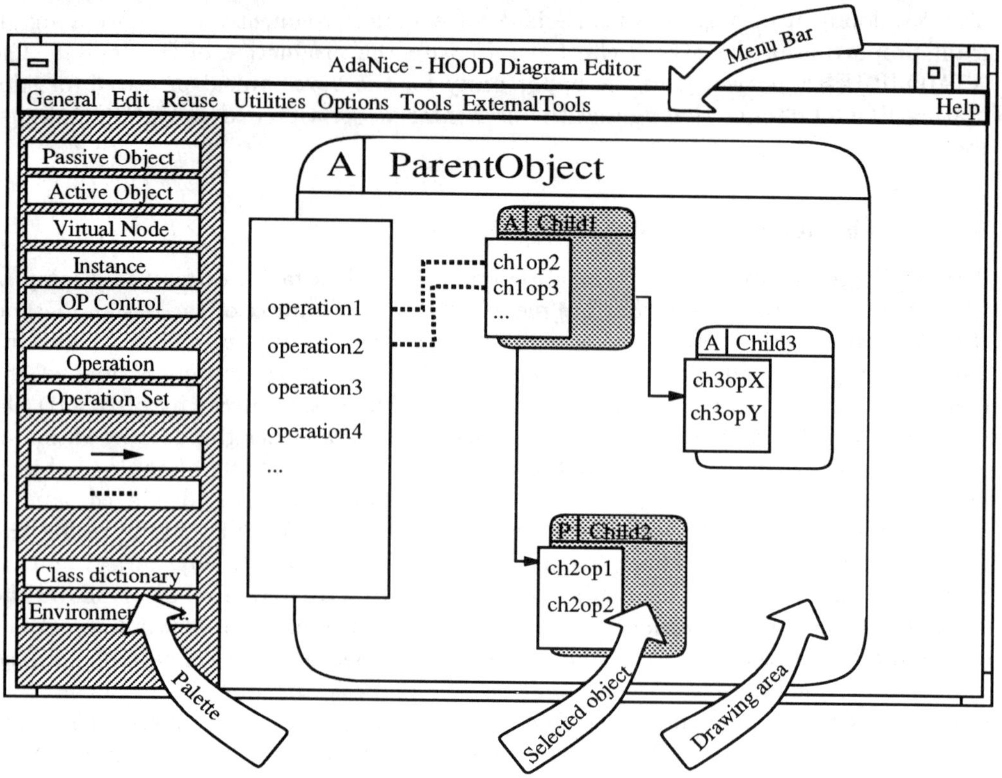

Figure 8.8 Each window maintained by the HOOD diagram editor consists of three main areas: the drawing area, the menu bar and the palette. The palette is used to select the kind of element to be placed into the drawing area; it is placed by clicking within the drawing area; AdaNICE then prompts the user to supply whatever parameters are needed. Several AdaNICE operations are based upon a previous selection of entities. For example, child objects *Child1* and *Child2* had to be selected before the creation of the *use* relationship between them. § 8.3.1 describes some of the more general operations contained in the menu bar.

the means for adding GSED time behaviour information to a HOOD design, and the second the animation of HOOD designs during a GSED simulation.

8.3.2 Defining time behaviour for GSED

The preparation for a simulation of a HOOD design involves the definition of the time behaviour of each HOOD object and operation of the design. Since AdaNICE is to be used as the graphical display of the final simulation, it is natural for it also to be used as the basis of dialogue for selecting those HOOD entities for which time behaviour is to be defined.

It proved essential to maintain a textual dialogue for the identification of objects

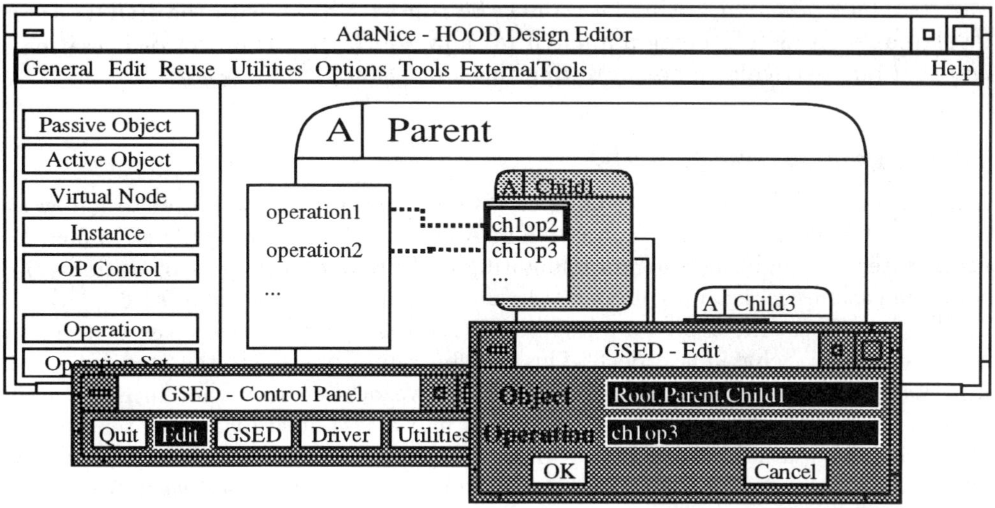

Figure 8.9 Once started from AdaNICE, GSED is primarily visible through its *control panel*—a window containing a number of control buttons, each of which offers a number of functions. In this diagram we see how AdaNICE acts as a graphical interface allowing the selection of HOOD entities as the basis of operations of *both* AdaNICE and GSED. The user has selected the edit operation of GSED, and a dialogue box has appeared whose parameters have been filled with the name of the currently selected operation, and the HOOD pathname of the HOOD object to which it belongs.

and operations, even though a graphical dialogue could have been used in most cases. Using the HOOD method, it is possible to specify not only those operations that form part of the external interface of an object, but also those that are used internally for the implementation of the non-decomposed leaf object of the design hierarchy. The time behaviour of these 'private' operations is an important part of a design simulator. However, 'private' operations are not shown in HOOD's graphical formalism, and consequently they could not be selected using the HOOD diagram editor.

Consequently, all of GSED's dialogue is based upon a textual name for each object and operation, with the name of an object being the path of named objects used to navigate to the object from the root of the AdaNICE subproject, and that of an operation being qualified with the HOOD pathname of the object of which it is a part. To ease dialogue, the parameters of operations are defaulted based upon any HOOD entity currently selected within AdaNICE's HOOD diagram editor.

The facilities of GSED were made available through a *control panel* window. Figure 8.9 shows this and demonstrates its use in the dialogue for editing the time behaviour of a HOOD operation. The cooperation between GSED and AdaNICE that underpins this dialogue is described in § 9.1.2.2.

8.3.3 Design simulation

§ 6.3.4 introduced the ideas behind preparing a simulation, and the production of a composite time behaviour object combining the time behaviour of a selection of HOOD objects. Once prepared, a simulation may be run by GSED, with the HOOD design displayed by AdaNICE being animated to show which HOOD object or operation is active at any particular moment during the simulation.

8.3.3.1 Animating the design

The purpose of animating a design is to give a visual means for a user to follow the progress of a simulation. The animation of AdaNICE driven by GSED is, in fact, the coordinated highlighting and unhighlighting of HOOD objects and operations. The communication necessary to support this animation is described in § 9.1.2.

The state of a time behaviour-enriched HOOD design is precisely the state of the composite time behaviour object. This can be reinterpreted as the state of the finite state machine modelling the currently active operation of the currently active HOOD object. Neither GSED nor AdaNICE had a graphical means for representing the time behaviour state machines of HOOD objects or operations. The only available graphical entities through which an animation could be visualised were AdaNICE's representations of HOOD objects and operations.

The basic graphical prerequisite for animation was for AdaNICE to support a means for highlighting and unhighlighting each HOOD object and operation, ideally in a way that was visually distinguishable from the selection of HOOD entities. Such a means was added to AdaNICE. The fact that time behaviour objects were not visually represented was considered to be a temporary limitation of the AdaNICE/GSED combination that could naturally be added to GSED in future versions.

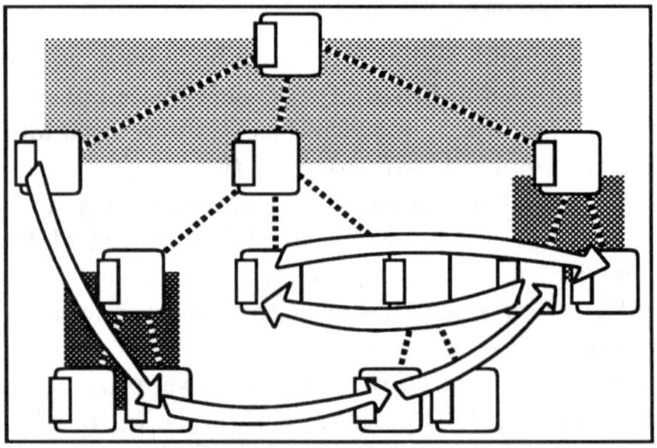

Figure 8.10 A typical control flow during a GSED animation. This diagram shows a HOOD decomposition tree—a root object and its hierarchical decomposition—during a simulation. Although the goal of a HOOD design is to neatly decompose a system into a hierarchy of design components, this formalises the flow of control between objects without greatly restricting it. This fact, combined with the inherent parallelism of HOOD systems, means that the time-linearised display of active objects may appear somewhat *ad hoc*. Another problem to be dealt with was that many 'visited' objects may not be currently displayed (shaded areas correspond to those decompositions currently displayed.)

8.3.3.2 Highlighting non-visible entities

In practice, the simple provision of a means to highlight the currently active HOOD entity proved to be inadequate for several reasons. The most immediate of these problems was that, due to the deliberately hierarchical nature of the HOOD method, a user rarely sees all HOOD objects on the screen at once.

Figure 8.10 shows a simulation in progress, underlining the fact that at any one time only a small proportion of the objects of a HOOD design might be displayed on the screen. In such a case, a decision had to be made as to whether any object should be highlighted at all, and if so which one.

The most natural means for highlighting a non-visible entity was to highlight the nearest enclosing (ancestor) object that was currently displayed, if any. If this was to be done, however, it would have been useful to visually distinguish an object highlighted as an ancestor of the currently active object from an object that was itself active.

The fact that the currently active HOOD entity was hidden was known only to AdaNICE, and so it was considered to be AdaNICE's responsibility to determine which entity to highlight. This subject is discussed in a little more detail in § 9.1.2.3.

8.3.3.3 Ability to navigate the design during an animation

The lack of visibility of many HOOD objects could result in a period of a simulation where the animation appeared to get stuck within a single object. This corresponded to either to a period where all activity was confined to objects nested within the highlighted object, or to a real problem, such as a deadlock, or a state which had no possible leaving transitions. In order to distinguish between these cases it proved important to be able to open new windows on the design to check whether activity was really continuing or not, and if not where the design had become stuck. This feature of the integrated toolset cost nothing to implement since GSED and AdaNICE were very well decoupled—opening new windows on child objects was actually a basic feature of AdaNICE, available with or without GSED.

8.4 RAPID ADDITION OF SIMPLE TOOLS—THE FORM INTERFACE

§ 7.8 described how an environment builder can complement the data schemas of well-designed, modular PCTE tools with organizational data schema fragments to generate an overall data schema that is relevant to the organisation that will use it. This freedom to extend the data schema is balanced by East's *Form Interface*, an East common service that allows simple, yet meaningful views—forms—to be added to the environment with very little effort.

8.4.1 Life without forms—the browser

The basic graphical 'shell' of East is known as the Browser. This tool supports one primary view of an object which displays an icon for each object linked to this central object, next to the link name of each link. The tool can be used to navigate around the object base and, since it is based upon the East-UIMS and properly represents all objects and links that it displays, allows all operations of each object and link to be started. The browser acts as a default view when no more meaningful view is available of a particular type of object—this tool provides a minimal interface to the object base but falls short of supporting the user in 'understanding' the object base.

8.4.2 The forms interface

Each entity of a logical image maintained by the East-UIMS has not only a logical type but may also represent a PCTE entity. The forms interface offers a simple library of basic structure schema components which can be used to generate a class of structure schemas and their corresponding presentation rules. A *form definition* consists of a structure schema (and presentation rules) together with a table describing how the elements of the structure schema map onto PCTE types. This mapping is used by a generic tool—the *form editor*—to query the object base and construct a view based upon a central object.

The library includes elementary components and constructors for displaying information to be found within the vicinity of the central object. These include:

- components for displaying fixed text and images
- components to display the attributes of nearby objects and links
- boxes that represent underlying PCTE objects
- lists used to display all of the links of a given type leaving a single object. Each element of the list may itself contain a number of other elements. Lists may be nested within lists.

New forms can be defined using an interactive tool known as the *form designer* and can be associated with specific object types in a similar way to DOCS document classes (see § 7.7.2), except that each object type may have many associated forms. Figure8.11 shows a simple form and the types of objects represented by it.

8.4.3 Forms as a replacement for the browser

Forms supported by the form editor feel very much like tools. They represent the object base and so allow the environment's operations to be started while at the same time supporting simple manipulations of the object base: components that display attributes allow these attribute values to be changed, the addition or removal of an entry from a list is accompanied by the creation or deletion of a link. By providing forms for most of the object types of the environment the browser is made largely redundant. Moreover, each of these forms continues to support the basic functionality of the browser while at the same time presenting the object base in a more meaningful manner.

It is the role of an environment builder to supply forms to cover the types that they introduce in organizational schemas. The effect of this is the rapid provision of a large set of organisation and process-specific 'tools'.

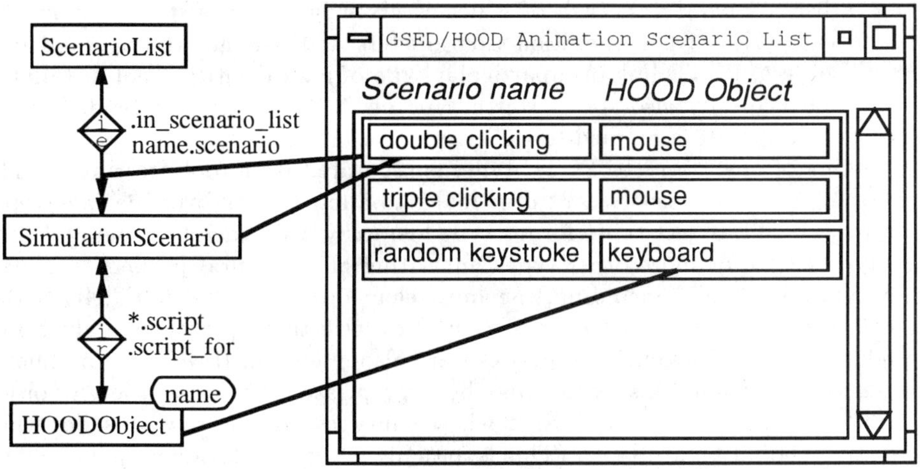

Figure 8.11 This diagram shows a form providing a view of a scenario list, an object type that was introduced in § 7.8.2. The form provides a list of scenarios, with each entry in the list *representing* one of the links of type *.scenario* leaving a central *ScenarioList* object. Each entry is itself made up of two fields, the first displaying the key attribute of the entry's *.scenario* link and representing an object of type *SimulationScenario*, and the second representing (and displaying the name attribute of) the HOOD object for which the scenario has been defined. Since forms are supported by the East-UIMS, all operations of the represented *SimulationScenario* and HOOD objects and *.scenario* links are available to the users of this form.

8.5 MAKING TOOLS AVAILABLE FROM THE East-UIMS

The East-UIMS is based upon a so-called entity/operation model, in which tools provide operations for the manipulation of certain types of PCTE objects and links (*entities*), and the user-visible menu of operations generated for a designated region of the screen includes all *operations* appropriate for any underlying PCTE entity that the region may represent (see § 8.1.3).

This section describes how tools are registered within the environment, and their operations made available as operations of particular types of PCTE entity. It goes on to describe how an operation interface can be added to a foreign tool through the provision of a *UI capsule*. Finally, some of the operations available within the Aerospace Environment are listed, including those of both native tools (such as RMT) and encapsulated foreign tools (such as the IDEF Toolset and AdaNICE).

The TICKLE system [CEG+91] offers an alternative approach for providing an object oriented interface for PCTE, dealing with the problems of operation attachment and binding tools to operations. However, this was primarily inspired by control integration needs and had no notion of user interface representation of PCTE entities.

8.5.1 Operation attachment and tool registration

The operations of any tool to be used in an East environment are registered through the provision of a *tool description*. A tool description includes the tool's *operation interface*: a list of operations, each of which is given in terms of its *signature*—the names and categories of the operation's parameters and whether the operand is to be a PCTE object, PCTE link or a particular type of logical entity. Tool installation documentation typically also states which type of PCTE entity is intended as the operand of each operation applied to PCTE entities.

The binding of operations to PCTE types is separated from tool description. This is done for a number of reasons, but principally to allow control over the *inheritance* of operations. PCTE object types form a type hierarchy, with each type being defined as a subtype of one or more other types, inheriting all structural properties of each ancestor type up to, and including, the most elementary type 'object'. Given that structural properties are inherited, it is natural to wish that operations—which may be considered to be behavioural properties—are also inherited. However, a number of highly generic operations exist which may be appropriate for a wide variety of object types and for which no single type exists whose subtypes are precisely those for which the operation should be available. (This is actually a detailed technical point related to the fact that the set of parent types of a PCTE object type is fixed when the type is created. Consequently it is impossible to create an object type to which such a new generic operation could be applied.)

Adding a tool to the environment therefore involves not only the registration of the tool and its operations, but also the identification of the PCTE types within the environment to which these operations should be applied. Examples of such operation/PCTE type bindings are given in the following sections.

8.5.2 User interface encapsulation

The East-UIMS assumes that all registered tools have an operation interface. This interface allows the East-UIMS not only to start each tool but to communicate with it allowing a single PCTE process to be reused to handle a succession of operations. Foreign tools—tools not based upon the East-UIMS—inevitably do not have such an interface, and can be provided with one in the form of a *UI capsule*. A UI capsule is itself a native East-UIMS tool, its primary role being to capture any parameters required for starting the tool that it encapsulates and to translate these parameters into a format appropriate for starting the tool.

There are essentially three classes of foreign tool which can be encapsulated:

non-interactive command line tools
Besides capturing and forwarding a tool's parameters, capsules of non-interactive tools must capture and display the results of the command, typically the *standard output* and *standard error* streams and the *exit status* of the tool.

interactive command line tools
Interactive command line tools, such as the UNIX *mail* tool, not only supply information on their output streams but have an open input stream allowing the user to supply commands. This requires the capsule to provide dialogue elements that map onto the commands of the underlying interactive tool, allowing the user to achieve all that he would have when using the encapsulated tool itself.

A well known system offering this style of encapsulation is SoftBench's Encapsulator (see [Cag90] and § 17.7).

graphical tools

Service	*Object type*	*Applied operation*
RMT	requirement	display_single_node
		display_text_view
		display_tree
DOCS	BehaviouralReq MiscReq PerformanceReq	edit
		print

Table 8.1 The operations of RMT and its installation within the Aerospace Environment

Tools maintaining their own windows can be started, as long as they are based upon the same underlying windowing technology as the East-UIMS (see § 8.1.4). Most graphical tools are treated just like non-interactive tools. However, this simple encapsulation has the drawback that if several requests are made that would all be supported by a single tool, a separate process would be started for each one, resulting in rapid consumption of memory and an associated reduction in machine performance. This can be avoided if, for example, the encapsulated tool maintains a standard input stream along which commands can continue to be passed.

The tool encapsulated by a UI capsule may itself be a data capsule (see § 7.6.2). These two capsules then combine to allow the use of certain non-PCTE non-East-UIMS tools within East. For some tools there is a considerable advantage to be gained from combining data and UI capsules to give a single multi-purpose capsule.

The design of a capsule is much like the design of any other East-UIMS-based tool, involving the identification of the operations that the tool supports and the PCTE object or link types to which these operations will be applied. While some tools have just a single *entry point*, others may be started in many different ways, each causing the tool to work in a different way. For example, the main tool of AdaNICE includes a HOOD diagram editor, an object definition skeleton (ODS) editor and an informal solution strategy editor. AdaNICE could be started so that it is immediately displaying a specific HOOD object or operation using any of these editors.

The encapsulation of a single tool may give rise to a number of operations. Naturally the encapsulation of a toolset involves the encapsulation of each tool of the toolset. However, some graphical tools may not have externally available entry points for all operations that they support. In this case a capsule will be unable to gain access to these 'hidden' operations, and will be limited to simply launching the tool. The cost of encapsulating a tool or toolset is therefore proportional to the total number of entry points within the toolset, and not to the total number of operations supported by the toolset. The apparent degree of integration of the tool into the environment may itself be related to the proportion of the tool's operations that exist as external entry points.

8.5.3 Requirements capture and non-functional specification—RMT

Being built upon the East-UIMS, the inclusion of RMT within the Aerospace Environment is achieved simply by registering the tool and applying its operations to the types that it manipulates.

Toolset	*Tool*	*Object type*	*Applied operation*
IDEF Toolset	model editor	IDEF_model	view_idef_model
	diagram editor	IDEF_diagram	view_idef_diagram
AdaNICE	HOOD diagram editor	HOODObject	view_hood_object
			view_informal_solution
			view_ODS
			make_into_subproject
		HOODOperation	view_hood_operation
		HOODsubproject	view_hood_subproject
			reintegrate_subproject
	SIF importer	HOODObject	import_SIF
		HOODsubproject	
		HOODproject	
	SIF exporter	HOODObject	export_SIF
		HOODsubproject	
		HOODproject	
	Rule checker	HOODsubproject	check_design_rules
		HOODproject	
	Document generator	HOODproject	generate_hood_document
		HOODsubproject	
		HOODObject	
	Code extractor	HOODsubproject	generate_system
KeyOne/C	KeyOne	CSource	edit_Csource
		CHeader	edit_Cheader
	KeyDoc	CSource	print_Csource
		CHeader	print_Cheader

Table 8.2 The operations of the IDEF Toolset, AdaNICE and KeyOne/C

RMT is built assuming the presence of one (or more) external document editors, used for supplying the content of requirements. Such a document editor is made available, without modifying RMT, by applying the operation that starts the document editor to each object type used to store requirement contents. Within the Aerospace Environment the document editor chosen was DOCS (see § 7.7) and three DOCS document classes were created for storing three different classes of requirement (see § 7.8.1).

The operation applications for the use of RMT within the Aerospace Environment are summarised in table 8.1.

8.5.4 Registration and encapsulation of the IDEF Toolset, AdaNICE and KeyOne/C

A number of East-UIMS capsules were needed to bring the IDEF Toolset, AdaNICE and KeyOne/C into the Aerospace Environment. As described in § 8.5.2, the entry points of each tool of each toolset had to be identified and an East-UIMS operation provided and registered within the environment for each one. Some of the operations identified are shown in table 8.2.

Service	*Object type*	*Applied operation*
Hyperlink	requirement	create_hyperlink
		follow_hyperlink
		delete_hyperlink

Table 8.3 The operations of the hyperlink service

8.5.5 The design verification tool GSED, and KeyOne-ODS

The GSED/HOOD toolset was entirely dependent upon AdaNICE—indeed, it did not make sense to start GSED in any other way than from AdaNICE. Consequently, it was inappropriate to provide East operations to make GSED available within the Aerospace Environment. GSED was indirectly available as a result of AdaNICE's availability.

Although KeyOne-ODS could have been started as an independent operation of a HOOD object, this would have involved developing not only an East-UIMS capsule, but also a PCTE capsule. AdaNICE not only allowed the calling of KeyOne-ODS from its user interface, but provided KeyOne with indirect access to the ODS which was stored in the PCTE object base. Consequently, KeyOne-ODS was not directly available through the East-UIMS, and had not otherwise been data encapsulated.

8.5.6 Operations for organizational data types from within the basic East infrastructure

Many tools were specifically designed to manipulate object types of which their developers had no specific knowledge. Tools such as this are referred to as *generic tools* and are the means by which organizational schemas are supported. The East infrastructure contains a number of these and they can be made available for use on specific types simple by applying their operations to particular PCTE types.

Examples of generic tools and services include:

- the Browser
- the Forms Interface
- the document editor DOCS
- basic version management operations
- the hyperlink service
- process related operations

All of these are made available as described above, and many require additional customisation.

An example of a generic service that can be made available for certain types of object is the hyperlink service, introduced in § 9.2.1, which offers means for supporting hypermedia-like browsing facilities throughout the environment. It is based upon operations for the creation, navigation and deletion of hyperlinks. The navigation of a hyperlink results in the display of the destination entity of the hyperlink in a view appropriate to the type of that entity. This view is identified in terms of an operation that opens the view.

Hyperlinks are used to partly meet integration opportunities 2 and 4 (listed in § 6.4.1), that is for the maintenance of traceability from requirements capture to functional specification, and from non-functional specification to architectural design. Both requirements capture and non-functional requirements are supported by RMT, and so the desired traceability is supported by the availability of hyperlink operations on the *requirement* object type.

The fact that the operations *view_idef_function* and *view_hood_object* are to be the default operations for viewing objects of type *diagram* and *HOODObject*, respectively is registered by the hyperlink mechanism (see § 9.2.2).

9

Control Integration

Within the Atmosphere project the term *control integration* was often used to cover what others [Was90, TN92] might separately refer to as *control integration* and *process integration*:

- control integration is related to the low-level mechanics of getting tools to cooperate towards the provision of a common service
- process integration is a higher level concept related to the degree to which activities that are performed by machines and humans combine together to achieve the larger goals of systems engineering.

The Aerospace Environment is based upon both control and process integration technologies.

Tools can be integrated pairwise using control integration mechanisms such as the point-to-point message passing of the Object Request Broker [OMG91a], but an environment is more easily extended if it is based upon message broadcast technology such as that in Field and SoftBench [Rei90a, Cag90]. Within the Aerospace Environment the primary examples of tight control integration between tools are those of AdaNICE with GSED/HOOD and KeyOne/ODS, as described in § 9.1. These examples are based upon the use of a common point-to-point communication package that is now integral to AdaNICE's architecture, and which will continue to allow AdaNICE to be extended with similar tools in this common manner.

A more general mechanism within the East framework supporting a specific class of integration between tools is the hyperlink service, which is introduced in § 9.2. Like other features of East that lead to tight, yet extensible, integration of tools, the hyperlink service is based upon East's entity/operation model. The separate registration of tool operations from the tools that provide them, as described in § 8.5, provides apparent control integration between East-UIMS-based tools simply by their use of the East-UIMS and the fact that the tools manipulate and represent common types of data. The use of an external document editor by RMT when RMT had no explicit knowledge of the editor to be used, or even of the fact that it was possible to edit the content of a requirement is an example of apparent control integration which was merely a feature of the underlying presentation integration technology.

The careful use of the PCTE data manipulation model when designing organizational data schemas has already been mentioned as a means of implicitly defining certain development processes (§ 7.1.5), as have some of the hazards inherent in schema

Tool Integration: Environments and Frameworks, Edited by D. Schefström and G. van den Broek

design which capture process assumptions. While East also has support for explicit, coarse-grained process modelling this support is not described in this book.

9.1 CONTROL INTEGRATION OF AdaNICE WITH KeyOne AND GSED

§ 6.2.4 described the HOOD method as being extensible. It is natural, therefore, for a HOOD toolset itself to be extensible. The AdaNICE toolset includes a package called IPCP (Inter Process Communication Package) which allows AdaNICE to start and communicate with *add-on* tools. Two tools were integrated with AdaNICE using this package during the ATMOSPHERE project: the GSED toolset, which could animate a HOOD design displayed by AdaNICE; and the ODS variant of KeyOne.

The IPCP package was based upon the communication facilities of X/Window. It was a stand-alone package developed for the precise goal of integrating AdaNICE with add-on tools, and its simple architecture reflected this goal.

9.1.1 The IPCP package

IPCP allowed the simple *extension* of a tool with other tools of which it had explicit knowledge. A parent process, typically AdaNICE, was able to start other tools as child processes in such a way that they could communicate with the parent, informing it of what they were doing, making requests of the parent, responding to requests from the parent, and so on.

While a single process could act as both the parent process for a set of child processes forming an IPCP *process group*, and simultaneously act as a child process for another group, this would really only have been of academic interest. IPCP solved the specific needs of integrating a specific class of tools and was never intended to support all forms of control integration. However, the recognition that a tool could be integrated with several other tools using a common mechanism was itself a useful generalisation.

9.1.1.1 Starting communication

IPCP communication was based upon the basic event management mechanisms of X/Window, where tool processes can receive input through logical devices called *windows*. Most windows are made visible on the workstation's screen and are subject to user-inspired *events*. However, they may equally well never be displayed and receive events raised by other processes. IPCP is based upon such *hidden* windows.

A process may raise an event within any window whose 'location' and 'identifier' it knows. Knowledge of which windows will be used for the communication between a parent and child process is therefore a prerequisite for such communication to take place.

Each IPCP process group had a single parent process and a number of child processes that had been started by the parent. Each of these processes had a *tool identifier*, and a pair of hidden windows to receive *request* and *reply* events. A *tool identifier* was supplied to a child process by its parent when the child was executed, along with the identifiers of the parent's request and reply windows. The child could then create its own request and reply windows and communicate their identifiers to its parent using a special class of request. Once this had been done, communication had been established and requests could be exchanged until the tools agreed to stop communication.

9.1.1.2 Passing and waiting for requests

Once communication was established between a parent and child process, requests could be sent at any time, and with any semantic that could be expressed as a null-terminated string. IPCP directed each request to the request window of the process having a given tool identifier, and the receiving process was told the tool identifier of the sender. In practice, the identifier of the recipient or sender was only of interest to the parent of an IPCP process group as only it could be in communication with more than one other process.

All IPCP requests included the tool identifier of the process sending or receiving the request, a request *type* and a null-terminated string containing the body of the request. The reply to a request itself had a given type and body, as well as a return value that indicated that a reply had been received, or that the reply had taken too long to arrive and that the request had timed out.

The way in which a request was passed is shown in figure 9.1.

9.1.1.3 Intended usage

Although it could be used for communication inside a variety of toolsets, IPCP was primarily developed to allow AdaNICE to talk with other tools. In this context, AdaNICE acted as the parent process of an IPCP process group.

IPCP supported the integration of tools based upon the passing of requests. Each request corresponded to a request by one tool for a service to be provided by the other tool or a reply to such a request. These requests are quite clearly *point-to-point* (see § 2.1), and correspond to the needs of providing specific functional cooperation between the tools.

The pairwise integration of two tools using a point-to-point mechanism involves the development of a set of requests supporting the required dialogue between the tools, and functions within each tool to respond to these requests. Often these functions require extensions to be made to the original tools. The class of extensions to a tool that seem reasonable and that do not change the fundamental nature of that tool, seems to be restricted to those that do not introduce a large *common state* between the two integrated tools. During the communication between a pair of tools, a certain amount of common state may be built up due to their cooperation. The higher the degree of a non-persistent common state, the tighter the coupling between the tools.

It was a clear design goal to keep the reliance on common state to a minimum. AdaNICE is a commercial tool, and while it may be desirable for it to be as apparently tightly integrated as possible with other tools, this should not be done at the expense of too tightly coupling AdaNICE to these other tools.

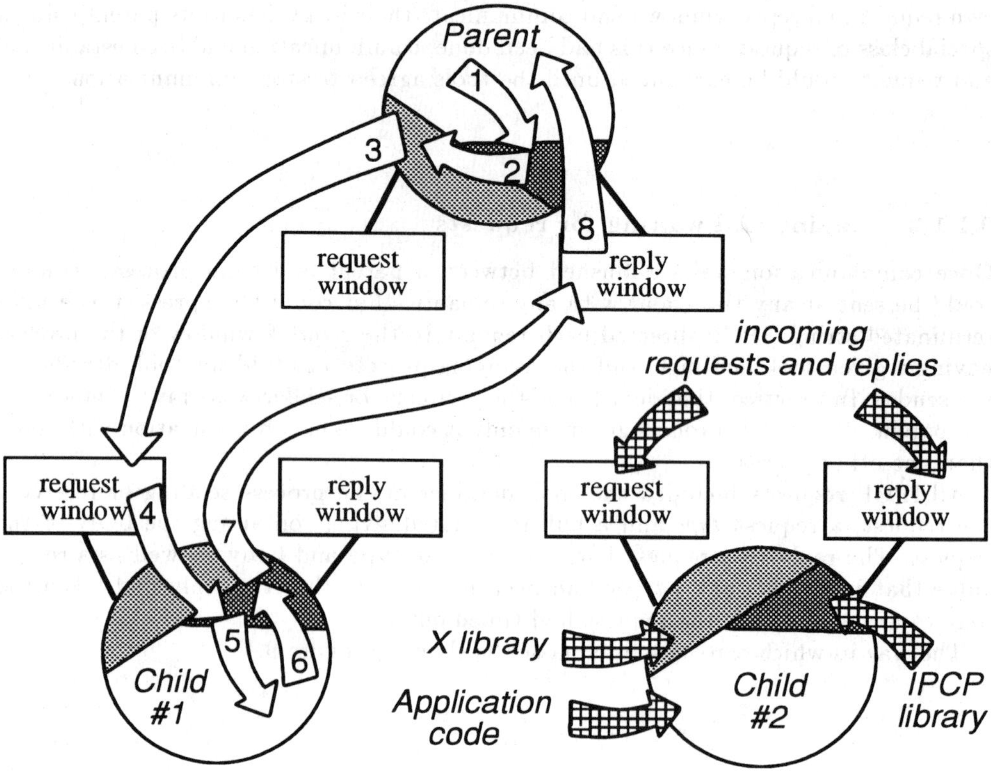

Figure 9.1 An IPCP process group has a leading process (*Parent*) and a number of child processes (*Child #1* and *Child #2*), each of which includes the IPCP library which is itself based upon X/Window. A process may make use of a service offered by another process (1) by making an IPCP request. IPCP converts this into an X/Window event (2) that is raised (3) within the *request window* of a tool that can fulfil that request. The event is decoded by IPCP (4) which invokes an IPCP *callback* (5) within the service provider. Once this callback is complete it returns control to IPCP (6) which then sends a reply (7) to the originating process by raising an event in that process's *reply window*. This event then gets decoded by IPCP resulting (8) in a reply to the original request.

9.1.1.4 Basic requests supported by AdaNICE

A minimal set of requests was developed that were seen to be of general use for the integration of AdaNICE with other tools. These foreseeable requests fall into three clear categories:

- those that allow a foreign tool to determine information about the state of AdaNICE, including which HOOD object or operations is currently selected.
- those that allow a foreign tool to translate AdaNICE's internal identifiers for objects and operation into a textual format and *vice versa*
- those supporting the internal concurrency control policy of the AdaNICE toolset.

AdaNICE is always started to work within the context of a HOOD *subproject*, which defines a context for the rest of an AdaNICE session. From this point on, the AdaNICE tools always perform the majority of their dialogue with the internal data handler in terms of *object identifiers* and *operation identifiers*. However, a number of tools need to communicate with the user in terms of the names of objects and operations. For this reason basic requests exist for translating between identifiers and names. The various ways of refering to HOOD objects and operations were introduced in § 7.4.3.

The final set of requests is particularly interesting as it highlights one of the difficulties of developing a tool which may exist in many different variants, each based upon a different database technology. The pre-ATMOSPHERE version of AdaNICE was based upon a proprietary database—the HOOD Project Library (HPL)—which supported concurrent access to its data by the various tools of the AdaNICE toolset by means of a particular locking policy. This policy was used to lock individual HOOD objects and supported two main lock values: *existence*, whose acquisition by one tool prevented other tools from deleting the locked HOOD object; and *object* whose acquisition prevented other tools from modifying the object in any way and at the same time allowed the acquiring tool to modify the object freely.

The set of lock values supported by a database affects the ways in which application code can protect itself, and consequently the precise values to be used for any particular operation of the application is database technology specific. The database handler interface of AdaNICE supported a fixed set of lock values—that of the HPL—and it was the responsibility of each database technology-specific data handler to provide these locks in terms of the lock values offered by its underlying database technology. The PCTE-based data handler coordinated the acquisition of PCTE locks. However, PCTE tools that needed to cooperate with AdaNICE, such as GSED/HOOD had to respect not only the lock modes enforced by PCTE but also those of AdaNICE.

The basic requests supported by AdaNICE are summarised in table 9.1.

9.1.2 Integration of AdaNICE and the PCTE-based tool GSED using IPCP

Three groups of requests are passed between the architectural design tool AdaNICE and the design simulation tool GSED. The first group allows AdaNICE to change the state of GSED, the second group is needed to allow the editing of GSED time behaviour objects (TBOs), and the third group supports the animation of HOOD designs.

9.1.2.1 The states of GSED/HOOD and state changing requests

As mentioned in § 8.3.2, GSED was started by selecting an entry within AdaNICE's *external tool* menu. Selection of this menu entry resulted in the display of the GSED control panel. This control panel itself had a control button allowing users to *Quit* GSED, an operation that implied the removal of the GSED window.

As far as AdaNICE was concerned, GSED could be in one of three main states: *not present* implied that no GSED process was associated with the current AdaNICE process; *hidden* implied that a GSED process existed but its control panel was currently hidden; and *visible* which implied that the control panel was visible. The intermediate

Tool	*Request*	*Inputs*	*Outputs*	*Tool state*
AdaNICE	get_selection	*(null)*	obj_id op_id	Based upon AdaNICE's current selection
	get_subproject	*(null)*	subp_name op_id	Based upon AdaNICE's current subproject
	id_to_path	obj_id op_id	obj_path op_name	
	path_to_id	obj_path op_name	obj_id op_id	
	id_to_name	obj_id op_id	obj_name op_name	
	find	obj_name op_name	obj_id op_id	
	place_existence	obj_id	*(null)*	caller gains an existence lock on the object
	place_object	obj_id	*(null)*	caller gains an object lock on the object
	promote_to_object	obj_id	*(null)*	the caller's existence lock is promoted to an object lock
	demote_to_existence	obj_id	*(null)*	the caller's object lock is demoted to an existence lock
	remove_lock	obj_id	*(null)*	the caller's object or existence lock is removed

Table 9.1 The basic IPCP requests supported by AdaNICE. Each request also has a number of error cases. The *return_status* output parameter is not shown.

Tool	*Request*	*Inputs*	*Outputs*	*Tool state*
GSED/HOOD	GSED_visible	*(null)*	*(null)* op_id	if GSED is in the state *hidden* it becomes *visible*.
	GSED_hide	*(null)*	*(null)* op_id	if GSED is in the state *visible* it becomes *hidden*.
	GSED_stop	*(null)*	*(null)*	if GSED is in the state *hidden* it exits.
AdaNICE	highlight	obj_id op_id style	*(null)*	the specified object or operation is highlighted in the given style.

Table 9.2 IPCP requests supported by GSED, and the single request added to AdaNICE in order to extend AdaNICE with GSED. As before, the *return_status* output parameter is not shown.

state '*hidden*' could be used to optimise runtime performance of the AdaNICE/GSED combination, implying that if GSED was called a second time the same process could be reused, thus dramatically reducing the reappearance time of GSED.

Beside the initial execution and establishment of communication with GSED AdaNICE could send requests that forced GSED to change state. These requests are shown in table 9.2.

9.1.2.2 TBO editing

§ 6.3.4 introduced the GSED toolset, and described the need for associating a time behaviour object (TBO) with each HOOD entity. § 8.3.2 described the dialogue for selecting the HOOD entity for which a TBO should be specified, and the fact that GSED was able to reuse the current selection of AdaNICE to simplify the user's dialogue.

Additionally, like all components of AdaNICE, be they built-in or add-on components, GSED has to request to place an AdaNICE *object lock* on each object before it modified it. GSED had therefore to send requests to set and release an object lock to protect each edit it made to an object's TBO, or to the TBO of any of the operations of an object.

The basic requests of AdaNICE were sufficient to support this dialogue and that allowing the generation of a composite TBO based upon the selection of those HOOD objects whose TBOs were to be included when preparing a simulation.

9.1.2.3 Animation related requests

As described in § 8.3.3, the animation of a HOOD design by GSED involved the highlighting and unhighlighting of HOOD *objects* and *operations*. This was coordinated by GSED, and indicates the HOOD entities that were currently active at each moment of the simulation.

A single IPCP request was added to AdaNICE to control the highlighting of HOOD entities—this is also mentioned in table 9.2. This allowed GSED to change the presentation style for a HOOD entity to indicate changes in the state of the entity during a simulation. GSED was also responsible for resetting the style of each object after a simulation.

§ 8.3.3 described a number of issues related to AdaNICE's response to these methods. Particular problems occurred when a request was made to highlight a HOOD object that was not currently displayed by AdaNICE. The design trade-off that had to be made was between the amount of knowledge that GSED had of the diagrams currently displayed by AdaNICE, and the difficulty for AdaNICE to calculate which entity to highlight upon the receipt of a highlight request from GSED. The solution adopted aimed at maintaining as much independence of the tools as possible. There are potentially a large number of ways of presenting HOOD designs, each of which could give rise to different animation difficulties. It was also conceivable that AdaNICE could subsequently be enriched with other ways of visualising design animation. Consequently, all requests sent by GSED were phrased in terms of the entities currently active in the simulation without any consideration of which entities are actually displayed—a choice that renders GSED as free as possible from the HOOD tool that it animates, and AdaNICE able to be animated by a variety of simulation tools.

At the time of writing, no attempt had been made to ensure the consistency of the composite TBO (simulator) and the design being animated: animations continued until they encountered a HOOD entity that could not be highlighted by AdaNICE—because it did not exist—before giving an error message. Indeed, a user could continue to edit the HOOD design with AdaNICE while a simulation was under way: it was not considered necessary for a prototype to prevent this.

9.1.3 Integration of AdaNICE and the non-PCTE-based tool KeyOne using IPCP

KeyOne was integrated with AdaNICE to act as a more powerful alternative to AdaNICE's Object Definition Skeleton editor. As described in § 8.3.1, KeyOne was made available to the user through AdaNICE's *external tools* menu.

With the combination of AdaNICE and KeyOne, the user was supplied with two means of viewing a HOOD object: the graphical format supported by AdaNICE's HOOD diagram editor, and the structured text format of KeyOne. To prevent the parallel inconsistent modification of a single object by these two tools, a number of states for KeyOne were established, and coordinated with AdaNICE's data handler's lock modes. Moreover, requests were introduced to allow the parallel display of a HOOD object by both tools, but with just one of them being used as editor at any one time.

The application of KeyOne's browsing capabilities to the HOOD method implied that any reference to a HOOD object within an ODS—such as the definition of a child object within its parent's ODS—could be followed to reveal the ODS definition of that object itself. This capability was based upon AdaNICE's *find* request.

9.1.3.1 The states of KeyOne-ODS and state changing requests

Unlike GSED, which was parameterless, the user of KeyOne-ODS always requested KeyOne after first selecting the HOOD object whose ODS was to be edited. As far as AdaNICE was concerned, KeyOne could be in one of just two main states: *not present*, implying that no KeyOne process was associated with the current AdaNICE process; and *present*, implying that a KeyOne process existed. Once present, KeyOne could display the ODS of several objects simultaneously, each in a separate window. Even if KeyOne was not currently displaying any windows it could remain present, assuring that subsequent calls to it avoided expensive reexecution time.

Additionally, each window currently displayed by KeyOne had two states: *displayed* and *edited*. These two states corresponded to whether AdaNICE or KeyOne was being used to edit the object. When a KeyOne window was first opened on a HOOD object, the state of the window was *displayed*. The requests used by AdaNICE to change KeyOne's state are shown in table 9.3.

9.1.3.2 KeyOne for displaying an ODS

When a request to open KeyOne to view a HOOD object was made, AdaNICE sent KeyOne a request to tell it to edit the ODS of this object. KeyOne then had to ask AdaNICE to prepare a UNIX file for it that contained the attribute that KeyOne must edit (as described in § 7.6.1), and request an AdaNICE *existence* lock on the object. KeyOne was then able to load and display the object, knowing that the HOOD object would not be deleted by AdaNICE while it was displaying it.

At this point, the KeyOne window was merely *displayed*, and remained so until the user first modified the ODS using KeyOne. Up to this point the user could continue making modifications to the object using AdaNICE. After each such change, AdaNICE sent a request to KeyOne, informing it that the object had changed, and that KeyOne should reload it. Consequently, all changes made by AdaNICE were automatically reflected in KeyOne's views.

9.1.3.3 KeyOne as an ODS editor

As soon as a modification was made to an object using KeyOne, however, KeyOne requested an AdaNICE *object* lock to be placed. This lock stayed in place until the ODS was saved through KeyOne, thus preventing any concurrent changes being made to the ODS by AdaNICE. The window was then in the *edited* state.

Unlike those modifications made through AdaNICE, which were automatically reflected in KeyOne, modifications to a HOOD object's ODS made using KeyOne were not automatically reflected in AdaNICE. There was a sound reason behind this choice: the syntax of the textual representation of an ODS allowed many semantic inconsistencies that were not allowed in the graphical representation. Consequently, to try and reflect changes made in the KeyOne-supported textual view immediately in the AdaNICE-supported graphical view would have implied imposing more semantic constraints from within KeyOne than would have been acceptable for a user of a *syntax-directed* editor.

The use of KeyOne to edit an ODS blocked the AdaNICE graphical editor until the user acknowledged finishing editing the ODS. Such an acknowledgement could be

Tool	*Request*	*Inputs*	*Outputs*	*Tool state*
KeyOne	KeyOne_display	obj_id	*(null)*	a new view is opened in state *displayed.*
	KeyOne_redisplay	obj_id	*(null)*	KeyOne must redisplay the given object.
	KeyOne_flush	*(null)*	*(null)*	KeyOne should close all open views.
	KeyOne_stop	*(null)*	*(null)*	KeyOne should exit.
AdaNICE	provide_ODS	obj_id	UNIX_path	AdaNICE creates a UNIX file containing a copy of the ODS of the requested object.
	save_ODS	obj_id	*(null)*	AdaNICE copies back a UNIX file that it previously created.
	check_ODS	UNIX_path	*(null)*	AdaNICE runs its rule checker on the given UNIX file.

Table 9.3 IPCP requests supported by KeyOne, and the requests added to AdaNICE in order to extend it with KeyOne. As before, the *return_status* output parameter is not shown.

made either by saving or by throwing away the changed ODS, and either could be done with or without the removal of the window in which the ODS was displayed.

To support various combinations of ending editing—with or without commit, with or without closing the window—a number of orthogonal requests were introduced into AdaNICE (see table 9.3), and coordinated by KeyOne. Finishing editing corresponded to a change of state of the window from *edited* to *displayed.* The closure of the window implied the removal of the AdaNICE lock that KeyOne had acquired on the HOOD object.

As a precursor to saving a set of changes, the user could check the validity of his changes. This was a pre-existing functionality of AdaNICE's basic ODS editor. Requests were added to support the application of AdaNICE's checking algorithm to an ODS being edited by KeyOne.

9.2 TOOL EXECUTION BY FOLLOWING HYPERLINKS

There is a wide body of literature devoted to the subjects of hypertext and hypermedia, a survey of which is presented in [Con87]. A principal goal of these systems is to allow for easy and rapid browsing through large quantities of information which, in the case of hypermedia, may combine text, graphical elements, images, video sequences, etc. One characteristic of hypermedia is, therefore, the ability to navigate between very different entities, each of which may be displayed and managed by very different software.

A typical goal of hypertext is to allow relationships to be maintained between arbitrary pairs of entities, however fine they may be. For example, if one electronic book were to make reference to a section within another then it would be considered desirable, within the hypertext community, to be able to *follow* the reference (the ***hyperlink***) within the text of the first electronic book and to immediately see the referenced text.

Given the large amount of information produced during system development and the number of formalisms and formats in which it is represented, the provision of a hypertext/hypermedia-like browsing style seems to be quite desirable. Examples often quoted include being able to see the declaration of a variable given any use of that variable; seeing the code that implements a given design element; following a chain of hyperlinks from a requirement through design and down to code to see the effect of changing requirements; and so on.

The ATMOSPHERE project presented an opportunity to further investigate the provision of a hypertextual capability within a software engineering environment.

9.2.1 Principals of the hyperlink mechanism

The key problems of providing a hypertextual interface turned out to be in its interference with version and configuration management, how to integrate a generic hypertextual capability with foreign tools, and how to associate a hyperlink with fine grain data—any data item other than an entire PCTE object—while ensuring the referential integrity of that hyperlink.

9.2.1.1 The prototype hyperlink mechanism

The creation of hyperlinks was controlled by an East operation which was applied to a number of object types (see § 8.5.6). Being applied directly to these PCTE types, hyperlinks could be created from an object of one of these types whenever that object was represented on the screen by an East-UIMS-based tool. The creation of the link involves the identification of a destination for the link, and the association of a comment that could be displayed to ease the selection of links during navigation.

An operation to follow hyperlinks was also available upon all object types from which hyperlinks could be created. This operation allowed the user to choose a link to follow from amongst those leaving the object, based upon the comments entered when each link was created. Following a link resulted in the display of the destination object in a view that was appropriate for that type of object. The appropriate view for each object type was identified in terms of the operation used to display that view. For example, if the destination object were to be of type *requirement* then the view displayed might be that produced by the *display_single_node* operation of RMT (see § 8.2.2).

The fact that the appropriate operations for viewing different types of objects would probably be supplied by different tools, and that these tools would inevitably be supplied by different suppliers meant that the hyperlink mechanism would be limited according to the degree to which each tool was integrated with the East-UIMS. It appears impossible to provide a hyperlink facility that would automatically work with all tools without requiring those tools to respect at least some basic conventions (such as *representation*).

9.2.1.2 Adding the hypertext facility to foreign tools

The operations for the creation, navigation and deletion of hyperlinks were all available whenever the objects to whose types these operations were applied were represented in a view. This level of integration of the hyperlink mechanism with an East-UIMS-based tool was achieved without building any direct support for the hypertextual mechanism whatsoever into the tool. However, a tool that did not support the East-UIMS's notion of representation could not support these operations.

At the other end of the link any East-UIMS operation could be used to display the destination object. Since a number of foreign tools (such as AdaNICE and the IDEF Toolset) were encapsulated to allow these tools to be started to view specific objects—IDEF0 diagrams displayed by the IDEF Toolset's diagram editor, and HOOD objects displayed by AdaNICE (§ 8.5.4)—these tools could appear tightly integrated with the hyperlink mechanism, if only for displaying the destinations of hyperlinks.

9.2.1.3 Associating links with fine grain data

The previous sections were phrased in terms of PCTE objects and object types. If hyperlinks were to be used to relate finer grain information, such as a reference to a specific diagram within one book from within another book, and neither the origin nor the destination was represented as a PCTE object, then a number of extensions would have had to have been made to the model.

The first extension would relate to the identification of the origin or destination *scope* of the hyperlink. While the East-UIMS is aware of regions of the user interface that represent PCTE objects or links, the identification of other possible scopes for hyperlinks can only be done by a tool which has some understanding of these scopes. The tool must provide an identifier for the scope which can later be used to highlight the scope whenever it is the destination of a hyperlink, or to allow the origin scope to be highlighted so that the presence of a hyperlink can be suggested to the user. Moreover, the operations for creation, navigation and deletion of a link need to be somehow associated with all potential origin scopes, and operations need to be provided allowing all potential destination scopes to be displayed.

At the time of writing the hyperlink mechanism was unable to handle fine grained origin and destination scopes. To illustrate the difficulty of this problem, imagine that the origin scope is the use of a variable within a source file, and the destination scope is the declaration of that variable within another file. Both files may be edited using a simple text editor, and are developed and therefore owned by different users. Moreover both files may continue to be edited after the creation of the link. The link cannot be specified in terms of the displacement of the destination scope within its source file (line L, character C) because this is likely to change if the file is edited; neither can the destination scope be defined by placing a label next to the scope within the destination source file, since that would involve the modification of a file to which the owner of the source file did not have write access.

It should be noted that many hypertext-like browsing facilities can be provided without explicit creation of persistent links. KeyOne is a good example of this, providing a comprehensive set of browsing facilities based upon its own understanding of the syntax of certain languages. Such facilities can be referred to as providing a *symbol-based* rather than a *link-based* hypertextual interface.

9.2.1.4 Interference with version and configuration management

Hyperlinks are used to provide quick means for navigating between arbitrary data elements. These links are essentially relationships between entities, and are subject to all of the same binding issues introduced in § 6.2.8. In particular, if a link is established between two entities that are independently versioned, the link will tightly bind the two specific versions of entities together, even when they may be independently used within different configurations.

This is a difficult issue to resolve, and is not further discussed in this book. It is suggested, however, that an inter-tool browsing capability could be partly supported by a broadcast message server such as those to be found at the centre of Field [Rei90a] and SoftBench [Cag90], possibly in combination with a symbol-based rather than link-based service.

9.2.2 The use of the hyperlink mechanism within the Aerospace Environment

The previous section described how the use of the hyperlink service relied upon the availability of the service's operations for each allowable origin object type, and the identification of a suitable operation for viewing each possible destination object type. In practice, however, it was easier to control the set of possible origin object types than the set of destination types and this implied that a default means for viewing unforeseen destination object types was required.

9.2.2.1 Controlling the set of hyperlink origin object types

Control over the availability of the hyperlink service for each object type was achieved through the East-UIMS's entity/operation model. The hyperlink service consisted of the three operations to create, navigate and delete hyperlinks, and so was enabled for a particular type of object by simply applying these operations to this object type.

There are quite strong arguments for whether the use of the hyperlink service should be limited to just a few object types or not. On the one hand, since hyperlinks are essentially unconstrained in origin or destination type their unrestricted use would allow the creation of links when no PCTE link type existed which had the desired semantic. On the other hand, being essentially semantic free, it is difficult to perform meaningful queries based upon hyperlinks, and there is always a danger that hyperlinks will be used in preference to PCTE links that more strongly capture the user's intentions, but that the user is simply unaware of. One means of facing this danger would be to provide a similar user interface for the creation and navigation of PCTE links and hyperlinks. Indeed, hyperlinks could appear almost as an afterthought within a common link creation and navigation operation.

The role of hyperlinks in the Aerospace Environment is quite clearly defined—to support a traceability from user requirement capture through to non-functional and functional specification, and from non-functional specification through to architectural

Tool	*Object type*	*Viewing operation*
AdaNICE	HOODSubproject	view_hood_subproject
	HOODObject	view_hood_object
	HOODOperation	view_hood_operation
IDEF Toolset	IDEF_model	view_idef_model
	IDEF_diagram	view_idef_diagram
East Browser	(*by default*)	show_icon_view
RMT	requirement	display_single_node

Table 9.4 Hyperlink destination viewing operations for the Aerospace Environment

design. The list of objects for which the hyperlink service was made available in the Aerospace Environment is given in § 8.5.6.

9.2.2.2 Views for all potential hyperlink destination object types

The creation of a hyperlink is controlled by an East operation. One of the parameters of this operation is the destination object of the hyperlink, and this parameter is filled using the dragging mechanism of the East-UIMS. Consequently, either the dialogue for creating hyperlinks would have to distinguish between valid destination object types for hyperlinks at link creation time, or any object that is represented by the East-UIMS may be supplied as the destination of a hyperlink.

The prototype hyperlink service did not support a limit set of destination object types for hyperlinks—unlike the control over origin object types that was cheaply obtained through the existing entity/operation model, restricting the set of destination types would have required introducing a degree of parameterisation that was not really needed for the prototypical investigation of the hyperlink concept.

However, the prototype did support the association of viewing operations with PCTE object types. The prime application of the hyperlink mechanism within the Aerospace Environment was to meet partly integration opportunities 2 and 4, that is for the maintenance of traceability from requirements capture to functional specification, and from non-functional specification to architectural design. Hyperlinks were used to provide the desired traceability, and so appropriate viewing operations had to be identified at least for the display of the target objects of these traceability hyperlinks.

The key object types within the tools that supported these methods are shown in table 9.4, together with the operations chosen as viewing operations for each of these object types. Figure 9.2 shows an example of the navigation of a hyperlink between a requirement displayed by RMT and a function displayed by the IDEF Toolset.

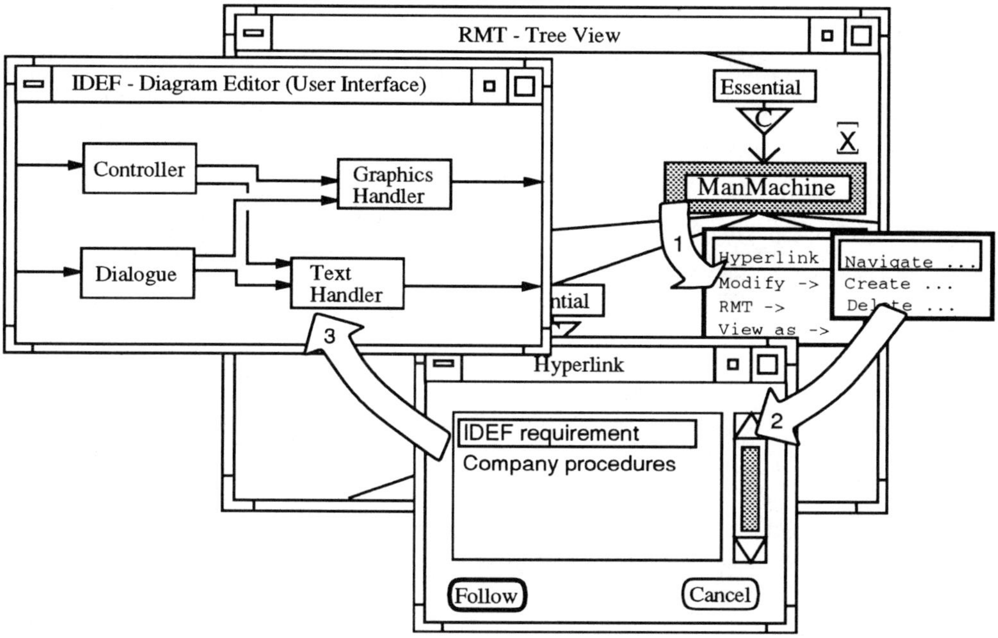

Figure 9.2 In this example, a request is made to follow any hyperlinks that may have been created from the requirement object labelled *Man Machine*, first by designating the region of the screen representing this requirement (1) and then selecting (2) the menu entry *Hyperlink* → *Navigate*. This results in the execution of the underlying operation *follow_hyperlink*, which displays a dialogue box to allow the user to choose amongst the hyperlinks leaving the object. A decision to see the corresponding *IDEF0 requirement* results in the display of the destination IDEF0 diagram, as displayed using the viewing operation *display_single_node*.

10

Summary and future directions

This description of the Aerospace Environment has discussed a wide variety of issues that affect environment users, tool developers and environment builders. This section seeks to summarise those issues and give a few pointers to the future of systems engineering environments and CASE tools. The conclusions of this section are in no way restricted to the aerospace domain.

10.1 CONSTRUCTING A SOFTWARE ENGINEERING ENVIRONMENT

The Aerospace Environment was produced by bringing a number of tools into the East framework and by using the generic tools of the East framework to build many 'lightweight' tools.

10.1.1 Environments modularity and the role of the framework

There are both immediate and innovative reasons for upgrading from software engineering using operating system-based CASE tools to software engineering using framework-based environments. Immediate benefits result from a simultaneous increase in the degree of integration between tools, the degree of uniformity across the user's development environment and the degree of freedom for the builders of environments to produce environments that are tailored to suit their needs. More radically, the introduction of appropriate framework technology should allow the fulfilment of a major goal of software engineering environment research: the exertion of environment-wide influence over the software process of those using an environment.

However, the use of a common framework in itself is not enough to ensure that even the first of these goals is achieved. Tools must not only be redeveloped to make use of the framework—they must be developed to behave as 'good citizens' within any environment based upon that framework. As in most societies, behaving as a 'good citizen' implies following the conventions of that society. Moreover, to find a role within a number of different environments, even if they are based upon similar conventions,

Tool Integration: Environments and Frameworks, Edited by D. Schefström and G. van den Broek

a tool should be as compatible as possible with the additional needs of each specific environment. This implies that the tool should fulfil a very well defined role and be prepared to rely on other components of the environment to perform other roles in their own way, even if those roles seem closely related to the tool's own role.

It is for these reasons that this description of the Aerospace Environment and East has constant themes related to the modularity of tools and the needs of the environment builder. If other issues, such as those deliberately not presented but listed below, had been presented in more detail, then these themes would have been even clearer.

10.1.2 Light weight *vs* heavy weight tools

To the end user of the Aerospace Environment, or another East-based environment, a 'form' seems to be a tool that is not only well integrated into the environment—it behaves like any other East-UIMS-based tool—but fulfils a clear functional role, yet to the environment builder, a form is not really a 'tool' at all—it was produced by the simple customisation of a generic tool. At best a form can be described as a *lightweight tool*, being both simple and cheap to produce.

However, at the time of producing the Aerospace Environment there were certain components of the environment that the environment builder could not generate so easily. These *heavyweight tools* included RMT, the IDEF Toolset, GSED/HOOD and KeyOne. It is natural, therefore, to ask the following questions:

"Are forms the only imaginable class of 'lightweight' tool?
What makes a 'heavyweight' tool 'heavyweight'?
Is it not possible to render more classes of tool 'lightweight'?"

The possibility of providing generic tools is one of the great advantages of building an environment upon a common, powerful framework such as the combination of PCTE and the East-UIMS. It is precisely these generic tools that allow end users to develop their own highly relevant environments, although they may remain unduly constrained by the heavyweight tools that they select.

10.1.3 'Ready to Use' models and Environment building

Finally, it is clear that there is a role for the professional *environment builder*. In much the same way that large information systems are governed by 'database administrators' (DBAs) who define and control the functionality of these systems through the development and control of the system's data schema, a tightly integrated and complete software engineering environment should be built and managed by someone skilled in the techniques of environment building.

An environment builder would analyse a software engineering organisation's development processes and select from the tried and tested elements of their own library of 'Ready to Use' components. However, since all software development organisations have their own peculiarities, many components would have to be developed specifically for each organisation.

10.2 SUBJECTS DELIBERATELY NOT ADDRESSED IN DETAIL

Within a limited amount of space it is impossible to address all software engineering issues. However, the deliberate decision not to devote sections to of all things the subjects of process, version and configuration management may seem surprising. This is especially true in the light of reports such as [BFW92] which reflect the wide felt opinion that these subjects are central to the field of software engineering environments.

10.2.1 Version and configuration management

ATMOSPHERE, being a large research project, inevitably ended up with many activities taking place in parallel. Even the team devoted to the investigation of supporting the aerospace domain was involved in such diverse activities as:

- extending existing engineering methods
- integrating together existing methods
- providing tool support for extended and integrated methods
- development of general strategies for the use of existing frameworks.

The resulting Aerospace Environment highlights this most clearly and would have to have undergone at least one more iteration of tool redesign for each of these parallel activities to influence the others. The clearest example of lessons that were learnt too late to make a full impact on the resulting environment are those in the areas of version and configuration management.

Despite considerable progress in previous projects (notably PACT [Tho89]) towards the development of a strategy for performing version and configuration management on PCTE, a few problems remained for the ATMOSPHERE project to solve. While the solutions found were not applied widely during the project itself, significant progress was made through the study of the Adele configuration management system (see § 6.2.8) resulting in the production of VMCM [BLM91] and the underlying convention for representing configurations—the *surrogate*. At the time of writing this increased understanding of CM on PCTE was being applied within East and other projects.

10.2.2 Process management and guidance

Watts Humphrey, author of a celebrated book on 'the Software Process' [Hum89], draws an interesting analogy between process technology and the automated processing of handwriting. The spirit of this analogy is as follows:

> It was a great dream of the image processing community to be able to analyse human handwriting and thus to allow handwritten text to be read as input into computers and wordprocessors. However, while it soon became clear that this was a highly ambitious task, all was not lost since it was noticed that there was much to be gained from storing and manipulating uninterpreted images of handwriting. A large industry has built up around this idea—just look at the prevalence of the fax machine.

> It seems that the management of software development processes is similar to the manipulation of handwriting. While much can be gained from a certain degree of process modelling, many details are best left to humans.

Most presentations of process support concentrate upon process modelling techniques and their enaction semantics. Each such technique allows the description and subsequent control of processes at any of a wide range of granularities. Some suggest a coarse-grained, task-based planning paradigm. Others aim to allow the 'micro management' of processes, in which every user-selected action changes the state of a 'process engine' and the next set of possible actions is calculated. However, the latter tends to lead to a need to understand detailed human behaviour patterns which is a problem comparable to that of analysing handwriting. As Humphrey suggests, this is probably a problem that is not worth solving.

The array of techniques available to the builder of an East-based environment includes the ability to define 'task templates' which allow the environment to provide users with guidance in following a defined process, as well as supporting project planning and providing a record of the development process. While 'task templates' and other aspects of the East framework that could be characterised as pure process technology have not been described in this book, an emphasis has been placed upon the many ways in which other parts of the framework can be used to support process choices. The dangers of tool developers building excessive process assumptions into their tools' data schemas have also been highlighted.

Part III

Process Control Systems Software Engineering Environment

Gerd Höfner
Siemens AG
ZFE BT SE 54
Paul-Gossenstr. 100
W-8520 Erlangen

Germany

Tool Integration: Environments and Frameworks, Edited by D. Schefström and G. van den Broek

11

Introduction

11.1 OVERVIEW

The environment integration approach of the Siemens subproject is an evolutionary approach. Based on a given framework and a couple of tools and toolsets constructed on top of this framework one objective of the subproject was a higher integration *between* the tools and toolsets, as well as a tighter integration of the tools *within* a toolset. The main goal however was the integration of the toolset to an *integrated environment.* (Along with the "technical" integration went the integration of the methods. Due to the fact that there is separate book on "Method Integration" [Kea92], only basic descriptions of the method integration are included here.)

The environment of the Siemens subproject supports the whole software life cycle. Section § 11.2 describes the used project model and gives an overview about the methods and tools that go along with the different phases of this process model.

The focus of the Siemens work done within ATMOSPHERE was on the early phases of the software life cycle, namely the requirement and the design phase (and the integration of these phases). Therefore, the subsequent chapters describe in detail how the integration of these phases was achieved.

Chapter § 12 describes the technical background, i.e. the integration framework and its components.

The use of a common user interface is one of the basic characteristics of the environment. Therefore chapter § 13 describes the user interface of this toolset and the way this common "look and feel" is achieved. Chapter § 14 on Control Integration describes the communication facility of the toolset and the way in which it is used to gain a tight integration between different tools. The object model of the environment and its definition language is explained in chapter § 15, Data Integration.

The chapter § 16 contains a summary and an outlook.

11.2 PROJECT MODEL

This chapter describes the project model of the Siemens system engineering environment. The project model considers the software life cycle and provides a time structuring for the software development process by organizing the development pro-

Tool Integration: Environments and Frameworks, Edited by D. Schefström and G. van den Broek

cess into successive phases. At the end of each phase defined results (milestones) exist. The results of a phase are the basis for the activities of the subsequent phase. The primary purpose of structuring a project into phases is to minimize the complexity of the project by organizing it into individual easy-to-handle subprojects, which can be processed separately or in overlapping periods of time.

A common approach to the implementation of such a project structure was defined by B.W. Boehm [Boe76] in his waterfall model. Its name (waterfall) indicates, that the results of a phase drop into the subsequent phase as in a waterfall. The opinions as to whether this model is adequate for modern software development differ. Common practise and literature [Sch89b] show, however, that it is still adequate for software project structuring.

The project model of our environment is an advanced version of the waterfall model, i.e. a helical model. Its individual phases are

- Analysis
- Design
- Implementation
- Test
- Integration / Acceptance

The phases are processed sequentially. It is, however, possible to move backwards within the model if modifications of the results of a previous phase are required.

As seen over an extended period of time a product in most cases passes several cycles of the project model: whenever the product is modified or updated, it passes the model again; this creates a helical process. This process is also called evolutionary software development [Sch89b].

The introduction of life cycle phases (management, development, documentation, test, production, putting into operation, counselling/training and field service) extends the waterfall model of Boehm in our process model (see figure 11.1).

The fields of action mirror the functional division of labour during the software creation process.

In a project, different tasks have to be carried out; these tasks require different knowledge and can be carried out independently of each other. The project model or a cycle of the model consists of a matrix. The columns of the matrix define the process phases, the rows define the fields of action. A matrix entry describes the activity (or the milestone) the field of action has to carry out in the respective phase.

This creates the structure as shown in figure 11.1.

In our project model, quality assurance is a process-wide, continously executed task. The results of the quality assurance measures are documented in test and acceptance reports.

At the end of each phase specific results must have been achieved. These results are called milestones (e.g. requirements specification, design specification, source code ...). The contents of the milestone have been defined in guidelines. Similarly, the steps leading to a milestone and the quality assurance measures which have to be carried out for a specific milestone (reviews, code inspection, etc.) are defined.

A detailed description of these guidelines and generation rules is given in a manual [AHS91]. The manual also contains the topics project and configuration management and thus covers the entire project model.

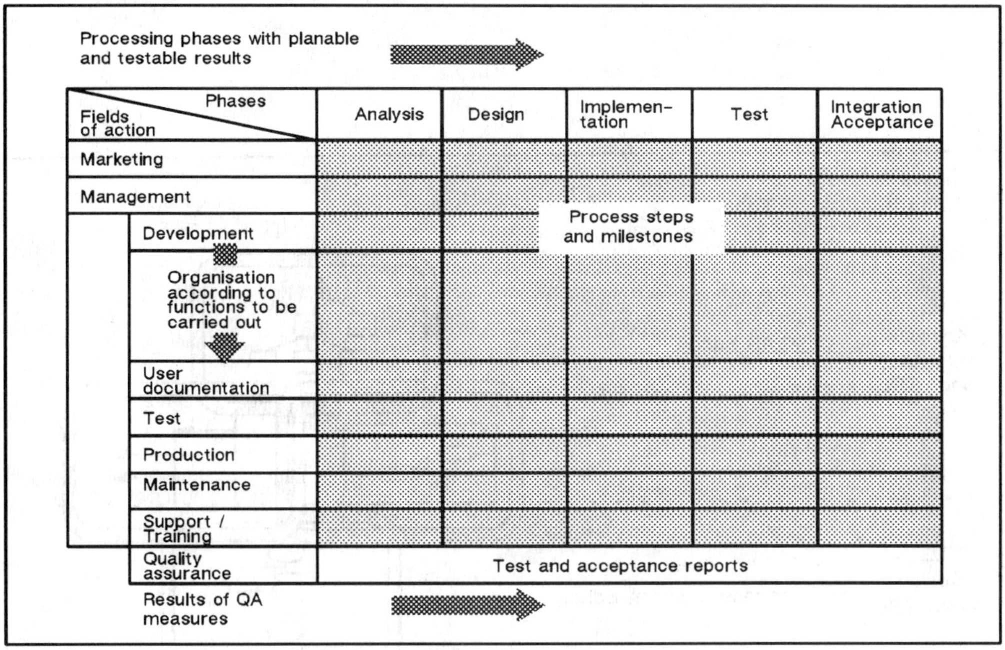

Figure 11.1 Functional job sharing within the project model

11.3 BASIS OF THE SIEMENS ENVIRONMENT

This section provides a brief summary of the methods and tools of the integrated system engineering environment used by Siemens and their position within the software life cycle (see figure 11.2). In sections § 11.4 to § 11.7 the methods and tools are described in more detail.

The basis of our environment are the methods **AKL** for requirements engineering and the design method **SDL**. The tools supporting these methods cover all phases of the project model.

The **KLAR editor** is used during system analysis to determine the requirements of the system to be created using the method AKL. Using the **Sequence Chart editor for sequence charts** processes and sequences of the communication between system components can be analysed. In the design phase the analysis results of the KLAR editor and the Sequence Chart editor are transformed into **SDL process diagrams** using the **Process Diagram editor**. Integration tools are available, which allow the conversion of results from the KLAR editor to sequence charts (**DAX/SC**, DAta eXchange KLAR to SC) and process diagrams (**DAX/PD**, DAta eXchange KLAR to PD) and from sequence charts to process diagrams (**SDL-IT**, SDL-Integration Tool). With the SDL-IT it is also possible to check automatically the consistency of analysis and design results. These tools are not shown in figure 11.2.

The analysis and design tools are suitable for the development of software and hardware systems as well as combined hard and software systems.

For automatic conversion of designs created with the SDL Process Diagram editor into implementations there are code generators for the languages C and VHDL (VHSIC

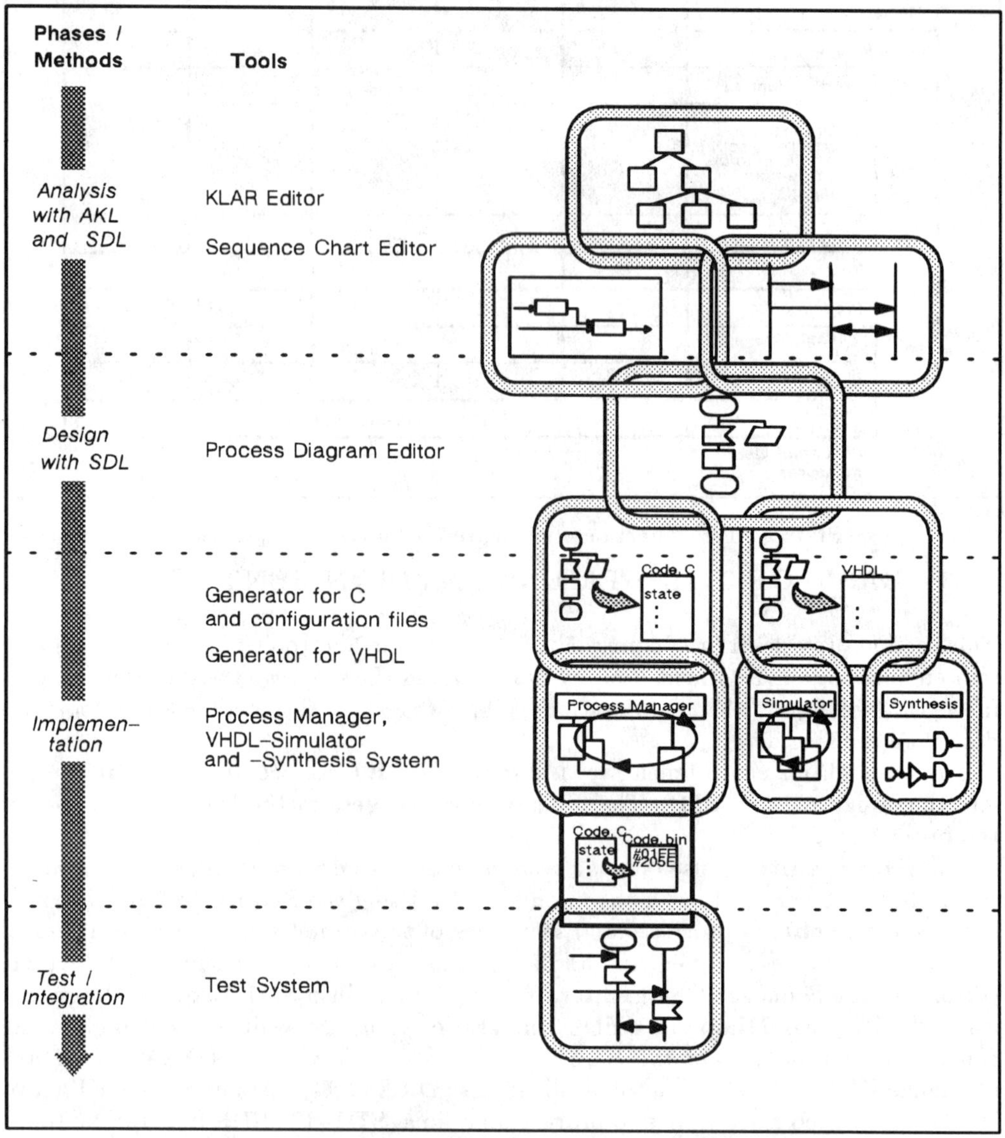

Figure 11.2 Tools and methods and their position within the life cycle

Hardware Description Language) as well as runtime systems (process manager) for various target systems.

Designs converted to VHDL can be simulated using a VHDL simulator and can be mapped to hardware using a synthesis system. The generation of software systems using the configuration management systems DSEE [DSE88] and UNIX-make / SCCS [SCC89] is supported by the automatic generation of configuration files.

The test system can be used at the SDL symbolics level to test the processes and to graphically visualize the execution in sequence charts. The required system behaviour as modelled with the KLAR, the Sequence Chart and the Process Diagram editor, can be compared to the actual behaviour visualized by sequence charts.

11.4 AKL - A METHOD FOR OBJECT BASED REQUIREMENTS ANALYSIS

AKL was developed in Siemens AG based on experiences using other methods like SADT (Structured Analysis and Design Technique [RS77]) and SA (Structured Analysis [DM79]). It may be considered as an enhanced version of these methods. The name AKL refers to the German term "Aufgabenklärung" for requirements analysis.

The AKL method addresses the following aspects:

- A system and its functionality are considered from different points of view, until all partners have a sufficient understanding of the problem to solve.
- The variety of possible interpretations of the results of an analysis is minimized.
- The requirements are structured and documented.
- AKL enables the system engineer to validate the final system concerning to the requirements described during the analysis phase.

AKL is supported by the KLAR editor which is part of our integrated programming support environment. In the following we briefly describe the AKL method. A more detailed description is given in [Kea92].

11.4.1 Basic Features of AKL

When a system is analyzed, there are always two complementary views: something has to be done ("what is to do"), and there must be somebody who does it ("who does?"). We will call "something that has to be done" a task and the "somebod" a component. Tasks correspond to the functions of the system. A component might be for example a person, some hardware-component or a software module. Both the system and the functionality of the system are iteratively decomposed. This dual inspection of a system, analyzing the funcionality and the components, is the basic idea behind the AKL method.

Most structured methods for requirements analysis like SA or SADT only follow a functional approach. The functions of a system and the dataflow between these functions is described. AKL includes such an SA-style functional analysis: the functionality of the system is decomposed into functions (called tasks) and each of these tasks may

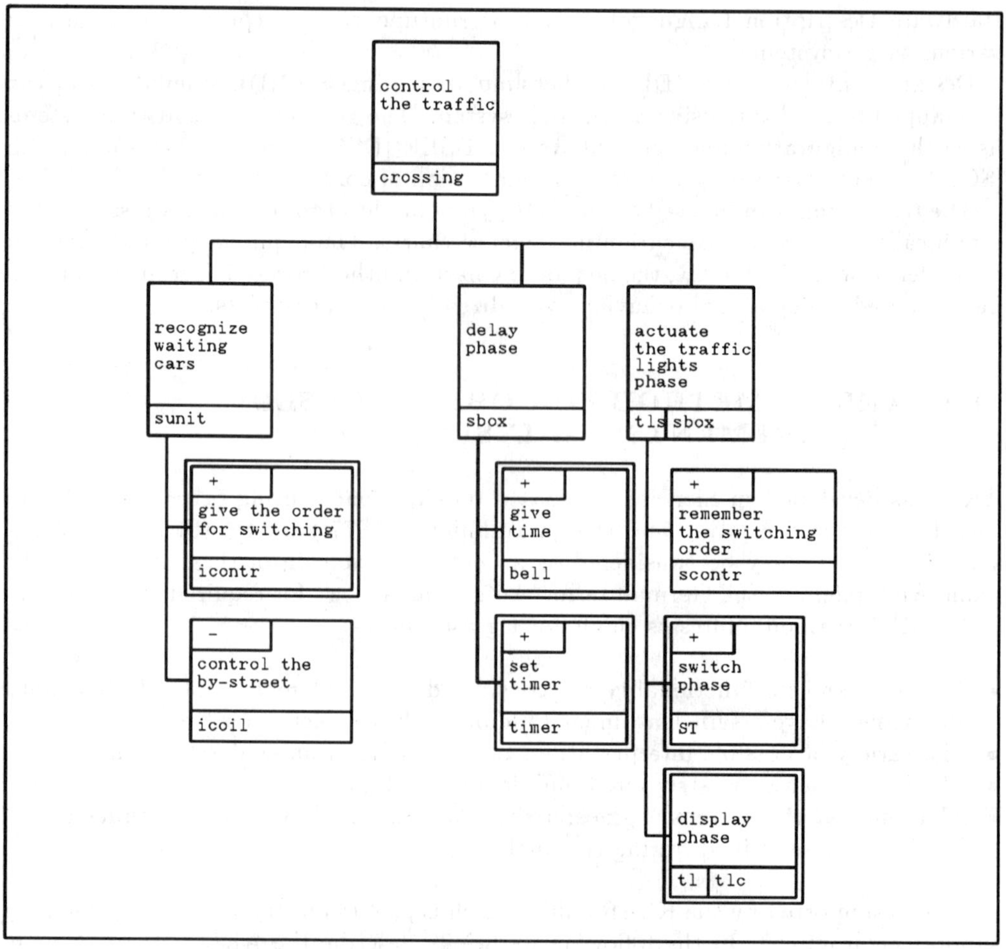

Figure 11.3 Example of a task tree diagram

be further decomposed into subtasks, etc. This results in a hierarchy of tasks. The hierarchy (it's a tree) is graphically represented by a tree diagram (see figure 11.3).

To each task a so-called interface diagram is attached (cf. figure 11.4). An interface diagram describes the datastreams between the subtasks. A datastream is either a dataflow in the sense of Structured Analysis or a control flow in the sense of Real Time Analysis (RT). Thus the interface diagrams are the analogue of SA/RT's data flow respectively control flow diagrams. The usual consistency condition holds: each input datastream of a task has to be consumed as an input by the subtasks and each output datastream of a task has to be generated as an output by the subtasks. Datastreams may ramify. The meaning of a ramification either is that the datastream has a substructure, or that the same datastream is simultaneously input for different tasks. To avoid this ambiguity the substructures of a ramification have to be named in turn.

The AKL method extends the functional approach to the analysis considered so far. The system analysist may also decompose the system into its components and each of

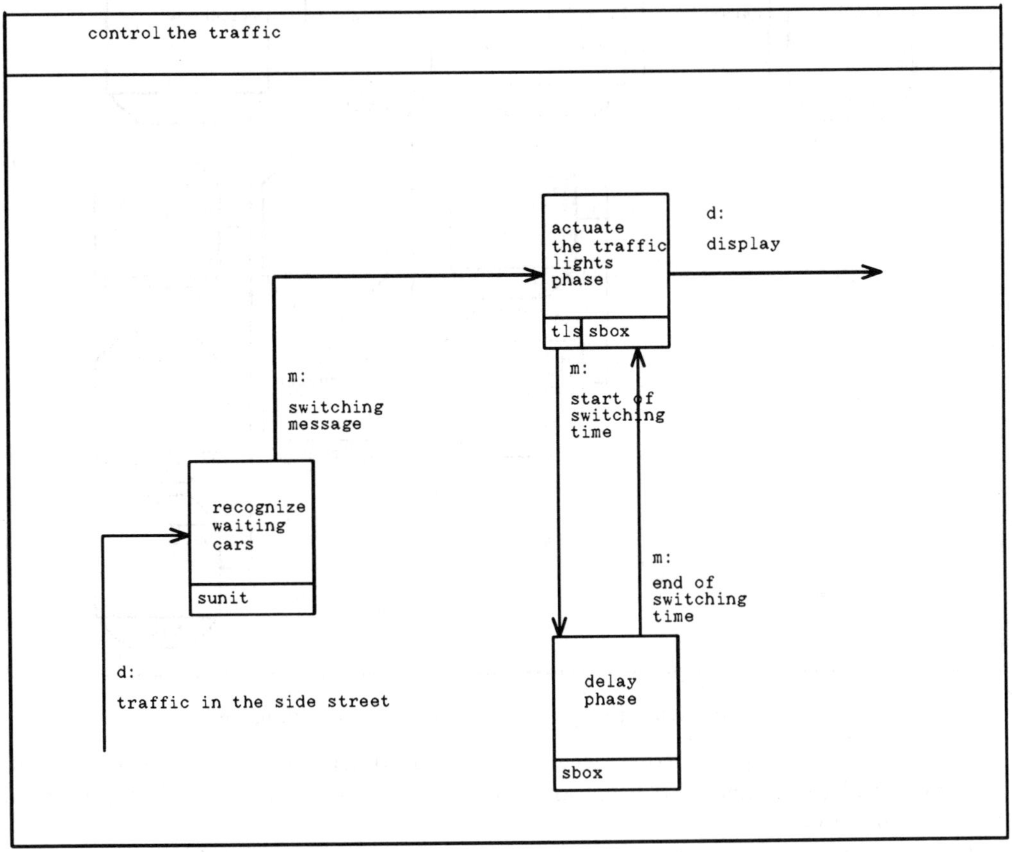

Figure 11.4 Example of an interface diagram

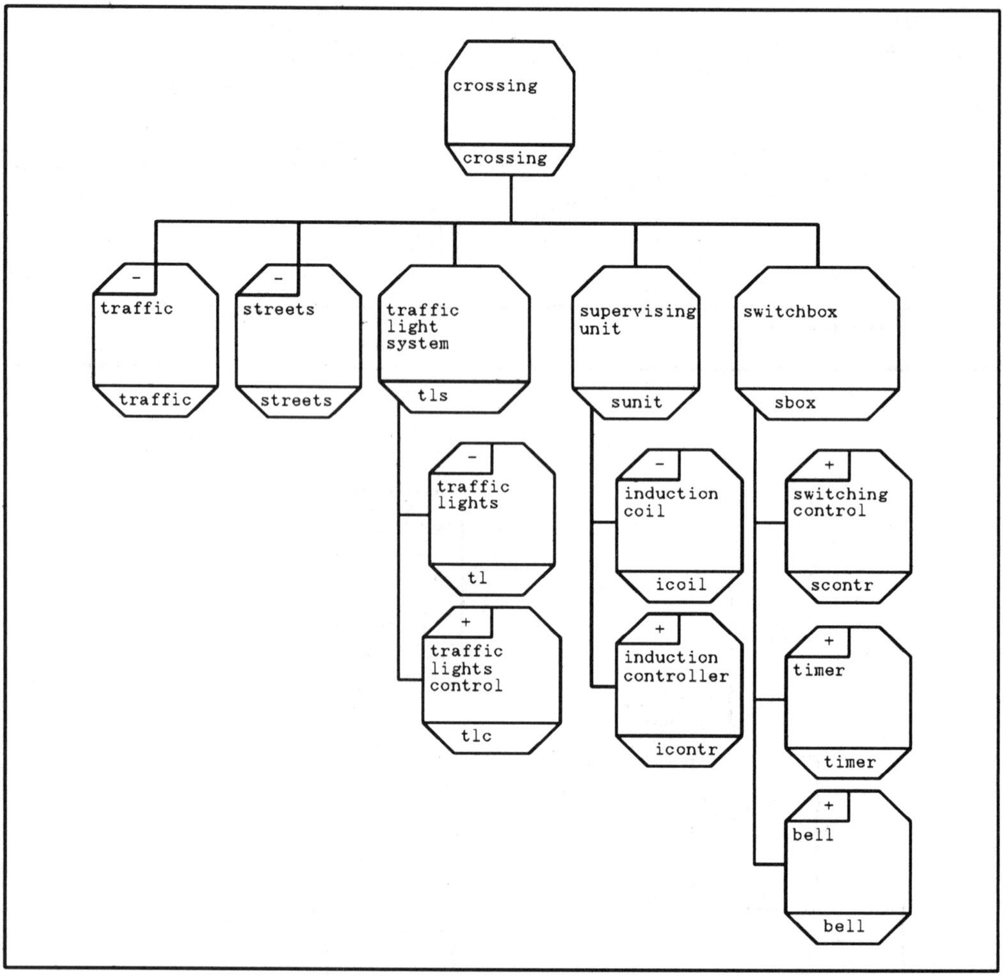

Figure 11.5 Example of a component tree diagram

these components may be further decomposed into subcomponents, etc.This results in a hierarchy of components. The hierarchy (it's a tree) is also graphically represented by a tree diagram.

It is also possible to assign an interface diagram to a component. Such an interface diagram describes the datastreams between the subcomponents. An analogous consistency condition as described above holds. Input datastreams of a component often represent an event on that component, and an event usually triggers the execution of a task. Thus interface diagrams may be very helpful for identifying tasks or splitting up a task into subtasks.

Both tasks and components form a part-of-hierarchy, and the tasks and the components are coupled. Each task is assigned to these components which are responsible for carrying out the task. Generally this assignment is not 1:1 but n:m. That means performing a task may involve more than one component, and a component may be responsible for several tasks. The assignment of tasks to components is displayed in the task tree diagram (see figure 11.3): each task is marked with the (short) name of the corresponding component. Short names for components are specified in the component tree diagram (see figure 11.5).

It is up to the system analyst whether he refines the hierarchy of tasks or the hierarchy of components in the next step. Both tasks and components are analyzed in parallel. Refining tasks and components (i.e. decompozing them) and assigning tasks to components we successively get a better and more detailed understanding of the system components and their functionality.

Of course the user of AKL may restrict himself to the functional approach. This simply means that he does not construct a component hierarchy at all. All tasks are assigned to the overall system in this case. Therefore AKL may be considered as a true extension of SA.

Since AKL considers in addition to the tasks the components / objects of a system which perform or are manipulated by these tasks, AKL integrates elements of object-oriented analysis (cf. § 15.5). That's the reason why AKL deserves the attribute "object based".

11.4.2 Steps of AKL

Usually the application of the AKL method is subdivided into several steps. There are four steps leading from the problem to the result of requirements analysis using AKL:

- embedding
- first refinement
- delimitation
- second refinement

In the following these steps will be explained:

- Embedding the system into its environment
  Each system has interfaces to its environment, and therefore it is influenced by the environment. For that reason the system has to be embedded into its environment. The meaning of embedding is the definition of a system, a superior system, containing the system to be developed. The analysis will not start on the essential system but on the superior system.
- First refinement and delimitation
  The superior system has to be decomposed (we also say "refined") both on the task side and on the component side. After finding new subcomponents we inspect them in order to find out whether they belong to the environment or to the system to be developed. We sign components belonging to the environment with a '-', and to the system to be developed with a '+'. If we can't decide wether a component gets a '-' or a '+', the component is marked with a '?'. The marks have to be transfered to the tasks: tasks whose associated components are all marked with '-' get a '-', tasks whose associated components are all marked with '+' get a '+'. All other tasks remain unmarked. This proceeding is called delimitation. We continue these two steps - refinement and delimitation - until each task and component is definitely marked with '+' or '-'.
  As a result all tasks and all components of the system to be developed are identified (namely all marked by '+') and all interfaces to the environment. The signs '+', '-',

'?' are so-called semantic properties (see below). Semantic properties are a special feature of AKL and may be used to put specific semantics on the objects handled in AKL (tasks, components, datastreams).

- Second refinement
  Having identified which components and tasks belong to the environment and which are to be developed, we focus on the latter ones. They have to be decomposed to specify the internal requirements of the planned system. The decomposition/refinement stops when the components correspond to implementable objects, e.g. modules, objects (in the sense of object-orientation) or SDL processes, or to objects, which can be reused or acquired. Analysis is not yet finished and has to be continued as long as there are tasks which are not assigned to one and only one component ("For every task it must be clear who does it.").

During the transition to the design components are interpreted as modules which may be implemented e.g. as modules, abstract data types, object classes or SDL processes. The assigned tasks correspond to functions within a module, with operations on an abstract data type, with methods of an object class, or with parts of SDL-transitions. In this way the dual view of AKL - considering tasks and components - can help to avoid many difficulties arizing during transition from analysis to design.

11.4.3 Semantic properties and descriptions

In AKL **semantic properties** may be attached to tasks, components and data streams. We used the semantic properties '+','-' and '?' to mark whether a component / task belongs to the environment or to the system to be developed. Semantic properties are attributes which can be used for a precise classification of tasks, components and data streams. They are either represented by a prefix to the name of a task / component / data stream (example: the prefix m: in m:switching_message may indicate that the datastream switching_message is a message between components) or by some graphical attribute (e.g. line-style) of a task/component-node in the corresponding tree diagram respectively by some graphical attribute of a datastream in the interface diagram.

The meaning of a semantic property and its representation is defined by the user of the AKL method. The only semantic properties in AKL with a predefined semantics are the earlier mentioned '+','-' and '?'. In general semantic properties provide the user of AKL with a great flexibility to put more semantics on tasks, components and datastreams.

AKL's semantic properties are adequate means to classify tasks, components and data streams. Additionally tasks, components and data streams may be described in more detail in so-called **descriptions**. A description may include text and graphics. It may contain for example a verbal description of the task / component / datastream, conditions for sequences, rules, algorithms ("Mini Specifications", "Control Specifications") etc.

11.5 SDL - A METHOD FOR DESIGN OF EVENT DRIVEN SYSTEMS

SDL (Specification and Description Language) is a design language standardized by CCITT (Comite Consultatif International Telegraphique et Telephonique) for the design of computer-based exchange systems [CCI88]. The name SDL expresses the objective to consistently transfer the specified, required behavior of a system (= specification) into a description of the actual behavior (= description) by detailing the specification.

The method originates from telecommunications (developed since 1972) and has been successfully used in this application domain for years. But SDL with its powerful modelling capabilities may equally well be used with great benefits in other application domains like e.g. industrial automation. Notice that the application of SDL is not restricted to the design of software. It may also be used for hardware and mixed hard/software systems (see § 11.7.4, VHDL Code Generator).

11.5.1 SDL - a brief description

Some of the basic features of SDL are the following:

- A system is modelled by use of objects called processes.
- Processes communicate via message passing (sending and receiving messages).
- A process has different states and additional local data.
- In each state a process is waiting for messages. An incoming message (an event) triggers some action. These actions usually cause a state transition in the process and therefore they are called "transitions".
- Each process is an instance of a process type. Process types correspond to the class concept in object-orientation. Instances of process types can be created dynamically at runtime.
- The reaction of a process to an event (the performed transition) depends on the type ("the class") of the process and on its actual state.

And because of these principles like instantiation, message passing, etc., SDL may be considered as an object-oriented method.

All actions in an SDL-specified system are triggered by events. Thus SDL-specified systems are event-driven. An event may e.g. be a user action like pressing a key or an alarm signal in a process control system.

SDL models parallel processes which communicate in an asynchronous way. Synchronous communication may also be easily modelled, if required. SDL is particularly well-suited to model distributed systems: because the processes only interact by exchange of messages, they are almost independent and therefore may be easily distributed, e.g. in a network.

The behavior of an SDL process may be briefly described: at any particular time an SDL process is in a well-defined state. It is waiting for events from other processes or the environment. If an event is received and this event is accepted in the current state of the process, the process starts a so-called transition (see above). This transition may change the state or terminate the process. The resulting state of a transition may be identical with the initial state.

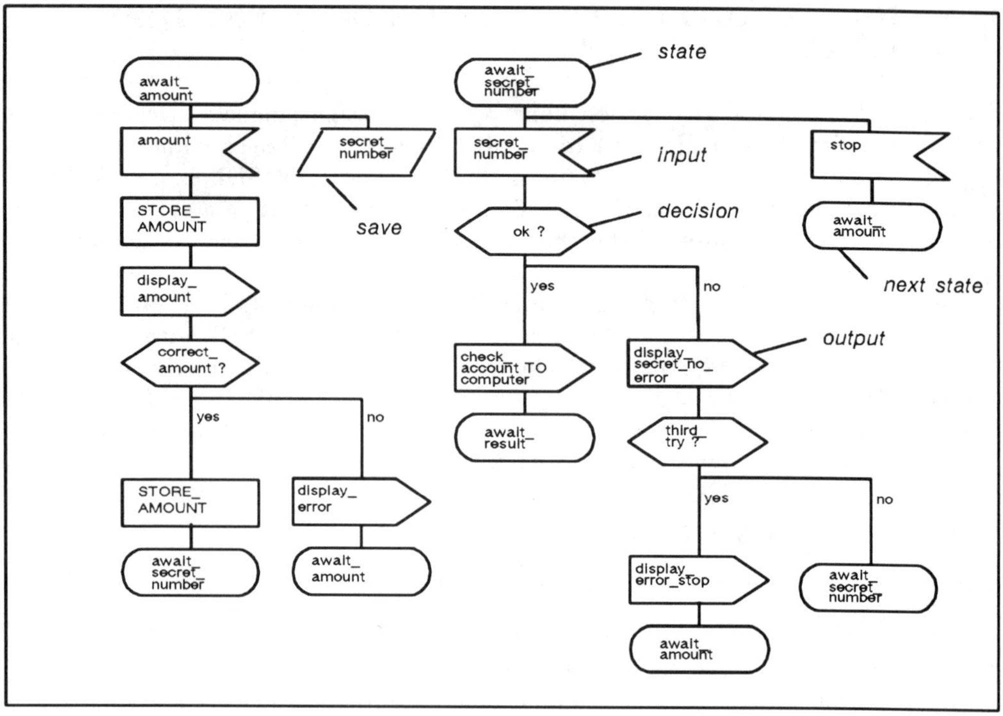

Figure 11.6 Part of a process diagram (two state diagrams)

The behaviour of an SDL process is described by state diagrams (see figure 11.6). For each state of a process there is one state diagram. It shows which events are accepted in this state and which transitions are performed as a response to the events. All actions during a transition are described in the state diagram as well as the state which is reached after the transition is finished. The collection of state diagrams of a process is called a process diagram. The process diagram shows the complete behaviour of an SDL process, from its creation and initialization to its termination. Process diagrams are exact specifications of the behaviour of SDL processes. Starting from these diagrams code generators (which are also part of our environment, cf. § 11.7.4) may generate the complete frames for a final implementation of the system.

In addition to the process diagrams SDL provides two more types of diagrams for system specification and description:

- Block Diagrams:
  They may be used to describe the static structure of a system by representing the SDL processes and the communication channels between them. We do not consider block diagrams here because the static structure may be described equally well by the AKL method, and in our environment it is usually done by AKL and the KLAR editor.
- Message Sequence Charts:
  These diagrams describe scenarios of typical communication between processes (including the environment). They give an overview about the communicational behaviour between parts of the system. Usually sequence charts do not cover all

possible sequences of communication. Thus they do not represent a complete specification, but they are very usefull in getting a complete understanding of the system and in expressing the communicational aspects of a system. Sequence charts may be applied during requirements analysis, and the resulting diagrams may equally well be used as test cases for testing the communication in the implemented system. Depending on the degree of detailing, three different kinds of sequences charts exist (see figure 11.7). The three types differ in the symbols which can be used within the diagram. A sequence chart in standard form may only consist of messages and dialog symbols showing the plain communication. A sequence chart in state form may also contain information about the states the processes are in, about tasks and decisions during a transition, etc. And a sequence chart in state input form additionally contains the information about the consumption of the messages; it shows at which time an incoming message causes a transition and in what order the events are consumed.

In our figures (process diagrams, sequence charts) we used graphical representations. These graphical symbols are standardized by the CCITT as the graphical form SDL/GR (**Graphic Representation**) of the language SDL. An equivalent alphanumerical representation called SDL/PR (**Phrase Representation**) is also standardized. These two representations can be transformed 1:1. SDL/GR visualizes the static structure and the control flow of the communicational behaviour of a system by graphical symbols. SDL/PR enables the portability of diagrams between graphical workstations and serves for archivation. Usually the graphical representation is preferred, because it is easier to learn, understand and handle. The core of our tool environment is powerful graphical editors for SDL/GR (see § 11.7.1 and § 11.7.2), and all diagrams shown in this section were created by these editors. The codegenerator of the environment internally converts the SDL/GR to SDL/PR as base for the codegeneration. But SDL/PR does not include the layout information of diagrams. An extension of PR called CIF (Common Interchange Format) which covers layout information has already beendefined (cf. § 15.3)). The editors can convert the CIF-format into their internal format of our toolset and vice versa. So the users of the SDL-method may work with tools of different vendors and the cooperation of working groups using different SDL-tools is possible.

11.6 TRANSFORMATION FROM AKL TO SDL

The transformation of the results of the analysis phase to the design phase is an essential problem in software development.

During the analysis phase "what has to be don" (tasks), and "who is going to do it" (components) is described. In the design phase it is defined "how" the components perform the tasks.

The most important aspect which has to be taken into account regarding the transformation is the consistent and complete passing of analysis results to the design. Repetitive manual entry of data which has been acquired before must be avoided, since such a process is error prone and may lead to inconsistencies.

The transformation cannot be fully automated since during design a different, lower

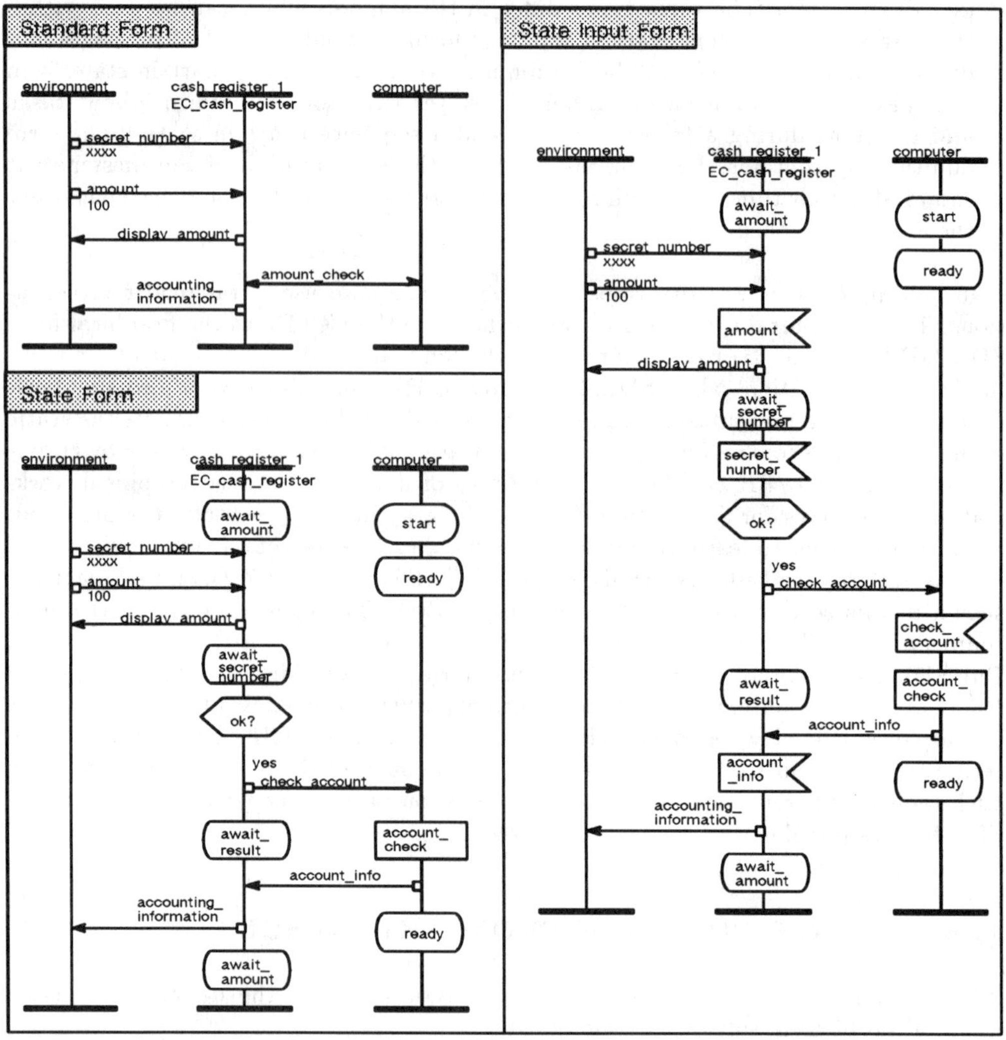

Figure 11.7 Example of the different sequence chart types

level of abstraction and a higher degree of detailing of the system is relevant. The fully automatic transformation of analysis results to design, which would provide suitable results, requires during the analysis phase, at least in part an approach to the system on a level corresponding to that of the design. The design phase would be integrated into the analysis phase, which is contradictory to the objective of structuring the development process into defined phases with precisely defined results (milestones, see § 11.2).

Because of the semantic gap between these phases, user interaction and creativity plus knowledge are essential for successful transformations.

The particular properties of the AKL method (and the KLAR editor) facilitate the transformation from analysis to design. The first and most difficult task of the transformation is to assign the tasks worked out during analysis to suitable modules (in the subsequent design using SDL these modules are the SDL processes). The assignment can be derived from the task-component assignment created during analysis. It is a prerequisite, however, that the components have been refined in such a way that they can be interpreted as parts of an implementation structure, as modules, objects, or SDL processes.

In SDL, the tasks assigned to an SDL process are parts of transitions; those data streams leading to a task are transformed to SDL inputs in the least complex case; data streams leading away from a task are interpreted as SDL outputs (see figure 11.8). However, the data streams may also be local data or states of a process. This decision has to be made by the user upon the transformation to the design, depending on his interpretation of the datastreams.

For each component to be implemented as an SDL process, the user has to search the assigned tasks with their data streams and has to convert them to SDL symbols. In this, he is supported by the tools (see § 11.7).

The conversion into SDL process diagrams is the creative process to be carried out by the user in which the results worked out during the analysis are directly passed to the design, i.e. without repeated data entry. But the user has to decide whether an AKL task corresponds to an SDL task or an SDL decision, which states have to be added to the SDL processes, etc.

Using sequence charts during the analysis phase to describe the communicational behaviour of the processes in addition to the AKL view, frames for the corresponding SDL process diagrams can be created directly from them (see § 11.7.3). A precondition for this is that besides the processing sequence the states of the SDL processes, decisions, tasks, etc., are also specified in the sequence charts.

These transformations (see § 11.7) - from AKL models to sequence charts and from sequence charts to process diagrams as well as the direct transformation from AKL to process diagrams (see figure 11.9) - are supported by the tools of our environment. Even if the transformation is finished, e.g. from AKL models to process diagrams, and changes are made afterwards in the AKL model, it is easy to transform the new or the changed AKL-parts to process diagrams. That is it is possible to make an incremental transformation, small changes on the AKL-side cause only small changes on the SDL-side.

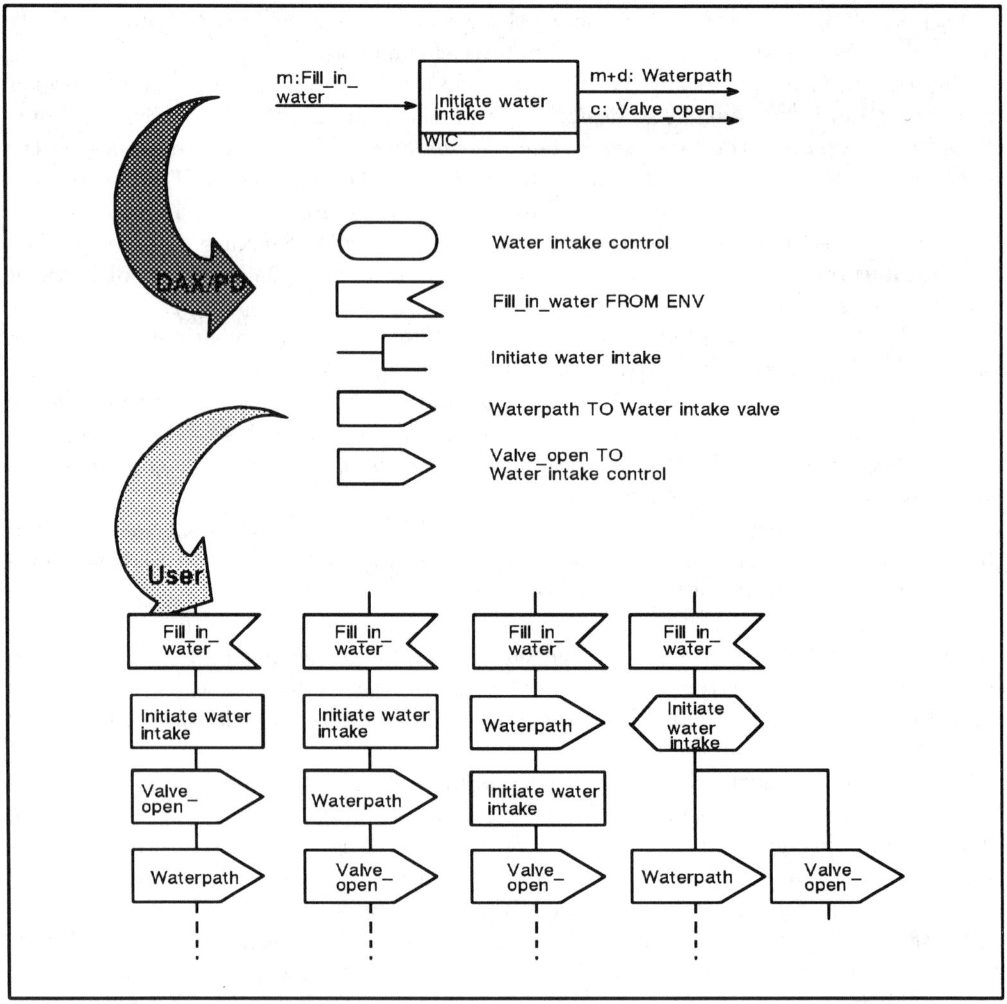

Figure 11.8 Mapping of the AKL results to SDL / possible layouts in SDL (excerpt)

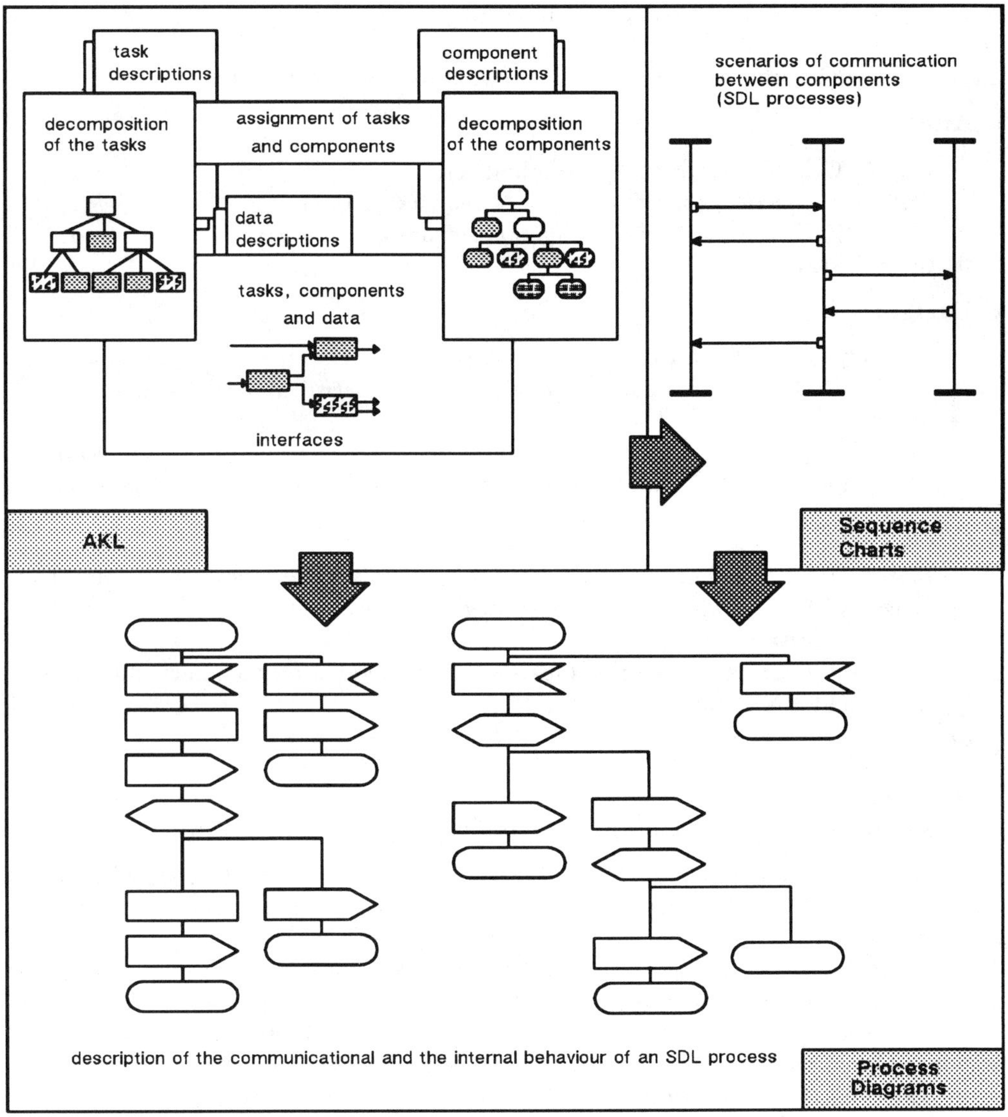

Figure 11.9 From AKL to sequence charts and process diagrams

11.7 SYSTEM ENGINEERING ENVIRONMENT

This chapter describes the individual tools of our system engineering environment and their integration. The chapter's structure mirrors the process model (see § 11.2). The tools are described in the order of their use within the phases of the model. A brief summary of the tools and their position within the life cycle has been given in § 11.3.

For the individual phases, the environment contains the following tools:

- **Analysis:**
  - *KLAR:* Graphic editor for the method AKL
  - *SC:* Graphic editor for the creation of sequence charts
  - *DAX/SC:* Transformer for the passing of data between the KLAR editor and the SC editor
- **Design:**
  - *PD:* Graphic editor for the creation of SDL process diagrams
  - *DAX/PD:* Transformer for the passing of data between the KLAR editor and the PD editor
  - *SDL-IT:* Integration tool for the generation of process diagrams from sequence charts, for consistency analysis and visualization between both representations
- **Implementation:**
  - *Generators* for the languages C and VHDL (VHSIC Hardware Description Language, VHSIC = Very High Speed Integrated Circuits)
  - Various *runtime systems* (process manager)
  - *Generators* for configuration files of the configuration management systems DSEE and UNIX-make / SCCS
- **Test:**
  - Graphic SDL *test system*
  - VHDL *simulator*, VHDL *synthesis system*

The editors, transformers, and SDL-IT use a graphic user interface and provide a consistent look and feel which allows the user to learn the functionality quickly and which helps to avoid user errors (see § 13.4).

The creation of diagrams is done in an object oriented way using context dependent menus, action buttons and forms in all editors. Each diagram is output in a separate window; this allows the user to manipulate several diagrams in parallel. Besides graphic standard functions such as move (via ghostframes), size, cut/copy/paste (even between windows), etc., they offer method specific functions and functions for the generation of documents. The extended functions of the editors are described in § 11.7.1 and § 11.7.2.

The editors KLAR, SC, PD, the implementation tools for C and UNIX and the test system are available as part of the integrated software engineering environment SIGRAPH-SET (Software Engineering Tools) by Siemens-Nixdorf Information Systems AG. Within SIGRAPH-SET there are additional tools available which complement and enhance the functionality of the tools described herein. Basically, these are tools for the modelling of data in accordance with the entity relationship model, pseudo code, project management and a basis component (SIGRAPH-SET-Basis). This basic component includes a graphic process model which can be customized to projects, connection to configuration systems, management of guidelines for the creation of milestones, etc.; all these could be described by the term auxiliary project support.

11.7.1 Analysis

11.7.1.1 The KLAR editor

The name KLAR insinuates that the use of the KLAR editor leads to clear results in the requirements analysis ("KLAR" is the German word for "clear"). The KLAR editor is used to create models of a system. A model consists of (see § 11.4)

- a diagram with the task tree,
- a diagram with the component tree,
- interface diagrams.

Beyond the graphic standard functions the KLAR editor offers the following functionality:

- Automatic consistency management between various diagrams
- Consistency checking
- User specific definition of semantic properties
- Document generation
- Provision of component task lists for the design

Automatic consistency management between various diagrams

The various diagrams of a model are not independent of each other. Several consistency rules apply; the KLAR editor makes sure that these rules are implemented:

- Tasks/components are represented in the tree and interface diagrams and have identical names in both diagrams.
- Each input datastream of a task must be consumed in the underlying interface diagram as an input by the subtasks and each output datastream of a task must be generated as an output by the subtasks.
- The short names of components are specified next to the related tasks and are identical to the short names next to the components.

Consistency checking

The KLAR editor checks the completeness of models ("have all the tasks, components and data streams been labelled and have they been given a description, have tasks been assigned to all of the components and vice versa?") and notifies the user of multiply used labels. Moreover, the consistency between models can be checked; a check is made whether a specific task which had been extricated as a separate model for separate processing corresponds to the root of the related model as far as labels and interfaces are concerned. This facilitates the structuring of projects into subprojects which can be more easily handled and understood.

User specific definition of semantic properties

For the marking of tasks, components and data streams with semantic properties, KLAR provides specific configuration files. In these files the user enters project or company specific semantic marks. This allows him to add problem specific semantic flexibility to the analysis.

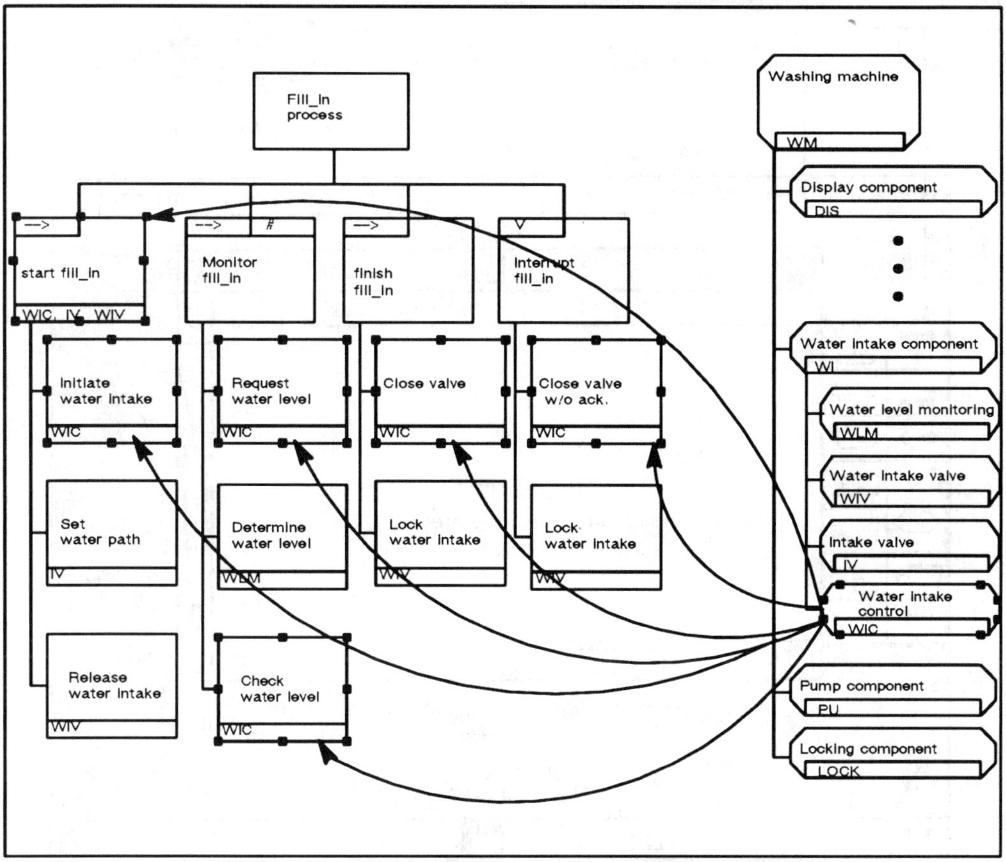

Figure 11.10 Relationship of components and tasks in AKL

Document generation

From the diagrams and the description of a model, documents for desktop publishing systems can be generated. The parts of such a document ("which diagrams and descriptions should be contained within the document?") can be selected by the user.

Definition and provision of component task lists for the design

Upon the transformation from analysis to design the user has to look up all the tasks and data streams related to each of the components and has to convert them to the corresponding representation of the design method (e.g. SDL process diagrams). This lookup is taken care of by the KLAR editor. A component can be selected and the tasks of this component are displayed (see figure 11.10).

For each component, a list of the related tasks and their data streams can be generated. This list can be written to a file in a defined ASCII format and can thus be used in other tools. The tools DAX (see § 11.7.3 DAX/SC and DAX/PD) for the reading in of results achieved in the KLAR editor make use of this facility.

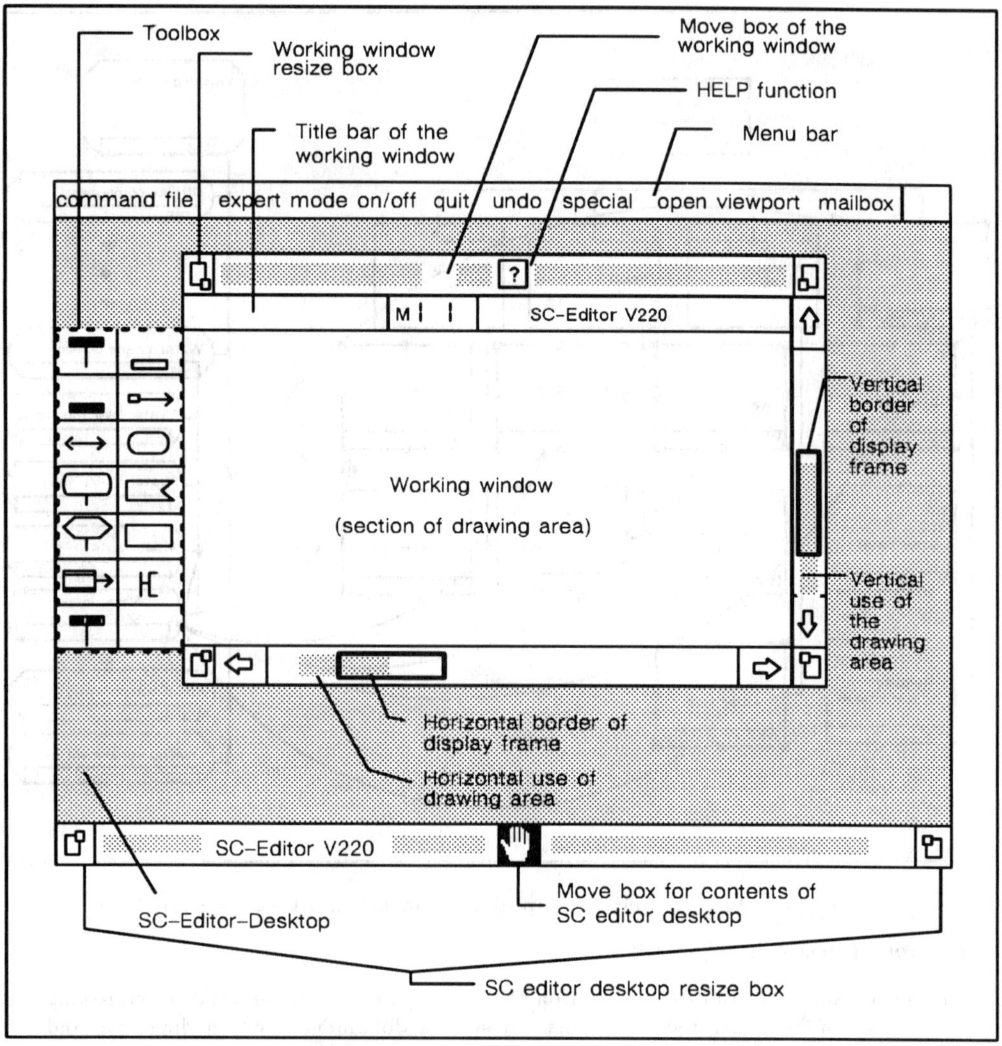

Figure 11.11 User interface of the SC editor

11.7.1.2 The SC editor

The SC editor is used for the generation of example communication processes (scenarios) as a supplement to the considerations made using the KLAR editor.
The user interface of the editors SC and PD resemble each other. In the following we describe their basic structure (see figure 11.11).

The action buttons in the menu bar trigger global functions and make global settings applying to all working windows. On the desktop of the editor an arbitrary number of working windows may be opened. In a working window a sequence chart is created within the drawing area, which is virtually unlimited. The working windows may be resized and moved within the desktop without restrictions. The positioning within the working windows occurs by means of scroll bars at the window borders or using the cursor keys. In the individual working windows the user is offered context specific menus providing the available operations with reference to the selected objects. Many operations may also be triggered using the tool box situated at the left hand border of the desktop. It is also possible to assign operations to keys and thus to operate the editor using the keyboard (expert mode).

Beyond the graphics standard functions, the SC editor provides the following functionality (a detailed description is given in [SCE]):

- Online help function
- Generation of various types of sequence charts
- Analysis of the created sequence charts
- Communication interface
- Command file connection
- Document generation via desktop publishing systems
- Generation of PR and CIF format

Online help function

By clicking on the question mark at the top of a working window, the online help function is called; it describes the executable functions of the editor.

Generation of various types of sequence charts

The editor distinguishes four types of sequence charts. The individual types use different symbols. There are sequence charts in the formats standard, state or state input and hybrid sequence charts. Sequence charts in standard format may only contain the symbols process instance, environment, message, dialogue, instance end and instance interruption. The different types can be checked for correctness by a separate function.

Analysis of the generated sequence charts

The order of the symbols in the sequence charts and the symbol labels are checked. In addition, it is checked whether there are deadlocks within the sequence charts. Positions which contain errors can be displayed in the working window.

Command file connection

Functions of the editor can be triggered by commands read in from a file (batch mode). It is possible to protocol the actions taken when drawing a sequence chart and to repeat the process step by step by reading in the corresponding command file. Moreover the command file is used to set parameters after starting the editor (symbol size, type size,...).

Communication interface

Commands may also be sent to the editor by other programs (e.g. the test system) via process communication. For this purpose the editor provides a communication interface. Via this interface the editor is also able to send commands which can be interpreted by other programs. The communication between the individual programs is handled by a communication server (see § 14.4).The protocol is described e.g. in [SCE]; this allows the communication of any tool with the SC editor, as it is required for an open interface. This functionality is used for the generation of sequence charts from other representations by the tools DAX/SC and SDL-IT; the test system uses this functionality for visualization purposes.

Document generation via desktop publishing systems

From sequence charts, documents for desktop publishing systems may be generated. The page layout of the diagram can be set in the editor. Alternatively, the diagrams generated may be printed directly.

Generation of PR and CIF format

In order to facilitate the exchange of sequence charts between editors provided by different suppliers, the editor is able to save diagrams in the textual formats SC-PR and CIF.

11.7.2 Design

For the design, the Siemens Environment contains a graphic editor for the creation of process diagrams using the SDL method (see § 11.5), an analysis system (PD-STAN), and an information system (PD-INFO).

11.7.2.1 PD editor

The user interface and the graphic standard functionality of the PD and SC editors resemble each other (see § 11.7.1). In the following we briefly outline the specific characteristics of the PD editor (a detailed description is given in [PDE]).

These features are

- Three symbol labelling levels
- Automatic syntax checking during diagram creation
- Local checks in diagrams and processes
- Project structuring by means of various storage modes
- Communication interface
- Interfacing with the generators of the implementation phase

Three symbol labelling levels

The symbols can be labelled on three levels: text, code and comments. This allows the subdivision of the design into frame design and detail design. The text level contains brief descriptions e.g. in order to introduce diagrams in a milestone document (e.g. specification of frame design). On the code level, codings are entered, e.g. C statements (detail design); during the transformation to the implementation, these codings are evaluated by the corresponding code generators. The comment level contains extended descriptions which may be used to e.g. explain the codings given on the code level or algorithms for the code level (transformation from frame to detail design).

Automatic syntax checking during diagram creation

It is made sure that according to the SDL method only syntactically correct process diagrams can be created. For example the PD editor only permits input and save symbols as successors to a state symbol.

Local checks in diagrams and processes

The created diagrams can be checked for completeness and correct labelling. For example for each state diagram a check is made whether all branches are terminated and whether all decision outputs have been labelled differently. In a process diagram, i.e. all state diagrams of a process, a check is made whether there is a state symbol for each nextstate symbol (completeness) and whether there is a nextstate symbol for each state symbol (reachability). These checks can be triggered at any time; during saving, they are initiated automatically. Errors can be displayed at the error positions within the diagram.

Project structuring using different storage modes

The diagrams may be stored to different directories. In addition, SDL procedures may be stored in procedure libraries and diagram parts may be stored in macro libraries.

Communication interface

The communication interface works identically to the one in the SC editor (see § 11.7.1). In the SDL tools DAX/PD and SDL-IT this functionality is used for the creation of SDL process diagrams.

Connection to the generators of the implementation phase

The process diagrams are the input for the generators in the implementation phase (see § 11.7.4). Using these generators an executable program can be generated from process diagrams almost automatically.

In addition to the PD editor there are two supplementary tools, PD-STAN and PD-INFO (see § 14.6). Both are technically independent of the PD editor and are called from a UNIX shell.

11.7.2.2 Static Analysis of process diagrams using PD-STAN

The Static Analysis checks the syntax and the static semantics of the process diagrams. Thus a check is made as to whether all messages sent in output symbols are consumed in input symbols too, and vice versa. If errors occur during the analysis, PD-STAN generates a command file which can be used to graphically visualize any errors in the PD editor.

11.7.2.3 Obtaining System Information using PD-INFO

PD-INFO can be used to output miscellaneous Information such as state transition tables, lists of any occurring symbols, etc.

11.7.3 Integration of analysis and design

Our environment supports the transition from analysis to design with three tools: DAX/SC and DAX/PD can be used to pass results achieved in the KLAR editor to the SC editor and the PD editor. The SDL integration tool (SDL-IT) supports the

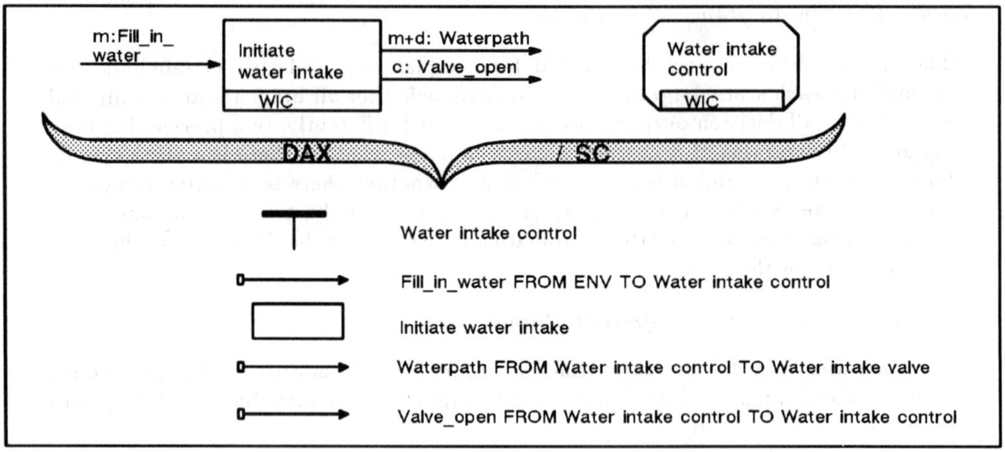

Figure 11.12 AKL-SC transformation of the DAX/SC

generation of process diagram frames from sequence charts, checks the consistency of sequence charts and process diagrams and visualises relationships between both representations.

Thus different alternatives are available for the transformation from analysis to design:
From AKL via sequence charts (DAX/SC) to the process diagrams (SDL-IT) and directly from AKL to the process diagrams (DAX/PD).

11.7.3.1 DAX/SC

In the analysis phase sequence charts are used to describe the system dynamics as a supplement to the AKL models describing the system statics. They can be used to describe in further detail the communication process between the system components defined in the KLAR editor. The transformation tool DAX/SC facilitates the use of the results achieved in the KLAR editor. The KLAR editor is used to select those components within the AKL model to be implemented as SDL processes. For each of these components DAX/SC creates the sequence chart symbols derived from the AKL model in state input format (optionally in standard format). From the data streams occurring in the AKL model as input/output at a component (more precisely: at a task of the component) messages are generated. For each component an SDL start symbol, an instance axis and an end of instance is generated. For each task assigned to the component a task symbol is generated. For the data streams leading to and from a task, a message, a state and an input symbol are generated. Moreover, DAX/SC resolves the to/from relationships of the data streams as far as possible on the basis of the available information; it specifies which SDL process a message is sent to or from (see figure 11.12).

DAX/SC graphically displays the generated symbols. By a mouse click the symbols can be included in the corresponding sequence charts created in the SC editor.

In the course of this conclusion the user defines the order of communication; in the

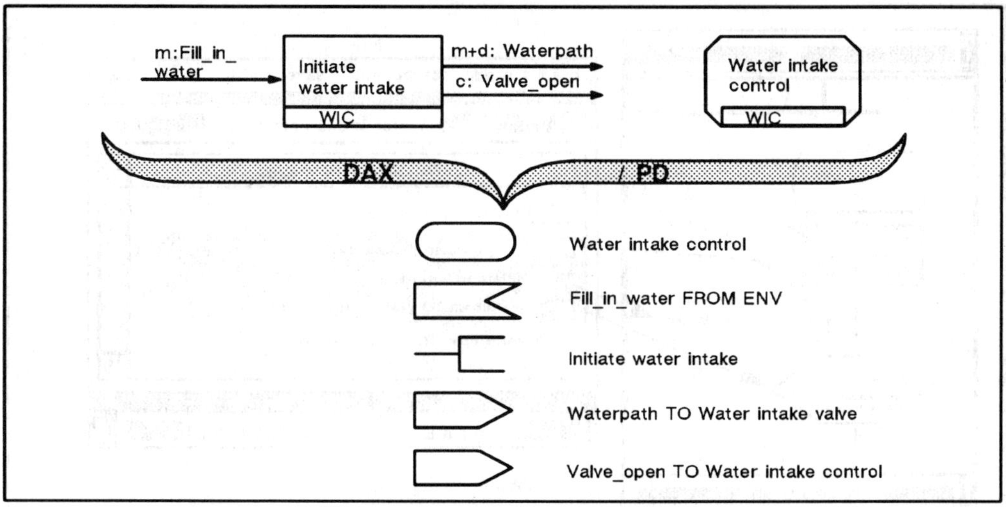

Figure 11.13 AKL-SDL Transformation of the DAX/PD

course of the generation of sequence charts in state input format the user defines the states and the time of consumption of the messages (as input).

When using special semantic properties in KLAR/AKL, which contain information on orders and conditions, automatically sequence charts may be derived from AKL models. A detailed description of these functions is given in [Gie91].

11.7.3.2 DAX/PD

The transformation tool DAX/PD supports the direct transition from the requirements analysis with the KLAR editor to the design of process diagrams using the PD editor. The KLAR editor is used to select those components within the AKL model to be implemented in SDL processes. For each of these components DAX/PD generates the SDL symbols which can be derived from the AKL model for use within the corresponding SDL process diagrams.

Actually, for each component an SDL start symbol and for each task assigned to the component an SDL comment symbol is generated. For the data streams leading to a task, an SDL input symbol and for data streams leaving a task an SDL output symbol is created. Moreover, DAX/PD resolves the to/from relationships of the data streams: it specifies which SDL process a message is sent to (output) or who a message (input) is sent from (see figure 11.13).

DAX/PD graphically displays the generated SDL symbols organized according to processes. By a mouse click the symbols can be included into the corresponding SDL process diagrams generated in the PD editor (see figure 11.14).

During this inclusion, the user has to make design decisions. He has to decide which inputs are processed in which states, whether the comment symbol is converted to a task or a decision symbol or whether the combination input/output is mapped to a local datum as a task.

If all symbols generated by DAX/PD are included, the user can be sure that all results achieved during the analysis phase with the KLAR editor have been included

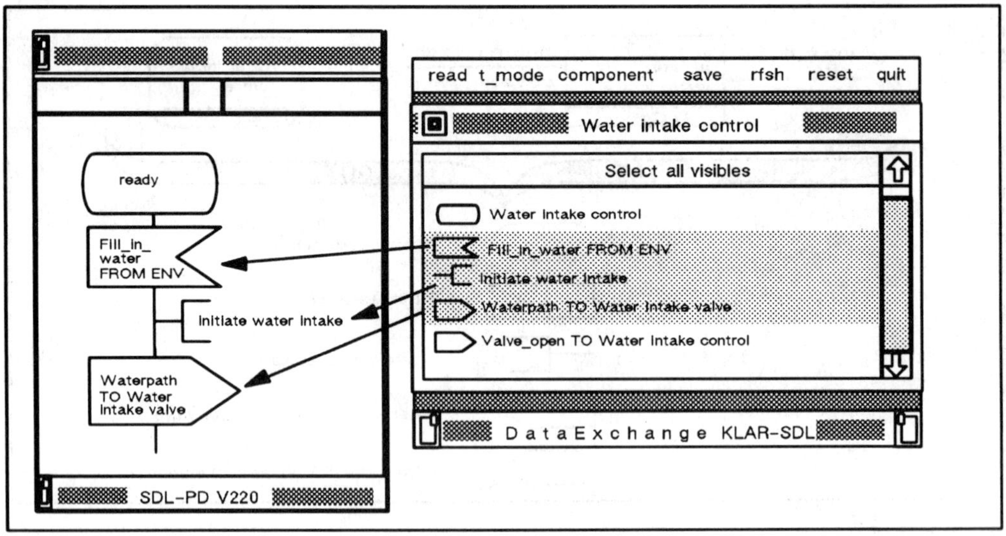

Figure 11.14 Interdependence between DAX-PD and the PD editor

into the design.
These functions are described in detail in [PDE].

11.7.3.3 SDL-IT

The SDL integration tool provides the interface between the SDL representations sequence chart and process diagram (see § 11.5). It allows the generation of process diagrams from sequence charts (transformation), the consistency check between these representations and the visualisation and animation of the results of the consistency check. These functions are described in detail in [GER+91].

Transformation

From a user defined group of sequence charts parts of state diagrams are generated (see figure 11.15). The user then completes these partial state diagrams in the PD editor. Since sequence charts in general do not describe the complete behaviour of a process, only parts of state diagrams can be generated; sequence charts only show typical communication scenarios. It is also possible that some information or symbols is/are omitted on purpose, which must not be omitted during the detail design of process diagrams. It is also impossible to automatically generate the appropriate branches in process diagrams, since the corresponding information in sequence charts is not always clear. Therefore, the user has to complete the partial state diagrams.

Consistency Check

Sequence charts and the corresponding process diagrams are checked for consistency (see figure 11.16). The meaning of consistency is:

- Any symbol sequences occurring on the instance axis of an SDL process in sequence charts have to occur on at least one valid path in the corresponding

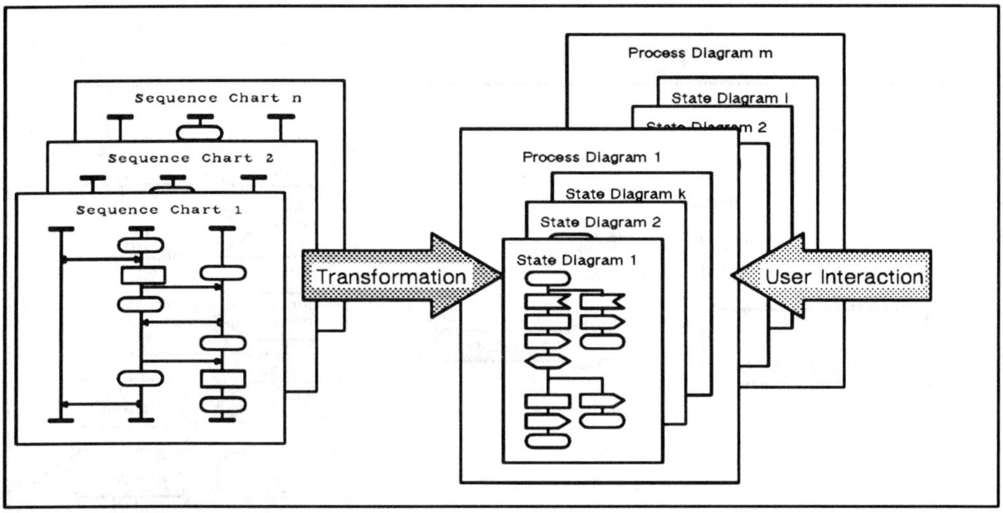

Figure 11.15 Transforming sequence charts to process diagrams

process diagram in an identical order (path matching). Both the symbols and their descriptions must be identical.

- With sequence charts in state input format additionally the processing order of the messages has to be identical to that in the process diagrams (queue consistency).

The sequence charts may be available in one of the formats standard-, state- or state input; the latter two formats may contain the SDL symbols start, task, create and decision result.
A successfully executed consistency analysis indicates that there are one or more paths within a process diagram which correspond to the symbol sequences on the instance axes of a sequence chart. It is impossible to derive information as to the correct modelling of the branches in process diagrams from the sequence charts, since branches normally depend on the local process data; therefore they have to be checked by the user; the animation helps him in this process.

Animation

The animation graphically displays the results of the consistency analysis in the editors SC and PD (see figure 11.17). Any inconsistencies encountered are also displayed. For the animation both editors and the animation tool are started. After the diagrams analyzed have been loaded, the execution of the symbol sequences are step by step indicated in the PD and the SC editor. In the case of decision symbols, the user can determine interactively which result branch is executed. Alternatively, he can leave this decision to the animation tool ("automatic" animation).

11.7.4 Implementation

Using the SDL implementation system it is possible to generate executable programs almost automatically from the design of a software system available as an SDL specification. This section describes the details of this generation step.

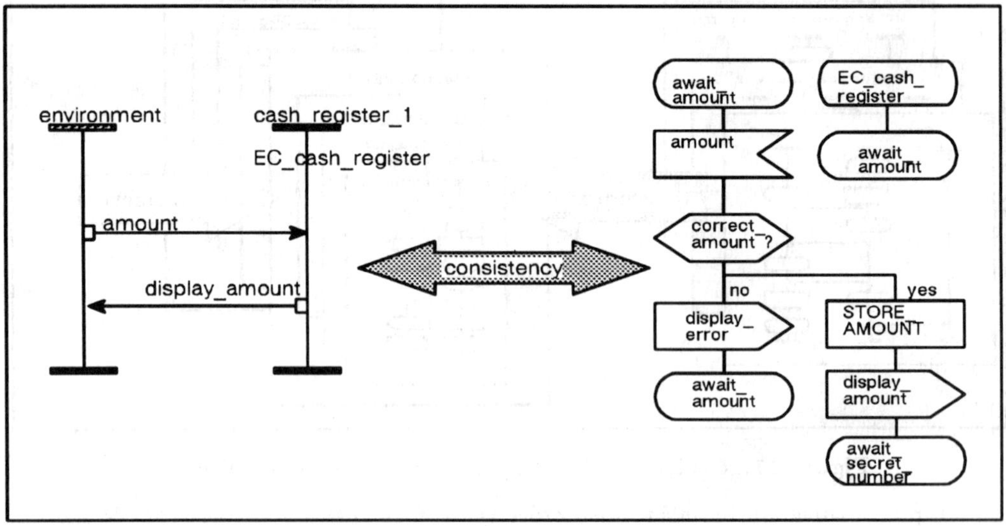

Figure 11.16 Consistency between sequence charts and process diagrams

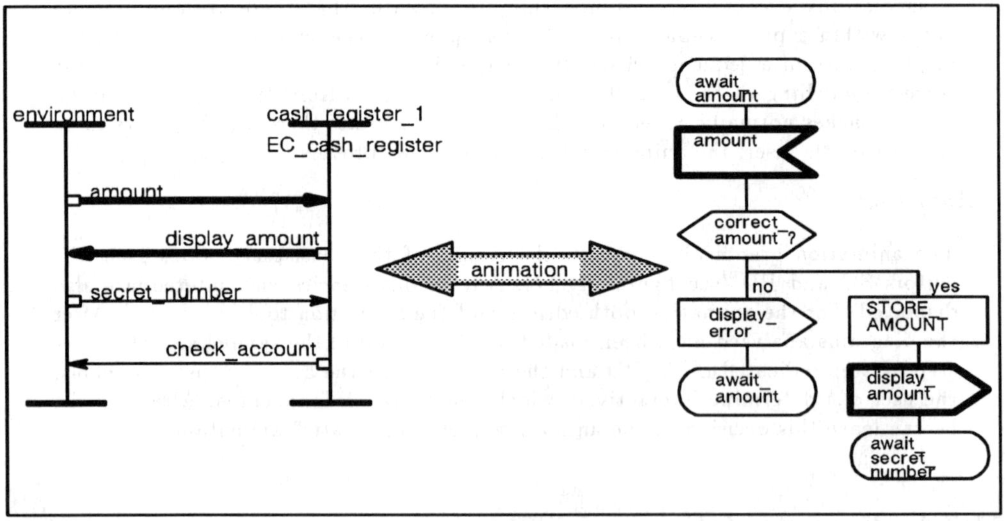

Figure 11.17 Example of an SC - PD Animation

The implementation system contains a code generator for the C programming language which creates C source code files from process diagrams. These source code files implement the individual SDL processes of the system. The C sources can be compiled with the C compiler and then be linked with the SDL runtime system; the finished product is an executable system. The runtime system, the so-called process manager, manages the SDL processes at runtime and controls the communication between the processes. In particular it manages the queues. There are process managers for various target systems, e.g. for UNIX and for SORIX, the real-time expansion of UNIX.

The execution of the individual steps of the system generation is done automatically on the Siemens Nixdorf WS 30 / Apollo using the DSEE configuration management system [DSE88] or, in general terms, on UNIX systems using the UNIX make feature [SCC89]. The implementation system contains a generator which automatically generates the configuration rules (model or makefile).

It is not possible to generate the entire system automatically from the SDL specifications. The code for tasks, decisions, type definitions of local data of a process, etc., must be provided.

The implementation system also supports the hardware development. Using a code generator, from SDL process specifications descriptions in the specification language VHDL are generated.

11.7.4.1 Generators for the automatic system generation

The automatic system generation may be carried out alternatively via Apollo-DSEE or via UNIX Make, depending on the system which is used to manage the process diagrams and the other implementation files.

In a configuration rule (model or makefile) dependencies and execution rules for the software systems are generated. The configuration rule defines the elements required for the generation and the activities to be carried out on the individual elements, e.g. upon initial generation of the system or following modifications in process diagrams.

When the configuration rule is processed, the generator is called for code generation, and the compiler and linker are called too. The result of this is an executable program.

11.7.4.2 C code generator

The C code generator generates compilable C code from the process diagrams and the additional implementation files. For each input branch of the process diagrams one C function and tables for the process manager are generated. The tables e.g. contain for each process all states, all input branches per state, etc.They allow the process manager the activation, coordination and monitoring of the SDL processes.

11.7.4.3 VHDL code generator

The VHDL code generator generates VHDL code from the process diagrams. VHDL is an IEEE hardware description standard ([IEE88]). This language facilitates the description of the structure, the data flow and the behaviour of hardware systems. It provides several ways for the description, similar to those of programming languages.

For VHDL there are simulators and hardware synthesis systems. The VHDL code generated can be used in two ways:

- Simulation of the VHDL description
- Conversion into hardware ([KGD90])

During the simulation the external stimuli (SDL inputs) are entered according to the flow in the SDL test system and the system execution and the reactions of the systems to these stimuli is indicated. In addition, external hardware components of which VHDL descriptions are available can be simulated together with the SDL specifications. By assigning times to tasks these simulators allow real-time simulation.

The VHDL synthesis systems generate netlists for the hardware or direct field programming gate arrays. This closes the gap between hardware design and implementation.

11.7.4.4 Process Manager

The process manager handles the central coordination of the parallelly executable processes and of the messages. This allows the decoupling of the processes specified in SDL of in general time consuming task switching and communication functions of a standard operating system.

The process manager can be considered a function library providing standard functions required by SDL to the user. This extends the standard function library of the language used in such a way that the required functionality is provided (e.g. concurrent processes, messages and state specific process activation, priority dependent message delivery, save mechanism). It is linked with the code generated by the code generator and the user specific codes to an executable program (SDL subsystem). Actually the process manager is an adapter between the operating system independent SDL specification and the operating system of the target computer (see figure 11.18). Therefore, it must be available on the target computer and must be adapted to this environment.

The SDL specification, i.e. the process diagrams, are entirely operating system independent; it is not necessary to modify it for such an adaption, since the communication on diagram level is carried out in a standard message format. Thus, so-called kernel functions and interface functions adaptable to the communication functions of the target system are available to the user. During porting to a target system, adaptions to specific requirements are also possible in the kernel functions, e.g. for optimization purposes.

This adaption of the process manager to the target operation system supports a Host / Target approach in software development: the system can be developed on convenient graphics computers (Host) up to and including implementation and test. The finished system is then transferred to the target system and is executed there.

11.7.5 Test

In the test and integration phase the SDL test system supports graphic high level debugging. The executable programs can be tested on the SDL symbolics level. The communication between processes is graphically visualized in sequence charts.

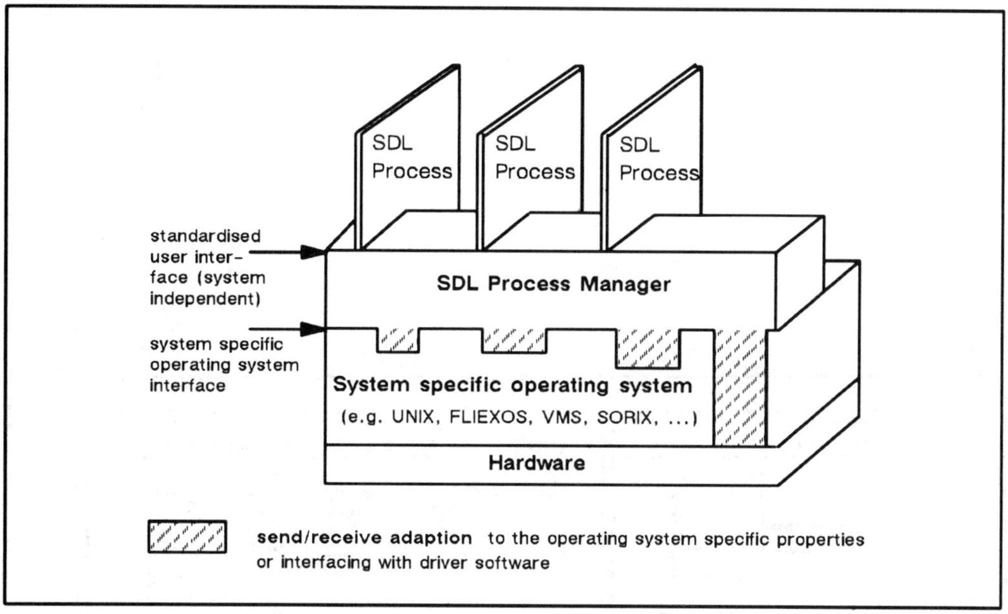

Figure 11.18 Process manager

The following functions are available:

- Graphic animation and visualization of processes in sequence charts illustrated with SDL symbols (extended sequence charts)
- Emulation of processes which have not yet been implemented and their environment
- Supplying the process instances under test with messages
- Tracing of SDL symbols
- Generating test data
- Setting break points within SDL processes

In addition, the visualization of the online process allows the verification with reference to the sequence charts and SDL process diagrams from the analysis and design phase (see figure 11.19).

For the execution of the test the SDL subsystems to be tested have to be started. Subsequently messages (test data) can be sent to the SDL processes individually or by means of a command file. The transitions triggered by this and the SDL symbol sequences executed can be represented online on screen and can also be written in a file for later evaluation.

If errors occur, the corresponding debugger can additionally be activated. Thus, test facilities are available on two different abstraction levels:

- Test on the logical SDL level
- Test on source code level

The test system commands are also sent to the SDL subsystem, which contains the SDL process under test. There, they are accepted and are processed by the process manager.

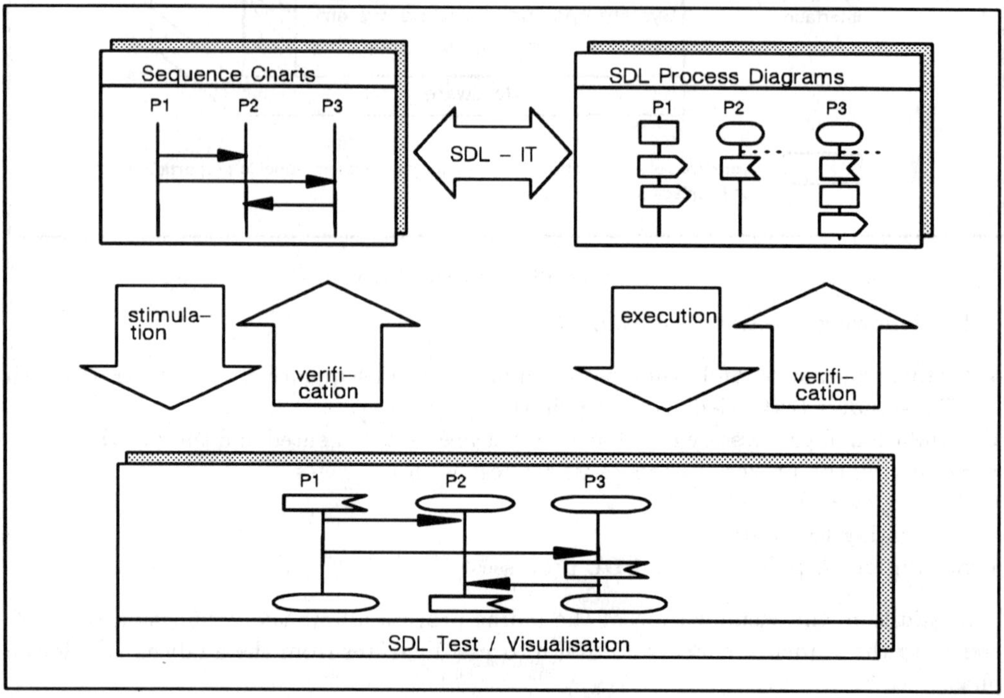

Figure 11.19 Relation between sequence charts, process diagrams and the test system

12

Environment Architecture

The integration approach of the Siemens environment can be regarded as a framework driven approach, that is starting from an already existing environment, new tools and toolsets were integrated by using services of a given framework.

All new tools and toolsets that were integrated into the environment within ATMOSPHERE are related to the SDL toolset. They are either a part of the SDL toolset itself or serve as a link from the analysis tool KLAR or to the toolsets of the implementation phase. Figure 12.1 shows the tools and (sub-) toolsets of the SDL toolset and their connection to other tools of the environment.

Central tools of the SDL toolset are the three diagram editors. From a technical point of view, these tools and their realization are also the most interesting tools regarding integration aspects. Therefore this chapter explains the architecture of the editors and the framework components. Because the next chapters describe certain integration aspects in more detail, the knowledge of the framework architecture is useful for understanding the integration approach.

12.1 OVERVIEW

The system architecture of the SDL toolset is characterized by its framework, which consists of two components. The DIATOOLS are a UIMS and provide all services for interaction with the user, including window management and input/output handling. TOROS is a system that includes services for managing graphic objects (such as lines, rectangles and edges), including drawing, rotation, zooming, etc., and general data management function (which is not only used for managing user interface objects, c.f. § 15.1).

Tools and toolsets are directly built on top of this framework with one exception: The three editors of the SDL toolset were built using an additional service layer, so the system architecture of the SDL editors can be seen as a layer model with the use of several framework services located in lower layers of the architecture. Figure 12.2 shows a simplified version of the layer model.

On top of the framework layer with its two main services the base editor layer is located. The base editor is a system of services that are common to all kinds of graphic

Tool Integration: Environments and Frameworks, Edited by D. Schefström and G. van den Broek

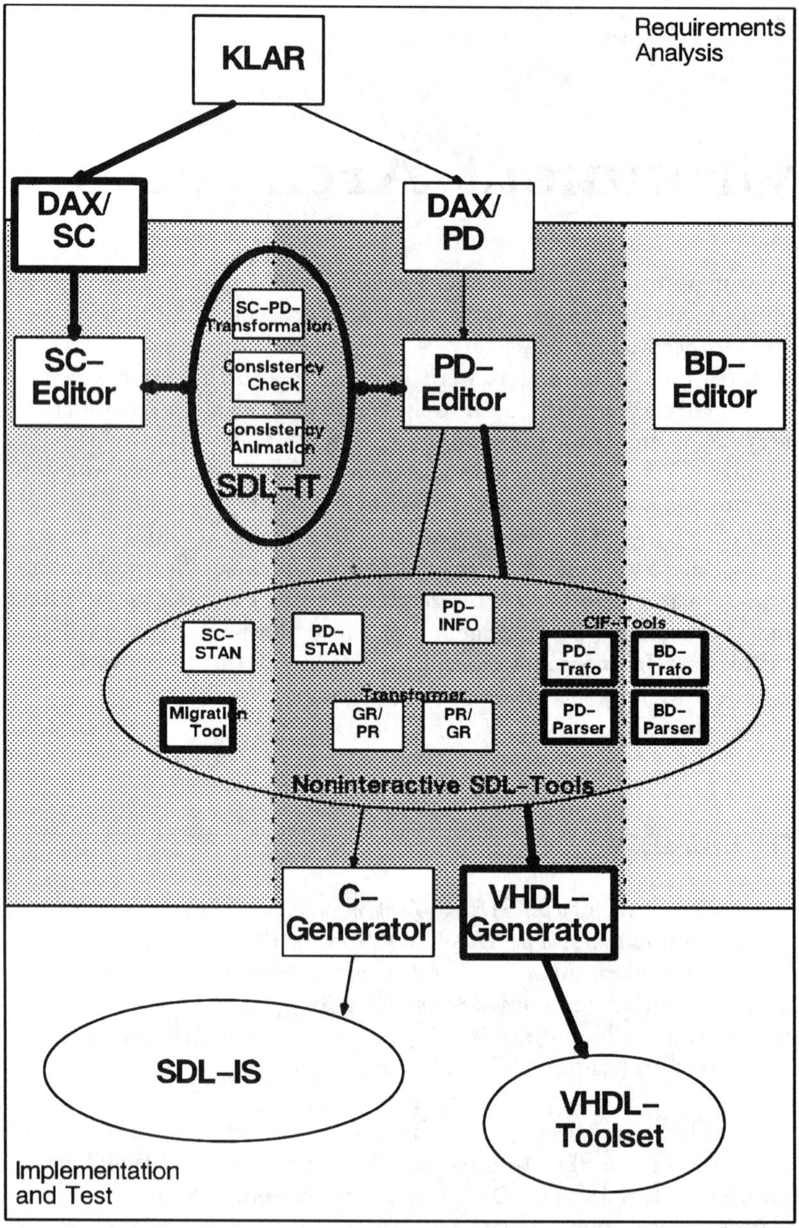

Figure 12.1 Every box stands for a single tool, tools within an oval belong to a toolset. The three shaded areas reflect the three different views/diagram types in SDL. Thick lines indicate that the tool/path was integrated within the ATMOSPHERE project.

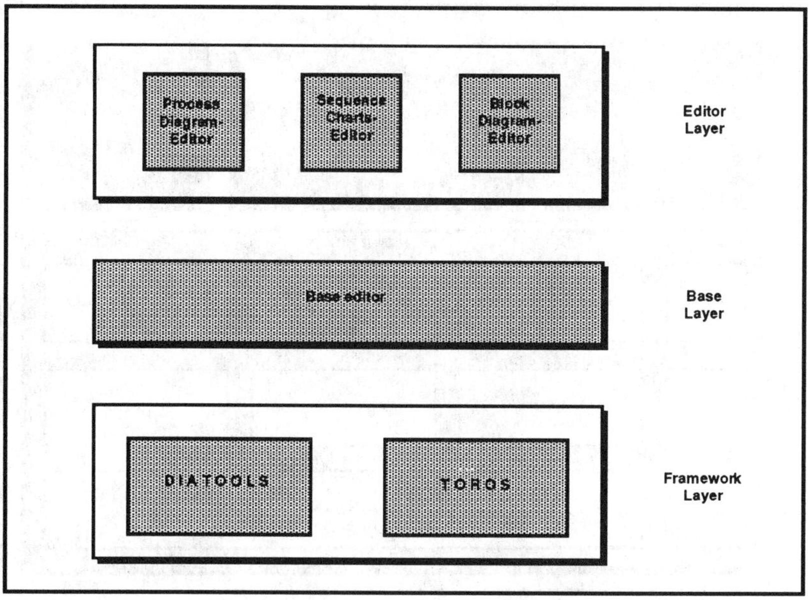

Figure 12.2 A simple layer model of the SDL editors

editors. For example, functions like command parsing, clipboard management, undo-support and communication services are located in the base editor.

On top of the base editor lies the editor layer. Here the editor specific extensions to the base editor are included. The three different SDL editors are called PD editor (Process Diagrams), SC editor (Sequence Charts) and BD editor (Block Diagrams).

12.2 FRAMEWORK ARCHITECTURE

Parts of DIATOOLS and TOROS work tightly together to form a suitable interface between the framework layer and the base editor. For better understanding of the combination, the architecture of both systems is described separately first.

12.2.1 DIATOOLS

The UIMS DIATOOLS consists of a set of homogeneous, combinable tools for the development and management of graphical user interfaces. Core of the DIATOOLS is the "DIAMON" (DIAlog MONitor), the application programmers interface with data structures and functions for defining and manipulating objects for graphical user interfaces. For the definition and testing of dialogue objects (desktops, windows, menus, forms etc.) in an interactive manner the tool "DIAEDIT" (DIAlogue EDITor) exists. This tool ensures the creation of a user interface independently from the other parts of an application. A couple of small tools complement these two main parts. These tools are either supplements of the DIAMON or "stand-alone-tools" which don't use any of the DIAMON functionality.

(An *application* in the sense of DIATOOLS is any system with a user interface

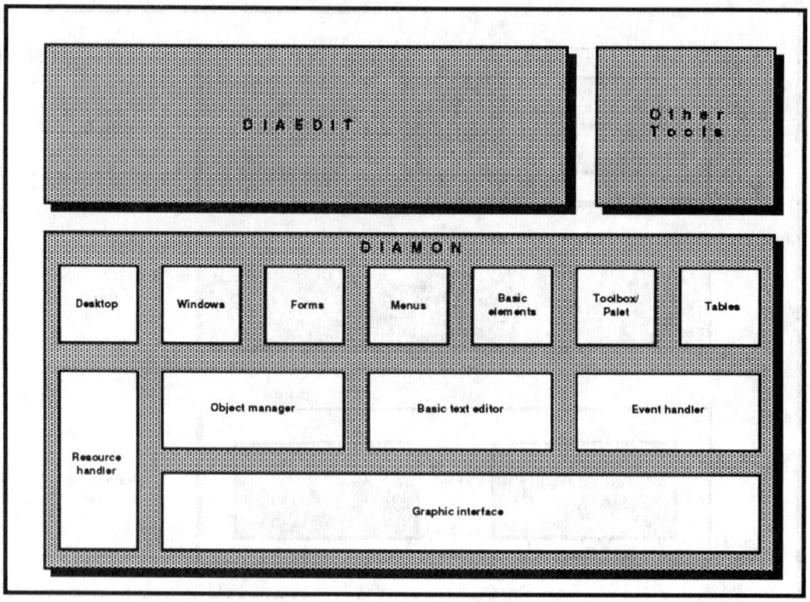

Figure 12.3 Architecture of the DIATOOLS

based on DIATOOLS, that is every application that uses the application programmer's interface DIAMON. The basic concepts and the use of the elements of the DIATOOLS are described in § 13.)

Figure 12.3 shows the architecture of the DIATOOLS. All dialogue objects are managed by corresponding DIAMON components (for example functions to create, show, hide and manage menus are summarized in the component "menu handler"). The overall application programmer's interface (the set of all interface functions of all components) consists of approximately 500 functions. With the means of these functions the application can dynamically create and manipulate all dialogue objects.

The DIAMON contains an own graphic interface called **graphic support**. The functions of this interface are also available for applications. The use of an internal graphic interface eases the porting of applications to other hardware platforms. Below the DIAMON graphic interface either X/Window [SG86] or GPR (the graphic interface of Apollo workstations) is used.

The **object management component** realizes the class of all common attributes and functions of the dialogue objects. It provides the other components with an interface to create and manipulate these graphic objects on the screen. This interface serves also as a facility for the application programmer to create his own dialogue objects. All objects are stored in a tree structure and the object management realizes the task of refreshing, supports moving and resizing of objects and allows changes in the object hierarchy. The storing of these (dynamic) data is done by the resource handler.

The **resource handler** enables the application to store persistent data. The static attributes of objects can be stored in a file (the object hierarchy is mapped to a binary format) or can be read from a file (the object hierarchy is restored from the binary information). Because usually the access to objects is realized with pointers and these pointers are lost when saving an object tree, the user can assign logical names to objects. After restoring of the object hierarchy it is possible to get a certain pointer again via the logical name of the object. The assignment of action routines also works with logical names, but the resolution of the names to pointers is done within the resource handler.

The **event handler** deals with all user input (keyboard, mouse movements, mouse keys, messages from other DIAMON applications, arbitrary user defined events) and dispatches the appropriate events to the objects, by calling object specific action routines. All predefined dialogue objects have special action routines which ensure the correct behaviour of the elements (such as opening a menu if the left mouse button is pressed) and call the user defined action routines.

The DIAEDIT is the tool for the interactive generation and testing of DIATOOLS user interfaces. It uses many functions and mechanisms of the DIAMON (in fact the DIAEDIT itself is a DIAMON application). The objects of the user interface that have been defined with the DIAEDIT are stored in a "resource file", which has to be loaded by the application at runtime. By means of DIAMON functions these objects can be shown on the screen. During the runtime of the application they can be treated as though they were created by DIAMON function calls during runtime, i.e. these elements can be dynamically changed. Therefore the creation of user interface objects with the editor (independent from the application code) and the creation of them during runtime is equivalent, the mixture of loading a resource file and generating new elements at runtime is also feasible.

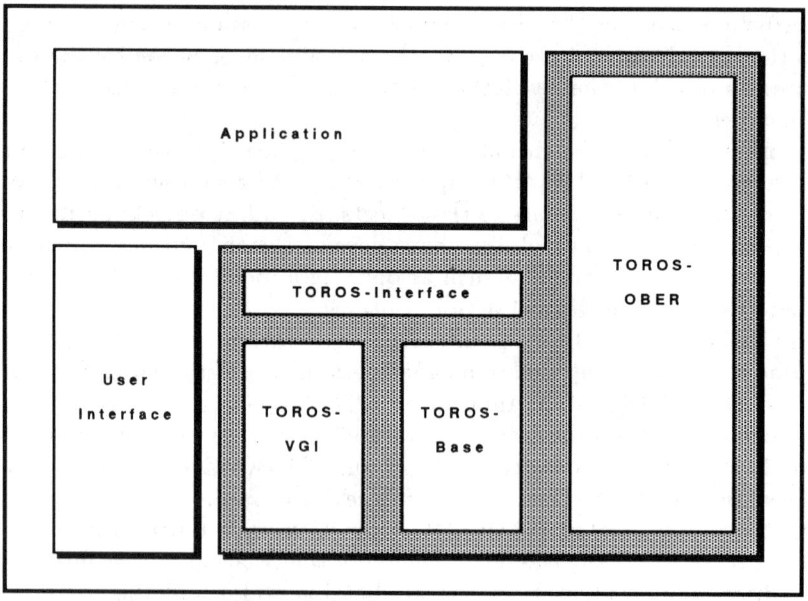

Figure 12.4 Architecture of TOROS

12.2.2 TOROS

TOROS (Toolkit for Object and Relation Oriented System) is a system for managing graphic objects such as lines, rectangles, circles, etc. and consists of four parts (figure 12.4).

For the definition of graphic objects and their attributes and methods a language called OBER (Object Based language for Engineering Requirements) is used. The TOROS-OBER compiler converts the textual object description into C files that programmers can use to integrate the object hierarchy into their system.

TOROS-Base deals with the storage and access of the object data, TOROS-VGI includes all objects and methods to create and manipulate any kind of net diagrams (for example Petri nets or SDL diagrams, for details see § 13.2). The application programmers interface to these two parts is called the TOROS interface and provides also access to the window handler of the DIAMON.

For both parts – TOROS-Base and TOROS-VGI – the OBER language was used to define the available classes (and also to refine some of these classes for use in the base editor and in the editor layer).

(For more detailed information about TOROS see § 15.1.)

12.2.3 Integration of framework services

A more detailed view of the system architecture with the focus on the framework layer is shown in figure 12.5.

The integration of DIAMON and TOROS is driven by TOROS-VGI, which uses parts of the DIAMON to provide its functionality to the next higher layer. That is

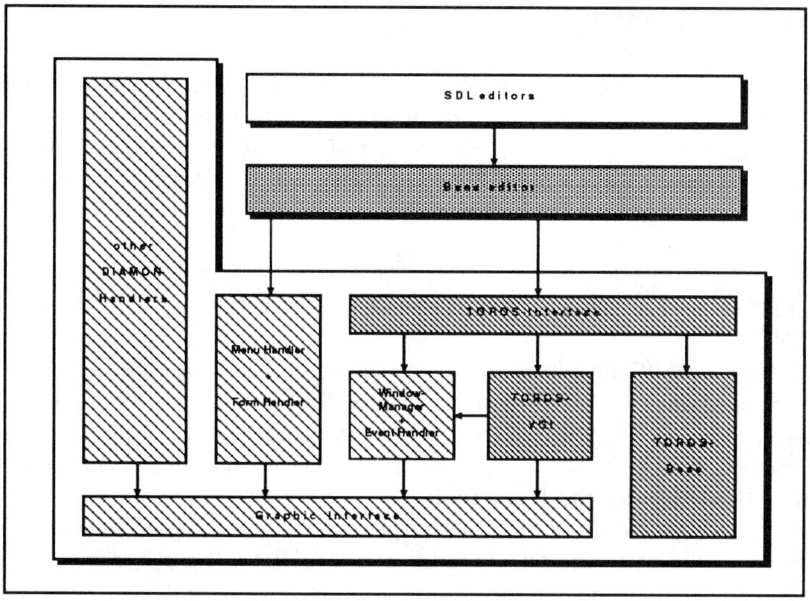

Figure 12.5 Architecture of framework components

the main input/output functions of the whole system are managed by TOROS-VGI by means of appropriate DIAMON mechanisms.

The graphic support interface of the DIAMON is not only used by DIAMON components but also from TOROS-VGI to realize low level graphic output for its high level graphic objects. In a similar way the TOROS interface has access not only to the functions of TOROS-VGI and TOROS-Base but also to the window manager and the event handler of the DIAMON.

Two other components of the DIAMON are used by the base editor for managing menus and forms. The rest of the DIAMON components are not directly used, but most of them are needed by other DIAMON components (these "internal DIAMON relations" are not shown in figure 12.5).

12.3 BASE EDITOR

The base editor provides common services that are needed in the editor layer. Among these services are the management of the three standard pop up menus and the provision of other high level input facilities that are used in every SDL editor (for details see § 13).

The objects of the base editor were described with OBER, for the management of these objects and the realization of advanced input facilites at runtime (command input, selection of objects etc.) the TOROS interface is used.

For managing menus and forms the base editor uses appropriate handlers of the DIAMON.

12.4 SDL EDITORS

To build a fully developed graphic editor, specific extensions to the base editor have to be created. These extensions distinguish one editor from another (different diagram symbols and different menu titles). For details of the different SDL editors see § 13.

The editor specific objects of the SDL editors were also described with OBER, for the management of these objects at runtime the base editor is used.

12.5 ARCHITECTURE OF OTHER TOOLS

All interactive tools of the environment are using the framework services in a similar way, as a consequence the architecture of these tool looks a lot like figure 12.5. The main difference is the *direct* use of the framework components (without the base editor layer), including the direct use of some other DIAMON handlers. This goes for example for the KLAR editor and the DAX tools.

The noninteractive tools of the environment don't have a graphical user interface. Therefore, they don't use the DIATOOLS or TOROS-VGI. But some of them use the object management component of TOROS to read data that was written by other tools or to write data that can be read by other tools. This especially goes for the transformer tools, which transform data from an ASCII-representation to TOROS format and vice versa.

13

Presentation Integration

13.1 DIATOOLS

The UIMS DIATOOLS is a set of homogeneous, combinable tools for the definition, test and management of graphical user interfaces. It provides standard dialogue objects and mechanisms to achieve a common look and feel for all applications built with DIATOOLS. It was developed by Siemens and is widely used within the company (and since DIATOOLS is a product, it is used within other companies as well). The decision for the DIATOOLS as the means to development the user interface of the environment was taken due to the fact that at the beginning of the SDL tools development (in the middle of the eighties) no other toolset with similar possibilities was available.

Core of the toolset is the "DIAMON" (DIAlog MONitor), an application programmers interface with data structures and approx. 500 functions for defining and manipulating user interface objects.

To allow the development of DIATOOLS user interfaces in an interactive way, the "DIAEDIT" (DIAlog EDITor) is used. It enables the developer to create the static parts of a user interface independant from the application code and provides support for the definition and test of DIATOOLS dialogue objects.

A couple of other tools complement these two main parts. Among these smaller tools are a browser for generated dialogue objects and a set of special user interface objects and mechanisms to realize functions that are common in many applications, e.g. load/save with a navigation facility and support for integrating on-line-help to DIATOOLS applications.

The available dialogue objects and their recommended use in a user interface of an application are described in an additional "styleguide" document [Zea88].

Figure 13.1 shows as an example the user interface of a texteditor that was developed with the DIATOOLS following the guidelines of that styleguide.

13.1.1 DIAMON

Software systems that use DIATOOLS to create their user interfaces are called DIATOOLS *applications*. The main principle of DIATOOLS applications is the use of a desktop. Every application has exactly one desktop (with a menu bar on the top) and all other dialogue objects are located inside this desktop. The desktop can be seen

Tool Integration: Environments and Frameworks, Edited by D. Schefström and G. van den Broek

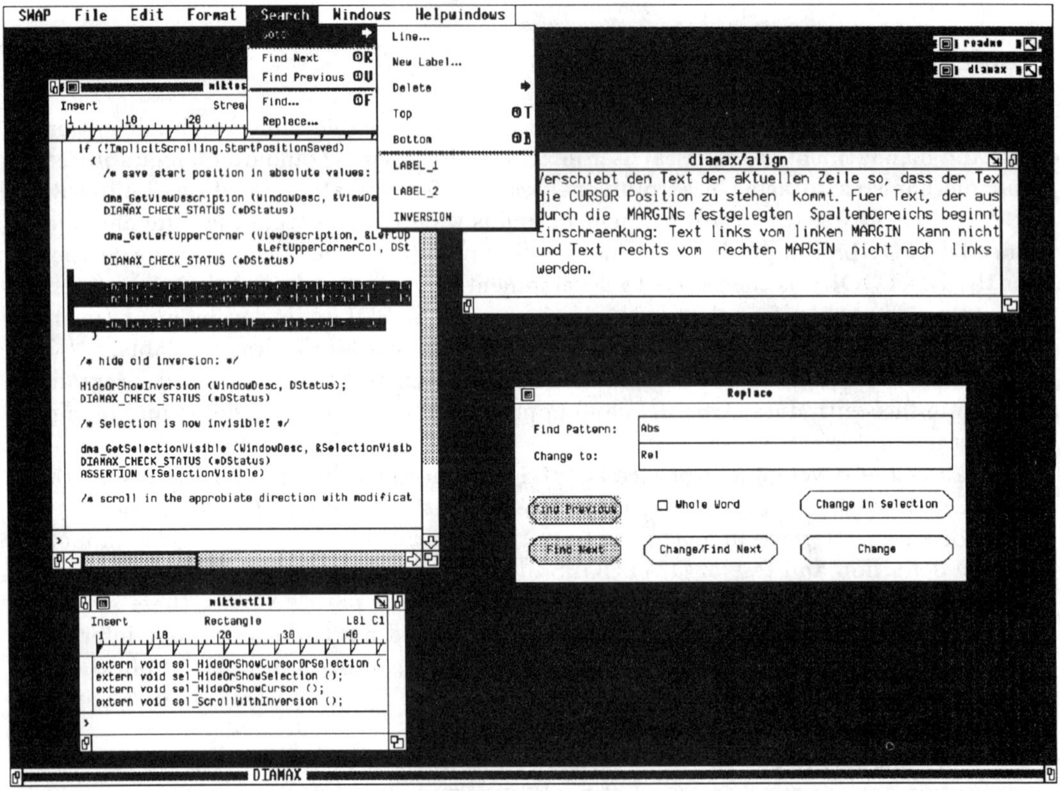

Figure 13.1 Example of a DIATOOLS application

as one large main window, which can be manipulated like any other window on the screen (for example by a window manager), but the windows, forms, etc., created by and used within the application itself can't be moved out of the desktop. That is all dialogue elements created by or belonging to that applications are only visible within the desktop. This concept has the advantage that the user always knows to which application a single window or form belongs. That advantage becomes important if more that one application is running at the same time on the same screen.

The drawback is the required size of the desktop, because to work efficiently within a desktop oriented application the desktop should have a certain size (large enough to show the working area and a large form without overlapping, for example). Because of that reason each desktop of an application covers a large area of the screen, which leads to problems if the user works with more than one application simultaneously, because it needs a lot of "popping" to skip from one application to another.

The other dialogue objects are similar to objects used in other UIMS (e.g. MOTIF or OPEN LOOK), the remaining part of this section gives a short description of the main DIATOOLS dialogue objects and their use:

- **A desktop** consists at least of a title, the desktop area and the menu bar. Optional elements are sizeboxes to change the size of the desktop and a scrollbox. Because the desktop shows only a view of a virtual indefinite area, the scrollbox enables the user to move the visible part of the desktop over the virtual part.
- The interaction between user and application (e.g. the visualization of the application specific objects) is done mainly by **windows**. The application has free access to the content of a window. Because several windows can be opened simultaneously and moved, resized and iconified arbitrarily, the application has a flexible possibility to structure and visualize its information.
  An arbitrary number of windows can be visible at one time at the desktop, but only one window is active. This window is not obscured by other windows and can be recognized by its grey titlebar. Other (optional) elements of windows are sizeboxes, closeboxes, infoboxes (to get informations about the window), helpboxes (to invoke the help facility), iconboxes and (vertical and horizontal) scrollbars.
- **Menus** serve mainly for the visualization and activating of commands, functions and modes. The DIATOOLS provide several kinds of menus (drop down menus, pull down menus, pop up menus). Menus are cascadable and can be manipulated dynamically (to change the title, font, size, number of columns, etc.). For every menu item a keycode (a "shortcut") can be defined.
- Because menus are not permanently visible (exept for the menubar), a special dialogue object called **palet** is available. It is visible on the desktop at anytime and enables one to set, modify and visualize modes (global states) of the application.
- If elements of a certain type (same shape or properties) are needed many times (e.g. the graphical elements of SDL diagrams), the **toolbox** is used. It consists of a set of graphic symbols. The user can take a symbol out of the toolbox by dragging it with the mouse and position it to the desired area of a window.
- **Forms** are used to communicate with the user. Either to ask him for additional input (e.g. parameters) in "dialogue forms" or to show him messages and results. Contrary to windows the application has no free access to the content of forms but has to use predefined dialogue objects. Within DIATOOLS two kind of forms

are distinguished: **Modal forms** are forms the user is obliged to fill in and to acknowledge. As long as a modal form is open, all actions outside the form are prohibited. A typical example is the acknowledgement of a warning. **Nonmodal forms** can be filled in at any time, i.e. the user can work with other forms, windows, etc. while a nonmodal form is open. A typical example is a search-and-replace form which is used in parallel with a text window.
The predefined objects that could be used in forms are subsumed by the term **basic elements**. Among these elements are text fields, single and multiple selection fields and action buttons. The text fields are realized with an integrated text editor. This editor supports different fonts, provides cut/copy/paste mechanisms and scrolling in single and multiple line text fields.

13.1.2 DIAEDIT

The DIAEDIT is a tool for the interactive generation and testing of DIATOOLS user interfaces. All elements of the DIAMON are supported by the DIAEDIT. By providing certain predefined elements the DIAEDIT also supports a set of guidelines from the DIATOOLS styleguide.

There are two modes. In the definition mode, the user can define new objects or change existing objects. In the test mode he can test the behaviour of the defined objects. The user can arbitrarily switch between the two modes, so the look and feel of new defined objects can be tested immediately.

During the definition work, dialogue objects can be created from a predefined set of elements or by copying and changing previously generated elements (e.g. elements from the user interface of another DIATOOLS application). The construction and manipulation of the elements is done in a graphical way with the mouse (and by filling in forms, if necessary).

The objects of the user interface are stored in a *resource file*, which has to be loaded by the application at runtime. With the means of DIAMON functions the generated dialogue objects can be shown on the screen. The elements will behave in the same way as in the test mode of the DIAEDIT because in both cases the DIAMON has the control over the objects. (In fact the DIAEDIT itself is a DIAMON application and therefore uses many DIAMON functions and mechanisms.) During the runtime of the application these objects can be treated like they were created by DIAMON function calls during runtime, i.e. the elements can be dynamically changed. The mixture of loading a resource file and generating new elements at runtime is also feasible.

From a functional point of view all user interfaces created with the DIAEDIT can be realized in an identical matter by the exclusive use of the application programmers interface of the DIAMON. But experience shows that the use of the DIAEDIT leads to a lot of advantages:

- *The design of homogeneous user interfaces is much easier.* This is achieved by providing the look and feel of basic objects and the combination of basic objects to more complex dialogue objects.
- *The user interface can be realized independently from the application.* Static aspects of dialogue elements (position, size, font, etc.) can be changed without touching the application code. This eases the prototyping of a user interface.

- *The user interface can be tested separately from the application.* The layout can be seen and some dynamic aspects can be assessed before a single line of code is written. This helps to detect design errors very early.
- *The user interface can be created by non-programmers.* The use of the editor is easy enough to enable the end-user of an application to tailor the interface to his specific needs.
- *The user interface or parts of it can be reused in other applications.* This also supports the goal of achieving homogeneous user interfaces, e.g. by building user interface libraries.
- *The user interface is easy to change.* Without great effort an existing interface can be changed, e.g. to alter the sequence of menu items or to get a different language version (without touching the application code).
- *With the use of the DIAEDIT the code of the application is reduced.* Due to the fact that the dialogue symbols are not created using DIAMON calls (which have to be coded in C) but loaded in binary format, the effort for maintenance decreases.
- *The creation of the user interface with the DIAEDIT is faster than programming the interface with the DIAMON.* Specifiying the layout of a complex form with a lot of information about position, size, hierarchy, etc., with the means of the application programmers interface not only increases the amout of code but also takes time to test the elements. E.g., adjusting elements to the desired position on the screen by giving pixel values as function parameters costs a lot of time compared to the possibility of simply moving the element with the mouse to that position.

The use of the DIAEDIT shortens the development time of an application significantly, but there is a restriction in the sense that only static aspects of the user interface can be described with it. The dynamic behaviour of a user interface has to be specified within the application code. The only support by the DIAEDIT is the assignment of forms and submenus to menu items (a form or submenu is automatically displayed after selecting a menu item). The description of a sequence of actions (like opening a form after clicking a certain button in another form) can't be done with the DIAEDIT, these dynamic aspects are "hidden" in the interaction between the appropriate action routines, i.e. they are contained in the code of the application.

13.2 TOROS-VGI

The main purpose of the TOROS-VGI (in the following only the term VGI is used) is the provision of mechanisms and objects to create and manipulate any kind of net diagrams. These kinds of diagrams are widely used in the domain of software engineering (i.e. petri nets, AKL diagrams, SDL diagrams) and provide good means to visualize complex relations.

Every diagram under control of VGI has its own (world-) coordinate system, which is (theoretically) indefinite in x- and y-direction. This frees the user from dealing with pixel calculation.

A window is a rectangular view of the coordinate system. Because VGI uses DIAMON windows, appropriate decoration elements are part of the window frame (e.g. boxes to close, iconify or resize the window, or scrollbars to change the view of the diagram). The content of a window consists of the drawing area and one line on the top for special purposes like displaying messages (e.g. error messages) or filenames and control elements for status indicators (e.g. insert/overwrite mode). The user can work with different views on one diagram simultanously. Every drawing area consists of up to 32 layers.

VGI distinguishes the following types of input events:

- **Locator**: position indicated by mouse or cursor motion keys
- **Choice**: keys (ASCII code of the pressed key) or mouse buttons (left/middle/right button, up or down). Mouse events within the indicator area of a viewport are distinguished from mouse events within the drawing area.
- **String**: a string is typed in via the keyboard and finished with the return key. If the echo mode is on, the string is shown in the message area of the viewport.
- **Rectangle**: spawning a rectangle with the mouse. Rubberbanding is supported. Result is the mouse position after releasing the left mouse button.
- **Pick**: direct input of an object by selecting it with the left mouse button.
- **Stroke**: input of a row of points, marked either by lines or by a rubberband

Two additional event types are closely related to the DIAMON, the **Menu** event (when the user clicks into the menubar of a desktop to open a menu) and the **Mailbox** event (when a communication event from another DIAMON application occurs).

There are three different input modes to control input events, the *request mode* (wait until an input from the requested type occurs and ignore inputs of other types), the *event mode* (input events are queued) and the *sample mode* (status, e.g. current position of mouse cursor). Not all of the modes are applicable to all input types.

The VGI provides its services by the means of a set of functions available to the application programmer (via TOROS-Interface). Besides basic functions (creation/initializing of objects, undo-support, etc.), a lot of functions exist to support graphical operations:

- Drawing of primitive graphic elements like polylines, polygons, circles, rectangles, arcs and splines and different kinds of text (with or without consideration of care returns, etc.)
- Manipulation of the graphical context (attributes): linestyle, linewidth, linecolour, fillcolour, interiorstyle, cornerstyle; different fonts, sizes, colours and orientation for text elements; support for drawing arrows, etc.
- Translation, zooming, highlighting (inversion) of objects
- Selection of objects, different kinds of "picking" an object (inside the rubberband, touched by the rubberband, etc.)
- Moving ghost pictures (shadows) of objects with the mouse cursor
- Grid support
- Support for routing of connections between graphic symbols
- User defined symbols, composed of sets of primitive graphic elements
- Geometric operations like rotate, reflect, stretch
- Printing

13.3 BASE EDITOR

Common services that are needed in different kinds of editors are concentrated in the base editor. The services are:

- *Common look and feel of the user interface*: the base editor uses TOROS-VGI and the DIAMON for realizing user interface objects like windows, menus, forms and so on. This ensures a consistent look and feel for all editors developed on top of the base editor.
- *Provision of common basic editor functions*: several common functions to be used within graphic editors are provided, divided into general ("global") functions, functions to perform on selected objects and functions to perform when no object is selected. These three groups of functions are mapped to three different popup menus, which appear automatically in the appropriate context.

  1. "Nothing selected" menu
     - Undo
     - Change view
     - Overview
     - Create symbol (empty submenu, filled by the specific editors)
     - Position to symbol
     - Show partition of print pages
     - Quit editor
  2. "Selected" menu
     - Highlight objects
     - Reset highlight
  3. "Global" menu
     - Change linewidth
     - Change font
     - Reset marks
     - Clear drawing area
     - Change scale
     - Allow keyboard input (yes/no)

- *Advanced input facilities*:
  - Definition of mouse buttons: left button for selecting objects (other selected objects will be deselected), middle button for popup menus, right button for adding/removing an object to/from the selection set

  - Selection of objects with a rubberband (all objects that are completely inside the rubberband rectangle form a selection set), deselection by clicking in an unoccupied area, automatic selection of connections between selected objects, automatic highlighting (inversion) of selected objects
  - Command input: the user can also execute menu commands by typing a key on the keyboard. For every menu item (and submenu item) one key is defined. The assignment of the keys can be done by the user. If a symbol is created with a key code, the symbol will be drawn at the current cursor position
  - Support for integrating editor specific menu items into the menu structure. The content (i.e. the name) and the sequence of the menu items can be changed.
  - A menu for reading editor commands from command files (an alternative means of input, see § 14)

- *Grid support*: when scrolling through a diagram (either with scrollbars or with blockcursor keys) a grid is supported, so that after every scrolling action the topleft corner contains one whole element. The last line/column before scrolling becomes the first one after scrolling. After resizing windows similar calculations take place.

13.4 SDL TOOLS

The SDL tools consist of a set of related tools, including three editors with interactive graphical user interfaces. The other SDL tools are called from within the editors or they work as simple transformers or analysis tools and therefore don't need an interactive user interface.

13.4.1 SDL editors

The three SDL editors were developed to support the graphical development of SDL systems, that is to allow the user the manipulation of the SDL diagram types *block diagrams*, *process diagrams* and *sequence charts* (see § 11.5). The names of the corresponding tools are *BD editor*, *PD editor* and *SC editor*.

All three editors are extensions of the base editor and therefore have not only a common look and feel regarding the user interface, but share as well some common services provided by the base editor. The use of the base editor leads to a unification of the user interfaces of all three editors regarding the following facts:

- All editors have a desktop with a menubar on top of it which contains some general menus and menu items.
- The window handling and the look and feel of the windows, the forms, the menus and all other dialogue elements is the same in all three editors.
- All editors use the same pop up menus in the same context.
- Although every editor deals with different kinds of diagrams (and therefore different kinds of objects), the way of manipulating these objects is the same (e.g. selecting, moving, copying, labelling of objects).
- Every editor uses the same mechanisms for the communication with other tools (see § 14).

- All editors provide the same way to execute prerecorded command sequences (see § 14.1).

Each editor has its own desktop with a menubar that provides the most general commands in drop down menus. All other commands can be reached by the means of pop up menus. Controlling the editors with the keyboard is also supported.

The user edits diagrams in windows (here called viewports). The elements of the appropriate diagram type are provided by a toolbox that contains icons of the editor specific symbols. These symbols can be selected and moved to the desired position of the viewport. Additionally each symbol can be created by selecting the appropriate menu item in a pop up menu.

The user interfaces of the three editors are very similar in general. To show the common functions and the differences of the three editors a short overview about the menu functions is given:

- The functionalilty of the **menubar** on top of the desktop is the same for all the editors. It contains menu items for the functions "undo" and "quit" as well as items for opening windows and enabling/disabling keyboard input. There are also submenus for handling the execution of command files and for communicating with other tools (see § 14.5.2). One submenu contains general functions like manipulating the current command file, showing the version number of the editor, and showing/hiding the object toolbox.
- When the user presses the middle mouse button over the status line of an arbitrary editor window, the **global menu** appears. It contains some general functions concerning the content and the properties of the appropriate diagrams. The global menus of the three editors differ in the position and the name of some functions. Because some functions are special to a specific editor, they appear only in the global menu of that editor.
  Common to all three editors are the "properties" submenu, which provides subsubmenus and functions to alter values for line width, font and highlighting, a submenu to set the scale for the diagram and two menu items for closing a window and deleting all objects of a window. In every editor there is at least one mechanism to select objects via command (select all, select all of one type, select last) and with the exception of the SC editor there is the possibility to use a grid to ease the alignment of objects. In the global menu of the PD editor there is an additional submenu for choosing different layers of text description, while in the global menu of the SC editor a submenu for the highlighting of message sequences exists.
- If no diagram object is selected and the user pressed the middle mouse button over the work area of an arbitrary window, the **ns menu** (nothing selected) appears. Like the global menu it contains general functions, but functions that are more often used than the functions of the global menu. The ns menus of the three editors differ in the position and appearance of some functions. Especially the ns menu of the PD editor contains more items than the appropriate menus of the other two editors.
  Common to all three editors are the "change viewport" submenu and "I/O functions" submenu on top of the ns menu. The "change viewport" submenu provides functions to change the position of the viewport (i.e. to show different views/parts of a large diagram) and to search symbols (by symbol number or by text). With

the means of the "I/O functions" submenu diagrams can be saved and read. Also common to all three editors is a submenu, which lists all the diagram elements (objects) that are available in the appropriate editor and a submenu to create, show and hide the numbering of diagram symbols.
Every editor provides a "paste" function and a "print" submenu in the ns menu, the SC and PD editors have a function to eliminate redundant lines, columns and bends from the diagrams and a function to analyze the diagrams. The PD editor checks the whole diagram, while the SC editor provides several kinds of syntactical checks (according to the four kind of SC diagrams). The last item of the PD editors' ns menu is a submenu, which handles the request of objects from the transformer tool DAX-PD (see § 13.5).

- If one or more diagram objects are selected and the user presses the middle mouse button over the work area of an arbitrary window, the **selected menu** appears. It contains functions that are applicable to selected objects. Again the three menus are slighly different and additionally the last menu items in each of the menus handle special functions of the appropriate diagram types.
  Common to all selected menus are functions and submenus to delete, cut, copy, move and resize objects, to edit a symbol text and to replace symbol text. To allow still consistent, but clearer layout of diagrams, the SC and the PD editor provide functions to stretch objects and edges. For recognizing causal structures in diagrams both editor support the visualization of predecessors, successors, concurrent objects, etc. Special to the PD editor is the possiblility to move, copy or exchange text from one text layer to another, to write all descriptions of a certain text layer into a file and to change the symbol type without losing the text information. An important additional function of the BD editor is a menu item, that opens a refinement window for a selected block.

For the realization of the dialogue objects that are not provided by the base editor that is TOROS-VGI the UIMS DIATOOLS was directly used (for several kinds of forms and toolboxes). This ensures the same look and feel also for these editor specific dialogue objects. Additionally there is a way to configure the user interface with the means of configuration files, which allows one to change the layout of the menus and the forms, so the user is not restricted to the predefined user interface configuration.

The link between process diagrams and sequence charts is another interactive tool that supports the SDL developer in achieving consistency between these different views of a SDL system. This tool has its own desktop, menus and forms (also realized with the DIATOOLS). It doesn't deal with the diagrams directly, but uses the communication facility of the SDL toolset to show the diagrams via the SC and PD editor.

13.4.2 Non-interactive SDL tools

Several non-interactive tools complete the set of SDL tools. Among them are two tools to analyze process diagrams and report the results of such an analysis. These tools can be called from the command line (and will then perform their work on a file) or they can be called from within the PD editor via the menu item "syntax" (and then will work on the current diagram in the PD editor).

Two other tools are transforming process diagrams from the standardized textual representation to the graphical representation and vice versa.

To support the transformation from the SDL Common Interchange Format (a company-independent graphical representation of block diagrams and process diagrams, see § 15.3) into the binary format for the editors, other transformer tools are available.

13.5 AKL SUPPORTING TOOLS

While the SDL tools enable the user to design a system, the KLAR editor covers the requirement phase of the software life cycle. (For details of the underlying method AKL see § 11.4.) For transferring the results of the requirement phase to the subsequent design phase, there are two DAX (DAta eXchange) tools which convert the system description made with the KLAR editor to SDL process diagrams and SDL sequence charts respectively. Because this conversion process requires some decisions made by the user, the DAX tools are also interactive tools.

All the tools are realized using framework components and therefore have a look and feel similar to the interactive SDL tools, that is they have a desktop with a menubar, pop up menus, forms, etc./.

14

Control Integration

The main aspect of control integration in the Siemens environment is the communication facility of the SDL toolset. By using this communication facility and the concept of command files, SDL tools (and other tools) are able to control the SDL editors from the outside. That is control of the tools is not only possible in an interactive way, but can be done by other tools by means of sending remote commands to the receiving tools.

This chapter describes the mechanisms of the communication facility in detail, beginning with the concept of command files and an overview about the communication model. After the description of the communication protocol and the role of the communication server, a couple of integration approaches used within the environment are described. Among these approaches are the integration of internal and external tools and the use and integration of stand-alone-tools in the Siemens environment (which form another aspect of control integration).

14.1 COMMAND FILES

The usual way of controlling an interactive tool is the selection of objects, commands, etc., by the user via keyboard, mouse, etc. Additional to this "internal" control mechanism, the Siemens environment provides a special means of external control. Every command that can be given in an SDL editor, has an external format, that is a number that identifies the command plus parameters that add necessary information like coordinates, file names, text strings, etc. For this external format, mouseclicks are also treated as commands.

By using this external format, command files can be created (using a normal "texteditor") which then can be executed within the appropriate editor. Additionally, every user has the possibility to record a whole editor session, which means all commands given by the user interactively during the work with the editor are written in their external format to a command file.

In the menubar of every SDL editor there is a menu called "commandfiles" which enables the user to select the following commands:

- **start**: a form appears in which the user has to specify the name of the command file that should be executed. Only one command file at a time can be open. During

Tool Integration: Environments and Frameworks, Edited by D. Schefström and G. van den Broek

the execution of a command file no interactive input is possible. If an error occurs or the command "return to dialogue" is found in the command file, the editor stops the execution and returns to the interactive mode.

- **continue**: by selecting this command the editor continues with the interpretion of the next command in the file after an interruption due to an error or the "return to dialogue" command has occured.
- **stop**: this command aborts the execution of a command file after an interruption. To reexecute it, the start command has to be given again.

Two arbitrary command files can be executed right after starting an editor. They have to be specified when starting an editor and enable for example the use of groupdependent default values for the editor in the first file without losing the possibility for the user to choose additional defaults for himself (in the second file). Other possibilities to use command files are

- to define command macros
- as a recovery possibility
- the remote control of tools
- to animate diagrams, etc.

One way in which the command files are used within the environment is the support for syntax checks of diagrams. During the check, the syntax analyzer generates editor commands in a special command file. After a syntax error has occurred the user can open this command file and by executing the generated commands from the analyzer the editor positions to the faulty symbol. The user can correct the symbol and then continue with the command file until the next error is shown or the command file is completely read. This way of treating syntax errors helps the developer to create correct diagrams more efficiently.

Another way of using command files is the distributed execution of commands, i.e. to send and execute commands or command files over the communication facility to another tool running on a machine located somewhere in the local area network. The next sections describe the communication mechanism of the environment in more detail.

14.2 COMMUNICATION MODEL

The communication model was mainly developed for the needs of the SDL toolset, but one goal was the generalization of the model for the use in other tools as well. In detail, the following requirements have been identified for the realization of the communication mechanism of the environment:

- All tools should be able to send and receive messages of varying lengths.
- Sending and receiving tools can run on separate workstations.
- It should be possible to receive messages from a sender not known to the receiver (open architecture).
- Different instances of the same tool should be able to communicate with each other and with other tools.

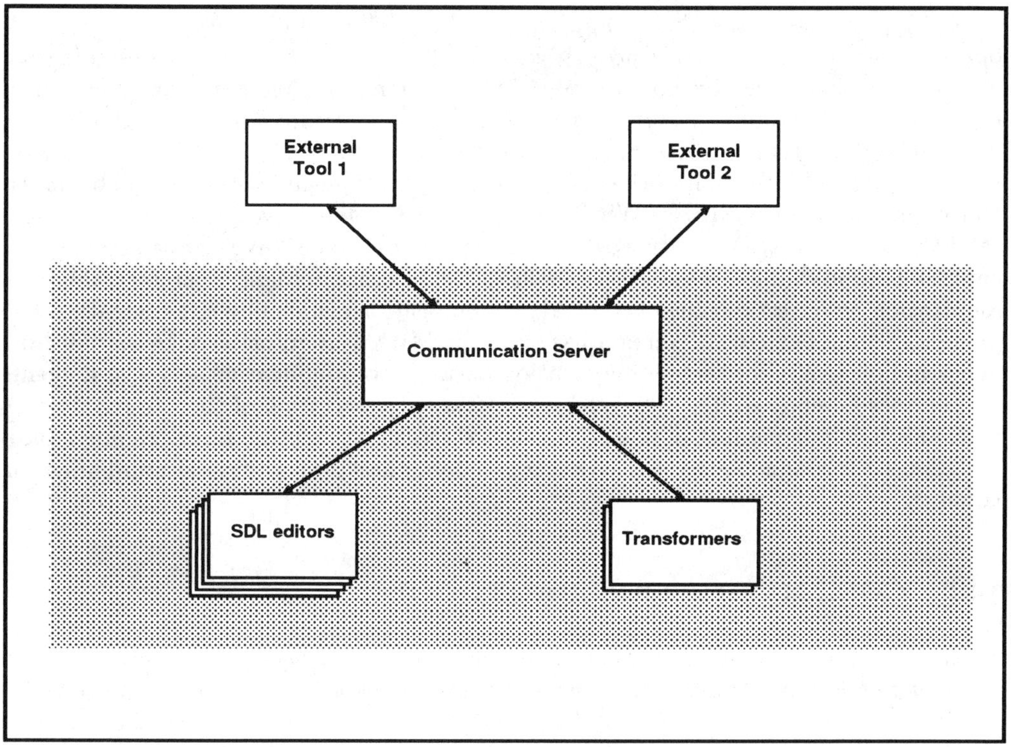

Figure 14.1 Model of the communication facility

- Sending and receiving should only be possible when communication is desired. Without opening the communication or after closing it the tools need not take care of incoming message events.
- It should be possible to build notifying mechanisms between two tools, even if they do not know each other.

Following these requirements, a communication model was developed. All tools of the environment can communicate within the local area network, the so-called *communication server* is responsible for managing the participants (clients) of the communication and for receiving and distributing the messages. There is special support for the communication between the existing SDL tools, but the model is not restricted to this toolset. Every tool running within the LAN can participate in the communication if it uses the predefined communication protocol. Two (or more) new tools can also define new protocols and use the server for the communication with each other.

The communication server is the link between different tools (clients) which want to communicate. As a deliberate design decision, a "point-to-point-communication" approach was chosen.

To communicate with another tool, the sender has to address the receiver explicitly and the server handles the correct forwarding of the message. In a ring of connected workstations there is only need for one communication server, i.e. it is not necessary to run the communication server on every workstation on which a client is running.

One application of the chosen approach is the sending of diagrams to other developers. If, for instance, several people work simultaneously with the process diagram editor (each one works on his own parts of a system), one of them can send a part of his current diagram to a certain developer (i.e. to a certain instance of the process diagram editor) without disturbing the other ones.

The technical realization of the communication mechanism was done in two equivalent ways. On Siemens Nixdorf WS 30 workstations it is based on the Mailbox Manager (MBX) system calls. On other workstations (Siemens Nixdorf WX 200 and SUN) the communication channel is based on sockets of the Internet domain. Therefore, the communication server establishes the initial communication channel by either creating and opening its mailbox (in the version based on the MBX system calls) or by establishing one common socket for the communication between communication server and clients (in the socket version). The following more detailed description of the communication mechanism is independent of one of the concrete realizations (the term "channel number" is used throughout the whole chapter to designate an identifiable communication channel).

14.3 COMMUNICATION PROTOCOL

Each tool (internal and external) can be adressed over a *logical device number* or a *channel number*. A certain logical device number stands for an appropriate tool, for example the PD editor has the number 1. For the interactive tools of the SDL toolset the logical device numbers from 1 to 7 are fixed and the numbers 8 to 9 are reserved for additional tools that may be included in a future version of the SDL toolset. The numbers 10 to 19 are free to use for other tools, which can choose their own logical device numbers. A channel number is used to distinguish between two or more instances of the same tool and is assigned by the communication server. As additional information the identification of the machine (node-id) on which a tool is running is also kept by the server. All this information about registered clients can be requested from the communication server (and can be shown in the SDL tools within a form).

Every message that is sent must identify the sender and the receiver (within the message header):

- logical device number of the sender
- channel number of the sender
- logical device number of the receiver
- channel number of the receiver

Usually the sender and receiver are identified by the logical device number. In that case the communication server completes the message header by filling in the channel numbers of sender and receiver. If there is more than one instance of a tool registered in the server (which then all have the same logical device number), the sender can adress a certain instance by setting the channel number of the receiver by itself. If it's set to the special value 99, the communication server will send the message to that instance which has most recently registered.

The messages that are sent between tools are not supposed to contain large data packages (the maximum length of a message content is restricted to 1146 bytes).

Instead, the contents of messages are used as command triggers and references (e.g. to command files). By this means it is possible to e.g. trigger the creation of a complex diagram by sending just the filename of a command file to the appropriate editor. About the format of the message content the sender and the receiver have to agree, i.e. they have to define their own protocol. If SDL tools are involved in the communication (either as sender or receiver, or as sender and receiver), then a particular protocol can be used. For this purpose there is a reserved area in the message header, e.g. a control flag which indicates several predefined ways of interpreting the message content:

- If the control flag is set to 0, the content of the message will be interpreted as *the name of an SDL command file* which will be executed after receiving the message. If an error appears while executing the command file, the editors stops, but the user can continue with the execution by selecting the "continue commandfile" item from the 'commandfile" menu. In this case there is no difference between executing a command file from within an editor or via communication mechanisms.
- if the control flag is set to 1, the content of the message will be interpreted as *a sequence of editor commands* which will be executed after receiving the message. If an error appears the editor immediately continues with the next command.

A third way of using the control flag is the communication between a special class of SDL tools (transformers) and the SDL editors (see § 14.5.3). In this case the control flag indicates certain types of messages like register the transformer to the editor, sending simple acknowledgements, etc.

The control flag is also used to indicate that the message contains the list of client information sent by the communication server (value "x"). In that case the message contains the following data:

- the number of clients
- for every client one entry consisting of:
  - the logical device number
  - the channel number
  - the node-id of the client machine
  - an end-of-client marker (newline character)
- an end-of-entries marker (NULL character)

Because the control flag is only used for the communication with SDL tools, tools that are not included in the SDL toolset and do not communicate with SDL tools (but want to communicate with other external tools via the communication server) are free to use the reserved area of the message header (e.g. the control flag) for their own purposes.

14.4 THE ROLE OF THE COMMUNICATION SERVER

The communication server is responsible for the correct distribution of the messages. It has to be started once if a communication is desired, subsequent attempts to start the communication server again are rejected. A tool which wants to communicate with

other tools has to open the communication by sending an open request together with its logical device number to the communication server. The communication server checks whether there are enough resources for that request. If the maximum number of channels is not occupied yet, the client will be assigned to a channel number and will be entered in the table of clients. The entries of the table of clients are arranged in order of the logical device numbers. If there is more than one request for the same logical device number, each entry for that number will get its own channel number and the entries will be arranged in chronological order.
The server supports two ways of communication between clients:

1. Sending via the channel number (direct addressing) or
2. Sending via the logical device number to the client who most recently opened the communication for that logical device number.

In both cases the server is informed about the send request. In the first case it redirects the message to the indicated channel number, in the second case it evaluates the corresponding channel number out of the table of clients and redirects the message to that channel.

The clients can request the current table of clients, to get the information about all other clients, who have opened the communication. Each entry consists of the logical device number, the channel number and the node identifcation of the client's workstation.

If a client wants to close the communication he sends a close request to the communication server. The communication server then deletes the corresponding entry from the table of clients.

14.5 INTEGRATION OF COMMUNICATION FACILITY INTO THE ENVIRONMENT

To integrate the communication facility into a tool, the tool programmer has to bind a special library to the application code. This section describes this communication library and two ways of using its functionality within the environment. One way is the use within the SDL editors and the other way shows the application of the communication mechanisms within transformer tools.

14.5.1 Communication library

For tools which want to communicate via the communication server a library of predefined functions exist. This library has to be bound to the application code. The following functions then can be used to communicate with other tools (which also have to use this library):

- **open_channel**: this function establishes the connection between the communication server and the calling client (register the client to the communication server). After an open_channel call an external tool is able to communicate with all clients known by the communication server. The desired logical device number of the tool must be given to the function. As a result the communication server delivers an identification handle that has to be used in subsequent communication calls (or a NULL if no channel can be opened).

- **send_msg**: this function is used to send messages to other clients or to the communication server itself. Messages that can be sent to the communication server are an implicit close (without using the close_channel function explicitly) and the request for the identification of all clients known to the communication server. The identification of the receiver must be specified in the header of the message.
- **receive_msg**: this function is used to receive messages from other registered clients or from the communication server itself (if a previous request for the identification of all clients was sent to the communication server). The distinction between messages received from a client or from the communication server is done by a control flag within the message header. A buffer in which the message can be written has to be provided by the receiving client. If no message is available, the function waits until one appears. As a result a status is delivered.
- **receive_cond_msg**: this function is the conditional form of receive_msg, i.e. it doesn't wait for a message if no one is available, but returns immediately with an appropriate status.
- **request_coord_list**: this function sends an explicit request to the communication server to send back a list of all clients that currently can participate in the communication, i.e. which tools are registered to the communication server. The return message (to be received by the sender via a normal receive_msg call) contains the overall number of clients and for each client the logical device number, the channel number and node identification.
- **close_channel**: this function indicates to the communication server that the client is no longer interested in communicating with other clients. The communication server removes the sender (and all the information attached to it) from its list of clients. If the tool subsequently want to participate in the communication again, another open_channel call is necessary.

In general there are no restrictions in using these functions, with two exceptions:

- the first command before sending or receiving any messages has to be "open_channel".
- the header of every message (11 bytes) is reserved and must contain certain information like sender and receiver identification or control flags (see § 14.3).

14.5.2 SDL editors

One way of using the communication facility is the general support of message exchange between tools done by the user of a tool. This kind of support is integrated in the SDL editors to give the user the freedom to send any kind of message, that is he is supported in using the functionality of the communication library. This support hides the communication protocoll by using forms, etc., to specify the receiver and the message itself.

The access to the communication facility within the SDL editors is done via a submenu of the menubar (see § 13.4), which provides the following items to support the user when he wants to communicate with other tools (because of the aspired freedom for the user, most of the library functions are more or less mapped to appropriate menu items):

- **open communication**: this command registers the tool as a communication client to the communication server. The logical device number (which is fixed) and the channel number (which is chosen by the communication server) of the tool are assigned automatically, so the user doesn't have to deal with this "low-level" information. Every tool has to give this command before it can send and receive messages. If the communication server is not running in the local area network, an error message appears.
- **close communication**: this command causes the communication server to remove the tool entry from its list of clients. The editor is no longer able to receive messages (until another "open communication" command).
- **send message**: when the user selects this menu item, a form appears in which the user has to fill in the message and has to specify to which tool resp. to which logical device and/or channel number the message should be send (and in the case of communicating with SDL editors whether the message contains commands or a command file name). After acknowledgement of the form the editor creates from the content of the form a message (with a header and a content) and sends this message to the communication server.
- **mbx only**: after selecting this item and acknowledgement of a confirmation form the tool can be controlled only via the communication interface, i.e. all mouse or keyboard events will be ignored. The tool remains in this mode until a "return to dialog" command was received.
- **show coord list**: this command opens a form which contains the table of client information known by the communication server. The table contains the assignment of logical device numbers to channel numbers and node ids.

14.5.3 Interactive transformers

The second way of using the communication facility within the SDL toolset is (semi-) automatic creation of diagrams. With the described mechanisms of the communication facility external tools are inter alia able to create diagrams automatically in the SDL editors. Such *transformer* tools can generate command files (that are internal descriptions of diagrams), which then are sent to the appropriate editor. The editor reads the command file and creates the diagrams automatically. In this way the creation of diagrams can be done without any user interaction.

In many cases this automatic creation is not desired or not feasable. Instead, the user wants to determine the kind of transformation and the layout of generated or transformed diagrams while he is working in an SDL editor. This requires the possibility to control parts of the external tool, for example the information which parts of a diagram should be transferred and to what position in the SDL editor. The DAX tools and the SC-PD integration tool are examples of such *interactive transformers* (see § 13). Simple converters from one data representation into another are also called transformers in the Siemens environment (see § 14.6).

The SDL editors support the connection to transformer tools with a set of special messages within the communication protocol. Transformers can register to an editor and can subsequently receive messages from that editor. Some of the messages are sent by user request, others are acknowledgements to transformer messages.

The usual communication between an editor and a transformer follows these steps:

1. After starting the editor and the transformer (and loading the diagram to be transferred into the transformer) both tools register themselves to the communication server.
2. Then the transformer registers itself to the editor by sending a special message to it. The editor now knows that a transformer wants to be informed about user requests.
3. The editor acknowledges the registration.
4. The user can now work with the editor in the normal way. Also during multiple requests to the transformer he can edit his diagram to correct or enhance it.
5. The user selects the part of the diagram that should be transferred within the transformer
6. By selecting either the item "cut" or "copy" from the "transfer request" submenu of the editor the user requests for the selected diagram portion. The information whether the diagram portion is moved (cut) or copied from the transformer, together with the coordinates where this portion should appear in the editor (the current mouse cursor position) is sent to the transformer.
7. The transformer generates from its selected diagram parts appropriate editor commands (with consideration of the mouse cursor position) and sends these commands to the editor.
8. The commands will be executed within the editor and the generated symbols appear at the desired position in a window of the editor. The editor doesn't know that the commands were generated by a transformer. If during the execution the special command "send acknowledge" is recognized, the editor sends the result of the last command to the transformer.
9. If the user stops the communication or quits the editor, the connected transformer receives a special quit message from the editor. It can react to this disconnection in any way, e.g. wait for interactive user input or quit itself.

14.6 NON-INTERACTIVE TOOLS

Another aspect of control integration is the use of smaller tools that don't need to interact with a user. In the Siemens environment there are several such non-interactive tools that can be called from the command line. They only need a set of call parameters to do their job. Most of these tools are simply converters which transform data from one representation into another (e.g. SDL descriptions from textual to graphical representation and vice versa). But two non-converter tools are special:

- PD-STAN is a tool that performs static analysis of SDL process diagrams. It works on files which the user has created with the PD editor. The tool analyzes diagrams, processes, libraries or complete systems. Besides writing the results in an analysis protocol the tool is able to generate a command file which - when it is executed in the PD editor - shows errors in a graphical way.

- PD-INFO is a tool that reports several kind of information about SDL processes, states and procedures in tables (e.g. state transition tables). Before using the PD-INFO tool the analysis tool has to be called, because PD-INFO works on the files of certain types of analysis results. Some input information is also gained from the process diagram files created with the PD editor.

Because the static analysis is a valuable function in the PD editor as well, there is a possibility to call the PD-STAN tool from within the editor. One implicit call is performed every time the user tries to save a complete diagram in a process library (only correct diagrams can be saved in process libraries). To analyze a diagram or process during editing an explicit call can be done using the menu item "syntax". In both cases the PD editor creates an appropriate call of the PD-STAN tool, depending on some internal information (kind of file to save, symbol under cursor when selecting "syntax", etc.).

The user need not to know that the analysis is actually done by a separate tool. He doesn't have to deal with call parameters, filenames, options, etc., because the editor knows from the context of the work which kind of analysis is appropriate and generates all the required parameters automatically.

The same goes for the results of an analysis. If errors have occurred during the analysis, the user does not to have deal with textual information about errors in protocol files. Instead, with the means of command files the editor visualizes the faulty parts of the diagram and the user can correct them immediately.

14.7 PROBLEMS/EXPERIENCES

Once a tool is registered to the communication server, messages from other tools may arrive asynchronously. There is no explicit notification mechanism. This concept allows the control of other tools in a "batch mode", but this turns out to be a drawback when a user interacts with the tool at the same time. The user of a SDL editor for instance has no possibility to prevent the execution of commands sent by another tool.

This problem arises from the way incoming messages are handled by the framework component DIAMON (see chapter § 13): When the communication server forwards a message to the receiver, the event handler of the DIAMON receives a special event (before an "open communication" command is given these events are ignored by the event handler). This event causes the execution of a predefined function (a so-called action routine). In the case of the SDL editors this action routine handles the receipt and interpretation of the message.

During the execution of the action routine all other events are ignored. That is when a communication event arises, no further work can be done until the message is received and treated. This fact can be seen in the way that communication events implicitly have a higher priority than normal events (mouse clicks, menu selection, etc.), which can lead to confusion. Consequently, if the communication mechanism is not used in the normal batch mode, participants of the communication must synchronize their actions very well. Every external tool that wants to participate in the communication has to provide such an action routine which handles the incoming messages and especially such a routine must be secure in the sense that no deadlock situation can arise, because while waiting for a communication event the user can't control the tool interactively and therefore he does not have the chance to stop the communication (or even the whole tool).

15

Data Integration

Integration of data within the Siemens system engineering environment is obtained by applying object-oriented implementation techniques and tools, in particular by using the same object-oriented data definition language (the same "object model" respectively the same "data model") and the same library of data management functions in all the tools. Each tool of the environment has its own database. The tools do not operate on a common database. But since all tools work with the same notion of objects and thus "speak the same language", the private database of a tool may be easily accessed by the other tools. It is easy to implement interfaces for the exchange of data between the various tools (see § 15.2), and this has been done as explained in more detail in § 11.7). There the integration across lifecycle phases of the toolset is discussed. In § 15.1 an overview about the object oriented implementation tool TOROS is given. In § 15.2 it is shown how data may be exchanged between different tools. The Common Interchange Format (PR/CIF) may be used for the exchange of data between SDL tools of different vendors. § 15.3 presents the transformation tools in the Siemens environment generating the CIF-format and transforming data in CIF-format into the database format of the environment. Aspects of version control, in particular the handling of existing data, when new versions of the tools are developed, are discussed in § 15.4, and object oriented aspects are considered in § 15.5.

15.1 OBJECT MODEL

All tools of the Siemens system engineering environment are implemented by use of TOROS (Toolkit for Object and Relation Oriented System, [DSV91, SD91]). TOROS is a hybrid development tool integrating various types and styles of programming. Its core is an object oriented programming system built on top of the procedural language C. TOROS provides the following facilities for application development:

- The C language as the basis.
- The data definition language (better class definition language) OBER (Object Based Language for Engineering Requirements) to be used for the definition of the object oriented part of an application.
- A precompiler for the OBER language, compiling OBER declarations into C.

Tool Integration: Environments and Frameworks, Edited by D. Schefström and G. van den Broek

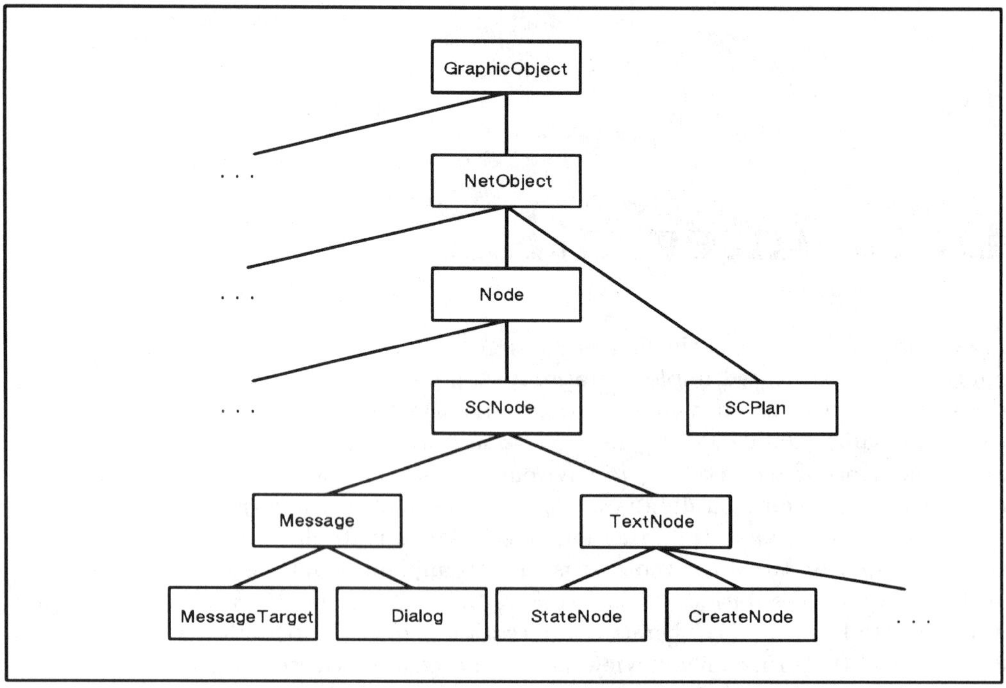

Figure 15.1 Part of the SC Editor's class hierarchy

- TOROS-BASE, a predefined hierarchy of classes with functions to manipulate and manage data.
- A flexible, fully compiled rule language.

The graphics library VGI (cf. § 13.2) is a TOROS class library and is also part of the TOROS environment. In an application the predefined class hierarchies TOROS-BASE and TOROS-VGI are extended by the application specific classes, for instance by the classes of the editor for sequence charts (cf. 15.2). The rule system of TOROS was not used in the development of the tools.

The OBER language satisfies all the requirements for a modern object oriented programming language. It provides

- declarative description of classes of objects,
- creation of class hierarchies with inheritance,
- creation of semantic networks,
- generation of runtime-readable meta-information (information about the structure of object classes),
- message passing.

The data definition language OBER is used to establish a class hierarchy, to attach procedures (methods) to the classes, and to describe the relations between objects. Figure 15.1 shows parts of the OBER class hierarchy of the implementation of the Sequence Chart editor.

Attributes are used to express the environment-independent property structure of classes and their objects. OBER adopts C's strict typing of attribute values, i.e. each

```
CLASS Message;
  SUBCLASS OF SCNode;
  ATTRIBUTES:   MESSAGE_POINTS: S[ ];
                MESSAGE_NAME: C[ ];
                MAX_ID: S;
  RELATIONS:    PARTNER: (R=B) -> (CreateNode), (Dialog);
  FUNCTIONS:    CHECK_COPY: check_copy_message();
                CHECK_MOVE: check_move_message();
                MODIFY: modify_message();
```

Figure 15.2 Example of an OBER class definition

attribute can assume only values of a specific C-type. The main data types of C (char, short, int, long, float, double) are permitted, as well as arrays of fixed or variable dimension of such types.

Relations serve to express relationships between objects, including objects of different classes. They thus describe the embedding of an object in its environment. In contrast to attributes, relations are object-valued variables. Since relations can take sets of objects as values, (1:n)-relations between objects can be represented. For instance, the symbols in a sequence chart are stored in a relation 'contains' defined in class SC_PLAN.

Facets are used to attach additional information to classes, attributes and relations. Facets are class specific variables and may be used, for instance, to express restrictions of the cardinality of a relation.

Messages are another type of class-specific variables. They are function-valued. If an object receives a message, the TOROS message handler invokes the function (method) declared in the corresponding message slot in the object's class. Methods are implemented as normal C-functions by the programmer.

An example of an OBER class definition, taken from the SC editor, is shown in figure 15.2.

The OBER precompiler output consists of

- definitions of the object structures,
- meta-information,
- symbolic identifiers for all defined classes, attributes, relations, facets and messages.

All the information contained in the class definitions is available at runtime for the application as so-called meta-information. The meta-information corresponds to the schema information in databases. Reading the meta-information the application knows at runtime about the structure of the object classes. For example it may ask for the names and datatypes of the slots of some class. The availability of meta-information is the basis for the data management functions provided by TOROS which are described below. It is also exploited in the solution for updating existing data when new versions of the tools are produced and the underlying class model changes ("schema evolution"). The generation of a complete meta-information clearly distinguishes OBER from other C-based object oriented languages such as C++ where almost no meta-information is accessible to the application at runtime.

The library TOROS-BASE comprises methods and functions to manage data. In this context data are objects, more precisely, instances of TOROS classes. For example, TOROS-BASE provides services for

- creating, copying and deleting objects,
- reading and writing attribute and relation values,
- handling bidirectional relations between objects,
- invocation of active values by write and read access to slots,
- storage: writing a backup copy of sets of objects to external media,
- loading: reading sets of objects from external media with restoration of all interconnections (relations).

The database functionality provided by the two latter services allows the working with persistent objects in an application. This is crucial for the development of the tools in the Siemens environment. Each created TOROS object is assigned to a so-called object set, and object sets can be saved to external (UNIX-)files, called object files, as in object databases, and such object files can conversely be read (loaded). When an object set is loaded the references (relations) to other loaded object sets are restored. The partition of objects into object sets is defined by the application. A binary format is used for the external object files to guarantee efficient saving and loading procedures. TOROS can provide general storage and loading functions for objects because the meta-information is available at runtime. From the meta-information the storage and loading functions obtain all the relevant information about the structure of objects (e.g. types of attributes).

All tools of the Siemens environment use these TOROS data management functions: AKL models, sequence charts, process diagrams, etc. are stored in TOROS object files. The tools therefore use the same model of objects, defined by the TOROS-language OBER. This fact facilitates the data integration in the environment.

Each tool has its own database consisting of TOROS object files, where the user data (about AKL models, sequence charts, process diagrams, ...) are stored. Today there is no underlying common database based on a uniform data model for all tools. Nevertheless the tools are closely integrated and may exchange data (cf. § 15.2). It is planned for the future to supplement the environment by a common database.

The tools do not directly provide multi-user support and LAN/WAN distribution. From our point of view good tools already exist to support these features, and the tools within the Siemens environment can interact with these tools. For example to solve multi-user problems occuring during cooperative work in teams you may put the TOROS-objectfiles into a project library of some configuration management tool like DSEE [DSE88] or SCCS [SCC89].

15.2 EXCHANGE OF DATA BETWEEN TOOLS

Since all tools of the Siemens environment are implemented by the TOROS system, they work with the same notion of objects and thus "speak the same language". We take advantage of this fact in the integration of the various tools. For example there is a tool integrating the editor for sequence charts (SC editor) and the editor for SDL process diagrams (PD editor). It is called SDL-integration tool (SDL-IT, see § 11.7.3) and, among other things, generates (partial) process diagrams from sequence charts. In the following it is sketched how the data are transferred from the SC editor to the PD editor by the tool SDL-IT.

The SC editor stores the data describing a sequence chart in a TOROS object set. There is a functional interface to these object sets, called SC-Handler, which provides access to the sequence chart data for other tools. Now the SDL-IT reads the information about a sequence chart in the corresponding TOROS object set by use of the SC-Handler, generates parts of process diagrams from this information and passes them to the PD editor. The resulting partial process diagrams may then be completed by use of the PD editor. The SC-Handler runs as a separate UNIX-process. The SDL-IT communicates with the SC-Handler by means of the communication facilities (see § 14). We mentioned a common database for the tools in the previous section. Of course, integration tools may get a lot of information from this database. But the functional interfaces like the SC-Handler will still be necessary for a really powerful integration tool. The reason is that these interfaces provide direct access to all data generated by the corresponding tool including graphical information. Tools like the SDL-IT as interactive tools with graphical interface which, for instance, allow objects to be transfer from one editor to another simply by mouse-click, require access to the graphical information (e.g. of a sequence chart). But of course it would not be possible to store also all the graphical data generated by a tool into a (e.g. relational) database without serious efficiency problems.

Another integration tool, DAX/PD (see § 11.7.3), enables the user to transfer results obtained during requirements analysis with the method AKL and the editor KLAR to design by SDL. Components become processes, data streams become messages between processes in this transfer. Basically the data from the KLAR editor to the PD editor are transferred as follows. The KLAR editor, implemented by TOROS, stores the data of an AKL model in a binary or, alternatively, in an ASCII-TOROS object file. DAX/PD gets the the data to be transferred from the ASCII-object file, generates parts of process diagrams from this information and, as the SDL-IT, passes them to the PD editor. The integration tool DAX/SC (see also § 11.7.3) works in a similar way. By use of this tool data may be transferred from the KLAR editor to the SC editor.

15.3 THE COMMON INTERCHANGE FORMAT FOR SDL

For the users of tools it is often desirable or even necessary to be able to exchange data between different toolsets and environments. Since SDL is a language with the standardized format SDL-PR ("phrase representation") for block and process diagrams, such an exchange was already possible to a certain degree in the past. But SDL-PR does not contain any layout information of the diagrams. And because the SDL-toolset with graphical interfaces has become more widespread in the SDL-community, the demand to exchange also layout information has also increased.

Therefore the Common Interchange Format (CIF) was defined [MW91]. It is a format for the layout and semantics of SDL diagrams. It uses SDL-PR for the semantics and a subset of CGM (Computer Graphics Metafile, cf. [ISO87]) for the layout information.

15.4 ASPECTS OF VERSION CONTROL

Usually documents and components of documents produced in a project (analysis, design documents, sources, ...) exist in several versions. These versions must be controlled. Thus in a project we have the need to control the versions of AKL models, sequence charts, process diagrams, ... produced by applying the corresponding tools.

The tools do not include functionality for controlling versions. But since the Siemens environment may be connected to any configuration system, each project may use its own configuration management for this purpose. For example, most projects working on Siemens Nixdorf WS 30 / Apollo Domain workstations use DSEE [Apo85] and administrate the different versions of models, charts and diagrams by putting the corresponding TOROS object sets into a DSEE project library.

Concerning versions there is another problem. New versions of the tools are developed. This usually means that the TOROS class model of the tool is modified, e.g. new classes are defined, attributes and relations are added or deleted. This means that the model of the data, the schema, is changed, and we have the problem that existing data produced previously by the tool, for example data on process diagrams, must be converted to the new data model (class model). How do we solve this problem of schema evolution in the Siemens environment?

The features of the TOROS system, in particular the generation of meta-information, allow a rather easy solution. For each tool, e.g. the PD editor, we implemented a transformation tool converting existing object sets to the data format of the new version. This program includes the meta-information of the old tool version and the meta-information of the new version. Thus it knows all about the old class model and all about the new class model at runtime, and it is now an easy matter for the tool to read an object set produced by the old tool version and transform it to an object set which corresponds to the class model of the new tool version. Therefore upgrading e.g. from SDL to OSDL from the PD editor's point of view is no problem, if the new object set is an extension of the old one.

The availabilibity of meta-information turns out to be very useful for an easy solution of this version control problem.

15.5 OBJECT ORIENTATION

In the first section the object oriented implementation of the environment was briefly discussed. In the second section it was sketched how object oriented analysis and design is supported by the methods AKL and SDL respectively the corresponding tools.

15.5.1 Support of object oriented analysis and design

Object oriented techniques for analysis and design are getting more and more popular in system development (see e.g. [CY90] and [SM88] on object oriented analysis).

The analysis and design tools of the environment support fundamental concepts of object orientation and may well be used for the analysis and design of object oriented systems. In fact all the tools were implemented in an object oriented way, and we developed the tools by applying the methods AKL and SDL and early versions of the tools during the analysis and design phase.

In contrast to the classical functional approaches to requirements analysis like SA or SADT, the analysis method AKL supports a dual view on functions and objects. The engineer not only describes the required functions (tasks) of a system but simultaneously also the objects (components) which perform or are manipulated by these functions. Both functions and objects form a part-of-hierarchy: A function may consist of several subfunctions and an object (a component) may consist of several subobjects (subcomponents). In addition each function is explicitly connected by a relation to those objects which perform this function. If a function is not performed by a unique object, the function has to be decomposed further and analysis has to be continued.

Hence, basically, what we do when applying the method AKL and the KLAR editor is to identify objects and their assembly structure and the services of objects. In Coad / Yourdon's terminology [CY90] this means to establish the "object layer", the "service layer" and essential parts of the "structure layer". Their "structure layer" usually also contains a classification structure reflecting class-member organization and generalization-specialization. Such a classification is not part of the method AKL, but you may use the KLAR editor to describe classes, instances and class hierarchies.

Therefore the KLAR editor and the underlying method AKL already include essential elements of object oriented analysis, and therefore we call them object based.

SDL on the other hand is an inherently object oriented method. Processes may be considered as objects and vice versa. The process type concept of SDL corresponds to the class concept in object orientation. Objects/processes communicate by exchanging messages. The reaction of a process to a message depends on the type (class) of the process (object). It also depends on the state of the process/object. An incoming message is considered as an event in the process and triggers a state transition. Though object oriented programming languages like C++ often do not have an explicit notion of state (the state is implicitly given by the current values of the instance variables), most authors on object oriented analysis and design agree that objects take on states during their lifecycle and that the behaviour depends on their state [SM88]. Process diagrams describe the dynamic behaviour of an object. Sequence charts may be used to describe the communication between several interacting objects.

What's missing in standard SDL and also missing in the Siemens system engineering environment today is the concept of class hierarchies (process type hierarchies) and inheritance. This defect will be remedied by the introduction of object oriented SDL (OSDL, see [MPBD87]).

16

Outlook and Conclusion

16.1 EXPERIENCES WITH THE SIEMENS SYSTEM ENGINEERING ENVIRONMENT

The main application areas of the Siemens system engineering environment are the domains of automation and telecommunication. Within ATMOSPHERE the environment was used in a pilot project dealing with telecommunication.

In order to be able to use the facilities of the tool chain from analysis to design, implementation and test in full and consistently, a custom process manager for the target operating system SORIX has been developed within the project (see § 11.7.4, Process Manager).

The experience gained in the pilot project with respect to the use of methods and tools - in particular on the basis of comparisons with previous projects which had been carried out without this support and systematics - were absolutely positive in two aspects: error free communication of the persons participating in the creation process and also with regard to software engineering criteria such as structuring, separate processability, clearness, automatic documentation creation, etc.

We also applied the methods AKL and SDL and early versions of the tools for the development of newer versions and of the integration tools. Beside these applications AKL and SDL the corresponding tools are used in several projects in automation and telecommunication as parts of the software engineering environment SIGRAPH-SET (see § 11.7). The experiences gained with the methods and the tools were positive in the same aspects as in the pilot project. That is productivity has increased

- by structuring the problems,
- by methodical proceedings supported by powerful tools,
- by earlier recognition of defects.

16.2 EXPERIENCES DURING THE DEVELOPMENT OF THE INTEGRATION TOOLS

The main problem during the development of the integration tools was the methodical question of how to transfer the results of one phase to the next, e.g. an AKL model to SDL process diagrams.

Tool Integration: Environments and Frameworks, Edited by D. Schefström and G. van den Broek

From the existing editors point of view like the KLAR and PD editors there arose no problems. The data of the diagrams created with these editors were available, and both editors have open interfaces to communicate with other tools. Therefore nothing had to be done on the editors.

16.3 OUTLOOK

What has to be done in the future is to extend the attribute "object based" of the methods to "object oriented". That is to extend the method AKL with the concept of class hierarchies (process type hierarchies), relations between objects and inheritance. As mentioned in § 15.5, OSDL is going to be standardized by the CCITT and so the object oriented aspects become part of SDL. The graphical editors like KLAR and PD will be enhanced by these additional features in the future.

For the implementation and test phase a code-generator for object oriented programming languages like C++ has to be developed as well as an object oriented test system.

The integration aspect - in addition to the transformation tools like DAX/SC and DAX/PD - will be supported by integrating a data dictionary as a common data pool for all of the tools within the environment.

Part IV

Communication Systems Software Engineering Environment

Ger van den Broek
Philips Research
Prof. Holstlaan 4
5656 AA Eindhoven
The Netherlands

Tool Integration: Environments and Frameworks, Edited by D. Schefström and G. van den Broek

17

Introduction

17.1 BACKGROUND

The "Communication Systems" subproject aims at improving the *current* way of working in the application area. This means that a rather evolutionary approach towards integrated environments has been adopted. The subproject followed the concept of "technology pull" in contrast to a "technology push". This means that (most of) the activities within the subproject are discussed (and agreed upon) with representatives of the intended user community (the Communication Systems product division of Philips Electronics). In this way acceptance by the user is facilitated and backed by senior management. The rationale of the introduction of an environment is based on:

1. One can recognize several application domains within the area of developing communication systems. However they have a lot of commonality.
2. Product and process quality are tremendously enhanced if the software development activities are carried out according to common methods and tools. Especially so, if the methods and tools are integrated (viz. using another method or tool introduces no discontinuity in the work).
3. The overall costs of the product division software development are expected to be less, if the business units within the product division use the same methods and tools offered. The benefits are:
   (a) Easier transfer of information, projects and software engineers.
   (b) Reduce the problems related to joint projects.
   (c) More efficient education and training programmes.
   (d) Developing and maintaining one software development environment is much cheaper.
   (e) Even smaller development centres can afford a software development environment.

The mission is to realize, within four years (1991 — 1994), a software development environment that can be applied by the various business units of the Communication Systems product division. Since there was no standard framework with industrial quality implementations available at the start of the project, tool development and integration activities are done in a way that implementation on different frameworks remains feasible. This resulted in an approach where the integration will be based on

Tool Integration: Environments and Frameworks, Edited by D. Schefström and G. van den Broek

intra tool-set integration and an environment is considered to be a set of tool-sets. Most of the tool-sets support a specific method in the analysis, design, realization or testing phase but they must be able to cooperate with a configuration management system. An evolutionary approach was taken to construct such an environment, starting from existing tool-sets, defining the required interoperability, and developing the required interfaces (filters or transformation tools). The intra tool-set integration is implemented using SoftBench, which concentrates on control integration across tool-sets and using OSF/Motif for the interactive tools. Data integration is still on the level of using files as a data exchange mechanism.

17.2 DOMAIN CHARACTERISTICS

Communication Systems are very complex systems which serve to provide a wide variety of communication services to a wide class of users. The classical role of communication services is to convey information from one place to another, but as communication systems have evolved over the years, many more tasks have been integrated into them — beginning with accounting, management of routing information and data-protection and security. Traditionally, stored-programme control systems contain already complex computer software subsystems. The introduction of computer networks at the location of the end users has led to a further level of integration — which means that by now personal computer networks, office automation computers and switching systems should all be considered part of the area of "communication systems". Although efficient algorithms and dedicated hardware play an important role, the most dominant characteristic of the application domain is the complexity of the systems. In particular, their specification is a most difficult task. For example in public telephony peculiarities of national networks (routing strategies, charging, national services and regulation, signalling systems, the integration with mobile radio) and the diversity of stored-programme control systems require both an accurate specification of what is wanted and an accurate analysis of what is offered on the market. These aspects motivate the study of specification methods that can ensure the efficient production of reliable specifications. It is also clear that the system specification and production processes themselves become more and more difficult to master; they require sophisticated methods and tools for system specification (formal methods like, e.g., COLD and LOTOS), system description (traditionally SDL) and configuration management.

Telecommunication applications are often extremely large and normally distributed over a heterogeneous hardware. Response time demands are forcing execution in parallel. Another important issue is the requirement for a high degree of reliability. The systems are long lived (30-40 years) and usually a large number of variants must be supported which puts extreme demands on their adaptability, maintainability and extensibility.

The development and maintenance of telecommunication applications is in itself a special problem. The development projects are very large and often distributed over several sites, sometimes in different countries, and in several cases even done by different companies. Which means that one must be able to cope with different organisational structures, different working procedures and different cultures. The maintenance is often also distributed over several countries. During operation, the system interacts with other systems developed by other parties.

These characteristics influence to a large extent the absorption of changes into the way of working and are the reason that changes are introduced in an incremental way (evolution not revolution).

The overall goal: "a single environment to support software development" does not immediately lead to a specification. A lot remains to be discovered and uncovered (and decided) during the construction of the SDE. That is the main reason why the an evolutionary approach is selected. In this way, the activities can be (re)directed to the requirements as they become apparent during the construction of the SDE.

The goals within this subproject from Atmosphere with respect to environment building and tool integration could be defined as:

- integration within tool-sets to enable a closer cooperation between tools (SDT)
- integration across tool-sets to support the concepts of method integration (SDL-VHDL, LOTOS-SDL, ASN.1-SDL and SDT-PKI)
- construction of a an environment consisting of a number of tool-sets (SoftBench based environment)

17.3 DEVELOPMENT PROCESS

The software development environment effort in communication systems products has increased significantly during the last ten years. In 1979, a strategic decision was made to develop a tailor-made software development environment for communication systems. The kernel of this development environment is the Specification and Design Language: SDL (see section 17.4). At the moment, a development environment exists at the business unit in Nürnberg, an environment which is fully accepted by the developers. In cooperation with the Information and Software Technology unit from Philips Research, steps are being taken to ensure the further evolution and introduction of this environment within other business units.

The development process can be seen as a number of consecutive phases. In the analysis phase (also called system design phase) a static refinement in blocks occurs. This refinement is normally done according to functional or hardware-oriented aspects, or a mixture of both. In the second phase the dynamics of the system are described by means of "interworkings" between these blocks. In this way the communication behaviour of the system is described. Depending on the complexity of the system, the blocks are refined in several sets until the level of "SDL-processes" is reached. Each design step contains static (blocks or processes) and dynamic (interworkings) descriptions. The static refinements result partly in the SDL data dictionary, while the final interworkings are further refined in detailed SDL process specifications. During the implementation phase a "virtual machine" is developed. This virtual machine is a collection of sequential procedures implemented in a conventional programming language. The complete code production is finally achieved by connecting different tool calls linking the SDL and the virtual machine layer of the software. The integration and maintenance phase are supported by additional tools as debugging and tracing tools as well as documentation tools.

During the development a large number of tool-sets or tools are used and data passed between these tools as files in a workspace which can be accessed by the tool-sets. This means that it is of great importance to have a consistent set of files. The configuration management procedures however depend to a large extent on the product structure and organizational procedures (see [Ber84, BD91]). A configuration management tool helps to maintain consistent configurations of source files. The files, needed in the workspace where the tool sets operate, can be extracted from the repository maintained by the configuration management system.

The main methodology is based on the following concepts:

- The methodology supports the the development process from the analysis phase to the maintenance phase. During the analysis phase mainly the SDL concept is used. From the design phase the methodology is supported by the formal SDL mechanism.
- SDL software has a clear three layer structure covering control, data manipulation, and run-time support.
- The methodology supports a clear separation of descriptions for control, data objects, and configuration.
- SDL as specification language is easy to learn and software written in SDL is easy to understand.

Currently the methodology is extended by the use of ASN.1. This methodology could be used for protocol oriented tasks. A set of tools is developed to support the translation from ASN.1 notation to SDL and C code.

17.4 THE FORMAL SPECIFICATION LANGUAGE SDL

SDL, the Specification and Description language is an international standard language for the specification and description of systems. It has been developed and standardized by CCITT (International Telegraph and Telephone Consultative Committee).

The development started in the 70s. The latest version is SDL 88 which is considered to have reached such maturity that any changes are not of current interest. Early versions of SDL have been in use for a long time. The experience from this use has contributed to the improvement of the language.

Within CCITT, the work with optional additions to SDL continues. An improved version with additional concepts will be presented at the beginning of 1992. The updated standard will be called SDL 92.

17.4.1 Field of application

Today SDL is mainly known within the telecommunications field. However, it has a broader field of application. The application areas of SDL can be summarized as follows:

- type of system: real-time, interactive, distributed
- type of information: behaviour and structure
- level of abstraction: overview to detail

17.4.2 The benefits of a specification language

Despite the long history of SDL, it is a fact that we see today only the beginning of the era of specification languages. It is widely accepted that the key to success of a system is a thorough system specification and design. This requires however a suitable specification language, satisfying the following needs:

- a well defined set of concepts
- unambiguous, clear, precise and concise specifications
- a basis for analyzing specifications for completeness and correctness
- a basis for determining conformance of implementations to specifications
- a basis for determining consistency of specifications relative to each other
- use of computer based tools to create, maintain, analyze, simulate and translate specifications

The use of a specification language makes it possible to analyze and simulate alternative system solutions, which in practice are impossible when using a programming language due to the cost and the time delay. A specification language offers a well defined set of concepts for the user of the language, improving his capability to produce a solution to a problem and to reason about the solution.

SDL has been defined to meet these demands. The language has a graphic syntax which is extremely intuitive. Even non-constructors can quickly obtain an overview of a system's structure and behaviour. A most important characteristic of SDL is that it is formal. The semantics behind each symbol and concept are precisely defined. But above all, the great strength of SDL is in describing large real-time systems. SDL provides the instrument with which to describe and understand the extra dimensions real-time applications possess compared with traditional applications: time and concurrent activities. SDL has been developed to enable people behind the technology to communicate with one another in an intuitive way, and to be able to understand what exactly is to be created, in a comprehensible manner. SDL provides the engineer with a whole battery of concepts to support the development process, concepts which we already use intuitively every day.

17.4.3 Main concepts in SDL

The two major properties of SDL are the ability to describe structure and behaviour. Structure can be subdivided into two concepts: static and dynamic structure.

The static structure or distribution of a system is defined in terms of Blocks and Channels, see figure 17.1. A Block is perceived as a module with the well known "black box" as its model. With concepts such as Block and Channels it is possible to define clear interfaces between structural units in a system. Blocks can reside in other Blocks, and this structural description can be recursively refined until, in the end, one is describing the dynamic structure.

The dynamic structure is defined with the help of the Process concept, an independent device which reacts to stimuli in the form of Signals (events), see figure 17.2. Signals travel through channels between blocks, and from one process to another via signal routes.

The system's behaviour is described within one or more processes. The model behind the processes is the Finite State Machine. A process is always to be found in a State.

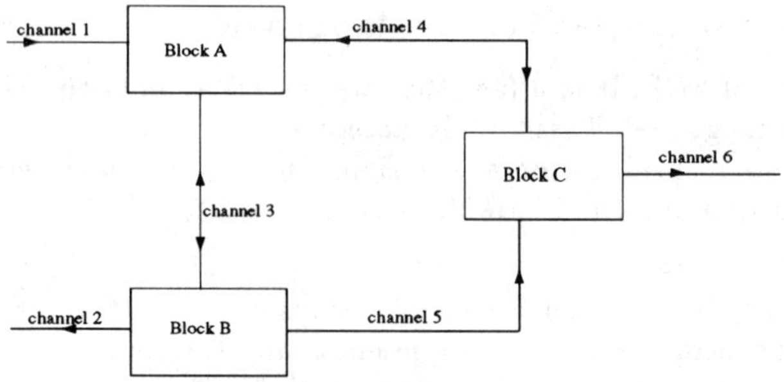

Figure 17.1 Static structure

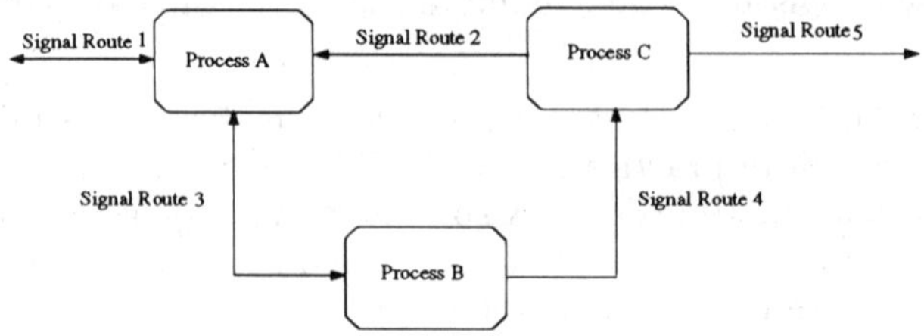

Figure 17.2 Dynamic structure

Via stimuli from its environment or from within itself, the machine is induced into transiting from one state to another. The model for the process is, moreover, further enhanced with a number of utilizable concepts. During transition a process can carry out such activities as the dynamic creation of other processes and procedure calls.

Signals are information carriers between processes. A signal in its simplest form is a semaphore or a flag which stimulates the process into transiting. Here the information is at a minimum. More information can be carried by the signals, from simple variables, via compound variable structures, to abstract data types. These abstract data types can contain not only a self-defined complex value-set, but also those functions which operate on this value-set.

Having a whole range of types of information carriers which the signals accept, facilitates the specification of higher forms of communication between coordinated processes and the system's environment. Signalling in SDL is by nature asynchronous; synchronous signalling is specified with the help of timers and a behavioural description in the process.

Figure 17.3 shows how the graphic notation for the finite state machine appears in SDL. The classic informal notation (of bows and circles) is used in the State symbols and the Flow-lines, however with a different appearance. Insignals have been encapsulated in a symbol with easily recognizable characteristics.

We can clearly see that if the process is in state A it will transit either for insignal S1 or S3. In the former, the process lands in state B, and, in the latter, in state C.

During transition, the process can communicate with itself or with other processes. This is represented by the output symbol. State, insignal and outsignal constitute the fundamental building blocks in the finite state machine.

In SDL, the diagramming facilities have been expanded, see figure 17.4, using more building blocks, so that more complex descriptions can be shown. Decision controls the

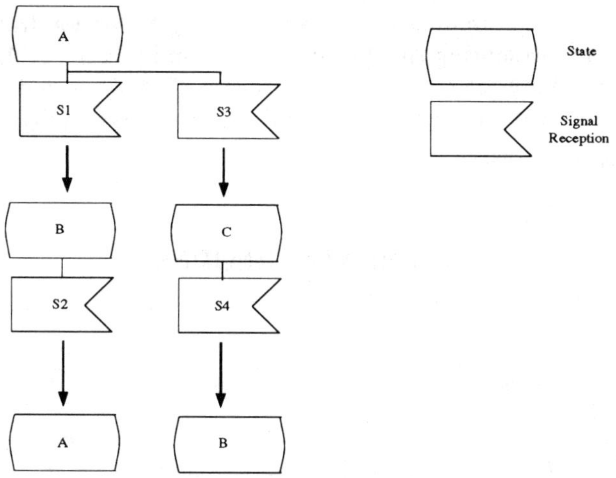

Figure 17.3 The SDL finite state machine

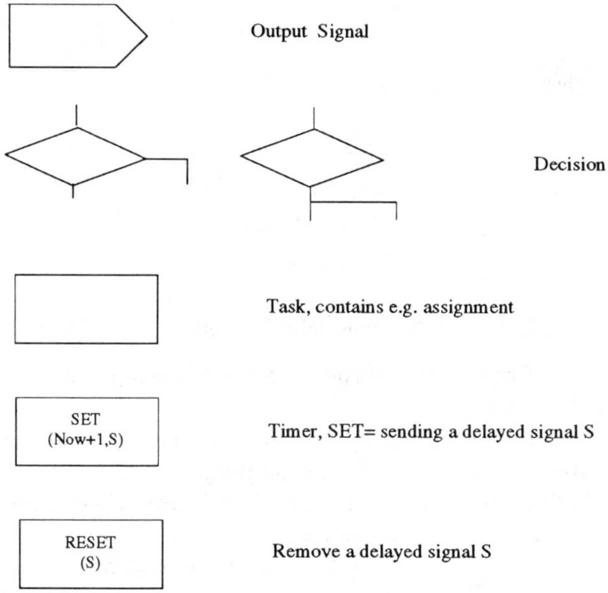

Figure 17.4 Extensions to the finite state machine symbols

route the transition takes depends on the evaluation of the logical expression contained within the symbol. This construction corresponds to the "case" and "if" statements in high level languages, the difference being that here we modulate a control flow's alternative routes, rather than a data flow's.

Assignment statements also have their direct equivalent in the Task symbol. A task can, for example, contain a variable assignment. The figure shows another example of assignment, namely a timer, an internal alarm clock, which is assigned a time. When a given time is reached in the system, the timer ensures that a signal is sent to the process. Using a timer, one can elegantly modulate a system's time-flow.

The dynamic structure of a system is also directed during transition from one state to another. The symbols representing this behaviour, shown in figure 17.5, are Create Request and Stop. Create Request creates a new process of the specified type, whilst Stop indicates that the process has reached its final state and is thereby terminated.

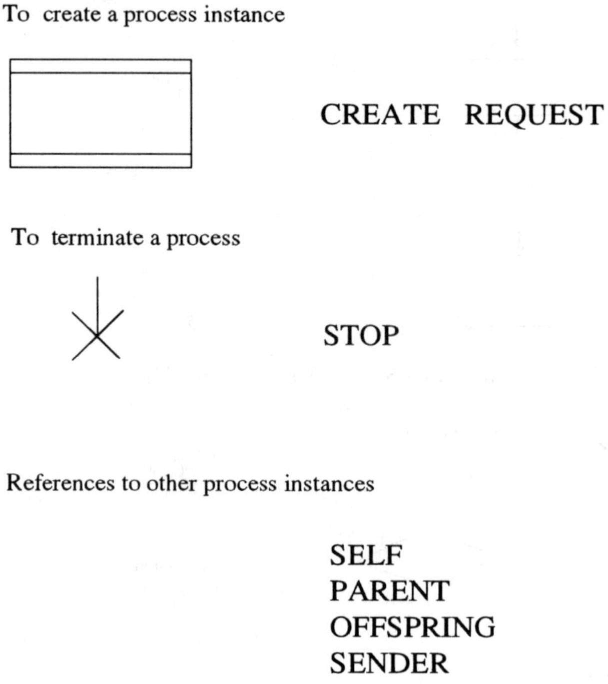

Figure 17.5 Dynamic symbols

There are also a number of predefined variables for referencing other processes, e.g. self, parent, offspring and sender.

In SDL the widely spread and accepted abstract data types have been chosen. These are to be found in most modern implementation languages. In their simplest form the concepts differ very little from such languages as Pascal, but when fully utilized the engineer has a powerful instrument at his disposal.

Figure 17.6 shows how the predefined type Boolean is defined with an abstract data type.

The user can also use the predefined data elements as integer, real, natural, boolean, character, charstring, duration, etc., and generators for handling of strings, arrays, records, etc.

17.4.4 SDL graphical and textual representation

SDL is available in two representations both standardized by CCITT. The textual form is mainly used as a transport format between different SDL-tools. The graphical form is used as the main input and output format for a user friendly interaction.

```
NEWTYPE Boolean;

LITERALS True, False;

OPERATORS
  ''NOT'':  Boolean -> Boolean;
  ''AND'':  Boolean,Boolean -> Boolean;
  ''OR'' :  Boolean,Boolean -> Boolean;
  ''=>'' :  Boolean,Boolean -> Boolean;

AXIOMS
  ''NOT'' (True) = False;
  ''NOT'' (False)= True;
  ''AND'' (A,B)  = IF A=False THEN False ELSE B FI;
  ''OR'' (A,B)   = IF A=True  THEN True  ELSE B FI;
  ''=>'' (A,B)   = IF A=True AND B=False
                   THEN False ELSE True;
```

Figure 17.6 Literals: enumerate the total value set that Boolean can accept
Operators: enumerate those operations which are valid for this type
Axioms: set up a framework for the results arising from the operations when these are applied to the value set.

17.4.5 SDL summary

The intention of this short introduction to SDL is to demonstrate SDL's features, which can be summarized as follows:

- The language supplies the engineer with concepts for an hierarchical structuring of the system, and describes behaviour at various layer levels. These concepts are necessary in order to provide the technology to enable the creation of these complex systems.
- Using blocks and channels we can define clear interfaces between modules. Signals define the information carriers which stimulate the process into transiting. Concurrency and the dynamic properties of a real-time system are exactly reflected in these terms.
- The language's graphical syntax provides an almost intuitive understanding of the system specification. This provides appreciable help in relating the customer's requirements to what the supplier believes can be realized.
- SDL is an international standard with a stable user base. This standard is expected to have a long life, and attracts strong support from both industry and organizations within the sphere of telecommunications.
- SDL is designed to facilitate SDL-handling tools. Such tools exist, for example SDT.
- Descriptions in SDL have a formal semantic model. This means that SDL specifications are analyzable, their descriptions can be simulated, and they can be translated into implementation languages.

17.5 SDL ENVIRONMENT

In this section an overview of the SDL environment as used within Philips Electronics. The following sections describe a number of tool-sets which combine SDL with other methods. Those tools have been developed and used within NOKIA. This split is the result of allocating topics to companies which for historical reasons use private dialects of SDL. This resulted in tool-sets which can not be used immediately by the other partners. There is a trend towards using standard SDL.

The software development environment effort in communication systems products has increased significantly during the last ten years. The CCITT has defined a language for Specification and Design Language (SDL) (see [CCI88] and section 17.4) of those systems. This language is now widely used and supported by tool-sets from several (mainly European) suppliers. Within the subproject "Communication Systems" the following SDL related tool-sets are used.

17.5.1 Initial environment

The initial Philips Electronics SDL environment consisted of a tool-set (the PKI tool-set) developed at "Philips Kommunications Industrie" at Nürnberg. These tools run on VAX/VMS systems and all the input must be prepared with a text oriented editor.

17.5.1.1 PKI tool-set

The PKI tool-set supports the implemention phase of the software development process. It contains tools that can create code for a number of run-time platforms. PKI SDL is based on the SDL80 standard. A PKI SDL specification is divided into Data Declaration Files (DDL) and SDL Transition Files. Information for the code generation tool on the target operating system and the target hardware is given in "configuration files". Figure 17.7 shows the tool-set in relation to the data.The implementation of the SDL specifications is given in the form of Virtual Machine (VM) procedures. The tool-set consist of:

- Basic tools:
  - The compiler SDLC which carries out syntax and semantic checks of SDL source and translates into object files and/or target language code.
  - A data dictionary generator (DDG) which reads and analyzes SDL Data Declaration Files. The data dictionary is used by all other tools.
  - A linker (TLINK) which produces code containing process information of the SDL process.
- Component tools which generate code for a particular SDL block or process and symbol information to enable tracing of SDL statements.
- Subsystem tools which generates tables containing information on local data of SDL processes and state tables for each process.
- Run time environments for several targets are available which provide services for inter process communication, memory management, timers and tracing.
- For testing an SDL debugger is available which provides interactive symbolic debugging on a host (VMS or PC) or on a target system.

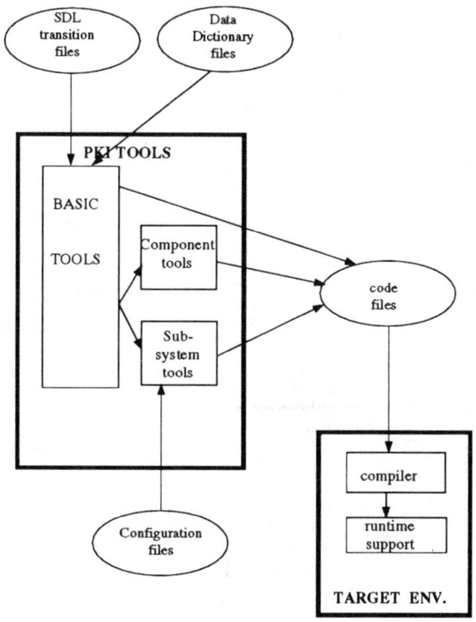

Figure 17.7 Initial Philips Electronics SDL environment

17.5.2 Extended environment

To benefit from the emerging technology such as graphical editors for SDL and checking facilities a commercially available tool-set (SDT) was selected. Since this tool-set is based on the SDL88 definition and the PKI tool-set on an older definition, a conversion tool (SPI) was needed to check and transform the data. Figure 17.8 shows the tool-sets in relation to each other. The new tool-set also contains code-generation, simulation and host-target support; these feature are not (yet) used for compatibility reasons with existing code. These facilities will be evaluated in the near future.

17.5.2.1 SDT

SDT is a design tool for producing system specifications in SDL88. The tool-set consists of tools that on the SDL level support the user in the various phases from documentation, verification and validation to implementation.

The *Graphical editor* is used to create the design of a system on such different levels as system block, sub-block, process, etc.

The *Analyzer* is used to check parts of a design or a full design of a system. Where errors are found, either syntactic or semantic, these are directly pin-pointed in the design. The Analyzer will also give warnings concerning the dynamic aspects of the designed system. Via the Analyzer, input and output of textual SDL (SDL-PR) is carried out.

The *Simulator* is a valuable complement to the Analyzer, allowing full simulation of the designed system. It gives the user a better understanding of how the system

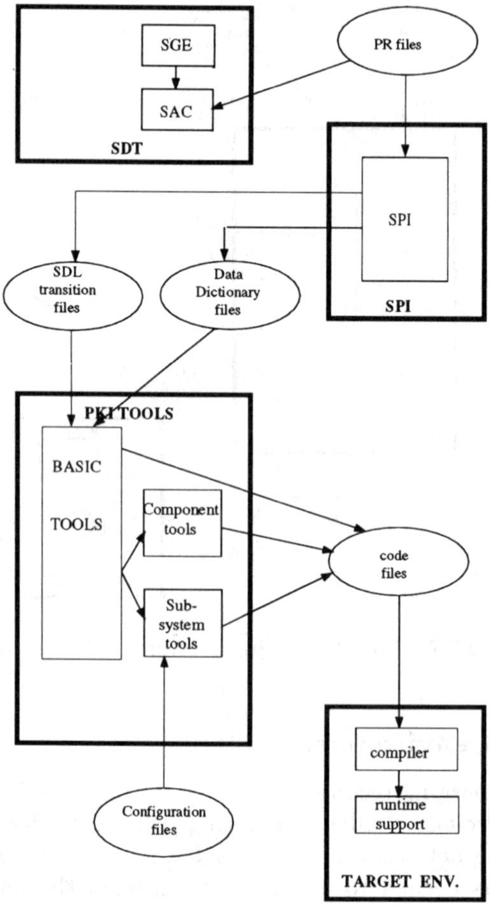

Figure 17.8 Extended Philips Electronics SDL environment

behaves. The Simulator may also be used as a symbolic debugger, by using facilities such as tracing, break-points, loging.

The *C-Code Generator* is the link from specification to implementation. Execution of produced code can be done in a host environment under control of the host operating system or in a target environment with a real-time operating system, or using SDT run-time kernel. The Simulator monitor can also be incorporated in the host and target executables.

The *Structure Browser* is the common base from which one can reach the other tools. With the Structure Browser, the user may navigate among the different design-units stored in the system. The tool always shows the updated hierarchical view of the SDL system.

Within the context of the project mainly the *Structure Browser*, the *Graphical Editor* (SGE) and the *Analyzer* (SAC) are used.

The SDL language will be extended with object oriented features and there is a proposal for a new standard in 1992. The OSDL tool-set is an extension of SDT and supports the proposed extensions.

17.5.2.2 SPI

The SDL—PKI Interface (SPI) uses the standardized CIF format that allows the user to combine the graphical editors and analysis tools in the SDT tool-set with the powerful code generation and simulation tools provided in the PKI SDL tool-set. In this way, a tool-chain which covers the design and the implementation phase has been created. The possibility of supporting other SDL front-end tools is under investigation.

17.5.3 Configuration management

The characteristics of the application area (large products, large teams, long term support, several variants) require that multiple product baselines are kept consistent during the development and maintenance phase as well as the post-development stage (generation, distribution, service).

Configuration management systems are sometimes used to enforce a process model (implemented through scripts) and to support co-operative work in the sense that developer workspaces are recognized and work from several developers can be merged to produce consistent configurations.

A lot of homegrown configuration management systems exist. Within the context of ATMOSPHERE , COMAC (a PHILIPS proprietary tool) has been exercised. COMAC is an acronym for **CO**nfiguration **M**anagement and **A**ccess **C**ontrol. The emphasis of COMAC is on managing *consistent* configurations. The results show that the SDL tool-sets can be combined with a separate configuration management tool. This is demonstrated by using a configuration management tool (CMD) which supports the software developer in his working context and an integrator which controls a repository with accepted configurations.

17.5.3.1 The CMD model

In general, the model consists of three parts:

1. File Archive
2. Developer Domain
3. Integrator Domain

The overall picture of these domains is shown in figure 17.9.

The model supports two roles:

1. Developer — a developer is a project member responsible for implementation of (a part of) a product.
2. Integrator — the integrator is a special project member. He checks all modifications made by the developers on consistency (in case of a successful build he will accept them). Furthermore, he performs integration tests (in case they are successful, an approve will be done by him).

A number of versions exists per file and each version has always has one of the following statuses:

Experimental: file version is controlled by the developer. This is the initial status of each file version.

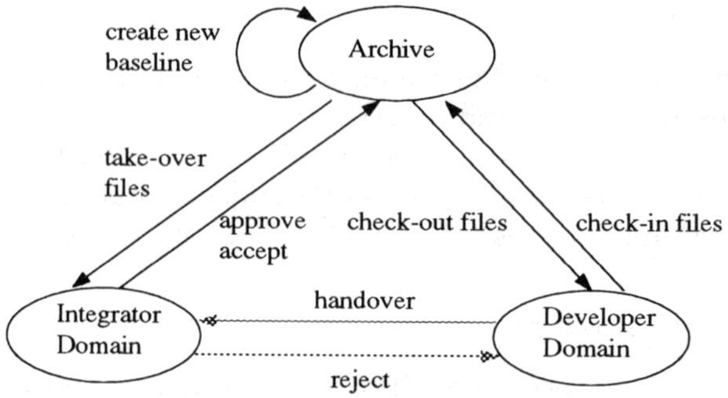

Figure 17.9 CMD domains

Handed_over: file version must be checked by the integrator. A file gets this status by means of the function hand-over.

Taken_over: integrator has taken over the handed-over revision of the file by means of the function take-over.

Rejected: integrator rejected the handed-over file.

Accepted: integrator checked that a compilation with the taken-over files succeeds. No further testing is done.

Approved: integrator accepted the handed-over file, which makes it part of the next approved configuration.

Removed: removal of a file from a configuration, the latest revision of the file gets the status "removed", except when it was "approved".

An approved configuration exists of approved objects, and therefore approved file versions only. The integrator can create a new approved configuration by approving the taken-over and already accepted objects. A new approved configuration then gets a label for identification. Furthermore, the integrator can accept taken-over objects (without actually approving them) in case a successful build can be done with them. Then the developers referring to the accepted configuration are always sure to refer to a (not tested) buildable configuration and will continuously get the updates at their disposal.

If the status of a file version changes, the version number of the file does not change. Each new revision starts with the status "Experimental".

The overall general picture of these statuses (per revision) is shown in figure 17.10.

All file transfer is done through the file archive. There is no file transfer directly between the developer and the integrator. Their direct communication is only information about (the result of) actions performed. The status of the files gives the necessary supplementary information.

17.5.3.2 CMD domains

File Archive One file archive, with a number of approved configurations, an accepted configuration (continuously updated) and a source file version container, exists per product version. The container only contains the history files of source objects. The container is used for change history and access control on source files. The approved

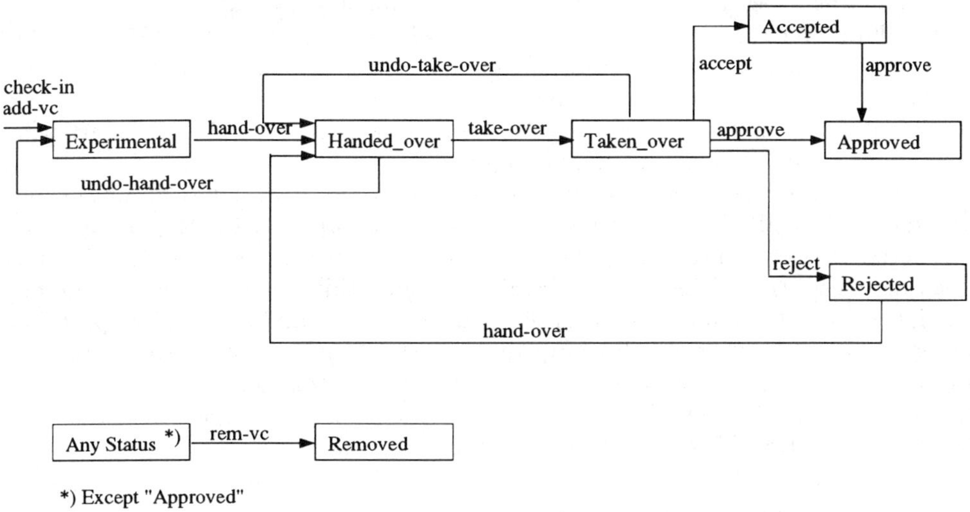

Figure 17.10 CMD statuses

configurations contain both the approved source files and the related derived objects. The accepted configuration consists of the latest approved configuration objects and all later accepted changes (and related derived objects).

When work starts on a new version, the container is filled with the latest version of the source files from the associated baseline (this is also the first approved configuration of the new version). This means that the container only contains the history between the originating baseline and the "current" moment. Furthermore, an "initial" approved configuration is constructed from these initial source files.

Developer's Domain The developer's domain contains the full product directory structure created by the "initialize" function. The developer will do all his development work in this directory structure.

All source file versions and derived objects of the approved configuration on which the initialize has taken place, that are necessary for the building process, are at the developer's disposal. However, the source files are not physically present in the developer's domain. Physically present will be only those source files that are explicitly requested by the developer, e.g. by means of the command check-out.

Integrator's Domain The integrator's domain also contains the full product directory structure created by the "initialize" function. The integrator will do all his work in this directory structure. The integrator always refers to the accepted configuration, because this also includes the already accepted changes.

All source file versions and derived objects of the accepted configuration on which the initialize has taken place, that are necessary for the building process, are at the integrator's disposal. However, the source files are not physically present in the integrator's domain. Physically present will be only those source files that are explicitly requested by the integrator, e.g. by means of the command take-over.

After taking-over the handed-over objects, he will build the product. If the build is successful, the taken-over objects can be accepted. If he tests the product using these taken-over objects he can either first accept them after the build (so all users can use these accepted objects) and then start the testing procedure, or directly start with testing. After completion of the test, an approve can be done.

After an approve, the accepted configuration is identical to the latest approved configuration, because all already accepted changes are also approved during an approve.

The necessary items in the integrator's domain for accepting a new baseline depends on the implementation of the baseline archive. Because this is not yet clear, no details can be given about the requirements on the integrator's domain for this. Most probably however, he will at least need a directory to extract all objects in the correct structure from the file archive with the product version to be accepted.

For the creation of a new file archive (for work on a new baseline) the integrator only needs a directory in which to create the file archive.

17.5.3.3 The CMD process model

In general there is no data (file) transfer between the developers and the integrator directly. Their direct electronic communication consists of information/confirmation messages only. The status information of the files is used for further identification.

Developer Cycle If a developer starts working, he will do an initialize of his development domain on the latest available approved configuration or the accepted configuration for the appropriate product version. The developer will then develop in a stable situation in case of reference to an approved configuration, otherwise he will continuously see the new accepted changes. The developer will get the complete product directory structure, all derived objects and source objects at his disposal. However, only those source files he explicitly requests (e.g. using check-out) will be physically present in his domain.

If a developer wishes to change an object, he must check-out this object. If required, first a set of files can be defined. At the moment of check-out the latest version is taken from the container and physically put in the developer's domain at the appropriate place. Two developers can not check-out a file simultaneously.

A developer can check-in his object back into the file archive, without influencing the work of any other developer (they develop in a stable situation, because the refer to all object versions of the approved configuration specified at initialization time). Thus, a developer can check-out and check-in objects as necessary, without having to wait for the integrator. The check-in is optional, because hand-over can be used to perform the check-in implicitly.

After completing changes on his objects, the developer can hand-over these objects to the integrator. The integrator is informed about the fact that a hand-over has been done. It is required however that the developer checks all his changes to the latest available approved or accepted configuration before handing the objects over (between the moment of initialize and the moment of hand-over the integrator can have approved changes made by other developers). In the case of reference to an approved configuration, the function catch-up is available, to change the reference (set at initialization time) to the latest available approved configuration. In the case of reference to the accepted configuration this is not necessary.

If the integrator rejects an object, the developer is informed, who can change the object (check-out and check-in) and hand it over again.

Integrator Cycle If an integrator starts working, he will do an initialize of his integration domain on the accepted configuration for the appropriate product version. The integrator will then continuously see all already accepted changes. The integrator will get the complete product directory structure, all derived objects and source objects at his disposal. However, only those source files he explicitly requests (e.g. using take-over) will be physically present in his domain.

After being informed by a developer's hand-over function, the integrator will take-over objects from the file archive (identified by the status "Handed_over").

He then can use the build function. After building he can accept or reject the object(s). In case of a further test, an approve can be done, to approve all already accepted changes and the current taken-over objects. Approve is always done on the whole product basis, accept and reject can be done of a finer grid than the grid of hand-over (e.g. a hand-over is done on a cluster basis, while a reject of a single component is done, if the integrator detects the problem in that object). After a reject, the cycle is repeated.

The integrator does not need the catch-up operation, because his domain is always up-to-date with the accepted configuration (except for the objects taken-over). The commands accept, reject and approve ensure this.

17.5.3.4 Implementation

In the current implementation of CMD the commands available to the developer and the intregrator are implemented as shell commands. In this way they can be used directly from the command line as well as from scripts. The commands are also encapsulated into SoftBench to replace the original SCCS based version management facility from SoftBench.

17.5.4 Eventhandling

EventHandler is a software tool that provides the members of a software development team with a quick and easy online facility to enter and manage problem reports and change requests about the products they are developing or maintaining.

17.5.4.1 The users and their roles

The team where *EventHandler* is used consists of one *event manager*, who is responsible for the management of the problem data, and several *team members*. These two roles constitute the actual users of *EventHandler*. There is a third role, *subscriber*, denoting persons who do not belong to the team and have no access to the system, but who may be mentioned on *EventHandler*'s mailing lists and thus may only receive mail. The three roles together constitute the *employees*. An employee is identified by a unique *employee_id* and has a role which can be *event manager*, *team member* or *subscriber*.

17.5.4.2 What is an event?

In the context of *EventHandler*, an *event* is the discovery of an unsatisfactory aspect of a software product. Examples of events are the detection of a programming error, the confrontation with a faulty behaviour of a product, the disappointing finding that a certain feature is missing and the discovery that the requirements specifications hide an annoying aspect for future users. These examples show that there are various kinds of events: events may concern *existing* as well as *planned* products; they may concern found *errors* as well as desired *enhancements*. However, *EventHandler* does not distinguish between types of events. Events may arise in the world of developers where software products are made or maintained, as well as in the world of customers where these products are used. *EventHandler* is typically intended for the developers' world. Events should be reported and documented so that they become manageable. *EventHandler* is a tool for documenting and managing events.

17.5.4.3 What is an Event Report?

An Event Report is a document assigned to one particular event. An Event Report is created by a member of the team to report an event. From then on *EventHandler* registers on the Event Report all follow-up decisions taken by the event manager and the work done by team members until the event has received sufficient attention and the case can be considered as closed. Thus in the end an Event Report contains the description of an event and the full history of its life.

17.5.4.4 The Event Report life cycle

The progress an Event Report has made in its life is characterized by the *status* of the Event Report.

EventHandler uses a *life cycle* of statuses and status transitions, which must be defined by the event manager, and thus can be adapted to the team's needs. The life cycle consists of exactly one begin status, one or more end statuses and any number of intermediate statuses. As it is not desirable to permit steps from any status to any other status, the allowable status transitions must be specified as well. The result must comply with:

- each status can be reached from the begin status
- an end status has no successor
- the begin status has no predecessor.

Thus an Event Report begins its life with the begin status and then steps from status to status until it reaches one of the end statuses. The event manager is the only authorized person to perform status changes, except in the case mentioned in section 17.5.4.5. *EventHandler* supplies a default life cycle. See figure 17.11.

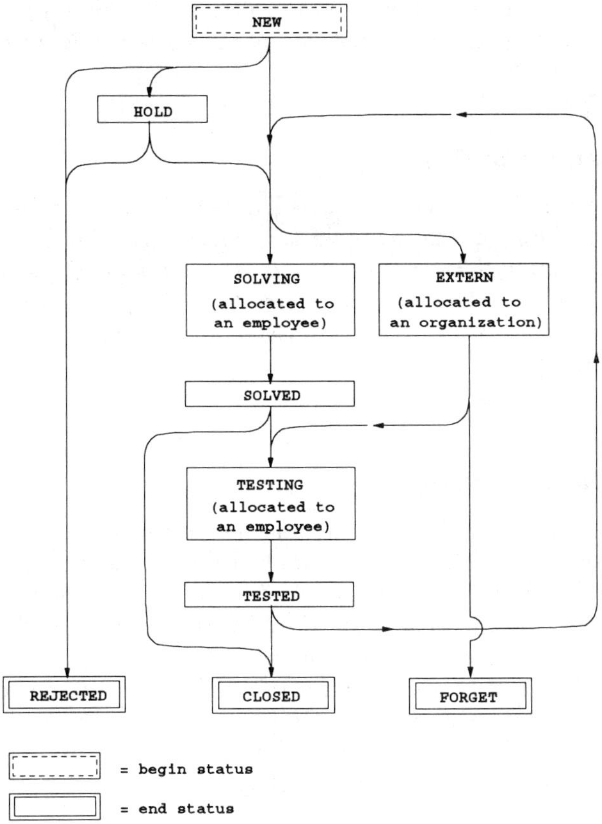

Figure 17.11 Example of an Event Report life cycle

17.5.4.5 Allocation of an Event Report

There may be some statuses in the life cycle which imply that the Event Report is *allocated* to a team member for doing some work concerning the event. Similarly, there may be some other statuses which imply that the Event Report is allocated to an external *organization*. The latter is meaningful when it is found that the reported event has its source in a product of an external organization. When the status of an Event Report is changed and the new status implies an allocation to a team member or to an organization, the event manager must specify to which team member or to which organization the Event Report is allocated.

A team member to whom an Event Report is allocated is allowed to perform exactly one change of status: from the current status to a permissable successor status.

17.5.4.6 Creating an Event Report

All team members are authorized to create a new Event Report. It consists of specifying the *title*, the *urgency*, the *product_discovered*, the *mail_always_list*, the *mail_now_list* and the *description*. *EventHandler* generates the contents of several other fields such as the *ER_id*, the initial *status*. The result is a new Event Report with the supplied information in the appropriate fields. The new Event Report consists of the header section and the first change section.

17.5.4.7 Updating an Event Report

Existing Event Reports can be updated by adding new information or changing existing information. Information that was not supplied upon creation can be supplied later (e.g. the *product_solved*). Information supplied upon creation may in some cases be changed later (e.g. the *mail_always_list*, specified by a team member when creating the Event Report, can be changed later by the event manager). The *status* can be changed and the *allocation* can be specified according to the rules explained in sections 17.5.4.4 and 17.5.4.5. Updating an Event Report always results in a new *change* section which is appended to the history of the Event Report. Information in existing *change* sections can never be changed. Adding remarks to an Event Report is discussed separately in section 17.5.4.9.

17.5.4.8 Automatic notification facility

Every time when an Event Report is changed (and the first time when it is created), *EventHandler* will send notifications to the persons appearing on the *mail_always_list* of the Event Report header and to the persons appearing on the *mail_now_list* of the current change. The first mailing list must be specified when the Event Report is created, the second when the change is made. *EventHandler* sends a copy of the Event Report (with the current change added to its history) to the persons on both mailing lists, using the electronic mail facility of the computer system on which it is running.

17.5.4.9 Adding remarks to an Event Report

A person who creates an Event Report or changes one of its attributes may enter a long text and use a preferred editor to describe the event or to justify the change. It is also possible to use this long text facility to suggest a solution or to make remarks without changing any of the other attributes of the Event Report. All team members are authorized to do this. The remarks are entered in the *description* field of a new change, which is appended to the history of the Event Report. The automatic notification facility takes care of the distribution.

17.5.4.10 Selecting the Event Reports to be included in a report

EventHandler offers facilities to select Event Reports on the basis of the attribute values. Attribute values may be specified as conditions. Event Reports that satisfy these conditions are shown in a condensed overview. Thus it is possible to select, say, all Event Reports that are created after a certain date or all Event Reports that have a certain status. Conditions can be *anded*, thus it is also possible to select all Event Reports that are created after the mentioned date *and* have the mentioned status. If the displayed selection is still too large, it can further be reduced by indicating on the screen (using cursor movement facilities) which Event Reports are needed.

17.5.4.11 Sorting the selected Event Reports

The sorting facility takes as input the selected Event Reports (as mentioned in section 17.5.4.10. It sorts the selected Event Reports with the aid of up to three *sort keys*. Several attributes can be designated as sort keys. For example, the selected Event Reports can be sorted in the (alphabetical) order of their *status* (first sort key) while the Event Reports with the same status are further sorted in the order of, say, their *date of last change* (second sort key).

The resulting sorted selection of Event Reports serves as input for the reporting facility (see section 17.5.4.12).

17.5.4.12 Generating reports

Three types of report can be generated:

overview (the same as mentioned in section 17.5.4.10). This produces one line of output per Event Report.

last change This produces the full 'last change' (the last change section added to the history) per Event Report.

full report This produces the full listing per Event Report.

The destination of the output can be the screen, a printer or a file. The *overview* consists of one line for each selected Event Report. A line is subdivided in *columns*, one for each attribute of the Event Report. If all columns are displayed, the line can become too wide for the output device. Some columns might not be of interest for the user. Therefore the reporting facility allows the user to specify which information of the Event Report must be included in the overview.

17.5.4.13 Help facility

EventHandler offers a context-sensitive help facility. Pressing the help key displays advice about how to proceed. The help facility consists of an extensive set of help texts and a mechanism to select the appropriate help text when the help key is pressed. The help texts associated with the *text_attribute* and the *date_attribute* are not included in the system. These must be defined by the event manager when initializing the system. All other help texts are supplied with the system.

17.5.4.14 Configuring and supporting the system

EventHandler requires several program settings to work with. These must be entered by the event manager. The following information must be supplied.

- Repository information: where must *EventHandler* store its data?
- Program settings: the names and roles of the employees; the names, versions, and platforms of the products on which the team works; the urgencies; the organizations to which Event Reports may be allocated; the settings for the text_attribute and date_attribute (including the associated help texts as explained in section 17.5.4.13 and the life cycle information as mentioned in section 17.5.4.4. In connection with the life cycle, there is a facility which validates if *EventHandler* can work with the new or modified life cycle.

Event Reports that have arrived at an end status can be exported to an archive repository.

17.5.4.15 Multi-user system

EventHandler is a multi-user system, thus several sessions may be active at the same time and it may happen that several users wish to update the same Event Report simultaneously. Also, when the event manager is updating program settings, it may happen that other users wish to create or update Event Reports which need these settings. *EventHandler* has the necessary provisions to prevent these situations from causing loss or inconsistency of stored data.

17.5.4.16 User interface

EventHandler has a user interface (further called UI) offering *forms* and *command lines* as means to interact with the system. The forms UI follows closely the OSF/Motif Style Guide[1].

The forms UI, which is invoked by means of a command line, makes use of menus (including pop-up menus and menu bars with pull-down menus) and data entry forms. All functions can be performed through the forms UI. The command line UI is included enable the use of scripts (a sequence of commands, stored in a file, and executed

[1] The OSF/Motif Style Guide is meant for graphical displays whilst *EventHandler* is designed for alphanumerical displays. Nevertheless, it was possible to implement the recommendations of the Style Guide to a large extent, using JAM, a *Forms Interface Management System*. JAM is a registered trademark of the JYACC Corporation.

by a single command). Through the command line UI all functions can be performed except entering the program settings.

17.5.5 Development platforms

A variety of platforms is used, varying from time sharing systems with character based terminals and PCs to UNIX based workstations in a network. The dominant platform, however, is still VAX/VMS with terminals. Usually these large VAX systems are configured in a cluster to achieve high availability, high performance and data sharing between computers. Terminals, printers, plotters, PCs, and sometimes also workstations, are connected to the computers using an Ethernet based local area network.

For communication between geographically distributed sites, a wide area network is implemented using proprietary networking software which offers file transfer and e-mail facilities in heterogeneous computer environments.

17.5.6 The integrated environment

At the start of the project no widely used framework could be recognized. So initially the cooperation between tool-sets was implemented using command procedures and filters which translate the data to be exchanged between tools. Within the tool-sets the integration of the tools depends on the supplier (e.g. Postmaster within SDT).

Since we now have a number of more or less independent tool-sets available, a next step towards a more integrated environment is taken. Due to the fact that a widely accepted mechanism for data integration is still not available, the emphasis is on the dimension of control integration and as mechanism the concept of a message server is exploited. As a framework to achieve such an integration SoftBench has been evaluated and used to construct an environment where different tool-sets can communicate with each other. This environment uses existing tool-sets from the SDL environment in use within Philips Electronics and SoftBench as an integration framework. The environment has been constructed by encapsulating SDT, SPI, PKI-tools, SDL based metrics, Configuration Management (CMD), Event Handling, and a documentation tool (Framemaker) into SoftBench. Figure 17.12 shows the global architecture of the integrated environment. Within the integrated environment, encapsulation of tools is used for:

- simple tool invocation (SDT)
- event/trigger based tool interaction (programming editor, builder, configuration management)
- remote execution (SDT, PKI-tools)
- reacting on a trigger based on the availablity of new files created by the PKI-tools.

The integrated environment offers the developer a view on his workspace by displaying the files in the *Development Manager*. The developer can select a file and invoke a default action or an action from an action menu. The actions available are dependent on the file type. By encapsulating existing tools, they can send *requests* or respond to *requests* sent by other tools. This can be used to synchronize tools with each other (e.g. an editor and a builder) or to invoke a tool automatically even on another system

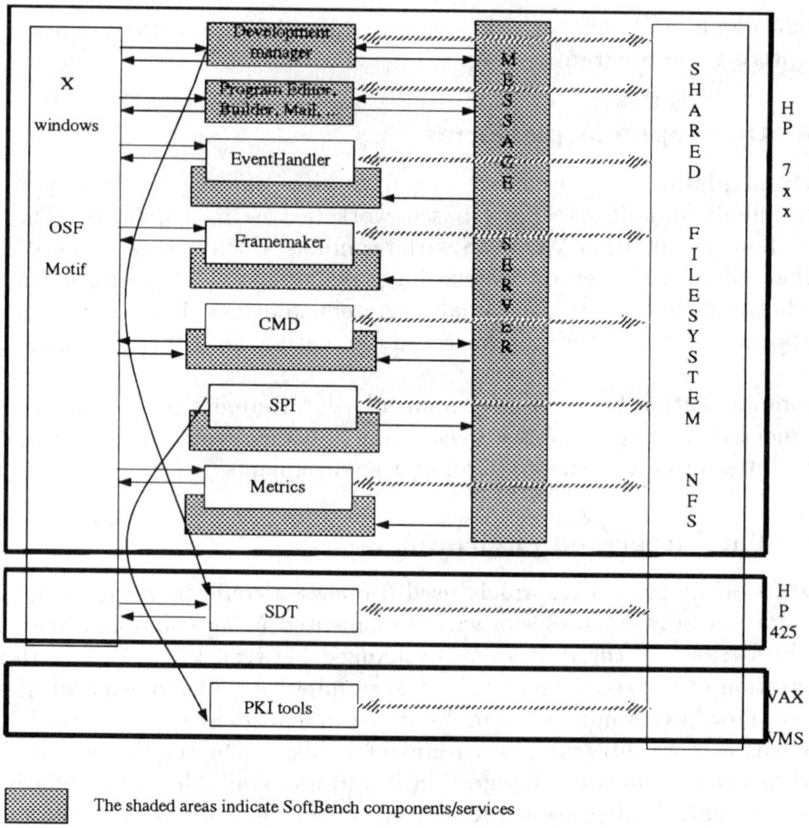

Figure 17.12 The picture shows the integrated environment. NFS is used as shared file system across three different platforms and OSF/Motif is used to have a common user interface on two of these platforms as well as to allow for remote display facilities. The SoftBench message server is used for tool-tool communication. The tools are indicated by small labelled boxes and encapsulated tools have large boxes around them. The arrows in the diagram show whether data flows from the tool itself or from the capsule which encloses the tool.

(e.g. SPI which invokes the PKI-tools). A complication however is that the tools are not available on a single platform. As desktop equipment for the developers an HP 9000/7xx workstation is selected, an HP 425 as server to execute SDT and a micro-VAX running VMS to run the PKI-tools. SoftBench is running on the user's desktop workstation and from this interface the user will have transparent access to all other tools. To enable data sharing NFS is used as a shared file system across all platforms.

17.6 ADDITIONAL INTEGRATED TOOL-SETS

To support method integration some tool-sets are implemented by NOKIA. Since these tools are based on NOKIA's dialect of SDL called TN-SDL they are not used in the integrated environment. The results and the approaches used however are worth to mention.

17.6.1 LOTOS-SDL tool-set

LOTOS (see [Kea92]) is, as SDL, a method to describe distributed systems by their states and changes of states. Both are based on the application of abstract data types and on message passing. LOTOS however uses a process calculus to describe processes and offers a clean and clear mathematical foundation. As described in [Kea92] one can integrate both methods to take advantage of the specific properties offered by each of them. Such an integration is supported by the following tools-sets. There are two tool-sets: the LOTOS-SDL tool-set and the LOTOS-SDL simulation tool-set. The tool-sets utilize a method where the interfaces to the functionalities of SDL blocks are described in an event-oriented formalism adopted from LOTOS. The method introduces an approach to SDL development where the interfaces of the blocks are defined early in the design process. The interfaces can be seen as parts of the overall protocol between the blocks involved. The LOTOS-SDL tool-set supports the use of the method. The verifier tool checks the conformance of an SDL block against its event-oriented interface definition. This is accomplished by exhaustively generating the state spaces of the event-oriented definition and the state machines of the SDL block and examining net morphisms of the two resulting reachability graphs.

The LOTOS-SDL tool-set also includes educational tools to support the adoption of the method: an event-oriented definition single-stepper and a translator producing SDL state machine skeletons from the event-oriented definition. The LOTOS-SDL simulation tool-set utilizes event-oriented definitions to support SDL simulation of parts of an SDL system being developed. This is accomplished by generating a test harness from the event-oriented definitions. As signal parameters are not described in the event-oriented formalism, it is used together with a test data language. The test harness is generated into SDL. This makes it easy to use in any SDL simulation environment and the developer can easily modify and refine the test harness to meet the simulation goals.

17.6.2 ASN-SDL tool-set

Nokia has developed two tools for automatic code generation for communication applications, namely the CASN Compiler for ASN.1 and TN-SDL Translator. ASN.1 is a high-level language standardized by ISO and CCITT for defining data types. The CASN Compiler for ASN.1 generates C type definitions and coding functions for values of these types from ASN.1 type definitions. TN-SDL is a language based on CCITT SDL-88 for defining and implementing processes of the DX200 switching system. The TN-SDL Translator generates C source code from a TN-SDL system definition. In order to integrate these two tools a third tool is needed. GENSDL CASN back-end is this tool. It connects the CASN Compiler and TN-SDL Translator as follows:

- It converts types defined in ASN.11 to TN-SDL and thus makes the use of types defined in ASN.1 much easier in TN-SDL systems.
- It enables the use of CASN coding services in TN-SDL systems.

17.6.3 SDL–metrics tool

Metrics means here the automatically measurable aspects of complexity. The theory and applications of software complexity metrics have been studied for more than fifteen years. Several studies have shown that a meaningful correlation exists between software complexity metrics and the number of changes made to the software or the number of errors found in the software. It is thus possible, in principle, to predict software units that are likely to be problematic. Unnecessary complexity may then be removed and remaining units with high complexity can be tested more thoroughly.

With SDL the use of metrics can start relatively early in the life cycle. Although it is clear that something has to be written before any metrics analysis can take place SDL descriptions can be analyzed relatively early if compared to traditional programming languages. The metrics tool will analyze TN-SDL, Nokia's SDL dialect.

17.7 SoftBench AS INTEGRATION FRAMEWORK

At the beginning of the project the facilities for data integration were not mature enough to host the existing tools on a repository such as PCTE. It was decided to concentrate on presentation integration (OSF/Motif) and on control integration. With respect to control integration, new technology based on the use of a *Broadcast Message Server* was emerging and it was decided to exploit this technology by using SoftBench as an integration framework. The product SoftBench can be described by the following two views:

- A set of software development tools (see [Ger90]). This view on SoftBench gets the most attention from marketing and sales, and most of the product documentation is oriented to this approach. The standard SoftBench product offers a language sensitive editor, program builder with a compilation error browser, symbolic debugger, code structure analysis tool, file-manager with source code management facilities and mail.
- An integration framework offering an architecture for a new generation of software development tools (see [Ger90]). This view emphasizes the facilities which are offered as an environment and covers technical concepts. The article on HP Encapsulator (see [Fro90]), the product documentation on HP Encapsulator and on configuring the development manager cover framework aspects as well. As a framework (or tool integration platform) SoftBench offers tool communication and control integration based on messaging concepts, distributed computing services, OSF/Motif appearance and behaviour, and integrated help facilities.

17.7.1 SoftBench: a framework for tool integration

In this view, SoftBench is considered as a framework for tool integration that offers:

- the possibility to integrate tools or tool-sets, in such a way that they can communicate with each other, and present a task-oriented environment to developers.
- the possibility to interchange tools, without the need to make changes to other tools, and have at least the same cooperation as the the original tools.

For the implementation of the framework, (industry) standards such as Posix, X/open, UNIX SVID (in the future OSF/1), NFS, ARPA networking, X/Windows and OSF/Motif are used. The framework offers facilities for:

- event driven **Tool Communication**.
  The communication is based on a message server concept, and offers bi-directional one-to-many or many-to-one communication. The tools communicate with each other according to predefined tool protocols, one protocol for each each class of tool. Each tool makes its operations available to other tools by means of these protocols. As long as a new tool fully supports the appropriate tool class protocol, that tool can be substituted for the original tool, and the other tools in the environment continue to operate with the new tool just as they did with the original tool. The protocols can be implemented hard coded in the tools, using a library of C functions, or by using Encapsulator to put a layer around an existing tool. Such a mechanism for communication between tools offers opportunities for task automation, programmatic testing, computer based training, and on-line help.
- working in a **Distributed Environment**.
  The message server facility from SoftBench can operate in a distributed environment as long as on each of the involved computer systems a subprocess control daemon is running. Based on this technique, *remote execution* is transparently available for the SoftBench user. Since NFS or RFS can be used, it is also possible to work with *remote data*. This allows the use of a file server as a common location for project data. Since SoftBench uses the X Window System, *remote display* capabilities are available. This gives the opportunity to run SoftBench, or an application within SoftBench, on remote systems.
- consistent **look and feel** based on OSF/Motif.
  The integration services, offered through Encapsulator, are based on a sub-set OSF/Motif. The user-interface model is based on the object-action model and offers a task-oriented view to the user. Native language support, based on the X/Open standard, is used.

The following three levels of integration can be used with SoftBench:

level 1: integration based on the modification of customization files. This addresses mainly tool invocation based on a default action connected to a file type and visibility in menus.

level 2: integration based on encapsulating tools. In this case the tools themselves are not modified.
For tools based on standard input/output, the user-interface is implemented using the menus and dialog facilities offered by the Encapsulator. It is also possible to define events and triggers to communicate with other tools.
For interactive tools with an X/Windows based user interface the tool can be encapsulated together, e.g., with preprocessing and postprocessing functions as file conversion or check-in/out.

level 3: integration based on the usage of the framework library. In this case the applications get dependent on SoftBench but the integration gives less run-time overhead and greater flexibility at implementation time.

The diagram in figure 17.13 shows a systems view of SoftBench.

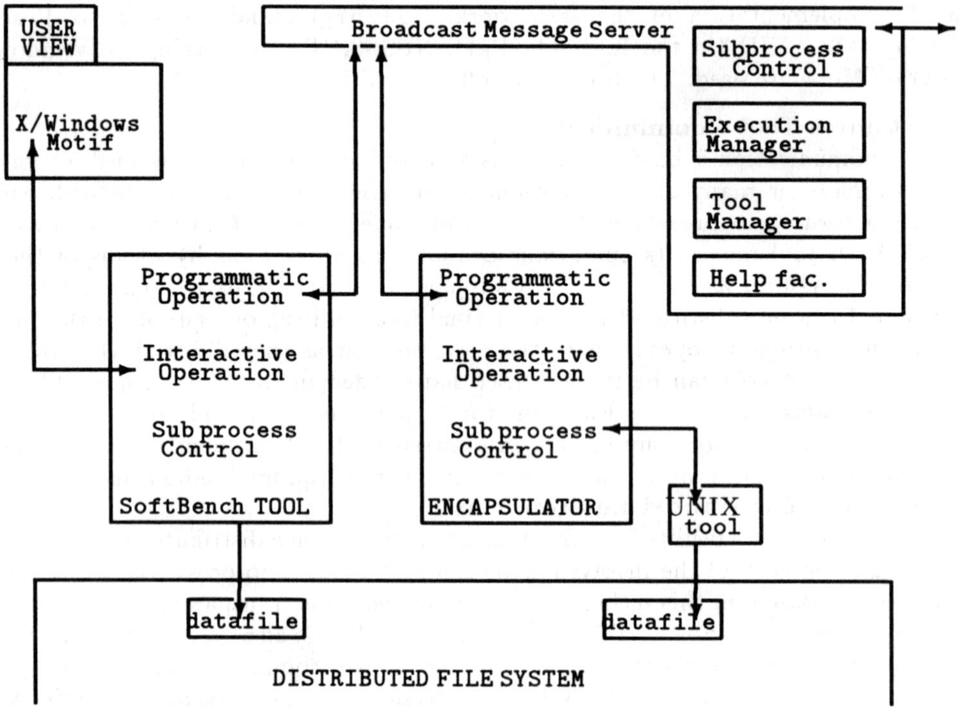

Figure 17.13 System view of SoftBench

17.7.2 SoftBench: a new generation of software development tools

As a tool-set for software development, the standard SoftBench product has the following characteristics:

- strong support for program construction, testing and maintenance. This is offered through the basic tool-set language sensitive editor, program builder with a compilation error browser, symbolic debugger, code structure analysis tool. These tools know of each other's existence and use messages to synchronize their views or to open files.
- possibility to automate tasks in the development process. In this way it is possible to hide procedural steps for the developer and to invoke them implicitly.
- easy to use task-oriented system. The system as such does not enforce a specific way of working. One can select a file from the window of the development manager, start up the editor or another action (related to the file type). One can also start up the source code browser, navigate through the source files, modify files and even start up the builder or debugger. A similar way of working can be started from the debugger. The user can request to "check out" or "check in" the currently used file using the configuration management tool.

In addition SoftBench offers facilities for:

Team File Management, to manage access to files within a software project. It is possible to reserve, lock, check-out a file and check-in the file after modifications. These actions can be performed explicitly, or they can be hidden from the developer and executed implicitly. Saving a file could result in an automatic check-in or a succesful build can start up an analysis tool to produce code metrics.

Team Communication, through electronic mail is very useful, but within SoftBench it is possible to automate the sending of mail, e.g. to communicate the result of a build.

17.7.3 Integration facilities offered by SoftBench

SoftBench offers several facilities to integrate tools into the environment. Those facilities will be discussed from a view of the following classes of users:

- end users, the software developers who need to develop a product.
- environment administrator, someone with a greater knowledge of the SoftBench internals.
- environment integrators, persons who want to encapsulate existing tools without access to source code.
- tool builders, persons who want to develop SoftBench native tools.

Before we discuss this in greater detail, some SoftBench concepts must be explained.

17.7.3.1 Tool classes

Within SoftBench tool classes are defined (such as CM, DOC, STATIC, EDIT, DEBUG, PM, ...). The intention is two fold: first within one tool class several tools for different kind of files could be defined (e.g. an editor for programming languages, a word-processor and a drawing tool all belong to the tool class EDIT), second a tool for a specific kind of file could be replaced by another tool (e.g. emacs and SoftEdit to edit program sources). It is of course important that tools which belong to a certain class have a number of *required general messages* and a number of *required and recommended class messages* in common. For each of the tool classes operational specifications are being produced. Those specifications describe the standard required messages, the standard recommended messages, and the tool specific messages independant of the implemention of the message system. It is the intention to have those operational specifications accepted for a number of tool classes by a group of tool vendors and vendors of message servers based framework components in the middle of 1992.

17.7.3.2 File types

The use of SoftBench depends highly on the object-selection-action model. To make this possible file types must be registered for SoftBench in a specific file and an action menu related to the file type should be defined. The information on file types is used by SoftBench to decide which tool to start for a specific file type by the execution monitor and to know which specific action menu, with the relevant actions available for this file type, must be displayed by the development manager. Entries in the file type definition file look like:

```
SDL System|          .ssy         SSYFILE    ssyClass
SDL Block|           .sbk         SBKFILE    sbkClass
SDL Process|         .spr         SPRFILE    sprClass
SDL Procedure|       .spd         SPDFILE    spdClass
SDL Substructure|    .ssu         SSUFILE    ssuClass
SDL Macro|           .smc         SMCFILE    smcClass
SDT Search List|     .ssl         SSLFILE    sslClass
ISDL|                .pr          PRFILE     prClass
FrameMaker|          .doc         FMFILE     fmClass
VMS Build|           .mms         MMSFILE    mmsClass
DCL|                 .com         DCLFILE    dclClass
TeX|                 .tex         TEXFILE    texClass
TeX Output|          .dvi         DVIFILE    dviClass
Picture|             .vec         VECFILE    vecClass
Picture|             .fig         FIGFILE    figClass
Build|               .makefile    BUILD      make
WBS|                 .wbs         WBSFILE    wbsClass
```

17.7.3.3 SoftBench startup

Besides the files with file type definitions and menu specifications, SoftBench also reads the resources from the X-windows environment and an initialization file either from the home directory or a system-wide default file.

A number of features from the SoftBench tools can be selected by means of the X resources, for instance which version management system to use (SCCS, RCS, or other CM tool), whether a request to edit a file should result in starting a new editor image or use the multi buffer facility from an already available editor, and default values for certain fields in dialog boxes.

The initialization files specify the tools which are available for that session, their tool class, the file types they can handle, their invocation commands and their scope (file, directory, host, or net). In this file one specify for instance that within the class EDIT the SoftBench program editor should be invoked for `.c and .h` files, `xemacs` for LaTeX files, a drawing tool for a `.vec` file and Framemaker for `.fm` files.

17.7.3.4 Customizing facilities for end-users

End-users have access to the X resource definitions and a local version of the SoftBench initialization file. This means that it is possible to make a selection of available tools or to have a different set of tools depending on the activity of a specific user and it is also possible to define personal preferences for default values.

17.7.3.5 Integration facilities for administrators

An administrator of a SoftBench environment can adapt the system-wide initialization file, can define new file types, add specific compilers to the environment (which can be selected by the user at build time), adapt a file (containing definitions of regular expressions to interpret the error message from a compiler) which is used by the error browser. Adding a cross compiler to the framework takes about one hour. Also the menu entries used by SoftBench could be modified to add new actions. One should have a good understanding of the way SoftBench operates to make those changes.

17.7.3.6 Integration facilities for environment integrators

Environment integrators can of course use the same facilities as the environment administrator but they also have a very powerful encapsulation facility available. Encapsulation means to put a "capsule" around an existing tool. In this way one can integrate an existing tool without changing the code. SoftBench has a companion product for this purpose which consist of an interpreter and a translator for a language EDL to some internal format. The syntax of the language is C-like. The most important features available in this context are:

- A number of widgets, to define windows, menus, lists, buttons, ...to implement a user interface consistent with other SoftBench tools.
- Message functions to communicate with the rest of the SoftBench environment.
- Event functions to define events and how to react on them. Events can come from the user, the encapsulated application (based on pattern matching), a message received from the message server or the operating system.
- Process control functions to start sub-processes and send commands (using a pipe or ptty interface to the process) to those sub-processes.

With these features, a very simple encapsulation can be realized to invoke a single command. One can also combine a number of commands in a single encapsulation and offer an advanced user interface and parsing of output from the encapsulated application (as done for SCCS). For a tool which has already a graphical interface one could add message facilities to communicate with the rest of the environment (e.g. interface to version management).

17.7.3.7 Integration facilities for tool developers

For tool developers who want to implement SoftBench hosted tools, a library is available with C and C++ bindings, offering the same functionality as EDL for the environment builders. Using this approach, one can of course also use Motif libraries and have the full freedom of a generic programming language. Another important advantage is, of course, performance since the code does not have to be interpreted.

17.7.4 Encapsulating applications

To encapsulate a tool into SoftBench is technically not a difficult task. One should realize however that, as in normal software engineering, immediately starting with coding is not the proper way of working. Constructing an integrated environment should be considered as a normal engineering cycle with requirement capture, specification, design, implementation, generation and installation aspects. On a tool level this results in the following steps:

- Requirements analysis and specification.
  - Understand the functionality of the tool. Which are available and could they be accessed?
  - How would a user use this tool? Would it be started from a command line, through the SoftBench toolmanager, by other tools?
  - Will the tool create, change or delete files which would be used by other tools as well?
  - Would the user want to access functionality from other tools through this tool?
  - To which SoftBench tool-class does the tool belong and does it need new file types to be defined?
- Design and implementation.
  - Define the actions which the tool will take. This could mean encapsulating more than one command or tool function in one encapsulation.
  - Define the user interface such as the menus, dialog windows, etc.
  - Define the message interface to the broadcast message server.
  - Define the triggers to respond to. Those triggers can come from the operating system (signals), messages, application events caused by the output from the encapsulated tool.
  - Create the online help information.
  - Adapt configuration files.
- Generation of the encapsulated tools in a format suitable for distribution . This means that all information needed to install the tool in a SoftBench environment should be grouped together.
- Installation procedures for the tool. Ideally tools must be able to be installed without explicit knowledge from other tools in the SoftBench environment.

Finally this would result in a well encapsulated tool in the SoftBench environment. Figure 17.14 shows how such a tool communicates with the environment. If the tool has an own graphical user interface it can communicate directly to the X-server. The box representing the encapsulated tool can be composed of several tools or commands, for instance a command which checks out a file from a configuration management repository, a tool (with its own graphical user interface) to modify the file, and another tool to perform some checking or translation into another format. The capsule around the tools can communicate with the user to set options, interpret exit codes or even interpret and display intermediate results.

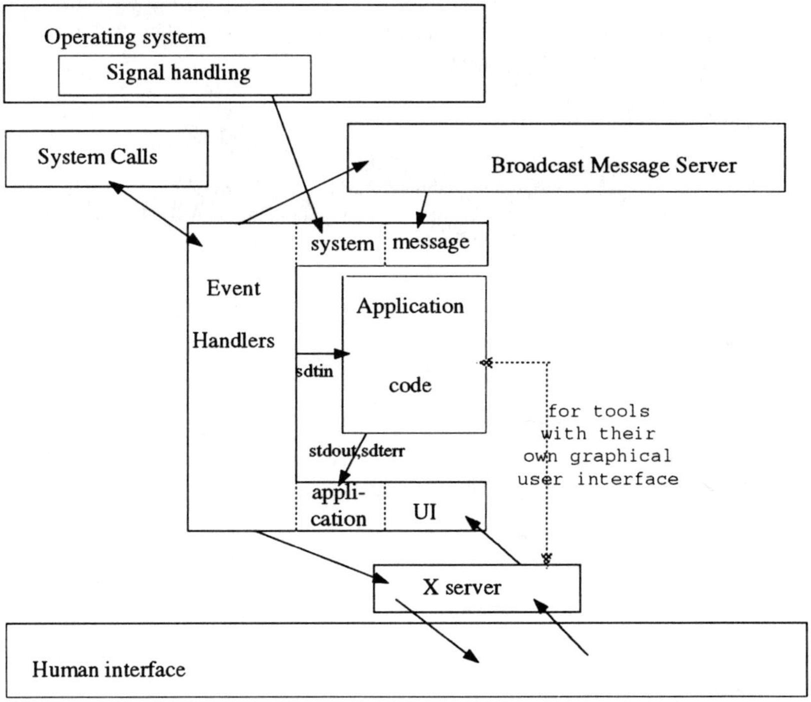

Figure 17.14 An encapsulated tool within SoftBench

18

Data Integration

The integration of tools requires that tools can access and understand each other's data. Since the SDE of the subproject "Communication Systems" is implemented as a set of co-operating tools or tool-sets, there exists no common repository for the data. The current state of practice is that the tools expect the data in the developers work space. To understand each other's data is another issue which can be discussed on the following levels:

- Data integration within tool-sets.
  This is usually the easiest since the supplier of the tool-set has full control of the representation of the data. The data integration within the SDT tool-set will be described as an example.
- Data exchange between tool-sets.
  For the integration between tool-sets one has to conform to common format such as CIF (common interchange format for SDL) and to develop tools which understand this format or develop translators from one format to the other. Meta tools as a parser generator can help in the implementation. Within the subproject a parser generator called Elegant is used to generate such interfaces. The tool SPI within the integrated SDT and PKItool-sets is an example of a translator which is implemented by using Elegant.
- Data integration in the integrated environment.
  At the moment SoftBench only supports the UNIX file system and offers no added value with respect to data integration. In the (near) future however a PCTE-based version of SoftBench will be available.

18.1 SDT

Managing SDL information is a complex task. Graphical data which is structured hierarchically together with other kinds of information should be managed both efficiently and flexibly. A fundamental entity in our data model is the SDL object which corresponds to a SDL diagram. A number of SDL diagrams may then compose a system.

This section is split into two parts: the first part describes the *local view*, which deals with the internal structure of a SDL object, the second part describes the *global*

Tool Integration: Environments and Frameworks, Edited by D. Schefström and G. van den Broek

view which describes how the SDL objects are stored and could be accessed by other tools.

The SDL object is the basic component for SDT on which data integration is achieved.

18.1.1 The local view

The requirement for an open-ended storage model for SDL objects is mostly a question of how information concerning one SDL diagram should be stored. The storage of SDL diagrams should allow the different tools to access common data, extend this data or remove data not needed anymore. In addition to the data kept within an SDL object, data may be divided into sub-objects or could be stored in a format accessible to other tools. This means that the SDL object can contain references to other objects, SDL objects or other types of external or internal objects.

Data handled by an SDL object are the entities which describe one SDL diagram. The data kept may vary from source code (both in gr-format and in pr-format) to information derived from the source code such as symbol tables. Other information that may be available is different types of control information for the SDT tools such as layout information.

In order to maintain the information, an SDL object is composed of a set of attributes and relations. The attributes are used for storing information corresponding to the current SDL object. References could be used to point to other SDL objects or external objects of another type such as executable objects or documentation objects.

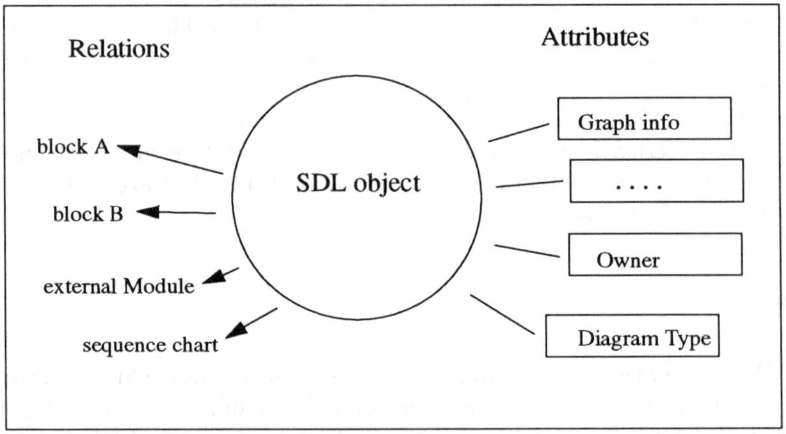

Figure 18.1 SDL objects, relations, and attributes

Both attributes and relations can be created and deleted dynamically. This means that when a new tool is added and it needs to store a new attribute or relation, this can be created using a new unique name without interfering existing tools. Already existing attributes can be shared with other tools.

By providing a type hierarchy system, operations concerning attributes and relations can be uniform. At the top level of this hierarchy components common to attributes and relations are found. The attributes are divided into two basic types: the sequence attribute and the elementary attribute. The sequence attribute is an attribute of arbitrary length and the contents of the attribute is accessed and retrieved in the same way as the contents of a binary file. The elementary attribute has a fixed size and its contents are accessed and retrieved in one single operation. New types can easily be introduced. A new type in the type hierarchy also implies that a new scope for that component type is created.

18.1.2 The global view

Avoiding hard binding of SDL objects is crucial for providing an open-ended environment. For that reason, a global view of SDL objects and their logical bindings is introduced. The SDL handle is the mapping between the logical SDL entity and the physical location of that entity in the environment. The handle to an SDL object should be implemented independent of the platform or environment. In order to be independent of a particular binding mechanism, SDT has its own model of how to implement the bindings between SDL objects. By dividing the world into two parts, an SDT world and an unknown (platform or environment specific) world, platform or environment specific binding mechanisms are avoided.

The SDL objects are stored in the environment in two logical areas, the original area and the working area (see figure 18.2).

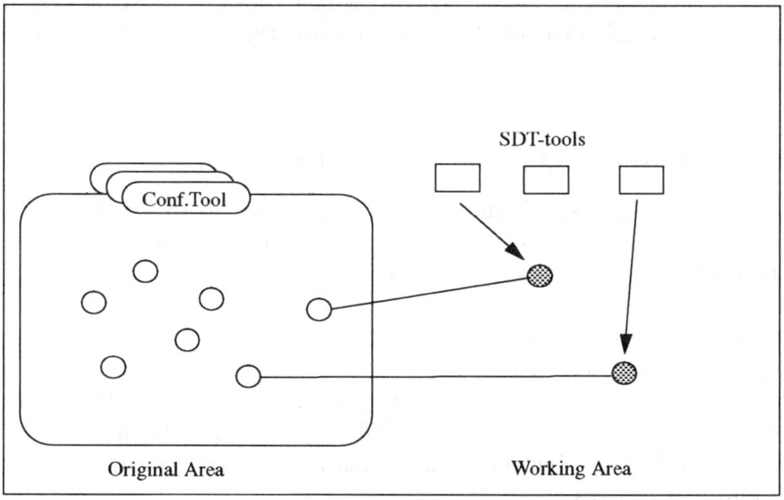

Figure 18.2 SDT tools and configuration management tools

The working area is where the user has his temporary SDL objects and in a file based environment this corresponds to the user's working directory. In the working area the SDT tools have full control over the bindings of the objects. The complexity of moving objects between the original area and the working area is dependent on the complexity of the organization of the objects in the original area.

In the original area access to SDL as well as other objects could be controlled by other tools such as a version management or configuration management system.

An SDL tool can not bind an object in the original area. Instead it is checked out into the working area where the user has full control. This is because it can neither guarantee the consistency of the binding nor understand or know the organization principles of objects in the original area.

In the simplest case - a file system - the original area is defined as a search hierarchy of directories, in which the hierarchy indicates the level of stability of objects. In such a file system, moving objects from the original area to the working area is the copy command in the file system.

18.2 SPI

This section describes the integration of the SDL Design Tool (SDT) developed by TeleSoft and the PKI tool-set developed by Philips Kommunikations Industrie AG (PKI) in Nürnberg. The integration is performed using the SDT-PKIInterface (SPI) developed by Philips Research.

The SPI is an interface that allows the user to combine the graphical editor and analyzer tools in the SDT tool-set with the powerful back-end tools provided in the PKI SDL tool-set, thus creating a software development environment.

SDT is based on SDL'88, while PKI-SDL is based on SDL'80. There are constructs in SDL'88 that can not be transformed to PKI-SDL. Therefore a subset of SDL'88, called Interface SDL (ISDL) has been defined, which contains all those constructs of SDL'88 that can be transformed to PKI-SDL. Figure 18.3 shows how the three tools relate to each other.

18.2.1 Integration of SDT and the PKI tool-set

The SPI checks if an SDL88 specification conforms to the translatable subset (ISDL) and if so generates the Data Declaration Files and SDL transition files, which are needed for the PKI tool-set. The sources of the virtual machine and the configuration files have to be supplied by the user.

The SPI is constructed in such a way that parts of an ISDL specification can be processed separately. To achieve this each SDL component should be stored in a separate PR file. The dates of these PR files are used to check which PR files have been changed since the last call of the SPI. The SPI only writes DDL and SDL files that really have been changed. In this way tools which rely on time stamps can be used to optimize the building process.

The SPI needs a separate PR file for every component, but SDT only generates a single file containing the complete ISDL specification. A tool called SPLITSYS has been implemented. This tool takes the PR file produced by the SDT Analyzer and splits it into separate PR files for each SDL component as required by the SPI.

Also the SPLITSYS tool only creates a new component file if the component has

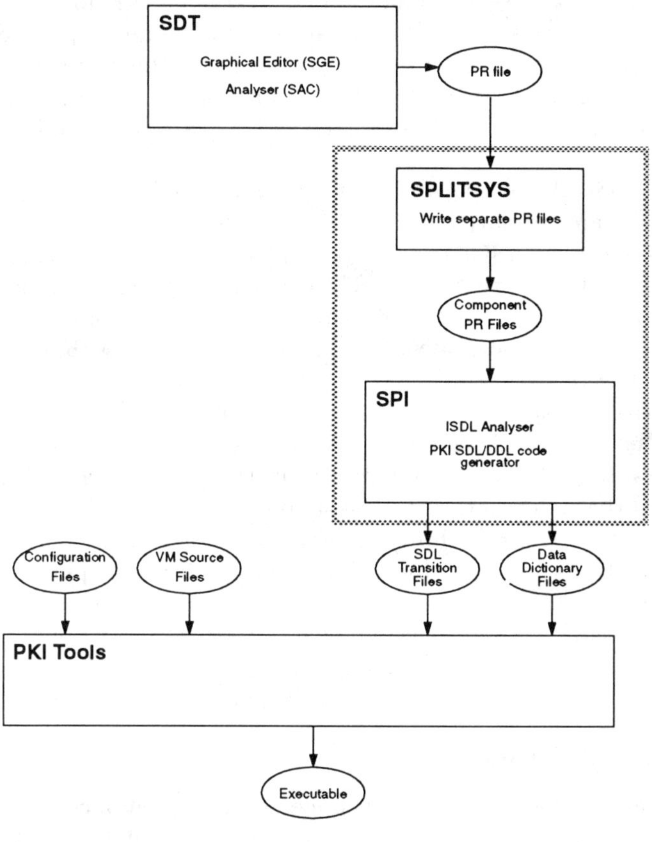

Figure 18.3 SDT-PKI Integration

been altered since the last time the tool was invoked. In this way it is possible for the SPI to determine which components are really changed.

18.2.1.1 Description of the technology used

The technology used to implement SPI and SPLITSYS is based on the use of a parser generator for Attributed Syntax Graphs (ASGs). The basic idea is to let the tools communicate in terms of a standardised form of ASGs, which are essentially generalized parse trees decorated with attribute information. This avoids the situation that a specific input and output format has to be defined for each tool. On the other hand, sufficient flexibility is required with respect to variations in syntax and attribute structure. This is obtained by providing a general scheme for defining classes of ASGs by means of *descriptors*, so called ASGDs.

ASGs can be viewed as abstract mathematical structures, which have an ASGD as their type. In order to develop a tool that takes an ASG as its input and/or produces an ASG as its output, we must be able to read and write ASGs to and from the storage medium that acts as the interface of the tools (i.e. a file system). This would imply that, for each given ASGD, we have to know the internal format according to which ASGs of that type are stored. This can be avoided by automatically generating read and write routines for ASGs from a descriptor. Furthermore, the routines to manipulate (create, inspect, modify, etc.) ASGs can also be automatically generated from the descriptor. Thus tool developers get the front and back ends of their tools for free.

The decision to model ASGs as graphs rather than trees is motivated by efficiency considerations. ASGs are primarily meant as an aid in developing efficient language processing tools. Restricting ASGs to tree structures could rule out a number of optimizations that are possible in processing ASGs (such as exploiting common subexpressions). The graph model allows the tool developer as much freedom as possible, while a restriction to tree structures can always be made (by excluding those operations on ASGs that disturb tree structure).

ASGDs can be used to specify the input and output of tools that process ASGs. A typical application is a tool that computes certain information associated with language constructs and adds it as an attribute in the output graph. The input and output descriptor of the tool will then be the same, except for the additional attribute in the output descriptor. The reusability of tools of this type is increased if they also accept input that contains more attributes than required by the input descriptor. The additional attributes should then be copied transparently to the output. This leads to a notion of *upward compatibility* for ASGs. These and related matters of implementation of ASGs are discussed in subsection 18.2.1.2.

18.2.1.2 Tooling with ASGs

In the SPI tool set all language processing is done using Elegant, a compiler generation tool kit. The acronym Elegant stands for **E**xploiting **L**azy **E**valuation for the **G**rammar **A**ttributes of **N**on-**T**erminals and the Elegant tools are developed by Philips Research within the ESPRIT-415 subproject (see [Auga] and [Augb]). An Elegant tool specification consists of:

1. a parser and attribute evaluation specification,
2. a scanner specification, used to generate an efficient token scanner,
3. a types specification, used to describe the types of the attributes of the grammar, the so-called semantic domains,
4. a code generation specification, used to generate the back end of the tool.

From a (well formed) ASGD it is easy to derive the various Elegant specifications.

- All tools processing ASGs use the derived types specification;
- Tools that acts as a transformer from one ASG to another, use two ASGDs from which two types specifications have to be derived.
- To read an ASG from the file system one uses the derived scanner and parser.
- To write an ASG to the file system one uses the derived code generation specification.

18.2.2 Lessons learned and recommendations

ASGDs form a good and compact way to describe a language for which a language processing tool is to be developed. At the moment this approach supported by Elegant is used for several applications. Amongst them are tools to process a formal specifications language (COLD). Also for describing the interface between two information exchanging tools ASGDs are suited.

Using a powerful compiler generator like Elegant is recommended strongly.

19

Control Integration

According to the dimensions of integration several techniques for control integration can be used. Within the context of this project we recognize the following:

- The use of scripts or command procedures to invoke a sequence of usually non interactive tools.
- The use of a message server to communicate between tools.

From the second approach we will describe two examples. First the communication between tools in a single tool-set (SDT). Within this toolset PostMaster is used by tools to communicate with each other. The result however is still a rather closed tool-set since PostMaster is a proprietary mechanism and is not made publicly available. The second example is the integrated environment which is based on SoftBench. This offers the facility of loosely coupling from tools and since this is commercially available it can be used by other tools as well.

19.1 TOOL COMMUNICATION WITHIN SDT

Tools within the SDT tool-set are integrated by means of control with a selective broadcast mechanism called "the PostMaster". The mechanism is used for instance for the communication between the simulator and the graphical editors to animate the execution.

The PostMaster model is an integration mechanism which describes how tools are integrated in order to achieve loose integration between functional components and at the same time provide a tightly integrated environment with a uniform user interface. This definition is extended also to cover the goal of making the environment externally open-ended by providing a simple but expressive interface to the internal structure and to the functionality of the tools of the environment.

The basic model is based on the presence of a PostMaster. Each tool in the environment knows the PostMaster and sends its state transitions in a message to the PostMaster. The PostMaster will distribute a copy of each message it receives to the tools which have subscribed to the current type of message.

No constraints on the message are set up. A message consists in its simplest form of a type name and a data part for the information sent together with the message. The information part of the message may be of arbitrary length and can contain any

Tool Integration: Environments and Frameworks, Edited by D. Schefström and G. van den Broek

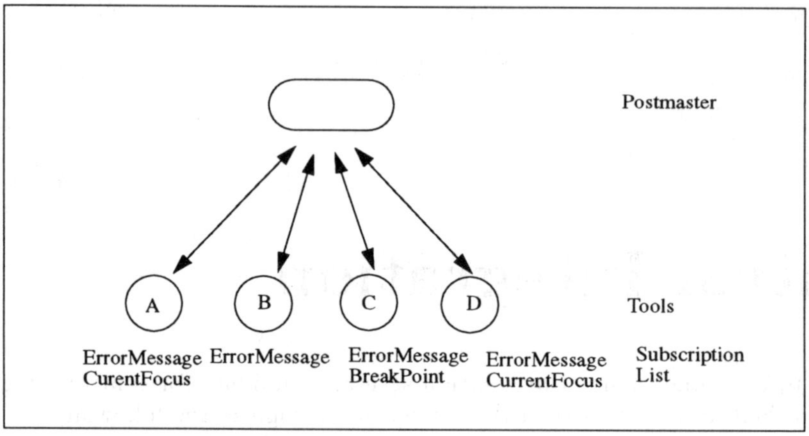

Figure 19.1 The PostMaster model

type of information, since it is regarded as a string of bytes from the point of view of the postmaster.

A tool may broadcast a message for two different purposes. The first is to notify others about a state transition that has taken place in the tool. This state transition may be a semantic error found during analysis or a notification from the debugger that a breakpoint has been reached. Common for these messages is that they are sent without knowledge of which tools have subscribed to that particular message. In other words the sending tool can not know whether any other tool performs any action corresponding to the message sent.

The second way a message can be used is for a request. An editor may request someone to set a breakpoint at a certain line. The editor broadcasts the SETBREAKREQUEST message with the current source line as information in the message.

If any tool subscribes on SETBREAKREQUEST messages it may as action set a breakpoint at the corresponding source code line. After the break point has been set, the tool may broadcast a notify message in order to tell the other tools of the environment that a new breakpoint has been set. The state transition in this case is that a break has been set to a specific source code line. Tools which subscribe on this type of message can perform an appropriate action, in the editor case e.g. highlight the line which contains the breakpoint. If for instance the debugger was not available at the time of the request for a breakpoint, no answer will be returned to the editor and thus no highlighting will occur within the editor display of the programme.

Note that the request message was not sent to a specific tool. The reason for not doing this is due to the model, a tool should not be aware of the existence or type of other tools. Using this approach, the notify and the request messages are similar. The tool selects the type of messages which shows his intent with the message.

The two examples show the strength of the PostMaster model. There are no dependencies whatsoever between the tools of the current environment configuration.

The advantage of using an explicit PostMaster is that a tool only knows the existence of the PostMaster and is not aware of the existence of other tools present in the particular configuration. New tools may easily be added and removed without interfering with the functionality of other tools.

The PostMaster model consists of a set of basic components. The overall behaviour of the model is defined in the configuration description documents which defines the flow of information within the model. The PostMaster distributes messages according to the definitions in those documents.

The composites of the model are the following basic components.

- A *message* in the system is an information carrier. The message type specifies the intention of the message and the corresponding information.
- Configuration descriptions in the PostMaster model are the *message and tool definition document* and the *subscription list document.*
- The *PostMaster* distributes the messages according to the subscription list.
- Tools in the model are those functional components of the environment which are uniquely identified by the PostMaster and have separate entries in the message and tool definition document. The tools use the *PostMaster's public tool interface* which is the functional interface for a tool to the PostMaster mechanism.

There are no restrictions on the tools. The basic interface consists of the following functions

- **InitConnection**
- **ExitConnection**
- **BroadCastMessage**
- **ReadMessage**

In addition to the four basic functions, a small number of support functions operating on the message queue list are available.

The PostMaster model does not provide any support for synchronous messages handling, instead it is entirely asynchronous. However, sometimes it is necessary to perform a request-reply. This is in SDT modelled as follows. A SendMessage function exists which has the same behaviour as the BroadCast function except that it directs the message to one receiver. The requester sends a BroadCast message, which could have a number of receivers. The receivers which reply do that with a SendMessage directed to the sender of the request message.

The PostMaster is implemented as a separate process. It is responsible for distributing messages according to the subscription list. An arbitrary number of tools may be connected to the PostMaster. Several PostMasters may be started and thus several instances of a session may be started. Messages are only distributed within the current session and other PostMasters will not be interfered with messages from other sessions.

A tool is expected to send an alive message (Alive) after it has done its internal initiation. Similarly, a tool is expected to send a stop message before it is disconnected with the PostMaster (StopNotify). This could either be initiated by a user who wants to exit the tool, or it could be requested from another tool via the message (Stop).

In the example below a brief example of a session is given.

```
InitConnection;
BroadCastMessage(Alive);
.. ReadMessage ... BroadCastMessage(xxx)..
Actions -- The main loop of the programme
BroadCastMessage(StopNotify);
ExitConnection;
```

The communication mechanism must be able to work with other event driven mechanisms i.e. window managing system. In our case we must comply with both the X-Window system on workstations and Microsoft Windows on PCs.

Mechanisms that allows the PostMaster to work independently of the used window event mechanism or in cooperation with the window system are provided. In this way a tool implementor may choose to use the functions of the PostMaster for his application in an efficient way. In the X-Window example he may choose to use a callback function similar to X callbacks whenever a PostMaster message has arrived.

19.2 TOOL COMMUNICATION WITH SoftBench

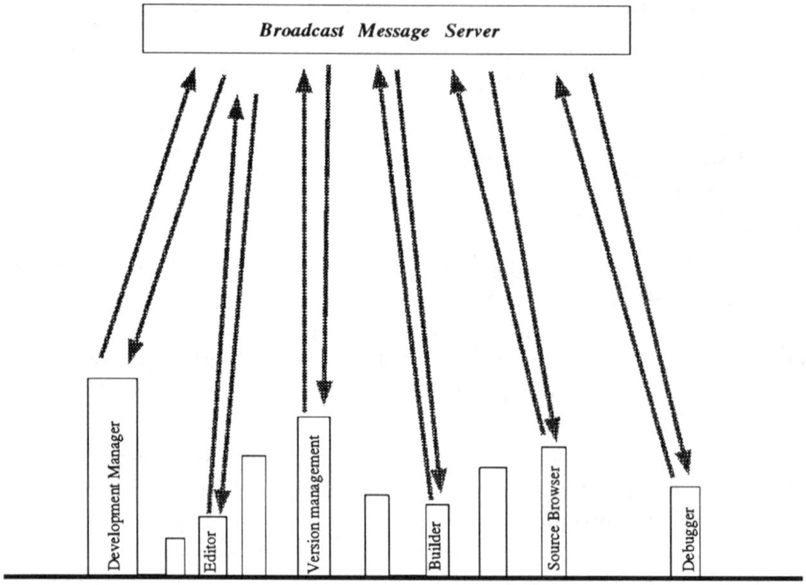

Figure 19.2 The broadcast message server

SoftBench uses a broadcast message for communication from tools with the SoftBench environment as well as for communication between tools (see figure 19.2). Within an integrated environment based on SoftBench control integration starts from the moment SoftBench is started. At that moment the broadcast message server (BMS), the tool manager and the development manager are started. The other tools are started either through the development manager by double clicking on a file name, which starts the default tool for that file type, or by selecting an action from one of the menus. The process is in both cases as follows:

1. A *request* message for a specific tool class is sent to the BMS.
2. The BMS checks whether the tool is already running within the required scope, if not the execution manager will start the tool using the information from the SoftBench initialization file.

3. When the tool is started it will inform the BMS and let the BMS know which messages it can send and what kind of messages it is interested in.
4. All inter tool communication is handled further by sending request messages, responding to requests from other tools and sending notification messages.

19.2.1 SoftBench message format

SoftBench messages use the following format:

sender id type tool-class name host dir file data ...

The fields in the message are seperated by white space (spaces,tabs, newline). An "*" in field means "not applicable" and an "-" means use the default.

The fields in the message have the following meaning:

sender a unique identifier of a running SoftBench tool
id a unique identifier for a message and any response to that message
type one of the three types of SoftBench messages: *Request, Notify, or Failure.* the corresponding values are R, N or F.

Request message is a message to the BMS to request an action from another tool. The requester does not wait for a reply but expects either a Notify message for succesful completion or a Failure message for failing the request.
Notify message is broadcast to notify interested tools of the succesful completion of a request.
Failure message to notify the failure of a request.

tool-class one of the tool-classes defined in the SoftBench initialization file.
name is the name of the action requested.
host, dir, file as a tripled form the context where the tool should operate.
data ... The data fields contain additional information that is specific to actions related to the message.

The following text is an example of the communication to start up the building tool and a number of messages which request actions from the builder.

```
Softbench.8 * N BUILD TOOL node user *
Softbench.8 30-519-node R MSG-SERVER ACCEPT * * N BUILD START node user
Softbench.8 31-519-node R MSG-SERVER ACCEPT * * F BUILD START node user
Softbench.8 32-519-node R BUILD START node user *
server 0-5-node N BUILD STATUS node user * * STARTING
Build.14 - N MSG-SERVER START
Build.14 1-5-node R MSG-SERVER ACCEPT * * R - STATUS - - - -
Build.14 2-5-node R MSG-SERVER ACCEPT * * N * FILE-MODIFIED * * *
Build.14 3-5-node R MSG-SERVER ACCEPT * * R BUILD BUILD-TARGET node user *
Build.14 4-5-node R MSG-SERVER ACCEPT * * R BUILD MAKEFILE-BUILD node user *
Build.14 5-5-node R MSG-SERVER ACCEPT * * R BUILD RUN-CMD node user *
Build.14 6-5-node R MSG-SERVER ACCEPT * * R BUILD SHOW-ERRORS node user *
Build.14 7-5-node R MSG-SERVER ACCEPT * * R BUILD PREVIEW-TARGET node user *
Build.14 8-5-node R MSG-SERVER ACCEPT * * R BUILD UPDATE-MAKEFILE node user *
Build.14 9-5-node R MSG-SERVER ACCEPT * * R BUILD MAKE-MAKEFILE node user *
Build.14 10-5-node R MSG-SERVER ACCEPT * * R BUILD SET-CONTEXT node user *
```

```
Build.14 11-5-node R MSG-SERVER ACCEPT * * R BUILD COMPILE-FILE node user *
Build.14 12-5-node R MSG-SERVER ACCEPT * * R BUILD DIRECTORY-BUILD node user *
Build.14 13-5-node R MSG-SERVER ACCEPT * * R BUILD FIRST-ERROR node user *
Build.14 14-5-node R MSG-SERVER ACCEPT * * R BUILD LAST-ERROR node user *
Build.14 15-5-node R MSG-SERVER ACCEPT * * R BUILD NEXT-ERROR node user *
Build.14 16-5-node R MSG-SERVER ACCEPT * * R BUILD PREVIOUS-ERROR node user *
Build.14 17-5-node R MSG-SERVER ACCEPT * * R BUILD SET-MAKEFILE-NAME node user *
Build.14 18-5-node R MSG-SERVER ACCEPT * * R BUILD START node user *
Build.14 19-5-node R MSG-SERVER ACCEPT * * R BUILD RESTART node user *
Build.14 20-5-node R MSG-SERVER ACCEPT * * R BUILD STOP node user *
Build.14 21-5-node R MSG-SERVER ACCEPT * * R - STOP  - - -
Build.14 22-5-node R MSG-SERVER ACCEPT * * R BUILD ICONIFY node user *
Build.14 23-5-node R MSG-SERVER ACCEPT * * R - ICONIFY  - - -
Build.14 24-5-node R MSG-SERVER ACCEPT * * R BUILD NORMALIZE node user *
Build.14 25-5-node R MSG-SERVER ACCEPT * * R - NORMALIZE  - - -
Build.14 26-5-node N BUILD STATUS node user * * READY
Build.14 32-519-node N BUILD START node user *
```

19.2.2 Exploiting a general message server

To be able to construct environments based on sending messages one has define some protocol. For SoftBench this protocol contains the following parts:

- *Standard Required Messages* which are expected to be understood and reacted upon by each tool. The list of "standard required messages" mentioned below is the minimum set. For each tool-class this set will be extended. The following "standard required messages" are defined:

  START a tool in a specific context
  STATUS request a tool to return its current status
  STOP request a tool to cleanup and exit
  SET-CONTEXT request a tool to change its context or a notification that the default context has changed
  FILE-MODIFIED to inform tools that a specific file or even the contents of a directory has been modified

- *Standard Recommended Messages* which are neat but not required. The list of "standard recommended messages" mentioned below is the minimum set. For each tool-class this set will be extended. The following "standard recommended messages" are defined:

  ICONIFY to request a tool to iconify all its windows.
  NORMALIZE to request a tool to return its windows to normal size.

- *Tool Class Specific Messages* which are specific for a tool class. Again these messages can be divided into required, recommended and tool specific messages.

Work is going on to define "standard" messages in the form of operational specifications for a number of tools classes such as: editors, documentation, project management, configuration management, static analysis, metrics, building, test, defect tracking. This is done by cooperation of the SoftBench suppliers and a group of tool suppliers organized in CASE Communiqué. The goal is to define those operational specifications independent of the underlying message server. This will make it easier for tool suppliers to conform to such a common set of messages and allow environment constructors to combine tools into an integrated environment and even have the option to choose between alternative tools.

19.2.3 Conclusions

Experience shows that an integrated environment is not constructed by gluing some tools together. One should really investigate in detail which tools will be used and make an analysis of the data flow between the tools. This should give the requirements for the encapsulations. Problems will occur if one wants to integrate tool-sets which do not make their primary functions (such as edit/view a diagram, navigation within such an editor) directly accessible or do not support messages to do this.

20

Presentation Integration

Within the pilot project, presentation integration was in the first instance not considered as a high priority issue. However, the workstation based tools use the industry standards X-Window and Motif. This new technology is now being used by individual tool-sets, such as SDT, and is also the basis for the SoftBench based integrated environment.

20.1 USER INTERFACE OF SDT

SDT is a set of tools of which some are highly interactive. The main components are the graphical editor, structure browser, analyzer, file-viewer and help tool. The user interface of SDT is based on the windowing technique. Every tool within SDT has an associated window where the application presents its results and the user can choose commands or manipulate objects.

To accommodate a common user interface for all tools within SDT and also to conform to standards, SDT has built its user interface on Motif and Microsoft Windows/Presentation Manager. This choice was quite natural when the choice was made as the SDT requirements for a user interface were modern windowing systems existing on both workstations and PCs. The two systems are quite alike which makes it possible to have a common view on the user interface when developing the SDT tools. By following the style guides for these environments, the learning time for a user of SDT is very small if he already is familiar with other applications in these environments. Even without previous experience these windowing systems are very intuitive and easy to use. Some important common aspects from the style guides are

- The use of menus and predefined menus (File, Edit) and menu commands (New, Open, Save, Exit, Undo, Cut, Copy, Paste).
- Direct manipulation of objects.
- The use of dialogues when the application needs additional information to perform a command. The ellipsis following a menu command indicates that a dialogue will be shown before the command is executed.
- A Help command should be available to give you online help.
- Favour the WYSIWYG concept if possible. The result on the screen (What You

Tool Integration: Environments and Frameworks, Edited by D. Schefström and G. van den Broek

See) should be as close as possible to the result you will get when things are printed on paper (Is What You Get).

- The user must be informed, e.g. by showing a clock cursor, when it takes a long time to perform a task.
- Every action can be undone by choosing the Undo menu command.
- Nothing is written to disk before you explicitly save it.

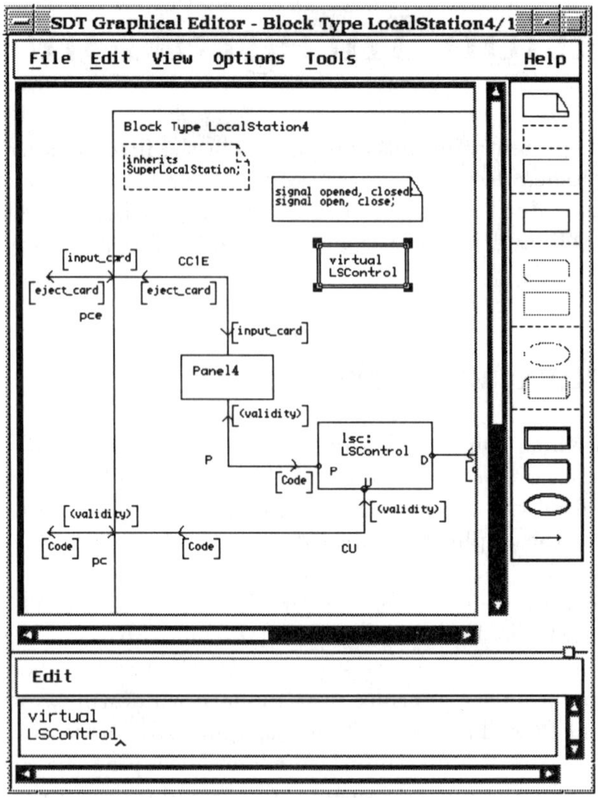

Figure 20.1 Window appearance of the SDT graphical editor

Every SDT tool uses a main window to work in. The tools use the direct manipulation technique. Objects are selected by clicking or using direction keys. Actions on selected objects are either done directly by using the mouse, double-clicking, dragging, shift-click, etc., or by choosing a command from a drop-down menu presented on the menu bar situated at the top of the main window. In the editor new symbols are placed on the diagrams by picking symbols from a symbol menu window.

The editing of texts in the graphical editor is a delicate user interface problem. Many graphic drawing applications use the direct manipulation technique for text editing, i.e. the text can be edited directly in the symbol, by clicking or dragging on the text and then typing from the keyboard. When using SDT often the size of text inside SDL symbols is small, as you need quite a lot of text and you do not want huge symbols. Due to the poor resolution of display screens the text is often very hard to read using the scale 1:1. This fact has led us to our choice of using a separate window for text editing. When an object is selected the associated text is presented in the text window. Here the text is easy to read and it can easily be edited using the standard means for the windowing system.

The different tools within SDT communicate with each other such that the user will always have consistent SDL information. For example a name-change in a reference symbol in the editor is immediately reflected in the browser's SDL hierarchy list. Another example is that a second analysis is only performed on changed diagrams relative to the first. More information on the communication mechanism within SDT can be found in the Control Integration section. A similar immediate response behaviour is used in the graphical editor when editing text. When the text is changed in the text editing window it is also drawn in the work area window. Due to performance problems, as it is very time consuming to draw graphics, there is a delay of one second between the drawing and the last text editing event.

A specific user interface question for the design of the editor is how much freedom the user should have when placing symbols on the work area. One approach is to use an automatic layout where the user only chooses the symbol sequence and flow-line couplings and the tool then arranges all the symbols. This can more easily be combined with a complete syntax-driven editor, where you have many restrictions and can only construct legal SDL diagrams. Another approach is the general drawing tool, where you have the freedom to place symbols, lines, etc,. anywhere on the work area. SDT uses an intermediate approach. Symbols and lines are placed on a grid and there are some restrictions on the placement of symbols, but the user still has freedom enough not to get frustrated on an automatic behaviour of the layout.

The user interface is implemented in a graphics package, a programming interface providing all the functionality needed in the different SDT tools. As of today there exist packages for Motif and for MS-Windows. By choosing the graphics package model, it will be relatively easy, if there is a need, to port SDT to other windowing systems.

20.2 USER INTERFACE WITHIN THE INTEGRATED ENVIRONMENT

The user interface within the environment constructed is based on the use of OSF/Motif. Within this section the user interface as used by the integration framework (SoftBench) is described and not from the integrated tools. Figure 20.2 shows how the user interface of some SoftBench tools.

All SoftBench tools are built using an OSF/Motif based widget library which does not contain all OSF/Motif facilities. With respect to presentation integration SoftBench offers the following facilities to the environment constructor or tool developer:

- customizable menus which are used by the development manager,
- encapsulation of existing tools (which use the standard input/ouput facilities from UNIX) to add an OSF/Motif based user interface for these tools,
- a library (C or C++) to create and use OSF/Motif based user interface objects for tools which are developed in C or C++.

The facilities offered in the C or C++ libraries are the same as offered by the encap-

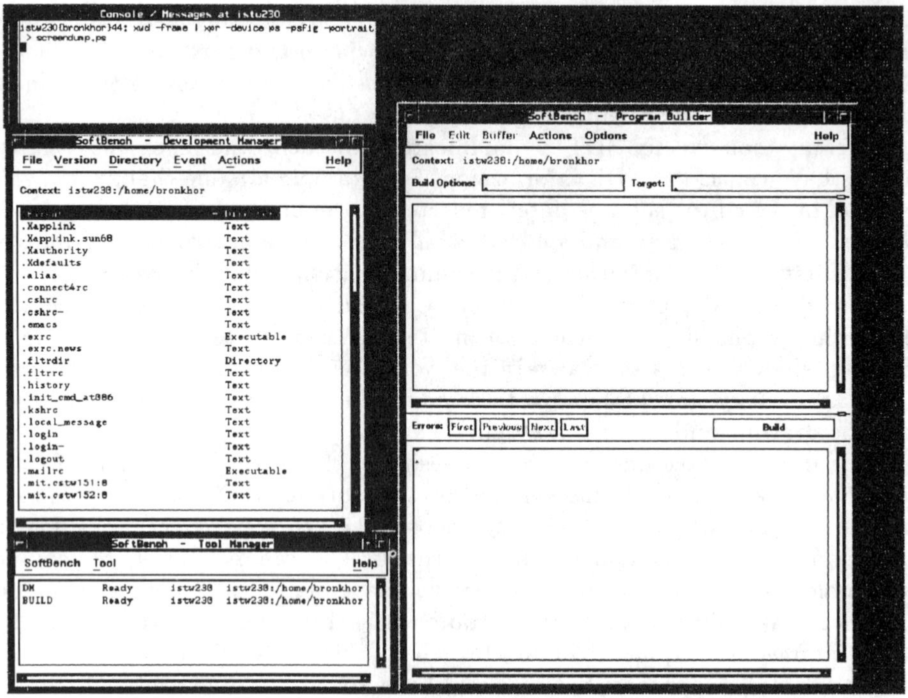

Figure 20.2 User interface of the SoftBench environment

sulation utility. The facilities contain functions for object creation, manipulation of the objects and manipulation of the attributes of objects. It is however also possible to use the full OSF/Motif libraries.

21

Examples of Integration between Tool-Sets

Besides the integrated environment described in this part it is also useful to describe some integrated tool-sets since they support the integration of methods. The method integration issues are discussed in [Kea92].

21.1 LOTOS-SDL TOOL-SET

This section covers the experience gained during the construction of the prototype SDL-LOTOS tools, the LOTOS-SDL tool-set, and the integrated LOTOS-SDL tool-set. The experience has been smoothly accumulated during the different phases but where the behaviour of the tools is explicitly described mainly the integrated LOTOS-SDL tool-set is used as an example. However, as the implementation of the integrated tool-set has not yet been completed at the time of writing this report some parts of the text are based on the design phase and do not necessarily correspond to the final implementation.

The goal of this report is twofold. Firstly, the tools are described in order to make it possible to use them as such or as submodules in other constructs. For this purpose the interfaces of the tools are explained, in enough detail to make the principle understandable. The exact grammars obeyed by the input and intermediate files are left to the design documentation of the tools. The second goal is to document the experience gained during the construction process. This is done in order perhaps to make it possible to avoid similar pitfalls in other constructs. For this purpose some problems encountered during the construction are listed and the chosen solutions and approaches explained. Also comparison with existing tools is included in order to point out that one should take a look at the existing tools before starting the construction of new ones. In addition to these the basis of the integration of LOTOS and SDL is described. The idea is to point out the similarity in the two formalisms.

The tool-set has evolved somewhat during the different phases. The main tendency has been to make the system more open, i.e. to split the tool-set into smaller units and to use clearly defined text files as the interfaces between the different modules. Among other advantages, this makes it easier perhaps to later combine the modules

Tool Integration: Environments and Frameworks, Edited by D. Schefström and G. van den Broek

in new ways. In addition there have been more practical changes. One was the change of the implementation language from C to Prolog. The shift was motivated by the feeling that the tools were rather experimental and a language on a higher level of abstraction makes it easier to change things even during the implementation phase.

21.1.1 Overall structure of the tool-set

The overall structure of the tool-set is illustrated in figure 21.1. Each tool is represented by a box. The inputs and outputs of the SDL state graph generator, the LOTOS labelled transition system generator, the graph comparator, and the model checker are made explicit in the figure. This explains also the interfaces between the tools, each oval corresponds to an ASCII file. The SDL specification is represented in the syntax of SDL-88, the state graph as a set of Prolog facts, the LOTOS specification in the syntax of basic LOTOS, and the labelled transition system again as a set of Prolog facts.

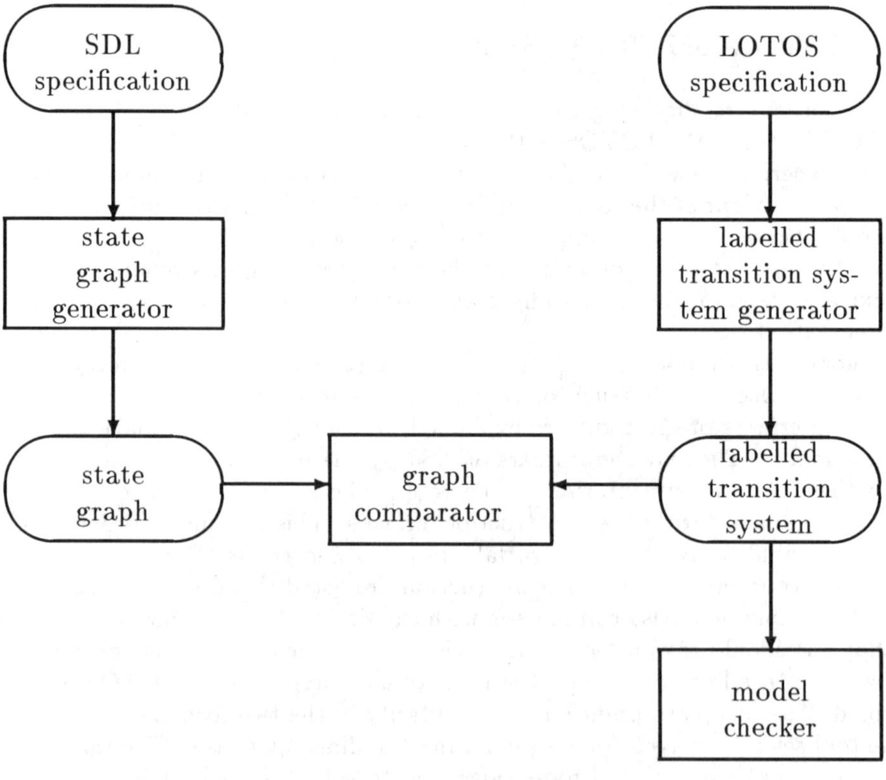

Figure 21.1 The overall structure of the tool-set. The ovals represent input and output of the tools, the boxes are the tools themselves. All input and output take place in the form of ASCII files.

21.1.2 Method integration

Both LOTOS and SDL are supposed to describe distributed systems where the system is determined by its states and changes of states.

Formalisms for describing distributed systems are usually composed of two parts, one for defining the control aspects and one for the data aspects. As far as the data part is concerned, LOTOS and SDL are both based on abstract data types defined by algebraic specifications and thus very close to each other. The current tools operate however on the so called propositional level where data is ignored and this similarity is thus not exploited. On the control level LOTOS and SDL are still quite similar, the main difference is the used model of communication. LOTOS is based on synchronous and SDL on asynchronous communication, i.e. message passing.

LOTOS is a process calculus where processes are represented as terms of an algebra. This offers a clean and clear mathematical foundation. SDL on the other hand is based on finite state machines which communicate with each other using message queues. One of the main advantages of SDL is the use of intuitive concepts like state, input, and output which together with the existing graphical form have made SDL very popular within the telecommunications industry.

The common basis of LOTOS and SDL is in the tools found on the level of the used computation model. The labelled transition systems of LOTOS processes are directed graphs where the edges are annotated with the actions in order to indicate the action sequences possible in the process. In a labelled transition system the emphasis is on the edge labels. Although the nodes are in principle labelled with processes these labels are normally ignored. In a state graph of SDL the interest is also on the labels of the nodes which describe the states of the system. A description of a state defines e.g. the values of the variables and the contents of the queues. The labels of the edges have a minor role in SDL state graphs, actually there seems to be no common agreement what the labels should be. The approach taken in the present tools is to use messages sent to and received from outside of the system as the labels.

Summarizing, on the execution model level LOTOS and SDL are quite similar, both are based on some forms of state graphs. In LOTOS the main emphasis is on the edges of the graph while in SDL on the nodes of the graph. It is worth noticing that most other formalisms also fall into the same category — some of them, e.g. Petri nets, see the edges and the nodes as equally important. Seen from a more practical point of view the tools are quite loosely coupled with each other, the main dimension of integration is data. All interaction between the tools takes place by reading files written by other tools and by writing files. The "external" interfaces of the tool-set consist of the CCITT recommendation language SDL-88 and the LOTOS language. There is very little integration on the control level, however the use of the different tools has been made as consistent as possible. Most of the tools are not interactive, they are executed by a command from the command line by giving a set of options and files as arguments. On the presentation level there is no additional integration between the tools.

21.1.3 Interfaces

Initially the prototype tools were constructed so that after reading the input files they kept most of the information inside. Later on human-readable intermediate files were found to be necessary and thus the tools were split into smaller units.

The representation of the intermediate files is highly influenced by the used programming language, i.e. Prolog. All the files are directly Prolog source code. This makes it possible to read them efficiently into the tools. Reading files character by character would in general be slower in any programming language. The representation as Prolog programmes (actually sets of facts) means that although the files are human-readable, they are in an, at least partly, parsed form.

21.1.3.1 Interfacing with the labelled transition system generator

The labelled transition system generator reads a specification of a LOTOS process and produces the labelled transition system for the process. The system is represented as a set of Prolog facts, each corresponding to one edge.

The input grammar of the LOTOS labelled transition system generator is extracted from [BB87]. It is described in more detail in the design document of the integrated LOTOS-SDL tool-set. The visibility rules are interpreted to be such that each process definition can see all the other definitions in the same description.

Actually there are two possibilities for the representation of the edges in the output of the generator. The one to be used normally uses unique integers as the labels of the nodes, the other one intended mainly for debugging purposes has terms corresponding to LOTOS processes as the node labels. The representation is chosen by a switch when the generator is run.

The algorithm used in the construction of the labelled transition graphs is fairly simple. For each behaviour expression defines a (possible empty) set of possible actions and remaining expressions. Now given an expression, its successors can be computed straightforwardly using the semantics. Further the successors of these new nodes can be computed by referring to the semantics and so on.

21.1.3.2 Interfacing with the model checker

In the early versions of the tools there was a "simulator" which could be used to wander in the labelled transition system of a LOTOS process. In the integrated LOTOS-SDL tool-set the simulator was replaced by a model checker which subsumes the simulator by offering more advanced ways to investigate the graph.

The name "model checker" is due to the fact that the labelled transition system is interpreted as a model of dynamic logic and the tool computes the truth value of formulae in a state of the system [Eme90a]. This activity can be described also as checking whether the system is a model of the formula. The model checker reads the labelled transition system of a LOTOS process as a Prolog programme and then interactively computes truth values of formulae given by the user in the initial node of the system.

The non-logical vocabulary of the queries is collected from the transition system. The edge labels are the atomic programmes of the dynamic logic in question. Relevant parts of the syntax of the formulae are adopted from the input language of

OTTER [McC90]. The exact description of the syntax of the formulae can be found in the design document of the integrated LOTOS-SDL tool-set.

The model checker is by no means restricted to labelled transition systems of LOTOS processes. It has also successfully been used for CCS agents and Petri nets. The basic structure also suits well for SDL state graphs but that adaptation has not yet been implemented as part of the LOTOS-SDL tool-set.

The model checker is based on an earlier idea of using dynamic logic as a general intensional logic and the actual model checking algorithm is developed from the one in Helsinki Logic Machine [NT87]. The dynamic logic used in the checker is RPDL described in [Har84]. In addition a state preserving translation from the temporal logic CTL into RPDL is valuable. The query language is thus actually a union of RPDL and CTL. The checker can be described as a top-down local model checker.

The model checker also contains an explanation facility. In addition to giving the truth value of the formula, it also gives a submodel of the original one as an explanation. The submodel has the property that the truth value of the formula is the same in it as in the original formula. The advantage of the submodel is that it contains only that part of the original formula which is relevant to the truth value of the formula and it is thus usually much smaller than the original one. The generated submodel is in the same form (set of Prolog facts) as the original formula and it can thus be used as an input to the model checker. This makes it possible to gradually focus one's interest in the relevant fragments of the model.

The main problems met during the construction of the model checker were performance problems. It took some care to write Prolog programmes which would run in the available memory space with large labelled transition systems.

21.1.3.3 Interfacing with the state graph generator

The state graph generator is probably the most complicated of the tools included in the tool-sets. The main difficulty is caused by the dynamic changes in the configuration of the SDL system. Processes can be created and killed on the fly and the addressing of the signal is also done dynamically. One additional difficulty is to find out what kind of information is needed in the graph, this was mainly found out by experimenting and adding when something was found to be missing.

The algorithm used to generate the state graph resembles the one used for generating the labelled transition systems for LOTOS expressions. The edges are defined by the semantics of SDL.

21.1.3.4 Interfacing with the graph comparator

The graph comparator reads two graphs which are in the form produced by the labelled transition system generator and state graph generator. The output of the comparator is a set of paths in the SDL state graph, again represented as Prolog facts. The given paths are the ones which violate the LOTOS specification. Unfortunately, the implementation of the comparator is not completed at the time of writing this and the exact output form is thus to some extent open. The design and test documents of the integrated LOTOS-SDL tool-set will include more details.

21.1.3.5 Inclusion in other environments

Because the individual tools in the tool-set are quite loosely coupled, it should be fairly simple to incorporate some or all of the tools in other environments. Also the interfaces described above were designed to be clearly defined and simple. This might in some cases cause some loss of efficiency but that was not considered to be very harmful.

Especially the LOTOS part, i.e. the labelled transition system generator, the model checker, and partly the graph comparator, could be used in environments for experimenting with LOTOS. This is because they carry out simple well defined tasks. The SDL part, i.e. the state graph generator, on the other hand doesn't solve a very clearly defined problem due to several design choices. These choices, e.g. ignorance of data, cause the resulting state graph to be incomplete and it depends on the usage whether this is acceptable or not.

21.1.4 Problems encountered

This paragraph covers some of the problems encountered during the construction of the tools. Part of the problems were quite practical by nature, e.g. the straightforward writing of Prolog didn't produce efficient enough programmes. Some other problems had a more elementary nature. For example, it was not at all obvious what kind of information should be included in the state graph of an SDL system.

21.1.4.1 Writing efficient Prolog programmes

Writing efficient programmes is not easy in any language. When performance becomes essential, the programmer has to understand the language quite deeply in order to make the correct choices concerning both data structures and algorithms. This also is true for Prolog, as R. O'Keefe puts it in [O'K90]: "Hacking your programme is no substitute for understanding your problem. Prolog is different, but not that different. Elegance is not optional."

The main point in writing good Prolog programmes is to make the predicates deterministic whenever possible. This saves a lot of memory because unnecessary choice points can be discarded. The same should be done also in the grammar rules, but in the implemented tools it wasn't. The problem with the Definite Clause Grammars normally included in Prologs will however shortly be viewed in this report.

21.1.4.2 Definite clause grammars

The parsing mechanism in Prolog has originally been designed for parsing natural languages where the framework is usually a bit different from formal languages like SDL or LOTOS. In natural languages sentences are in general short but can have several different parse trees. In formal languages, on the contrary, the strings to be parsed can be very long but usually have a unique parse tree.

In contrast to e.g. the parser generator YACC, the Definite Clause Grammar mechanism in Prolog only carries out a straightforward transformation of the grammar rules into Prolog rules. This has the advantage that e.g. the debugger and cross-referencer can be directly applied also to the grammar code, but on the other hand it means that the resulting parser is based mainly on brute force, i.e. on trying to apply the grammar rules in the order they are given. Unfortunately, the produced clauses can normally not take advantage of the indexing mechanism in Prolog.

The definition of a process in basic LOTOS is usually quite small, usually some tens of lines, but an SDL specification can be quite large, perhaps tens of thousands of lines. This implies that from the performance point of view the scanner and parser for SDL are the critical points, for both execution time and memory consumption. In fact, measurements confirm this belief, the SDL scanner seems to take a major part of the execution time in the tools.

There are mechanisms with which a set of grammar rules can in some cases be made deterministic but these have not so far been applied in the LOTOS-SDL tools. The mechanism implements a kind of look-ahead such that the choice of the grammar rule can be made deterministically based on the look-ahead token.

21.1.5 Conclusions

It was felt that all the aspects mentioned in this report were important to the successful construction of the LOTOS-SDL tool-set. As general guidelines the following items can be extracted:

- make experiments with existing tools already before starting the design of the new ones,
- start with simple prototypes to detect the possible flaws in the ideas involved, and finally
- make the tools efficient enough to be practical.

21.2 CASN-SDL TOOL-SET

21.2.1 Architecture of GENSDL

GENSDL CASN back-end is implemented according to the guide-lines given in the document [Tur91b] (background material). Routines found in the CASN Back-end Toolbox, BET, (background material) are used extensively in the implementation. BET offers e.g. routines for handling internal data structures and routines for environment independent I/O. The general structure of GENSDL is as follows (see figure 21.2):

1. Command line parsing and initialization.
2. Reading of syntax trees into internal buffers.
3. Generation of TN-SDL definitions. The following is repeated until all types which are visible in one ASN.1 module or which are reachable are defined.
   (a) Walk through a syntax tree and find the next visible or reachable type.
   (b) If the type has component types, define components recursively. In this way TN-SDL types are defined before they are used.
   (c) Define the type itself.

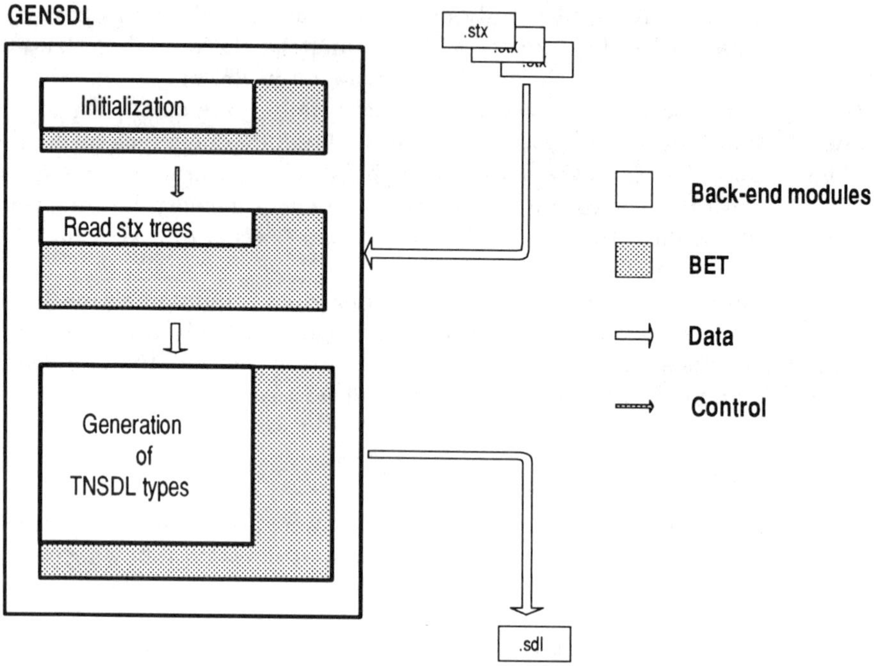

Figure 21.2 Structure of GENSDL back-end

21.2.2 Integration aspects

Data integration is achieved at the source code level (ASN.1.1 definitions files, C source and header files, TN-SDL definition files). The only binary files are syntax trees, but they are used only to pass information between CASN and GENSDL and thus considered to be internal. Used data files are presented in the following subsections. Figure 21.3 shows the flow of data between the different parts of the tool-set.

21.2.2.1 Input of CASN

The CASN input consists of one textual ASN.1 definition file and binary syntax tree files for previous compilations, if any.

The ASN.1 definition is as presented in [OSO]. In addition there can be options for CASN Compiler within ASN.1 comments. The options affect generation of C types. The options and their use is described in [Nok91] (background material). Besides CASN Compiler options there are a few back-end options which have meaning for GENSDL back-end only. The effect of CASN Compiler options and back-end options to the TN-SDL type declarations is described in [Tur91a].

We were forced to make a few restrictions to ASN.1 type definitions for TN-SDL systems. This is due to differences between CASN Compiler and TN-SDL Translator.

These restrictions are as follows:

- Use of nested structures is not allowed if certain special CASN code generation

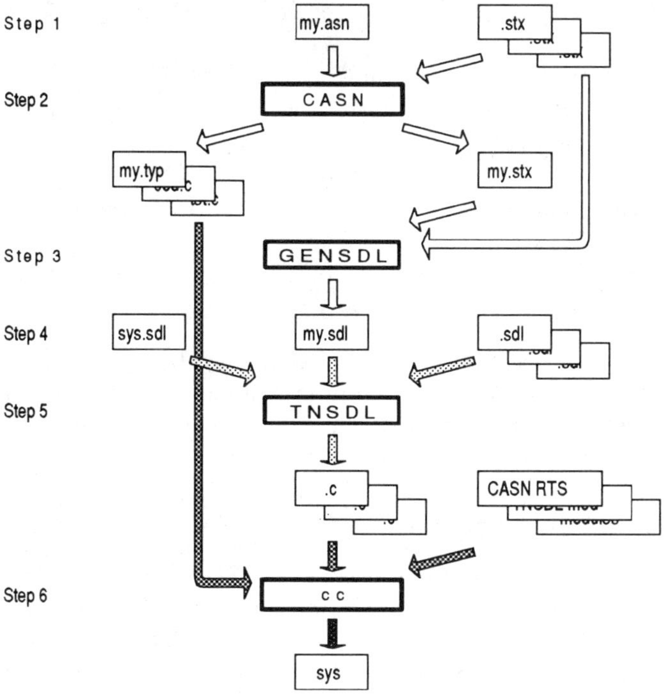

Figure 21.3 Use of GENSDL with CASN and TN-SDL

options are used. This restriction is due to the differences in code generation and was considered to be very easy to get around.

- No support for REAL type. Real type was dropped because the implementation of CASN and TN-SDL reals differs. This restriction was considered to be a minor one because no real types are used in TN-SDL systems at the moment.

Other problems in the integration of ASN.1 and TN-SDL types together with solutions to these problems are presented in [Tur91a]. Almost every solution involves use of CASN and/or GENSDL options.

21.2.2.2 Output of CASN

The CASN output consists of three kinds of files:

1. C source files;

    - coding functions for visible and reachable ASN.1 types found in a module definition. (&cod.c) and
    - test functions for visible and reachable ASN.1 types found in a module definition. (&tst.c)

2. C include files;

- C type definitions for visible and reachable ASN.1 types found in a module definition (&.typ), [1]
- other definitions (&.def, &.tab) and
- function prototypes (&cod.ext, &cod.usr, &tst.ext, &tst.usr).

3. Binary syntax tree file (&typ.stx, used by GENSDL)

Document [AKT91] (background material) contains more information about generated files.

21.2.2.3 Input of GENSDL

The GENSDL input consists of one or more CASN syntax trees which contain ASN.1 module definitions. One of them is the topmost module i.e. it contains the definitions which are to be converted into TN-SDL. The others, if any, contain exported definitions which are used in the topmost module directly or indirectly.

21.2.2.4 Output of GENSDL

The GENSDL output consists of one textual TN-SDL definition file for the topmost module. The file name is derived from the module name (first five letters) and an sdl suffix, e.g. *mymod.sdl* for module MyModule. The TN-SDL type definitions are almost equivalent to C type definitions generated by CASN. The few differences are due to the restrictions in TN-SDL and they are described in [Tur91a].

21.2.2.5 Input of TN-SDL translator

The TN-SDL type definitions generated by GENSDL are used as a part of the TN-SDL system definition. Other parts of system definition are outside of scope of this document.

21.2.2.6 Output of TN-SDL translator

The GENSDL generated TN-SDL definitions are translated into C type definitions. The generated C types are bitwise compatible with the CASN generated C types.

GENSDL is a command line driven program. Options are prefixed with a hyphen and consist of an option name and an option value. Option names are similar to those of CASN. Options consist of information about directory paths and commands for TN-SDL type generation.

GENSDL has only one mandatory argument, file prefix of the topmost ASN.1 module, e.g. *mymod*. Example:

```
\GENSDL{} -S=stx -H=sdl -SUBRANGE=0 mymod
```

GENSDL reads syntax tree(s) from the syntax file directory (default is current directory) and generates a TN-SDL definition file into the include file directory (default is current directory).

[1] "&" stands for the file prefix, i.e. the first five letters of the ASN.1 module name, e.g. *mymod* for a module MyModule.

The presentation integration is not important with GENSDL because GENSDL is a command line driven program whose input is a set of automatically generated binary files and output is a file to be used as input for another tool.

21.2.3 Use of CASN and GENSDL tools with TN-SDL

The use of CASN and GENSDL tools with TN-SDL can be separated into six steps (see figure 21.3).

1. Making of ASN.1 definitions. Documents [Nok91], [AKT91] and [Tur91a] contain necessary information about how to declare types and how to use CASN and GENSDL options in order to get wanted TN-SDL type definitions.
2. Generation of C type definitions and coding functions with CASN Compiler. Run the CASN Compiler once for each ASN.1 module definition. The modules must be compiled in bottom-up order. CASN generates C type definitions and coding and test functions for those types and a syntax tree which is used in later compilations and in TN-SDL type generation.
3. Generation of TN-SDL type definitions with GENSDL. Run GENSDL once for each module definition. GENSDL generates TN-SDL type definitions which are equivalent to CASN generated C type definitions.
4. Making of a TN-SDL system definition. Include generated TN-SDL type definitions together with pre-defined TN-SDL type definitions for CASN (asntype.sdl) in the TN-SDL system definition. Types found in the generated files can be used as any other TN-SDL types. If there is a need to encode and decode these generated types then CASN generated coding functions can be used.
5. Generation of the TN-SDL system with TN-SDL Translator. Run the TN-SDL Translator to generate the TN-SDL system. Translation and generated C source files are described in [LRKT91].
6. Compilation of the TN-SDL system. Compile and link the following C modules together:
   - TN-SDL generated system functions.
   - Other TN-SDL modules (background material).
   - CASN generated coding functions and CASN runtime system (background material) if ASN.1 coding services are used.
   - Other modules, if any.

21.3 SDT AND CODE GENERATION

To produce an executable program, the SDL system is entered into the analyzer tool set. If the system is syntactically and semantically correct a program is generated in C source code. The C-Code Generator uses all aspects of the SDL specification to generate complete C code. This code is then compiled by a C compiler and linked together with an SDL run-time library and with the C runtime library, to form the executable program. This production process is completely automated and is performed by the analyzer. Technically, a “make file” is generated by the C code generator together with the C code. By starting the make facility with this make file, the analyzer is able to initiate the compilation and linking of the generated program. This is true when code is generated for the host machine. For targets the user has to be involved, as parts of this process are unknown to us.

Figure 21.4 shows the steps in the production of an executable programme from an SDL system description.

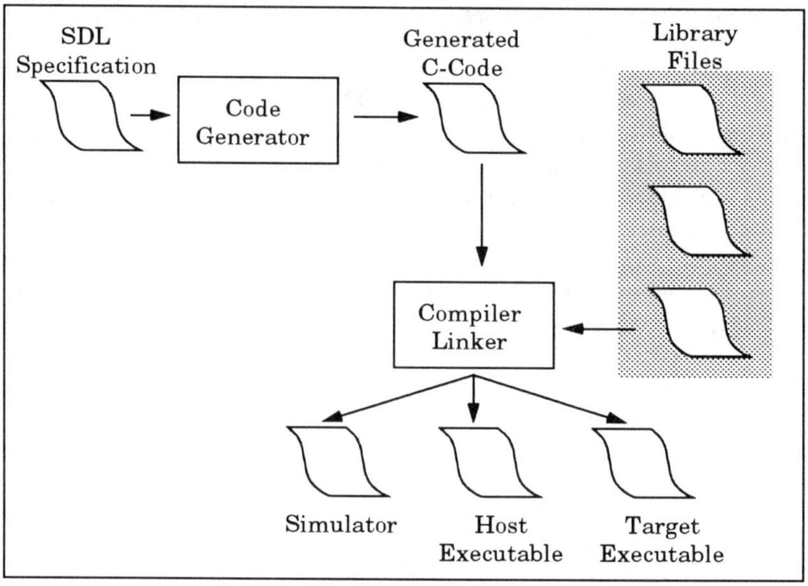

Figure 21.4 Generation of host or target executable

A very important aspect of the production process is that the generated C code should never be changed. If the executable programme does not behave as expected, then the input to the process, i.e. the SDL description should be changed and the new C code should be generated, compiled and linked. In this way it is possible to guarantee that the SDL graphs, that is the documentation, are consistent with the executing programme. Of course, it also means that the code generator has to be very flexible, so there will be no real need to make changes in the generated code. How this flexibility is achieved is discussed below.

Generator flexibility is, when implementing real applications, of most importance in the following areas:

- Possibility to include C together with the SDL specifications, for example, to improve performance for time critical parts of the application.
- Flexible control of the execution of the SDL system.
- Possibility of adopting the generated code to I/O and real-time functions in the target hardware.
- Flexible connection to user specified environment signals and/or user programmes.

The language SDL does not in itself contain everything necessary to describe an implementation of an application. With SDT it is possible to use directives, inserted in the specification as SDL comments, to give supplementary information to the code generator (example: /* number sign DIRECTIVE*/). Directives are for example used for:

OP, ADT Giving implementations of abstract data types. This is mainly intended to give C implementations of the operators in the abstract data types, but can also be used to specify the full implementation of the abstract data type, including the type definition, how to perform assign and equal operations and so on.

CODE To include C code in SDL tasks. Actions which are impossible or difficult to describe in SDL can be coded directly in C, and this code can be included in an SDL task.
To include declarations of any kind written in C. In this way types, functions, variables, and so on, declared in C can be included in the generated C code.

INCLUDE To include C files in SDL specifications.

NAME, SDL Mapping between SDL and included C code. Using the above mentioned directives, it is possible to have declarations in both SDL and C, and actions both in SDL and C. It is then necessary to be able to use names declared in SDL or C, in actions in SDL or C. The suitable mapping functions are provided to make this possible.

PRIO To give priorities to processes or signals so the user can control the execution of the system.

SEPARATE To inform the code generator how to divide the generated system into files.

WITH To inform the code generator that user defined and/or predefined units shall be linked together with the generated program.

The parts of the library depending on the underlying system/hardware have been identified and placed in a module of their own. By the possibility of changing the implementation of these base functions, the user can port the whole SDT runtime environment to any hardware that has a reasonably good C compiler available, preferably ANSI-C. Examples of such functions are:

- Allocate and deallocate memory.
- Read the clock or handle hardware timeouts.
- Read and write signals and characters.
- Enable and disable interrupts.

To connect external SDL environment signals the user has the possibility of inserting the signals in the I/O driver routines. The system will see the signals as any other SDL signal in the system so in the specification all can remain on an SDL level.

21.3.1 The execution model

The execution of the generated program is based on a runtime model that contains the following major components (see figure 21.5):

- The generated code, which mainly represents the behaviour of the SDL processes, i.e. the state machines.
- The library containing SDL oriented types and functions including runtime functions dependent on the underlying system/hardware.

- The environment routines In and Out, which may be supplied by the user and which represent the connection between the state machines and their environment.
- Interrupt routines or drivers to handle external events, including functions dependent on the underlying system/hardware.

An executable programme will also contain C library functions from the library of the C compiler system.

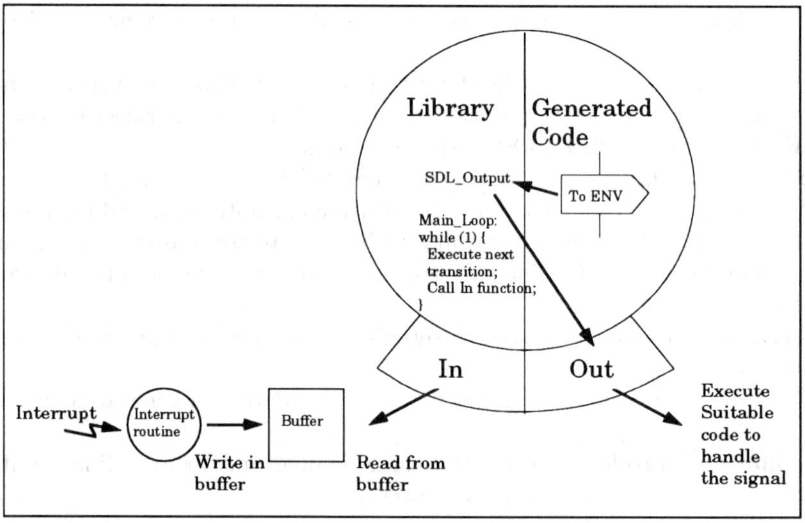

Figure 21.5 The execution model

The main loop, which is an endless loop located in the library, will execute one transition at a time, sequentially. To select the order in which process instances may execute their transitions, the priorities of the processes are used, or the priorities of the signals that are to be received. This means that the next transition to be executed will always be the transition with highest priority, but also that a transition is executed to its end before the next transition can be started.

If a signal is sent from an SDL process to the environment of the SDL system, the library function handling outputs of signals will call the environment routine Out, with the actual signal as parameter. In the Out routine the user can examine the signal for its type, the sending and receiving process, and the signal parameters and can then perform the actions necessary to physically implement the signal sending. In this way the implementation of external activities has been divided into two parts. First the logic part where a state machine decides to send a signal to the environment, and then a second implementation part where this signal is transformed to its actual implementation.

Receiving information from the environment can be implemented in several ways, using different implementations of the In routine. In figure 21.5, a model using interrupts is presented. In this case the reception of information is divided into three steps. First an interrupt will tell the application that some information from the environment has become available. The interrupt routine, which is automatically called, can then receive the information and store it in a buffer. The second step of receiving information is performed by the In routine. This routine is called from the main loop between transitions, and checks in the buffers to see if any information has been received. If so the information is transformed to SDL signals and sent to the SDL system. In the third step these signals cause transitions where appropriate actions can be taken in the SDL system.

The environment routines In and Out are the place where the conversion between external events and SDL signals is done. The actual code in these routines depends on the event that causes a signal to be sent to the SDL system and the actions that are performed as a result of a signal sent from the SDL system. Examples of such actions are writing information to a specific memory address or to a port, communication with another computer in a network, or with another operating system process within a computer, using some communication mechanism (for example TCP/IP, UNIX pipes). In the case of a communication protocol, such as the one mentioned, it is usually possible to remove the interrupt level in the model discussed above since that level is handled by the communication protocol.

This runtime model is frequently used by people working with the state machine concept in the development of embedded systems. Numerous applications have been developed using this kind of model, including time critical systems.

It is worth noting that the model described above does not require any operating system or executive for a micro computer target. It is possible to run the code on a naked machine.

21.4 SDT HOST-TARGET SUPPORT

A successful port of an SDL application, generated by SDT to an arbitrary target computer system, requires the ability to debug the application code at different levels of abstraction. Debugging must in these cases be performed both at the SDL level, the implementation language level, in our case "C", and ultimately at the assembler level. This in turn results in a list of requirements put on the application generator and debug tools. These requirements are: the ability to perform debugging in a heterogeneous language and computer environment; the ability to handle Real-Time and concurrent multitasking mechanisms; etc. Traditionally this set of requirements are not met in any single tool but involves the use of different debug tools, and hence different methodologies for different aspects of system test and debugging.

With the introduction of tools like SDT many of the above mentioned aspects are obtainable in one integrated development tool. In SDT these are:

- SDL-level debugging, both in the development host and the target system.
- "C"-level debug support in the development host and limited support in the target system.
- Simulation of real-time multitasking behaviour in the host development system.
- Simulation of real-time multi-system interaction in the host development system.

Among the other features of SDT's debugging capabilities are graphical traceback to the SDL graphs, both in simulation and debugging mode. Another feature is the possibility to shorten development time by allowing concurrent independent development of the SDL-application and the code needed to implement the External SDL Layer, and the lower layers, see below.

The debugging mechanisms are based on the application execution model developed for SDT. The basic static execution model requires the system under test to adhere to our layered model, see figure 21.6. This model consists of 3 software layers, where the upper layer (Application layer) has two components, the SDL-application itself and the SDL-runtime library. The SDL-application consists of:

1. the SDL-code, transformed by SDT into compilable "C"-code;
2. a runtime library that consists of a utility/scheduler package, a debug-monitor package and a user configurable "C"-file (sctOS.c) where the user, if required, may insert extra "C"-code to transform six calls from the utility package into proper calls to the virtual target machine.

The "Virtual target machine" is the target computer system software/(hardware) interface as seen from an application.

The second layer (the External SDL Layer, (ESL)), is normally supplied by the user except when simulating the application on the development host. The ESL interfaces upwards (to the application and R-T libraries) via the External SDL Interface (ESI), and downwards via the Virtual Machine Interface (VMI). The reasons for the ESL, is to have a place to insert the code required to perform the necessary type/sort conversions, between the SDL- and the C-world, of SDL-signals in a controlled manner and to provide the user with a VMI, i.e. an interface where the user has full control of the implementation.

The third (lowest) layer is the Virtual Machine Layer (VML) and is optional if the target machine is equipped with an operating system/executive of some kind.

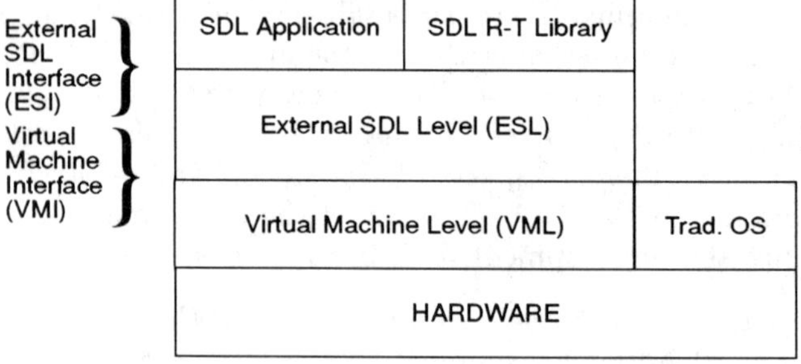

Figure 21.6 Different layers in the static execution model

The typical debug/system-integration activities supported by SDT are described in the following subsections.

21.4.1 Functional debugging of state-machine implementations

SDL-application debug during its development phase. This is done in the development host environment and SDT provides all the tools required for the debug sessions. That is, with the aid of SDT, a user can automatically transform the SDL-diagrams into "C"-code, compile it and link it with the supplied, preconfigured (for the host environment), SDL-runtime libraries. An SDL-system generated in this manner has the following properties:

- It can be executed from SDT, with full user control. Full control in this context means that the user may for example step through the execution symbol by symbol or set breakpoints for the execution while at the same time being able to follow the execution path graphically in the system specification diagrams.
- Simple variables and other types of entities like signal queues may be inspected and optionally altered interactively by the user.
- Fault conditions can be simulated by interactively manipulating queues, processes, etc.
- Signals to-and-from the SDL-system environment, i.e. the ESL may be simulated and analyzed.
- The whole debug session can be logged onto a file for later analysis and stimuli to the system-under-test may be input from a prepared command file, in order to simplify regression test on a system or a part of a system.

21.4.2 System level debugging

SDT enables multi SDL-system interaction analysis, including certain timing effects. A typical sample case where this is an important aspect of debugging is test of communication protocols. This feature gives the user the possibility of debugging both the receiving and transmitting ends of a communication link before any actual test system is available. SDT's PostMaster mechanism, described in section 19.1, is providing the test-system intercommunication mechanisms, which otherwise may be time consuming to implement by a user. All the properties under section 21.4.1 above are applicable in this case as well.

21.4.3 Interface code debugging

Once the SDL-application system level diagram has been produced, this document provides the basis for developing the External SDL Level of code, and the optional layer below it. By inserting conditionally compiled code, that uses host console I/O, in the places where the actual writing-to and reading-from the target VMI is done, the user can test the ESL/VML code separately in the actual target environment (with the aid of for example an In-Circuit Emulator, in which case SDT has provided information, in the "C"-source code, to back-track execution to the appropriate SDL-diagram and symbol, see section 6.4 below), or simulate it together with the SDL-application in the host environment. The addition of conditionally compiled code is normally of the order of 1 (one) line of "C"-code per external SDL-signal. An addition which is very limited and greatly enhances the testability. The major benefit of this activity is that the user can verify the ESL functionality in a controlled manner.

21.4.4 Target debugging

Provided the user has access to the source code for the SDL-runtime libraries, he may now choose to cross-compile the "C"-code generated from SDT, the runtime libraries (both the utility/scheduler file and the debug/monitor support file) and his ESL/VML code. After linking these together he may either download the code into the target system or programme the code into EPROMs (or similar devices). Provided a "dumb" terminal is connected to the target system it is now possible to debug the system on the SDL-level using the same command interface as used by the internal SDT simulator mechanism. The functionality offered is almost the same as under section 21.4.1, above, with the exclusion of the graphical trace utility, and possibly the logging utility. The latter depends on whether the target system is equipped with a file I/O device or not.

21.4.5 Integration test

The last step in system development/debugging/integration is normally to run the produced code in the target environment either directly or under In-Circuit Emulator control to try out initialization routines, response times, etc. This phase is partially supported by SDT. The support given is in the nature of references generated into the SDL-application "C"-code which enables the user to back-track the execution to the proper SDL-symbol(s), and hence obtain a better understanding of the behaviour of the executing code. To utilize this feature the user must provide at least a target system source code debugger or a similar device.

22

Observations and Future Outlook

OBSERVATIONS

The development environment described in this project is intended to support existing development teams with an existing software base. The projects rely on a large volume of already existing application code which must be maintained and improved. This means that changes in methodologies, tools and even the computer infrastructure must be based on an evolution instead of a revolution. To the original environment new tools are added and where needed tools to transform data (glueware) are added. Such glueware is needed when data formats between tools differ. To produce such glueware the use of a parser generator for abstract syntax graphs has proven to be very useful.

The extended environment consists of a tool-chain of tool-sets and the next set step was to construct an integrated environment of those tool-sets. For this integration a framework (SoftBench) is used which offers the developers an SDL integrated environment based on loosely coupling tools using messages to request services from other tools. This development environment runs on a heterogeneous network of workstations and mini computers to enable the use of existing tools. This integration activity showed that using such a technology as a broadcast message server is technically not a big problem but the following observations can be made:

- The process of constructing such an integrated environment is an engineering process in itself and needs a specification, design, implementation, testing, generation and installation phase. To take full advantage of such an environment *all* tools which are used by the developers should be integrated.
- The introduction of such an integrated environment needs a lot of attention since it influences human ways of working from human beings and as such it can be compared to automating, for instance, a salary administration or even introducing a logistic system. As such it has an impact on working procedures and on the organization since new roles will be defined. An additional complication can be that the tools and the integration of tools are realized using technology (software) which is familiar to the users.

Tool Integration: Environments and Frameworks, Edited by D. Schefström and G. van den Broek

- The functionality of an integrated environment should reflect the level of maturity of the development group, especially with respect to process integration. One needs a well defined and accepted process before it can be automated.
- To enable fruitful integration the primary functions of a tool should be directly accessible. Preferably these functions should be available through standardized messages and not only by human interaction through a top level browser from the tool-set.
- Standardization of tool interfaces through a common set of messages makes integration easier and offers flexibility in tool selection.
- Standardization in data formats will reduce the need for glueware and is needed to achieve real data integration between tools.
- When shared repositories are used standardization of schemas is also required to achieve a fruitful data integration between tools.

FUTURE OUTLOOK

Upgrading the SDL-based tool-sets to support SDL-88 is planned (this will reduce the need for some glueware) and the extension of SDL with object-oriented features will have an impact in the future. Standardization on data exchange formats (CDIF), standardization of messages for inter tool communication (CASE Communiqué), standardization of schemas for shared repositories and the availability of repositories (PCTE) which offer extendible schema definitions (which offer a powerful typing mechanism on objects as well as relations) will make construction of more powerful integrated environment possible. A lot of activities are going on and will produce results in the next couple of years. An example this can be the North American PCTE Initiative (NAPI). A consortium founded to work together with ECMA on the evolution of PCTE, to implement a public domian version of PCTE and to organize a validation suite to check the conformance of implementations. However in practice one should be aware that interoperability with existing tools will always be needed. In the meantime we should not wait for the ultimate solution but exploit the available technology now.

To plan and realize the evolution of the required technology and of frameworks to support the construction of integrated environments a close cooperation of platform vendors, framework suppliers, tool suppliers and the user community is needed. The ultimate goal is to solve the user needs. The challenge is to combine the forces to realize this, not for software development in isolation but also in combination with other engineering disciplines such as IC design, PCB design, mechanical design and ultimately also with logistics and manufacturing preparation.

Part V

Hardware Engineering Environment

Maria Brielmann, Elisabeth Kupitz, and Susanne Rudolph
CADLAB[1]
Bahnhofstraße 32
W-4790 Paderborn
Germany

[1] Joint Venture of Siemens Nixdorf Informationssysteme AG and University of Paderborn

Tool Integration: Environments and Frameworks, Edited by D. Schefström and G. van den Broek

23

Introduction

23.1 Rationale, objectives and approach

Future computing systems will be faced with increasing requirements regarding their functionality, reliability, and performance. This holds not only for technically oriented systems, but also for the so–called commercial systems (e.g., for financial institutes, insurance companies, or retail stores). In addition, the available time to satisfy these increasing requirements is steadily decreasing. To remain competitive, advanced computer aided support of the system engineering process becomes indispensable for industrial development departments. For system parts to be realized by hardware the use of hardware synthesis methods will greatly decrease the design time and design effort, allowing the exploitation of alternative hardware realizations to improve the hardware realizations with respect to the stated requirements. Furthermore, to meet the stated requirements the behaviour of a system has to be assessed from the beginning and, accordingly, system analysis and evaluation have to be performed during the whole system engineering process, i.e., during system design, realization and operations.

In the past remarkable results have been achieved in the area of system modelling and evaluation as well as in the area of hardware engineering. Many advanced high level synthesis methods and tools have been developed during recent years, but presently only lower level synthesis tools starting with a register transfer description of the hardware are used to some extent in industrial environments. The application of high level design synthesis that starts with an algorithmic description of the hardware which abstracts from the hardware architecture will be an important push towards real system engineering, where the starting point is a homogeneous description of the entire system behaviour and even the distinction between hardware and software realization of the system constituents is open.

The situation for evaluation and analysis tools is similar. Although the importance of evaluation techniques during the development of computing systems is well recognized, appropriate methods and corresponding tools unfortunately are used less than in other engineering disciplines. One of the main reasons is that the design process is not considered as a unit, and hardware modules and software components are designed and developed separately. Real world practice, however, has shown that qualitative and quantitative evaluation of system behaviour is necessary at all stages of development. Being aware of these deficiencies and industrial needs, analysis and evaluation

Tool Integration: Environments and Frameworks, Edited by D. Schefström and G. van den Broek

techniques have developed enormously since the late seventies. Especially at universities and research institutes, there have been notable improvements in the field of modelling and evaluation techniques which have already been integrated in tools sufficiently mature for industrial use.

Difficulties with all tools, both synthesis and analysis tools, available on the market arise from the fact that they stand more or less isolated and, probably therefore, are not widely used in industrial practice. This situation rationalizes the plan to build an "Integrated System Engineering Environment" for the development of information technology as a long term objective.

The strategy to achieve this objective follows an incremental and partly parallel approach in order to make advances within several areas. Therfore, the system design and development process itself as well as the provision of the necessary tools for its support in appropriate, integrated sub-environments have to be regarded. Additionally, some progress is necessary for the required integration technology (framework) before being able to supply a full blown "Integrated System Engineering Environment", which supports and eases the development of todays information technology systems throughout the whole life-cycle.

23.1.1 Contribution of the work under study

The work described here contributes to help in moving towards the above mentioned objective. It has been performed within ATMOSPHERE by four parties: Siemens Nixdorf Informationssysteme AG, Cadlab[1], and the Universities of Dortmund and Strathclyde. This specific contribution is reflected by the dual role Cadlab plays within this context: on the one hand, Cadlab acts as supplier of appropriate integration technology, i.e., of major components of an advanced framework, the JESSI Common Framework [Ste92, Kat92], which provides flexible and open services for the integration of arbitrary tools/toolsets, both internal and external to SNI. On the other hand, Cadlab also acts as a supplier of advanced system engineering tools to be integrated using this technology.

The Hardware Engineering Environment, whose integration is described here, consists of the Hardware Synthesis System (HWSS) [RS91] for the design of digital integrated circuits, the CIRCAL verification tool [BMMM91], and a performance evaluation toolset, consisting of the tools HIT [BMW88, BS87] and BEMO [Mey89] (for a more detailed description of the tools see section 23.3). The integration of these tools has been performed by using the integration technology provided by the JESSI Common Framework. As this toolset has a strong hardware engineering component the integration efforts described here are mainly driven by hardware engineering requirements.

23.1.2 Overview on contents of report

In the remainder of this section first the role of hardware engineering in the system engineering process (see section 23.2.1) is described. The tools provided by the Hardware Engineering Environment concentrate on the design phase rather than on other

[1] Cadlab is a joint venture of Siemens Nixdorf Informationssysteme AG and of the University of Paderborn

phases like requirements engineering or hardware production. Therefore, the general principles of hardware design are explained in more detail (see section 23.2.2). This subsection is especially recommended for those readers, who are not familiar with hardware engineering. Afterwards the tools and the resulting architecture of the Hardware Engineering Environment are introduced (see sections 23.3, 23.4).

This introduction is followed by a discussion about the three integration dimensions: data, presentation, and control. For each of these integration dimensions at first the underlying integration technology is described. Afterwards, the experiences and the major achievements gained during the integration of the Hardware Engineering Environment are discussed for each integration dimension. The main part of the integration work described here is based on data integration. Therefore, the data dimension is considered first in chapter 24. Chapter 25 deals with presentation integration. Control integration is described last (see chapter 26), because it is based on the work done for data and presentation integration. The description of the integration approach under consideration here is closed with a conclusion.

23.2 UNDERLYING PROJECT MODEL

In this section the hardware development process will be described. In the first part of this description general remarks on the role of hardware design in system engineering and a brief comparison between the development of software and hardware systems will be given. In the second part the hardware design process will be explained in more detail.

23.2.1 The role of hardware design in system engineering

The system development process can be split up into several phases. Since the interfaces and expected results of the different phases can be clearly defined, the entire process can be controlled more easily. At the end of each phase only the defined results have to be checked to decide whether the process has been successful so far. This subdivision should also help to provide data consistency and to define distinct interfaces for information flow. Usually the system development process consists of six phases (a more detailed description can be found in [HNS86]):

1. During the *requirement phase* the requirements for the system are collected.
2. During the *specification phase* the requirements for the system are analyzed with respect to the solution techniques and a detailed specification of system functionality, performance, and structure is elaborated. Additionally the interfaces to the surrounding system and the test procedure should be determined.
3. The system development is started with the *system design phase*. The main development direction is top down (see section 23.2.2). At first, the design is described in a coarse manner. The elements of this coarse description are refined during several steps until they are defined using elementary functions and their interconnections. Often, block diagrams are used to describe the decomposition of the design. The control flow is for example defined with the help of Nassy–Schneidermann diagrams. The development of the modules, which are defined during the decomposition pro-

cess can be distributed to several designers. Errors, which are made during this phase, are very difficult to overcome, because they are usually found very late.

4. During the *implementation phase* the modules building up the design are constructed and tested. The coding of the modules can either be done in a graphical and symbolic manner or with the use of procedures. In the past, the graphical description was mostly used for hardware design whereas procedures were used for software development. But nowadays the hardware is also described more and more with the help of procedural languages. Usually, the design phase and the implementation phase are executed with many iterations, so that often they are not clearly separated. The coding of the modules is followed by a compilation process. The result can be an executable program or the data needed for the fabrication of the system. During compilation the syntactical correctness of the design is checked.
5. During the *integration* and *verification/validation* phase the elements of the system are combined and the functional correctness is checked. This means also examining whether the requirements, which have been collected during the requirement phase, are fulfilled by the developed system. Software is usually checked for correctness by running a set of test programs that were defined and coded during the previous phases. The most common method for validation of hardware designs with respect to their "behaviour" is simulation. Also some verification tools like CIRCAL are emerging, but unfortunately they are not widely accepted. For performance evaluation, besides simulation, quantitative analysis techniques based on queuing networks theory and Markov chain analysis are also used.
6. During the *production phase* the system is transferred from the development environment to the production environment. The product management ensures that the system is ready for use. For software development the result is a usable and released software product. For hardware development the system has to be fabricated. The result, for example a chip, has to be tested for fabrication faults.

Usually, it is not possible to follow these phases purely sequentially, because some key functions have to be described in detail before the design can be further developed. Therefore, the top down and bottom up methods are usually merged resulting in the so-called yo-yo method. Additionally, the design is often partitioned to get parts which can be handled more easily ("divide and conquer"). The different parts can also be in different phases of the development process. Therefore, concurrent engineering techniques are necessary ensuring the correct development of the whole system (the term concurrent engineering was defined by the Institute for Defense Analysis IDA [W+]).

Some differences between hardware and software development can be found. For example, usually, software is described by data and control flows, whereas hardware is described by a graphical representation of the functional blocks. But this difference is fading out more and more. Nowadays, a lot of hardware description languages exist to describe the data and control flow of hardware and the use of graphical representation methods of software is increasing. Other differences are the number of abstraction levels, verification methods, test preparation, and production.

For software development only a few levels of abstraction exist: the description in a high level programming language and the code of a design. For hardware development several additional levels of abstraction exist (see section 23.2.2).

For software development the fabrication of the design means to copy the code, whereas for hardware development, e.g., a chip has to be produced. The production is a very expensive process. A lot of equipment is needed and in contrast to software the hardware fabrication process produces a relatively high rate of material faults. This is the main difference between hardware and software production, also causing a number of other distinctions. For example, no different releases of a chip exist. If the chip is correct and manufactured, no further changes are made. For the development of a successor chip usually a redesign is necessary.

The verification of a software design is done by compilation (syntactical correctness) and the resulting code is tested (functional correctness), whereas for hardware design the verification of the real product would require fabrication of a chip. As this is too expensive, the testing of hardware is split up into two phases: the validation of the design process and the fabrication test. The validation of hardware designs is done by simulation to avoid the fabrication of an incorrect piece of hardware. If the design is correct, the piece of hardware is fabricated. During the production, e.g., of an integrated circuit, stochastical faults may occur. Therefore, after fabrication, the chip has to be tested again.

In the following section the hardware design process (phases 3, 4 and 5) will be described in more detail, because the tools of the environment described here do not concern the other phases of the hardware development process.

23.2.2 The hardware design process

In this section the hardware design process will be described to show which integration technology is useful for the integration of tools from this domain. A more detailed description can, for instance, be found in [Ram89].

The hardware design process (phases 3, 4 and 5 of section 23.2.1) usually consists of two types of activities (see figure 23.1):

- generation
- checking

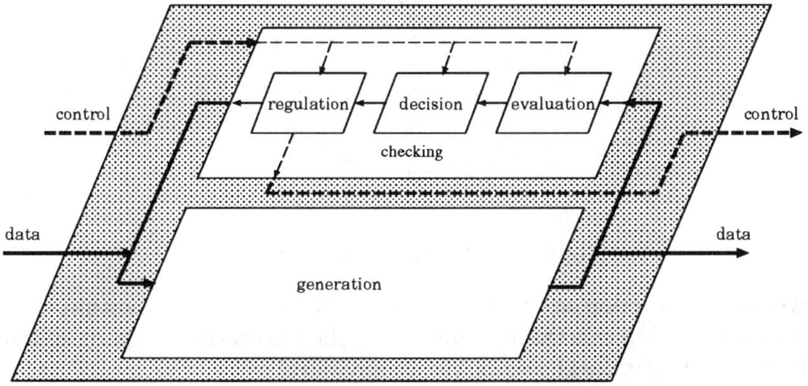

Figure 23.1 General model of the hardware design process [Ram89]

During the *generation phase* the design of a certain piece of hardware is done whereas in the *checking phase* it is tested whether the resulting description fulfils given constraints. These constraints may concern area, timing, performance, etc. The checking phase can be further split up into an *evaluation*, *decision*, and *regulation phase*. First, it has to be checked, whether the constraints are fulfilled, for example with a performance evaluation tool, and, if not, which of them are violated. Then it has to be decided whether the constraints or the design should be changed and what these changes should look like. In the regulation phase the decision has to be executed. This process is repeated until the actual constraints are fulfilled. As input to this process a description of the digital system in a "design language" (for instance VHDL, CDL, Waveforms, ...) and some control information are used. The results of this process are design documents describing the hardware. These documents and some output of the checking phase can be stored in a data base or file system.

This model is very simple and only fits for small parts of complex design processes. Such complex design processes can be handled by using the two general paradigms *divide and conquer* and *abstraction*. Divide and conquer means the decomposition of a problem and the composition of partial problem solutions. The problem is broken down into smaller pieces (divided), each of which can be more easily handled (conquered). After solving the subproblems, the solutions have to be combined to get a solution of the whole problem.

Levels of abstraction are a widely used concept for system design. On each level of abstraction several different descriptions of the same piece of hardware are needed, for example the description of the circuit behaviour is quite different from the description of its structure or geometrical realization. Therefore different views have to be introduced into the model of the design process. Figure 23.2 contains the Y-chart introduced by Gajski [GK83], which is a well-known representation of the relations between levels of abstraction and views.

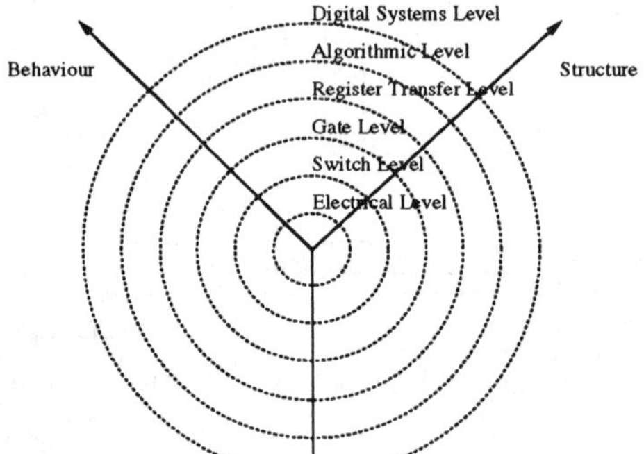

Figure 23.2 The Y-chart of Gajski

The levels of abstraction are represented by concentric circles within the chart. At each level of abstraction several descriptions of the hardware design on different views exist. The Y-chart of Gajski shows the behavioural view, the structural view, and the geometrical view. They form the three axes of the chart. But for hardware design, some additional views might be necessary, for example a view for testing or a floorplan view.

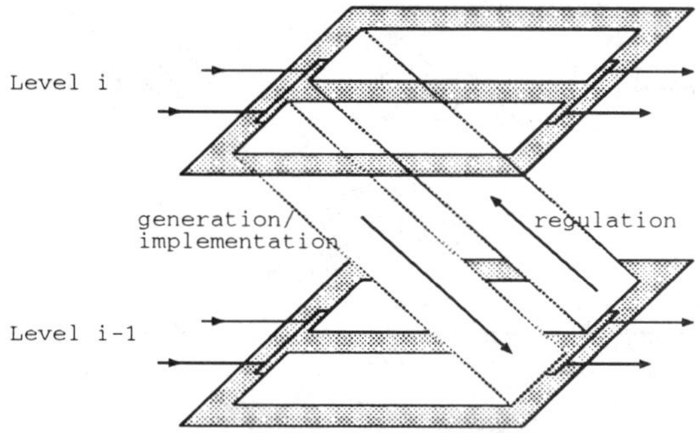

Figure 23.3 Refined design process [Ram89]

Table 23.1 contains the levels of abstraction and examples of the description concepts that are usually used during the design of digital systems.

	Level	Behavioural Entities	Structural Entities
5	*Digital Systems*	interface descriptions	processors, connections
4	*Algorithmic*	concurrent algorithms	modules, data structures
3	*Register–Transfer*	operations, bitstrings	ROMs, PLAs, ALUs, registers
2	*Gate*	Boolean equations	combinational elements like nand, nor ...
1	*Switch*	discrete equations	transistors & their connections
0	*Electrical*	differential equations	electrical parts & their connections

Table 23.1 Levels of abstraction and their description concepts

The model of the design process depicted in Figure 23.1 can be applied independently to each level of abstraction, resulting in completely disjoint processes. Replacing the inter-level activities with intra-level activities spanning over different levels leads to a connection of these disjoint processes. Figure 23.3 shows how this connection can be achieved.

Here, the description of a design at one level of abstraction is generated using the description at the next higher level. The first step going down from one level to the other is called implementation. This step substitutes the generation phase mentioned at the beginning of this section. If this step is done by hand, it is necessary to verify whether the result is a correct implementation of the description on the next higher level.

Additionally, the result of this activity has to be tested against the constraints that have to be satisfied at this lower level of abstraction, for example with a performance evaluation tool. If these constraints are not met it will be attempted solve the problems first at the current level via modification and optimization of the description. But if it

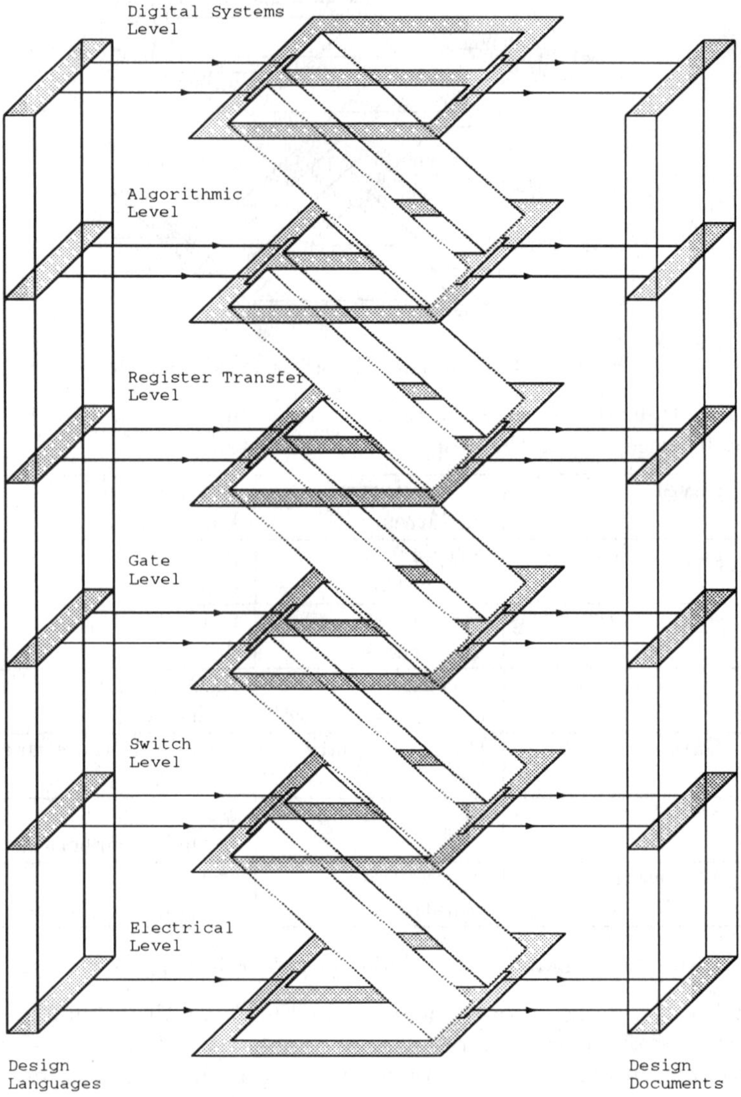

Figure 23.4 Design process model [Ram89]

is not possible to implement the object at the lower level with respect to all existing constraints, the only way to create a correct design is to go back to the higher level and to make some modifications there. This means, that regulation has to be carried out on the previous level of abstraction.

This method of generating a description at a lower level of abstraction by implementation and regulation can be used between all different levels of abstraction. This is shown in figure 23.4. The inter-level activities do not have to connect adjacent levels of abstraction. Also direct transformations, for example from the algorithmic level to the gate level, are possible. It can also be seen that the activity flows up and down until a stable version of the final layout of the chip is created. It is possible to enter the design process at each level of abstraction by supplying a description in an abstraction level-specific design language (for example VHDL, Schematic, diagrams, CDL, Waveforms). These descriptions are used by tools or by the designer to develop the design, i.e. to create descriptions of the design in multiple views, which can be used as input for further design steps, that may modify the descriptions or produce new ones. Usually, they are stored as documents in a file system or database. These documents may themselves serve as input descriptions.

While going up and down through the different levels of abstraction, alternative descriptions (versions) of the same piece of the design (design unit or cell) are created. Hence different implementation alternatives have to be carried out, eventually down to the electrical level, to find out which alternative is the best one with respect to the given requirements.

Besides different levels of abstraction and views, composition and decomposition play an important role in simplifying the design process. This means that usually a hardware design is developed hierarchically. The design is decomposed into smaller pieces to reduce the complexity. This reduction makes it easier for design tools to handle the resulting subdesigns. These subdesigns can be handled, almost independently, in parallel.

The model of the hardware design process depicted in figure 23.4 abstracts from this partitioning process and the resulting concurrency. In practice, it is not the case that the entire design is developed at one level of abstraction and completely implemented at the next lower level. Usually, it happens that some design parts are further developed to lower levels of abstraction than others at one point in time.

After this partitioning and after the development of the layout of the different parts the pieces of the circuit have to be composed to get a result for the whole circuit. This divide and conquer approach and the resulting reduction of problem complexity usually increases design efficiency (with respect to computation time).

The hierarchies that concern the structure of a circuit are of great importance. Stepping down the different levels of abstraction they become more and more detailed reflecting the whole development process. Furthermore, these hierarchies are used to split up the work, so that it can be done by several designers. Each piece of the design can be developed independently from the others, even at different sites of a company. Only the level within the decomposition hierarchy that combines these pieces has to be fixed, ensuring that the interfaces of the different pieces of the design are defined. The individual designers are not allowed to change these fixed interfaces defined at the combining level of the design (see also section 26.3).

Figure 23.5 shows the refinement of the structure of a hardware design during the design process. At first, a top module is created, which might consist of several hardware modules described at algorithmic level. With the behavioural description of these hardware modules as input a new structure is built up and the resulting modules are described at RT–level (Register–Transfer–level). The behavioural description of the RT–modules can be used by logic synthesis tools. These tools produce, after a few steps, modules at gate level. At each level of abstraction, several decomposition levels are possible, for example, a RT–module might consist of several other RT–modules.

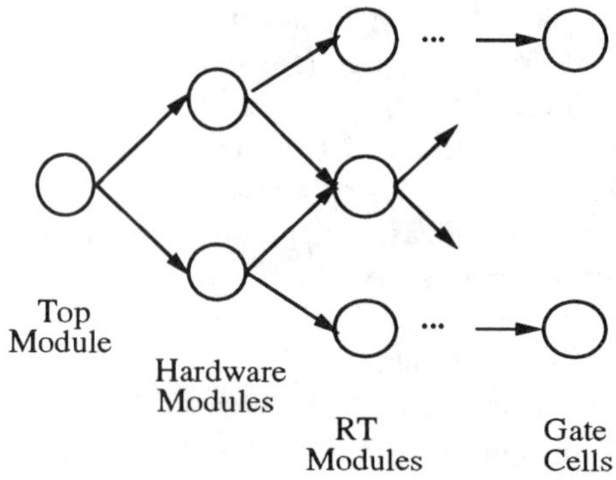

Figure 23.5 Decomposition hierarchy

23.3 DESCRIPTION OF THE TOOLS TO BE INTEGRATED

In this section those tools under consideration for integration will be described. First an overview of their role in the hardware engineering process will be given. This overview will show which integration possibilities for these tools exist in principle. After a brief discussion of the integration benefits the tools and the chosen integration approaches will be described in more detail.

23.3.1 Classification of the hardware engineering tools

Within the Hardware Engineering Environment several tools responsible for different tasks within the hardware development process exist. Two groups of tools can be distinguished according to the phases of the design process (see figure 23.1). The Hardware Synthesis System comprises tools for the generation phase between two adjacent levels of abstraction. It starts from a behavioural description at the algorithmic level and transforms it into a description at the electrical level in a stepwise manner (the assignment of the different tools to the levels of abstraction is shown in section 23.3.3). The tools CIRCAL, HIT, and BEMO may be used during the evaluation phase (see figure 23.1). Figure 23.6 shows how the tools work with respect to the levels of abstraction. One task of CIRCAL is the verification of the synthesis results at one level versus the specification at a higher one. Additionally it can be used for simulation and constraint checking at one level of abstraction. The tool HIT does performance analysis using the description at only one level of abstraction, which can be any of the levels previously mentioned. BEMO (not shown in Figure 23.6) starts after the fabrication of the developed piece of hardware. It evaluates the performance of already existing hardware.

23.3.2 Integration benefits

Integration of a verification tool like CIRCAL with the Hardware Synthesis System would allow the verification of hand performed changes to hardware designs, known to be correct after synthesis. The tools of the Hardware Synthesis System and CIRCAL work on two levels of abstraction, respectively: the tools of the Hardware Synthesis

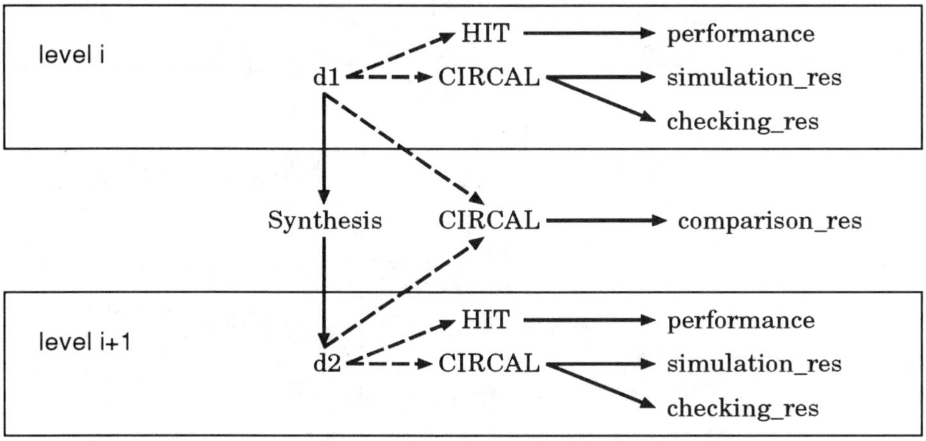

Figure 23.6 Assignment of the tools to the levels of abstraction

System transform the description on one level of abstraction to the next lower one, whereas CIRCAL could be used to verify this transformation. The integration of these two toolsets mainly concerns the data aspect. The goal of this integration is the definition of common design data formats to be used by CIRCAL and the Hardware Synthesis System. They would enable CIRCAL to read the data produced by the Hardware Synthesis System without data transformations and to compare it with the results of some manual design changes, in order to verify the manual changes. The data integration described in section 24 is a first step towards this goal.

By moving from behavioural descriptions of hardware designs (e.g., VHDL) to HIT, a combination of functional–oriented description techniques with quantitatively–oriented model specification techniques will be reached. This transition enables the connection of HIT with any tool of the Hardware Synthesis System: the description of the design on one level of abstraction will be transformed into a HI–SLANG description (at the moment this has to be done by hand), which then can be analyzed by HIT. The results of HIT are used to decide whether the performance constraints of the design are fulfilled. If not, the design has to be changed.

The BEMO tool will mostly be employed after the design and production of a system in order to check if the stated (performance) requirements of the whole system are met. Its load simulation output, however, can in principle be used as input load to run HIT models of already existing systems, but which for arbitrary reasons should be evaluated. Here, again, the integration enables the tools to use the same data without copying it.

23.3.3 The Hardware Synthesis System

The objective of the Hardware Synthesis System [RS91] is to transform functional hardware descriptions at the algorithmic level into netlists of standard cells, which can be further processed by the layout synthesis and assembly tools. The target architecture for chip layouts produced by the Hardware Synthesis System is a set of synchronous hardware modules coupled via asynchronous communication modules. Figure 23.7 shows the synthesis tools and the synthesis flow disregarding repetitions and cycles. On the right hand side of the figure the synthesis steps are mapped to the levels of abstraction.

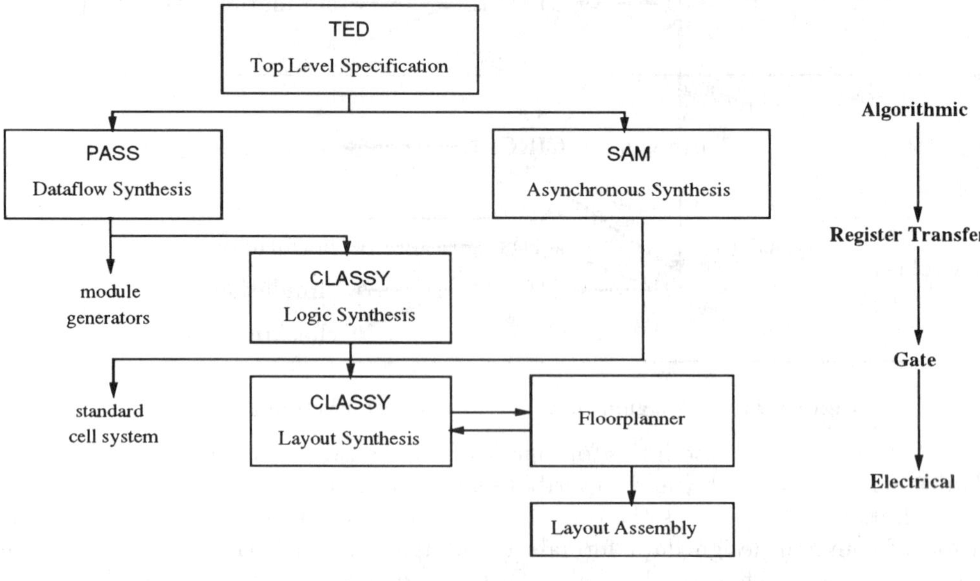

Figure 23.7 Overview of the Hardware Synthesis System

By TED (Top Level Structure Editor) the user specifies which modules make up the hardware to–be–synthesized, which modules should contain clocked hardware, which modules should contain synchronization hardware, and how the modules are connected.

From a specification of the synchronization hardware SAM (Synthesis of Asynchronous Modules) [RS91] generates a netlist of library cells. The PASS (Paderborn Synthesis System) [Ewe90, EG90] dataflow synthesis generates an RT–structure (Register Transfer) from a specification in the dataflow language PEDAL. Module generators like CLASSY (CadLab ALU Synthesis SYstem) [BL91] generate a network of library cells for each RT–module.

The layout synthesis part of the module generator CLASSY [BVL90] estimates the size of different layout versions for an RT–module from the netlist and the information in the cell libraries. A floorplanner selects one of the alternatives. Subsequently, the layout synthesis part of CLASSY generates the layout for the RT–module.

Finally, a layout assembly tool assembles the layouts for the RT–modules to a layout for the entire chip. The layout assembly uses the floorplan created by the floorplanner and performs local routing.

23.3.3.1 The Top Level Structure Editor

TED (Top Level Structure Editor) is the entry point of the Hardware Synthesis System. This editor allows one to define the module structure of the hardware at the top level. In addition to this structural partitioning a functional partitioning is done, i.e., it is specified which modules should contain clocked hardware and which should contain synchronization hardware. With TED the interfaces of the modules are graphically described by ports. All the variables representing these ports are type–checked.

TED generates algorithmic interface descriptions for the defined modules. They can be further processed by the subsequent design tools SAM and PASS. In fact, the interface descriptions are included in the behaviour descriptions used as input by those high level design tools.

23.3.3.2 Synthesis from dataflow descriptions

The task of PASS is the synthesis of RT–structures from dataflow descriptions. The synthesis starts with an algorithmic description of the module behaviour including the interface description of TED. These algorithmic descriptions are specified in the dataflow language PEDAL. From an algorithmic description an analyzer generates a dataflow graph. The dataflow graph is the central data structure in the synthesis with PASS.

The scheduler assigns to each operation of the dataflow graph a start time, a delay time, and a hardware component. The allocation phase maps components of the dataflow graph to the hardware resources. Each edge corresponds to a register and each node to an operation. This symbolic allocation is transformed into a real allocation. PASS minimizes the number of inserted lines and multiplexers. A new allocation method was developed that maps the scheduled dataflow graph on to a partitioned bus structure. The main idea is that switches allow a temporary separation of bus segments into independent partitions, and that the buses are laid out in parallel. The advantage of this interconnection structure over a multiplexer or standard bus structure is the drastic decrease in layout space without loss of parallelism. In typical examples the space was reduced by a factor of 2.

From the just obtained register and processor allocation the RT–structure is generated. To simplify the test of the RT–structure a graphical simulator was developed. Furthermore, PASS also generates RT–structures in the TREEMOLA [BS90] file format.

In parallel to the data path synthesis a finite state machine is generated, based on the schedule, and a micro program is generated, based on the processor and register allocation.

23.3.3.3 Synthesis of asynchronous hardware

The synchronization hardware which is necessary for the communication between modules will be synthesized by SAM (Synthesis of Asynchronous Modules). The synchronization hardware to be synthesized by SAM has to be specified in a separate module using a specific input language.

The input language is translated into a labelled Petri net. The language that is recognized by this labelled Petri net defines the behaviour at the interfaces of the asynchronous hardware. This language corresponds to traces introduced by van de Snepscheut [Sne85]. The alphabet from which the language is formed contains a symbol for each value change that is possible at a port. The Petri net specification is input for the further synthesis. The synthesis takes place in 5 steps:

1. Optimization of the Petri net based on the net structure.
2. Partitioning of the Petri net into subnets.
3. Optimization of the subnets based on reachability analysis.
4. Transformation of the subnets into subnets with predefined properties.
5. Covering of the subnets by predefined library elements.

Steps 2 and 3 may be iterated. To ensure that the Petri net transformations produce well defined results the trace–like Petri net language is used. Petri net transformations are defined such that they preserve the Petri net language.

The result of the SAM synthesis is a netlist of cells from a specific cell library. For each library element a Petri net model exists. This model is used for the last synthesis step. The structure of the cell library is related to the libraries described in [BKKR86, BKR85]. Furthermore, an intermediate hardware architecture for the asynchronous modules is defined. This hardware architecture consists of an interconnection of asynchronous automata. The asynchronous automata themselves are realized by an interconnection of library cells.

23.3.3.4 Logic and layout synthesis from RT–structures

An RT–structure, as synthesized by PASS, describes the behaviour of the various RT–modules and the interconnections between these modules. There are different types of RT–modules such as RAMs, ROMs, PLAs, ALUs, registers, multipliers, etc. Module generators create the layouts of the various RT–modules. The module generator CLASSY (CadLab ALU Synthesis SYstem) is used for ALUs. The input of CLASSY is a behavioural ALU description, in which every combination of operations from a given large set is allowed. From this input CLASSY first automatically synthesizes an array of bit–slices.

Subsequently logic optimization is performed on the single bit–slices. Because logic optimization is performed on the bit–slices instead of the entire ALU, the optimization is efficient and produces regular circuitry. Novel algorithms were implemented that perform logic optimization on logic with a symbolic input. This enables CLASSY to delay the encoding of the control signals of the ALU until after the logic synthesis. This leads to better encodings and hence smaller logic. A comparison of the results with results of existing approaches shows significant improvements.

Finally, a regular layout is generated that is made up of bit–slices. The layout synthesis part of CLASSY is based on a layout style where bit–slices are realized by one or several rows of standard cells. This specific layout style allows the generation of very compact layouts.

23.3.3.5 Floorplanning and layout assembly

The sizing functions calculated for the RT–elements are used to build up a floorplan for the whole design. The floorplan fixes a sizing point of the sizing function of the RT–elements. This size should not be exceeded during the layout development. By selecting a sizing point for the RT–elements the floorplan and the size for the bit–slices are also fixed. The layout of the RT–elements is generated by placement of the gate design units within these columns and by a routing process.

After the layout generation for the RT–elements the layout development for the toplevel hardware modules and the whole design is possible. This is done in a bottom–up manner using the instantiation hierarchy in the floorplan view.

For data exchange between CLASSY and the floorplanning and layout assembly tools an EDIF like format [Uni90] is used.

23.3.3.6 Intra toolset integration

For the Hardware Synthesis System not only an integration with the other toolsets but also an intra toolset integration is possible. Figure 23.8 shows the data flow within the Integrated Hardware Synthesis System. In section 23.4 the architectural principles of the integration within the framework are explained.

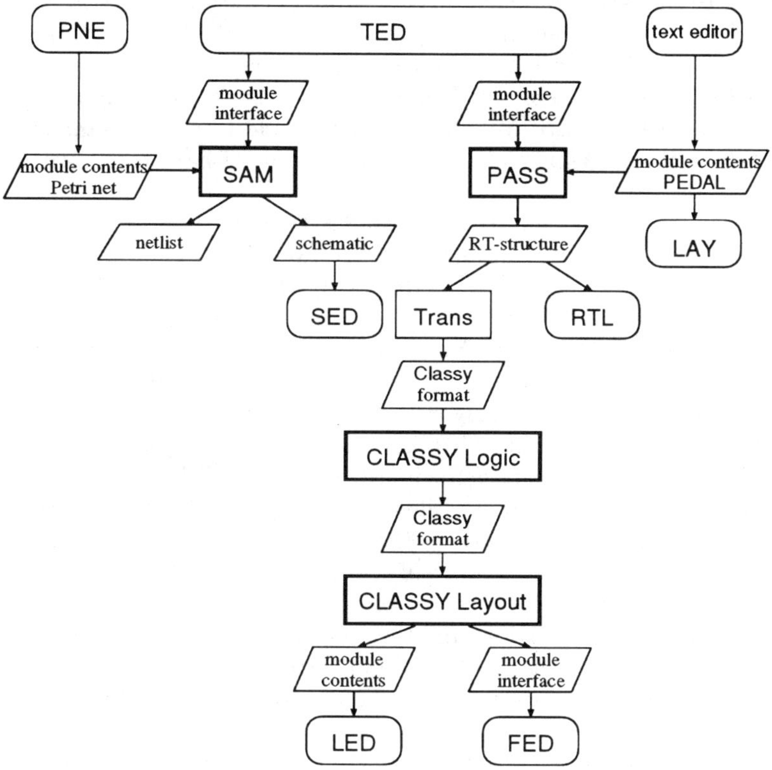

Figure 23.8 Dataflow within the integrated Hardware Synthesis System

The Integrated Hardware Synthesis System also consists, in addition to the tools mentioned in the previous sections, of some editors and transformers. For the production of the input descriptions not only TED, which is responsible for the top level structure, but also a Petri net editor PNE and a text editor are integrated. The descriptions produced by these editors are used by the specific high level synthesis tools SAM or PASS. SAM produces a netlist and a schematic, which can be used by the schematic editor SED as input. The input description for the tool PASS can be visualized by the editor LAY and its output, the description of the RT–structure by the editor RTL. This RT–structure can be used by a transformer, which produces a description in the input format for the logic synthesis phase of CLASSY. During this phase an intermediated description is created, which is used by the layout synthesis phase of CLASSY. The results of this phase are interface and contents descriptions of the modules. The interface description can be used by the floorplan editor FED for the visualization of the floorplan, whereas the contents description is used by the layout editor LED.

23.3.4 The CIRCAL verification toolset

CIRCAL is a verification formalism developed by Milne in the early 80s, specifically for the analysis of digital systems; a fact which is reflected in its name — **CIR**cuit **CAL**culus. It consists of two distinct parts *(i)* a set of core operators and *(ii)* a set of derived laws. The laws are based on the semantics of the core operators, defined using a labelled transition system. While CIRCAL is similar in many ways to other process algebras such as CCS [Mil89b], it contains additional mechanisms which make it particularly well suited to modelling the behaviour of hardware [Mil89a].

In order to provide an effective, engineer friendly means of using CIRCAL the CIRCAL language has been embedded within XTC (eXTended C), a high level, interpreted, general purpose programming language [McC91b]. This embedded language is called XCIRCAL [McC91a]. Access to the CIRCAL process algebra and the toolset is provided through XCIRCAL, bringing to the designer the power of high level programming language constructs such as functions, loops, enumerated types and structures. Through XCIRCAL the designer gains access to the operators of the language which allow both circuit description and rigorous behavioural analysis to be conducted. Thus, for example, it is possible within XCIRCAL to describe a netlist of interconnected cells, and to derive the *total* composite behaviour from the individual component behaviours expressed in CIRCAL. Furthermore, the designer is then able to analyze the resultant behaviour. This analysis typically takes the form of *(i)* verification of specification versus implementation *(ii)* simulation or *(iii)* constraint checking. XCIRCAL provides an easy entry route for those designers already familiar with conventional hardware description languages such as VHDL, and through the automatic verification technology, allows the opportunity for the application of formal techniques without the need for mathematical expertise. An overview of the data flow within the toolset is given in figure 23.9.

The top section illustrates the types of commands available to the designer, and the lower section the generated results which are possible. The commands supported by XCIRCAL have been split into a number of categories, the first three of which support the definition, simulation and manipulation of circuit behaviours. The last category, "display commands", represents those requests for behaviours, simulation results, etc. to be displayed. These commands are the designers route to controlling which parts of the generated output are displayed. For a full description of all the available commands the interested reader is referred to [McC91a]. The "CIRCAL kernel" section of the diagram collectively describes those tools available to the designer through XCIRCAL commands. Communication between these facilities and XTC is supported by a procedural interface.

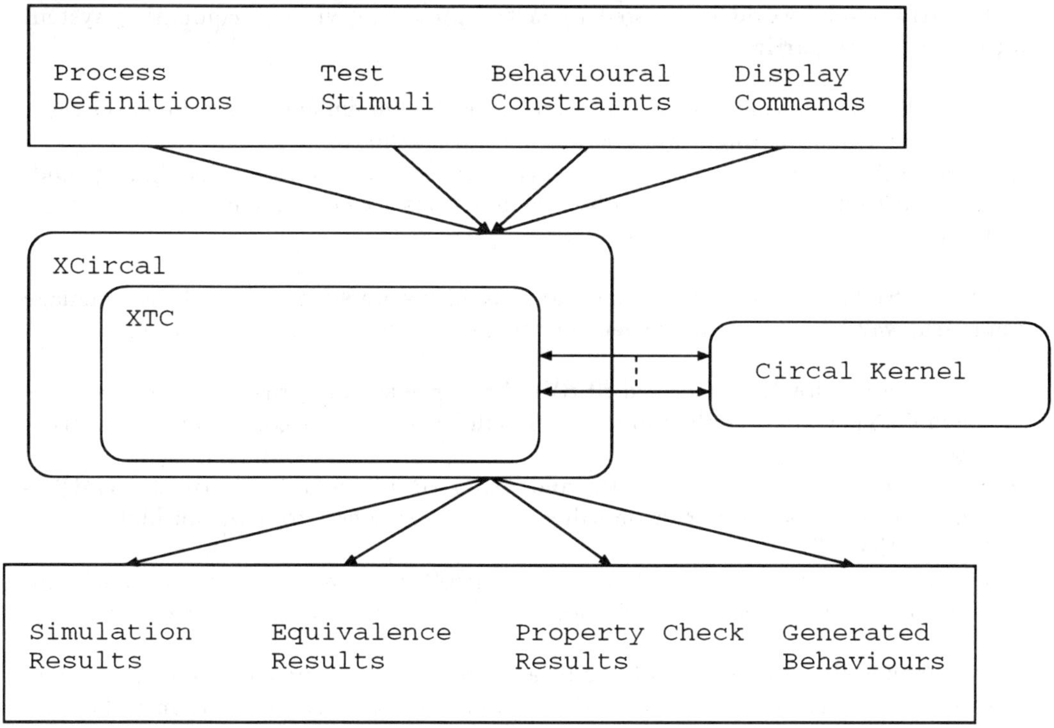

Figure 23.9 CIRCAL toolset overview

23.3.5 The hierarchical evaluation tool HIT

HIT (see [BMW88, BS87]) is a comprehensive software tool supporting the model–based evaluation of computing system performance. HIT models exhibit a highly structured view of the systems to be assessed, based on (vertical) functional hierarchies and (horizontal) modularization as employed in modern software engineering and hardware architecture approaches. Analysis of HIT models is provided by analytic–algebraical, analytic–numerical, exact and approximate techniques, and by discrete–event simulation. Both model description and model analysis utilize the model structure for convenient problem specification and efficient evaluation respectively. Particular emphasis is placed on decomposition and aggregation options and on a mixed (heterogeneous) use of different analysis techniques. Although originally developed for evaluating computing system performance, HIT also lends itself to the analysis of "similar" systems such as communication and office systems, transport and logistic systems and others of the specified system type. More particularly, HIT allows for

- the specification of models of dynamic, discrete–event, stochastic systems using a particular model description language, HI-SLANG via a normal text editor, and/or a graphical user interface, HITGRAPHIC;
- the performance analysis of correspondingly specified models using a variety of techniques of the simulative, analytic–algebraical and analytic–numerical type.

The HIT model world is tailored upon the prevailing view of computing system structures which partitions a system

- vertically, into a sequence of layers and levels, communicating via function calls, and jointly representing a hierarchy of virtual machines;
- horizontally, into independent, mutually well protected, information–hiding modules, each one realizing some subset of functions to be provided at a particular level.

The HI-SLANG specification maintains, as far as possible, a high level language approach, well known to and convenient for the user community of the tool:

- Conventional functions (termed SERVICEs) serve as "patterns" for processes "to–be–run". They are described in terms of high level language control and data structures.
- SERVICEs can be packaged into and exported by modules (termed COMPONENTs). These services can be called by other services from within higher layer COMPONENTs.
- Options for initiating processes in time–controlled or event–controlled mode complete the specification capabilities for describing systems of parallel processes.

Disjoint specifications of models (to be analyzed) and experiments (to be performed with these models) greatly increase the flexibility of use. HIT evaluation techniques include the following approaches:

- stochastic discrete–event simulation with appropriate statistical result evaluation;
- exact result evaluation for "separable networks" (with product–form solution) and approximate evaluation techniques for both "large" separable and certain "non–product–form" networks;
- numerical evaluation of Markov chain representations of more general models;
- submodel analysis and aggregation with the objective of generating "equivalent" higher level representations called aggregates, to be used in structured and/or heterogeneous (total model) evaluation.

The implementations of these techniques are contained in the HIT solver library. The selected solver is linked to the generated code of the HI-SLANG compiler. The resulting analyzer yields the performance values of interest as results. An overview of the HIT architecture is given in figure 23.10. Note that the term "User Interface & Model Base" is used to characterize the following options for a HIT user interface and a model base supporting storage and retrieval of (parts of) models and analysis results:

- use of a normal text editor and UNIX commands as user interface and use of a normal file system for input and output (e.g., results),
- use of OMA, a model base including a simple user interface,
- use of HITGRAPHIC, a graphical user interface including a model base.

All these alternatives can be used separately but this is not obligatory.

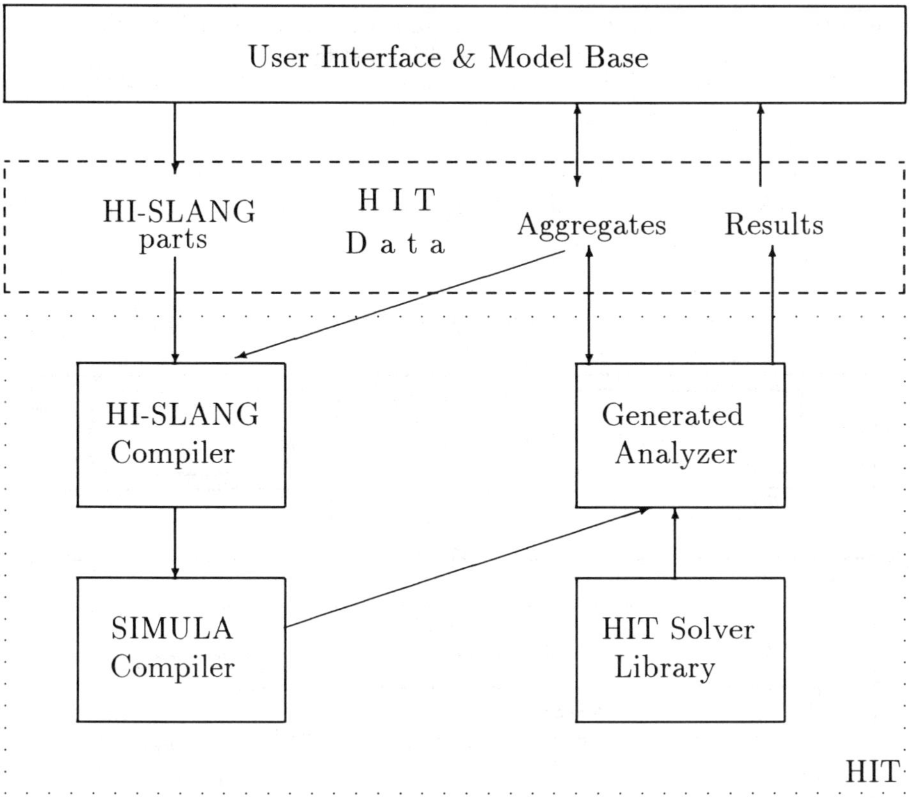

Figure 23.10 HIT architecture

23.3.6 Description of the benchmark monitor BEMO

For the performance evaluation of computer systems usually different loads are used. These loads are simulated on the computer system to be evaluated and the performance of the system is measured. The load can consist of real applications, or synthetic loads, or a composition of them. For the evaluation different measurement tools like software and/or hardware monitors are used.

The benchmark monitor BEMO is a load simulator for the performance evaluation of computer systems running UNIX. BEMO can be used for performance evaluation as well as for benchmarking. A load description for BEMO can be purely synthetic, but it may also contain real applications. Thus, BEMO is a tool to produce defined and reproducible load on UNIX systems. Different loads can easily be specified for the evaluation of system components or for getting performance information in comparison with other systems. For these tasks BEMO offers a number of elementary load programs which claim special system resources (CPU, disk, terminal, network, ...) and which can be combined in an arbitrary way. The benchmark monitor is mainly used for

- performance evaluation of the system components,
- creation of a defined basic load for the evaluation of real applications,

- simulation of the load produced by real applications to get information about the performance of the system even in early design stages,
- comparison of different systems based on standard loads (benchmarks),
- control of user defined test and load programs.

A load simulation with BEMO can be divided into three independent parts (see also Figure 23.11): definition of the load to be simulated, execution of the load simulation, and evaluation of the simulation results.

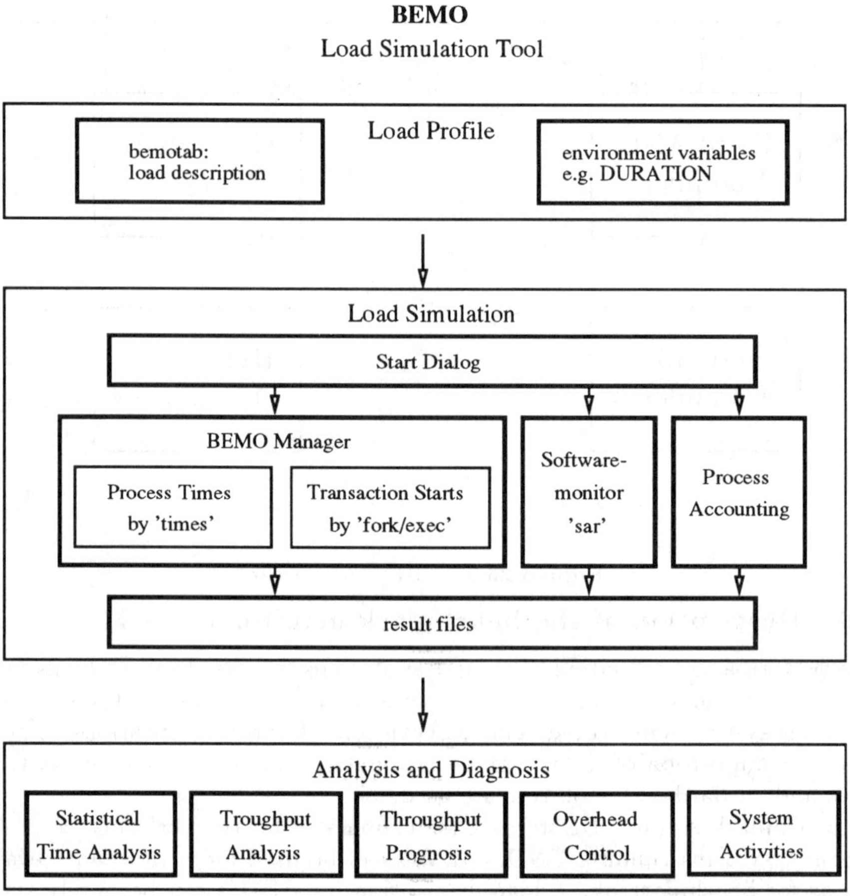

Figure 23.11 BEMO overview

For the load simulation with BEMO at first the commands creating the load and the stimuli matrix of the simulation have to be defined. The specification of the load has to be entered into a table called bemotab. The load is produced by the execution of commands on the system to be evaluated. These commands can be divided into single commands and composed commands. Single commands are usually program calls with options and parameters. The user can choose between single commands offered by BEMO, elementary load programs, user defined programs, and commands of the operating system. A composed command consists of an arbitrary collection of elementary load programs. With the specification of the time interval of the calls and with additional accompanying information for the simulation, these commands are combined to applications. Several applications together with the BEMO environment variables (e.g. the duration of the simulation run) describe the load profile.

The simulation run is controlled by the BEMO manager. It starts the separate load applications under consideration of the load profile. For each of the load applications a process is created. If several applications are assigned to one working place, only one of them can be active at the same time. During the simulation run all information is noted in special result files. The execution times of the applications are automatically measured by using the system call times(). Additionally, the UNIX tools sar (System Activity Report) and the Process Accounting can be invoked to get more information for the evaluation of the simulation results.

After the simulation run several analysis and diagnosis facilities for the evaluation of the system behaviour under the given load exist. Depending on the previously selected measurement programs information of the BEMO processes (Process Accounting) or of the System Activities (sar) can be evaluated in addition to the process execution times. With the Overhead Control the load caused by BEMO can be calculated. The standard evaluation offers information about the average response time and the targeted and actual number of starts for the load programs and the resulting throughput of the application. During Throughput Analysis, in addition to the standard output, the nominal and actual throughput are compared and statements about the average lead delay are given. The Statistical Time Analysis determines the statistical properties of the processing times of the load programs. This includes the calculation of the average, variance, standard deviation, minimum, median, and maximum quantiles. For the evaluation of the time distribution the range between minimum and maximum process time is split up into several parts based on the number of measurement data. Thus, irregularities can be detected. Based on these evaluations eventually existing bottle necks can be detected or performance estimations for larger loads can be calculated (Throughput Prognosis).

23.3.7 The approach for inter toolset integration

The tools described in this chapter are responsible for the implementation of system parts, especially of hardware, specified at one level of abstraction on one or more deeper levels and the verification and evaluation of these steps. The integration of the different tools eases the cooperation between them (see also section 23.3.2). So the result is a homogeneous system for the development of integrated circuits in this case.

In order to get such an integrated system, much effort has to be spent for data integration because hardware design is very data intensive, and because a different data format exists for each (view, abstraction level)–pair. Moreover, the size of each design element can vary between a few hundred bytes and many gigabytes, the latter corresponding typically to a generated chip layout. Therefore, it is necessary to use a database, which is able to keep such a large number of data units of much differing sizes. The data units should be stored at a well defined place in the database, where they can be found by all tools using them. Thus, a data schema for the administration of the data units is required, which defines a retrieval path for each data unit. This data schema should also be useful for configuration management and access control.

In future, it should also be possible for more than one tool to work on the same data unit at the same time. Hence, the database should also be able to manipulate the data within the data units. Consider, for example, an editor and a checking tool running on the same data unit. Whenever changes have been made within the editor, these changes have to be evaluated by the checking tool. Possible errors can be automatically highlighted within the editor if the checking tool is allowed to write on the graphical data of the editor. No explicit communication between the two tools is needed for the realization of this parallelism if a database with two levels of granularity is used, one level storing data units and the other used to administer these data units. The communication can then be realized by events that are triggered automatically.

The different views and levels of abstraction lead also to requirements for presentation integration. Different kinds of information are stored in the data units describing different views and levels of abstraction of the design. Thus, the graphical representations of these kinds of information are also different. Therefore, a number of different editors, each one responsible for only one kind of graphical representation, are needed. But it is undesirable that each editor has its own look and feel, i.e., editors should resemble each other as much as possible. The tools of the Hardware Synthesis System have the task to transform the descriptions of one level of abstraction to the next lower level. This means that their tasks are similar. Accordingly, a first step towards presentation integration would be to offer similar user interfaces for these tools. But during the development of these user interfaces, it has to be considered that also analysis tools should also be able to have user interfaces with the same look and feel.

To integrate the design process the control dimension also has to be regarded. One aspect is the support of the process flow. The large number of different descriptions of the same design complicates the storage of a special data unit at the correct place in the data schema. For tools this problem is solvable. The schema paths of their input and output data can be hardcoded. But if a designer wants to do a design step by hand, it is necessary to know where to find and store the data. That means that he/she has to know where they are in the database. Therefore, some help is necessary. Additionally, some help is required for the invocation of the tools. The designer has to know which tool to use for which design step and what input data the tool needs. Again, some guidance would be useful.

Another aspect of control integration is the communication between different tools. Some mechanisms have to be offered for information exchange. This point becomes very important if more than one tool works on the same data at the same time. All the tools working on shared data have to be notified about every change of this data.

When writing this chapter not all of the previously mentioned concepts had already been realized. For data integration the definition of a common administrative data schema has been completed. All of the tools have been integrated using this data schema, but are still working on their own specific data format for the detailed design data. For the transformation of these private data formats converter tools are needed, which have only been implemented for the Hardware Synthesis System. Only the editors are tightly integrated into the JCF–OMS.

Concerning presentation integration a common look and feel of the tools and editors of the Hardware Synthesis System has been achieved. The other tools of the environment use the standard graphical Desktop of the JCF and their private user interfaces.

Regarding control integration the most important aspect is the reflection of the typical design process within the administration data schema. For support of the design process the Synthesis Control Editor is provided, which shows the database objects already created and which allows one to invoke the tools on these objects. Basic mechanisms for communication between the tools are already provided, but will only be used when tightly integrating some of them.

23.4 ENVIRONMENT ARCHITECTURE

Within this chapter the architecture of the Hardware Engineering Environment is explained. The JESSI Common Framework (JCF) is used as a basis for the integration work done so far. Its object management system JCF–OMS offers important facilities to realize the approach for data integration described later on. Thus, at first, the architecture of the JESSI Common Framework is described. Additionally it is shown which parts of the framework are used and what the resulting overall architecture of the environment looks like.

23.4.1 Architecture of the JESSI Common Framework

The global architecture of the JESSI Common Framework was defined regarding the following goals: the system should be designed modular, high performant, and user configurable. Under these constraints a global architecture was defined. This architecture can be seen under setup, startup and runtime conditions.

23.4.1.1 Setup view

Part of the framework is a basic data schema of the logical database, which is a part of the physical database logically separated from other parts. For example, the data of the Hardware Engineering Environment would be stored in such a logical database, whereas the data of other application domains would be stored in other ones. This schema information is necessary for the proper working of the Desktop and design management components.

Objects, relations, attributes, user roles, and all object relevant methods (pop–up menus) of the Desktop are defined via TIDL (tool integration description language). This information is compiled via the TIDL compiler and filled into the database. This setup must happen in single user mode.

The schema can be changed by an administrator to influence the pop–up menus which belong to specific object types or to extend the schema via domain specific parts. It is essential that such a schema change is only possible before the creation of a logical database. Later on, schema changes are not supported. In general, changing the schema can only be done as a database administrator in a single user mode.

23.4.1.2 Startup view

When starting the framework, the Desktop reads some files which can again be used to customize the behaviour of the system. JCF provides the following customization features:

- Parameters (colours, shapes, etc.), pull–down menus and the display of object attributes can be customized by using the extended X–resources mechanism.
- Scenarios, which are the link between the Desktop menus and the rest of the functionality in the system (design management, data handling and common basic services) can also be changed or extended.

23.4.1.3 Runtime view

Per logical database one data handling server is present (see figure 23.12). Together with the database clients, it handles all data traffic to avoid inconsistencies resulting from the concurrent access of the database. Multiple framework instances (Desktop instances) access all the same data handling server if they use the same logical data base.

When a user starts the JCF Desktop, a process will be executed, which contains:

the graphical part of the Desktop :
This is the main user interface of the framework which covers most of the functionality. It handles the display of the objects and all user interaction. Customization of this part is possible during setup or startup.

all scenarios :
In order to perform a user–request via a selected object–method combination a so–called "scenario" is executed by the Scheme engine. A scenario is a Scheme script combining user interface actions with design management calls. As described previously all scenarios are loaded into the Desktop during startup or when accessed for the first time.

the Scheme engine :
It interprets the scenarios and provides a Scheme interface to the underlying components (design management, data handling, common basic services). A powerful set of routines for handling of X and OSF/MOTIF interfaces is present.

the design management :
The design management controls all meta data accesses to the database and thereby guarantees consistency in the database. By exchanging basic information with the tool server via IPC (Inter–Process Communication), start and control of tools is done.

the data handling interface (client) :
This interface is needed by the above mentioned components for data storage. Via IPC it is connected to the central data handling server.

the common basic services interface :
It contains functionality for the help service and the error handling service which can be used by all other components of the framework. This interface handles all traffic to the help server and the error handling server via an IPC interface.

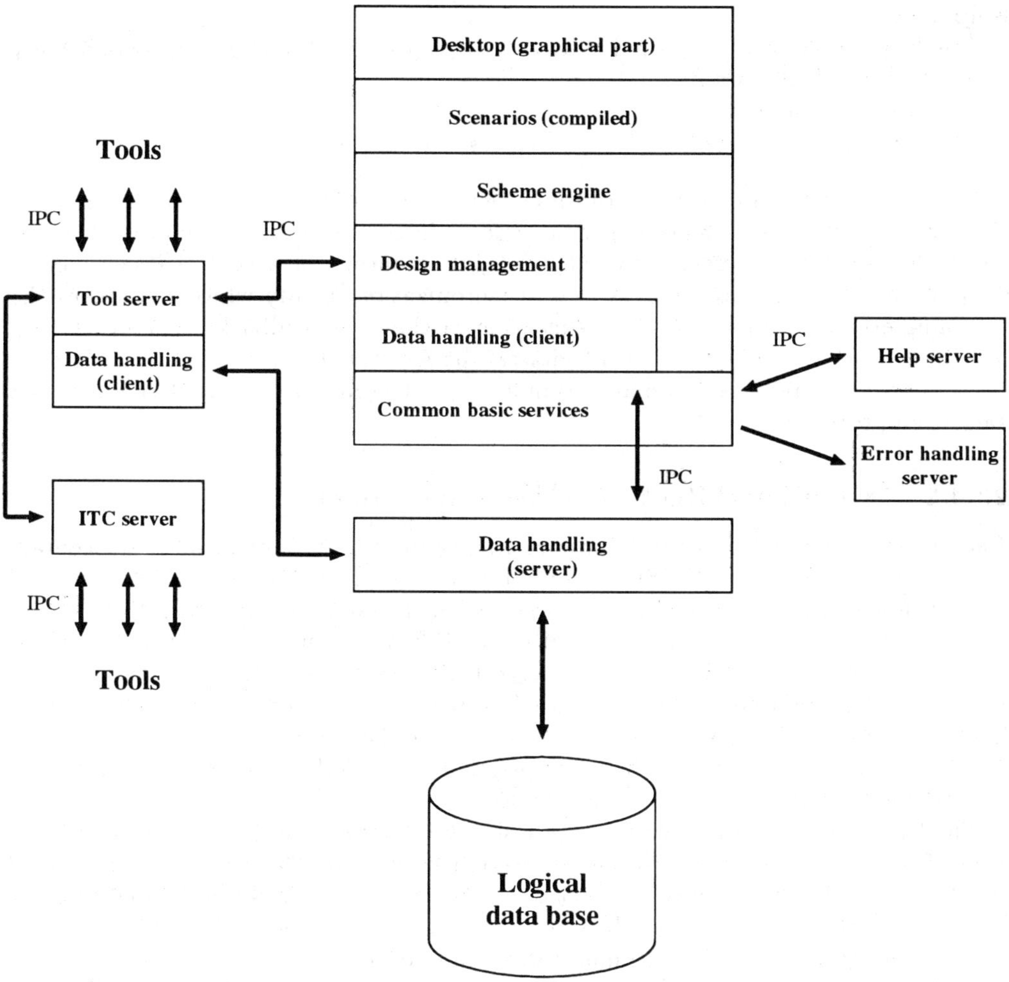

(*IPC: Inter–Process Communication; ITC: Inter–Tool Communication*)

Figure 23.12 Global architecture of the framework (runtime view)

Besides the Desktop connected process, other processes are present which have the following functionality:

tool server :
The tool server exchanges information via IPC with the design management to handle parallel tool runs. Via IPC only basic information is exchanged. The rest of the information is held for both communication partners in the database.

ITC server :
The ITC (Inter–Tool Communication) server manages communication between tools, between tools and framework services, and between framework services. The difference between IPC and ITC is that IPC is used for low level, internal process communication, e.g., for large data (tool and data handling server). ITC is used for notification and request, e.g., control data (control integration of tools).

help server :
The help server provides functionality to display short and long help texts for any application which uses it.

error handling server :
The error handling server collects all errors and logs it.

Beside the partitioning of the runtime view into functional blocks and processes, the processes themselves have a specific concept in common. For every process which has to handle asynchronous input channels, the concept of a central event loop is introduced. The event loop serves as a synchronization facility which dispatches the incoming events to allow serialized execution of the event callbacks. The event loop has three different input sources. Events can be generated via user actions, via data handling actions and via communication actions. The number of input channels can vary from process to process.

23.4.2 Overall architecture of the environment

The overall architecture of the Hardware Engineering Environment does not contain all the components of the JESSI Common Framework. The main reason is that not all of the framework components were available when the integration work started. Therefore, mainly the database component of the JCF has been used. For the construction of the user interfaces of the Hardware Synthesis System a prototype user interface management system not included in the JCF has been utilized; for HIT and BEMO, TIDL and the Desktop have been used as well, since their integration started later and has become much easier using these components. The resulting overall architecture of the environment is depicted in Figure 23.13.

The frame of the environment consists of a database system (the database component of the JCF) and a user interface management system. The tools to be integrated can be assigned to three classes. Most of the tools can be tightly integrated into the frame and belong to the class *Tool*. To visualize the results of these tools *Editors* are also integrated. For the communication and control of these tools and editors a *Control Tool* exists. The batch oriented tools can be integrated in two ways. A *tightly integrated tool* uses the data provided by the database as internal data structure. An *encapsulated tool* keeps working on the file system. Only its input and output files are stored within the database. These files have to be exported before the tool can start its work and imported after finishing the work. In order to enable *tightly integrated tools* to work on data produced by *encapsulated tools* a *Converter Tool* is needed, which feeds these data into the database.

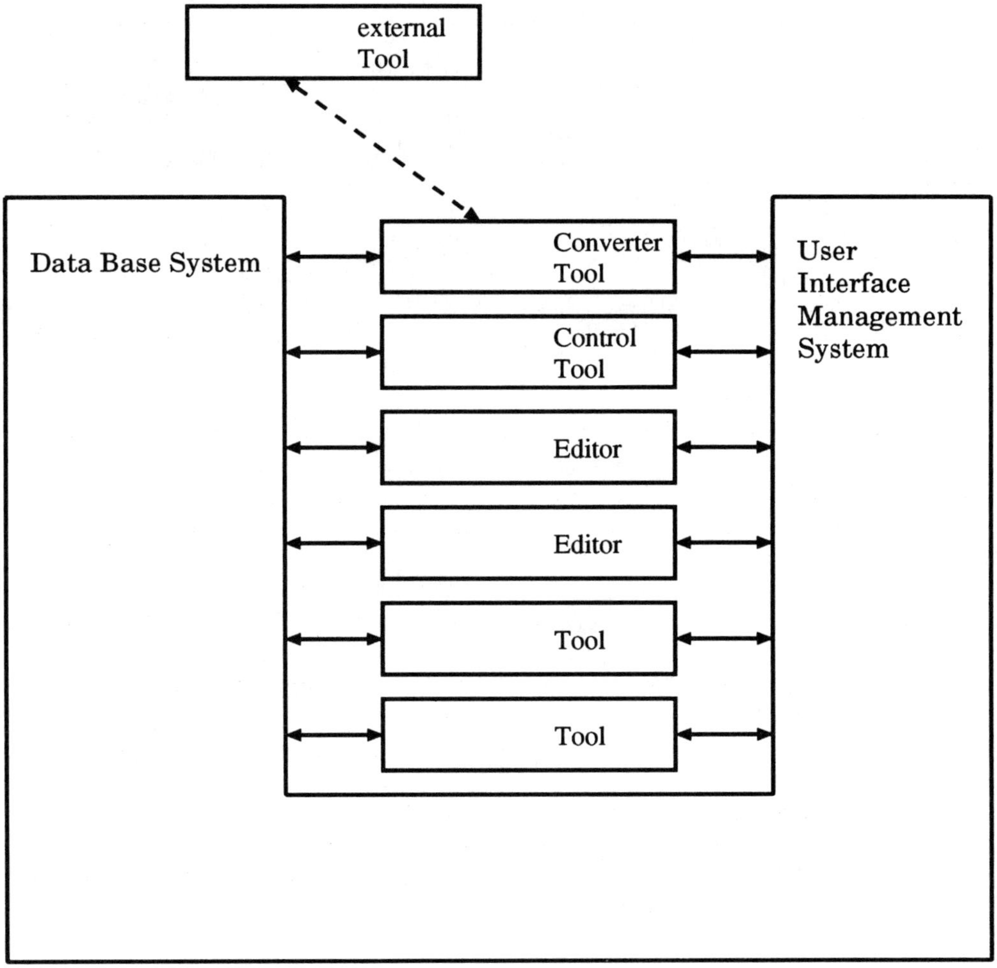

Figure 23.13 Overall architecture of the Hardware Engineering Environment

24

Data Integration

As described in section 23.3.7 data integration plays an important role for hardware design tools. All the different descriptions of one piece of hardware on several views and levels of abstraction have to be handled. Additionally, it should be possible for more than one tool to work on the same data unit at the same time (see section 23.3.7). Therefore, a database is required, which offers the possibility to handle data units of different sizes and which supports two levels of granularity. These requirements are fulfilled by the JESSI Common Framework – Object Management System (JCF–OMS).

Additionally, it has to be defined how the different descriptions of the pieces of hardware are organized in the database and how meta data for administrative tasks have to be stored. Consequently, a common *administration data schema*, responsible for the administration of data units, has to be developed and mapped on the first level of granularity of the JCF–OMS. As this data schema will be shared by various tools, it should not be optimized according to the requirements of a specific tool, but be generally applicable and easily extensible for future needs. Accordingly, the administration data schema should be oriented towards requirements resulting from the general design process to guarantee system openess. This approach is followed for the integration described here.

Currently the tools listed in section 23.3 only share a common administration data schema. In the future, more than one tool should be able to work on the same data at the same time. Therefore a common *design data schema* has to be developed and mapped to the second level of granularity of the JCF–OMS, in order to enable the JCF to offer consistency mechanisms. This design data schema containing the design data needed by the tools should cover different design views. It additionally should help to save data conversion efforts. Instead of adapting a new tool to a variety of private data formats, the tool should be able to use this well defined common data format as runtime data structure.

The data integration approach described here is based on the JCF–OMS and its services, which therefore are described first. Afterwards, the requirements for an administrative data schema, resulting from the hardware design process as described in section 23.2.2, will be listed. In the following paragraphs an administrative data schema is defined, which fulfils all these requirements. At the end of the data integra-

Tool Integration: Environments and Frameworks, Edited by D. Schefström and G. van den Broek

tion description it is shown how configuration management is done based on the data schema.

24.1 OVERVIEW OF THE JESSI COMMON FRAMEWORK OMS

The JCF–OMS [M+92] provides a procedural interface that supports data integration as well as control integration. Data in the database can be shared by several tools. Multiple reader/writer access to the data is synchronized by the database system. Furthermore, the database system offers mechanisms for tool communication (Inter–Tool Communication and Events). For detailed and complete information about the JCF–OMS the reader is referred to [Kac90] and [Cad90].

JCF–OMS is conceived as a database kernel system supplying simple, atomic mechanisms for data modelling and data manipulation. These mechanisms are generic in order to be able to support a wide range of applications. Thus, applications may be associated directly with the JCF–OMS or data models/interfaces. For example, the Entity Relationship Model of a higher level may be realized above it.

24.1.1 The internal data model of the JCF–OMS

The administration and design data schemas mentioned above will be mapped onto the IDM (Internal Data Model) of the JCF–OMS. In IDM the "real world" (e.g., digital circuit design) is modelled by objects which can be related to other objects. The properties (attributes) of an object are formally defined by an object type. All objects of one object type have the same structure, which is associated with this object type. Hence, an object has to be created as an instance (occurrence) of exactly one object type.

Object types are defined as a set of attribute types for holding data. An attribute type specifies the underlying data type and, if necessary, the range of values of the attribute. These types can be specified by the user.

Between two object types, even between identical ones, the formal definition of relation types is possible. The relations, which are the instances of the relation types, may be considered as edges between two objects, which are the instances of the object types. When an edge is attached between two objects, the definition line and the access line of the relation are set. The definition line specifies the direction and the access line defines the accessibility of an edge. Accessibility means that objects can be accessed along edges in both or only in one direction.

IDM relation types are a very simple, yet powerful means of realizing relations efficiently. However, e.g., attributed relations cannot be realized by IDM. The remedy for these limitations is to use objects for building relations. Typically such relations are modelled with objects of type ECO or PO which will be mentioned below.

In general, relation types of the IDM always allow the establishment of n:m relations. This may be understood as follows: if a relation type is defined between the object types *type1* and *type2*, then an object *object1* of object type *type1* may be attached to several objects of object type *type2*. Vice versa, an object *object2* of object type

type2 may be related to several objects of object type *type1*. Objects and relations are shown in figure 24.1.

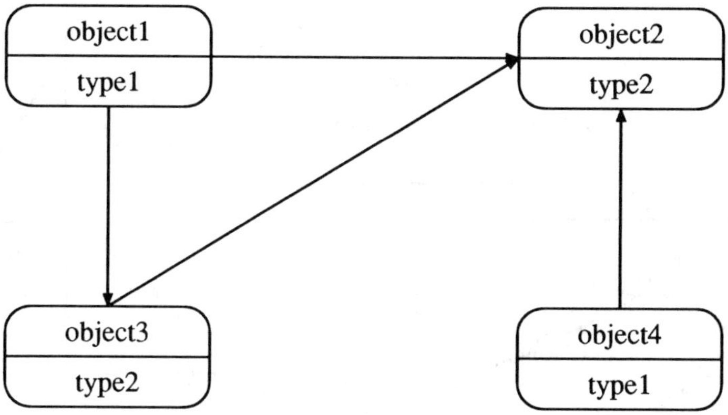

Figure 24.1 Objects and their relations

The construction of complex objects by an "is–contained–in"–relation is supported by the IDM via the structured complex objects (SCOs).

Using SCO types, object types and associated relation types can be composed to form a higher level typed object [BB84]. The object types contained in an SCO are referred to as primitive object types. An instance of such an object type is called a primitive object (PO). The definition of an SCO excludes the property of "being–contained–in" for complex object types. The result is that the object granularity strictly consists of two levels: there are complex objects and primitive objects. IDM allows the creation of relations between primitive objects and complex objects. This makes it possible to express "is–contained–in" hierarchies.

The complex objects and the relations between them form a complex object graph. Analogously to this complex object graph, within a structured complex object there generally exists one graph of primitive objects. The internal data model is shown in figure 24.2.

Any SCO is taken to be a cluster by the OMS, i.e., a cluster is the physical collection of data (e.g., design objects) to one unit that can be handled in an efficient way. When an SCO is opened, the graph of primitive objects pertaining to this SCO is loaded into the data base system's main memory. This supports efficiently the kernel operation methodology of design tools.

The graph of complex objects may also contain, besides the SCOs, unstructured complex objects (UCOs). In contrast to the SCOs, the UCOs do not contain a graph of primitive objects but a byte string of arbitrary length which is uninterpretable for the database system. Uninterpretable means that the database system knows neither the structure nor the content of the byte string. With regard to this aspect, UCOs are indeed comparable to the files of a file system. Due to this fact, UCOs may be used to support tool encapsulation. Like SCOs, UCOs also have the cluster property.

In addition IDM provides two more basic types of complex objects:

- ECO (Empty Complex Objects) which do not contain further components, e.g., for modelling attributed relationships,

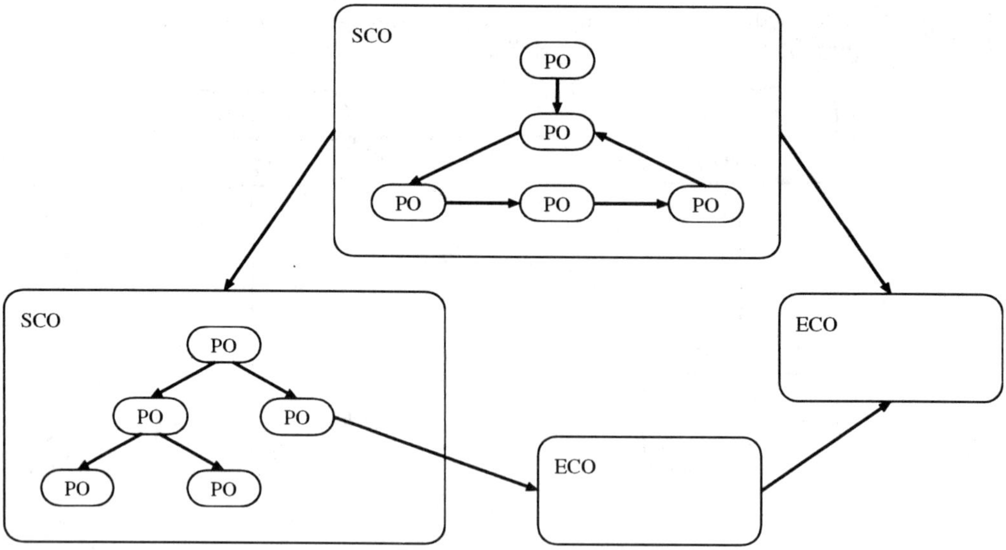

Figure 24.2 Internal data model

- XCO (External Complex Objects) used as links to objects located outside the database in the underlying file system, e.g., for system resources that must also be visible to other applications.

24.1.2 Further concepts

In addition, IDM contains concepts which go beyond the modelling of data and relations. Among others, these are event handling (see section 26.1) and version handling.

With the version handling of IDM the user is allowed to create different versions of one object. In general, these different versions can be used for different purposes (e.g., different versions of a digital circuit). To handle the versioned objects IDM provides a corresponding functionality to the user (e.g., an administration of current objects, especially a functionality to get the current version object of all versions of one object).

24.2 REQUIREMENTS FOR AN ADMINISTRATIVE DATA SCHEMA

A first step towards data integration is, as mentioned before, the development of an administrative data schema enabling the administration of the data in the same way by all of the tools. The requirements for an administrative data schema can be found by analyzing the design process as described in section 23.2.2. Usually, digital systems are composed of a number of parts which we call design units. In the development process of digital systems a lot of different descriptions may exist for each part of the design. During the design process descriptions at all levels of abstraction and for each view are produced. All these descriptions have to be handled by the data schema. Accordingly, there must be a way to store descriptions of different views and different levels of abstraction within the data schema.

This leads to the following requirements:

REQ 1: different levels of abstraction,
REQ 2: different views.

During the process of implementation (generation) and regulation between the levels of abstraction alternative descriptions of the same piece of the design may be created. It might be necessary to carry out several of these alternatives to find out which one is the best with respect to the whole circuit. Therefore, the global data schema must be able to hold these alternative descriptions of the same piece of the design and to offer efficient access to description parts belonging to one alternative of the design unit. In other words: the administrative data schema must handle

REQ 3: alternative realizations of designs.

Additional requirements result from the decomposition/composition activities. Usually, a design is developed hierarchically. The design is decomposed into smaller pieces to reduce its complexity. This reduction eases the handling (or understanding) of the total design for a designer as well as for a corresponding tool. Of course, the different parts finally have to be composed or configured to get a description of the total digital system. This hierarchy, resulting from the decomposition process, is called the *instantiation hierarchy*. One level within this hierarchy is built up by the instantiation of smaller pieces of hardware. Thus, the data schema has to reflect

REQ 4: instantiation hierarchies.

But the hierarchy built up at higher levels of abstraction sometimes is not useful at lower ones, because it is necessary for some tools to repartition the design and to build up a new instantiation hierarchy [Nie83]. The new hierarchy may not use all the modules or design units that exist in the old hierarchy. In some cases new design units may be created to structure the design units and modules of the design in a different manner.

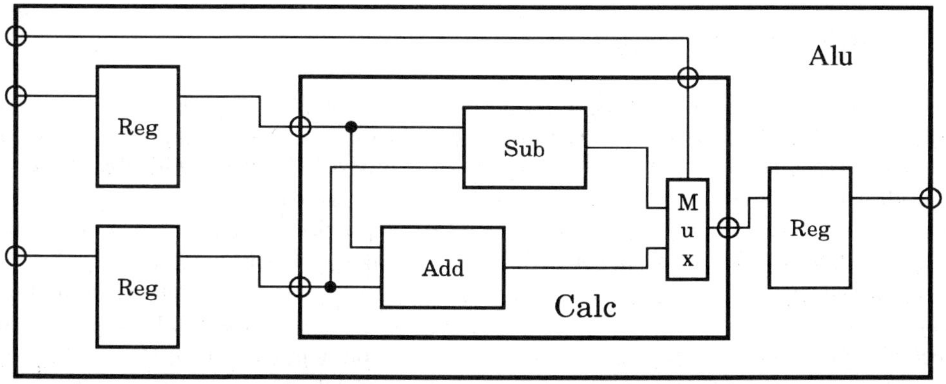

Figure 24.3 Register transfer structure

Figure 24.3 contains as an example the hierarchy of a design at RT-level in the structure view. This hierarchy may not be useful for constructing the floorplan, thus requiring a repartitioning of the design. An instantiation hierarchy in the floorplan view, which may result from this repartitioning, is shown in figure 24.4. The new hierarchy is not as deep as the old one, and design unit Calc is not needed.

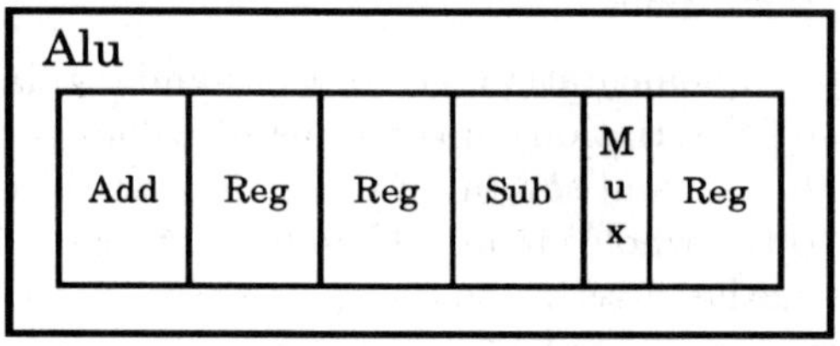

Figure 24.4 Floorplan

This example illustrates the necessity of another requirement:

> **REQ 5:** different non isomorphic instantiation hierarchies within different views.

In addition, the instantiation hierarchies within different alternative realizations of a design may also differ. For example, the design unit Calc might not be needed or the inclusion of new design units might be required within an alternative register transfer realization. Therefore, the following requirement also exists:

> **REQ 6:** different instantiation hierarchies within different alternative realizations.

Because the instantiation hierarchy can be very deep, it is inconvenient and time consuming for a designer to find the data needed. The whole hierarchy tree has to be walked through, because it is not known where the data describing a special module can be found. Thus, a static hierarchy is needed that eases the retrieval of the data and that is independent of the hardware design process. This hierarchy should be of a small restricted depth. Thus, an administrative data schema should contain a:

> **REQ 7:** static access hierarchy.

If different alternatives of design units are stored, configuration aspects become very important. Imagine a design unit composed from different sub-designs (REQ 4). For each sub-design there may be several design alternatives (REQ 3), which can really be used alternatively. Some or all of these sub-design alternatives may be composed from sub-designs as well, resulting in a high number of possible configurations of the total design. But for hardware design it is difficult to find out which alternative realizations of the sub-design can be combined. If a designer uses a piece of the design during definition of another one, it is necessary to know quite well which alternative of this piece will fit. Therefore, the configurations have to be defined during the development of a design and have to remain fixed. To manage this there has to be a mechanism to select special design alternatives along the instantiation hierarchy. This mechanism is called:

> **REQ 8:** configuration management.

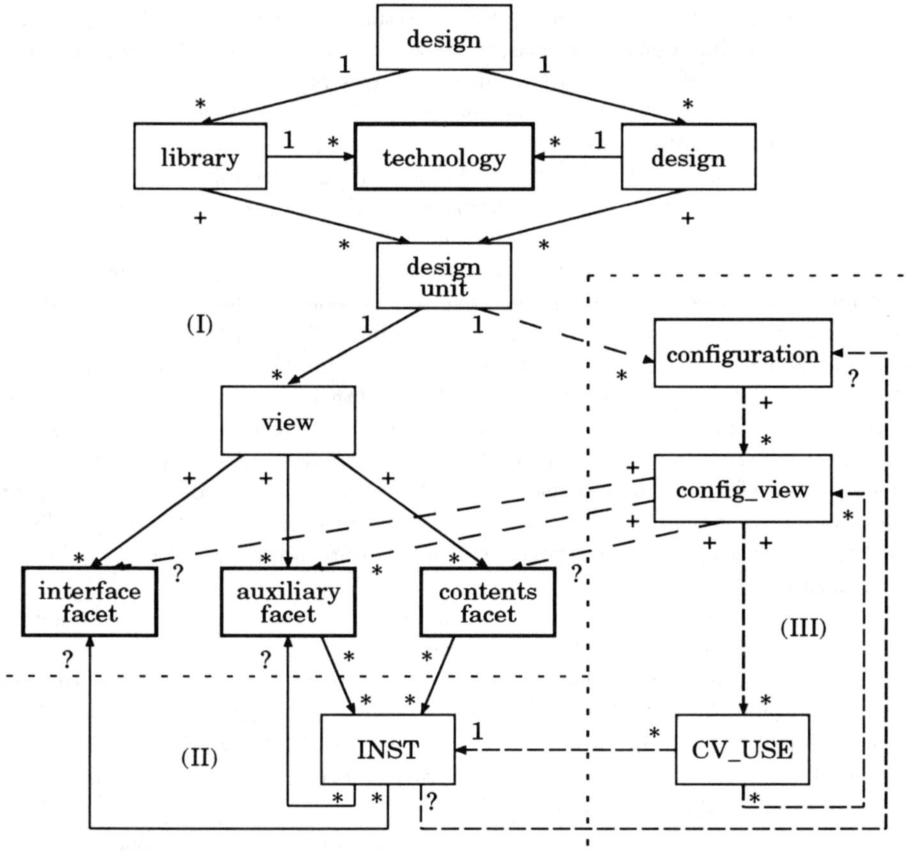

1) For each INST object at least one father must exist: a contents or an auxiliary facet.
2) For each INST object exactly one son must exist: one interface or one auxiliary facet.

Figure 24.5 The administrative data schema

Additionally, some general requirements for the common data schema can be listed: The schema should be easily extensible for tool-specific needs and it must be possible to reuse design parts. Moreover, the granularity of design data should at least enable distinction of interface and contents parts of design units.

24.3 THE ADMINISTRATIVE DATA SCHEMA

A data schema, that fulfills all requirements listed, is depicted by figure 24.5. The following kinds of symbols are used here: boxes represent different classes available mainly for data structuring purposes. Only objects of classes depicted in bold style contain the real data, comparable to files. The arrows (both solid and dashed) denote father–son relationships, which can have arbitrary semantics (e.g., part of, type of). The number at the end point of an arrow gives the number of sons the father may have (a "*" is used if there is no restriction, a "+" means: at least one, and a "?"

means: at most one), while the start point is attached with the number of fathers a son may have, and thus denotes whether the son can be "reused" by another father.

The following kinds of symbols are used here: boxes represent different classes available mainly for data structuring purposes. Only objects of classes depicted in bold style contain the real data, comparable to files. The arrows (both solid and dashed) denote father–son relationships, which can have arbitrary semantics (e.g., part of, type of). The number at the end point of an arrow gives the number of sons the father may have (a "*" is used if there is no restriction, a "+" means: at least one, and a "?" means: at most one), while the start point is attached with the number of fathers a son may have, and thus denotes whether the son can be "reused" by another father.

Figure 24.5 is divided into three segments, separated by dotted lines. The largest segment represents a *static access hierarchy* (*I*), which enables direct access to different design units. At the bottom the subschema for *instantiation hierarchies* (*II*) follows, which enables storing of hierarchical designs. Moreover, on the right-hand side the *configurations subschema* (*III*) is given. This graphical description of the data schema can easily be transformed to that used by EXPRESS (an object oriented information modelling language developed for the exchange of product model data, see [SS91]), but for this paper the selected representation is more appropriate to emphasize all points of interest.

In the following sections these subschemas are explained in detail, and hereafter the use of the schema is illustrated. However, the specification of concrete data for central design management tasks, like creation or modification dates or authors of objects, is of minor interest here. Such data is stored in additional attributes, which can be used for objects of any kind, whether they contain design data or not. Within the figures of the following subsections some object types occur more than once for a better illustration of the mechanisms.

24.3.1 The static access hierarchy

The main part of the access hierarchy is similar to EDIF [EDI87]. EDIF is an ASCII–format, which is used to interchange data between different tools. This format mainly reflects a static part–of hierarchy. This hierarchy, built up of *designs*, *libraries*, *cells*, and *views*, is reflected in the schema developed for the integration of the hardware design tools. But the schema described here has some additional features, because it should offer the possibility for other tools outside the scope of hardware synthesis to be integrated into the environment. In the schema the term "cell", used in hardware design and EDIF terminology, is replaced by "design unit" to reflect the ability to handle general designs beyond the scope of hardware engineering.

Figure 24.6 shows this static access hierarchy. The object classes are represented by vertices and the relations are represented by edges. The vertices are named with the class they stand for. The schema distinguishes the following object classes:

entry:
An object of this class is used as an entry point for the data of the integrated tools. For this purpose a special root is created. Thus, data of other tools not belonging to the integrated environment can also be stored within the data base. Only one object of this class exists.

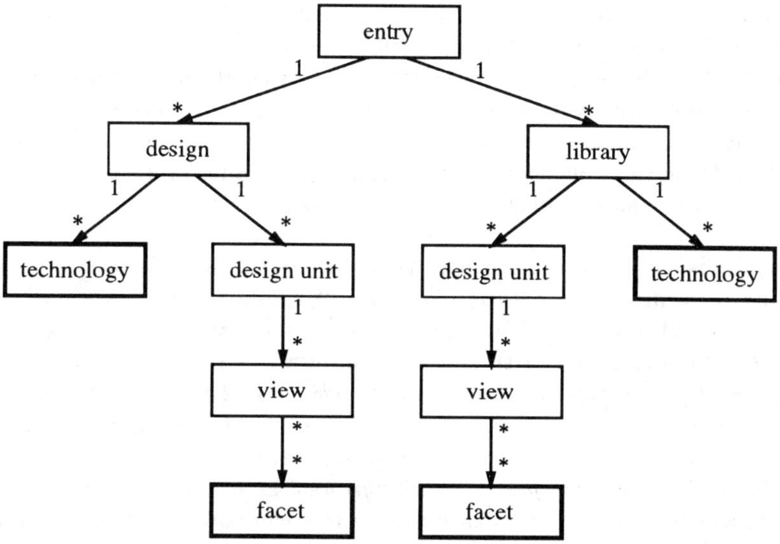

(*The number at the end point of an edge A* ⟶ *B denotes how many successors of class B an object of class A may have and vice versa. The star at the end points or start points means that any number of successors or predecessors is allowed.*)

Figure 24.6 Static access hierarchy

design:
Objects of this class serve as an entry point for all data of a design. This means that the descriptions of different design units that are used and developed for a special design can be found below this object. Several objects of this class may exist within the database. Another possible way to use an object of this class is to characterize a task for a particular group of people. It might be possible that the design units developed to solve this task can be used to construct a complete integrated circuit.

library:
Objects of this class have the task of grouping predefined design units, which can be reused to simplify the design process. Different objects of this class may exist to group design units of different technologies or design units used by different tools.

technology:
Objects of this class contain data describing the technology (CMOS, NMOS, Bipolar, ...) of the *design* or *library* the object belongs to. Additionally, design rules that have to be fulfilled during the design process are stored within the *technology* object. Several objects may exist per *design* or *library*.

design unit:
A *design unit* object represents a part of a design. For example, it contains the description of a control unit, data path, ALU, register, NAND, NOR, etc. It is created by a designer or by a tool. The enumeration of possible objects of this class shows that a *design unit* is able to contain descriptions of subcircuits of varying complexity. For each *library* or each *design* several *design units* may exist.

view:
Objects of this class specify the design view that the descriptions of the *design*

unit grouped below the *view* belong to. The *views* behaviour, structure, geometry, etc. can be distinguished. For some tools special *views* are necessary. Ideally, all tools would use the same format where the information they need is the same. In this case only one system wide description would be necessary for each view. However, in reality, most tools need their own representation of the data. Hence, in addition to the *system views* containing descriptions in a unified format, tool–specific descriptions, so–called *tool views*, are necessary.

facet:
Objects of this class contain the real data, e.g., in the Hardware Synthesis System, describing a circuit. They can be realized as UCOs, which are simple byte strings comparable to files, or as SCOs, which contain data structured as a graph of POs. Thus, a *facet* holds a part of the description of a *design unit* in one *view*. Usually, three types of *facets* exist per *view*: an *interface facet* type, a *contents facet* type, and an *auxiliary facet* type. The *interface facet* holds the interface of the *design unit* described. Usually, descriptions of *design units* at higher levels of hierarchy only refer to the *interface facet* of a *design unit* at a lower hierarchical level. The *contents facet* contains the realization or implementation of an *interface facet*. If it is not possible to select between interface and contents, the data can be stored in an *auxiliary facet*. *Facets* of these three types contain the description of a *design unit* within one *view*.

The objects that contain real data are *facets* and *technology* objects. The other objects are used for structuring reasons.

24.3.2 Alternative realizations of design units

The schema described so far is similar to EDIF. It fulfills the requirements for a static access hierarchy (REQ 7) and for different views (REQ 2) as mentioned in section 24.2. The problem here is that it is not possible to identify alternative descriptions which belong together. The alternative realizations or configurations of a *design unit* mentioned in REQ 3 determine for each *view* one of the *interfaces* and one of the *contents facets* available for that *design unit* as well as for every *design unit* used. Therefore, the selections are specified top–down along the instantiation hierarchy (see section 24.3.4). Choices made at a higher level affect the choices that need to be made at lower levels due to REQ 6.

This mechanism can be expressed by a structure recursion, which can roughly be written as:

$$K_D := \sum V_D \qquad V_D := I_D + C_D + \sum_{I \in C_D} V_{D_I}$$

Thus, a configuration K_D of a design unit D consists of several views V_D. Each such view consists of an interface I_D and (+) contents C_D of that design unit, as well as views V_{D_I} for all design objects D_I, which are instantiated in the selected contents facet ($I \in C_D$). As a result a tree of facets is obtained.

To include this mechanism into the schema some extensions have to be made. A new object class *configuration* is defined to handle alternative descriptions, which may consist of several views. For example, an alternative description of the behaviour of a design unit leads to an alternative structure. That means the task of *configuration* objects is to identify alternative descriptions of different views which belong together. Usually, the *configurations* of *design units* in a *library* cannot be changed by a designer once they are used in a *design*.

To preserve the access hierarchy a new branch has to be created, which is attached to the *design unit* object. As mentioned above a *configuration* may consist of several views. Therefore, a new class *config_view* belonging to a *configuration* has to be introduced to represent the views.

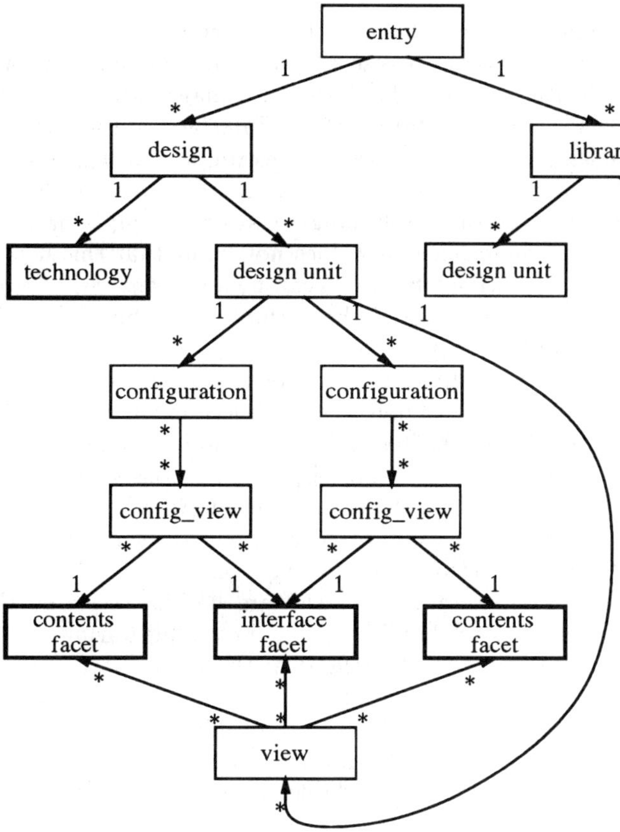

Figure 24.7 Configurations

Figure 24.7 shows an instance of the resulting conceptual schema. Objects of the class *design unit* may have successors of two classes: the class *view* and the class *configuration*. A *configuration* itself consists of *config_view* objects. Objects of the classes *view* and *config_view* that belong to the same design unit have the same *facets* as successors. The difference between them is that objects of the class *config_view* are only allowed to have one successor of the *interface facet* type and the *contents facet* type, whereas objects of the class *view* may have several of them. Within figure 24.7, the *view* has been moved to the bottom, because the path *configuration*, *config_view* is more important for tools working with the data schema.

Constraints concerning *configuration* and *config_view* depend on the design environment. For example, two different description formats for the behaviour of design units might exist in an environment. Hence, in the refinement of the schema two *tool views* are needed to hold the behavioural description. But for one *configuration* only one of the *tool views* should exist. Constraints like this can only be defined for a special design environment.

24.3.3 Reuse

An advantage of the schema described above is that *facets* may have more than one predecessor. Accordingly, it is possible to use the same description within different *configurations*. For example, the interface of a *design unit* may be the same for different *configurations* where only the implementation of this interface is different.

Additionally, *config_views* can also be reused. For example a *design unit* may have two different floorplan representations but the *behaviour view* may be the same. But for *designs* under development this reuse is dangerous. For example, if the designer simply changes the *behaviour config_view* and does not know that this description is also used within another *configuration*, the result can be an inconsistent *configuration* of the *design unit*. Therefore, this reuse should be performed carefully. If fixed versions of objects are reused, this problem does not arise.

One way to solve this problem would be to implement a mechanism for consistency management. Whenever data is to be changed such a mechanism would detect if the data is reused and, if so, copy the old version of the data and inform all the users about the change, for example by marking the using objects as inconsistent. The designer responsible for the *design* using the data then has to decide whether to use the old or the new version. This decision could be supported by a mechanism, which offers some information about the differences between the two versions.

Another aspect of reuse, very common in hardware design, concerns the use of predefined design parts which are stored in libraries. For example during layout design, library cells are often used to compose the layout of the entire hardware. However, hardware composition is a much more complex process than simply writing some composition scripts. Thus, layout synthesis tools are usually provided to do this job. Such tools in contrast to composition scripts have to "understand" the input format and to produce a specific output format readable for the user and usable for the production process.

24.3.4 The instantiation hierarchy

With the previously presented mechanism a designer can only develop a static access hierarchy. However, it is also necessary that support is provided for designs containing many levels of hierarchy. As pointed out in section 24.2, it must also be possible to generate different hierarchies within different views. Consequently, a relation between *config_views* or between *facets* is necessary. Relations between *design units* or between *configurations* would not be sufficient, as then all *views* of a *design unit* or *configuration* would have the same instantiation hierarchy. In the following paragraphs the instantiation mechanism within the schema is presented followed by an example, showing how it works for a particular design.

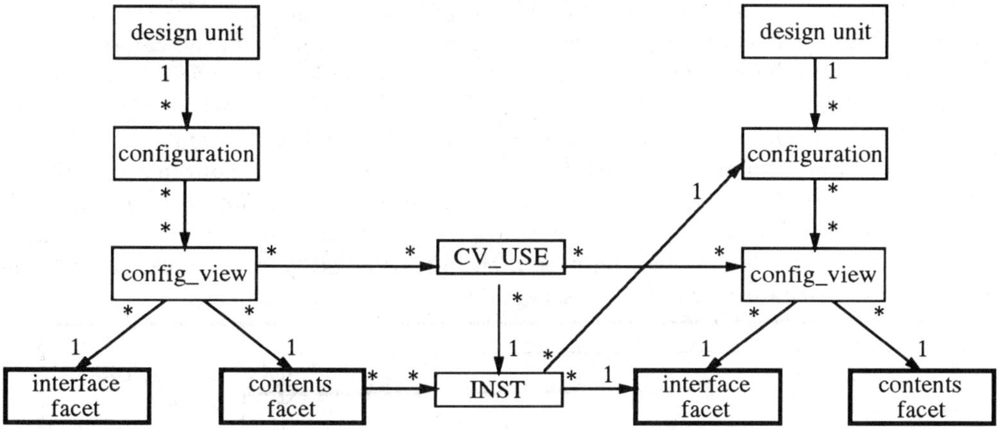

(The question-mark at the end points or start points means that zero or one successor or predecessor is allowed.)

Figure 24.8 Instantiation

To generate relations from one *facet* to another, each from different *design units*, a new class of object called *INST* is used (see figure 24.8). With these relations between *facets* we can represent exactly which element within a specific *facet* instantiates which *design unit* (if the structure of the instantiating *facet* is known by the database, i.e., the context of the instantiation remains visible.) This is also important if tools that work with primitive objects are to be integrated using this administrative data schema.

It is permitted to instantiate a *design unit* (a *facet*, respectively) more than once within another *facet* and one *design unit* may be instantiated by different *facets* to provide maximum reuse. Only reuse of *design units* belonging to the same *design* or to *libraries* is allowed, as otherwise consistency problems may arise. For example, if a *design unit* of a foreign *design* is instantiated, and the designer who owns this *design unit* changes the description without knowing that anyone else uses this *design unit*, the designer would consequently not inform the user of the *design unit* that any changes have been made. Obviously however, such changes would have some influence on the users of the altered *design unit* resulting in inconsistent and unpredictable behaviour.

Within one *view* it is possible to instantiate *design units* that are not instantiated in any other *view*, for example *design units* specially created for this *view*. Additionally, it is legal to instantiate *facets* belonging to different *configurations* to hierarchically describe different *views* of a *design unit*. For example, the *structure view* might instantiate *design units* in a configuration *C1*, and the *floorplan view* might instantiate *design units* in a configuration *C2*. Hence, the instantiation hierarchy is specific for each *view*.

The *interface facet* of a *design unit* is instantiated out of *contents facets* because at a higher hierarchical level only the interface is important. But, usually, it is not sufficient to know which *facet* is instantiated because a *facet* can be used by different *configurations*. Therefore, an edge from the *INST* object to the *configuration* is added.

According to the formula of section 24.3.2 the *config_views* refer, in addition to the *interface* and *contents facet*, to the *config_views* of all those *design units* which are instantiated in the *contents facet*. For this purpose a so-called *CV_USE* object (Config_View_USE) connects a *config_view* with both an *INST*ance, and the *config_view* for that *INST*. The reference to the *INST* is necessary to show which *INST* is configured by that *CV_USE*. The *CV_USE* object provides a way to express, which combinations of *interface* and *contents facets* are selected in the hierarchical description of one *config_view*. (This is explained further by an example later.) This approach avoids the copying of the *contents facet* for each *configuration* context, as would be necessary if only the *INST* object and the pointer to the *configuration* were used. The following examples (which have already been presented in section 24.2) will motivate the chosen instantiation mechanism within the schema.

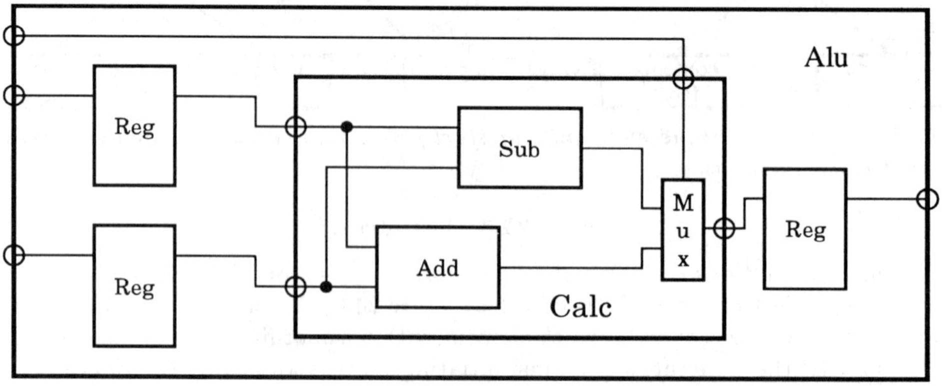

Figure 24.9 Structural description of a design

Figure 24.9 shows a design unit *Alu* (arithmetic logic unit) in the *structure view* using four design units: one *Calc* (calculator) and three *Reg* elements (registers). The *Calc* itself also contains several design units: one *Add* (adder), one *Sub* (substractor), and one *Mux* element (multiplexer). Hence, the design uses three hierarchy levels with the *Alu* at the top, the *Regs* and the *Calc* at the next level and the other design units at the bottom. Figure 24.10 contains the same design with the same functionality within the *floorplan view*. Here only two levels of hierarchy are used. Usually, in the *floorplan view* the instantiation hierarchy is changed to get better results; for example in figure 24.10 the hierarchy level corresponding to the *Calc* element is omitted.

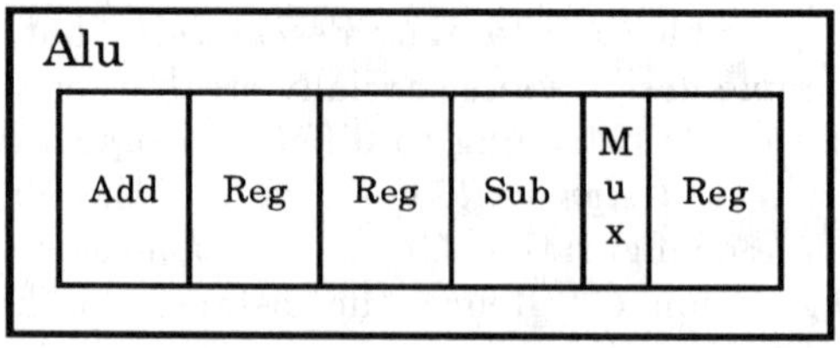

Figure 24.10 Floorplan of a design

Figure 24.11 shows the schema representation of the example of figures 24.9 and 24.10. Six *design units* (*Alu, Reg, Calc, Add, Sub, Mux*) have to be created (*Sub* and *Mux* are not shown in the figure). For each of them one *configuration* object and the description of the *structure view* (*contents* and *interface facet*) exist. Instance objects

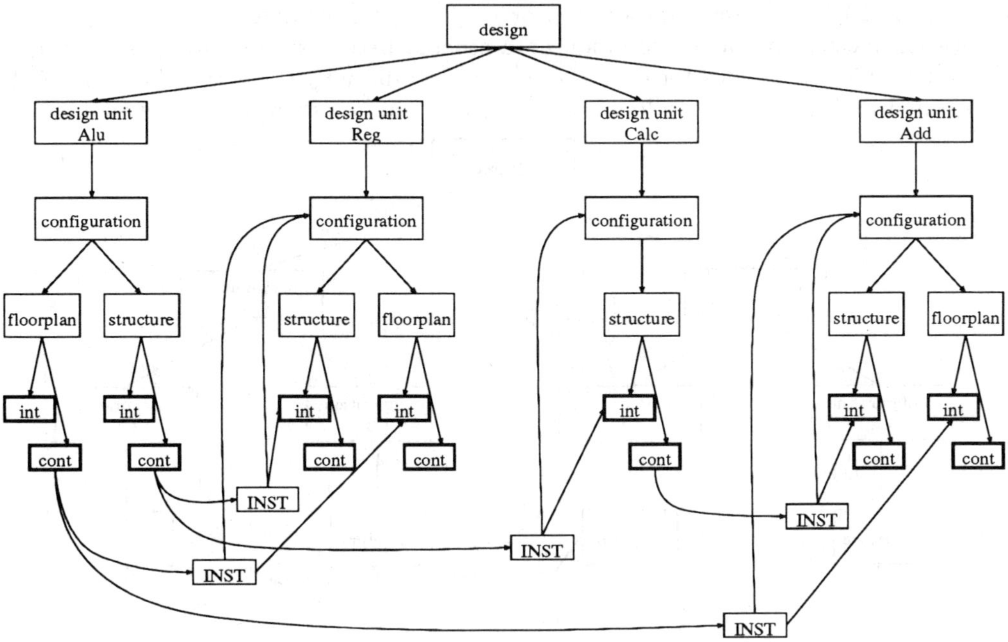

$(int = interfacefacet, cont = contentsfacet)$

Figure 24.11 Schema representation of the previous example

($INST$) are referenced by the *contents facets* of the *design units Alu* and *Calc* to represent the instantiation hierarchy. They refer to the *interface facets* of the *design units Reg*, *Calc*, and *Add*. For the representation of figure 24.10 the *view floorplan* has to be introduced. Each of the *design units* (except *Calc*, which is not used for the floorplan) has an *interface* and a *contents facet* in the *floorplan view*. Here, only two instantiation levels are used: the *contents facet* of *design unit Alu* instantiates the *floorplan interface facets* of the *design units Reg* and *Add*.

It is not always necessary to use both $INST$ and *CV_USE* for the instantiation. Depending on the application only one of them may be necessary. Figure 24.12 shows an example illustrating the benefit of the *CV_USE* mechanism. Here, only the schema representation of the *design units Alu* and *Calc* is shown and only the relations of interest are depicted. For each *design unit* there are some (versions of) *interface* and *contents facets* available, which are selected by the *configurations*. The two *configurations* of *Alu* instantiate different *configurations* (and *contents*) of the *design unit Calc* out of one *contents facet*. One *CV_USE* object connects the *structure views* of the *configurations C1* and *C3*, and one *CV_USE* object connects the *structure views* of the *configurations C2* and *C4*. Only one $INST$ance object belonging to both *CV_USE* objects is necessary to connect the *contents* and *interface facets* of the two *design* units. If the selection of the *configurations* had been done by a pointer from the $INST$ object to the instantiated *configuration*, two $INST$ objects would have been necessary: one for each *configuration*. This would have required that the *contents facet* of the *Alu design unit* be copied, which could potentially be an expensive operation if a large amount of data is involved.

In figure 24.12 only one kind of *view* or *config_view* is depicted. However, the configuration mechanism of the common data schema becomes particularly powerful, if several kinds of *views* exist for *design units*. This is especially the case if the *views* of all integrated tools are stored under each *design unit* and are then configured en–bloque.

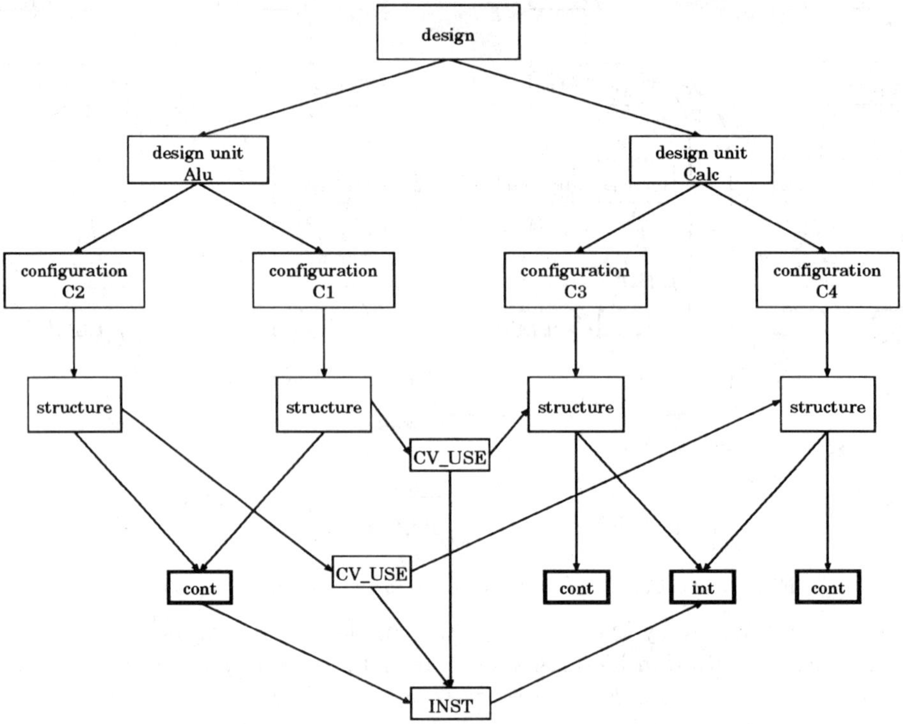

Figure 24.12 Configurations using *CV_USE*

The use of an additional edge pointing from the *INST* object to a *configuration* is helpful for a tool that works on more than one *view* using the *INST* relation. Figure 24.13 shows an example where it is necessary to identify the *configuration* that belongs to the instantiated *facet*.

In this example the *views floorplan* and *layout* are used. The *floorplan* of the *design unit Alu* consists of *design unit Reg* and several other *design units*, which are not shown in the figure. Consequently, the *interface facet* in the *floorplan view* of the *design unit Reg* is instantiated by the *contents facet* in the *floorplan view* of the *design unit Alu*.

After the development of the floorplan, a layout construction tool tries to create the description within the *layout view* using the hierarchy. This is possible, because the floorplan is the result of a decomposition phase and the layout is the result of a composition phase both using the same hierarchy. Therefore, the composition tool itself will use the hierarchy of the *floorplan view* to find out which design unit has to be handled next. This means that the instantiation hierarchy in the *layout view* can be developed bottom–up.

In the example of figure 24.13 the layout construction tool wants to create the layout of the *design unit Alu* using the layout of the *design unit Reg*. But the *interface*

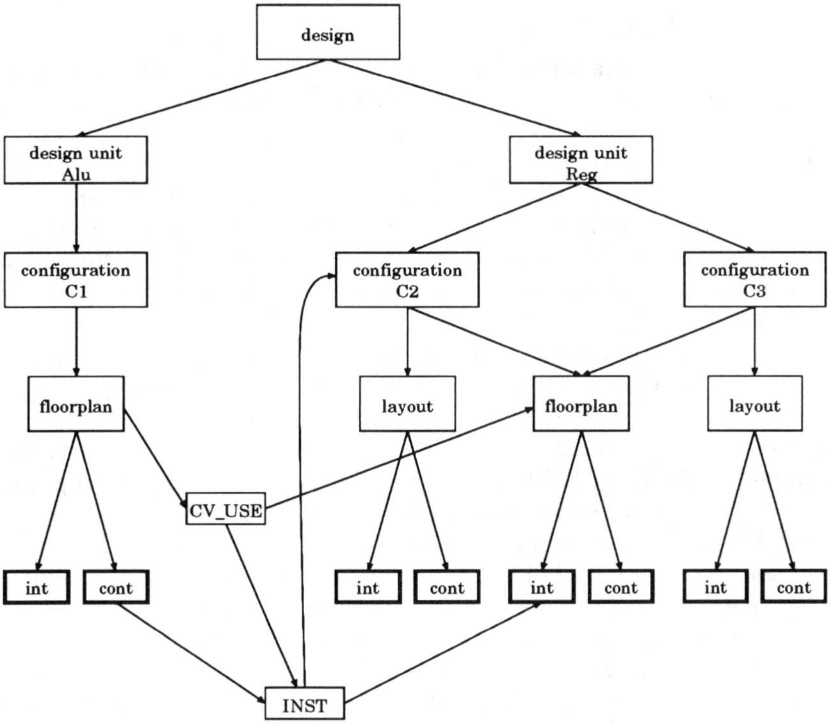

Figure 24.13 Combination of instantiation and configuration

instantiated in the *floorplan view* of the *design unit Alu* belongs to two *configurations*: *C2* and *C3*. Each *configuration* has its own layout. Therefore, it is important to document which *configuration* of the *design unit Reg* is used to construct the *layout* for the *configuration C1* of the *design unit Alu*. The arrow pointing to *C2* solves this problem for composition tools that do not have a specific *configuration* as entry to the instantiation hierarchy. It is worth noting that the *CV_USE* relationship alone does not solve the problem because of the reuse of the *floorplan view* object.

24.3.5 Different instantiation hierarchies within different views

As mentioned in section 24.2, different *views* might need different hierarchies. For example, the hierarchy built up in the *structure view* on RT–level might not be useful for the layout construction of a floorplanner (see figures 24.3 and 24.4). This does not concern the static access hierarchy, which is a part–of hierarchy valid for the whole design. The instantiation hierarchy (or hierarchies) can change within different *views*. However, each instantiation hierarchy has its own entry point.

Construction of different instantiation hierarchies within different *views* is straightforward because the instantiation hierarchy belongs to a specific *view*. Thus, no ambiguity is possible.

24.3.6 Repartitioning

Within the hardware domain tools exist that not only use the instantiation hierarchy developed previously, but also do some repartitioning and generate a new instantiation hierarchy within the schema. This new hierarchy is only relevant for these tools and the hierarchies within the previously existing *views* remain important for the current *configuration* of the *design*. Some *design units* of the old hierarchy might not be used and some new *design units* might be created. In the section which explained the instantiation mechanism an example of this was described, where a floorplanner does some repartitioning on the instantiation hierarchy of the *structure view* (see figures 24.9 and 24.10).

A tool can distinguish between the two hierarchies because they refer to different *views*. Figure 24.11 shows the representation of the two instantiation hierarchies for the *design units Alu*, *Reg*, *Calc* and *Add* within the schema.

The *design units* that already exist in the *structure view* are not newly created for the instantiation hierarchy built up by the floorplanner. Thus, the top *design unit* and the leaf *design units* will remain in both views. The *design units* that exist in both hierarchies get a new *view*, the *floorplan view*, and new *facets* describing the *design unit* in this *view*. This holds for the *design units Alu* and *Reg* in figure 24.11. If one or more *floorplan config_views* already exist within a *configuration*, an additional *floorplan config_view* has to be created in a new *configuration*.

If a new hierarchy is created some *design units* that are at the same level in the existing hierarchy may be at different hierarchical levels in the new one. For this reason, new *design units* have to be created. These *design units* are solely described within the *floorplan view*. The *structure view* will not be created for them. Usually, the *behaviour view* would also not be generated for such *design units*, because the designer has no real idea what they do.

In the bottom–up process of layout assembly the tools will use the hierarchy of the *floorplan view*. The *design units* that are only described in the *structure view* will not be considered. This means, that these *design units* are described in the *structure view* or the *behaviour view*, but not in the *floorplan* and the *layout view*. On the other hand, the *design units* that are created by the floorplanner will not be described in the *structure view* and the *behaviour view*. Hence, it is necessary to make a distinction between these two types of *design units* to know which *views* are defined for which *design unit*. For this reason the *design units* created during the partitioning process are called *top–down design units*, whereas the *design units* created by the floorplanner are called *bottom–up design units*. A third class of *design units, top,* is defined to fix the entry point of the instantiation hierarchies.

24.3.7 Implementation of the data schema

The administration data schema is implemented using the JCF. It determines which complex object types and which connections between complex objects of these types (edges in the complex object graph) are allowed. Furthermore, it defines which attributes are permitted for complex objects of a specific type, and what the default values of these attributes look like.

During the design of the data schema, it was also considered by which tools the data should be used. To support data sharing, information needed by different tools is also distinguished in the data schema. This is achieved by defining special types for objects that contain data for different tools. An example showing the refinement of the data schema for CIRCAL can be found in [BKM+92].

Furthermore, the implementation of object types also considers the communication mechanisms, especially events (see also chapter 26). Events can for instance be used to check consistency conditions. If objects with the same information content need different consistency checking facilities it might be reasonable to define different complex object types and events with different event procedures for these object types. Then the database system automatically chooses the right event procedure for consistency checking of those objects depending on their type.

The common schema does not depend on the JCF, but can be used for other frameworks and object management systems as well. Only the data schema has to be mapped on the data model of the underlying object management system. However, some general requirements have to be considered, when selecting a special object management system. For example, a lot of different files, very small and very large ones, have to be stored. Hence, the use of a relational database would lead to a very bad performance. Additionally, the object management system must offer two levels of granularity, in order to enable more than one tool to work on the same data at the same time. (In section 23.3.7 this has already been explained in more detail.)

25

Presentation Integration

As described in section 23.3.7 presentation integration was mainly done for the tools of the Hardware Synthesis System. These tools have similar tasks in the hardware design process, which eases the development of similar user interfaces. But also the analysis tools have been regarded, so that the concepts can easily be transferred to them. For the tools HIT and BEMO presentation integration was achieved by using the standard JCF Desktop and defining common icons, object attributes, access methods, method groups and client groups using a common TIDL script.

Presentation integration has the objective of creating user interfaces which are nearly the same for all tools of an environment. Several requirements for such a common user interface can be fixed:

- unified look and feel,
- simple control (i.e., easy to learn),
- direct command entering by pointing device or by keyboard,
- unified command classification, e.g., separation between display commands and data modification commands.

The most important aspect for presentation integration is reaching a unified look and feel. The first step to reach this is to use "standards" for the development of the user interface. For the integration of the Hardware Synthesis System the user interface is implemented with X/Window and OSF/Motif software/standards. For the development of the user interface the Cadlab User Interface Management System (UIMS) described in the following sections is used. Its use should simplify the development of user interfaces, which fulfill the requirements listed above.

25.1 THE USER INTERFACE MANAGEMENT SYSTEM

The User Interface Management System (UIMS) was developed to support the presentation integration of several applications (see [GKKK86, GKK+88]). It guarantees the uniformity of the user interfaces of all integrated tools by providing special services. Not only newly developed tools, but also existing tools can be integrated.

The integration of two different groups of tools is supported. The first group consists of graphical interactive tools; for instance, editors. Batch oriented tools build up the second group.

Tool Integration: Environments and Frameworks, Edited by D. Schefström and G. van den Broek

Through presentation integration the integrated tools should be standardized with respect to their user interface. Simple control of the tools should also be possible. These requirements are fulfilled by the UIMS, which supports the realization of several features for the dialogue with the user. Thus, the tool programmer is relieved from implementing the same dialogue mechanisms for several tools repeatedly. The dialogue is controlled by a context free grammar [ASU86]. By using this grammar the dialogue syntax is standardized and a simple specification of the dialogue syntax is possible.

Furthermore, the UIMS supports the handling of graphical information which is very important for graphical applications. The application programmer is therefore freed from implementing the details of graphical output and standard operations on graphical data, such as zooming, selection and redraw. Routines for graphical output on a screen or on a plotter are available. A well defined data structure containing the graphical information is used as a basis for the realization of such graphic operations.

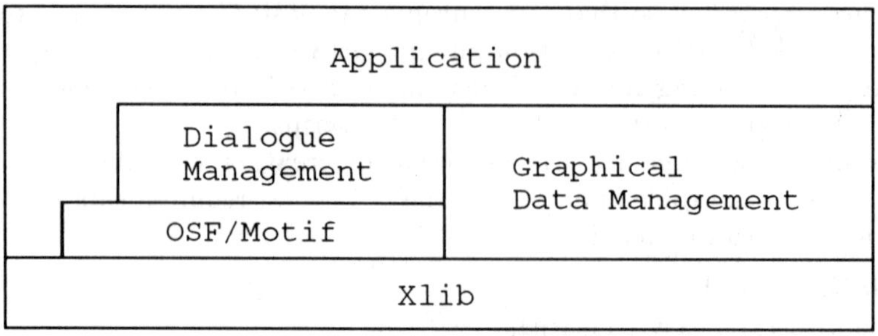

Figure 25.1 Layered model of the UIMS

Figure 25.1 shows a layered model of the UIMS. The basis of all services is built up by the X/Window system and the Xlib interface. The graphical data management is directly based on the Xlib, whereas OSF/Motif contributes to the realization of the dialogue management. The application programmer has the chance to use both, dialogue management and graphical data management. As only the Hardware Synthesis System is currently integrated with respect to presentation integration, OSF/Motif and the Xlib interface can also be used by the application programmer. For an overall integration system direct use of OSF/Motif and Xlib will be prevented, so that the resulting user interfaces will be more uniform.

25.1.1 Overview of the components of the UIMS

As shown in figure 25.2, the UIMS consists of the modules Interpreter (INT) for the dialogue management, the LGM (Low Level Graphic Module) and the GDS (Graphical Data Structure) for the graphical data management.

The Interpreter is the central part of the UIMS. It consists of a context free grammar with corresponding actions. The Interpreter controls the user dialogue and can get input from several sources. Those sources are for instance user interactions, macro files or scripts, and other tool processes. User interactions by pointing device or by keyboard are first processed by the X/Window system and OSF/Motif. Each user interaction may trigger an X–event. The X–event starts an application specific procedure, which has to be defined by the application programmer and is implemented in

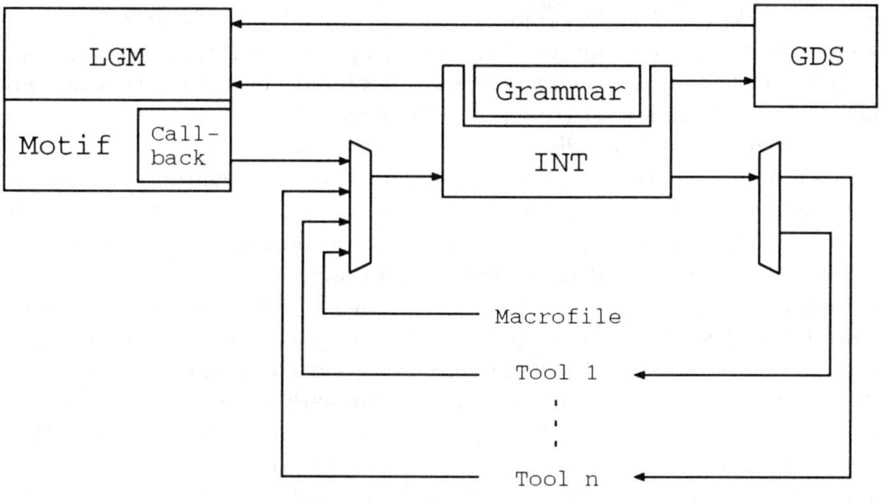

Figure 25.2 UIMS components

C. The procedure is called a "callback" procedure. It converts the X–event into one or more tokens for the Interpreter. If the Interpreter gets input from macro files or other tools, this input is passed by channels to the Interpreter and transformed into tokens by specific services.

As mentioned above the Interpreter can get input from several sources. As the Interpreter is not able to process the tokens in parallel, if inputs arrive from multiple sources, an appropriate scheduling strategy has to be realized for token processing. A default strategy is provided.

When the Interpreter receives (a set of) tokens, it activates a corresponding function, which has access to the GDS or to the LGM. If the Interpreter receives tokens as a result of a user interaction, this function may also activate another tool or tool command.

The GDS comprises a hierarchical data structure for graphical data and a library of routines for access and manipulation of this data structure. For the realization of the graphical output the GDS passes the graphical data to the LGM. The LGM offers routines for graphical output.

The modules mentioned above are described in more detail in the following sections.

25.1.2 LGM - Low level Graphic Module

This module provides a procedural interface for graphical output in windows built with X/Window, the so–called graphic edit fields. For this kind of window the LGM offers special functions which ease the graphical output. Compared to the Xlib interface, the LGM has higher functionality.

The LGM offers the following extensions:

- World–coordinates are used instead of window–coordinates.
  The origin of the window–coordinate system depends on the graphical window. As a result of this, all coordinates of graphical objects have to be changed if the area seen in the display window of a graphical editor is moved. If a world–coordinate system is

used actions like moving and zooming do not change the coordinates of the graphical objects. The world–coordinates of the LGM are integers. Every graphic edit field has an associated *graphic transformation*. A graphic transformation determines a translation, a rotation, a mirror and a scaling operation, that are used to transform world–coordinates into coordinates of the X Window system.

- A set of graphical primitives and corresponding drawing routines is offered.
  The graphical primitives are points, lines, rectangles, arcs, polylines, circles and text. Some primitives can be drawn as contour or filled with a pattern (see below).
- A related graphical context exists for every window.
  The graphical context is composed of a number of attributes which describe the appearance of the graphical output. Some of the attributes are pen, pattern and font as well as the colour of foreground and background, and the grid.
  Some graphical primitives, e.g., lines, are drawn with a pen. A pen is a rectangular area. The lower right corner of the pen is fixed when the first point of the line is chosen. The upper left corner of the pen follows the line.
  Graphical primitives which form the boundary of geometric areas can be filled with a variety of styles (pattern). Patterns are defined by the X–data structure *Pixmap*.
  In the area of a graphic edit field a grid can be drawn. Position and colour of the points of the grid are given by the graphical context.
  The foreground and background colour of a window can be changed with the graphical context.

For the integration of tools belonging to the Hardware Synthesis System the LGM is used to realize the display window. Within this window, the design data are graphically represented. While using the LGM, the application programmer is freed from filling in the details of graphical output for each drawing operation.

25.1.3 GDS - Graphical Data Structure

The GDS comprises a hierarchical directed graph as data structure for graphical data and a library of routines for access and manipulation of this data structure. The data structure is optimized for region queries to allow fast retrieval of graphical objects according to given coordinates. This feature is especially important for graphical applications, since a large amount of interaction with graphical applications is the selection of objects by a pointing device, e. g., by a mouse. Hence, for each selection the objects specified by a set of coordinates have to be determined.

The GDS provides library functions for different kinds of region queries to find out all graphical objects whose bounding boxes

a) lie totally within a specified rectangle, or
b) have at least one common point with a specified rectangle.

This allows fast selection of graphical objects because groups of objects can be selected without selecting each single object.

The GDS hierarchy provides two levels of data granularity, graphical elements and graphical objects. At the lower level graphical elements describe graphical primitives such as lines, rectangles, and so on. Graphical primitives directly correspond to LGM drawing routines. The data for the graphical output is stored in structures which contain information about the graphical elements (objects), and their appearance on the screen. For example, lines have colour, thickness and type (e.g., solid, dashed, dotted).

At the upper level graphical objects are either composed of graphical elements or of graphical elements and other graphical objects. In the latter case, the graphical information is hierarchically organized as a directed graph. For instance, let there be a graphical object A containing two other objects B and C. C again is composed of three objects: B, D, E. The result is a graphical structure as shown in figure 25.3. These concepts allow the reuse of existing graphical descriptions by multiple references (instantiations) of the same graphical object. All library functions can either work on the total graph or on a single object of the hierarchy.

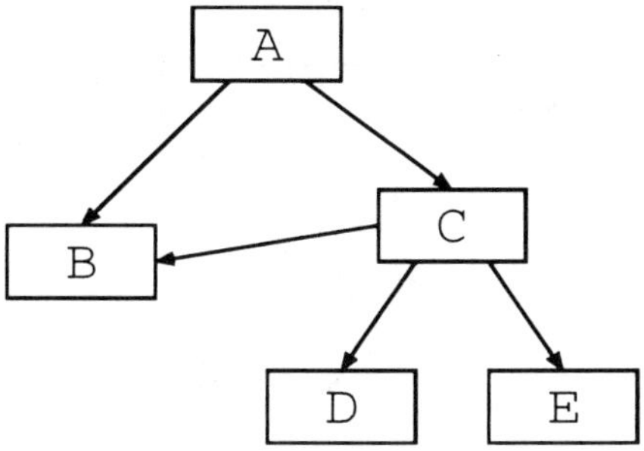

Figure 25.3 Hierarchical structure

Deep integration of the GDS into the JCF yields many advantages. To achieve deep integration the hierarchical graphical data structure described above is mapped onto the data model of the JCF–OMS. The objective of this integration is to store graphical data and other design data in a non–redundant manner. If the GDS were not integrated, for example, two hierarchies for a schematic (the graphical representation of a netlist) would exist: the graphical hierarchy and the netlist hierarchy. Here the problem of consistency arises. If, e. g. , the netlist is changed an update of the graphical hierarchy is necessary. With deep integration this consistency problem will be solved because the two hierarchies will be merged into one. Consistency can then be automatically monitored via events.

25.1.4 INT - INTerpreter

The Interpreter is the central part of the UIMS. It is responsible for interpreting the user input and activating the corresponding tool actions. The Interpreter consists of a parser, an event scanner, and several scanners for the tool processes (see figure 25.4).

The parser is specified by a context free grammar [ASU86] to which the corresponding actions are linked as so–called attribute functions. From this description C–code for the dialogue part can easily be generated by existing parser generators. The parser can get input from several channels, each channel having its own scanner. The scanner converts the messages on the channel into tokens for the parser.

As the event scanner is responsible for processing the user's actions it represents a special kind of scanner. User interactions via a pointing device, or keyboard, are converted into X–events by the X–Server. X–events are queued in the event queue.

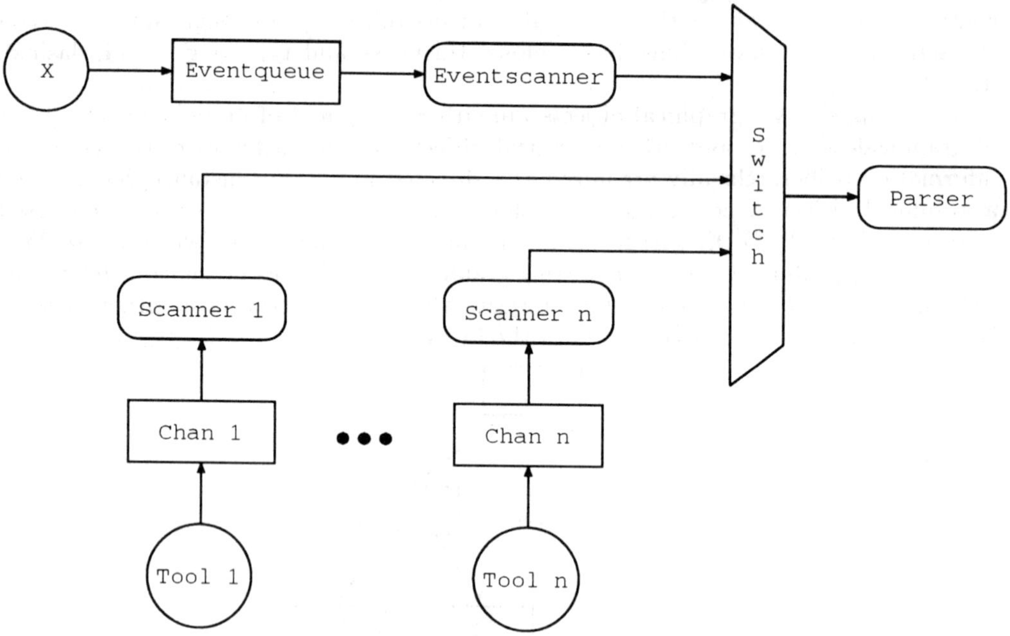

Figure 25.4 Structure of an Interpreter

The event scanner removes an X–event from the queue and generates one or more tokens. The parser is only able to process tokens sequentially. In case inputs arrive from multiple sources an appropriate scheduling strategy has to be realized.

Either the Interpreter is part of an interactive tool, for instance an editor, or a tool is encapsulated by the Interpreter. In the latter case, the Interpreter acts like a graphical shell establishing the interaction between a user and a tool. This helps to provide a unified graphical user interface for existing tools also that currently have an ASCII interface without adapting their code. In this case, user input from the screen is first passed to the Interpreter. The Interpreter translates the input into the tool–specific syntax and then sends the result by specified communication channels (usually "standard in") to the tool.

Tool outputs are processed similarly but in the opposite direction: from the tool to the Interpreter shell and then to the user. For the tool this shell is transparent. In this scenario the name " Interpreter" really denotes the task of this shell.

The editors of the Hardware Synthesis System are implemented using the first approach. To provide a unified graphical user interface for the batch oriented synthesis tools, compatible with the interface of the editors, the second approach is also used.

According to the two approaches described above the Interpreter can call attribute procedures for the following tasks:

- to draw graphical data on the screen (LGM),
- to communicate with the tools attached to it,
- to manipulate data stored in the GDS.

If a new tool is to be integrated, a grammar must be designed, or an existing grammar has to be extended. In most cases an existing grammar can be copied and changed. The attribute functions for this grammar must then be implemented and a new Interpreter program has to be generated. The attribute functions have to be implemented in C.

For constructing a tool grammar, several grammar parts concentrating on command structure and dialogue mechanisms are provided. These are used by the tool programmer to guarantee uniformity among all tools. Grammar parts for the following dialogue mechanisms are provided:

- command activation (menu, keyboard),
- parameter input (textmasks, keyboard),
- object selection / coordinate specification,
- command structuring (nesting of commands).

Thus, a tool programmer's main task consists of personalizing these mechanisms within special commands. For a better understanding consider the following productions and actions describing the nesting of commands. The productions are written in BNF [ASU86], with the actions enclosed in {...}.

```
cmd_group_i ::=  <cmd_id_i> <object_cmd_j_nesting> <cmd_end>
                 {finish cmd i}

<object_cmd_j_nesting> ::=   empty
                           | <object_selections> <cmd_group_j>
                             <object_cmd_j_nesting>

cmd_group_j ::=  <cmd_id_j> <object_selections> <cmd_end>
                 {finish cmd j}

cmd_id_i ::=  <cmd_selection> <cmd_name_i> {init cmd i}

cmd_id_j ::=  <cmd_selection> <cmd_name_j> {init cmd j}

cmd_selection ::=  <menu_activation> {activate menu}
                   <menu_selection>
                   {deactivate menu; refresh screen}

object_selections ::=   <object_selection>
                        {function call for initiated cmd}
                        <object_selections>
                      | empty
```

This example shows a grammar fragment, through which a tool programmer can be restricted to use command nesting with a maximum depth of two. This however is not a general restriction of the UIMS and can be changed by substituting the corresponding grammar fragment. The tool programmer can now describe the tool commands by simply specifying groups of commands which can be nested in other groups of commands with the restriction stated above of only one level of nesting. This specification is done by writing productions in BNF and then describing the appropriate actions for each command.

As the provided grammar fragments must be used by all interactive tools, easy adaptation to special user requirements is possible. If, for instance, a user group wants to use keyboard input instead of menus for command activation this can easily be implemented by changing the grammar part for *cmd_selection* and generating the dialogue part of all tools from this new grammar.

25.2 WINDOW LAYOUT

Besides configuring the command syntax and realizing the commands using this UIMS a unified layout of the user interfaces has to be defined. Figure 25.5 shows how the user interfaces of the tools within the Hardware Synthesis System look.

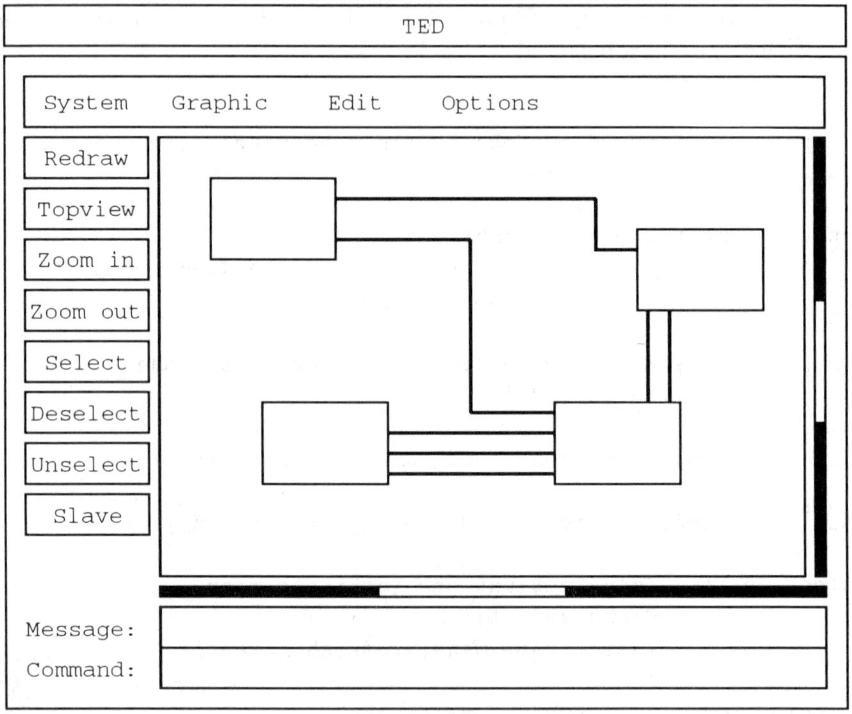

Figure 25.5 Common user interface

The user interface shown in figure 25.5 consists of a display window, commands, and message lines for ASCII input and output. Within the display window, the elements of an object can be displayed and new elements can be drawn. To ease the command input, special buttons and pull–down menus are used. Additionally, command entering by keyboard and ASCII output of user messages are possible. The commands are split up into two classes. The commands which do not change any data can be found in a row on the left side of the display window, because they are used very often. On top of the display window groups of data modification commands can be found. Here, the commands like drawing of lines can be found. These commands are not used as often as, for example, the "select" command which is used by nearly all drawing commands. Therefore, the use of a pull–down menu for each group seems to be the best solution. The groups should be unified for all tools. This means, if one group (or a subset) is used in more than one of the tools, then all commands belonging to this group (or subset) should have the same command syntax and meaning for all tools. If one of the tools subsequently needs an additional command, this command should be put into an additional tool–specific group.

At the bottom of the display window a line for messages can be found. Here, the user can be informed what to do next, or about an error that occurred. Additionally, there exists a line for entering commands by keyboard if the user does not like using the pointing device.

26

Control Integration

As described in section 23.3.7 the control dimension is also important for hardware design tools. Control integration has two aspects. One aspect concerns the information exchange between different tools, enabling one tool to perform tasks for another tool. In the environment described here information exchange is supported by the JESSI Common Framework (JCF). The other aspect is to support automation of the design process. Thus, we will describe how the design process is supported in our environment.

26.1 COMMUNICATION MECHANISMS

One aspect of control integration is the communication between different tools. Some mechanisms have to be offered for information exchange. This issue becomes very important if more than one tool works on the same data unit at the same time, as every change of common data has to be reported to all of the tools working on this data. In the environment described here the communication mechanisms of the JCF are used.

The JCF provides two mechanisms for communication, the Event Trigger Mechanism and the Inter–Tool Communication System. The Event Trigger Mechanism allows integrity and consistency management of data objects and object relationships in the database. The Inter–Tool Communication System is especially desirable in interactions where high performance is expected and a small amount of data needs to be transferred. The Inter–Tool Communication System allows the exchange of information about actions performed on data objects stored outside the Object Management System. The JCF implementation follows the inter–tool communication guidelines published by the CAD Framework Initiative, CFI (see [CFI91]).

26.1.1 The JCF Event Trigger Mechanism

JCF events represent mechanisms for controlling consistency and semantics of data objects. Moreover, they serve to automatically start actions for further processing of a given object. The Event Trigger Mechanism can be seen as a powerful tool for the external extension of the database functionality.

To ensure the integrity and consistency of objects and object relationships in the Object Management System, operations are supplied which enable the user to react

Tool Integration: Environments and Frameworks, Edited by D. Schefström and G. van den Broek

on certain events. Events of this type are defined by a user program for the execution of certain OMS operations, e.g., the manipulation of a certain object. The user binds a user function (callback function), which he/she has previously defined, to the occurrence of such an event. As soon as the event occurs, the callback function is called by the Object Management System. The user function is automatically provided with some information such as the identifier and type of the object and the function which triggered the event. The user function can then react in the way the user desires (perform various operations on data such as manipulation, examination, etc.).

Events may be locally defined and processed in an application process. However, they may as well be distributed or identified across process borders. Thus, a concurrent user process can react to actions of another process. The reacting process may wait either actively or passively for the occurrence of events in the processes under its supervision.

There are three classes of events: pre–events, post–events and asynchronous events. With pre–events (post–events) the callback function is executed *before* (*after*) the function which triggers the event. With asynchronous events, no statement is made about the order of the callback function and the function which triggered the event. Events get an identifier from the Object Management System when they are defined. This identifier may be used to activate or deactivate event handling at run time. In addition the capability to trigger events can be disabled and enabled. For examples of the use of this mechanism see [KK91].

26.1.2 The Inter–Tool Communication System ITC

Inter–Process Communication enables tools to coordinate actions and share data without accessing persistent data. This capability is especially desirable in interactions where high performance is required, and where a small amount of data needs to be transferred between tools. Examples are: cross–highlighting between a simulator and a schematic tool or displaying simulation error markers on a schematic.

The information transferred in a cross–highlighting scenario is small, and is only relevant as feedback to the user. It does not have to be saved in persistent data storage, and it must be transferred quickly for the user to perceive smooth execution of the design process.

Additionally, an Inter–Tool Communication System ITC should be designed for interoperability and interchangeability of tools in order to increase productivity and to allow customization of a user environment.

The Inter–Tool Communication subsystem of the JCF provides the ability for tools and services to communicate with each other and to control each other. This communication is done via messages and point to point data streams.

Messages:

The message handling component of ITC allows tools and services to communicate with each other by messages that are controlled and routed through a central message server. In order to allow tool interoperability and interchangeability, the sender of a message neither needs to know who the receiver will be, nor does the receiver need to know who has sent the message. The context of the receiver and of the message determines delivery. A message is broadcasted and matched against registered contexts. A message can be received by multiple tools which have expressed interest.

Messages serve two purposes. A notification message announces a change of state, which may be of interest to other services or tools, and hence this kind of message is typically delivered to more than one tool. For this reason, the ITC message system is sometimes called a multi–cast message system. A request message, on the other hand, is meant to cause some action to occur and is delivered to one tool. This action may be merely used to return some data, or to change the state of the receiver, too.

The mechanism by which messages are delivered is based on a callback; as messages come into a tool, the ITC system will invoke specific application functions based on the type of message.

Point to Point:

The ITC also supports dedicated point to point communication paths which are often more efficient for sending large amounts of data or extremely high frequency messages between two tools. This architecture is a direct communication link between two concurrently running tools. The applications themselves must agree on the semantics of the messages that are passed between them.

26.2 USE OF THE COMMUNICATION MECHANISMS

Even at the present level of integration in the Hardware Engineering Environment, the communication mechanisms described in the previous section can be used. Concepts of the use of these mechanisms have been published in [KK91]. These concepts contribute to the openness of the integrated system by decoupling the tools. For example, the message channels can be used for task activation to reach a decoupling of the Hardware Synthesis System tools. The details will be described later on.

For the future, parallel access of data structures by different tools will be more important. This means, for example, that while a designer edits the schematic of a design, a checking tool might test in parallel whether the schematic is correct. Here the event triggering mechanism of the JESSI Common Framework can be used.

In the following paragraphs the future use of the communication mechanisms is explained in more detail. Therefore, first, the resulting system architecture is illustrated followed by a description of the propagation of data changes and of the tool activation mechanism.

26.2.1 System architecture

The overall environment architecture and the communication mechanisms described above lead to the system architecture depicted in figure 26.1. This figure also includes in addition to figure 23.13 information about the usage of events and messages. The other elements of the architecture have been explained in section 23.4.

All tools read and write shared data in the database. This read and write access is not depicted. The dashed arrows denote communication via messages, the solid arrows represent event procedures that read or write the database. Solid arrows directed from the database to a tool show that the tool has read access to the database in event

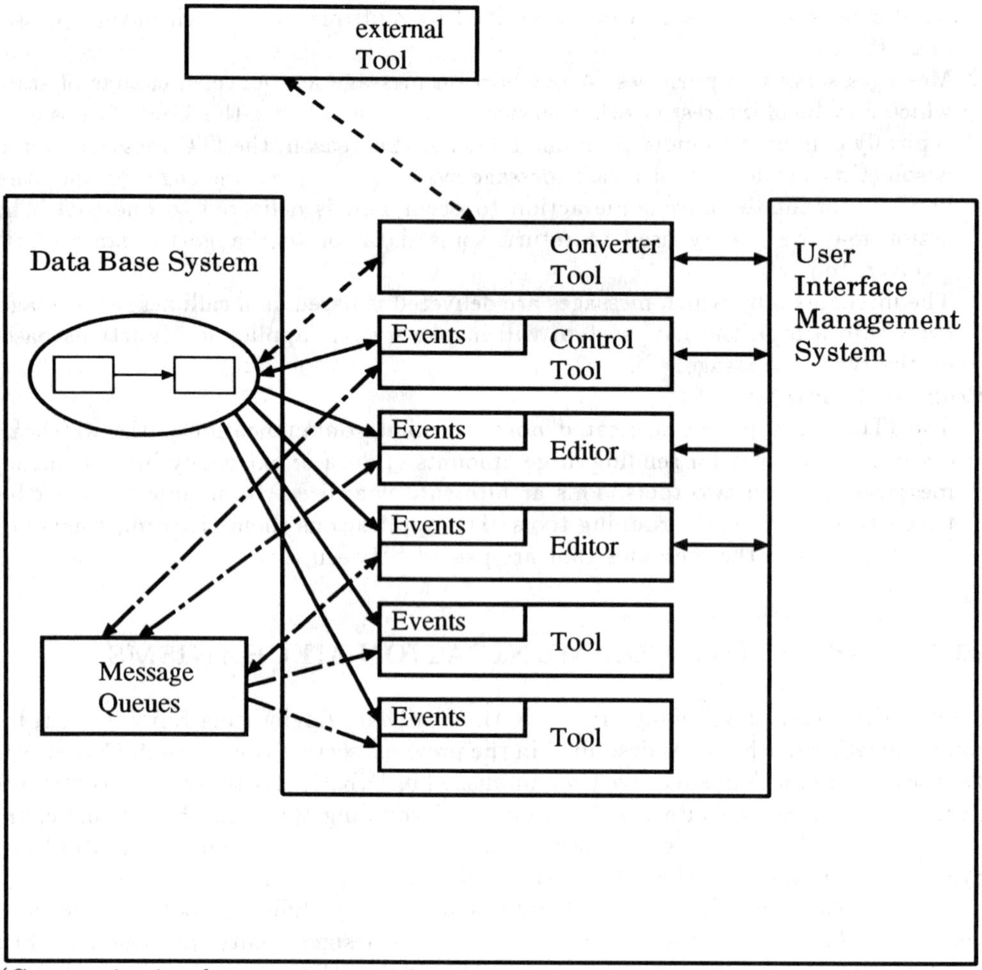

(Communication between integrated tools and the user interface is no longer necessary.)

Figure 26.1 System architecture including the communication mechanisms

procedures (callback functions defined for an event). Bidirectional solid arrows show that read and write access to the database is allowed in event procedures. In event procedures the editors and the synthesis tools have only read access to the database. For consistency reasons only the control tool has read and write access to the global data via event procedures.

Communication with the user interface is only necessary for the control tool and the editors. A direct communication to the integrated tools is not necessary, because the user interaction to these tools is handled by the editors. But, of course, for already existing tools direct interaction with the user is not forbidden.

Figure 26.1 also shows how external tools are coupled to the data base via a converter tool. In this case the arrows mean the usual read and write operations, not events. The data is extracted from the data base and transformed into an ASCII or binary representation needed by the external tool. This representation is stored in the file system. The data in the data base is usually not online updated by the external tool. Therefore, as long as the external tool works on these files the relevant data in the data base has to be locked for other tools, even for read access. This locking is not necessary if tools directly use the common data in the data base and online consistency is maintained via events.

26.2.2 Propagation of data changes

As the editors and the tightly integrated tools (see section 23.4) will also share data of fine granularity in the data base no explicit data exchange is necessary between the tools. But, for instance, the editors have to be informed when an update of their local data, the screen, is necessary due to a change of the global data in the database that was caused by a synthesis tool, for instance. This kind of information is exchanged via *events.*

By means of events online consistency checking is also performed. For all database accesses that might destroy consistency an appropriate event is defined. The event procedure may either maintain consistency by performing the necessary changes to other data, or if this is not possible an exception handling can be activated. Two kinds of events can be distinguished:

- *central events* triggered only in one process, in the control tool,
- *decentral events* triggered in several tools (processes).

Central events are used to update global data stored in primitive or complex objects. For this data a common schema must exist. To avoid data inconsistencies it has to be guaranteed that updates of the global data are always performed when necessary and that event procedures triggered by concurrent tool processes are synchronized. If the central events were distributed over several data processing tools this would be a very hard job. Each time a new process is activated or an existing one is stopped it has to be checked whether all the processes involved in updating global data structures are active. Therefore these events are defined in the control tool only. As this tool is active anyway, no restrictions for the other tools have to be considered. Another advantage is that concurrent data modifications of different tools are synchronized in this way, simply by sequential execution of the event procedures in the control tool. As the central events are triggered in one process they arrive in a certain order. In this order the event procedures are executed. Hence it cannot happen that one process performs only part of its update. Then a second process starts its update. The second process cannot succeed because of the inconsistencies left by the first one due to its interruption. Afterwards the first process also cannot continue due to the changes caused by the second one.

Decentral events are used to update local runtime data. They can be triggered in several tool processes, for instance, if a change of the common data schema necessitates update of the local tool data. Inconsistencies cannot appear when the tool is not running, because in that case the local data would not exist. Synchronization of concurrent modifications activated by events happens in the same way as described for the central events. The event procedures are executed sequentially in the respective tool process in the order the events are triggered for that process.

The following example very roughly explains the event mechanism. A detailed example for the use of events can be found in [KK91]. Suppose a layout editor defines an event for create, delete, or write procedure calls on graphic objects in the layout data schema. In this case the event procedure would for instance be a redraw of the screen. This kind of event is defined in all editors. It guarantees that whenever a tool creates, deletes, or writes a graphic object this change can be online displayed by the corresponding editor. The editor does not have to watch whether any tool performs such changes. This is automatically done by the database system. By this automation feature a decoupling of editors and integrated tools is reached. An editor does not have to know which tool performs a data change. Vice versa a tool does not have to know which editor displays a certain piece of information.

26.2.3 Tool activation

Tool activation occurs via logical message channels. To reach a decoupling between the editors and the integrated tools, messages are always distributed via a central message dispatcher located in the control tool. This message dispatcher is easily configurable via a message distribution table. Suppose a user enters a command to route a special area via the layout editor. The layout editor sends this message to the control tool. In this case the destination of the message is a router. The configuration of the message dispatcher determines which specific router is used to execute the command. The editor does not have to know which tool executes the command and would not notice any change of the dispatching algorithm. Hence simply by the means of process configuration it is possible to allow a user driven selection of tools and design algorithms. Also the configuration of design strategies is facilitated, e.g., whether for layout assembly first a placement tool and afterwards a router should be activated or whether placement tool and router should interact during execution of the assembly task.

26.3 PROCESS MODEL/WORK PROCESS SUPPORT

Work process support in our environment is based on the data schema. The design flow for hardware development is well understood and reflected within the data schema, so that tools responsible for the work process support can use this knowledge. For example, information about the next step within the work process can be elaborated out of the design flow.

As an example, the design flow of the hardware synthesis process and its influence on the data schema is illustrated in this section. The development of the instantiation hierarchy and of the different views is explained. Iteration steps which might be necessary during the design process are not examined because they lead only to new configurations, which, with respect to the schema representation, are of little interest. Within the figures only a few previously existing objects are shown as otherwise these figures would be too complicated. The newly created objects are added after each step. For a description of the different tools see section 23.3.3.

At the beginning of the design process a new *design* object and a *Top* design unit, as an entry point for the design, are created. Additionally, a first configuration object

(*Top configuration*) is automatically generated. With the help of TED (Top Level Editor, see section 23.3.3) as an input medium, the designer partitions the *Top* design unit into top–level hardware modules. The resulting structure and the interconnection of the modules are stored in the *contents* facet of the *structure* view. These hardware modules can be processed by the high level synthesis tools of the Hardware Synthesis System.

Each hardware module has to be represented by a new design unit. In figure 26.2 the design unit *Pass1* is used as an example for such a hardware module. For each of these design units its external characteristics and its behaviour have to be defined. For this reason an *interface* facet of the *structure* view and a description in one of the toolviews *Pass* or *Sam* have to be created by the designer. From this tool-specific description of the behaviour the system view *behaviour* can be extracted. Figure 26.2 shows this first instantiation hierarchy.

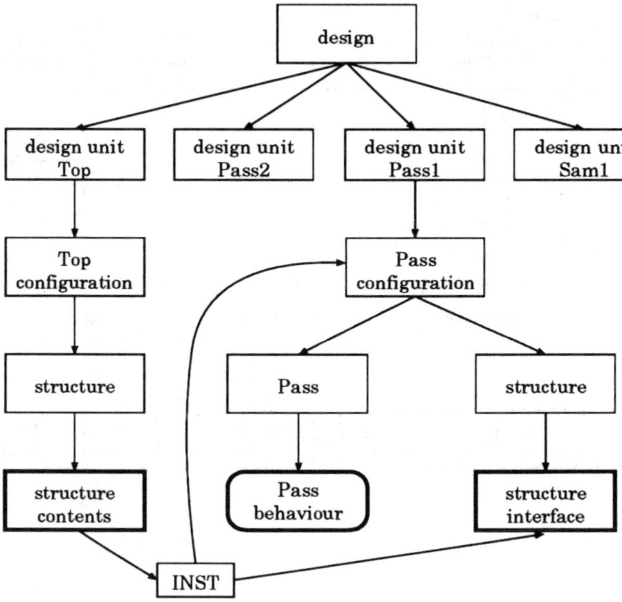

Figure 26.2 Structure of the modules at top level

At this point it is possible to distribute the different design units to several designers. For example, the design unit *Pass1* can be further developed by a different designer than the design unit *Pass2*. However, the designers are not allowed to change the *interfaces* of the design units. These descriptions have to remain unchanged, because they are used for the construction of the *Top* design unit. The different designers use the description of the behaviour of one of these modules as an input for the high level synthesis tools (PASS or SAM, see section 23.3.3). These tools execute a new partitioning phase and split up the top–level modules (e.g. design unit *Pass1* in figure 26.3) into RT–elements, for instance registers, ALUs, multiplexers, etc., and define their interconnections. This results in a description of the hardware module in the *structure* view at the RT–level. Therefore first the *Dataflow* view of the top–level module *Pass1* is created. With the help of this description the RT–structure can be developed. During this process some RT–elements are created which have to be represented by new design units, here *Alu*, within the data model. To each of these design units a configuration, *Pass_rt* or *Sam_rt*, is attached. This configuration contains the *interface* facet of the *structure* view and the description of its behaviour in the corresponding toolview (*CLASSY data*). All these descriptions are produced by the high level synthesis tools. The interconnection of the RT-elements is stored in the *contents* facet of the *structure* view of the top–level hardware module *Pass1*, i.e., the *structure interface* facets of the RT-elements (here *Alu*) are inserted into the instantiation hierarchy. If it is not possible to partition the top–level hardware module in one step additional levels have to be added to the instantiation hierarchy.

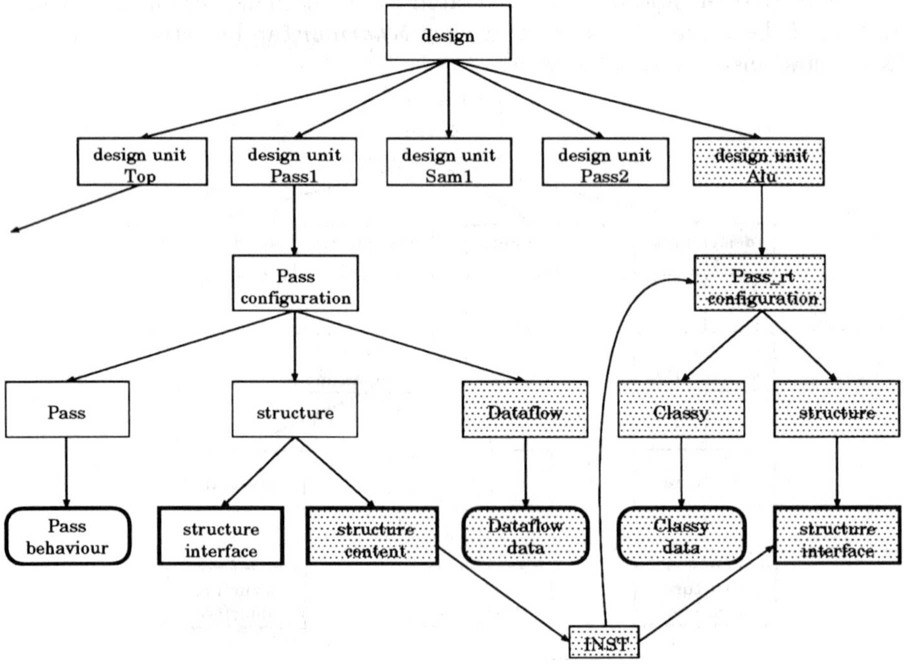

Figure 26.3 Instance of the data schema after the high level synthesis step

Again, the created design units can be further developed by different designers. For example, the design unit *Alu* can be developed separately from other RT–elements on the same hierarchical level. Only the structure interface description and the behaviour description have to remain unchanged to guarantee the correctness of the design units of the next higher level.

With the help of the behaviour description within the toolview *Classy* the module generator CLASSY partitions the RT–element into bitslices, which consist of gates stored in libraries. The layout of these library elements is used to construct bottom up the layout of the bitslices of the RT–modules (here *Alu*), of the top level modules (here *Pass1*), and finally of the *Top* design unit. Figure 26.4 shows the resulting schema representation of the design units *Top* and *Pass1*. For the design unit *Pass1* the *interface* and *contents* facets in the *layout* view have been created. This *interface* is instantiated by the *layout contents* of the *Top* design unit following the instantiation hierarchy of the *structure* view. This facet is entry point to the layout description of the whole design.

Other synthesis tools and their views can be integrated into the data schema and the design flow in a similar manner.

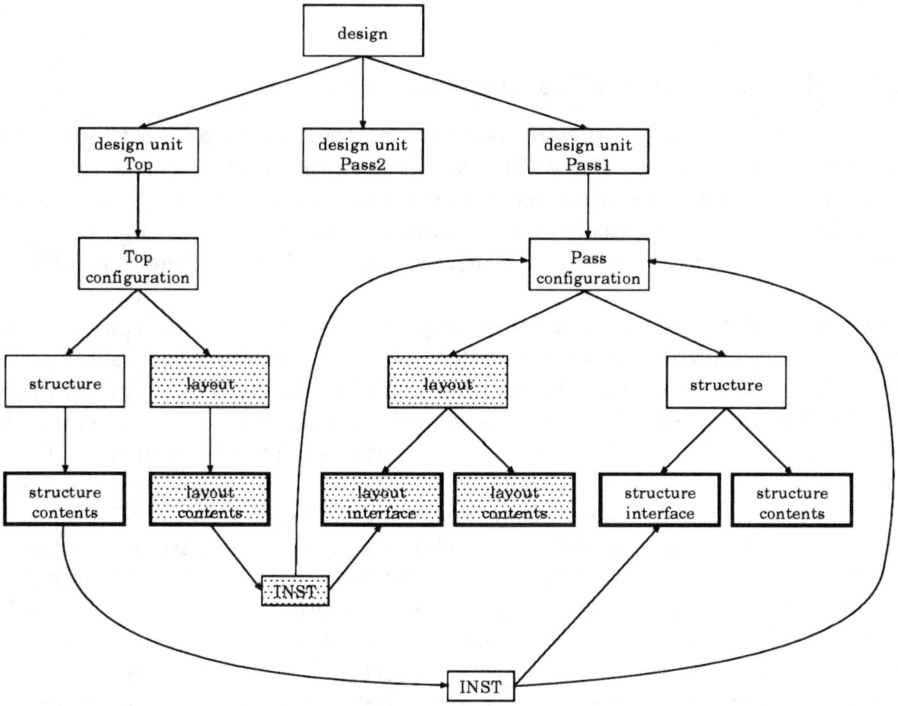

Figure 26.4 Instantiation hierarchy within the layout view

26.3.1 Cooperative work and scalability

As described in the previous section cooperative work and scalability are supported during the work process. Each time a new hierarchical level with new design units is created, the development of these new design units can be distributed over several designers, each one working independently from the others. Only the description parts elaborated during the partitioning process have to remain unchanged. During the development of the different design units it is not necessary that the different designers work on the same database. The work can even been done at different sites of a company or in different companies or countries. If it is not possible to develop a design unit without changing the descriptions worked out during the partitioning process, the designer responsible for the composition of the design units has to be informed, so that the other designers can be informed about necessary changes. This can, for instance, be done by using the communication mechanisms of the JESSI Common Framework.

The management of cooperative work is, at this time, done by the designers themselves without tool support. However, a clear knowledge about the problems involved exists. Thus, every designer is able to decide if alterations to his/her work would lead to problems for the development of the total design.

26.3.2 Methods supporting the work process

For the integration of the Hardware Synthesis System the Synthesis Control Editor (SCE) (see figure 26.5, see [BKM+91]) was implemented which offers the user the option to select input data in the database and to invoke a special tool to work on this data. It is also easy to integrate other tools, for example system engineering tools, in a loose manner. The editor is implemented with OSF/Motif and the X/Window system.

For the manipulation of the data items every object in the data base can be displayed graphically. To visualize the data schema (see section 24.3) not only single objects are represented but also their relations to others. Within the SCE the representation of objects and the displayed relations is called *path*. A *path* starts with the entry object as defined in the static access hierarchy. The path consists of a sequence of related objects. Objects are related if they belong to two object classes that are adjacent with respect to the access hierarchy or if they have been combined by an INST or CV_USE-relation. The hierarchy set up with these relations is the instantiation hierarchy.

Objects that are connected in these ways will be called successors or predecessors depending on the direction of the relation (the relations are established as father $\longrightarrow$ son relations). To distinguish between the direction of relations two symbols are used for the access hierarchy: a *cons_of* $\boxed{\rhd}$ and a *part_of* $\boxed{\lhd}$ symbol. Furthermore a *use* $\rhd$ symbol is provided to represent the instantiation hierarchy, the *user defined* $\bowtie$ symbol represents a user defined relation between objects of any class.

There exists only one valid path at a time. It keeps track of the navigation operations done by the user and allows selection of any of its components. The layout of the user interface of the SCE is similar to the general window layout described in section 25.2. The only difference is that the *graphic area* is subdivided into the *path area* and the *display area*. In the path area, the current path is displayed. The display area contains the actual objects for navigation. When navigating through the object hierarchy the predecessors or successors are visualized here.

In addition to the manipulation of the objects in the database, editors and tools can also be invoked. First the user has to select a configuration object. This is possible in the *path area* as well as in the *display area*. Next, the tool to be called is selected. An editor of the Hardware Synthesis System, for instance TED, or a tool such as the synthesis tools PASS, SAM, CLASSY, etc., may be selected. For a flexible reconfiguration of the list of editors and tools a special file is evaluated by the SCE.

This mechanism enables the encapsulation of tools. When the configuration object is selected and a tool is called, which does not work on the database, all needed facets belonging to the configuration are exported into the file system. The tool is now able to do its work. When it has finished the work, the resulting files are imported into the database. Encapsulation also provides a means to integrate tools that cannot be changed, because their source code is not available.

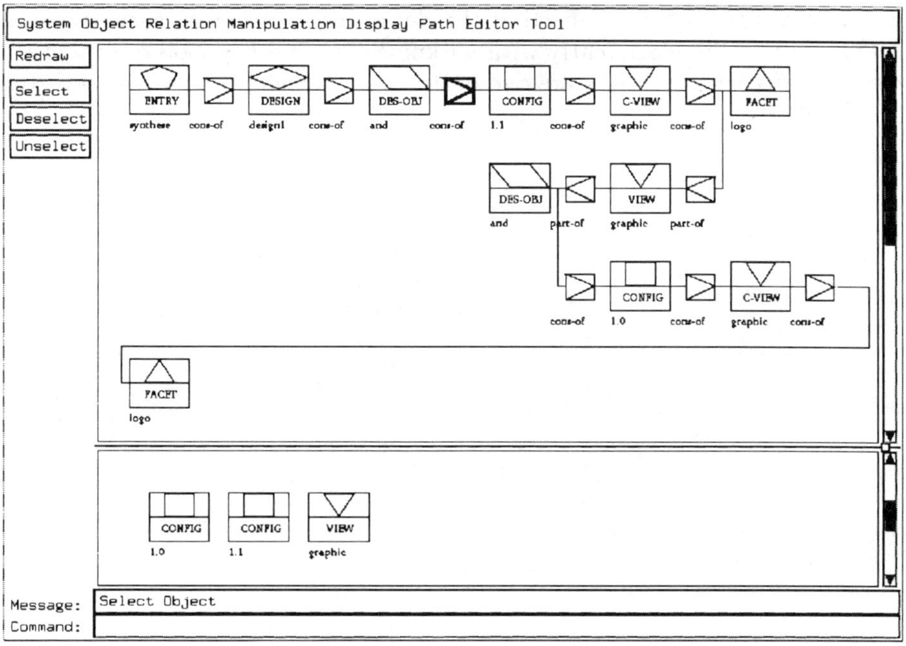

Figure 26.5 Example of a path in the SCE

26.3.3 Future work

As described above the large number of different descriptions of the same design complicate the determination of the correct place (with respect to the data schema) to store a specific object in the database. For tools this problem is solvable. The storage paths of their input and output data can be hardcoded. But if a designer wants to do a design step by hand, some help is necessary for data retrieval and schema conform storage of new objects. Additionally, some help is required for the invocation of the tools as the designer has to know which tool can be used for which design step, and furthermore, what input data the tool needs. Hence, some guidance would be useful.

Another aspect of future work concerning the design process is the implementation of consistency management. Using the knowledge about data manipulations in terms of the data schema, the definition of preconditions for execution of a specific tool is possible. By these preconditions rules may be defined that, for example, prohibit the execution of a specific tool whenever its execution may cause any data inconsistencies.

An example of such a rule may, for instance, be the case that a designer wants to call PASS a second time on the the *PASS_rt configuration* of design unit *PASS1*. This is possible without any danger if none of the RT–elements (e.g., design unit *Alu*) created by the previous run have been further processed by CLASSY or other module generators. This condition can be checked for instance for the *Alu* by examining the views and facets of this design unit. The condition is true, if no other objects than those depicted in figure 26.3 are attached to the *PASS_rt configuration* of the *Alu*. If this condition is false, and the designer calls PASS in spite of this fact, at least the possibly inconsistent data objects can be marked. Such a mechanism is especially valuable to support teamwork.

If a common data schema reflecting the design process exists, such rules can be defined for each tool independently without knowledge of other tools or tool execution sequences. Such central services are one of the main benefits that we expect from our integration efforts.

27

Conclusions and Outlook

In the previous chapters the integration of tools for system and hardware development has been shown. An overview of the hardware development process in general has been given and its differences from software development have been discussed followed by a description of the environment and its tools. After this introduction the three integration dimensions data, presentation, and control have been highlighted.

For data integration a common administration data schema was developed. It is responsible for the organization of the tool data and eases the exchange of data between different tools. The data schema was implemented with the help of the services provided by JESSI Common Framework (JCF), which offers facilities to define and work with data schemas on top of its Object Management System (OMS). The data schema is not dedicated towards requirements of special tools. Consequently, new tools can be easily integrated into the environment. Furthermore, it forms a basis for central management tasks, like consistency management, design auditing, configuration management, work process support, and support of cooperative work.

For presentation integration some ideas on how to reach a common look and feel are shown. A User Interface Management System has been described, which was used to implement the user interfaces of the tools of the Hardware Synthesis System, but can also be used for the presentation integration of the other tools of the environment.

The section on control integration covers the aspects of communication mechanisms and work process support. The communication mechanisms offered by the JCF are explained and it is shown how they are used. Additionally, it is described how the data schema reflects the work process. This eases the implementation of tools for work process support. For the manipulation of the schema objects and the invocation of the design tools a special control tool has been presented.

With these mechanisms an integrated Hardware Engineering Environment was constructed. The isolation of the different tools or toolsets was overcome. However, some topics for future work remain. For example, some additional work is required for consistency management and user/designer guidance. Additionally, tools supporting the other central management tasks mentioned above (e.g., configuration management, work process support, ...) should be provided. Concerning presentation integration the user interfaces of all the tools of the environment should be unified to reach a common look and feel throughout the whole environment. A large area for future work is the white box integration of the environment. This requires support of common mecha-

Tool Integration: Environments and Frameworks, Edited by D. Schefström and G. van den Broek

nisms for the structuring of the design data itself. Such a common data structure leads to a reduction of data conversion effort. Additionally, this would make it possible for different designers or tools to work on the same data at the same time. For example, during manual layout construction within an editor a design rule checker would be able to check the correctness of the constructed layout in parallel. This mechanism also simplifies the implementation of common tasks like consistency management and further support of cooperative work.

During the integration work described in the previous chapters a lot of experiences were gained. The generality of the integration approach has been shown through the integration of different tools not only from the hardware domain. Thus, the experiences will also be used to integrate tools from other areas of system engineering into the environment.

References

[AHS91] Siemens AG. *AUT-Handbuch fuer Software-Engineering*, 1991. Bestellnr. 6ZA6100-0UP10-8BA2.

[AKT91] A. Ahtianen, S. Kesti, and M. Turunen. *CASN Compiler User Manual.* Nokia Research Center, Computer Communications, Espoo, Finland, 1991.

[Apo85] Apollo Computer Inc., Chelmsford Ma. *Apollo: Domain Software Engineering Environment (DSEE) Reference Manual*, 1985.

[ASU86] A.V. Aho, R. Sethi, and J.D. Ullman. *Compilers, Principles, Techniques and Tools.* Addison Wesley, 1986.

[Auga] L. Augusteijn. Elegant language definition. ESPRIT-415 subproject. Technical Report D0335.

[Augb] L. Augusteijn. The Elegant scanner generator. ESPRIT-415 subproject. Technical Report D0282.

[BB84] D.S. Batory and A.P. Buchmann. Molecular Objects, Abstract Data Types, and Data Models: A Framework. In *Proc. of 10th Int. Conf. on Very Large Data Bases*, 1984.

[BB87] T. Bolognesi and E. Brinksma. Introduction to the ISO Specification Language LOTOS. *Computer Networks and ISDN Systems*, 1987.

[BD91] E. Bersoff and A. Davis. Impact of life cycle models on Software Configuration Managemnt. *Communications of the ACM*, August 1991.

[BEM91] Belkhatir, Estbublier, and Melo. Adele2: A Support to Large Software Development Process. In *First International Conference on the Software Process, Redondo Beach, California, USA*, October 1991.

[Ber84] E. Bersoff. Elements of Configuration Management. *IEEE Transactions on Software Engineering*, January 1984.

[Ber87] D. Bernstein. Database Systems for Software Engineering. In *Proceedings of the 9th International Conference on Software Engineering*, 1987.

[BFW92] A.W. Brown, P.H. Feiler, and K.C. Wallnau. Understanding Integration in a Software Development Environment. Technical Report CMU/SEI-91-TR-31 ESD-9-TR-31, Software Engineering Institute, Carnegie-Mellon University, Pittsburgh, USA, January 1992.

[BKKR86] R. Brück, T. Kathöfer, B. Kleinjohann, and F.J. Rammig. Synthesis of Modular Controllers from Algorithmic Descriptions. In *Proc. of DAC*, 1986.

[BKM+91] M. Brielmann, E. Kupitz, R. Milczewski, S. Rudolph, and J. Stroop. Access and Visualization Methods. ATMOSPERE Development Phase Internal Result I4.2.2.2.2.1, 1991.

[BKM+92] M. Brielmann, E. Kupitz, D. Mallon, F.J. Stewing, and N. Weißenberg. A Common Data Schema for Tool Integration. In *Proc. of the CAD'92*. Springer–Verlag, 1992.

[BKR85] R. Brück, B. Kleinjohann, and F.J. Rammig. Synthesis of Modular Controllers from CAP/DSDL Descriptions. In *Proc. of CHDL*, 1985.

[BL91] F. Buijs and T. Lengauer. Synthesis of Multi–Level Logic with one Symbolic Input. In *Proceedings of the European Conference on Design Automation*, February 1991.

[BLM91] K. Berrada, F. Lopez, and R. Minot. VMCM, A PCTE-based Version and Configuration Management System. In P.H. Feiler, editor, *Proceedings of the 3rd International Workshop on Software Configuration Management*, Trondheim, Norway, June 12-14, 1991. ACM Press.

[BM91] E. Bertino and L. Marino. Object-Oriented Database Management Systems: Concepts and Issues. *IEEE Computer*, April 1991.

[BM92] A.W. Brown and J.A. McDermid. Learning from IPSE's Mistakes. *IEEE Software*, 9(2):23–28, March 1992.

[BMMM91] A. Bailey, G.A. McCaskill, J. McIntosh, and G.J. Milne. The Description and Automatic Verification of Digital Circuits in CIRCAL. Technical Report HDV-15-91, University of Strathclyde, Glasgow, Scotland, May 1991.

[BMT88] Boudier, Minot, and Thomas. An overview of PCTE and PCTE+. In *Proceedings of the ACM Software Engineering Symposium on Practical Software Development Environments*, November 1988.

[BMW88] H. Beilner, N. Mäter, and N. Weißenberg. Towards a Performance Evaluation Environment: News on HIT. In *Proc. 4th Int. Conf. on Modelling Techniques and Tools for Computer Performance Evaluation*, 1988.

[Boe76] B. Boehm. Software Engineering. *IEEE Transactions on Computers*, 1976.

[Boe81] Barry W. Boehm. *Software Engineering Economics*. Prentice-Hall, 1981.

[Boe88] Barry W. Boehm. A Spiral Model of Software Development and Enhancement. *IEEE Computer*, May 1988.

[Boo87] Grady Booch. *Software Engineering With Ada*. Benjamin-Cummings, 1987.

[Bou90] J-Ph. Bourguignon. Structuring for Managing Complexity. In R.J. Mitchell, editor, *Managing Complexity in Software Engineering*, volume 17 of *IEE Computing Series*. Peter Perigrinus Ltd, 1990.

[BRS91] Bannon, Robinson, and Schmidt, editors. *Proceedings of the 2nd European Conference on Computer Supported Cooperative Work*, Amsterdam, October 1991. Kluwer Academic Publishers.

[BS87] H. Beilner and F.J. Stewing. Concepts and Techniques of the Performance Modelling Tool, HIT. In *Proc. 1st European Simulation Multiconference*, volume I, July 1987.

[BS90] R. Beckmann and W. Schenk. The TREEMOLA Language Reference Manual. Report 364, University of Dortmund, November 1990. Version 4.0.

[Buh83] R. Buhr. *System Design with Ada*. Software Series. Prentice-Hall, 1983.

[Bux80] J. Buxton. *DoD Requirements for ADA Programming Support Environments, STONEMAN*. DoD High Order Language Working Group, February 1980.

[Bux84] J. Buxton. Rationale for Stoneman. In Barstow, Shrobe, and Sandewall, editors, *Interactive Programming Environments*. McGraw-Hill, 1984.

[BVL90] F. Buijs, P. Vogelgesang, and T. Lengauer. Flexible and Optimizing ALU Synthesis. In *IFIP Working Conference on Logic and Architecture Synthesis*, 1990.

[CAC91] Collaborative computing. CACM, December 1991. Special issue.

[CAC92] Hypermedia. CACM, January 1992. Special issue.

[Cad90] Cadlab. IDM - Programmer's Reference Manual. Cadlab Object Management System Release 2.2 OMS-RM-01-00002-02.02, Cadlab, 1990.

[Cag90] M.R. Cagan. The HP SoftBench Environment: An Architecture for a New Generation of Software Tools. *Hewlett-Packard Journal*, pages 36–47, June 1990.

[CAP92] CAP Gemini Innovation, 118, Rue de Toqueville, 75017 Paris, France. *Process Weaver - General Information Manual*, 1992.

[CCI88] CCITT Recommendation Z100: Specification and Description Language SDL. ITU General Secretariat- Sales Section, Place des Nations, CH-1211 Geneva 20, 1988. Blue Book, Volume X.1.

[CEG+91] T. Collins, K. Ewert, C. Gerety, J. Gustafson, and I. Thomas. Tickle: Object-oriented description and composition service for large scale software engineering environments. In *Proceedings of Third European Software Engineering Conference, ESEC ' 91*, Milan, Italy, October 1991.

[CF88] ed. C. Fernstrom. *ESF Design Guideliness and Architecture*. ESF Consortia,

Hoehenzollerndamm 152, D-1000 Berlin 33, Germany, 1988.

[CFI91] CFI. Inter–Tool Communication Architecture. Document Number 55, CAD Framework Initiative, 1991. Version 0.9.

[Che76] P.P. Chen. The Entity-Relationship Model—Toward a Unified View of Data. *ACM Transactions on Database Systems*, 1(1):9–36, March 1976.

[CLO+90] Conradi, Lie, Osfjord, Westby, Ambriola, Jaccheri, and Liu. *Software Process Modelling in EPOS*, volume 436 of *Lecture Notes in Computer Science*. Springer-Verlag, 1990.

[Cod70] E. Codd. A Relational Model of Data for Large Shared Data Banks. *CACM*, June 1970.

[Com91] Multimedia Information Systems. IEEE Computer, October 1991.

[Con87] J. Conklin. Hypertext: An introduction and survey. *IEEE Computing*, 20(9):17–41, September 1987.

[Con89] EAST Consortium. EAST Overall Architecture. ESF, Hohenzollerndamm 152, D-1000 Berlin 33, Germany, September 1989.

[CR92] J. Cybulski and K. Reed. A hypertext-based software-engineering environment. *IEEE Software*, March 1992.

[CY90] P. Coad and E. Yourdon. *Object Oriented Analysis*. Prentice Hall, Englewood Cliffs, N.J., 1990.

[Dar91] Susan Dart. Concepts in configuration management systems. In *3rd ACM Conference on Configuration Management, Trondheim, Norway*, 1991.

[DM79] T. De Marco. *Structured Analysis and System Specifiaction*. YOURDON Inc., New York, 1979.

[Dow87] Mark Dowson. Integrated project support with istar. *IEEE Software*, November 1987.

[DSE88] Apollo Computer Inc., Chelmsford, Massachusetts. *Engineering in the DSEE Environment*, 1988.

[DSV91] H. Delfs, P. Suda, and S. Verplaetse. Objekt- und regelorientierte Programmierung in C mit TOROS. *unix/mail*, 1991.

[dV92] E. de Vespierre. CIDL. Sema Group, Brussels, Belgium, 1992.

[Eas92a] SFGL. *Data Model Design Guide*, 1992.

[Eas92b] SFGL. *Environment Cusomisation Guide*, 1992.

[ECM90] ECMA. Portable Common Tool Environment (PCTE). Technical Report ECMA-149, European Computer Manufacturers Association, Geneva, Switzerland, December 1990.

[ECMer] ECMA. A Reference Model for Frameworks of Software Engineering Environments (Version 2). *ECMA Report Number TR/55 (Version 2), NIST Report Number SP 500-201*, 1991 December.

[ECS91] *Proceedings of the 2nd European Conference on Computer Supported Cooperative Work* , Amsterdam, October 1991.

[EDI87] EDIF. EDIF Version 2.0.0, EDIF Steering Committee. Technical report, Electronic Industries Association, Washington, 1987.

[EG90] C. Ewering and G. Gerhardt. PASS: High–Level Synthesis. In *EUROMICRO 90, 16th Symposium on Microprocessing and Microprogramming*, August 1990.

[EG91] M. Eike and W. Gruber. Aus Alt Mach Neu: Alte Software mit Neuem Gesicht. *TOPIX*, April 1991. Köln, Geramany.

[EGR91] C. Ellis, S. Gibbs, and G. Rein. Groupware - Some Issues and Experiences. *CACM*, January 1991.

[Eme90a] E. Emerson. Temporal and Modal Logic. In J. van Leeuwen, editor, *Handbook of Theoretical Computer Science, Volume B, Formal models and semantics*, Amsterdam, 1990. Elsevier Science Publishers.

[Eme90b] GIE Emeraude. *General User Documentation*, v12 edition, 1990.

[ES90] M. Ellis and B. Stroustrup. *The Annotated C++ Reference Manual*. Addison Wesley, 1990. ANSI Base document.

[ESF89] ESF Technical Design Group, Hohenzollerndamm 152, D-1000 Berlin 33, Germany. *ESF Technical Reference Guide*, 2.0 edition, 1989.

[ESF91] ESF Technical Design Group, Hohenzollerndamm 152, D-1000 Berlin 33, Germany. *The ESF Software Bus - An Overview*, 1991.

[Est85] J. Estublier. A Configuration Manager: the ADELE Database of Programs. In *Proceedings of the Workshop on Software Engineering Environments for Programming-in-the-large*, pages 140–147, Harwichport, June 1985.

[Ewe90] C. Ewering. Automatic High–Level Synthesis of Partitioned Busses. In *Proceedings of the Int. Conf. on Computer Aided Design*, November 1990.

[Fei91] P.H. Feiler. Configuration Management Models in Commercial Environments. Technical Report CMU/SEI-91-TR-7 ESD-9-TR-7, Software Engineering Institute, Carnegie-Mellon University, Piitsburgh, USA, March 1991.

[Fel79] S.I. Feldman. Make—A Program for Maintaining Software Programs. *Software—Practice and Experience*, 9(4), April 1979.

[FO89] C. Fernstrom and L. Ohlsson. The ESF vision of a Software Factory. In *Proceedings of the International Conference on System Development Environments and Factories*, 1989. Berlin 9-11 May.

[FO91] C. Fernstrom and L. Ohlsson. Integration Needs in Process Enacted Environments. In *First International Conference on the Software Process*, Redondo Beach, CA, USA, October 1991.

[Fro90] B.D. Fromme. HP Encapsulator: bridging the Generation Gap. *HP Journal*, June 1990.

[Ger90] C. Gerety. HP SoftBench: a new generation of Software Developement Tools. *HP Journal*, June 1990.

[GER+91] G. Gries, R. Endres, M. Raff, A. Westphal, and B. Barthelmes. Functional Specification of the SDL-Integration Tool. ATMOSPERE ID: I2.2.2.1.6.1-pap-1.0-SIE-GG, 1991. Final Version 1.0.

[Gie91] H. Gierszal. Requirements Specification of the DAX/SC. ATMOSPERE ID: I2.2.2.1.2.1-rpt-1.0-2i-HG, 1991. Final Version 1.0. Industrial Informatics GmbH.

[GK83] D. Gajski and R.H. Kuhn. Guest Editors Introduction. *IEEE Computer*, December 1983.

[GKK+88] K. Gottheil, G. Kachel, T. Kathöfer, H.J. Kaufmann, et al. The Cadlab Workstation CWS - An Open Generic System for Tool Integration. In F.J. Rammig, editor, *Tool Integration and Design Environments*. North–Holland, 1988.

[GKKK86] K. Gottheil, H.J. Kaufmann, B. Kleinjohann, and E. Kupitz. A User Interface Management System for Generating Unified Tool - User Interfaces. Cadlab Report 4/86, Cadlab, 1986.

[GM90] A. Gustavsson and P. Madsen. The Postmaster Model - The SDT Tool Integration Mechanism. TeleLOGIC AB, Box 4128, 203 12 Malmo, Sweden, 1990.

[Gro89a] HOOD Working Group. *HOOD Reference Manual*. European Space Agency, Noordwijk, Netherlands, 3.0 edition, September 1989.

[Gro89b] HOOD Working Group. *HOOD User Manual*. European Space Agency, Noordwijk, Netherlands, 3.0 edition, December 1989.

[Har84] D. Harel. Dynamic Logic. In D. Gabbay and F. Guenthner, editors, *Handbook of Philosophical Logic, Volume II: Extensions of Classical Logic*. Reidel Publishing Company, Dordrecht, 1984.

[HHHW91] Howard, Hewitt, Hubbold, and Wyrwas. *A Practical Introduction to PHIGS and PHIGS Plus*. Addison Wesley, 1991.

[Hix90] D. Hix. Generations of User-Interface Management Systems. *IEEE Software*, September 1990.

[HNS86] E. Hörbst, M. Nett, and H. Schwärtzel. *VENUS: Entwurf von VLSI–Schaltungen*. Springer–Verlag, 1986.

[Hon88] Honda. Support for Parallel Development in the Sun Network Software Environment. In *Second International Workshop on Computer-Aided Software Engineering*, Cambridge, MA, USA, July 1988.

[Hum89] W. Humphrey. *Managing the Software Process*. SEI Series in Software Engineering. Addison Wesley, 1989.

[IEE88] IEEE Standard VHDL Language Reference Manual. Institute of Electrical and Electronics Engineers, 1988. IEEE Std 1076-1987.

[IEE89] IEEE Software, special issue on User Interfaces, January 1989.

[IEE91] *Proceedings of the 1st International Conference on the Software Process*, Redondo Beach, CA, October 1991. IEEE Computer Society Press.

[IEE92] Integrated CASE, Special issue of IEEE Software, March 1992.

[Inf85] The Rational Idea of Commercial Ada. InformationWEEK, November 1985.

[ISO87] Information Processing Systems - Computer: Graphics Metafile for the Transfer and Storage of Picture Description, Information , 1987. ISO/DIS 8632.

[Jac75] M. Jackson. *Principles of Program Design*. Academic Press, 1975.

[Jac83] M. Jackson. *System Development*. Prentice-Hall International, 1983.

[JCF91] Jessi-Common-Framework Architecture Specification. Siemens-Nixdorf, 1991.

[Kac90] G. Kachel. IDM - An Overview of the Data Model. Cadlab Report 13/90, Cadlab, 1990.

[Kat90] R. H. Katz. Toward a Unified Framework for Version Modeling in Engineering Databases. *ACM Computing Surveys*, December 1990.

[Kat92] T. Kathöfer. The JESSI–COMMON–FRAME Project - Sub–project Development -. In M. Newman and T. Rhyne, editors, *Proceedings of the 3rd International Workshop on Electronic Design Automation Frameworks*, 1992.

[KCTT91] R.K. Keller, M. Cameron, R.N. Taylor, and D.B. Troup. User Interface Development and Software Environments: The Chiron-1 System. In *Proceedings of the 13th International Conference on Software Engineering*, Austin, Texas, USA, May 13-17, 1991. IEEE Computer Society Press.

[Kea92] K. Kronlof and et. al. *Method Integration: Concepts and Case Studies.* John Wiley, 1992.

[KGD90] M. Koster, M. Geiger, and P. Duzy. ASIC Design Using the High-Level Synthesis System CALLAS: A Case Study . In *Proc. of the ICCD*, Cambridge MA, 1990.

[KK91] B. Kleinjohann and E. Kupitz. Tool Communication in an Integrated Synthesis Environment. In *Proceedings of the 2nd European Design Automation Conference*, Amsterdam, 1991.

[Kro92] Klaus Kronlof. *Method Integration: Concepts and Case Studies.* Wiley International, 1992.

[LC84] D. Leblang and R. Chase. Computer-Aided Software Engineering in a Distributed Workstation Environment. In *Proceedings of the ACM Software Engineering*, Pittsburg, PA, USA, April 1984. Symposium on Practical Software Development Environments.

[LCI+91] Linton, Calder, Interrante, Tang, and Vlissides. *InterViews Reference Manual.* Stanford University, Center for Integrated Systems, Room 213, Stanford, CA 94305, 3.0.1 edition, 1991.

[LHKB91] Lieven, Hallman, King, and Bienemann. ATMOSPERE Environment Integration - ProMod Architecture. Systemhaus GEI, October 1991.

[LLOW91] C. Lamb, G. Landis, J. Orenstein, and D. Weinreb. The ObjectStore Database System. *CACM91*, October 1991.

[LRKT91] M. Lindqvist, E. Ruohtule, E. Kettunen, and M. Tuominen. *The TNSDL Book.* Nokia Telecommunications, Espoo, Finland, 1991. Draft Edition.

[LV89] M. A. Linton and J. M . Vlissides. Unidraw: A Framework for Building Domain-Specific Graphical Editors. In *Proceedings of the ACM SIGGRAPH/SIGCHI User Interface Software and Technologies '89 Conference*, Williamsburg, Virginia, November 1989.

[M+92] A. Meckenstock et al. Concept and Architecture of a Distributed Object–Oriented Database Kernel. Cadlab Report 13/92, Cadlab, 1992.

[McC90] W. McCune. *OTTER 2.0 User's Guide.* Argonne National Laboratory, Argonne, 1990. Report ANL-90/9.

[McC91a] G.A. McCaskill. The XCircal User Guide and Reference Manual. Technical Report HDV-18-91, University of Strathclyde, Department of Computer Science, 1991.

[McC91b] G.A. McCaskill. The XTC Language Reference Manual. Technical Report HDV-14-91, University of Strathclyde, Department of Computer Science, 1991.

[Mey89] L. Meyer. BEMO - A Load Simulator (in German). In G. Stiege and J.S. Lie, editors, *Messung, Modellierung und Bewertung von Rechensystemen und Netzen, Proceedings, 5. GI/ITG-Fachtagung.* Springer Verlag, Berlin, September 1989.

[Mil89a] G.J. Milne. Describing and Simulating Complex Systems. Technical Report HDV-6-1989, University of Strathclyde, 1989.

[Mil89b] R. Milner. *Communication and Concurrency.* International Series in Computer Science. Prentice Hall, 1989.

[MOPT88] Munck, Obendorf, Ploedereder, and Thall. An Overview of DOD-STD-1838A, The Common APSE Interface Set. In *Proceedings of the ACM Software Engineering Symposium on Practical Software Development Environments*, Boston, MA, USA, November 1988.

[Mor88] Morgan. Configuration Management and Version Control in the Rational Programming Environment. In *Proceedings of the Ada-Europe Conference*, Munich, June 1988.

[MPBD87] B. Moller-Pedersen, D. Belsnes, and H.P. Dahle. Rationale and Tutorial on OSDL: An Object Oriented Extension of SDL . *Computer Networks*, 13(2), 1987.

[MS] McKinley and Schaefer. *DIANA Reference Manual.* Intermetrics Inc., Bethesda, MD, USA, draft 4 edition. IR-MD-078.

[MW91] P. Madsen and O. Wiegert. A Common Interchange Format for SDL, 1991. preprint.

[Nie83] C. Niessen. Hierarchical Design Methodologies and Tools for VLSI Chips. In *Proceedings IEEE*, volume 71, January 1983.

[Nok91] Nokia Research Center, Computer Communications, Espoo, Finland. *CASN Compiler Reference Manual*, 1991.

[NT87] I. Niemelä and H. Tuominen. Helsinki Logic Machine: a system for logical expertise. Technical report, Helsinki University of Technology, Espoo, Finland, 1987.

[Obj91] Object Design Inc., 1 New England Executive Park, Burlington, MA 01803. *ObjectStore Reference Manual*, 1991.

[O'K90] R. O'Keefe. *The Craft of Prolog.* The MIT Press, Cambridge, Massachusetts, USA, 1990.

[OMG91a] OMG. The Common Object Request Broker: Architecture and Specification. *Draft 91.8.1*, 26th August 1991.

[OMG91b] Class Definition Language Specification. Object Management Group, 1991. Produced by Sun Microsystems and Hewlett-Packard.

[OSO] ISO/IEC 8824: Information Technology- Open Systems Interconnection - Specification of Abstract Syntax Notation One.

[Ovu91] Workflow Management Software: The Business Opportunity. Ovum Ltd, 7 Rathbone Street, London W1P 1AF, England, 1991.

[PAC89] PACT. Public Type Definitions. Technical report, ESPRIT Project 951, September 1989.

[PDE] Siemens Nixdorf Informationssysteme AG, W-8510 Fuerth-Bislohe. *Benutzeranleitung SIGRAPH-SET-SDL-ED.* Bestellnr.E80850-A623-X-A1.

[Per89] D.E. Perry. The Inscape Environment. In *Proceedings of the 11th International Conference on Software Engineering*, Pittsburgh, PA, USA, May 1989.

[Pfa85] Pfaff, editor. *User Interface Management Systems*, Berlin, Germany, 1985. Springer-Verlag.

[Qui87] Vincent Quint. *Une Approche de l'Edition Structurée des Documents.* PhD thesis, L'Université Scientifique, Technologique et Medicale de Grenoble, May 1987.

[Ram89] F.J. Rammig. *Systematischer Entwurf digitaler Systeme.* Teubner Verlag, Stuttgart, 1989.

[Rat86] Application of the Rational Environment to Lifecycle Software Development.

Rational, 1501 Salado Drive, Mountain View, CA 94043, 1986. White paper.

[Rei90a] S. Reiss. Interacting with the FIELD Environment. *Software Practice and Experience*, 20, June 1990.

[Rei90b] S. P. Reiss. Connecting Tools Using Message Passing in the Field Environment. *IEEE Software*, July 1990.

[Rip88] K. Ripken. Automated Support for Design and Documentation of Large Ada Systems. In *Milcomp'88 Conference*, London, UK, September 1988.

[Roc85] A. Rockstrom. An Introduction to the CCITT SDL. Swedish Telecom Administration, 1985.

[RS77] D.T. Ross and K.E. Schoman. Structured Analysis for Requirements Definition. *IEEE Transaction on Software Engineering*, 3(1), 1977.

[RS91] F.J. Rammig and B. Steinmüller. Cadlab Annual Report 1990. Cadlab Report 19/91, Cadlab, 1991.

[SCC89] Hewlett-Packard Co. *UNIX SysV Programmer's Guide. Volume II, Chapter 9*, 1989.

[SCE] Siemens Nixdorf Informationssysteme AG, W-8510 Fuerth-Bislohe. *Benutzeranleitung SIGRAPH-SET-SC*. Bestellnr.U5433-J-Z97-1.

[Sch88] Schefström, D. Delaying Commitment - an Essay on the Nature of Development Work. Skargardsvagen 10b, 951 90, Lulea Sweden, 1988.

[Sch89a] Schefström, D. Building a Highly Integrated Development Environment Using Preexisting Parts. In *IFIP '89*, San Francisco, CA, USA, September 1989. North-Holland.

[Sch89b] A. Schulz. Software-Lifecycle- und Vorgehensmodelle. *Angewandte Informatik*, 4, 1989.

[Sch90] Schefström, D. Projections from a decade of CASE. In *Proceedings of the AdaEurope Internation Conference*. Cambridge University Pres, 1990.

[Sch91] Schefström, D. The Arcs Experience. In *Proceedings of the 3rd European Software Engineering Conference*, Milan, Italy, October 1991. Springer Verlag. LNCS 506.

[SD91] P. Suda and H. Delfs. TOROS, a System Integrating Object- and Rule-Oriented Programming in a C / UNIX-Environment . *Structured Programming*, 12(4), 1991.

[Ser90] An Introduction to GemStone and OPAL. Servio Logic Development Corporation, 1990.

[SFG91] EAST Environment. SFGL, 14, Rue de la Ferme - 92100 Boulogne, France, 1991.

[SG86] R.W. Scheifler and J. Gettys. The X Window System. *ACM Transactions on Graphics*, 5(2), 1986.

[Sim91a] I.D. Simmonds. C Development in a PCTE-Based Environment. In S.I. Feldman, editor, *Proceedings of the International Workshop on Unix-Based Software Engineering Environments*, Dallas, Texas, January, 1991.

[Sim91b] I.D. Simmonds. 'Duplicates'—A Convention for Defining Configurations in PCTE-Based Environments. In P.H. Feiler, editor, *Proceedings of the 3rd International Workshop on Software Configuration Management*, Trondheim, Norway, June 12-14, 1991. ACM Press. The concept of *duplicate* has since been renamed *surrogate.*

[SM88] S. Shlaer and S.J. Mellor. *Object Oriented Systems Analysis: Modelling the World in Data* . Prentice Hall, Englewood Cliffs, N.J., 1988.

[Sne85] J.A.L. van de Snepscheut. *Trace Theory and VLSI Design*. Springer Verlag, 1985.

[SS] R. Snodgrass and K. Shannon. Supporting Flexible and Efficient Tool Integration. Dep of Computer Science, Univ of North Carolina, Chapel Hill, NC 27514, USA.

[SS91] P. Spiby and D.A. Schenck. *EXPRESS Language Reference Manual*, 1991. ISO TC184/SC4/WG5.

[Ste92] B. Steinmüller. The JESSI–COMMON–FRAME Project - A Project Overview.

In M. Newman and T. Rhyne, editors, *Proceedings of the 3rd International Workshop on Electronic Design Automation Frameworks*, 1992.

[SUN89] The Network Software Environment. Sun Microsystems, 2550 Garcia Avenue, Mountain View, CA 94043, USA, 1989.

[Tel92] TeleSoft, 5959 Cornerstone Court West, San Diego, CA 952121-9891 USA. *TeleUSE User's Guide*, 1992.

[Tho89] M.I. Thomas. Version and Configuration Management on a Software Engineering Database. In *Proceedings of the 2nd International Workshop on Software Configuration Management*, pages 23–25, Princeton, New Jersey, October 1989. ACM Press.

[TN92] M.I. Thomas and B.A. Nejmeh. Definitions of Tool Integration for Environments. *IEEE Software*, 9(2):29–35, March 1992.

[Tra88] Will Tracz. Software Reuse: Emerging Technology. IEEE Computer Society, 1988.

[Tur91a] M. Turunen. CASN SDL-Specific Back-end, User's guide. ATMOSPERE ID D4.3.1.8.1.1-guide-1.0-NOK-MT, 1991.

[Tur91b] M. Turunen. How to make CASN back-ends. Technical report, Nokia Research Center, Computer Communications, Espoo, Finland, 1991.

[Uni90] Universistät Kaiserslautern. *PLIF Sprachbeschreibung*, November 1990. SFB 124.

[Uni91] Unicom Ltd, Brunel Science Park, Cleveland Rd, Uxbridge, Middlesex, UB8 3PH, UK. *Computer Supported Cooperative Work - The Multimedia and Networking Paradigm*, 1991.

[VB] J. Vlissides and C. Brauer. Ibuild User's Guide. unidentified part of Interviews distribution.

[Ver91] Versant Object Technology Corporation, 4500 Bohannon Drive, CA 94025, USA. *Versant System Reference Manual*, 1991.

[W+] R.I. Winner et al. *The Role of Concurrent Engineering in Weapons System Acquisition.* IDA, Alexandria, Va. IDA Report R–338.

[Was90] A. Wasserman. Tool Integration in Software Engineering Environments. In F. Long, editor, *Software Engineering Environments*, number 467 in Lecture Notes in Computer Science, pages 138–150, Springer-Verlag, Berlin, Germany, 1990.

[Wei87] M. Weiser. Source Code. *IEEE Computer*, November 1987.

[Wid91] J. Widen. Baseline Chapters of Arcs 2.0 Documentation Set. Telesoft, San Diego, CA, USA, 1991.

[WM92] Alan W.Brown and John A. McDermid. Learning from IPSE Mistakes. *IEEE Software*, March 1992.

[YC79] Yourdon and Constantine. *Structured Design.* Prentice-Hall, 1979.

[Zea88] R. Zellner and et al. Gestaltung der Benutzungsoberfläche, Richtlinie. Siemens AG, 1988.

Index